Beginning RSS and Atom Programming

Danny Ayers
Andrew Watt

WILEY

Wiley Publishing, Inc.

Beginning RSS and Atom Programming

Published by
Wiley Publishing, Inc.
10475 Crosspoint Boulevard
Indianapolis, IN 46256
www.wiley.com

Copyright © 2005 by Wiley Publishing

Published by Wiley Publishing, Inc., Indianapolis, Indiana

Published simultaneously in Canada

ISBN-13: 978-0-7645-7916-5
ISBN-10: 0-7645-7916-9

Manufactured in the United States of America

10 9 8 7 6 5 4 3 2 1

1MA/RZ/QU/QV/IN

For general information on our other products and services or to obtain technical support, please contact our Customer Care Department within the U.S. at (800) 762-2974, outside the U.S. at (317) 572-3993 or fax (317) 572-4002.

Wiley also publishes its books in a variety of electronic formats. Some content that appears in print may not be available in electronic books.

Library of Congress Cataloging-in-Publication Data

Ayers, Danny.
 Beginning RSS and atom programming / Danny Ayers, Andrew Watt.
    p. cm.
 Includes index.
 ISBN-13: 978-0-7645-7916-5
 ISBN-10: 0-7645-7916-9 (paper/website)
 1. Internet programming. 2. Web site development. 3. MPLS standard. I. Watt, Andrew, 1953- II. Title.
 QA76.625.A93 2005
 006.7'6—dc22
                              2005003120

About the Authors

Danny Ayers is a freelance developer, technical author, and consultant specializing in cutting-edge Web technologies. He has worked with XML since its early days and got drawn into RSS development around four years ago. He is an active member of the Atom Working Group, the Semantic Web Interest Group, and various other Web-related community groups and organizations. He has been a regular blogger for several years, generally posting on technical or feline issues. Originally from Tideswell in the north of England, he now lives in a village near Lucca in Northern Italy with his wife, Caroline, a dog, and a herd of cats.

I dedicate my contribution to this book to my wife, Caroline, and our four-legged companions, who have tolerated my air of irritable distraction these past few months. Okay, actually for several years now.

Andrew Watt is an independent consultant and computer book author with an interest and expertise in various XML technologies. Currently, he is focusing primarily on the use of XML in Microsoft technologies. He is a Microsoft Most Valuable Professional for Microsoft InfoPath 2003.

I dedicate my contribution to this book to the memory of my late father, George Alec Watt, a very special human being.

Credits

Acquisitions Editor
Jim Minatel

Development Editor
Kezia Endsley

Technical Editor
Brian Sletten

Editorial Manager
Mary Beth Wakefield

Vice President & Executive Group Publisher
Richard Swadley

Vice President and Publisher
Joseph B. Wikert

Project Coordinator
Erin Smith

Graphics and Production Specialists
Karl Brandt
Lauren Goddard
Jennifer Heleine
Amanda Spagnuolo
Julie Trippetti

Quality Control Technicians
Susan Moritz
Carl William Pierce
Brian Walls

Proofreading and Indexing
TECHBOOKS Production Services

Acknowledgments

Danny Ayers: Many thanks first of all to Andrew for getting this book started and more generally for his encouragement and role model of good-humored determination. Thanks to Jim Minatel for all the effort that went into making this project happen and for his diplomacy when I needed to be nagged out of procrastination. Many thanks to Kezia Endsley for taking care of the translation from Broad Derbyshire to U.S. English and to Brian Sletten for keeping a keen eye on technical matters (and remembering my birthday!).

I am extremely grateful to all the people who have helped me personally with various issues throughout the book. Unfortunately, if I were to thank them individually this would read like an Oscars ceremony screed. Worse, I'd also be bound to forget someone, and that just wouldn't be nice. I can at least show a little gratitude in my ongoing appreciation of their work, some of which will hopefully have been reflected in this book. More generally, I'd like to thank the developers behind the Web, RSS, Atom, and related technologies for providing such a rich seam of material to draw on and helping my own learning through mailing-list discussions and blog conversations. The material is alive out there! Finally, I'd like to thank the reader for showing an interest in a field that I personally believe has a lot to offer everyone and is certain to play a significant role in the shaping of at least the Web landscape over the next few years. Be inquisitive; be creative.

Andrew Watt: I thank Jim Minatel, acquisitions editor, for patience above and beyond the call of duty as the writing of this book took much longer than we had all originally anticipated. I also thank Kezia Endsley for helpful and patient editing and Brian Sletten for his constructive and assiduous technical assessment.

Contents

Contents

Contents

Contents

Contents

Contents

Contents

Contents

Contents

Contents

Contents

Contents

Contents

Contents

Foreword by Dare Obasanjo

As I write these words, a revolution is taking place on the World Wide Web. The way people obtain, store, and manipulate information from the Web is fundamentally changing thanks to the rise of information feed formats such as RSS and Atom. I discovered the power of RSS in early 2003.

Like most people who spend time online, I read a number of Web sites on a daily basis. I noticed that I was checking an average of five to ten Web sites every other hour when I wanted to see if there were any new articles or updates to a site's content. This prompted me to investigate the likelihood of creating a desktop application that would do all the legwork for me and alert me when new content appeared on my favorite Web sites. My investigations led to my discovery of RSS and the creation of my desktop news aggregator, RSS Bandit. Since then, RSS Bandit has been downloaded more than 100,000 times and has been praised by many as one of the most sophisticated desktop applications for consuming information feeds.

The concept behind information feed formats is fairly straightforward. An information feed is a regularly updated XML document that contains metadata about a news source and the content in it. Minimally, an information feed consists of an element that represents the news source and that has a title, link, and description for the news source. Additionally, an information feed typically contains one or more elements that represent individual news items, each of which should have a title, link, and content.

Information feed formats have a checkered history. There were several attempts to get such a simple metadata format on the Web in the 1990s, including Apple's MCF, Microsoft's CDF, and Netscape's RSS format. It wasn't until the rise of Web logging and the attendant increase in micro-content sites on the Web that people began to embrace the power of information feeds. The use of information feeds has grown beyond Web logging. News sites such as CNN and the New York Times use them as a way to keep their readers informed about the issues of the day. Radio stations like National Public Radio use them to facilitate the distribution of radio shows to listeners in a trend currently called "podcasting." Technology companies like Microsoft and IBM use them to disseminate information to software developers. Several government agencies have also begun using information feeds to provide news about legislative schedules and reports. It seems as if every week I find a new and interesting Web site that has started publishing information feeds.

In this new world, developers need a guide to show them the best ways to navigate the information feed landscape. Danny Ayers and Andrew Watt have created such a guide. This book is full of practical advice and tips for consuming, producing, and manipulating information feeds. It not only contains useful code samples that show practical examples but also explains many of the concepts of information flow that are crucial to understanding the ongoing revolution in distribution of content on the Web. I only wish I had a book like this when I started writing RSS Bandit two years ago.

Dare Obasanjo
RSS Bandit creator: http://www.rssbandit.org/
Program Manager, MSN Communication Services Platform
http://blogs.msdn.com/dareobasanjo

Foreword by Greg Reinacker

In the beginning, there was e-mail. E-mail was an exciting new way of communicating with others, and as it became ubiquitous, it revolutionized the way we work.

The World Wide Web represented the next revolutionary change in the way we communicate. Individuals and companies could now put information on the Web for anyone to see on demand, essentially for free. As the tools for the Web achieved critical mass and Web browsers were on every desktop, the Web became an essential part of our work and play.

But by themselves, both of these technologies have their problems. E-mail suffers from spam, which costs companies millions of dollars every year. And while the Web is an amazing resource, the information we want requires that we go look for it rather than it coming to us.

Syndication technologies (including RSS and Atom) provide the critical next step. By providing a simple way to publish information in a well-known, structured format, they enable the development of many new applications.

I first got involved with these syndication technologies, and RSS in particular, in 2002. At the time, RSS was in many ways a niche technology; it was becoming popular for Weblogs, but not many large commercial publishers had RSS feeds, with the *New York Times* being the most notable early RSS adopter. In my early work with RSS, I talked to many potential publishers, and almost universally, their response was "What is RSS? And why should we care?" And the situation wasn't much better for users, who would ask, "Where can I find more feeds?"

The landscape has changed dramatically since then. Nearly all Weblog publishing tools support either RSS or Atom, and Weblogs themselves have enjoyed major exposure in the mainstream media. Recent research shows that the majority of Internet users read at least one Weblog, and a large and growing number use some form of aggregator to read syndicated content. And commercial publishers have embraced RSS enthusiastically; the largest publishers are either supporting RSS on their sites or investigating how they should support it. When we ask publishers about RSS now, the question is no longer "What is RSS?" but rather "Can you help us with our RSS strategy?" And for users, the question is no longer where they can find more feeds but rather how they can best sort through the millions of available feeds to find the content they're looking for.

There is a large ecosystem of tools and services surrounding these syndication technologies. Small and large companies alike are building search engines, aggregators, publishing tools, statistics-gathering services, and more. Users can find the information they want and have it delivered to them on their desktop, on the Web, in their e-mail client, on their mobile phone, or even on their TV. You widen your distribution channel dramatically by simply building feeds for your content.

And with the advent of podcasting, video blogging, and the like, multimedia content within feeds is becoming more and more common. For the first time, people at home can use inexpensive tools to create audio or video for their audience and have it nearly instantly distributed to subscribers on whatever device they choose to use.

Major portals such as Yahoo! and MSN now support adding RSS feeds into their user experience, bringing this kind of technology to millions of users. Users can now add a favorite Weblog to their My Yahoo! pages as easily as they can add headlines from a major news service.

Enterprise RSS use is also taking off in a big way. Companies are using RSS internally for all kinds of information distribution. From project management Weblogs to RSS-enabled CMS, CRM, and ERP systems to RSS-aware source control and configuration management systems to RSS-enabled internal portals, companies are finding that these syndication technologies are making their employees and partners more productive.

Many software vendors who build publishing systems and other tools are working on adding RSS support to their products, and this trend shows no signs of slowing. In addition, a huge number of internally created applications contain or generate information that could be ideally distributed via RSS or Atom. Unlocking this information from these systems and distributing it to the people who can use and act on it is an important task. One of the most effective ways to do this is to write code to generate RSS/Atom feeds from these systems.

This book is about helping you understand RSS and Atom, navigating the maze of different versions of these protocols, and demonstrating ways to create and use these feeds. As you proceed through the book, you'll probably think of more places where you could create feeds to expose information to your users. And you'll learn that it's usually quite easy to create these feeds. By doing so, you open yourself up to the whole ecosystem of tools and services that have been created for these syndication technologies and the millions of users who use them.

First there was e-mail. Then there was the Web. Now there's RSS.

Greg Reinacker
Founder and CTO
NewsGator Technologies, Inc.
gregr@newsgator.com

Introduction

RSS and Atom are increasingly important technologies that enable users to have efficient access to emerging online information. There are now several million active information feeds (estimates vary) that use RSS and Atom. Many of those feeds, perhaps the large majority, are created automatically by tools used to create weblogs. Such feeds contain information on topics as diverse as XML, individual software products, cats, Microsoft, the Semantic Web, business information, and pop music.

Millions of users across the globe are increasingly using *aggregators*, software that allows subscribing to information feeds and display of new information as a more efficient way to remain up to date on subjects of interest than the former approach of manually browsing multiple Web sites. Businesses increasingly use information feeds to keep up to date on their markets, the activities of their competitors, and so on.

RSS and Atom information feeds have moved from being the plaything of a few to becoming an essential business tool. Understanding the detail of information feed formats and how to manipulate information feeds will be foundational to many upcoming pieces of software. This book aims to equip you with the understanding and skills to understand information feed formats and to use RSS and Atom feeds effectively in the software you write.

Whom This Book Is For

This book is for people who know that they and the people they write software for are going to fight an ongoing battle to find the information that they need in the ever-increasing volumes of electronic information that floods cyberspace. They know that the user's need to find information is crucial to the user's business success and that those who write effective software to help users manage information flows will likely succeed where others fail.

Beginning RSS and Atom Programming is intended to help you understand the issues that face the user community and, by extension, the developer community. By understanding user needs you will be better placed to write software to meet those needs. RSS, in its various versions, and Atom are useful tools to help you provide software that helps your customers to process information efficiently and effectively.

In addition, you will be introduced to the details of the widely used feed formats, the various versions of RSS and Atom that are already in use or are upcoming. You will also be shown many practical techniques using RSS to create and manipulate information feeds.

To use and process information feeds effectively you need to gain a grasp of many issues. This book is called *Beginning RSS and Atom Programming* because, without assuming that you already know things that you may not yet know, we take you step by step through the thought processes and skill building that enable you to get started working effectively with information feeds. In the latter part of the book, you will see some fairly advanced use examples of information feeds in action.

We don't assume any detailed knowledge of the various information feed formats or any deep programming skills. We hope you have had at least some programming experience because that will make progress through the book easier. Since we use several languages in the example projects, you are likely to find some code in a language that is familiar to you and some that is not. The descriptions of each project aim to make the example projects accessible to you, even if you have had negligible programming experience in any particular language. On the other hand, if you haven't done any programming with languages such as Python, PHP, or C#, some of the examples may feel pretty demanding and may need careful study on your part so that you grasp what is really going on.

Similarly, if you have no previous knowledge of XML and RDF, we try to introduce you to such topics in a way to make it possible for you to use and understand the example projects, but since these technologies have some tough aspects, you may need to spend some time on grasping unfamiliar topics.

What This Book Covers

This book attempts to provide you with a practical understanding to create useful functionality to control information flow today and also to stimulate your imagination to see what is possible tomorrow.

The user perspective is put up front early in the book. If you understand users' needs, then you can take intelligent decisions in the software that you write to meet their needs.

The various versions of RSS and Atom, including their document structures, are introduced and described. Understanding the feed formats is an essential first step in knowing how to use and manipulate them.

We discuss current aggregators and online tools both in terms of the useful things that they already do and the points where they, in our opinion, fail to fully meet the grade as far as some users' needs are concerned.

You are introduced to the tools available for developers who use languages such as Java, Python, and PHP. With that foundation you are then ready to move on to applying that knowledge and using those tools to create projects that create, manipulate, and display information feeds.

The practical chapters later in the book provide working code examples to demonstrate key software techniques used in feed publication and reading. RSS, Atom, and related formats are used alongside various protocols and can be seen in action as common languages across a wide range of applications. Generation, publication, reception, processing, and display of feed data are demonstrated. In these chapters, you will find code snippets, utilities, and full mini-applications. These aim to provide insights into the huge range of applications associated with syndication on the Web, from blogs, podcasting, newsreaders, and Wikis to personal knowledge bases and the Semantic Web.

Generally, the code is written so that you will be able to see how things work, even if you aren't familiar with the particular programming language used. You may want to build on the mini-applications, but chances are once you've seen an example of the way things can be done, you'll want to do them better yourself, in your language of choice using your tools of choice. Add your own imagination and you'll be able to explore new territory and create applications that haven't even been thought of yet.

How This Book Is Structured

The following briefly describes the content of each chapter:

❑ Chapter 1 discusses how information feeds change how users have access to new online information. Information feeds bring access to new information to your desktop rather than your having to go looking for it.

❑ Chapter 2 discusses the nature of the World Wide Web and how technologies that led to information feeds developed.

❑ Chapter 3 discusses issues relating to content from the content provider point of view. Why, for example, should you give your content away?

❑ Chapter 4 discusses issues relating to the viewpoint of the content recipient. Among the issues discussed are the user needs for access to data.

❑ Chapter 5 discusses how some information derived from information feeds needs to be stored for long periods.

After Chapter 5, there is a shift to examining individual technologies that you will need to understand in order to create and manipulate information feeds.

❑ Chapter 6 discusses the essentials of XML. Both RSS and Atom information feeds must follow the rules of XML syntax.

❑ Chapter 7 discusses Atom 0.3

❑ Chapter 8 discusses RSS 0.91 and 0.92. Both of these specifications avoid XML namespaces and RDF.

❑ Chapter 9 discusses RSS 1.0, which uses both XML namespaces and RDF.

❑ Chapter 10 discusses the modules that allow RSS 1.0 to be extended.

❑ Chapter 11 discusses basic concepts of RDF, including how facts can be represented as RDF triples and serialized as XML/RDF, as in RSS 1.0.

❑ Chapter 12 introduces RSS 2.0, which has XML namespaces but not RDF.

❑ Chapter 13 introduces the Atom 1.0 specification, which, at the time of writing, is under development at the IETF.

❑ Chapter 14 discusses some tools that create information feeds automatically.

❑ Chapter 15 discusses several desktop aggregators currently available or in beta at the time of writing.

❑ Chapter 16 discusses options for long-term storage of information.

❑ Chapter 17 discusses issues relating to online aggregators or aggregator-like tools.

After Chapter 17 we move to applying our growing understanding of the tools and technologies used in information feeds to a range of projects. Each of the following chapters contains sample code designed to give you a practical insight into the techniques under discussion.

❑ Chapter 18 briefly introduces a range of programming toolkits, several of which are used in the projects in the rest of the book.

❑ Chapter 19 provides a technical overview of the different components found in syndication systems, in particular looking at the HTTP server and client.

❑ Chapter 20 looks at the model behind information feeds from several different viewpoints, from a simple document through XML to object-oriented and relational approaches.

❑ Chapter 21 examines various approaches to storing feed data, from XML documents through SQL databases to RDF (Resource Description Framework) stores.

❑ Chapter 22 looks at the common details of applications that consume information feeds, covering important aspects of the HTTP protocol and simple XML techniques.

❑ Chapter 23 goes deeper into the issues facing the developer of applications that will consume feeds, looking at approaches to dealing with poor-quality data.

❑ Chapter 24 moves to the publishing side of syndication, discussing factors common among content management systems and demonstrating how feeds can be produced.

❑ Chapter 25 introduces two key XML technologies, XQuery and XSLT, and demonstrates how these can be powerful tools for the RSS/Atom developer.

❑ Chapter 26 looks at the design of client applications used in content authoring, subsystems closely associated with information feeds.

❑ Chapter 27 discusses what's needed to build a tool to aggregate information from multiple feeds, providing a simple implementation.

❑ Chapter 28 looks at the requirements of a desktop aggregator, with a demonstration application showing how a programmer might get started building such a tool.

❑ Chapter 29 discusses social applications of syndication and in that context demonstrates how applications could exploit feed data alongside FOAF (Friend of a Friend) information.

❑ Chapter 30 looks at using information feeds for publishing multimedia content, using a simple "podcast" recording application as a demonstration.

❑ Chapter 31 explores some of the other formats and protocols that help connect the space around information feeds.

❑ Chapter 32 takes a brief look at the possible future of information feeds.

What You Need to Use This Book

RSS and Atom can be used in a wide range of settings. Therefore we provide you with example projects using a range of programming languages, including Python, Java, PHP, and C#.

Virtually all the tools used in this book are available for download without charge from their respective authors. Links to useful sites are provided in Chapter 18 and in the individual chapters where we put specific tools to use.

Conventions

To help you get the most from the text and keep track of what's happening, we've used a number of conventions throughout the book.

Try It Out

The *Try It Out* is an exercise you should work through, following the text in the book.

1. Each *Try It Out* usually consists of a set of steps.

2. Each step has a number.

3. Follow the steps through with your copy of the database.

How It Works

After each *Try It Out*, the code you've typed will be explained in detail.

> **Boxes like this one hold important, not-to-be-forgotten information that is directly relevant to the surrounding text.**

Tips, hints, tricks, and asides to the current discussion are offset and placed in italics like this.

As for styles in the text:

❑ We use *italics* for new terms and important words when we introduce them.

❑ We show keyboard strokes like this: Ctrl+A.

❑ We show file names, URLs, and code within the text like so: `persistence.properties`.

❑ We present code in two different ways:

```
In code examples we highlight new and important code with a gray background.
```

```
The gray highlighting is not used for code that's less important in the present
context, or has been shown before.
```

Source Code

As you work through the examples in this book, you may choose either to type in all the code manually or to use the source code files that accompany the book. All the source code used in this book is available for download at `www.wrox.com`. When at the site, simply locate the book's title (either by using the Search box or by using one of the title lists) and click the Download Code link on the book's detail page to obtain all the source code for the book.

Because many books have similar titles, you may find it easiest to search by ISBN; this book's ISBN is 0-7645-7916-9.

After you download the code, just decompress it with your favorite compression tool. Alternatively, you can go to the main Wrox code download page at www.wrox.com/dynamic/books/download.aspx to see the code available for this book and all other Wrox books.

Errata

We make every effort to ensure that there are no errors in the text or in the code. However, no one is perfect, and mistakes do occur. If you find an error in one of our books, like a spelling mistake or faulty piece of code, we would be very grateful for your feedback. By sending in errata you may save another reader hours of frustration, and at the same time you will be helping us provide even higher quality information.

To find the errata page for this book, go to www.wrox.com and locate the title using the Search box or one of the title lists. Then, on the book details page, click the Book Errata link. On this page you can view all errata that has been submitted for this book and posted by Wrox editors. A complete book list including links to each book's errata is also available at www.wrox.com/misc-pages/booklist.shtml.

If you don't spot "your" error on the Book Errata page, go to www.wrox.com/contact/techsupport.shtml and complete the form there to send us the error you have found. We'll check the information and, if appropriate, post a message to the book's errata page and fix the problem in subsequent editions of the book.

p2p.wrox.com

For author and peer discussion, join the P2P forums at p2p.wrox.com. The forums are a Web-based system for you to post messages relating to Wrox books and related technologies and interact with other readers and technology users. The forums offer a subscription feature to e-mail you topics of interest of your choosing when new posts are made to the forums. Wrox authors, editors, other industry experts, and your fellow readers are present on these forums.

At http://p2p.wrox.com you will find a number of different forums that will help you not only as you read this book, but also as you develop your own applications. To join the forums, just follow these steps:

1. Go to p2p.wrox.com and click the Register link.

2. Read the terms of use and click Agree.

3. Complete the required information to join as well as any optional information you want to provide and click Submit.

4. You will receive an e-mail with information describing how to verify your account and complete the joining process.

You can read messages in the forums without joining P2P, but in order to post your own messages, you must join.

After you join, you can post new messages and respond to messages other users post. You can read messages at any time on the Web. If you would like to have new messages from a particular forum e-mailed to you, click the Subscribe to this Forum icon by the forum name in the forum listing.

For more information about how to use the Wrox P2P, be sure to read the P2P FAQs for answers to questions about how the forum software works as well as many common questions specific to P2P and Wrox books. To read the FAQs, click the FAQ link on any P2P page.

Part I

Understanding the Issues and Taking Control

Managing the Flow of
Information: A Crucial Skill

RSS and Atom are about information. More specifically, they are about information flows. They exist in a complex setting that involves many technical issues. Some of these issues are heavily programming orientated, and we will write about them at some length in later chapters of this book. However, there are many other factors that are important in considering the use of RSS and Atom, including interface issues and human usability issues. These issues are important determinants in how RSS and Atom information feeds are best used and influence when and how they work most effectively.

Your success in a rapidly changing information-oriented society is going to depend, at least in part, on how well you handle the flows of information that reach your computer, whether it is a traditional desktop machine, a laptop, or some other device. Similarly, the success of the software you create will depend on how much it helps your users meet their information needs.

> **The processing of information is undergoing a major paradigm shift with progressively wider adoption of RSS in its various versions and the emerging Atom format. The existence of automated information flows is changing fundamentally how we access and use information.**

RSS and Atom are simply two tools that enable developers to provide better access to information for users. One of the big changes that RSS and Atom are bringing about is improved access to all kinds of information for many types of users. It is no exaggeration to say that there is a prospect of everybody with Internet access being able to access all the information that they can handle. The changes in information flow that are already under way are immense. How we handle the flow of information is becoming increasingly important.

RSS and Atom don't exist in a vacuum. They are parts of a larger picture of information management. This chapter gives you a broad overview of several of the important issues that impact the use of information.

#### Chapter 1

In this chapter, you learn:

- ❑ How changes in information flow are taking place
- ❑ How to think about your information needs
- ❑ How to think about the information needs of your customers

New Vistas of Information Flow

The existence of RSS and Atom information feeds, or information flows, are opening up new possibilities in how information can be shared and accessed. Because information is easier and easier to access, software developers and software users must begin thinking about new and different issues.

> In this chapter, and elsewhere in the book, the term *information flow* refers to the notion of movements, or flows, of information. The term *information feed* refers to the more specific notion of flows of information that use RSS or Atom.

The Information Well and Information Flow

For newcomers to the world of information feeds, the terminology and concepts can be far from clear. This section explains our view of some of the changes that have begun and presents them within the larger context of technological changes that have taken place in various localities over hundreds of years. The changes in information flow will take place in a much shorter time span, but we hope the analogy will be helpful to newcomers to this field.

In the sections that follow, we use the analogy of how access to water and supply of water has progressed over time to illustrate what might otherwise seem a very abstract overview of information supply and management.

The Information Well

Consider that water was, and in some places still is, drawn from a well. Access to Web-based information until recently was similar to how a villager in a remote African village accesses water. It had to be done repeatedly and each time one sought out information, he or she had to take time to get to the source of the information. We had to go there every day that we needed information or wanted to see if there was new relevant information available, just as someone has to carry water from the well each time it was needed.

In an information society we need information to survive. Going individually to single Web sites or Web pages to check for updated information is an inefficient use of time. It is a strategy that is deficient in that we only go to places we already know.

Search engines can help reduce the inefficiency of that approach, because we can go to the Google site, or similar search engine, to look in one place for all the new information. Again, since the same search might be done repeatedly, the process is potentially inefficient.

Facilities in browsers, such as bookmarks, help to alleviate the repetitive nature of visiting individual Web sites. More recent features, such as the capability in Mozilla Firefox to open a folder of bookmarks with a single click, help to alleviate the repetitive nature of resuming online research at a particular point in the search.

Fundamentally, though, we are walking each day, or several times each day, to the online information well.

The Information Flow

Most of us live in homes where water comes to us, rather than us having to travel to the water. It makes a lot of sense that information, too, should flow to us. It avoids the repetitive actions of going to visit individual Web sites and, if done well, achieves easier, more efficient and more effective access to information.

Naturally, to set up information flows in an appropriate way takes time. Hopefully, the time spent customizing the information flows you see will be a largely one-time inconvenience, a little like the one-time inconvenience of laying water pipes. Because information is not a single entity, as water is, the situation is more complex and the analogy is too simple. But I hope that you see that having information flow to users is potentially much more efficient than having the users visit individual Web sites multiple times a day.

The Information Flood

At times, once information flows have been set up, typically using RSS or Atom information feeds, the problem is not in accessing information but being overwhelmed by the volume of information.

There are also parallels with the quality of water and of information. After a flood or tsunami water is plentiful but not all water is usable. Just as we want to find clean water in such a situation so, when dealing with information, do we need to assess information quality and reliability.

The flow of information is becoming an overwhelming flood. At the time of writing the number of information feeds is measured in millions. The total number of feeds may be approaching 10,000,000 of which roughly half may be active. Estimates vary. The reality is that nobody really knows exactly how many feeds there are. It is clear that the number is so large that the individual user has to have mechanisms to prevent the flood of information from preventing them from locating the information they need.

Managing Information

Efficiently and effectively managing information is a crucial skill both for individuals and for businesses. In a highly competitive business environment, efficiency in handling information is a key competitive tool. Businesses (or individuals) that handle information inefficiently compared to their competitors will fall behind.

The ability to locate relevant information in a timely and efficient way can help you succeed in the information economy in which we all now have to work. Several general questions are important with regard to the how information is best handled.

What Do You Want to Do with Information?

Information is not, of course, identical to water but the parallels continue. Just as you might want to use some water for drinking and some for washing, so some information is relevant for a particular purpose and some is not. One of the fundamental steps in information management is to define what you want to do with the information you access.

One line of thinking about information feeds is that the information that is brought to you is purely of transitory interest. In other words, it's temporarily useful and not worth storing. It's news, and will be replaced later today or tomorrow or next week by other information. That line of thinking looks on information as essentially disposable. However, it's not as simple as that. The following sections explore different responses to individual pieces of information.

Browse and Discard

For some information you will very likely simply want to browse the headlines and discard the information (or allow it to be replaced automatically when a feed is updated). Information such as conventional news headlines might fit this category. The majority of them are likely to be skimmed, many are likely to be of little interest if any, and much of the associated content will be left unread. A small proportion of the information (which will likely vary according to your situation) will be sufficiently interesting or relevant to be worth reading. However, much of it won't be of interest and you won't want or need to see it again.

The browsing of headlines is, perhaps, an inescapable chore. Many of them will be irrelevant, but it is possible to scan a large quantity of headlines in a short period of time. Keeping this irrelevant information for lengthy periods of time is not an issue.

Read

Some information will be more important or interesting and you will want to read it. Only after you have begun to read it will you be in a position to assess its current and possible future relevance to you.

Depending on the pressures on your time, you might not have time to read an entire article. Alternatively some articles you read may have content of more than transitory interest. The question of whether and how to keep the information comes into the picture. You have, explicitly or implicitly, to decide whether you want to keep it. Not all tools currently available make that process of longer-term retention of information easy. If you keep it, where are you going to put it so that it is easily retrieved and accessed when you want to review it?

Study and Keep

Some types of information, or information from certain sources, you might want to study in detail and want to keep, perhaps indefinitely. Long-term storage of this information is a significant issue. How should you group items? What search functionality is available in different tools that you can use for storage?

With these different information needs, you must find tools that give you ways to handle all these information types.

Taking Control of Information

You have specific information needs. Chances are you won't find a single tool that meets all of those needs.

> The term *aggregator* is used here for a piece of software that collects, or aggregates, information feeds. Typically you will be able to use an aggregator to subscribe to selected information feeds. Some aggregators have a built-in Web browser.

Aggregators have weaknesses and strengths just like any other class of applications. For example, when you open NewzCrawler or several other aggregators, in their default configurations, they will pop up a frenetic flurry of "pieces of toast" in the right side of your screen, over screen real estate that you might be using for another purpose. Whether listing screens of information that the aggregator has brought to you justifies the visual intrusion will depend on how you use information feeds. If you are interested in information being absolutely up to the minute you will probably want to review new information as soon as it is available and so some visual indication that new information is available is an advantage. Alternatively, you may be keeping a watching brief on a topic and don't need instant notification of new information. You need to be able to configure an aggregator, at an appropriate level of granularity, to give you information that you really want to see and avoid intrusion with information that isn't of a level of importance that justifies interrupting what you are currently doing.

Determining What Is Important to You

There is no shortage of information out there. In fact, the problem in many information domains is that there is too much information. Techniques for finding relevant information are key to successful and effective information flows.

So where do you find useful information? That's a topic we will return to in Chapter 4. For now, your bookmarks and Google searches are obvious places to start. If those pages match your interests there is a reasonable, or better, chance that any information feeds for those sites will also contain information that is interesting and relevant to you.

Avoiding Irrelevant Information

With increased amounts of available information, there is a growing need to filter out information that is not relevant to you. Time spent scanning headlines can be significant. Time spent exploring the "Oh that looks interesting" items can consume inordinate amounts of time, but not actually achieve anything useful.

One way to avoid, or reduce, irrelevant information is to choose carefully what feeds you subscribe to. However, many feeds contain diverse information and only a relatively small proportion of the information may be of direct relevance to you. Some aggregators enable the user to create filters so that certain types of post are hidden or only posts that contain keywords specified by the user are displayed. These techniques reduce the amount of irrelevant information, but at the risk of excluding interesting information present in the information feed.

If the topics of interest to you are rapidly changing ones and having a lead, however slender, over your competitors is a key issue, you might be willing to pay the price of screening all new feed items. For example, you might be a stock trader and want to be aware of rapidly changing stock prices, to help you buy or sell at an advantageous price. In this case, screening a stock ticker feed might be preferable in some circumstances to missing out on a key lead that happens not to use the key terms that you have put on your watch list. I don't think there is any way to avoid this trade-off of scanning time versus the risk of missing interesting material.

Determining the Quality of Information

One of the important issues of online information is whether or not it is trustworthy. There are many levels of trust. For example, it would a mistake to give your bank account details in response to an e-mail without checking very carefully that the e-mail is from a legitimate source. But trust in the context of information feeds is likely to consist more of the idea of a source of information being reliable for accuracy rather than moral trustworthiness.

However, there are situations where trust comes into play. If you are reading the blog of a corporate blogger, how can you know whether or not he or she will give you an honest view? Being a corporate blogger is a difficult position. The blogger, almost inevitably, needs to more or less toe the company line. But if the corporate blogger does that too tidily then he or she is unlikely to retain readers for long. Over time, a reader has to form a judgment about whether the individual blogger is trustworthy.

Judgment of a more technical nature comes into play if you are following a blog about possible upcoming technical trends. Does the blogger have a good grasp of technical trends? Does he or she have a track record of getting things right in the past? To apply the water metaphor again, is the water of good quality or not?

Information Flows Other Than the Web

The issues regarding access to information are not new. Some have been present for centuries, but in different forms than those of the present day. Access to information today is unprecedented. A century or two ago it is almost unthinkable that anyone except the privileged few would have had access to the amount of information available on the Web today. In fact, even the richest and most powerful in society would operate in deep ignorance compared to average citizens in today's world.

This section briefly explores some information-related issues that have contributed to the success of other information media over the centuries. Depending on nature of the information conveyed, any proposed solution that uses RSS and Atom must be examined in the light of the strengths of more established media. Sometimes there will be no contest. For example, books cannot be in print instantly in the way that an RSS or Atom information feed can be available globally almost instantly after it is created.

Users, typically, won't care whether an information flow uses RSS or Atom. They want their information needs met. Seeing things from the user's point of view is key to designing and implementing quality information flow solutions.

Books

Books have been around for some 500 years. There must have been good reasons to keep a pretty stable format for such an extended period. One possibility is that no superior technology came along during that time. Until the advent of radio that was, perhaps, true. Another factor is that a book has a huge convenience factor that online reading can't yet match. Try reading online during a power outage. During a power outage a computer becomes a useless piece of metal and plastic. Yet the low-tech book can, at least during daylight hours, continue to be read as normal.

Books still offer advantages for very large documents, because you can easily create your own bookmarks. In Web pages you have to rely on bookmarks that the document author has created. In addition, many people simply don't want to read for sustained periods of time onscreen. Books are more convenient to read for long periods of time. Many people simply don't like reading text onscreen for long periods.

Magazines

Magazines have, typically, different content from many non-fiction books. The articles are typically shorter, although often longer than a typical technically orientated blog post. Will information feeds, if a suitable business model can be found, increasingly replace magazines? I suspect that process is already happening. I used to subscribe to several computing-related magazines. Currently I subscribe to two. The others fell by the wayside, in part because I increasingly found them repeating information that I had seen on the Web or in information feeds some weeks earlier. The two magazines that I continue to subscribe to have what I would view as relatively meaty technical articles. I guess that similar articles are available online, but there is something satisfying about reading something in print rather than onscreen.

Newspapers

Newspapers, with rare exceptions, publish on a much faster timescale than a typical book or magazine. Twenty-four hours later that same newspaper and its content may have been discarded, used to wrap fish and chips (at least in the United Kingdom), or be burned or composted.

As mentioned elsewhere, handling news is where some protagonists of information feeds see their only role — providing information that is up-to-date and essentially disposable. Information feeds can compete with, and exceed, the speed of publication of newspapers.

Attitudes toward newspapers are slowly changing. People are finding more of the up-to-date information on the Web, through blogs and online news sites. The issue of reliability of information again features highly when choosing an online source of information. An increasing number of people are beginning to replace their newspapers with their newspapers' corresponding Web sites or a diverse range of online news sites. Surveys, such as the Online Publishers Association Generation study (`www.online-publishers.org/pdf/opa_generational_study_sep04.pdf`), suggest that newspapers are potentially under threat from online media including aggregators. Some data (for example, `www.wired.com/news/culture/0,1284,65813,00.html`) suggest that in some age groups newspaper subscriptions can't even be given away for free anymore.

Broadcast Media

Broadcast media have characteristics that are different from any paper-based media such as books, magazines, and newspapers. They can achieve instant coverage of chosen issues but suffer from a linear manner of presentation. For example, if I want a weather forecast from my favorite radio station I need to be listening at the exact time it is broadcast. Sometimes that is inconvenient for me. An online source of that information is more convenient.

Broadcast media also have significant production costs and other production issues. This has, for such practical reasons, limited the number of broadcasters. In some countries a business model of broadcasts serving up audiences to advertisers has been prominent. Blogging and the dissemination of blogged information through information feeds have greatly reduced production costs and therefore have opened up an online analog of broadcasting to a potentially wide audience.

The Web and Information Feeds

The Web when it was first widely available was in a way both wonderful and at the same time difficult to use. I first used the Web in 1994 in a text-based browser. At that time finding information was, as I recall, slow and clumsy. There was no Google although there were search facilities. Just finding my way around what then seemed to be a flood of information was intimidating and slow, in part because I had to navigate in a way wholly unlike anything I had done when using books, library catalogs, and so on. I can still remember the feelings of finding something interesting then, a little later, being totally unable to find it again. Tools have changed in the intervening decade and my familiarity with the metaphor of the Web means that things I found clumsy and disorientating in the early days are now routine.

Similarly, the arrival of information feeds will, I expect, seem confusing to some audiences. Currently I think it's likely that those using information feeds are largely a technically literate audience. When a wider, less technically literate, audience has information feeds made available to them, the usability of aggregators and other tools will be key factors in uptake. If the aggregator or other tool is hard for a beginner to use, then it is likely to lose out in market share to more usable products, whatever positive attributes your product may otherwise have.

New Information Opportunities

The existence of RSS and Atom and their use on a wide scale bring exciting new information opportunities. The aim, typically, is that you distribute information to significant numbers of people through an information feed. A host of issues then arises. How do you get your site or feed noticed? How do you keep the interest of those who subscribe to your feed? Such issues are similar to those that affect every Web site, but in an information feed the importance of the headline or title is crucial. If that doesn't catch the attention of users as they scan a list of titles, readers will be drawn into viewing your blog entries or Web pages. Getting people to subscribe to the information feed is essential but it's not enough. You need to be able to draw them into the content that lies behind the headlines.

New Information Problems

With increased flows of information one practical problem is how to handle the flood of information that is available to us. Some ubergeeks, Robert Scoble of Microsoft being one (`http://radio.weblogs .com/0001011/`), claim to review several hundred information feeds each day. At the time of writing, Scoble claimed to review 957 feeds each day.

Most users of information feeds won't attempt to follow that number of feeds, since doing so will demand a substantial time commitment each day. Many users will simply not be able to devote the required amount of time to scan and absorb relevant information.

The Need to Keep Up-to-Date

The knowledge that your competitors, in whatever field you work, can have access to essentially unlimited information flows can create a feeling of having to keep up. That pressure to keep up combined with the practical difficulties of absorbing and handling such continual large flows of information can cause so-called information anxiety. Attempting to monitor an unrealistically large number of information feeds can produce so-called *feed fatigue*.

Distractions

Another human factor in information feed management is distraction. If you subscribe to large numbers of feeds it is all too easy to spend time exploring articles or blog posts that are interesting but probably not directly relevant to what you do. When you have large numbers of diverse feed subscriptions, being disciplined and not following distracting posts can be far from easy. This issue is not dissimilar to the reasons that some companies banned employees from surfing the Web during working hours. The costs to companies of distracting information feed items could be substantial.

Summary

Information flows are likely to be the key to efficient information management over the next several years. Delivery of information through RSS and Atom information feeds opens up new opportunities for delivery of content to users. At the same time, the volume of information that's delivered to users through information feeds raises new issues of information management for individuals and for businesses; for example, how to select reliable information and how to cope with large numbers of feed items.

In this chapter you learned that...

❑   RSS and Atom provide a new metaphor of access to Web-based information—instead of going to the information well, user can now access information as easy as piped water in their homes.

❑   Selecting appropriate information is key to efficient information management.

❑   New issues arise as the spectrum of users who will use aggregators moves from being a highly technical audience to a more general one.

Exercise

1.   Review the bookmarks and favorites in the browser(s) that you use to see which sites provide information that you might want to include in an information feed. Consider how you might need to filter the information from some sites so that you get the information that you want.

Where Did Information Feeds Start?

The precise date when information feeds started is debatable depending on which aspects of information feeds or similar technologies are viewed as seminal. This chapter takes the view that information feeds started with the My Netscape portal, which aggregated content from many sources in a portal that could be customized by the user. The My Netscape portal provided a way for users to have a customized Web page where the information that interested them was what they saw. On the vast majority of Web sites at that time the information presented to a user was standardized for all users and what the user saw was the information that the Web site author chose.

For users to be able to define the information that was presented to them was a fairly radical departure from the previous situation on the Web, whereby users were largely passive recipients of information. Even when, the user saw only Web pages with non-customized content there was limited interactivity, such as clicking on hyperlinks and, of course, a user could choose which sites to visit. However, when users were able to influence or determine page content, things began to change.

In this chapter you learn about:

❑   The history of information feeds

❑   The history of the various versions of RSS

The Nature of the Web

My Netscape didn't occur in a vacuum. Several other technologies and factors were required to be in place for the customization of content to be possible.

Many factors are essential to the creation and delivery of information feeds. Some of those factors are related to the invisible infrastructure of the Web; others to its more visible parts.

HTTP

The existence of a physical network infrastructure was, of course, essential to being able to move information feeds around once they were created. In addition a transport protocol, or pair of transport protocols (in this context TCP/IP), needed to be in place. All information on the Web is sent in TCP/IP packets. On a physical system that's not totally reliable, the use of TCP/IP produces a remarkable approximation to reliability.

Over those protocols HTTP, the Hypertext Transport Protocol, is in place. When information feeds are retrieved by a browser or by an aggregator, retrieval is done using HTTP. For example, the URL for the information feed for my blog is located at `http://www.tfosorcim.org/blog/index.rdf`. HTTP is used in retrieving the RSS 1.0 document, which constitutes the information feed document for the blog.

If the physical and software infrastructure had not been in place, it would not have been possible to implement generally available information feeds, at least not in the way that they were implemented.

HTML

HTML, the HyperText Markup Language, was also a key part in the use and acceptance of information feeds. HTML, and more recently XHTML, has been the display format chosen for the Web pages represented as items in an information feed.

Converting RSS (and later Atom) information feeds to HTML was a relatively straightforward task. Scripting languages, such as Perl, were familiar to many programmers. And software modules were created which allowed the creation of HTML (or XHTML) from RSS and, later, Atom. Some software modules use XML parsing (discussed in more detail in the next section), whereas others treated an information feed as text. When faced with a malformed feed that didn't meet the well-formedness constraints of XML (discussed in Chapter 6), the use of regular expressions can support appropriate handling of the character sequences in the information feed and an HTML page can be created that the aggregator or a Web browser can display to the user.

XML

If an RSS or Atom feed has been created correctly, then the information feed document should be well-formed XML. In that case the feed document can be parsed using widely available XML parsers and each component part of the feed document can be displayed according to choices specified by the author of the aggregator or by the user.

XML software tools are available for many platforms. For example, XSLT transformations can be used to transform all or part of the feed document in ways to make it suitable for display.

Polling the Web

An aggregator polls a specified URL, using HTTP, to find an information feed. Once the feed document has been retrieved, it is parsed and, depending on the approach taken by the aggregator writer, all or parts of the retrieved information is displayed to the users. Figure 2-1 shows the appearance of the information feed from `www.tfosorcim.org/blog/index.rdf` in Mozilla Thunderbird 0.9.

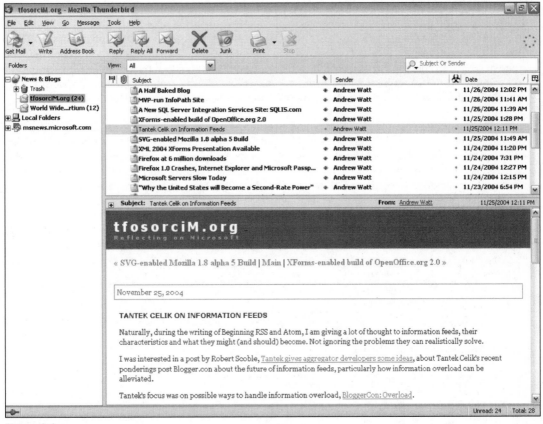

Figure 2-1

As you can see in the following code snippet, the information item contains information about a blog post. From that information the aggregator creates a display. The content of the `title` element is displayed in the highlighted line in the upper part of Thunderbird, together with the content of the `dc:creator` and `dc:date` elements. The content of the `dc:date` element is formatted in a way that makes it more acceptable to the human reader. Thunderbird doesn't display the content of the `link` element or the `description` element. The content of the `link` element is a URL used to retrieve the blog post and display it in the bottom pane of Thunderbird.

```
<item rdf:about="http://www.tfosorcim.org/archives/000277.html">
<title>Tantek Celik on Information Feeds</title>
<link>http://www.tfosorcim.org/archives/000277.html</link>
<description>Naturally, during the writing of Beginning RSS and Atom, I am giving
 a lot of thought to information feeds, their characteristics and what they
 might (and should) become. Not ignoring the problems they can realistically
 solve. I was interested in...</description>
<dc:subject>Information Feeds</dc:subject>
<dc:creator>Andrew Watt</dc:creator>
<dc:date>2004-11-25T12:11:09+00:00</dc:date>
</item>
```

The appearance of the same information feed item in RSS Bandit is shown in Figure 2-2. As you can see, the contents of the `item` element are processed in a noticeably different way. In the highlighted line in the upper pane, the contents of the `title`, `dc:date`, and `dc:subject` elements are displayed. The content of the `description` element is displayed in the lower pane. The content of the `link` element is displayed toward the top left of the RSS Bandit window. The content of the `dc:creator` element is displayed toward the upper part of the lower pane, together with the content of the `dc:date` and `title` elements, all laid out in a way that makes for ease of reading by a human reader.

The information feed simply supplies a number of feed items. In RSS 1.0 they are contained in `item` elements and their associated child elements. How an aggregator or similar software module processes and displays those basic pieces of information is what serves to differentiate one aggregator from another. As we discuss elsewhere, ease of use of aggregators and ease of customization are likely to be significant determining factors differentiating successful from less successful aggregators. They all receive the same information from the RSS and Atom feeds to which a user subscribes.

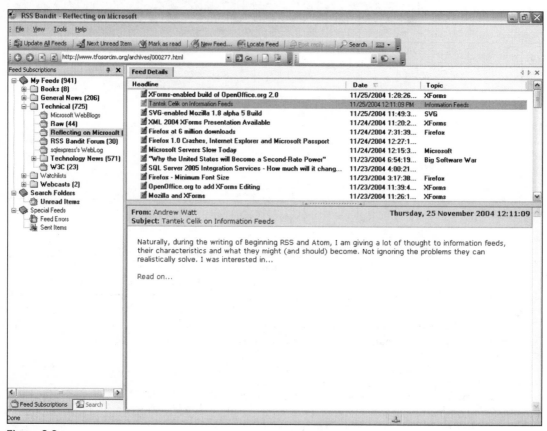

Figure 2-2

Precursors to RSS

This section briefly describes technologies that led to RSS and Atom. Some of the technologies mentioned contained key concepts that have been carried forward into RSS and Atom.

MCF and HotSauce

One way of looking at information feeds is as metadata that informs users about the content available for viewing. Work on information feeds, in that sense, began to reach a wider audience in the mid-1990s. The Meta Content Framework (MCF) was intended to provide information about content available on Web sites, on FTP sites, and in relational and other databases. MCF was intended to document the relationships among objects. It was a research project, associated with Apple, but it was intended to have practical outcomes.

> **Information about MCF is located at** `www.xspace.net/hotsauce/mcf.html`, **and information about HotSauce is located at** `www.xspace.net/hotsauce/`.

The MCF research project led to a product, HotSauce, which allowed Apple users to browse Web sites that had MCF data. In 1996, HotSauce seemed set for growth, but a change of management at Apple led to a loss of momentum in the MCF project and the associated HotSauce metadata browser. Some key staff then left the project.

While the MCF project at Apple languished, the concepts of MCF were developed further in an XML context to create the Resource Description Framework (RDF).

Netscape Channels

One of the individuals associated with Apple's MCF project was Ramanathan Guha, who moved to Netscape around the time that support for MCF from Apple management lessened. Around the same time interest in the embryonic XML specification was growing. The XML specification became a W3C Recommendation in February 1998. In addition, MCF was one of the technologies used to formulate the RDF specification at the W3C. RDF used XML as one of its serialization formats. RDF was used by Netscape in version 0.9 of RSS. At that time RSS stood for *RDF Site Summary*.

> **At the time of writing, a copy of the My Netscape documentation relating to RSS 0.90, apparently copied from the Google cache of the original, was accessible at** `www.purplepages.ie/RSS/netscape/rss0.90.html`.

For reasons that aren't entirely clear to the outside observer, Netscape lost interest in RSS, partly perhaps because of unease about how RDF did or didn't fit into an information feed document. At the time RDF was pretty new, and many who created software for the Web were only beginning to adjust to the existence of XML. Also, taking RDF on board seemed to some a step too far to expect software authors to accept. In the end My Netscape used RSS 0.91, which didn't use RDF. The My Netscape portal site closed in April 2001.

We will return to the various versions of RSS in a moment after a brief look at a similar Microsoft technology of that era, the Channel Definition Format (CDF).

The Microsoft Channel Definition Format

Like RDF Site Summary 0.90, CDF used the then-embryonic XML. A March 1997 Microsoft document, located at `www.w3.org/TR/NOTE-CDFsubmit.html`, contains a description of CDF.

Like RSS, CDF had a `channel` element which, among many other child elements, included a number of `item` elements.

CDF was intended to serve a similar purpose as Netscape's RSS. Microsoft envisaged users subscribing to channels that Microsoft would supply. My recollection of CDF was that it felt as if it were information being pushed at me by Microsoft. The use of the term *webcasting* by Microsoft contributed to that feeling. I didn't feel that it was information that I was choosing. It felt much more as if it were information that Microsoft was telling me that I should have. I was, at the time, very resistant to that notion. I suspect that others shared that sort of feeling, and uptake of CDF was poor. In the end Microsoft abandoned CDF.

> We think there is a very significant lesson to be learned there for creators of information feeds today. The feed creator needs to give the users the feeling that they are in control. Some creators of feeds are currently attempting to push advertisements into feeds in a way that disguises those advertisements. In time, users will rebel against that approach, just as they have done with pop-up advertisements in Web pages. With so many choices of information available to each user, any feed creator who attempts to push unwanted information at users will quickly lose his audience.

RSS: An Acronym with Multiple Meanings

The following sections briefly describe some salient points about the various versions of RSS that were proposed or released. The history is a little confusing, not least because the versions were not released in the order that the version numbers might suggest. The following table summarizes the chronology.

Technology	Version	Date	Company
RSS	0.9	March 1999	Netscape
RSS	0.91	June 2000	UserLand
RSS	1.0	December 2000	RSS-Dev Working Group
RSS	0.92	December 2000	UserLand
RSS	2.0	September 2002	UserLand
Atom	0.3	December 2003	Mark Nottingham

RSS 0.9

RDF was pivotal to RSS 0.9, as the name RDF Site Summary indicates. After some resistance to the perceived complexity of RDF, RSS 0.91 made an appearance.

RSS 0.91

The term RSS 0.91 is used for two distinctly different flavors of RSS. First, historically, was the Netscape version, which was RDF Site Summary. A little later, when UserLand became involved, RSS was then *Really Simple Syndication*.

The UserLand version of RSS 0.91, which is described in more detail in Chapter 8, continues in widespread use. It was designed to be simple to use by the standards of June 2000. Its simplicity made it easy for automated tools to create RSS 0.91 feeds which, no doubt, contributed to its initial and continuing popularity.

RSS 1.0

The way that RSS 0.9x progressed, or failed to progress according to your viewpoint, meant that many in the information feed community who had been attracted by the potential of the RDF-based Netscape flavor of RSS were looking for a flavor of RSS that had the metadata and semantic Web possibilities that RDF brought to the scene.

The enthusiasm for the possibilities for more-sophisticated use of metadata than was possible with RSS 0.91 led to the development of the RDF-based RSS 1.0. RSS 1.0 is described in more detail in Chapter 9.

RSS 0.92, 0.93, and 0.94

Three further 0.9x versions of RSS were specified by UserLand. Of those three versions, version 0.92 was released only a couple of weeks after the RSS-Dev Working Group had released the RSS 1.0 specification.

At that point UserLand was championing RSS 0.92, Really Simple Syndication, and the RSS-Dev Working Group was championing RSS 1.0, RDF Site Summary. By any realistic criteria the RSS world was a political minefield and technically, at least for the newcomer to the minefield, a confusing mess. Given the politics and differences in technical approach of the different versions of RSS it is amazing that there has been such rapid growth in adoption of information feeds. The relative simplicity for an aggregator author creating tools that can accept feeds in essentially any of the flavors of RSS (and later Atom) has likely been a significant factor ensuring the survival of the varied formats used for information feed documents.

Versions 0.93 and 0.94 are essentially of historical interest only.

RSS 2.0

RSS 2.0 was released in September 2002. Its lineage is the UserLand 0.9x family. A newcomer to the field might assume that RSS 2.0 was the replacement for RSS 1.0, which is not the case. The two specifications exist in parallel.

RDF was part of RSS 0.9 and RSS 1.0. RSS 0.91, 0.92, 0.93, 0.94, and 2.0 did not use RDF.

Use of RSS and Atom Versions

The use of RSS 0.91 has persisted surprisingly well, considering that it was nominally replaced by version 0.92 in December 2000 and RSS 2.0 in September 2002. This chapter was written in October 2004, when RSS 0.91 remains in widespread use.

Total information feeds at the time of writing are thought to be approaching 10 million, of which maybe half are active. In order to gain some impression of the relative usage of various versions of RSS and Atom, we used the feeds listed on the Syndic8.com Web site. Given that the numbers of registered feeds is small relative to the total estimated number of feeds, there has to be some uncertainty about exact proportions of usage of the different versions.

RSS 0.91 remains a frequently used information feed technology among the feeds listed on Syndic8.com. RSS 0.91, 1.0, and 2.0 and Atom 0.3 all have widespread usage. RSS 0.92 has significant usage but perhaps an order of magnitude less than the other four technologies just mentioned.

The following table summarizes one set of data, gleaned by exploring Syndic8.com, about the usage of different versions of Atom and RSS current at the time of writing.

Technology	Version	Number of Feeds
Atom	Pre-IETF	20,470
RSS	0.91	41,444
RSS	0.91fn	2
RSS	0.92	1,489
RSS	0.92d2	0
RSS	1.0	15,801
RSS	2.0	37,771
Total Feeds		**80,129**

You may notice that the total number of feeds, 80,129, is less than the sum of the feeds for individual versions. We are not sure as to the cause of the discrepancy. In part it may arise because some feeds provide information in more than one format. However, the purpose of showing the table is simply to capture the relative market share of different flavors of RSS and Atom late in 2004.

Despite the uncertainties about the figures, however, it seems clear that Atom 0.3 (the pre-IETF version), RSS 0.91, RSS 1.0, and RSS 2.0 are the dominant information feed technologies. RSS 0.92 is fifth in the pecking order, an order of magnitude lower than RSS 1.0.

If you want to do a similar analysis on Synic8.com to estimate how market share has changed since this chapter was written, visit the Syndic8.com Web site, select the Feeds link, and use the search facilities to specify format and version to explore how numbers have changed.

Summary

In this chapter you learned that...

- ❑ Information feeds use Internet protocols such as HTTP and TCP/IP.
- ❑ MCF and CDF were precursors of RSS and Atom.
- ❑ Several versions of RSS are still in widespread use.

Exercises

1. Visit Syndic8.com and check out the usage of different flavors of language used in information feeds registered with Syndic8. Use the Search facilities on the Feeds page. This will allow you to see whether usage of different versions of RSS and Atom have changed much since this chapter was written.

2. In your favorite aggregator(s) look for the pieces of information that were displayed in Figures 2.1 and 2.2 to see how the tools you favor handle the information from the elements inside an item element.

The Content Provider Viewpoint

Let's begin with a question that many content providers find difficult to ask: What is the business aim in creating content? You need to know the answer to that fundamental question if you are to design and create your content appropriately and effectively. In practice, many people create content corresponding to their interests and then ask themselves what they can do with it. Whichever way you approach the issue of content creation, when you supply content to users through information feeds, you must consider issues relevant to all content as well as issues specific to content provided in information feeds.

Assuming that you have made the decision to give your content away, how do you go about ensuring that your content is read by as many people as possible?

In this chapter you learn:

- ❑ Why many content providers are often delighted to "give their content away"
- ❑ What content might be appropriate to include in a feed and considerations in how to present it effectively to the user
- ❑ How to maximize the number of users who will find your feed
- ❑ About issues that influence whether RSS and Atom will increase or decrease your site's visibility
- ❑ About issues relating to advertising in RSS feeds

Why Give Your Content Away?

One of the questions raised from time to time in RSS and Atom communities is the question of why content providers should give their content away. The answers relevant to you or your business depend importantly on the business model you have chosen.

Information can be a valuable commodity. Regardless of whether you are creating content as a hobby or as part of your job, it costs money to create it, either directly when you pay someone to write it, or indirectly when time spent creating content could be spent doing other things for your business, such as writing code. Why then should you, as a content provider, consider giving away that content without payment? Of course, the same question could apply to the existence of a Web site. Why would you give its content away to anyone who happens to visit it?

Two broad reasons come to mind as to why you might give content away through an information feed:

❑ It is good advertising or publicity for you or your business.

❑ It's a hobby.

Assuming that the first of the two reasons just mentioned is the motivating factor for you, there are many reasons that can make it a sensible choice to give content away. The following list contains some of the more specific reasons that may be relevant for you to consider.

❑ Everyone else is doing it. As users increasingly use information feeds to find information relevant to their needs, if you don't have an information feed then you will be at a competitive disadvantage.

❑ It can increase the flow of traffic to your site.

❑ It can increase awareness of your company, product, or Web site. If your content is highly visible in a particular topic area then visibility through an information feed can be a useful form of free advertising.

❑ The existence of an information feed can influence search engine rankings. It can do this indirectly depending on how other sites link to your own. The more your site is known the more links to it are likely to be made.

Taken together, these reasons make it important for many businesses to put content online through an information feed.

Selling Your Content

Many content providers will give their content away for nothing, recognizing the direct and indirect benefits for their businesses of increased online exposure. However, some types of information may have sufficient business value that the information feed can be made available on a paid-for subscription basis.

Some online magazines charge for access to information. It seems likely that as information feeds become accepted more widely that it will be increasingly difficult for online magazines, other than specialized ones, to justify charging for access to content. Using one of the various online tools described in Chapter 17, users will be able to identify quickly which information feeds contain emerging information relevant to their interests. Because that information will be more than enough to satisfy the information needs of most users, the need to have paid-for subscriptions regarding similar content becomes problematic.

Creating Community

Information feeds impact the creation of communities in several ways. If you can reach a significant number of users and induce them to subscribe to your feed the community can, potentially, grow rapidly. The down side of that scenario is that a competing community, if it publicizes itself effectively, may equally quickly attract your community away.

Another factor is that an information feed is a pretty impersonal form of "community." If a user is only scanning item titles from your feed at the same time as he is scanning item titles from several others, it might be difficult for your feed to stand out.

Content to Include in a Feed

A fundamental question when creating a feed is what parts of the information on your Web site, blog, or other information source you want to make available in an information feed. How you present it is also important.

The Importance of Item Titles

If you look at your information feed from the viewpoint of a new or recent subscriber, you will realize that they may spend most of their contact with your feed simply scanning the feed item titles. If the only thing in your feed that a user may see to draw them in to your site is the list of item titles, it is hopefully clear that you need to think carefully about what goes into the item title.

It is important to give users information to draw them into your site. An item title like "XYZCompany announces XYZ product" is much less likely to draw in a user who has never heard of XYZProduct than an item title like, "XYZProduct relieves information overload by novel filtering." You may choose not to even mention the product, instead using a title like, "Approaches to solving information overload."

Conflict is always an effective way to draw some users into a site. Disagreement somehow always seems more lively than everybody quietly agreeing about a topic. Which of the following titles would you read, "Experts argue over Microsoft's XML implementation" or "XML is accepted by everybody"?

Of course, you need to be sure that your Web page content's quality and coverage matches what is promised by the title. There is an old established principle of crying wolf. Item titles that lead to boring Web pages can have a similar effect. Users disappointed by previous item teaser titles might simply avoid looking at your most important blog posting or product announcement of the year.

Internal Links

If your item titles promise an interesting read, they are likely to draw users into your site. The first paragraph on each Web page or blog post is crucially important in keeping them on your site. If that first paragraph is boring or doesn't hint at more interesting material to come later in the post, then it is very easy for a visitor to leave your site.

Another useful technique is to include at least one relevant link to another page or post in your site that is relevant to the current topic. If the reader is genuinely interested in that topic you may keep them on your site for some time. Placing relevant internal links in the first paragraph of a page or post can make it easier to keep a user in your site.

One Feed or Several?

There are several reasons why you might want to think about how many feeds to create for your site.

One consideration is the volume of information. If you are running a personal blog on a single topic you may very likely want to include all your posts in a single information feed for that blog. On the other hand, if you are, for example, IBM or Microsoft, or even one division within a company of that size, the volume of information relating to that division's Web site and various blogs could be totally overwhelming. If subscribers to your information are not to be overloaded with information it makes a lot of sense to split the information into several information feeds.

Another, albeit less important, consideration is the issue of which versions of RSS and Atom aggregators can handle. Most of the popular aggregators will handle any well-written feed document in any of the versions of RSS and Atom, and many of the aggregators will also handle a range of malformed feed documents.

Structuring Topics

How do you best structure the content within a feed? If you have a technically oriented feed, assigning feed items to an individual topic may be straightforward. However, if you like to mix technical content with other content, perhaps photos of your cats (see, for example, www.dannyayers.com), you may want to add a "personal" or "pets" topic so that readers interested in only technical content can skip such personal content or readers interested in getting to know the blogger better can easily spot such items.

Blogging Tools

Many information feeds are now created automatically using tools such as Movable Type (see www .movabletype.org/). This means that many content creators don't need to bother with the details of how to create an information feed.

In Movable Type, for example, you simply type desired content in the appropriate box, adding HTML elements where necessary (see Figure 3-1).

Figure 3-1

When the post is published to the Web site, the necessary markup is created for each post. The following example shows the feed `item` automatically created in the RSS 1.0 feed for the post in Figure 3.1:

```
<item rdf:about="http://www.tfosorcim.org/archives/000288.html">
<title>SQL Server 2005 Webcasts Next Week</title>
<link>http://www.tfosorcim.org/archives/000288.html</link>
<description>As mentioned in an earlier post, SQL Server 2005 Developer Webcasts,
  there is a raft of SQL Server 2005 webcasts next week. Visit SQL Server Developer
  Center to sign up for any remaining available places....</description>
<dc:subject>SQL Server 2005</dc:subject>
<dc:creator>Andrew Watt</dc:creator>
<dc:date>2004-11-29T10:23:04+00:00</dc:date>
</item>
```

If your Web site is not a blog then you will need to become familiar with the techniques for creating an information feed. Commonly used techniques including so-called *self-scraping* (where a tool examines the content of Web pages and makes decisions about how they can be presented as feed items) and *feed integration* (where you integrate a software module that can generate RSS or Atom into the server-side scripting technologies that assemble your Web pages).

Wikis

Wiki software may, depending on the implementation, provide automatic creation of information feeds, or require you to add an appropriate software module to the relevant scripting language.

Publicizing Your Information Feed

We have discussed what should go in the information feed(s) that you create. But the best information feed in the world is essentially useless if nobody knows it's there. So, by one technique or another, you need to decide on an audience and go out there and attract their attention.

Deciding on a Target Audience

Who do you want to see the information contained in your information feed? There is no point sending information to the wrong audience, for example, sending information about the practicalities of pregnancy to an audience that is made up mostly of 80-year-old men. It's quite simply unlikely to be relevant to their needs.

If the creation of an information feed is an integral part of your business strategy then you should have fully thought through the business purpose of the information feed. In that circumstance you are likely to have a pretty clear idea of who you want to be reading the information feed — people who may become customers for the products or services that the business offers.

If you have an existing customer base or belong to a community in some other sense, you can use those existing contacts to attract subscribers to your information feed. Of course, for that to succeed on an ongoing basis you will need to create a good number of good quality blog posts or Web pages over a worthwhile period of time, sufficient to make a potential subscriber believe that your information feed can offer him interesting content on an ongoing basis.

Building on an existing customer base in a way that gets you word-of-mouth (or word-of-fingertip) publicity can be key in building up interest in your information feed and its site. If your site offers something useful to a significant number of users it is likely that visitor numbers will grow quickly. If you have, for example, a software utility to give away that will bring visitors once, you need to give careful thought to how you keep visitors interested so that they will subscribe to your feed.

Registering with Online Sites

There are several online sites that facilitate the discovery of information feeds. The choice of which site or sites you should actively register likely needs ongoing monitoring. Sites are coming and going, and jockeying for position by offering services which they hope will lead to greater visibility of their site to those who want to publicize individual information feeds.

One of the longer established online registries exists at Syndic8.com (located at `www.syndic8.com/`). To have your site registered on Syndic8.com you need to create an account, then submit basic information about the site and its information feed. Syndic8.com then monitors the site's feed over a short period, to ensure that the feed is active, before it is accepted for listing.

It is an open question whether it is worth registering with individual sites using the technique just described. Other sites such as Technorati.com and Feedster.com allow you to register your site more easily.

As far as I am aware there are no publicly available numbers that indicate which registries (sometimes called *directories*) are the most used. That means that prioritizing the sites with which to register becomes a matter of guesswork, based partly on the buzz around individual sites.

How Information Feeds Can Affect Your Site's Visibility

Only a year or two ago it was a reasonable assumption that adding an RSS or Atom feed that another site would syndicate (the more sites the better) would lead to the visibility of your site increasing. There was relatively little competition. Competition is now becoming more intense and the intensity of competition is likely to increase further.

Now that information feeds are much more widespread, you need to give careful thought, as mentioned before, to how you use an information feed effectively. There is a practical limit to how many feeds any one individual can monitor, whether it is 10, 100, or 1000 feeds. You are competing with other information feeds for space in the user's aggregator. Unless you plan to have intermittent big attractions you will need to keep a flow of content going and that, in reality, is a potentially significant time and resource commitment.

Advertisements and Information Feeds

If you give your content away then you need, by one method or another, to make some income to cover direct costs of creating a site and your time investment, assuming that the site or blog is not simply a hobby. Paid advertising is one way to do that. Of course, if you are using an information feed as a way to attract attention to your company's products or services, then it may be undesirable to add external advertising to the site. You likely don't want information about a competing product appearing on the page where your wonderful new product is announced.

You can add advertisement items to the information feed itself. One site that is currently doing that is Lockergnome, `www.lockergnome.com/`. Personally, I find advertisement items included in an information feed to be as welcome as pop-up and pop-under advertisements on a Web site. It is one reason why I stopped subscribing to Lockergnome's information feed.

If your information feed is to be designed to be a source of significant income from advertising then you will need to attract, for most topics, substantial numbers of visitors. For some products or topic areas payment for click-throughs can be quite rewarding, but for many areas you will need large visitor numbers to make anything near a worthwhile income from a blog or Web site.

If you have a special, high-quality site and can attract good visitor numbers then Google AdWords, `https://adwords.google.com/select/`, can provide a useful source of income. One advantage of Google AdWords is that they are usually pretty carefully targeted ads with no intrusive graphics. People welcome the opportunity to click a Google AdWords sponsored link since the relevance of the advertisement is very high for the topic that they are reading about on a site.

Power to the User?

The pull aspects of information feeds means that it is very easy for a user to simply walk away from your information feed, if they find the presence of advertisements or the way you (or the provider of advertisements) use advertisements in an information feed.

Because one of the purposes of using information feeds is to save time, users are very likely not to want to have irrelevant advertisements placed in their line of thought as they scan titles in an aggregator, whether on the desktop or online. Clicking on what appears to be an interesting information feed item only to find out that it is a link to an advertisement is something almost everyone finds very irritating.

Filtering Out Advertisements

The Abilon aggregator (`www.abilon.org`) and the related ActiveRefresh Web news center (`www.activerefresh.com/`), both of which are described in more detail in Chapter 15, allow the use of filters on information feeds. One possible use for such filters is to prevent the display of advertisements. To set a filter that will, for example, filter out advertisements that use the term AdSense in the text of the ad, you simply create a filter such as the one shown in Figure 3-2.

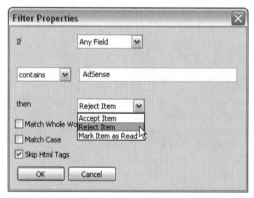

Figure 3-2

After a filter has been created it shows the action to be taken when specified text is found in specified parts of the feed items (see Figure 3-3). Filters can be ordered and combined to create fairly complex decision logic. If you want to continue to a particular feed and you know which advertisements it is using then it is usually pretty easy to block undesired advertisements.

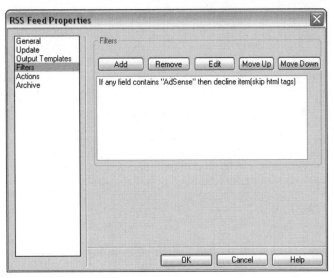

Figure 3-3

Summary

In this chapter issues relevant to the content creator were discussed. You learned that...

- ❑ Giving content away can make good business sense.

- ❑ It is important to make the titles of feed items informative, since it is those titles that a user scans in a desktop aggregator.

- ❑ You need to tailor the content of the information feed to your intended audience.

- ❑ You need to consider carefully whether it is appropriate to include advertising in your information feed.

Exercise

1. If you have an existing information feed that is ready for public viewing, then I suggest you pop along to sites such as Technorati.com, Feedster.com, and Syndic8.com and add your information feed. (Some blogging tools offer automatic connection to one or more online sites. You may want to check which sites you already automatically inform of new posts added to your blog.) As part of your monitoring of the success of your feed you may want to check your server logs to see how your information feed is being used. Individual server software will vary in the information provided.

The Content Recipient Viewpoint

For many practical purposes the content recipient is the most important individual in any information flow. The ultimate purpose of an information feed is to meet the information needs of the content recipient. When you create an information feed it is very important, particularly as competition in this sector increases, that you think carefully about what effect the information that you include in your feed has on users.

The use of information feeds hasn't always recognized the pre-eminence of user information needs. The history of information feeds included such false starts as channels, using the Microsoft Channel Definition Format which, in the view of some users, attempted to impose on the content recipient the content owner's perspective of what data is important. As a result, there was substantial resistance to channels in some contexts.

The reality now is that users have a lot of choices in terms of where they get information from that it is imperative to tailor your information feed to avoid the impression that you are imposing information on users. To succeed in an information environment where there is enormous choice of products and sources of information, the content and the way it is delivered and displayed must meet the content recipient's information needs. You must create information feeds as if the customer is king. Why? Because that is the reality.

In this chapter you learn:

- ❏ About the importance of changes in access to information
- ❏ Which issues impact the content recipient
- ❏ How to find wanted information
- ❏ How to exclude unwanted information

Access to Information

People today who have Internet access have access to quantities of information that probably weren't even dreamed about a couple of decades ago, except by perhaps an exceptional few. The recent changes in how we access information have quickly changed our views about information in radical ways. The effect is comparable in reach to the changes in communication that took place a century ago when the telephone began to enable people to communicate directly and instantly with people living hundreds or even thousands of miles away. Those changes in communication are something we now take for granted, as I suspect we already take for granted the more recent massive changes in how we access information.

With the arrival of the telephone you could make contact with someone living hundreds of miles away. Today I can access information online that I might have had to travel long distances to find, assuming that I had the time, interest, or funds to travel to the universities or major libraries where the information was stored. Traditional information stores are only patchily making their historic stores of information online, but as they continue to do so, information access will change even more.

Perhaps, more relevant to the traditional uses of RSS and Atom is information that has only recently been made available. This can include new information which, conventionally, we call news but also includes any other information that is available for the first time or in a new form. If the content is relevant to your information needs you are likely to want to know about it, however the information might be classified.

As aggregators begin to move into a second generation, we anticipate that users will become more demanding of them. They will want them to be able to do the basic tasks such as subscribing to a feed, updating a feed, filtering a feed and so on as a matter of routine. One of the issues that will differentiate successful aggregators from "also rans" is the way that they meet user needs for convenience.

Convenience

Convenience in accessing information is a growing issue. Convenience in using the interface is one reason why Google has succeeded. More frequently than with any other search engine relevant information is returned to the user. So, over time, Google has moved from being a quaint multicolored search site to being the dominant force in the online search market.

In the aggregator market there are several issues that seem to be crucial in this regard. In other words, we are arriving at a time when the following functionality is not simply essential in a commercial aggregator but also needs to be adjustable to user needs in a convenient and granular way:

- ❑ Subscribing to a feed
- ❑ Updating a single feed or all feeds
- ❑ Customizing frequency of automatic updates
- ❑ Customizing which feed items are displayed onscreen
- ❑ Storing information for the longer term

One other facility that is currently absent from desktop aggregators is the capability to subscribe to information by topic. Some online tools offer that functionality already but with the lower convenience factor characteristic of an online interface.

Timeliness of Access

The timeliness of feeds that will meet your needs will vary according to various criteria. If you are following a topic but don't need to make immediate active use of the information in a feed you may want an aggregator simply to aggregate information so that you can review it at some convenient time. Possibly you won't want the aggregator to display the title or synopsis of each information feed item as soon as it is retrieved.

On the other hand, if regular, timely monitoring of new information is essential so that you can take action in response to changing information you will probably want information to be displayed as soon as it is available. However, that too may vary with changing circumstances. For example, if you are active in the stock market and trading conditions are particularly volatile you may need information frequently, perhaps every minute at particularly frenetic periods of trading. Most of the time stock prices won't be changing fast enough to make such frequency appropriate.

As a developer you need to provide functionality that can be customized to meet changing user information needs.

Timeliness and Data Type

Certain types of data will, almost inevitably, require frequent access to the relevant information feeds. For example, a stockbroker or financial consultant may routinely require minute-by-minute access to information about stock prices. Fruit growers might require a weather feed to get the very latest weather data and forecast for frost or other significant weather.

Other types of data may, for some users at least, never be appropriate to be displayed on arrival. For example, if you follow a couple of dozen blogs daily then it's likely you won't want intrusions on your screen each time a blog post happens to be retrieved in an information feed. Therefore the aggregator software that you write would benefit from an option to customize behavior to display the arrival of new information feed items.

Timeliness and Data Source

The issue of timeliness and data type is one for aggregator developers. However, another factor relating to timeliness applies to feed creators. The question is whether a feed provides information often enough and close enough to real time to allow a user to make decisions based on the information contained in the feed. For example, if you are trading stocks looking only for long-term gains it may not be important to you that stock prices in a feed are 15 minutes out of date. If, however, you hope to make a profit by anticipating minute-by-minute changes in stock prices then access to information essentially in real time becomes very important.

A real-time information feed has resource implications on the server that produces it if the number of subscribers to the feed becomes too large. If you produce a feed that is accessed, say, every minute by many or most subscribers then careful resource planning is essential, including careful planning for failure. If subscribers are paying significant sums to have access to quasi real-time information then very close to 100 percent reliability is likely to be essential for many users.

Newsreaders and Aggregators

The evolution of any class of software is often accompanied by changes in what any term actually means. The terms newsreader and news aggregator are no exception to this axiom. Some people in the information feed space use the term *aggregator* to refer only to online tools and use terms such as *desktop clients* to refer to what we would term aggregators. Others use the term *newsreader* for similar software.

We prefer the term *aggregator* for tools, whether desktop and online, which allow a user to aggregate information from various feeds inside one interface. Essential functions, as mentioned earlier, include subscribing to individual feeds and displaying recent information from such feeds. Aggregators are considered in more detail in Chapter 15.

Aggregating for Intranet Use

Managers will want to follow closely any information that appears on the Internet about their company, its products, its performance, its prospects, and so on. Similarly, information about competitor companies and products will also be of great interest. Customized aggregators allow a corporation to retrieve and monitor information directly relevant to its business needs, which may not be possible, at least in the past, with publicly available tools.

Some companies will outsource the creation, deployment, and maintenance of custom aggregators in order to ensure that all relevant employees receive the information relevant to their individual role in the business.

Custom aggregators may provide additional business value by creating an interface to the retrieved information that suits the needs of individual employees.

Security and Aggregators

Many of the most widely used information feeds are publicly available. To subscribe, the user simply enters into the aggregator a URL that's either the URL for the information feed itself or the URL for a Web page where the aggregator can use autodiscovery to find the information feed URL.

> *Autodiscovery* **is the process of using information inside the header of a Web page to locate the information feed relevant to that Web page.**

Security of the feed information is rarely a concern in such circumstances, because the purpose of the feed is to make information available to others. However, where the information that is contained in a feed is confidential, reliable means of authentication and authorization are needed. Many aggregators don't provide the facility to authenticate, perhaps because they have been designed with the dominant paradigm of publicly accessible information feeds in mind.

Password-protected news feeds could be of wide use. For example, companies could inform employees or business partners of relevant information. Of course, that task can also be done through e-mail. However, an information feed (at least for the moment) seems a way of avoiding the continual noise of spam that haunts in-boxes of e-mail clients. Software companies could keep beta testers informed of new features, new builds, and so on using a private information feed.

At the moment many potential tasks for secure information feeds could equally well be done using e-mail. However, information feeds seem likely to be less vulnerable to spam, due to the pull model of an aggregator or other client actively having to retrieve information. Those who produce information feeds would have an excellent incentive to keep their information feeds free of spam since allowing spam to contaminate a feed could lead to a rapid loss of subscribers.

Paid-for information feed subscriptions also need a secure base. Legitimate subscribers would need a way to be identified so as to avoid giving away information intended to be sold.

Directories

As the volume of RSS and Atom information feeds has snowballed in recent years the need for mechanisms to provide content consumers with a way to access manageable amounts of information about available feeds increased in importance. Just as a telephone directory enables users to cope with a vast number of telephone numbers, so directories of information about information feeds became increasingly important.

If your aim in producing an information feed is simply to share information with people you already know, or if it's not too important to attract new readers, then you may not want to spend time considering how you can make your feed more visible. For many creators of feeds, however, maximizing visibility is a key aim.

To increase the chances that people unfamiliar with your blog or Web site will pick up an information feed you need to make sure that your feed is listed in the places in which people look for feeds. Online sites such as Technorati.com, Feedster.com, and Syndic8.com provide places where you can make the existence of your feed known. So if people search for terms that occur in your feed, your feed will pop up at the top of the list of potentially matching feeds. Just as a few years ago there was a scramble among Web site authors to find techniques to make a Web site visible in conventional search engines, so now there is the beginning of exploration of how best to do this with online directories of information feeds.

Some blogging tools, for example Movable Type, provide ways to connect to online directories of information feeds. If you are blogging using a blogging tool such as Movable Type check the supported functionality in your blogging tool. Some functionality may already be built-in. Other functionality may need to be added by, for example, pasting code into the relevant file. Depending on the tool used and its version you may need to watch the pinging dialog box, which may occur after you decide to publish a draft post. If there is no automatic contact after each post to sites such as Technorati.com, Blogger.com, and Feedster.com, then you will need to register manually at such sites or paste relevant code snippets into your blogging tool to ensure that your site is featured when users carry out searches there.

Having looked at publicity from the feed producer point of view, let's now look at the user perspective.

Chapter 4

Finding Information about Interesting Feeds

If you are using an aggregator, how do you go about finding information about the type of information feeds that are available for topics that interest you?

The Known Sites Approach

A simple, but not particularly efficient, technique is to browse your favorite Web sites and look for the RSS, Atom, or other information feeds offered on the site. Depending on how the site author has approached the idea of making the information feed available, you may find icons or text links on individual Web pages that indicate that a feed is available. Figure 4-1 shows a text link and an XML icon on www.dannyayers.com/. The text link is on the right of the screen and is moused in the figure. The XML icon below it links to the same RSS 1.0 file.

On large sites, you may find that a very large number of feeds are offered and you will need to make a careful choice to keep the volume of information to manageable levels.

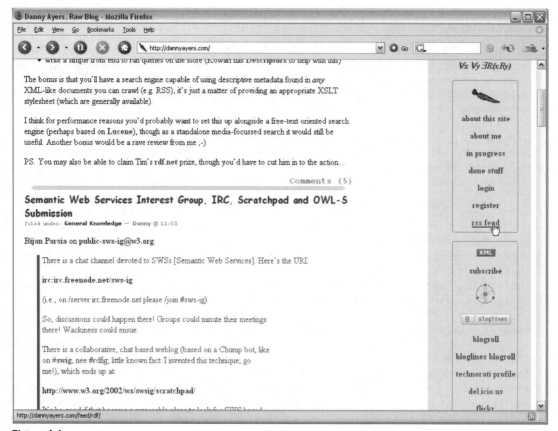

Figure 4-1

Some sites, including www.tfosorcim.org/blog/ at the time of writing, do not automatically include an icon to display a link to the feed. However, using browsers such as Firefox, you can make use of autodiscovery functionality that's normally found only in dedicated aggregators. Figure 4-2 shows the appearance of the "Reflecting on Microsoft" blog with the icon at the bottom right of the Firefox window indicating that an information feed has been found by autodiscovery. The user has the option to create a *live bookmark*, which is a term used in Firefox to indicate bookmark folders that store items from information feeds rather than, as is normally the case, individual Web pages.

Many dedicated aggregators also have autodiscovery features. Figure 4-3 shows the entry of a URL for www.tfosorcim.org/blog/ in the Abilon aggregator, which is described further in Chapter 15.

The Blogroll Approach

Many regular bloggers list somewhere on their blog a list of blogs that they themselves read. This list is called a *blogroll*. Some sites simply include a list of links, whereas others map out that list inside a section labeled blogroll. Figure 4-4 shows the blogroll on Chris Anderson's blog.

Figure 4-2

Figure 4-3

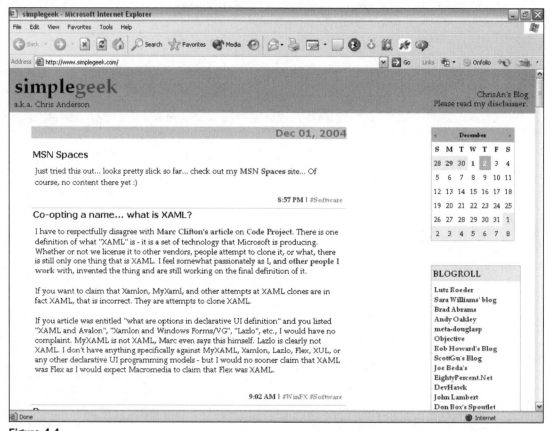

Figure 4-4

The Directory Approach

Online directories such as Technorati.com provide search facilities that enable you to search all blogs that Technorati is following. Simply enter a search term into the Technorati.com home page and, in time, a list of relevant blogs will be displayed. Figure 4-5 shows an example, where I had carried out a search for OOoFf, a boxed product that combines OpenOffice.org and Firefox.

Figure 4-5

Filtering Information Feeds

When you start using information feeds, the process of finding feeds with enough relevant information can be a source of anxiety. Using the techniques described in the preceding section you can very quickly find that you have far too much information available to you, not all of which may be relevant. Particularly when an information feed contains a range of information, only some of which is relevant to you, there is a need to filter the data to keep the displayed information to what interests you. Currently only some aggregators, including Abilon and ActiveRefresh, support filtering.

Filtering Blogs

At the risk of stating the obvious, blogs vary enormously in how narrow or broad is the range of subjects which they attempt to address. Some blogs focus tightly on a single topic, perhaps a single product. For example, the MSDN blogs of the Microsoft Infopath team (`http://blogs.msdn.com/infopath/`) and SQL Express team are not very focussed on a single product. At the other end of the spectrum blogs like Reflecting on Microsoft (`www.tfosrocim.org/blog/`) and Danny Ayer's blog (`www.dannyayers.com`) range far and wide over a diverse range of topics directly or indirectly related to software that we are working with or thinking about. For a user who has a specific set of topics of interest, the capability to filter the content on blogs with heterogeneous content would be very useful. Some aggregator tools, such as Abilon, offer the capability to filter information feed items based on the presence or absence of chosen keywords. Filtering is discussed in more detail in Chapter 15.

Summary

The user is the most important person in the information flow. Making your information available to the user in a way that's convenient for him to use is crucial. Publicizing your information feed, for example by registering with online directories, helps improve visibility of your site and helps to increase visitor numbers. Those same registries are useful for end users to discover sites where topics relevant to them are actively being posted.

You learned that...

❑	The user viewpoint is important and should guide you as to the creation and content of your information feed.

❑	User convenience may distinguish successful aggregators from their less successful competitors.

❑	Publicizing your feed on online sites such as Technorati.com helps to maximize your audience.

Storing, Retrieving, and Exporting Information

Many information feed users seem to assume that the information contained in the feed is of purely temporary interest or value. Sometimes that assumption is true, since some types of information are of purely transitory interest. Other pieces of information are of more lasting significance and are therefore more important than a lot of what comes to you from the various feeds to which you subscribe.

Information that is of short-term significance is reasonably handled either by ignoring an item in a list of items in a feed or by simply reading the item linked to a topic in a feed aggregator. Often you will simply allow such an item to be deleted automatically after the feed has been updated, at whichever interval the user or the software's default settings have specified.

However, it isn't always the case that information is of value for only a short time. If you are choosing information feeds carefully then it is likely that some, perhaps many, of the items you see or read in information feeds will be of more lasting interest for you. The question then arises as to what you do with that information. Since feeds are about helping you to be efficient and effective in finding information, shouldn't tools such as aggregators also help you be effective in retaining interesting information and help you to find it again when you need it?

Much of this chapter is presented from the user's point of view. When you develop information feed-based applications you will want to consider which of these user needs you will want to support in your application.

In this chapter you learn:

❑ About the need for storing some information derived from selected items contained in information feeds

❑ How you can use Onfolio 2.0 or OneNote 2003 to store information from interesting feed items

❑ About issues related to information retrieval

❑ About exporting information

Storing Information

One of the fundamental questions you must ask yourself, as a user, is what you want to store. Of course, there will be much larger volumes of information contained in information feeds that you choose not to read or to store. But, for the more valuable information, what parts of that information do you want to keep?

Do you want to store URLs? Or do you want to store the original information (or selected parts of it)? Or do you want to provide some sort of audit trail or citation system that allows you to store both the content and a URL and date that signify where the content came from. Needs vary among users, so solutions are likely to vary too.

Storing URLs

If you choose only to store URLs, one convenient approach is to use the bookmarks functionality in your favorite browser, for example the Bookmarks folder in Firefox or the Favorites folders in Internet Explorer.

Whether this is an appropriate approach will partly depend on the type of information that you want to link to and how long you anticipate that it might be of interest. If you have used the World Wide Web for more than a short time you will have seen the problem of broken links—that is, when you click a bookmark, the content that you previously were able to link to is no longer there. This can be because a domain has been sold or abandoned, or because a Web site has been restructured or content has for an assortment of reasons been deleted. So you must decide if it's enough to keep a link to a Web page that may not exist when you next try to access it, or if you need to keep a local copy of content.

One intermediate solution for Web pages that have recently disappeared or been edited is to use the version of the page cached by Google. To access a Google cached page simply go to `www.google.com/` and enter appropriate search criteria. For many pages, Google maintains a cached version. Figure 5-1 shows the mouse pointer over the link to the cached version of a page on SQL Server 2005.

Storing Content

Versions of Web pages in the Google cache are generally short lived after the original version of the page is deleted or edited. If capturing information exactly as you saw it is important, the only reliable way is to keep a local copy of the information.

There are various approaches to local storage of information, including simply saving a Web page locally or storing Web pages or information they contain in a relational database management system. Several products now incorporate ways to save Web content, which you may first have seen in the context of an information feed. A little later in the chapter, we cover a couple of software products that support local storage of information.

Storing Static Files

One of the simplest ways to store Web pages is to use the capabilities of your Web browser. Most Web browsers include functionality to save individual Web pages. In Firefox, for example, you choose the Save Page As option on the File menu to save an individual Web page.

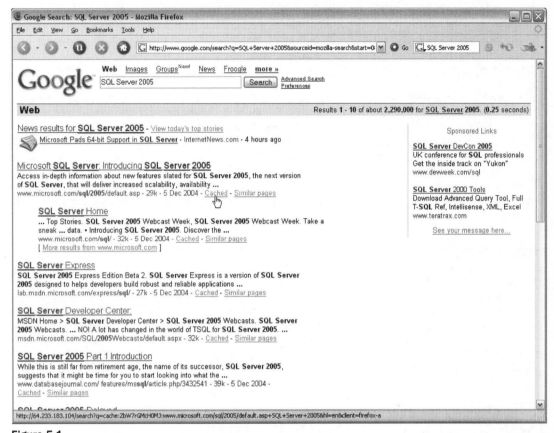

Figure 5-1

Saving individual Web pages may be satisfactory for small-scale storage of information. But it can become a cumbersome way to find information when the number of individual files starts to rise. When difficulties begin to arise about how to find information it's natural that other more flexible and powerful solutions demand to be considered.

Relational Databases

When storing many types of data, it is likely that you would choose a relational database management system. Relational database management systems also potentially offer an appropriate place to store significant amounts of information from information feeds.

Most relational database management systems offer advantages over storage in the file system. If you want to store information on a department or company basis rather than on an individual basis, a relational database management system offers more scalability, and more reliability and built-in functionality to back up all the applicable data. An RDBMS solution provides a solution to accompany information feeds targeted at corporate rather than individual information needs.

Storing information in an RDBMS typically requires significant amounts of custom programming, depending on the RDBMS you choose and the language or languages that you feel comfortable programming in. Solutions of that size and complexity are beyond the scope of this book. However, Chapter 24 describes a different use of RDBMS—the use of MySQL as the backend for a content management system.

However, some RDBMS products are beginning to offer functionality that would make aggregation of items from information feeds a simpler process. For example, at the top end of the range, the new SQL Server 2005 Integration Services (due to be released to market a few months after this book is published) can handle well-formed RSS or Atom information feeds as XML input, using Integration Services' XML Task. The flexibility of the Data Transformation Pipeline in Integration Services would allow an IS developer to store information feed items after filtering or any desired custom transformation. This gives the opportunity to feed items from a range of RSS and Atom information feeds into a SQL Server database. Such an approach, although not cheap, would allow retrieval of relevant information using conventional search and SQL Server's full-text search capabilities.

RDF Triple Stores

If you are using RSS 1.0, which is based on the Resource Description Framework (RDF), you might choose to store information (or at least some information) as RDF triple stores. RDF is described in Chapter 10. Conceptually, the relationship between objects can be expressed as an RDF triple and they can be stored for later use. Several languages support using RDF triples. The Python RDFLib includes a TripleStore object. Such triples can be serialized in several ways. One option is serialization as RDF/XML. Such RDF/XML files can then be stored in the file system or, assuming that the XML is well formed, in a native XML database or as columns that contain the xml datatype in SQL Server 2005.

Two Examples of Longer-Term Storage

Having briefly looked at some possible approaches to department- or corporate-level storage of information from information feeds, this section looks at two currently available solutions, one in beta and one in a released product. Both solutions give an indication of possible approaches to long-term storage of information from information feeds.

One, Onfolio 2.0, includes conventional information feed aggregator functionality. The other, OneNote 2003, provides an easy way to capture information from Web pages, possibly derived from information feeds.

Onfolio 2.0

At the time of writing Onfolio 2.0 is an early beta. Therefore the functionality described here could change before product release. If you want further information about Onfolio 2.0, visit www.onfolio .com/. Onfolio can be run as a standalone window, shown in Figure 5-2, or it can be used in either Internet Explorer or Firefox.

Figure 5-2

Onfolio 2.0 has three tabs. The Collection tab contains folders of Web pages. This allows you to group, and store locally, Web pages of interest for later retrieval. The Feeds tab enables you to set up information feeds. The Search tab enables you to search for and retrieve information.

You can add individual Web pages, which you may have found using an information feed, to a folder in the Collections tab. Figure 5-3 shows the first step involved in adding the specification for the Netscape version of RSS 0.91 to the Information Feeds folder, which we created earlier.

You have the option to capture only the link or to create a copy of the Web page locally, as shown in Figure 5-4. If you choose to capture only the link, the problems of broken links, as described earlier in this chapter, can occur.

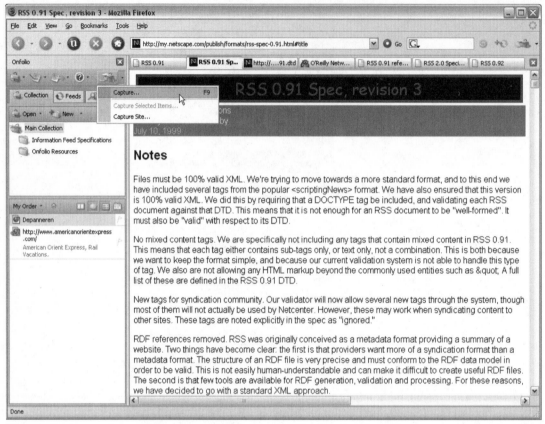

Figure 5-3

Figure 5-4

Figure 5-5 shows the Onfolio deskbar with the main information feed specifications added to a custom folder. Clicking any of the items opens the local copy of the page for viewing.

Figure 5-5

Adding information feeds to Onfolio is straightforward. On the Feeds tab you can access a context menu to add a new feed. Simply paste the URL of the feed document into the wizard as shown in Figure 5-6 to add a new feed.

Figure 5-6

After the feed is added, the recent items from the feed are displayed together inside the browser that is hosting Onfolio. Figure 5-7 shows the feed displayed in Firefox.

Onfolio was shown in this demonstration not because its support of feed functionality is unusual, but because the way that it allows longer-term storage of information from information feeds is unusual.

OneNote 2003

OneNote's functionality overlaps only slightly with that of Onfolio. OneNote is designed primarily as a note taking or information capture tool. But one very useful piece of functionality is the capability to capture complete Web pages or selected content from Web pages. Figure 5-8 shows a page from my blog in the RSS Bandit aggregator.

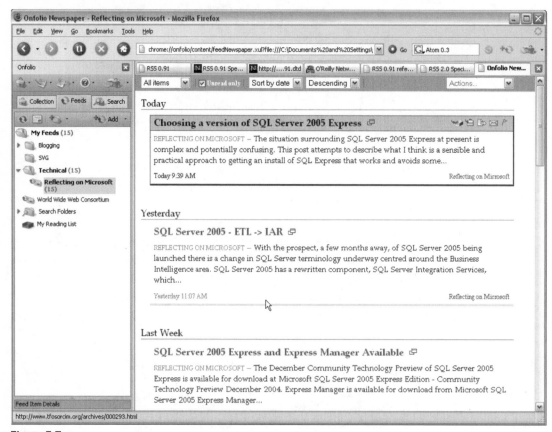

Figure 5-7

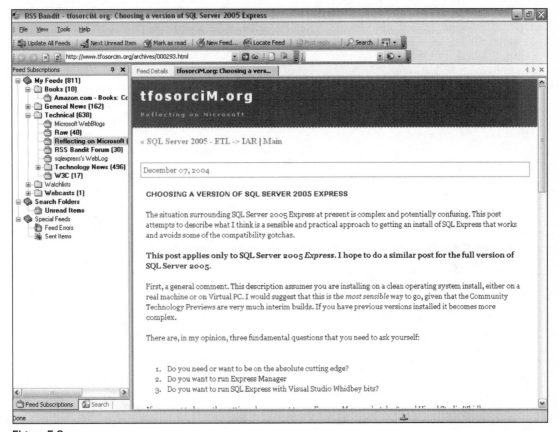

Figure 5-8

If you select text and then drag the selected text to the OneNote icon on the taskbar, the OneNote application will open (assuming that it is already running). You can then paste the content into a OneNote page, as you can see in Figure 5-9.

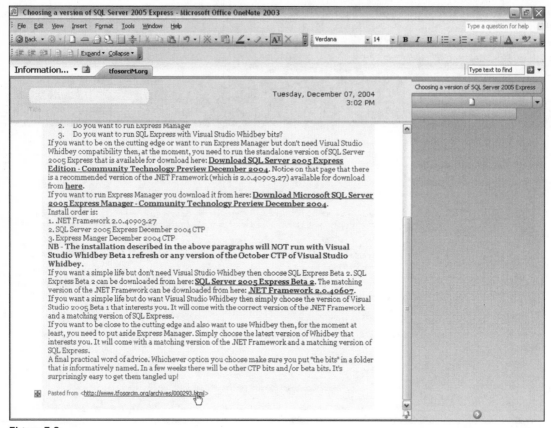

Figure 5-9

Notice in Figure 5-9 (toward the bottom of the page) that when the page originates in RSS Bandit the URL from which the text is pasted is automatically added as a live hyperlink. If you copy a page from an aggregator that doesn't use Internet Explorer, this functionality isn't available. An additional step of manually copying the URL is needed.

If a page has a layout that you want to capture, Onfolio captures the actual Web page complete with layout. If your emphasis is simply on text and image content, OneNote will capture all you need. We will return to information retrieval from OneNote 2003 a little later in this chapter.

Retrieving Information

If you have found useful information and stored it in some form of data store, then at some future date you want to be able to find the information again. The larger the volume of information that you store the more important it becomes to have effective and efficient data retrieval mechanisms in place. If you have saved Web pages to the file system and created meaningful folders you may simply need to browse to find the information that you want. However, tools like Onfolio and OneNote 2003 provide search capabilities to help you find the information that you want.

Search in Onfolio 2.0

In Onfolio 2.0 the Search tab supports search of saved Web pages or information feeds. If you choose to search saved Web pages you can search across all saved Web pages or a selected folder. Figure 5-10 shows the result for a search term "Atom" in the Information Feeds folder that was created earlier. As you can see in the Onfolio pane one matching result is returned. If that is clicked the locally saved version of the Web page is displayed in the main part of the browser window.

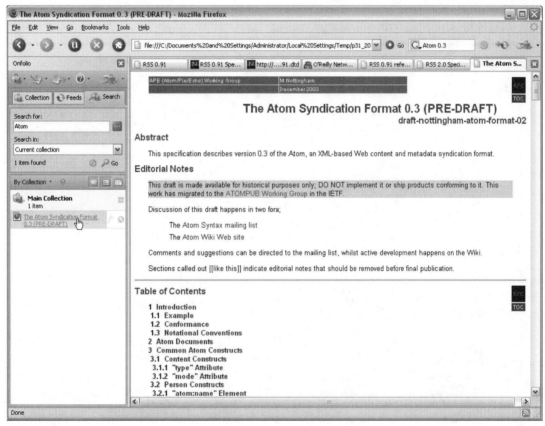

Figure 5-10

Search in OneNote 2003

OneNote also supports searching across text in saved Web pages, as well as text entered into OneNote in other ways. This approach allows information that originally came from information feeds to be smoothly integrated with information from other sources. For example, a student who is doing a project on a particular topic can enter lecture notes, personal notes from books, and information from information feed items into OneNote and then retrieve the information, irrespective of how it was originally captured. Figure 5-11 shows the results of a search for SQL Server 2005, which was the topic of the blog post captured earlier from RSS Bandit.

In this sample search only one page is returned in the current section. Notice in the lower right that the scope of the search can be narrowed or broadened as required. Notice in the upper part of the Page List task pane (the right of the screenshot) that a proximity search is being used. In this example, OneNote searches for the word *SQL*, which is near *Server*, which is near *2005*.

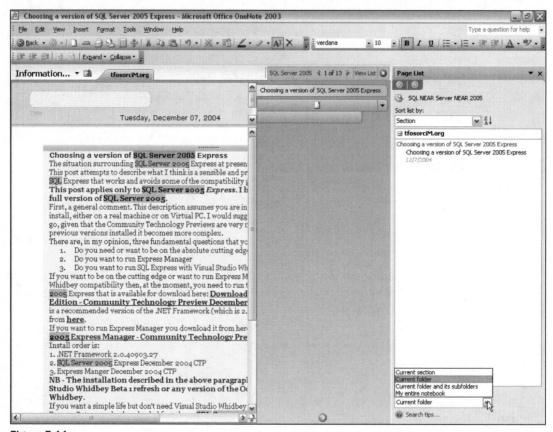

Figure 5-11

Exporting Information

If you have gone to the trouble of collecting information, perhaps complete with its source URL, date, and so on you may want to use that information as part of a report or some other document. If that is the case, you will want to export it to a word processor or similar text manipulation tool.

Exporting in Onfolio 2.0

Onfolio offers ways to export or otherwise share information that you found in the search for Web pages that contain the search term Atom. Figure 5-12 shows the options to export to files or to XML. Exporting in this manner can enable sharing with colleagues.

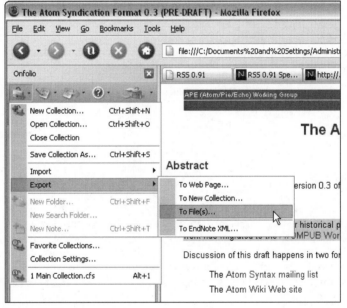

Figure 5-12

Alternatively, you can forward captured information by e-mail to colleagues, as shown in Figure 5-13.

Exporting in OneNote 2003

The text or images that you capture in OneNote 2003 can be exported to Microsoft Word, copied and pasted, or e-mailed to colleagues using Outlook 2003.

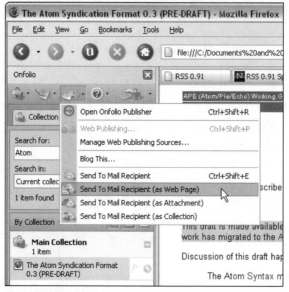

Figure 5-13

Summary

Some information retrieved from information feeds can be of temporary use only, whereas other information is of potentially lasting value. Such information can be captured in a variety of ways, ranging from saving individual files to the use of an enterprise relational database management system. You saw examples of storing Web pages using Onfolio 2.0 and OneNote 2003. Information in such pages can be searched for or shared with colleagues. Tools such as Onfolio 2.0 and OneNote 2003 allow information derived from information feeds to enter business workflows in ways that are easy to use and which add to the value of the information.

Specifically, you learned that...

❑   Information can be stored as URLs or as local copies of Web pages.

❑   Relational databases can provide storage suited to corporate needs.

❑   Products such as Onfolio 2.0 and OneNote 2003 can facilitate storing selected information from information feeds.

Part II
The Technologies

Essentials of XML

Extensible Markup Language (XML) is fundamental to several of the languages and technologies considered in this book. Most RSS and Atom feeds will be written in well-formed XML. Many tools that consume RSS and Atom feeds will depend, at least partly, on XML parsers to process the incoming feeds so that they can be processed and subsequently presented in an appropriate way for consumers of the feed.

It's not impossible to work in the information feed area with zero knowledge of XML, but it's pretty difficult and not advisable. Some aggregator tools will process malformed feeds that are "almost XML" but not quite using regular expressions or you can write similar tools using regular expressions rather than XML to process the text. In reality, if you want your data to be available to the largest possible audience, it's advisable to produce well-formed XML in your own feeds. To do that, if you are not relying totally on some tool to create XML for you automatically, you need at least a basic understanding of XML.

The purpose of this chapter is to provide readers unfamiliar with XML with the basic knowledge to enable well-formed and valid documents to be created. If you have worked with XML before you may want to skip through this chapter quickly as a refresher. If you already have done anything beyond the simplest hand coding with XML you will probably have the necessary understanding of what it takes to write and understand XML markup.

In this chapter you will learn:

- ❏   What XML is
- ❏   How to write a well-formed XML document
- ❏   How to use XML namespaces
- ❏   How to provide autodiscovery of feeds

What Is XML?

XML is an abbreviation for eXtensible Markup Language, which is normally written as Extensible Markup Language.

Understanding XML is reminiscent of the apocryphal story of how the elephant appears to blind people. Some felt the trunk, some the legs, some the tail, each arriving at a different impression of what an elephant is. Similarly, XML appears to be different things to different people who come to XML from different perspectives.

The following list describes several aspects of XML or viewpoints of it, each of which has at least some truth associated with it:

- ❏ XML is a machine-readable and human-readable way to describe a document.
- ❏ XML is a markup language.
- ❏ XML is a metalanguage.
- ❏ XML documents contain a sequence of Unicode characters.
- ❏ XML documents are a serialized representation of a logical model.
- ❏ XML is a format to create structured documents.
- ❏ XML is a semi-structured data interchange format.

XML is primarily targeted at machine readability. It has the advantage that it is also human readable. It is, for example, much easier for a human being to read the following code than a binary representation of even a simple document. At the same time, an XML parser will happily process such documents.

```
<SimpleDocument>
 <Message>Hello World!</Message>
</SimpleDocument>
```

XML documents are written in markup similar to HTML. Like HTML, XML markup uses angled brackets to indicate elements, which can have attributes. XML elements and attributes are discussed a little later in this chapter.

XML is not really a language but more a metalanguage that describes how the syntax of other languages are to be written. RSS and Atom are application languages that use the syntax rules of the XML metalanguage, although you may find feeds that resemble RSS and Atom but are not well-formed XML. Colloquially, RSS and Atom are said to be written in XML.

Any XML document consists of a sequence of Unicode characters. The following shows a skeletal RSS 0.91 document written in XML. A typical RSS 0.91 document has elements nested inside the `channel` element.

```
<rss version="0.91">
 <channel>
  <!-- This comment is a placeholder. -->
 </channel>
</rss>
```

Viewed as a text document, the preceding markup is simply a sequence of Unicode characters. Behind that serialization format, most developers can easily see a hierarchical logical structure. There is an `rss` element at the top of the hierarchy with a `channel` element nested inside it and an XML comment nested inside the `channel` element.

Viewed from the perspective of documents with no formal structure, an XML document seems like a structured document. Viewed from the precisely defined structures and relationships of a relational database management system, an XML document seems semi-structured. Arguably, of course, the XML document is a more richly, more flexibly structured document. That has the advantage of making XML suitable for tasks that represent hierarchical relationships and relationships which vary in detail from one instance to another. The disadvantage for traditional relational database developers is that they have to learn a new set of skills and that, until recently, powerful tools for management of large XML data sets were in short supply. Because most information feeds are relatively small in size, there is a large range of suitable tools available for manipulation of XML that can be applied to the task of processing information feeds.

One of the characteristics of any markup document that is genuinely XML is that it is *well-formed*. Well-formedness is a term introduced with XML 1.0 that describes several required characteristics of a legal XML document.

> The specification for XML 1.0 is, at the time of writing, in its third edition. See `www.w3.org/TR/2004/REC-xml-20040204/`.

The following list briefly describes some of the necessary characteristics of a well-formed XML document. Several of the bullet points will be discussed and demonstrated later in the chapter.

- ❏ An XML document has exactly one document element.
- ❏ All XML element names must follow the rules for naming XML elements.
- ❏ All XML elements must have paired start and end tags (or be written, when appropriate, as an empty tag), and the name in an element's end tag must match the name in the element's start tag.
- ❏ XML elements must be nested correctly.
- ❏ In any XML element each attribute name must be unique.
- ❏ All XML attributes must use paired single quotes or paired double quotes to contain the attribute's value.
- ❏ XML attribute values must not contain the < character.
- ❏ XML comments must not include the character sequence -- (two successive hyphens) except in the initial delimiter and final delimiter of the comment.

The following sections describe the parts of an XML document most relevant to RSS and Atom.

XML Declaration

The XML declaration is optional in the XML 1.0 specification but should be present. If an XML declaration is present it must be the first item in the XML document and must not be preceded by even a single space character.

```
<?xml version="1.0"?>
```

Strictly speaking, the XML declaration isn't an XML processing instruction although its syntax closely resembles an XML processing instruction.

If an XML declaration is present it must have a `version` attribute. It may also, optionally, have a `standalone` attribute and an `encoding` attribute. If no `encoding` attribute is specified the default encoding is UTF-8.

The following form of XML declaration specifies explicitly that XML version 1.0 is being used, that the characters in the document are using UTF-8 encoding and that the document is standalone, which means that it does not rely on accessing any external markup.

```
<?xml version="1.0" encoding="UTF-8" standalone="yes" ?>
```

XML Names

XML elements and attributes, which you will look at in the following sections, are formed of characters that must follow certain rules.

An XML name for an element, attribute, or namespace prefix that you create must not begin with the sequence of characters x, m, and l in that order in any combination of case. Those sequences of characters at the beginning of an XML name are reserved for W3C use, for example in future versions of the XML specification or as the indicative namespace prefix of the XML namespace (see also www.w3.org/XML/1998/namespace).

An XML name can begin with a letter, an underscore character, or a colon character. However, in practice, it is best to avoid using a colon character in any XML name, except when used as the separator between a namespace prefix and the local part of the name.

XML Elements

All XML documents have at least one element, called the *document element* or, sometimes, the *root element*.

In RSS 0.91, for example, the document element, which is the `rss` element, is written as follows. It has a single `version` attribute:

```
<rss version="0.91">
 <!-- More content goes here. -->
</rss>
```

All other elements must be nested inside the document element. For example, in an RSS 0.91 element the child element of the `rss` element is the `channel` element. To be properly nested, the start tag of the `channel` element must come later than the start tag of the containing `rss` element. Correspondingly, the end tag of the `channel` element must come before the end tag of the containing `rss` element, as shown in the following example:

```
<rss version="0.91">
 <channel>
 <!-- Other RSS 0.91 elements would go here. -->
 </channel>
</rss>
```

By convention, elements contained inside the document element are indented. This makes seeing the structure of the XML easier for human beings, but whitespace (such as indenting) does not affect the logical structure which an XML parser creates from an XML document.

Generally speaking, the ordering of elements in an XML document is significant. For example, the following simple document,

```
<book  title="Beginning RSS and Atom Programming">
<chapter>
 <number>6</number>
 <title>Essentials of XML</title>
 <content><!--Content goes here.--></content>
</chapter>
</book>
```

is a different document from

```
<book  title="Beginning RSS and Atom Programming">
<chapter>
 <title>Essentials of XML</title>
 <number>6</number>
 <content><!--Content goes here.--></content>
</chapter>
</book>
```

as far as an XML parser is concerned. This is due to the difference in order of the `number` and `title` elements, which are child elements of the `chapter` element.

Elements may have zero or any number of attributes. An element cannot have more than one attribute with the same name.

XML Attributes

XML attributes, which are written in the start tag of an XML element, provide additional information relating to the XML element. In the following simple document the `book` element has a single attribute, the `title` attribute, the value of which indicates the title of the book. The `chapter` element has two attributes, a `number` attribute and a `title` attribute, whose function should be obvious.

```
<book title="Beginning RSS and Atom Programming">
<!-- Other chapters go here. -->
<chapter number = "6" title ="Essentials of XML">
<!-- Chapter content goes here. -->
</chapter>
</book>
```

The ordering of attributes inside a start tag does not matter. From the point of view of an XML processor, the chapter element specified with the number attribute first,

```
<chapter number = "6" title ="Essentials of XML">
```

is identical, logically, to the chapter element with the title attribute specified first, as shown in this example:

```
<chapter title = "Essentials of XML" number = "6">
```

Similarly, an attribute's value can be written with paired single quotes as delimiters,

```
<book title = 'Beginning RSS and Atom Programming'>
```

or with paired double quotes as delimiters,

```
<book title = "Beginning RSS and Atom Programming">
```

and be logically equivalent. It is an error to use one single quote and one double quote character as the delimiters of an attribute value. The delimiters must be paired.

Whitespace inside the start tag of an element can be used to lay out markup, including how attributes are displayed. For example, the chapter element that you saw earlier can be written with additional whitespace, such as

```
<chapter
number = "6"
title ="Essentials of XML">
```

without changing the meaning.

XML Comments

XML comments are written in the same way as HTML comments. The initial delimiter is the character sequence <!-- and the ending delimiter is the character sequence -->. An XML comment must not contain two successive hyphens except as part of the initial delimiter or final delimiter.

Predefined Entities

The predefined entities in XML differ substantially from those available in HTML. The implicit DTD declarations of the five XML predefined entities are listed here:

```
<!ENTITY lt     "&#38;#60;">
<!ENTITY gt     "&#62;">
<!ENTITY amp    "&#38;#38;">
<!ENTITY apos   "&#39;">
<!ENTITY quot   "&#34;">
```

When used in an XML document, each entity is preceded by an & character and followed by a semicolon. The < entity represents the < character. The > entity represents the > character. The & represents the & character. The ' entity represents a single quote and the " entity represents a double quote character.

The file Entities.xml uses each of the five predefined entities:

```
<?xml version="1.0"?>
<document>
 <statement>The integer 5 is &lt; 10.</statement>
 <statement>The integer 10 is &gt; 5.</statement>
 <statement>The ampersand, &amp;, is written as &amp;amp;.</statement>
 <statement>Using apostrophes to quote: &apos;This is a quote.&apos;.</statement>
 <statement>Using double quotes to quote: &quot;This is a quote.&quot;.</statement>
</document>
```

Figure 6-1 shows the appearance when Entities.xml is opened in Internet Explorer. Notice how the entity is replaced in the display by the corresponding character.

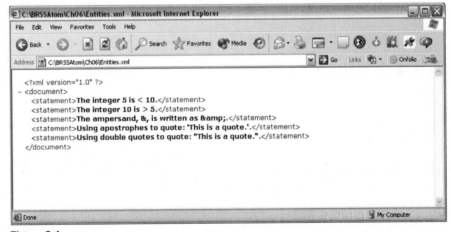

Figure 6-1

Character References

Unicode character references can be used in the content of XML elements. In the following sample file, CharacterRefs.xml, character references are used to replace one of the predefined entities shown earlier:

```
<?xml version="1.0"?>
<document>
 <statement>The integer 5 is &#60; 10.</statement>
 <statement>The integer 10 is &#62; 5.</statement>
 <statement>The ampersand, &#38;, is written as &amp;amp;.</statement>
 <statement>Using apostrophes to quote: &#39;This is a quote.&apos;.</statement>
 <statement>Using double quotes to quote: &#34;This is a quote.&quot;.</statement>
</document>
```

Notice that in the final two `statement` elements that one of the pairs of single quotes and double quotes is specified using a character reference and its matching partner is specified using a predefined entity. Figure 6-2 shows the appearance in the Internet Explorer browser.

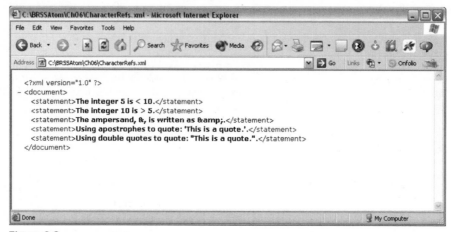

Figure 6-2

XML Namespaces

The XML 1.0 specification does not specify any element names since it is a metalanguage. Individual XML application languages can, therefore, be created by anybody. One result of the freedom to create languages that use XML syntax is that naming clashes can occur. For example, how would you distinguish the `table` element in the following two code snippets?

```
<table>
 <number_of_legs>4</number_of_legs>
</table>
```

and

```
<table>
<tr><td>First cell</td><td>Second cell</td></tr>
<table>
```

Very likely you would conclude that the `table` element in the first snippet refers to a piece of furniture and the `table` element in the second code snippet refers to an HTML or XHTML table.

An XML processor cannot use the number of legs associated with a table or its content of `tr` elements to decide which table element is intended. Another mechanism to distinguish between the two table elements is needed. The mechanism that the W3C chose to use is XML namespaces.

The Namespaces in XML Recommendation specifies a technique to distinguish XML elements by associating the element's name with a URI. The technique uses a special attribute to do so.

> **The Namespaces in XML Recommendation is located at** `www.w3.org/TR/REC-xml-names/`.

In the following code, the `rdf` namespace prefix of the `RDF` element is associated with the namespace URI `http://www.w3.org/1999/02/22-rdf-syntax-ns#`. This is the namespace URI (also called a *namespace name*) for the Resource Description Framework (RDF), which is used in the RSS 1.0 specification.

```
<rdf:RDF
   xmlns:rdf="http://www.w3.org/1999/02/22-rdf-syntax-ns#"
   >
```

The following namespace declaration uses a special prefix, `xmlns`:

```
xmlns:rdf="http://www.w3.org/1999/02/22-rdf-syntax-ns#"
```

Remember that names beginning with `xml` are reserved for W3C use. In this case the namespace prefix `xmlns` is reserved for use in namespace declarations. The namespace declaration consists of the special `xmlns` namespace prefix followed by a colon character followed by what will become the namespace prefix associated with the URI that follows. In this example, the namespace prefix `rdf` is associated with the namespace URI `http://www.w3.org/1999/02/22-rdf-syntax-ns#`.

Namespace URIs don't guarantee that element names and other names can be distinguished but the length of a typical URI makes a namespace clash orders of magnitude less likely.

When you create feed documents in RSS 1.0, RSS 2.0, or Atom the issue of XML namespaces becomes of real practical importance. For example, the document element of the RSS 1.0 feed for my blog, `www.tfosorcim.org/blog/`, includes the following start tag for the document element, `rdf:RDF`:

```
<rdf:RDF
   xmlns:rdf="http://www.w3.org/1999/02/22-rdf-syntax-ns#"
   xmlns:dc="http://purl.org/dc/elements/1.1/"
   xmlns:sy="http://purl.org/rss/1.0/modules/syndication/"
   xmlns:admin="http://webns.net/mvcb/"
   xmlns:cc="http://web.resource.org/cc/"
   xmlns="http://purl.org/rss/1.0/">
```

As you can see, not only is the `rdf` namespace prefix declared but four other namespace prefixes are included in namespace declarations. The final namespace declaration specifies that elements in the document that are not preceded by a namespace prefix are associated with the namespace URI `http://purl.org/rss/1.0/`, which is the namespace URI associated with RSS 1.0 elements.

In the RSS 2.0 feed, `http://dannyayers.com/feed/rss2/`, for Danny Ayer's blog there are namespace declarations, including the RSS 1.0 content module.

```
<rss version="2.0"
 xmlns:content=http://purl.org/rss/1.0/modules/content/
  xmlns:wfw="http://wellformedweb.org/CommentAPI/">
```

So elements from the RSS 1.0 Content module can be used in the RSS 2.0 feed but still be recognized as belonging to that module.

> **The Firefox 1.0 browser fails to display the namespace declarations in the previous feed document. They are displayed correctly in Internet Explorer.**

HTML, XHTML, and Feed Autodiscovery

When using a desktop feed aggregator, it is fairly straightforward to paste in the URL for an information feed. But it's also useful to be able to find the RSS or Atom feed on a web page without the process of copying and pasting the URL of the feed.

The HTML or XHTML `link` element provides a way for autodiscovery of information feeds.

On Danny's blog, `http://dannyayers.com/`, the main page is written in XHTML 1.0. You can be sure that it is XHTML 1.0 because the document element associates element names that have no namespace prefix with the namespace URI for XHTML 1.0.

```
<html xmlns="http://www.w3.org/1999/xhtml">
```

The following XHTML elements are contained inside the `head` element:

```
   <link rel="stylesheet" type="text/css" media="print"
  href="http://dannyayers.com/print.css" />
   <link rel="alternate" type="application/rss+xml" title="RSS 2.0"
 href="http://dannyayers.com/feed/rss2/" />
   <link rel="alternate" type="text/xml" title="RSS .92"
 href="http://dannyayers.com/feed/rss/" />
   <link rel="alternate" type="application/atom+xml" title="Atom 0.3"
  href="http://dannyayers.com/feed/atom/" />
```

The first `link` element contains a standard link to a cascading style sheet (CSS). The other three link elements use the `rel` attribute of the `link` element to indicate that it has a purpose that is alternate to styling.

Notice that the `type` attribute has a different value for the RSS 0.92, RSS 2.0, and Atom 0.3 feeds, because these are different document types. Of course, because these are separate documents, the respective documents for each format also each have their own URL, which is specified in the `href` attribute.

Similarly, my blog, `http://www.tfosorciM.org/blog/`, has a link element that specifies the location of its RSS 1.0 feed.

```
<link rel="alternate" type="application/rss+xml" title="RSS"
  href="http://www.tfosorcim.org/blog/index.rdf" />
```

Software that's aware of this convention can search the head section of an HTML or XHTML web page for `link` elements that follow this pattern. If they find an information feed in a dialect of RSS and Atom that they understand, they can then process that feed and present it appropriately to users.

The Firefox browser, shown in Figure 6-3, uses autodiscovery to populate the RSS button shown in the extreme bottom right of my blog.

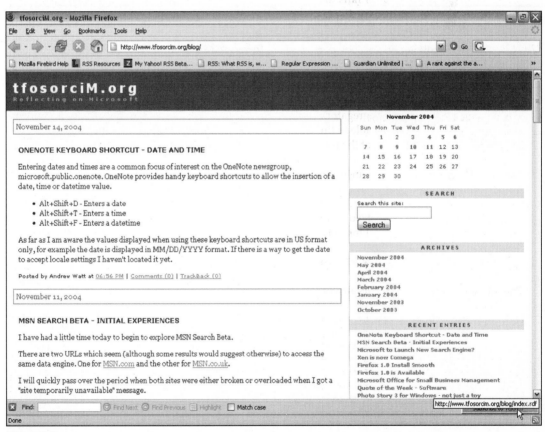

Figure 6-3

Notice that the URL in the lower-right corner of the figure is the one shown earlier in the link element of the web page.

Summary

In this chapter you learned that...

❑ RSS and Atom documents should be written as XML.

❑ There are rules for how a well-formed XML document is written.

❑ XML namespaces are used to avoid naming collisions.

❑ The link element is used in information feed autodiscovery.

Exercises

1. Is the following line of code part of a well-formed XML document?

```
<rdf:RDF xmlns:rdf="http://www.w3.org/1999/02/22-rdf-syntax-ns#'>
```

2. Can XML names begin with numbers?

3. Is the following well-formed XML?

```
<xmlDocument>
<!-- The content goes here. -- -->
</xmlDocument>
```

Atom 0.3

Atom 0.3 is an XML-based specification that defines a syntax for information feed documents. Atom 0.3 was developed in response to the confusing terminology and versioning of the various flavors and approaches used in RSS. The individual versions of RSS are discussed in Chapters 8, 9, 10, and 12.

Disentangling the name/acronym/version confusion inherent in RSS seemed a desirable step to some, with the possible hope that a single information feed specification could be created. Atom 0.3 was one specification that resulted from the perceived need to do something about the RSS name confusion.

Of course, while some saw Atom as possibly simplifying the multiplicity of specifications used in information feeds, others saw the addition of yet another specification for information feeds as adding to the existing complexity, making it necessary for those developers who write aggregators to accommodate even more variants of information feed document types. Whichever view you take, Atom 0.3 is here and it is used widely. Whether it will stay in common use or will shortly be replaced in daily use by the anticipated Atom 1.0 specification is presently still an open question.

> At the time of writing, Atom 0.3 is in widespread use by many thousands of information feeds, but its specification document now carries a "do not implement" label. By the time you read this book, Atom 0.3 may have been replaced, officially at least, by Atom 1.0, which is described in Chapter 13. Whether Atom 0.3 will follow RSS 0.91 in continuing to be widely used long after it is officially deprecated remains to be seen.

In this chapter you learn:

- ❑ What Atom 0.3 is
- ❑ About the structure of an Atom 0.3 document
- ❑ About the use of modules with Atom 0.3

Introducing Atom 0.3

Atom 0.3 is a specification for information feed documents. It was completed in December 2003 and has grown rapidly in use since then. Strictly speaking, the Atom 0.3 specification was never "completed." However, the December 2003 version Atom 0.3, is essentially a snapshot of a specification in development which entered practical use almost immediately after its publication.

The success of Atom 0.3 was partly due to its emergence during the general rapid growth of information feeds. Despite being quite early in its development, its popularly was the result of support from some big hitters in the blogging space. For example, Blogger.com adopted Atom 0.3 as its standard information feed format. That support alone added many thousands of Atom 0.3 feeds.

It is likely that soon after this book is published, Atom 1.0 will reach a stable state. However, the blogging and information feed communities have a history of continuing to use supposedly deprecated specifications. So it is possible that use of Atom 0.3 will continue long after the IETF officially blesses Atom 1.0.

The Atom 0.3 Specification

The Atom 0.3 specification document is primarily of historical interest, which is a point that the specification itself asserts. However, in practical terms at the time of writing Atom 0.3 is widely used, therefore if you are constructing an aggregator it is quite likely that for some time to come you will need to be able to parse Atom 0.3 information feeds.

The Atom 0.3 specification is located at `www.mnot.net/drafts/draft-nottingham-atom-format-02.html`. If you take time to read the specification document you will see that there are several places where it is ambiguous and in some places also includes comments that indicate that further development of those aspects of the specification was anticipated. Some of the ambiguities inherent in the specification are, inevitably, reflected in the content of this chapter.

The move of the embryonic Atom specification to the auspices of the IETF means that Atom 0.3 exists in a cyberspace void, widely used but officially now deprecated.

The Atom 0.3 Namespace

Atom 0.3 uses XML namespaces. Each Atom 0.3 element is associated with the namespace URI `http://purl.org/atom/ns#`. Typically, the Atom 0.3 namespace is declared in the start tag of the document element of an Atom 0.3 information feed, the `feed` element.

```
<feed version="0.3" xmlns="http://purl.org/atom/ns#">
```

Atom 0.3 Document Structure

Atom 0.3 documents are XML documents. They should have the associated mime type `application/atom+xml`. An Atom 0.3 document is allowed to include a `DOCTYPE` declaration, but many feed documents will not have one.

The following example shows a simple example Atom 0.3 document. We will discuss the parts of its structure in the following sections. As you examine the structure, notice the importance of the `feed` and `entry` elements.

```xml
<?xml version="1.0" encoding="utf-8"?>
<feed version="0.3" xmlns="http://purl.org/atom/ns#">
  <title>This is a simple sample Atom 0.3 Information Feed</title>
  <link rel="alternate" type="text/html"
   href="http://www.XMML.com/"/>
  <modified>2004-12-08T14:30:00Z</modified>
  <author>
    <name>Andrew Watt</name>
  </author>
  <entry>
    <title>Some interesting stuff</title>
    <link rel="alternate" type="text/html"
     href="http://www.XMML.com/2004/12/08.html"/>
    <id>tag:www.XMML.com,2004:12:999</id>
    <issued>2004-12-08T14:30:00Z</issued>
    <modified>2004-12-08T14:30:00Z</modified>
  </entry>
    <entry>
    <title>Some more interesting stuff</title>
    <link rel="alternate" type="text/html"
     href="http://www.XMML.com/2004/12/09.html"/>
    <id>tag:www.XMML.com,2004:12:1000</id>
    <issued>2004-12-09T14:30:00Z</issued>
    <modified>2004-12-09T16:30:00Z</modified>
  </entry>
</feed>
```

The feed Element

The document element of each Atom 0.3 document is the `feed` element that is in the Atom 0.3 namespace. The `feed` element must have a `version` attribute. For Atom 0.3 the only permitted value of the `version` attribute is `0.3`. The `feed` element should have an `xml:lang` attribute which specifies the human language used in the content of the information feed.

The start tag of the `feed` element must have at least one namespace declaration for the Atom 0.3 namespace:

```
xmlns="http://purl.org/atom/ns#"
```

However, sometimes you will see start tags for an Atom 0.3 feed, looking like the following:

```
<feed version="0.3" xml:lang="en">
```

However, the more correct form is:

```
<feed version="0.3" xml:lang="en" xmlns="http://purl.org/atom/ns#">
```

The child elements of the `feed` element are `title`, `link`, `author`, `id`, `generator`, `copyright`, `info`, `modified`, `tagline`, and `entry`.

The title Element

The `title` element is a child element of the `feed` element. It provides a human-readable name for the information feed. The `title` element is required, and each `feed` element can have only one `title` child element.

The link Element

A `feed` element must have at least one `link` element child but may have more. A link element has `rel`, `type`, and `href` attributes. The `rel` attribute specifies the relationship, the `type` attribute specifies the mime type, and the `href` attribute contains a URL.

The most usual form of the `link` element indicates an HTML or XHTML Web page that is associated with the information feed.

```
<link rel="alternate" type="text/html" href="http://www.XMML.com/"/>
```

The `link` element was one aspect of Atom 0.3 that I feel needed additional clarification. Given the nature of the typical use of the `link` element it was never clear to me why this should be specified as *alternate*. It seemed, in part at least, to carry over HTML-based perspective on links.

The author Element

The `author` element contains information about the person who is the creator of an information feed or of an information entry. Every Atom 0.3 information feed must contain an `author` element, except in the situation where each `entry` element has an `author` child element.

If there is a single author of individual entries, the feed author can choose whether there is one author element which is a child element of the `feed` element or can specify an author in each `author` element of `entry` elements. It is allowed to include both options in the same feed document, but it is not allowed to have more than one `author` element which is a child element of the `feed` element.

When there are multiple authors associated with a blog or other source of content, it would be appropriate to indicate routinely authorship of individual entries using `author` elements as child elements of the `entry` element.

The id Element

An Atom 0.3 feed may optionally contain an `id` element as a child element of the `feed` element. If present, there is only one `id` element, which is a child element of the `feed` element. Other `id` elements, one per `entry` element, can occur as child elements of the `entry` element.

The purpose of the `id` element is to provide a globally unique identifier for a feed or an information feed entry. One approach is to include a domain name and a timestamp. Assuming stability of ownership of a domain and accuracy of timestamping, this should provide a unique value.

The generator Element

The `generator` element is optional. If present it contains information about the software, often a blogging tool, that was used to generate the information feed. The `generator` element, optionally, has a `url` attribute whose value is a URL which should be capable of being dereferenced to a resource which is relevant to the generator used. Typically this will allow the user to navigate to a Web site containing information about the generator software if it is exposed as a clickable link by an aggregator. The `generator` element may, optionally, contain a `version` attribute that specifies the version of the generator software.

Bloggers who use the WordPress software to produce Atom 0.3 feeds will have a feed containing a `generator` element similar to the following one:

```
<generator url="http://wordpress.org/" version="1.2">WordPress</generator>
```

The copyright Element

The `copyright` element is optional. If present it contains a human readable copyright statement. The Atom 0.3 `copyright` element is not intended to contain machine-readable copyright information.

A `copyright` element typically conveys information similar to the following:

```
<copyright>Copyright John Smith 2004</copyright>
```

It might also contain information such as an e-mail address to allow the copyright holder to be contacted for uses other than those implicitly granted by public availability of the information feed.

The info Element

The `info` element is optional. The `info` element is intended to convey human-readable information, according to the specification but the most common use that I have seen is to contain machine-readable information about MIME type, such as in the following example:

```
<info mode="xml" type="text/html">
```

The modified Element

The `modified` element is a required element and must occur exactly once as a child element of the `feed` element. The content of the `modified` element is a date and time value, similar to the following example:

```
<modified>2004-12-08T20:53:38Z</modified>
```

It is not compulsory to include a time zone in the date and time value but, if present, the time zone must be UTC, Coordinated Universal Time, which is indicated by the final `z` in the content of the example `modified` element.

The tagline Element

An Atom 0.3 feed may contain a `tagline` element. The `tagline` element contains a human readable tagline or similar information for an information feed.

The entry Element

Individual entries in an Atom 0.3 information feed are contained in `entry` elements. Nominally, the `entry` element is optional but an Atom 0.3 information feed with no `entry` elements isn't useful for much.

> The term *entry* is used in Atom 0.3 to describe the concept known as an *item* in the various versions of RSS. An *entry* or item is, essentially, information about a blog post, a news story, and so on.

The Atom 0.3 specification allows any elements in any XML namespace to be included as child elements of the `entry` element. This provides great scope for flexibility. For some feed readers this may pose problems in processing certain elements in namespaces unfamiliar to a particular aggregator. However, because many aggregators will simply ignore elements of which they have no knowledge, a common effect is that not all information in an Atom 0.3 entry element may be displayed.

The following sections describe child elements of the `entry` element. The order of child elements of an `entry` element has no semantic significance.

The title Element

Each entry must contain exactly one `title` element. The content of the `title` element will, typically, match the name of the corresponding blog entry or news item, as shown in the following snippet:

```
<title>Semantic Web Applications and Perspectives (SWAP)</title>
```

The link Element

Each Atom 0.3 entry must contain at least one `link` element with a `rel` attribute having the value of `alternate`. The `href` attribute of a `link` element will, typically, link to a blog post or news item at the URL specified as its value.

```
<link rel="alternate" type="text/html"
    href="http://dannyayers.com/archives/2004/12/08/semantic-web-applications-and-
    perspectives-swap/"/>
```

The author Element

Each Atom 0.3 entry must contain an `author` element, except in the situation where there is an `author` element that is a child element of the `feed` element.

Often the `author` element is written with a child `name` element as shown in the following example:

```
<author>
  <name>John Smith</name>
</author>
```

The contributor Element

An Atom 0.3 entry may be written by more than one person, therefore the contributor element is available as an optional element to record information about a contributor to a feed entry.

The id Element

Atom 0.3 expects each feed entry to be identified by a globally unique identifier. The id element fulfils that expectation. Typically, the content of the id element is a URL that uniquely identifies the feed entry, as in this example:

```
<id>http://dannyayers.com?p=2251</id>
```

Or it includes a URL and timestamp, in various forms:

```
<id>tag:www.XMML.com,2004:12:999</id>
```

As long as the content of the id element has a high probability of being globally unique you are free to use whatever content you choose.

The modified Element

Each Atom 0.3 feed entry must contain exactly one modified element. The content of the modified element is a date and time value that must express the time as a time using the Coordinated Universal Time, UTC, time zone, indicated by a z as the final character of the value.

```
<modified>2004-12-08T14:30:00Z</modified>
```

If no created element is present for the entry it is assumed that the date and time at which the feed entry was created are the same as the date and time contained in the modified element.

The issued Element

Each Atom 0.3 feed entry may, optionally, contain one issued element. The content of the issued element is a date and time value that may express the time as a time in a time zone.

```
<issued>2004-12-08T14:30:00Z</issued>
```

The created Element

The created element, which is an optional element, contains a value that includes date and time parts. If a time zone is specified it must be UTC, Coordinated Universal Time.

The summary Element

The summary element is optional. If present, it contains a short summary or description of the feed entry. The content of the summary element is intended for human consumption.

The content Element

The `content` element contains, as its name indicates, the content of the feed entry. Typically, an entry will have one `content` element but the Atom 0.3 specification allows more than one `content` element to be present in an entry.

Using Modules with Atom 0.3

Atom 0.3 uses XML namespaces for the elements in the Atom 0.3 namespace. This means that XML namespaces can also be used unambiguously to incorporate elements from other namespaces in an Atom 0.3 document. This means that Atom 0.3 can be extended, as needed, with modules of elements from other namespaces.

The following example, which shows the start tag of the `feed` element of an Atom 0.3 feed, demonstrates how complex an Atom 0.3 document can become:

```
<feed version="0.3" xmlns="http://purl.org/atom/ns#"
 xmlns:dc="http://purl.org/dc/elements/1.1/"
 xmlns:rdf="http://www.w3.org/1999/02/22-rdf-syntax-ns#"
 xmlns:rdfs="http://www.w3.org/2000/01/rdf-schema#"
 xmlns:sy="http://purl.org/rss/1.0/modules/syndication/"
 xmlns:admin="http://webns.net/mvcb/"
 xmlns:dcterms="http://purl.org/dc/terms/"
 xmlns:content="http://purl.org/rss/1.0/modules/content/"
 xmlns:foaf="http://xmlns.com/foaf/0.1/"
 xmlns:cc="http://web.resource.org/cc/" xml:lang="en">
```

Prominent among the modules indicated by the above namespace declarations are modules that are part of the Dublin Core Metadata initiative. This allows the inclusion of information about pieces of metadata, like topics to which a blog post relates. A post can be relevant to multiple topics.

```
<dc:subject>Knowledge</dc:subject>
<dc:subject>Blogging</dc:subject>
<dc:subject>Programming</dc:subject>
```

In addition, combinations of RDF and Dublin Core allow associations between information resources to be expressed. The following example indicates a reference to the Semantic Web Applications and Perspectives meeting:

```
<dcterms:references
    rdf:resource=http://semanticweb.deit.univpm.it/swap2004/program.html
    dc:title="Semantic Web Applications and Perspectives (SWAP)"/>
```

The extensibility of Atom 0.3 allows information to be expressed in ways that parallel but expand on the official Atom 0.3 approach. For example, an Atom feed will likely have an `author` element, but it also allows information about an author to be expressed using, for example, the Friend of a Friend (FOAF) approach:

```
<foaf:maker>
 <foaf:Person>
 <foaf:nick>Danny</foaf:nick>
 <foaf:mbox_sha1sum>669fe353dbef63d12ba11f69ace8acbec1ac8b17</foaf:mbox_sha1sum>
 <foaf:homepage rdf:resource="http://dannyayers.com"/>
 <rdfs:seeAlso
   rdf:resource="http://dannyayers.com/archives/author/site-admin/foaf.rdf"/>
 </foaf:Person>
</foaf:maker>
```

Many aggregators will not know how to process such information but, if processing functionality is available in the tool chosen by the user, relationships can be explored which cannot be expressed in Atom 0.3 syntax.

Summary

Atom 0.3 is an XML-based syntax specification for information feed documents. Atom 0.3 is widely used but its future is uncertain at the time of writing due to the development at the IETF of Atom 1.0. Atom 0.3 allows the use of XML namespaces and so extension modules can be included in an Atom 0.3 information feed document.

In this chapter you learned that...

❑   Atom 0.3 is widely used but is likely, officially at least to be replaced by Atom 1.0 in due course.

❑   The document element of an Atom 0.3 feed is the feed element.

❑   In an Atom 0.3 document feed items are called *entries* and are contained in entry elements.

❑   Atom 0.3 uses XML namespaces so elements from other namespaces, for example FOAF (Friend of a Friend), can be included in an Atom 0.3 information feed document.

Exercises

1.   Open the Atom 0.3 feed from www.dannyayers.com and examine its content. The Atom 0.3 feed is located at http://dannyayers.com/feed/atom/. You can see how WordPress creates an Atom 0.3 document.

2.   Compare the structure of an Atom 0.3 feed with an RSS 1.0 feed. You can use the Web service that converts Atom 0.3 to RSS 1.0 at http://cavedoni.com/2004/02/rss1. Enter the URL of an Atom 0.3 feed at http://dannyayers.com/feed/atom/. Compare the structure of the RSS 1.0 feed that is produced by the original, for example, by opening the Atom 0.3 feed in another Firefox tab or browser window.

RSS 0.91 and RSS 0.92

Part of the quirky history of RSS is that the version numbers seem not to correspond with the stability of RSS versions. You might expect versions numbered as 0.91 and 0.92 to have been beta versions that would have been superseded long ago by version 1.0. But, RSS 1.0, which is described in Chapter 9, takes a very different approach than the one used in RSS 0.91 and 0.92. So, despite the version numbering indicating a temporary draft, both RSS 0.91 and 0.92 are still in daily use, alongside RSS 1.0 and RSS 2.0.

This chapter is being written in the final months of 2004, and many tens of thousands of sites are still using RSS 0.91 for their information feed and a substantial but smaller number are using RSS 0.92. Using these versions of RSS works, so perhaps it's an entirely reasonable decision for the person creating the feed because RSS 0.9x successfully performs the necessary task of making the information feed available in a form that most, perhaps all, aggregators can process.

As discussed in Chapter 2, RSS 0.9x did not lead to RSS 1.0, at least not directly. RSS 0.91 and 0.92 are distinctly different technologies from RSS 1.0, which is described in Chapter 9. RSS 2.0, which is described in Chapter 11, is a more direct descendant of RSS 0.9x.

In this chapter you will learn:

- ❑ What RSS 0.91 is
- ❑ About the RSS 0.91 document structure
- ❑ What RSS 0.92 is
- ❑ About the RSS 0.92 document structure

> RSS 0.9 is not discussed in this chapter because it is of historical interest only. If you want to access archived information about RSS 0.9 see, for example, `www.purplepages.ie/RSS/netscape/rss0.90.html`.

What Is RSS 0.91?

RSS 0.91 is a term that's been used to refer to versions of RSS from Netscape and from UserLand. Because the Netscape version is essentially dead, the description of RSS 0.91 in common usage and in most of the remainder of this chapter focuses on RSS 0.91 as defined by Dave Winer in `http://backend.userland.com/rss091`.

The UserLand flavor of RSS 0.91 aimed for simplicity and consciously avoided using XML namespaces, RDF, and XML schemas (specifically a document type definition [DTD], because W3C XML Schema did not exist at the time). This avoidance of complexity made the creation of RSS 0.91 documents pretty simple for those creating a feed, but at the expense of loss of metadata (due to the removal of RDF), loss of the ability to validate a feed at source (no DTD means you can't validate), and loss of the possibility to add modules (because XML namespaces were avoided). For the creation of simple information feeds RSS 0.91 did the job simply and easily. And it still does. Such ease of use was, perhaps, a significant factor in the initial rapid adoption of RSS.

Netscape was the originator of RSS. RSS in its Netscape flavor stood for RDF Site Summary, but in its version 0.91 Netscape dropped RDF, citing lack of RDF tools as a significant factor. However the Netscape 0.91 specification had a full XML DTD to accompany it and required validation against the DTD. The specification is located at `http://my.netscape.com/publish/formats/rss-spec-0.91.html`.

After Netscape essentially moved on from the My Netscape portal they dropped active interest in further development of RSS. And Netscape RSS 0.91 dropped out of the RSS scene, other than on historical grounds.

The RSS 0.91 Document Structure

Each RSS 0.91 document should follow the rules specified at `http://backend.userland.com/rss091`. One of the significant considerations in the UserLand flavor of RSS 0.91 was simplicity.

> **If you want to validate RSS 0.91 code, you can use the online Feed Validator located at** `http://feeds.archive.org/validator/`.

Each RSS 0.91 document is, or should be, a well-formed XML document. Criteria for well-formedness of XML documents were summarized in Chapter 6, "Essentials of XML."

In the following sections, certain elements are described as required. This refers to the description in the RSS 0.91 specification. Some aggregators treat individual elements as optional, whatever the official position in the specification might be. The `image` element is an example. It is said to be required in the specification but is not used by some aggregators.

The rss Element

The document element of an RSS 0.91 document is the rss element. All other elements in an RSS 0.91 document are nested inside the rss element. Each rss element which is the document element of an RSS 0.91 document has a required version attribute with the only allowed value being 0.91.

The start tag of the rss element is, therefore, written using paired double quotes as

```
<rss version="0.91">
```

or using paired single quotes as

```
<rss version='0.91'>
```

The channel Element

An rss element can have only a single child element, which is the channel element. The channel element has no attributes.

Required Child Elements of channel

The channel element must have the following child elements. The RSS 0.91 specification does not state if the items must be contained in the following order:

❑ title: This element contains the name of the web site, blog, and so on. It is ambiguous whether this should be the title of the home page, some content on the home page or what. Because it's a text title, it probably isn't crucial what it contains, as long as the content of title makes sense to the human reader. Text content is a maximum of 100 characters. In practice, it's wise to keep it shorter to ease display in an aggregator.

❑ link: A URL which identifies the web site, blog, and so on, which was named in title. Maximum length is 500 characters. The URL must begin with the character sequence http:// or ftp://.

❑ description: A description of the web site, blog, and so on up to 500 characters in length.

❑ language: A code for the language used in the content of the feed. The codes for language in RSS 0.91 are specified at http://backend.userland.com/stories/storyReader$16. They are similar to the language codes used in any XML language.

❑ image: Contains information about the icon for the information feed. Further information on the content of the image element is contained in a following section.

So a minimalist RSS 0.91 document would look like the following document, MinimalistRSS091.xml:

```
<?xml version="1.0"?>
<rss version="0.91">
 <channel>
  <title>An Interesting Web Site.</title>
  <link>http://www.XMML.com/default.svg</link>
  <description>Learn interesting things on this web site.</description>
  <language>en-us</language>
```

```
<image>
    <url>http://www.XMML.com/somePath/filename.jpg</url>
    <title>A description of the image.</title>
    <link>The URL to which the image should link.</link>
</image>
</channel>
</rss>
```

This document isn't useful for very much since there are no item element children of the channel element.

Optional Child Elements of channel

Optionally, the channel element may have the following child elements. I have listed the item element as an optional element since it is not listed as a required element in the RSS 0.91 specification. In practice, of course, an RSS feed with no items is of little use or interest to the recipient.

❑ copyright: Contains copyright information for the feed. The maximum length is 100 characters.

❑ managingEditor: Contains the e-mail address of the contact person for enquiries about the content of the feed. The suggested format is *name@domain.com (firstname lastname)*. The content has a maximum length of 100 characters.

❑ webMaster: Contains the e-mail address of the webmaster or other person responsible for the technical aspects of the feed. The content has a maximum length of 100 characters.

❑ rating: The PICS (Platform for Internet Content Selection) rating for the feed. The maximum length is 500 characters. PICS allows parents or teachers to identify content which may not be suitable for viewing by children. Further information about PICS is located at www.w3 .org/PICS/.

❑ pubDate: The publication date and time for the feed content. The date time values contained in the pubDate element should conform to the RFC822 specification (see http://asg.web .cmu.edu/rfc/rfc822.html). The relevant part of RFC822 specifies how a date time value is written.

❑ lastBuildDate: An RFC822 value that indicates when the feed was last changed.

❑ docs: Contains a URL which specifies the location of the RSS 0.91 specification. Typically, it would point to http://backend.userland.com/rss091.

❑ skipDays: Lists weekdays on which the user agent should not attempt to access the feed. Each day on which the feed should be skipped is listed in its own day element. For example, a feed which is not changed at the weekend might use the following value in the skipDays element:

```
<skipDays>
 <day>Saturday</day>
 <day>Sunday</day>
<skipDays>
```

❑ skipHours: Lists hours, measured on a 24-hour clock centered on Greenwich Mean Time (now often referred to as Coordinated Universal Time, UTC) during which the user agent should not attempt to access a feed. Each such hour is specified in an hour element. A feed based in the UK which is not updated between midnight and 06:00 might specify the following value:

```
<skipHours>
 <hour>24</hour>
 <hour>1</hour>
 <hour>2</hour>
 <hour>3</hour>
 <hour>4</hour>
 <hour>5</hour>
 <hour>6</hour>
</skipHours>
```

❏   textInput: Allows the display of an input text box and submit button, and may associate the value entered in the text box with a server-side application.

❏   item: The key element in a feed, which contains individual news items or other information items.

The image Element

The image element contains three required child elements and two optional child elements.

❏   url: Contains a URL which is the location of a graphic image, such as a GIF or JPEG. The maximum length of the URL is 500 characters. The URL must begin with the character sequence http:// or ftp://. This is required.

❏   title: Contains a description of the image. Typically the value of this RSS title element will be used in the alt attribute of an HTML/XHTML img element. This is required.

❏   link: Contains a URL to which the image should be linked. Often this will be the same URL contained in the link element which is the child element of the channel element. The URL must begin with the character sequence http:// or ftp://. This is required.

❏   width: Contains the width in pixels of the displayed image. Often this is 88 pixels. Maximum value is 144 pixels. This is optional.

❏   height: Contains the height in pixels of the displayed image. Often this is 31 pixels. Maximum value is 400 pixels. This is optional.

The textInput Element

The textInput element allows the creation of an input text box and a submit button. A common use has been to enter text to be processed by a CGI script.

The following list shows the child elements of the textInput element. Each of these is required if the textInput element is present.

❏   title: Contains the label for the submit button. The maximum length is 100 characters.

❏   description: Contains a description of what the textInput element does. The maximum length is 500 characters.

❏   name: Contains the value of the text object which is passed to a CGI script. Maximum length is 20 characters.

❏   link: Contains the URL of, for example, a CGI script. The maximum length of the URL is 500 characters. The URL must begin with the character sequence http:// or ftp://.

The item Element

The `item` element contains the information about each news story or other information item. In practice all feeds will have at least one `item` element, although in theory an RSS 0.91 document with no `item` elements is possible.

The `item` element has two required child elements and one optional child element.

❑ `title`: Contains a title for a particular information item. The maximum length is 100 characters. This is required.

❑ `link`: Contains a URL that allows linking to the Web page containing the story, blog entry, and so on. This is required. The URL must begin with the character sequence `http://` or `ftp://`.

❑ `description`: A description or extract from the information item. This is a maximum of 500 characters in length and must not contain markup such as HTML or XHTML. This is optional.

The following is a fictional RSS 0.91 document that contains several of the optional elements:

```
<rss version="0.91">
  <channel>
    <title>A Fictional Example RSS 0.91 Feed</title>
    <link>http://www.XMML.com/</link>
    <description>Describes what the site is about.</description>
    <language>en-us</language>
    <copyright>Copyright 1891-2005, XMML.com.</copyright>
    <managingEditor>nobody@XMML.com</managingEditor>
    <webMaster>webmaster@XMML.com</webMaster>
    <lastBuildDate>24/12/2005</lastBuildDate>
    <docs>http://backend.userland.com/rss091</docs>
    <image>
      <title>TheXMMLGraphic</title>
      <url>http://www.XMML.com/images/whichDontReallyExist.gif</url>
      <link>http://www.XMML.com</link>
      <width>88</width>
      <height>31</height>
    </image>
    <item>
      <title>Breathing is good for you!</title>
      <link>http://www.XMML.com/FictionalFeed/BreathingIsGood.html</link>
      <description>Keep doing it several times a day. It really is good for
you.</description>
    </item>
    <item>
      <title>Drinking is good for you too.</title>
      <link>http://www.XMML.com/FictionalFeed/DrinkingIsGood.html</link>
      <description>If you don't drink, you prunify. It's well known. So don't get
too dry.</description>
    </item>
    </channel>
  </rss>
```

Introducing RSS 0.92

In December 2000, UserLand produced a specification for a further version of RSS, version 0.92, information about which is located at `http://backend.userland.com/rss092`. All new features in RSS 0.92 are optional, so any RSS 0.91 document should be parsable as an RSS 0.92 document.

The RSS 0.92 specification followed the RSS 1.0 specification (which had taken an RDF-based route) by a couple of weeks.

The RSS 0.92 Document Structure

The changes to existing elements were minor:

- ❑ The value of the `version` attribute of the `rss` element is `0.92`.

- ❑ The limits on the length of content of RSS 0.91 elements are removed.

- ❑ The `language` element, which was required in RSS 0.91, is optional in RSS 0.92.

- ❑ The `title`, `link`, and `description` elements which are child elements of the `item` element are all optional.

- ❑ Entity-coded HTML is allowed in the content of the `description` element which is a child element of the `item` element.

RSS 0.92 has four new elements: `source`, `enclosure`, `category`, and `cloud`.

New Child Elements of the item Element

The `source`, `enclosure` and `category` elements are new optional child elements of the `item` element.

- ❑ `source`: The content of the `source` element is the name of the RSS feed from which the item was obtained. The `source` element has a `url` attribute whose value is the URL of the feed for the site from which the item was obtained. The purpose of the `source` element is to allow the original source of a feed item to be identifiable.

- ❑ `enclosure`: The `enclosure` element is an empty element. It has three required attributes: `url`, `length`, and `type`. The `url` attribute contains the URL for the enclosure, the `length` attribute contains its size in bytes and the value of the `type` attribute indicates the MIME type of the enclosure. The value of the `url` attribute must be an HTTP URL.

- ❑ `category`: The `category` element has a single required attribute, `domain`. The value of the `domain` attribute should contain the name of a taxonomy or classification. The value of the `category` element is a hierarchical list separated by forward slashes. The hierarchical list belongs to the taxonomy specified in the `domain` attribute.

One view of how the `enclosure` element would be used was to signify audio and video enclosures that would be downloaded in computer "dead time," that is when the user isn't using it. By downloading between, say, midnight and 06:00 large enclosures can be available from the hard disk to give a responsiveness which would be unattainable in real time.

The category element would appear like this:

```
<category domain="http://www.XMML.com/someFictionalClassification/">
/Markup/XML/RSS</category>
```

The cloud Element

The cloud element is an empty element with five required attributes. The purpose of the cloud element is to support the publish-and-subscribe metaphor, which was developed by UserLand using XML-RPC and SOAP. The domain attribute is a URL indicating the address of the cloud (a term used to refer to the publish and subscribe system). The port attribute specifies the port which the user's system is using. The path attribute specifies the path of a listener. The registerProcedure attribute specifies a procedure to be registered with the cloud. The protocol attribute specifies a protocol, such as XML-RPC, to be used.

```
<cloud domain="www.XMML.com/someWebService/" port="80"
  path="/XML-RPC"
  registerProcedure="somethingInteresting.rssPleaseNotify"
  protocol="xml-rpc" />
```

Summary

RSS 0.91 and 0.92 aimed for simplicity in use. They avoided the use of XML namespaces, Resource Description framework (RDF), and the use of a formal schema. The simplicity of RSS 0.9x likely contributed to the early adoption and its continuing popularity.

In this chapter you learned that...

❑   RSS 0.91 and 0.92 were specified by Dave Winer of UserLand.

❑   The document element of each RSS 0.9x specification is the rss element, which is not in an XML namespace.

❑   A channel element is the only allowed child element of an rss element. The rest of an RSS 0.9x document is contained inside the channel element.

❑   Items in an RSS 0.9x feed are contained in item elements.

Exercises

1.   Create a simple RSS 0.91 document and check its validity using the online validator located at http://feeds.archive.org/validator/. You will need to be able to upload the document to a publicly accessible URL using, for example, an FTP client.

2.   Does RSS 0.91 use XML namespaces? Can you explain why the relevant design decision may have been taken?

RSS 1.0

RSS 1.0 uses the Resource Description Framework (RDF) and thus it stands for RDF Site Summary. RSS 1.0 takes a different philosophical and technical approach from UserLand RSS 0.9*x* and RSS 2.0, neither of which uses RDF.

RSS 1.0 returned RSS to its early roots at Netscape by using RDF. However, UserLand RSS 0.91 dropped RDF. The absence of RDF simplified authoring of RSS but reduced its robustness in capturing and expressing relationships among pieces of metadata. The working group who created RSS 1.0 favored the expressiveness of RDF for metadata at the expense of some loss of simplicity in authoring information feed documents.

> **The Resource Description Framework (RDF) is described in Chapter 11.**

One of the philosophical divides in the information feed communities continues to revolve around the use or avoidance of RDF. It isn't the purpose of this chapter to take sides in that debate, but simply to describe for you the fundamentals of RSS 1.0 so that you can, if you want, create an RSS 1.0 feed by hand, or so that you can understand an RSS 1.0 document that serializes RDF via XML.

In this chapter you learn:

- ❏ What RSS 1.0 is
- ❏ About the RSS 1.0 Document Structure
- ❏ About how real-world RSS 1.0 appears

What Is RSS 1.0?

RSS 1.0 uses the RDF to specify an information feed and its metadata. Each RSS 1.0 document is recognized as a valid RDF document. RSS 1.0 is a specification that followed UserLand RSS 0.91 in time and, by a short time, preceded RSS 0.92. The emergence within a month of each other of RSS 1.0 and RSS 0.92 exhibited a deep split at the time in the communities interested in RSS about which aspects of RSS were more important. Broadly speaking, the RSS 1.0 camp favored the potential to handle metadata using RDF (all RSS 1.0 documents are RDF documents), whereas the RSS

0.92 camp favored an approach that continued the simplicity of authoring seen in RSS 0.91. The reality is that divergent views continue to be strongly held by many of the original protagonists.

The RSS 1.0 specification is available online at `http://web.resource.org/rss/1.0/spec`. Discussion about the RSS 1.0 specification takes place on the RSS-Dev mailing list. Further information is located at `http://purl.org/rss/1.0/mailinglist/`.

The following sections briefly introduce important characteristics of RSS 1.0. RSS 1.0 is RDF. It uses XML namespaces and it allows the use of modules that provide a flexible extensibility mechanism. Each of these aspects is considered in more detail in the following sections.

RSS 1.0 Is RDF

RSS 1.0 uses the RDF to express relationships between resources. One of the ways that RDF does that, when serialized as XML, is with liberal use of the `rdf:about` attribute.

For example, the `channel` element (which is in the RSS 1.0 namespace) has an `rdf:about` attribute, which indicates the URL of the blog or other online resource that the RSS 1.0 information feed relates to. The following line of code assumes that the RDF namespace has already been declared and that the namespace prefix `rdf` is used:

```
<channel rdf:about="http://www.tfosorcim.org/blog/">
```

Similarly, each `item` element (which is also in the RSS 1.0 namespace) also has an `rdf:about` attribute:

```
<item rdf:about="http://www.tfosorcim.org/archives/000293.html">
```

The value of the `rdf:about` attribute is a URL. RDF uses URLs to associate pieces of information. An underlying assumption is that each URL or URI is unique.

Other aspects of how RDF is used in RSS 1.0 are discussed later in this chapter when we look in more detail at the structure of an RSS 1.0 document.

> **More detailed information about the Resource Description Framework can be found in Chapter 11.**

RSS 1.0 Uses XML Namespaces

The use of XML namespaces in RSS 1.0 was pretty much inevitable once the decision was made to express RSS 1.0 as a valid RDF document. To assert unambiguously that elements and attributes in an RSS 1.0 document are RDF elements and attributes, XML namespaces cannot be avoided.

```
<rdf:RDF
  xmlns:rdf="http://www.w3.org/1999/02/22-rdf-syntax-ns#"
  xmlns:dc="http://purl.org/dc/elements/1.1/"
  xmlns:sy="http://purl.org/rss/1.0/modules/syndication/"
  xmlns:admin="http://webns.net/mvcb/"
  xmlns:cc="http://web.resource.org/cc/"
  xmlns="http://purl.org/rss/1.0/">
```

The previous example shows several namespace declarations on the start tag of a typical `rdf:RDF` element. Two are directly relevant here, whereas the others are namespace declarations for RSS 1.0 modules, which are discussed in Chapter 10.

The RDF namespace is declared using the following namespace declaration:

```
xmlns:rdf="http://www.w3.org/1999/02/22-rdf-syntax-ns#"
```

The RSS 1.0 namespace is declared using the following namespace declaration:

```
xmlns="http://purl.org/rss/1.0/"
```

This namespace declaration allows RSS 1.0 elements to be expressed without using a namespace prefix on each RSS 1.0 element. When attributes from the RDF namespace are used on elements in the RSS 1.0 namespace they are typically identified by the `rdf` namespace prefix. For example, an `image` element has an `rdf:resource` attribute, indicating the URL where the image can be accessed.

```
<image rdf:resource="http://www.XMML.com/images/SomeSmall.gif" />
```

RSS 1.0 Uses Modules

The use of XML namespaces opens up new vistas of extensibility in RSS 1.0 that weren't possible in RSS 0.9x. In RSS 0.9x all elements were in no namespace so there was no clean way to specify unambiguously that particular elements were RSS elements and that other elements belonged to some other specification or module. RSS 1.0 removes that potential for ambiguity about where an element belongs. Typically, elements that form part of an RSS 1.0 module will be identified by an XML namespace declaration. For example, the following namespace declaration specifies elements that are part of the Dublin Core metadata.

```
xmlns:dc="http://purl.org/dc/elements/1.1/"
```

RSS 1.0 modules are discussed in more detail in Chapter 10.

The RSS 1.0 Document Structure

RSS 1.0 has several differences in document structure from those in RSS 0.9x, which you saw in Chapter 8.

The following markup shows a bare bones RSS 1.0 document. It is included in the code download as `BareRSS1.0.xml`.

```xml
<?xml version="1.0"?>

<rdf:RDF
  xmlns:rdf="http://www.w3.org/1999/02/22-rdf-syntax-ns#"
  xmlns="http://purl.org/rss/1.0/">

  <channel rdf:about="http://www.XMML.com/Feed.rdf">
    <title>XMML.com</title>
```

```
      <link>http://www.XMML.com/</link>
      <description>
      The description of the information feed would go here.
      </description>

      <image rdf:resource="http://www.XMML.com/images/SomeSmall.gif" />

      <items>
        <rdf:Seq>
          <rdf:li resource="http://www.XMML.com/2005/03/19.html" />
          <rdf:li resource="http://www.XMML.com/2005/03/20.html" />
        </rdf:Seq>
      </items>

  </channel>
  <image rdf:about="http://www.XMML.com/images/SomeSmall.gif">
    <title>XMML.com</title>
    <link>http://www.XMML.com</link>
    <url>http://xml.com/images/SomeSmall.gif</url>
  </image>
  <item rdf:about="http://www.XMML.com/2005/03/19.html">
    <title>What happened on March 19th</title>
    <link>http://www.XMML.com/2005/03/19.html</link>
    <description>
    This item describes what happened on March 19th.
    </description>
  </item>
  <item rdf:about="http://www.XMML.com/2005/03/20.html">
    <title>What happened on March 20th</title>
    <link>http://www.XMML.com/2005/03/20.html</link>
    <description>
     This item described what happened on March 20th.
    </description>
  </item>
</rdf:RDF>
```

Let's look in more detail at the structure of the RSS 1.0 document. An XML declaration is optional but desirable in each RSS 1.0 document. The document element of each RSS 1.0 document is the `rdf:RDF` element, with the namespace prefix `rdf` being used to signify that the `rdf:RDF` element is an element in the RDF namespace. The start tag of the `rdf:RDF` element has at least two namespace declarations, one for the RDF namespace and the other for the RSS 1.0 namespace.

```
<rdf:RDF
   xmlns:rdf="http://www.w3.org/1999/02/22-rdf-syntax-ns#"
   xmlns="http://purl.org/rss/1.0/"
 >
```

Typically, if RSS 1.0 modules are used, other namespace declarations will also be present in the start tag of the `rdf:RDF` element.

The channel Element

The `channel` element is one of four permitted child elements of the `rdf:RDF` element. The others are `image`, `item`, and `textinput`.

The `channel` element can contain `title`, `link`, `description`, `items`, `textinput`, and `image` elements as its child elements. The `title` element contains the title of the information feed. The `link` element contains a URL that, typically, is the URL for the site or page associated with the information feed. The `description` element contains a short description of the information feed. The `items` element is described later. The `image` and `textinput` elements are optional. Each is described later, since a similarly named element can occur as a child element of the `rdf:RDF` element.

```
<channel rdf:about="http://www.XMML.com/Feed.rdf">
  <title>XMML.com</title>
  <link>http://www.XMML.com/</link>
  <description>
  The description of the information feed would go here.
  </description>
```

The content of the `channel` element is significantly different from the content of the `channel` element in RSS 0.91. In RSS 1.0, the `item` elements are not child elements of the `channel` element. Instead, an `items` element contains references to individual `item` elements in the information feed that are child elements of the `rdf:RDF` element and are sibling elements of the `channel` element.

The items Element

The `items` element is, essentially, a table of contents for the information feed. The sequence of information items is contained inside an `rdf:Seq` element which is a child element of the `items` element.

```
<items>
  <rdf:Seq>
    <rdf:li resource="http://www.XMML.com/2005/03/19.html" />
    <rdf:li resource="http://www.XMML.com/2005/03/20.html" />
  </rdf:Seq>
</items>
```

Each item in the information feed is referenced using an `rdf:li` element. The `rdf:li` element has a `resource` attribute whose value is a URL. The item being referenced has an `rdf:about` attribute whose value is the same URL.

The first `rdf:li` element in the preceding sample code,

```
<rdf:li resource="http://www.XMML.com/2005/03/19.html" />
```

contains the same URL as an `item` element, later in the document. The `rdf:li` element and the `item` element are associated since the URL in the `resource` attribute of the `rdf:li` element has the same value as the URL in the `rdf:about` attribute of the `item` element.

```
<item rdf:about="http://www.XMML.com/2005/03/19.html">
  <title>What happened on March 19th</title>
  <link>http://www.XMML.com/2005/03/19.html</link>
  <description>
  This item describes what happened on March 19th.
  </description>
</item>
```

The image Element

The `image` element is an optional child element of the `rdf:RDF` element. It contains an `rdf:about` attribute whose value is a URL that contains the location of an image associated with the information feed. The same URL is contained in the `url` element that is a child element of the `image` element. The `title` and `link` elements contain a title for the image and a link to the Web site associated with the information feed.

```
<image rdf:about="http://www.XMML.com/images/SomeSmall.gif">
  <title>XMML.com</title>
  <link>http://www.XMML.com</link>
  <url>http://xml.com/images/SomeSmall.gif</url>
</image>
```

The content of the `title` element can be used as alternative text when the information feed is rendered in HTML or XHTML. The content of the `url` element will, typically, be used as the value of the `src` attribute when the image is rendered in HTML or XHTML.

The `image` element, which is an optional child element of the `channel` element, has the same attribute and allowed child elements.

The item Element

The `rdf:RDF` element has one child `item` element for each item in the information feed. Each `item` element is referenced from the corresponding `rdf:li` element, which is contained in the `items` element, which, in turn, is a child element of the `channel` element, as described earlier in the section on the `items` element.

```
<item rdf:about="http://www.XMML.com/2005/03/19.html">
  <title>What happened on March 19th</title>
  <link>http://www.XMML.com/2005/03/19.html</link>
  <description>
  This item describes what happened on March 19th.
  </description>
</item>
```

Each item element must have an `rdf:about` element with a URL value that matches the value in the `resource` attribute of an `rdf:li` element, otherwise the item cannot be referenced as part of the information feed.

The title, link, and description elements, which are child elements of each item element, serve the obvious purpose. The title and link elements are required child elements. The description child element is optional.

The textinput Element

The textinput element enables you to input text to be used server side to provide input to search functionality, for example. The textinput element, which is a child of the rdf:RDF element must, if it is present, be referenced by a textinput element, which is a child of the channel element.

The textinput element, a child of channel, looks like this:

```
<textinput rdf:resource="http://search.XMML.com" />
```

The corresponding textinput element, which is a child of rdf:RDF, looks like this:

```
<textinput rdf:about="http://search.XMML.com">
  <title>Search XMML.com</title>
  <description>Search XMML.com's information.</description>
  <name>Search</name>
  <link>http://search.XMML.com</link>
</textinput>
```

The title, description, name, and link elements are all required child elements. Notice that the URL value of the rdf:resource attribute in the textinput element inside the channel element must match the URL value of the rdf:about attribute in the textinput element which is a child element of the rdf:RDF element.

Some Real-World RSS 1.0

Having looked at the basics of RSS 1.0, it's time to take a look at some real-world RSS 1.0. On the home page of the World Wide Web Consortium (www.w3.org/), you can find a link to the RSS 1.0 feed for the W3C home page. At the time of writing, the RSS feed is available at www.w3.org/2000/08/w3c-synd/home.rss. Figure 9-1 shows the appearance of the RSS feed page in the Firefox browser, when styled for human consumption on a date during the writing of this chapter.

The page looks suspiciously like a simple HTML or XHTML Web page, with no markup in sight. If you use the View Page Source option, you can see what is happening behind the scenes. Figure 9-2 shows some of the RSS 1.0 code for the page.

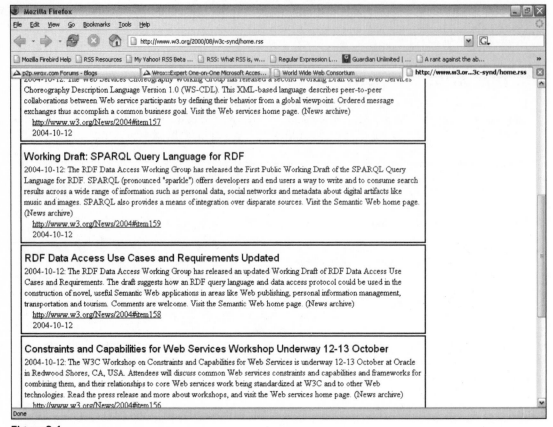

Figure 9-1

In the second line of the feed, you can see that there is an `xml-stylesheet` processing instruction that specifies how the content of the RSS 1.0 information feed is to be styled. The stylesheet linked to the information feed by the processing instruction produces the specific visual effect that you see in Figure 9-2. On the following line, you can see the `rdf:RDF` element's start tag with multiple namespace declarations.

The code for the W3C RSS feed on the relevant date is in the code download in the file `W3C_Home_20041021.rss` if you want to examine it all.

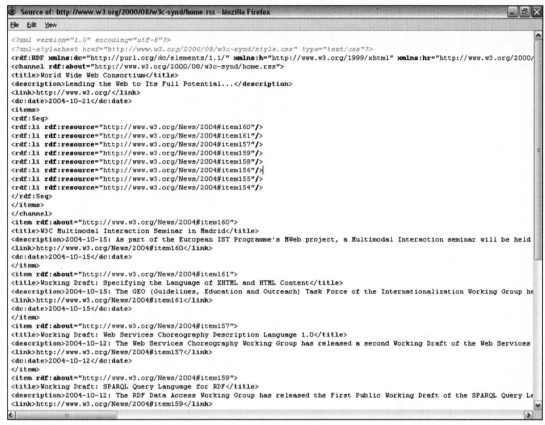

Figure 9-2

The W3C, by default, formats the RSS feed as shown in Figure 9-1. However, individual aggregators will format the data in different ways, in part influenced by user preferences in individual tools. Figure 9-3 shows the feed shown in Figures 9-1 and 9-2 in the RSS Bandit aggregator.

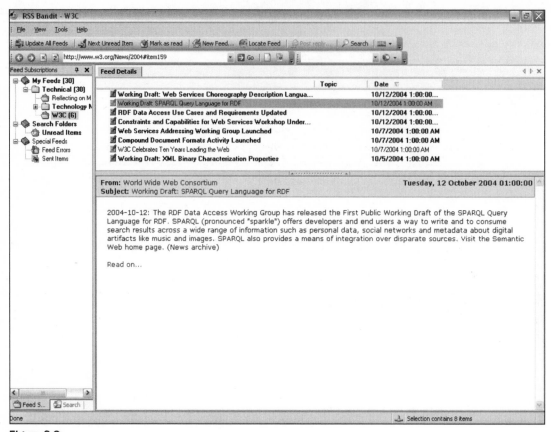

Figure 9-3

Summary

RSS 1.0 takes a different approach to information feeds than the emphasis on simplicity in RSS 0.9x. RSS 1.0 uses the RDF and uses URLs contained in RDF attributes to associate pieces of metadata. RSS 1.0 uses XML namespace declarations to allow elements to be in the RSS 1.0 and RDF namespaces. XML namespaces also allow RSS 1.0 to include RSS 1.0 Modules, which are described in Chapter 10.

In this chapter you learned that...

❑   RSS 1.0 uses the Resource Description Framework (RDF).

❑   The document element of an RSS 1.0 document is the `rdf:RDF` element.

❏   The `channel` element contains, among other things, a table of contents for feed items. That table of contents is contained in an `items` element.

❏   Each feed item is contained in an `item` element. Each `item` element is associated with a corresponding `rdf:li` element which is a child of the `items` element.

Exercise

1.   Examine the RSS 1.0 feeds located at `www.w3.org/2000/08/w3c-synd/home.rss` and `www.tfosorcim.org/blog/index.rdf`. Examine the structure of the current contents of those RSS 1.0 feeds. Notice, in particular, how URLs are used to associate parts of the document structure.

RSS 1.0 Modules

One of the innovations in the RSS 1.0 specification, compared to the 0.9x versions of RSS, was the introduction of XML namespaces that provide the foundation for the use of modules in RSS 1.0. The use of XML namespaces allows the use of RSS 1.0 elements together with elements from the Resource Description Format (RDF) namespace in a single RSS 1.0 document. More importantly, the use of XML namespaces also allows the use of elements from namespaces other than RSS 1.0 and RDF in a single document.

The availability of additional elements allows specialist information feeds to be created. All that is needed is that the aggregators and the generators of such feeds choose a predictable structure for the specialist elements. Aggregators intended for general usage may simply ignore a module of unknown elements or, if the module is important, may choose to process the module and add the data contained in it in an appropriate way.

A significant advantage of the availability of modules is that the RSS 1.0 specification can be extended without the core specification having to be revised. This means that development of new types of documents based on RSS 1.0 can be carried out without having to achieve a consensus among the full range of RSS 1.0 users.

In this chapter you learn:

- ❑ About the use of modules in RSS 1.0
- ❑ What the official modules in RSS 1.0 are
- ❑ How additional modules can be included in RSS 1.0 documents

RSS Modules

Having modules available in RSS 1.0 has several advantages. The core specification is simple and can stay simple, even when specialist groups choose to extend RSS 1.0 documents for non-standard purposes. Without extensibility mechanisms it would be necessary for the RSS 1.0 specification to be superseded in order to allow any new elements to be added to the specification. Only elements that meet with widespread approval would be likely to be added. Minority or specialist interest groups would find it difficult to have their needs for additional elements met.

Assuming that they select an XML namespace that won't lead to naming collisions so that the specialist modules are simply ignored by other aggregators, there is no reason for other groups to object. Specialist aggregators can be designed that process documents with the new extensions. This provides a flexible way to allow interested parties to exchange information of particular interest via information feeds while allowing normal aggregators to display typical information item data to ordinary users.

RSS modules are widely used in RSS 1.0 information feeds. The following example shows part of the RSS 1.0 information from my blog, `www.tfosorciM.org/blog/`. Notice that multiple namespace declarations are present on the start tag of the `rdf:RDF` element. Some of these extension modules, such as Dublin Core, Content, and Syndication, are described in detail later in this chapter. Each of those modules is an official RSS 1.0 module.

```
<?xml version="1.0" encoding="iso-8859-1"?>

<rdf:RDF
  xmlns:rdf="http://www.w3.org/1999/02/22-rdf-syntax-ns#"
  xmlns:dc="http://purl.org/dc/elements/1.1/"
  xmlns:sy="http://purl.org/rss/1.0/modules/syndication/"
  xmlns:admin="http://webns.net/mvcb/"
  xmlns:cc="http://web.resource.org/cc/"
  xmlns="http://purl.org/rss/1.0/">

<channel rdf:about="http://www.tfosorcim.org/blog/">
<title>tfosorciM.org</title>
<link>http://www.tfosorcim.org/blog/</link>
<description>Reflecting on Microsoft</description>
<dc:language>en-us</dc:language>
<dc:creator></dc:creator>
<dc:date>2004-11-11T19:07:15+00:00</dc:date>
<admin:generatorAgent rdf:resource="http://www.movabletype.org/?v=2.661" />
```

The RSS 1.0 Official Modules

RSS 1.0 has three official modules, Content, Dublin Core, and Syndication. The Dublin Core and Syndication modules were included in the original version of the RSS 1.0 specification in December 2000. The Content module was added in March 2001.

> **The official specification of RSS 1.0 modules is located at** `http://web.resource`
> `.org/rss/1.0/modules/`.

The RSS 1.0 specification was developed on the RSS-Dev mailing list. Further information on RSS-Dev is available at `www.yahoogroups.com/group/rss-dev/`. Modules are categorized as *Proposed* if they are under discussion by the mailing list. If they are adopted by the mailing list, or an appropriately authorized subgroup, they can be adopted as *Standard*. Proposed modules are listed at http://web.resource.org/rss/1.0/modules/proposed.html.

The Modules specification encourages modules to be tightly focused to fulfil a single clearly defined purpose. This tends to lead to rather simple individual modules without bloat of unnecessary or rarely used elements.

RDF Parser Compatibility

RSS 1.0 information feed documents are also RDF documents, as the rdf:RDF document element indicates. The modules specification encourages authors of modules to use a syntax that can be parsed by generic RDF parsers. To that end, elements in modules containing XML elements that aren't written as RDF should contain an indication of how they are to be parsed. So elements from the Dublin Core could be specified as follows:

```
<dc:creator rdf:parseType="Literal">
  <name>
    <firstname>John</firstname>
    <middle_initial>D.</middle_initial>
    <lastname>Smith</lastname>
  </name>
</dc:creator>
```

The rdf:parseType attribute indicates to an RDF parser that the content of the element should not be interpreted.

In practice, many aggregators will simply use XML parsing for RSS 1.0 documents. Similarly, many feed creation tools will focus more on the XML aspects rather than the RDF syntax compliance. This means that RDF compatibility of modules can be problematic in some circumstances.

Module Compatibility

Poorly structured modules could confuse the interpretation or structure of elements in the core RSS 1.0 specification or in other RSS 1.0 modules. The Modules specification requires, however, that no module is allowed to make modifications to elements in the core specification or in other modules. This approach ensures consistency of structure of elements in core RSS 1.0 and in other modules.

The Content Module

The Content module is intended for the description of the content of Web sites and is intended to allow content in multiple formats to be specified.

When elements in the RSS 1.0 Content module are used in an RSS 1.0 document, the Content namespace must be declared. Typically, this is done by including an XML declaration for the namespace URI on the start tag of the rdf:RDF element of the information feed document.

```
xmlns:content="http://purl.org/rss/1.0/modules/content/"
```

The content:items Element

The `content:items` element contains one or more `content:item` elements, with a structure similar to the following markup. The `content:items` element is used inside an RSS 1.0 `channel` element or `item` element. Notice that the `rdf:Bag` element (whose content is unordered) is used rather than the `rdf:Seq` element (whose content is ordered).

```
<content:items>
 <rdf:Bag>
  <rdf:li>
   <content:item>
    <!-- Content of content:item goes here. -->
   </content:item>
  </rdf:li>
  <!-- More content:item elements can go here. -->
 </rdf:Bag>
</content:items>
```

The content:item Element

The `content:item` element can be written in two ways. One uses an `rdf:about` attribute, the other does not. The syntax for the former syntax variant is:

```
<content:item>
   <!-- information about the item goes here -->
</content:item>
```

When an `rdf:about` attribute is present, the `content:item` element is written as follows:

```
<content:item rdf:about="http://www.XMML.com/items/content.html">
   <!-- information about the item goes here -->
</content:item>
```

The `content:item` element can have three child elements: the `content:format` element, the `rdf:value` element, and the `content:encoding` element.

The `content:format` element is required. It is an empty element. Its `rdf:resource` attribute indicates the format of the content. For example, if the content is written in XHTML 1.0 and is written to conform to the XHTML Strict DTD, the following appears:

```
<content:format rdf:resource="http://www.w3.org/TR/xhtml1/DTD/xhtml1-strict" />
```

If the content was a Scalable Vector Graphics (SVG) document the `content:format` element is written as follows:

```
<content:format rdf:resource="http://www.w3.org/2000/svg" />
```

The `rdf:value` element is required if the `content:item` element is written without a URI. The `rdf:value` element contains the content. The encoding of the content is specified using the optional `content:encoding` element. If the content of the `rdf:value` element is written as unencoded XML, the `rdf:parseType` attribute should be used to specify to an RDF parser how the content is to be processed.

```
<rdf:value parseType="Literal">
  <!-- The content goes here. -->
</rdf:value>
```

The `content:encoding` element is optional. When present, it uses an `rdf:resource` attribute to indicate what encoding is used. For example, if the content is well-formed XML, the following syntax is used for the `content:encoding` element:

```
<content:encoding rdf:resource="http://www.w3.org/TR/REC-xml#dt-wellformed" />
```

> **The Content module is specified at** `http://web.resource.org/rss/1.0/modules/content/`.

The Dublin Core Module

The Dublin Core module uses elements from the Dublin Core Metadata Initiative.

When elements in the RSS 1.0 Dublin Core module are used in an RSS 1.0 document, the Dublin Core namespace must be declared. Typically, this is done by including an XML declaration for the namespace URI on the start tag of the `rdf:RDF` element of the information feed document.

```
xmlns:dc="http://purl.org/dc/elements/1.1/"
```

The elements of the Dublin Core module can be used as child elements of the RSS 1.0 `channel`, `item`, `image`, and `textinput` elements.

The traditional way of writing Dublin Core elements is with simple text as content. For example, an article about woodworking might be written as follows:

```
<dc:subject>Woodworking</dc:subject>
```

The way that RSS 1.0 modules are constructed it is possible to extend them further. Typically, as just demonstrated, the `dc:subject` element can contain a simple text value. However, the module specification illustrates how a more formal taxonomy can be incorporated as a rich content model for the `dc:subject` element. Notice how the `rdf:about` and `rdf:value` attributes are used to provide RDF-based specification of the meaning of the subject. The following code assumes that the `taxo` namespace prefix has been declared elsewhere.

```
<dc:subject>
   <taxo:topic rdf:about="http://dmoz.org/Arts/Crafts/Wood_Craft/Woodworking/">
      <rdf:value="Woodworking" />
   </taxo:topic>
</dc:subject>
```

This approach allows semantics to be simple (either by using a literal text value or the value of the `rdf:value` element) or richer for those user agents that can process the richer semantics.

The following table lists the elements of the Dublin Core module, together with a brief description of their uses. The content of each element can be a simple text literal or can use the `taxo:topic` element to provide richer content semantics. The formal definition of Dublin Core elements is located at `http://dublincore.org/documents/1999/07/02/dces/`.

Dublin Core Module Element	Description
`dc:contributor`	An entity that has made a contribution to the content of a resource. Examples include a person or company.
`dc:coverage`	Indicates concepts such as geographical location or time period to which the resource refers.
`dc:creator`	An entity responsible for creating a resource. Examples include a person or company.
`dc:date`	A date that typically indicates the date of the creation or publication of a resource.
`dc:description`	A description of the content of a resource. This can consist of, for example, a summary or table of contents.
`dc:format`	Indicates the physical presentation of the resource. Often this is a MIME type.
`dc:identifier`	An identifier intended to be unambiguous. Examples include a URI or an ISBN.
`dc:language`	The language used in the content of the resource. Examples include `en` and `en-us`.
`dc:publisher`	An entity responsible for making a resource available. Examples include a person or company.
`dc:relation`	A reference to a related resource.
`dc:rights`	Contains information about intellectual property rights.
`dc:source`	A reference to another resource from which the present resource is derived in whole or in part.
`dc:subject`	The topic of the content contained in a resource.
`dc:title`	The title of the resource.
`dc:type`	The genre of the resource.

> **Information on the Dublin Core module is located at** `http://web.resource.org/rss/1.0/modules/dc/`.

The Syndication Module

The RSS 1.0 Syndication module is intended to convey information about the frequency of publication of an RSS 1.0 information feed. The Syndication module elements are intended to perform a similar function to the skipDay and skipHour elements of the UserLand flavor of RSS 0.91.

When elements in the RSS 1.0 Syndication module are used in an RSS 1.0 document, the Syndication namespace must be declared. Typically, this is done by including an XML declaration for the namespace URI on the start tag of the rdf:RDF element of the information feed document. Typically, the sy namespace prefix is used for elements in the namespace for the Syndication module.

```
xmlns:sy="http://purl.org/rss/1.0/modules/syndication/"
```

The Syndication module specifies three elements: the updatePeriod, updateFrequency, and updateBase elements.

The updatePeriod element specifies how often an information feed is updated. Allowed values are hourly, daily, weekly, monthly, and yearly. If the updatePeriod element is absent or if it is empty, the value daily is assumed.

The updateFrequency element specifies how often the information feed is updated during the period specified in the updatePeriod element. The expected value of the updateFrequency element is a positive integer. If the updateFrequency element is absent or if it is empty, a value of 1 is assumed.

The updateBase element specifies a datetime value that indicates the date and time on which the publishing schedule is based. The value of the updateBase element takes the form yyyy-mm-ddThh:mm.

> **The specification of the RSS 1.0 Syndication module is located at** http://purl.org/rss/1.0/modules/syndication/.

An information feed that's updated twice daily is specified as follows:

```
<sy:updatePeriod>daily</sy:updatePeriod>
<sy:updateFrequency>2</sy:updateFrequency>
```

Similarly, an information feed that's updated weekly is specified like this:

```
<sy:updatePeriod>weekly</sy:updatePeriod>
<sy:updateFrequency>1</sy:updateFrequency>
```

If an updateBase element is specified, the day of the week and the time of updating (assuming that weekly means exactly 168 hours apart) can be specified. December 13, 2004 is a Monday. So the following markup specifies a weekly update at 16:00 on a Monday:

```
<sy:updatePeriod>weekly</sy:updatePeriod>
<sy:updateFrequency>1</sy:updateFrequency>
<sy:updateBase>2004-12-13T16:00</sy:updateBase>
```

You can also specify a timezone in the value of the `updateBase` element. The following indicates an information feed based in the UTC (GMT) timezone with a weekly publication timing as described in the previous example.

```
<sy:updatePeriod>weekly</sy:updatePeriod>
<sy:updateFrequency>1</sy:updateFrequency>
<sy:updateBase>2004-12-13T16:00+00:00</sy:updateBase>
```

When the Syndication module is used in the information feed for a blog, the `updateBase` element is rarely used, because updating of a blog is rarely as regular as the publication of an online magazine is.

In reality, most blogs are updated on a pretty sporadic basis. The primary use of the `updatePeriod` and `updateFrequency` is more to discourage aggregators from putting an unnecessary load on the server that supplies the information feed, rather than any realistic description of the precise periodicity with which a blog is updated.

Including Other Modules in RSS 1.0 Feed Documents

Modules not included in the RSS 1.0 specification can be included anywhere in the RSS 1.0 document, provided that the namespace declaration for the module has been declared correctly. Examples from two widely used modules are described in the following sections.

Adding the Namespace Declaration

The namespace declaration is probably best included in the start tag of the `rdf:RDF` element. The XML 1.0 specification does not require that, but having all namespace declarations on one start tag makes it easier to see the namespaces used in a complex information feed document. So putting the namespace declaration on the start tag of the `rdf:RDF` element is good practice.

The Admin Module

Many blogging tools and similar feed creator tools use the Admin module to indicate the nature of the tool used to create the information feed. The namespace declaration of the Admin module is written as follows:

```
xmlns:admin="http://webns.net/mvcb/"
```

When using WordPress, the Admin module appears like this:

```
<admin:generatorAgent rdf:resource="http://wordpress.org/?v=1.2"/>
```

The FOAF Module

The FOAF, Friend of a friend, module is used to indicate relationships between human beings. The namespace declaration is written as

```
xmlns:foaf="http://xmlns.com/foaf/0.1/"
```

The following is an example from Danny Ayer's Web site of how the FOAF module can be used:

```
<foaf:Person>
  <foaf:nick>Danny</foaf:nick>
  <foaf:mbox_sha1sum>669fe353dbef63d12ba11f69ace8acbec1ac8b17</foaf:mbox_sha1sum>
 <foaf:homepage rdf:resource="http://dannyayers.com"/>
 <rdfs:seeAlso xmlns:rdfs="http://www.w3.org/2000/01/rdf-schema#"
rdf:resource="http://dannyayers.com/archives/author/site-admin/foaf.rdf"/>
</foaf:Person>
```

Summary

RSS 1.0 uses XML namespaces. All RSS 1.0 documents include elements from two XML namespaces — the RSS 1.0 namespace and the Resource Description Framework namespace. The RSS 1.0 specification identifies three official modules available for use in RSS 1.0 documents — the Content module, the Dublin Core module, and the Syndication module. Groups interested in adding other, possibly more specialized, modules are free to add such modules to RSS 1.0 documents, provided that they are used in permitted places in the structure of an RSS 1.0 document.

In this chapter you learned that...

❑ To use RSS 1.0 modules the appropriate namespace declaration must be made.

❑ RSS 1.0 has three official modules: Content, Dublin Core, and Syndication.

❑ The Content module can be used to specify the nature of the content of a Web site to which an information feed refers.

❑ The Dublin Core module contains information about the author, publication date, and so on of an information feed.

❑ The Syndication module contains information about the frequency of publication of an information feed.

❑ Modules other than the official RSS 1.0 modules can be used in RSS 1.0 information feed documents.

RDF: The Resource Description Framework

The Resource Description Framework (RDF) is intended to provide a way of representing metadata related to resources and the relationships of those resources with other related resources. Typically, resources are located on the World Wide Web or are conceptually identifiable using a Uniform Resource Identifier (URI).

More simply put, RDF is information about information or, if you prefer, data about data. But what does that mean? RDF isn't the data itself; it tells you something about the data. For example, the phrase "Hello World!" is used widely in beginning programming tutorials. We can say something about that phrase — that it's in the English language — without changing the phrase and without the idea of "English language" being part of the data. The idea of saying that "Hello World!" is written in English is a simple piece of metadata. It's not part of the data, that's simply "Hello World!" but it tells us about a characteristic of the data. In the context of an information feed, metadata includes publication date and author information.

Is it worth collecting metadata in information feeds? For some people and some uses of information the answer is "No." For others the answer is "Yes." In the context of information feeds, the split in philosophy between those who view information that's contained in information feeds as, essentially, disposable and those who view that information as potentially of lasting value becomes an important determinant of opinions on RDF. If you don't see items in information feeds as worth keeping then adding metadata, particularly metadata in RDF, to the feed is just a hassle. If you see items in information feeds having potentially lasting value, it makes sense (at least in some circumstances) to make the additional effort of adding RDF metadata to the feed. Those who see information feeds as conduits for disposable information often have little or no time for the idea of using RDF in a feed.

In this chapter you will learn:

- ❑   What RDF is
- ❑   How RDF is relevant to information feeds
- ❑   How an RSS 1.0 document is structured as XML/RDF

What Is RDF?

Fundamentally, RDF is a format or framework to represent metadata. More specifically, RDF is intended to provide information about properties of resources on the World Wide Web or resources identified by URIs and relationships among such resources. RDF can be used to refer to resources unambiguously, if globally unique URIs are used to express the logical connections among resources.

To understand what RDF is about, take a look again at what metadata is and how it can be expressed.

Simple Metadata

Metadata is data about data. You can say that "Hello World!" is written in English. You don't need to use RDF to express that. For example, in RSS 0.91, you could write:

```
<rss version="0.91">
  <channel>
    <!-- Other elements here. -->
    <language>en</language>
```

The content of the RSS 0.91 `language` element contains that piece of metadata that implicitly states that the content of the `channel` element is written in English. Somewhere else in the same document you might find the following:

```
<item>
  <description>Hello World!</description>
```

The content of the `description` element is pretty obviously in English to any human reader. But how is a machine to know that? What is the method of connection between the content of the `language` element and the content of the `description` element? The logical connection is contained in what I call *structural semantics*. The structure of the document is used to make the connection. All the content of the `channel` element is written in English. And that's adequate when dealing with single documents. But what happens when parts of information feed documents are shredded and used in other documents? The RDF approach is to use URIs to indicate a logical connection between pieces of information.

Simple Facts Expressed in RDF

To get a handle on how facts are expressed in RDF, you can first express the fact that "Hello World!" and the other content of the channel is written in English in a semi-formal form. You can express the idea as follows:

```
The channel's language is English
```

Similarly, you could say:

```
This chapter's author is Andrew Watt
```

Expressing ideas in this way is natural to human beings but poses significant difficulties for machine processing. A more formal, machine-understandable, model is needed to express even such simple ideas in ways that can reliably be understood by software.

The RDF Triple

In RDF, the fundamental way to conceptualize a fact is through the *RDF Triple*. To convey a fact, three pieces of information are needed: a subject, a property, and a value. To express a fact, you need these three pieces of information.

In the following example, the subject is `chapter`, the property is `author`, and the value is `Andrew Watt`.

```
This chapter has the author Andrew Watt
```

To express the same notion in a more generalized, abstract way, consider this:

```
[The subject] has [a property] with this [value]
```

The subject is the thing being described; in this case the subject is this chapter. In RDF jargon, the subject is a *resource*.

The property is some characteristic of the resource. For example, it might be an attribute of the resource, or some relationship of the resource. In RDF jargon the property is called a *predicate*.

The value corresponds to a value of the predicate. In RDF jargon the value is called the *object*.

So, you can rewrite the preceding generalized form as

```
[The resource] has a [predicate] with this [object].
```

For many newcomers to RDF the jargon does get in the way. If you find it easy to think that a subject has a property with a particular value, you might initially find it difficult to think in terms of a resource having a predicate with an object. Personally, I find it much more natural to think in terms of subject, property, and value. But whoever said that computing was natural?

Now that you know the terms that RDF uses for the concepts that are part of the simple statement,

```
This chapter has the author Andrew Watt
```

how can you identify which chapter you are talking about? It's fine to use the term "This chapter" inside this chapter, but how can you refer in an unambiguous way to this chapter from other chapters inside this book or other books or other places that aren't books at all? To solve this problem, RDF uses URIs.

Using URIs in RDF

URIs are used to identify resources. So how can you use a URI to help identify which chapter you mean by the term "this chapter"?

What URI should be used? This book is published by Wrox Press. So, in constructing a URI, it seems a good choice to start with `http://www.wrox.com`. Of course Wrox publishes many books. So you need a way to identify the book. Using the last six digits of the ISBN, `579169`, seems a reasonable approach.

Then you need a way to uniquely refer to the chapter. Because this is Chapter 11, use `chapter11`. A URI to identify uniquely the resource that is this chapter could reasonably be `http://www.wrox.com/579169/chapter11/`.

So the statement can be rewritten as

```
http://www.wrox.com/579169/chapter11/ has the author Andrew Watt
```

The author (which is the predicate) can also be represented by a URI, perhaps `http://www.wrox.com/579169/chapter11/author/`. It becomes a bit clumsy in English to recast the previous statement using two URIs in it, but they fit nicely in the RDF way of looking at this — the *directed graph.*

Directed Graphs

In RDF the directed, labeled graph is the default way to express an instance of the RDF data model. Because the RDF triple describing the author of this chapter is a simple example based on the RDF data model, you can express it as a simple directed, labeled graph. Figure 11-1 shows a directed, labeled graph that expresses as an RDF triple the notion that Andrew Watt is the author of this chapter.

Figure 11-1

The resource is shown on the left in the round cornered rectangle. It's a *node* representing the resource and identified by the URI you chose earlier. The predicate (the URI representing the author) is shown as a URI, which labels the *arc,* which connects the resource node to the object node.

An RDF triple can be represented by two nodes and an arc connecting them. There are three varieties of node, only two of which are used in Figure 11-1. The *uriref* type of node uses a URI reference, in this case to uniquely identify a chapter in a particular book (this chapter in this book). The *literal* node contains the name of this chapter's author.

Directed labeled graphs can, of course, be much more complex than shown in Figure 11-1. For example, it uses literal text to represent the name of the author. But because this same person has written other chapters and other books you might want to use a URI to uniquely identify him. The literal value `Andrew Watt` is ambiguous. There might be hundreds of people with the same name. If he is identified by a URI, his relationships to other chapters in this book and to other books can be explored, as can his gender, eye color, and so on.

If the various pieces of information were available publicly and appropriately associated with a unique URI such as `http://www.andrewwatt.com/theguy/` then an RDF processor could bring those pieces of information together in a way that allows you to build up a picture of the characteristics and relationships of the person.

Identifying people as objects and resources can seem a bit unnatural. It's also not usually convenient for human beings to identify each other by URIs. But on a global network some unique identifier is needed if related pieces of information are to be unambiguously associated. The URI provides a machine-processable solution.

How RDF and XML Are Related

It doesn't take much imagination to realize that sending directed graphs across the Internet isn't, typically, a very practical solution. In order to express the RDF model (which we won't discuss in detail because the purpose of discussing RDF in this book is to help you understand its use in RSS 1.0) and send it across the wire, you need a way to serialize the RDF model. *Serialization* is the creation of a series of characters to represent the model. One way to do that is to serialize RDF as XML, which is called RDF/XML.

All the RDF elements and attributes that you saw in RSS 1.0 documents or markup fragments are written in RDF/XML.

You saw earlier that a URI is used in the arc of a directed graph. Having seen that, the way that parts of an RSS 1.0 document are related might now become clearer. Inside the `channel` element you will see an `items` element whose content represents the table of contents of an information feed:

```
<items>
  <rdf:Seq>
    <rdf:li resource="http://www.XMML.com/2005/03/19.html" />
    <rdf:li resource="http://www.XMML.com/2005/03/20.html" />
  </rdf:Seq>
</items>
```

Each of the two `rdf:li` elements has a `resource` attribute that contains a URI. Somewhere else in the same document, you find the following markup relating to one item in the information feed:

```
<item rdf:about="http://www.XMML.com/2005/03/19.html">
  <title>What happened on March 19th</title>
  <link>http://www.XMML.com/2005/03/19.html</link>
  <description>
  This item describes what happened on March 19th.
  </description>
</item>
```

Putting this in terms of the RDF triple, you could say the following:

```
The [item in the TOC] has a URI http://www.XMML.com/2005/03/19.html associated with
    [the content of an item element]
```

I hope you can see that the connection expressed in the preceding two pieces of RSS 1.0 markup is an XML-based way of expressing the relationship between the item in the TOC and the item elsewhere in the information feed document. In other words, the URI in the `rdf:resource` and `rdf:about` attributes corresponds to the arc of an RDF directed graph.

What RDF Is Used For

RDF, as mentioned earlier, is intended to provide a framework for machine processing of resources on the Web. RDF can be used in many situations, including those in the following list:

- ❑ **Resource discovery:** RDF can improve the relevance of resources returned by search engines.

- ❑ **Cataloging:** RDF can allow relationships between parts of the content of a Web site or other source of information to be represented more meaningfully.

- ❑ **Intelligent agents:** RDF can be used to facilitate the exchange of information between information systems.

- ❑ **Intellectual property:** RDF can be used to express intellectual property rights for documents or collections of documents.

One widely used piece of software that uses RDF under the covers is the Mozilla browser and its associated Firefox and Thunderbird companion products.

RDF and RSS 1.0

Having briefly introduced some foundational parts of RDF, it's time to look in a little more detail at the use of RDF elements in RSS 1.0. The document element of each RSS 1.0 document is an RDF element, the rdf:RDF element.

Each of the child elements of the RSS 1.0 rdf:RDF element, that is the channel, item, image, and textinput elements, must have an rdf:about attribute. The values in such rdf:about attributes are used to associate two elements in different parts of the RSS 1.0 document.

For example, each item listed inside the items element has an rdf:resource attribute:

```
<items>
 <rdf:Seq>
  <rdf:li resource="some_URI" />
  <!-- Other rdf:li elements can go here. -->
 </rdf:Seq>
</items>
```

The URI specified in each rdf:resource attribute must match the URI specified in an item element elsewhere in the RSS 1.0 document:

```
<item rdf:about="some_URI">
 <!-- child elements of the item element go here. -->
</item>
```

Typically, the URI specified in these two attributes is a URL that specifies the location from which the resource associated with the URI can be retrieved. Formally, it is the link element, which is a child of the item element that contains the URL that allows the item to be retrieved. Often, however, the URI associating the rdf:li and item elements is character for character identical to the URL which is the content of the link element.

The rdf:Seq element is used inside the items element since a sequence of items is being specified. Typically, the order of items inside the rdf:Seq element will be used by an aggregator to determine display order for the information feed items. In RSS 1.0 the rdf:Seq element is used in preference to the rdf:Bag, because the content of rdf:Seq is ordered, unlike the content of rdf:Bag.

RDF Vocabularies

RSS 1.0 documents, because they are RDF documents, can be processed by RDF processors. More often, they are processed by information feed aggregators that treat the content pretty much as XML rather than RDF or might limit awareness of RDF to the previously described association between `rdf:li` elements and `item` elements.

However, other RDF vocabularies can be included inside RSS 1.0 documents. These vocabularies are covered in the following sections.

Dublin Core

The Dublin Core RSS 1.0 module, described in Chapter 10, is an RSS-standardized version of the wider Dublin Core Metadata Initiative, which is expressed in RDF.

Full information about the Dublin Core Metadata Initiative is located at `http://dublincore.org/`.

FOAF

You saw earlier in this chapter how RDF can express relationships between a resource, its properties, and their values. RDF is also well-suited to capture information about human relationships. The Friend of a Friend specification which, at the time of writing, is undergoing development, attempts to capture and express information about human relationships in ways that can be expressed in markup or visually.

The FOAF specification is located at `http://xmlns.com/foaf/0.1/`. The version number, 0.1, indicates that the FOAF specification is very much at an early stage of development.

The following markup is contained in the RSS 1.0 information feed for Danny Ayers and attempts to express some information about Danny:

```
<foaf:Person>
  <foaf:nick>Danny</foaf:nick>
  <foaf:mbox_sha1sum>669fe353dbef63d12ba11f69ace8acbec1ac8b17</foaf:mbox_sha1sum>
  <foaf:homepage rdf:resource="http://dannyayers.com"/>
  <rdfs:seeAlso xmlns:rdfs="http://www.w3.org/2000/01/rdf-schema#"
rdf:resource="http://dannyayers.com/archives/author/site-admin/foaf.rdf"/>
</foaf:Person>
```

There is a person whose nickname is Danny. You will sometimes see a `foaf:name` element used to express the same notion. This person has a homepage located at `http://dannyayers.com`. The person has a `foaf:mbox_sha1sum` property with a value of `669fe353dbef63d12ba11f69ace8acbec1ac8b17`.

Other FOAF elements such as `foaf:img` can be used to associate this person about whom you already have learned something with a visual representation of that person. The more FOAF elements are used the more you begin to build up a picture (forgive the pun) of the person. The `rdfs:seeAlso` element allows machines to access additional RDF-based information about the person. This begins to put in place the pieces of information that allow machine-based association of information. The processing of FOAF data enables the beginning of a machine-based version of the World Wide Web, with the URI-based information being the machine-targeted equivalent of hyperlinks in HTML or XHTML Web pages.

At present, most people don't use FOAF in their information feeds. Many aggregators don't yet handle FOAF markup. In time, perhaps, associations between people can be followed in aggregators. You might want to express the notion of a query as follows, "Find information feeds of people who Danny Ayers has expressed a relationship with and who also blog or write on RSS and Atom." You can do something similar to this now by visiting various sites and manually reviewing the blogroll, adding some individuals to your chosen information feeds, and so on. However, just as viewing Web pages is evolving from manually visiting sites to automatically following information in sites using information feeds, so it seems possible in the not-too-distant future you might follow relationships between people using FOAF or some similar specification.

RDF Toolkits

Tools to make use of RDF are becoming more widely available. This section briefly describes some RDF tools.

Jena

Jena is an open-source project that is developing a Java API for RDF. Detailed information about the Jena project is located at `http://sourceforge.net/projects/jena/`. It provides an RDF API, an RDF parser (ARP), an RDF query language (RDQL), an OWL (Web Ontology Language) API; and rule-based inference for RDFS and OWL. A mailing list for discussion of Jena is located at `www.yahoogroups.com/group/jena-dev`.

Redland

Redland is a multilanguage API for RDF. At its heart it is written in C. The C code is wrapped in APIs for languages such as Python, Perl, PHP, and Java. Detailed information on Redland is available at `http://librdf.org/`.

RDFLib

RDFLib is a Python library for manipulating RDF. RDFLib includes an XML/RDF parser and serializer and a triple store. Further information on RDFLib is located at `www.rdflib.net/`.

rdfdata.org

There is still relatively little RDF data available on the Web. One useful source of RDF data is the Web site at `http://rdfdata.org/`, which lists sources of RDF data that you can access across the Web.

Summary

The Resource Description Framework, RDF, provides a way for machines to process *metadata*, which is data about data. RDF provides a data model that uses the notions of *resource*, *predicate*, and *object* together with URIs to uniquely identify a fact. Facts are represented by RDF triples. RDF triples can be written in XML-compliant documents as RDF/XML. RSS 1.0 uses RDF to represent relationships between components of an RSS 1.0 information feed document. RSS 1.0 information feed documents can be extended using RDF-based modules that allow representation of additional associations between resources in RDF.

In this chapter you learned that...

- ❑ RDF is used in RSS 1.0 and provides a way to associate pieces of information using URIs.
- ❑ RDF relies on a data model that uses the concepts of *resource, predicate,* and *object.*
- ❑ RDF/XML is the typical way to serialize the RDF data model.

RSS 2.0: Really Simple Syndication

RSS 2.0, Really Simple Syndication, was announced in August 2000. It follows a line of inheritance from RSS 0.9x. RSS 2.0, unlike RSS 1.0, makes no use of the Resource Description Framework (RDF). However, RSS 2.0 does move one step closer to the RSS 1.0 approach, in that XML namespaces are adopted.

Any RSS 0.91 document is supposed to be a legal RSS 2.0 document. At least if the value of the version attribute were changed to a value of 2.0 it might be legal. In practice, many aggregators will process the information feed document without taking account of the value of the version attribute of the rss element. The variations in the versions of RSS have taught many authors of aggregator tools to be generous in what markup is accepted for processing. Therefore, any discrepancy in the value of the version attribute is unlikely to cause a practical problem in the majority (or perhaps all) of aggregators.

In this chapter you will learn:

- ❑ What RSS 2.0 is
- ❑ How to structure an RSS 2.0 document
- ❑ What RSS 2.0 extensions are and how to use them

What Is RSS 2.0?

RSS 2.0 is, at the time of writing, the latest version of the development tree of RSS. It passes through the UserLand version of RSS 0.91 and RSS 0.92. In common with RSS 0.9x, RSS 1.0 avoids the use of RDF. It seems reasonable to conclude that the avoidance of RDF is partly a result of Dave Winer's preference for simplicity and his assumption that RSS feeds transmit information of largely transitory interest. Recall from Chapter 11 that those who see information feeds as conduits for disposable information don't see the value of using RDF in a feed, because metadata is unimportant for those developers who see information feeds as containing disposable, transitory information.

The changes in RSS 2.0 from RSS 0.92 are, with one exception, fairly minor. For example, there are a few new elements and a few changes regarding what particular elements should contain. The one substantive change in RSS 2.0 is the use of XML namespaces. Using XML namespaces opens up possibilities for extending RSS 2.0 using modules.

> **The RSS 2.0 specification is located at** `http://blogs.law.harvard.edu/tech/rss`.

XML Namespaces in RSS 2.0

RSS 2.0 uses the XML namespaces technique specified in the Namespaces in XML recommendation, located at `www.w3.org/TR/REC-xml-names/`.

Because versions 0.91 and 0.92 of RSS don't use XML namespaces, all the elements associated with those specifications are, inevitably, not in any XML namespace. Therefore, unlike the situation with RSS 1.0 where a namespace URI is defined, in RSS 2.0 all the RSS elements are in no namespace.

The availability of XML namespaces allows RSS 2.0 documents to use elements from other namespaces, provided that an appropriate namespace declaration has been made. For example, you can use the Dublin Core module described in Chapter 10.

New Elements in RSS 2.0

There are several new elements in RSS 2.0. Each is briefly described in the following list. The use of these new elements is described in more detail in the discussion on RSS 2.0 document structure.

- ❑ `author`: An optional child element of the `item` element
- ❑ `comments`: An optional child element of the `item` element
- ❑ `generator`: An optional child element of the `channel` element
- ❑ `guid`: An optional child element of the `item` element
- ❑ `pubDate`: An optional child element of the `item` element
- ❑ `ttl`: An optional child element of the `channel` element

The RSS 2.0 Document Structure

The RSS 2.0 document structure has many similarities to the structure of RSS 0.91 and RSS 0.92 documents. For convenience, if you choose to implement RSS 2.0 only, the document structure is described without requiring you to cross-reference the chapter on RSS 0.91 and 0.92.

The rss Element

The `rss` element is the document element of an RSS 2.0 document. It has a required `version` attribute with a value of `2.0`. Supposedly, RSS 0.91 and 0.92 documents are legal RSS 2.0 documents but they have a different value for the `version` attribute. In practice this works, despite the different and theoretically illegal values in the `version` attribute in RSS 0.91 and 0.92 documents, because many aggregators ignore the value in the `version` attribute.

If you are writing an RSS 2.0 document, the start tag of the `rss` element should be written as follows:

```
<rss version="2.0">
```

You can also write it using single quote marks:

```
<rss version='2.0'>
```

The `rss` element has a single child element, the `channel` element. All content of the information feed document is contained in the `channel` element.

Notice that there is no namespace declaration on the preceding `rss` start tag. For consistency with RSS 0.91 and 0.92, the elements of RSS 2.0 are in no namespace. This has the advantage of backwards compatibility but does mean there is a risk of naming collisions. In practice, the risk of naming collisions is slight because most non-RSS 2.0 elements likely to be found in an RSS 2.0 document are in a namespace, which allows the aggregator or other user agent to distinguish those elements from RSS 2.0 elements.

The channel Element

The `channel` element is the only permitted child element of the `rss` element. The `channel` element has no attributes. The remainder of an RSS 2.0 document consists of child elements or descendant elements of the `channel` element.

The following child elements of the `channel` element are required in all RSS 2.0 documents.

- ❑   `title`: Contains the name that refers to the information feed. If the information feed refers back to a Web site or blog, the value of the `title` element is typically the name of that site or blog.

- ❑   `link`: Contains a URL that allows linking to the Web site or blog that's associated with the information feed.

- ❑   `description`: Contains a brief description of the information feed.

A minimalist RSS 2.0 document would therefore look like the following document:

```
<rss version="2.0">
 <channel>
  <title>Reflecting on Microsoft</title>
  <link>http://www.tfosorcim.org/blog/</link>
  <description>The Reflecting on Microsoft blog discusses issues relating to
  specific Microsoft products as well as the much larger issue of the competition
  between the proprietary and open-source approaches to software
  development.</description>
 </channel>
</rss>
```

This document is of little value in an aggregator because it contains no item elements. Surprisingly, the item element is optional in RSS 2.0 although, in practice, a typical RSS 2.0 document will have several.

The following elements are optional child elements of the channel element. Some elements, which have their own child elements, are discussed further following the list.

- ❑ category: This element contains information about the categories of information contained in the information feed. There can be several category elements as child elements of a channel element.

- ❑ cloud: This element has several attributes that contain information specifying how a connection can be made to a cloud, allowing subscription to an information feed to be always up to date.

- ❑ copyright: This contains copyright information relating to the feed.

- ❑ docs: This contains a URL pointing to the RSS 2.0 specification.

- ❑ generator: This contains information about the software that was used to produce the information feed.

- ❑ image: This contains information so an aggregator can locate an image (in GIF, JPEG, or PNG format) to display in connection with the information feed.

- ❑ language: This contains a two-letter language code, with optional extensions. Example values are en and en-us.

- ❑ managingEditor: This contains the e-mail address of the contact for queries about editorial content.

- ❑ pubDate: This contains the publication date for the feed.

- ❑ rating: The PICS (Platform for Internet Content Selection) rating for the channel.

- ❑ skipDays: This contains information indicating to an aggregator the days of the week when a feed is not expected to be updated.

- ❑ skipHours: This contains information indicating to an aggregator the hours when a feed is not expected to be updated.

- ❑ textinput: This displays a text box to allow the users to input information for processing on a server, typically (if the textinput element is present) on the server from which the feed originates.

- ❑ ttl: This contains information about the period of time before the aggregator should check for new content.

- ❑ webMaster: This contains the e-mail address of the contact for queries about technical issues relating to the information feed.

Several of the previous elements are shown in the example RSS 2.0 document later in this chapter.

The image Element

The image element specifies an image that can be displayed along with the channel in an aggregator or other user agent. The image element has the following required child elements:

❏   link: The value of this element is a URL representing the feed or Web site.

❏   title: This describes the image. If the feed is being rendered as HTML, the content of the title element may be used as the value of the alt attribute of the img element in HTML/XHTML.

❏   url: The content of this element is a URL that specifies the location from which the image can be retrieved.

The link element, a child of the image element, is required, although it seems simply to duplicate the content of the link element child of the channel element. The RSS 2.0 specification is not clear about the consequences should these two link elements contain different URLs.

There are three optional child elements of the link element:

❏   description: This contains a short description of the image. The specification suggests that it be used in the title attribute of the link in the corresponding HTML.

❏   height: This contains the height of the image in pixels.

❏   width: This contains the width of the image in pixels.

The cloud Element

The cloud element is a child element of the channel element. The attributes of the cloud element are used to specify a Web service that implements the rssCloud interface. A useful way to look on a cloud is as a Web application. A cloud acts as a central coordinator for subscriptions to an information feed. Instead of an aggregator polling a server at specified intervals (often hourly) the cloud (the coordinator) informs subscribed users when a change has taken place.

A cloud element would appear similar to the following markup:

```
<cloud domain="rpc.sys.com" port="80" path="/RPC2"
  registerProcedure="myCloud.rssPleaseNotify" protocol="xml-rpc" />
```

The textinput Element

The textinput element allows a user to enter text to be sent to a server-side process, such as a CGI script. Some people question the appropriateness of the textinput element, seeing that such functionality belongs more appropriately inside an individual Web page.

❏   description: This contains a short description of the text input area.

❏   link: This contains a URL which specifies a server-side process, for example a CGI script, to which the text entered by the user is sent.

❏   name: This contains a name for the text in the text input area.

❏   title: This contains the label for the submit button associated with the text input functionality.

The item Element

The item element may occur any number of times in an RSS 2.0 information feed document. Its child elements are described in the following list. The specification is unclear about whether or not these child elements are required. In practice, you can use which child elements you want and omit those you don't. There are theoretically some situations in which you could be in conflict with the wording of the RSS 2.0 specification but this won't arise with real-world items with a title and at least some content.

- ❑ author: This contains an e-mail address for a person with responsibility for authoring the content of the item.

- ❑ category: An item element can have multiple category element children. The content of the category element is information about a category into which the content of the item may be assigned. Each category element has an optional domain attribute, the value of which may specify a taxonomy to which the content of the item belongs. For example, in an item about XML the domain might be "markup languages."

- ❑ comments: This contains a URL of a Web page where a user can enter comments about the item.

- ❑ description: This contains a summary of the item or, in the case of items with a relatively small amount of text, might contain the full text of the item.

- ❑ enclosure: This contains information specifying a media object associated with the item. This is an empty element with three attributes. The url attribute contains a URL from which the media object can be retrieved. The length attribute specifies the size of the serialized object in bytes. The type attribute specifies the media type of the object.

- ❑ guid: This contains a value that uniquely identifies the item. The RSS 2.0 specification does not specify rules intended to achieve uniqueness. One typical approach is to use a URL from which the item can be retrieved. In that situation the guid element is likely to have an isPermaLink attribute with a value of true.

- ❑ link: This contains a URL that can be used to retrieve the full text of the item. When the item contains its full text in the description element, the link element is optional; otherwise, it is required.

- ❑ pubDate: This contains information about when the item was published. It includes both date and time components.

- ❑ source: This contains information about the channel (perhaps on another site) that the item originally came from. It has a url attribute that contains the URL for the source information feed. The content of the source element is, typically, the title of the feed.

- ❑ title: This contains a title for the item.

An example item element is shown in the following example RSS 2.0 document.

An Example RSS 2.0 Document

Having looked at the individual parts of the document structure of an RSS 2.0 document, you can now take a look at a sample RSS 2.0 document that happens to contain my first author blog post on Wrox.com.

```
<?xml version="1.0" ?>
<rss version="2.0">
<channel>
<title>Wrox P2P Blogs - Andrew Watt</title>
<ttl>60</ttl>
<description>Wrox.com P2P Community Blogs</description>
<link>http://p2p.wrox.com/blogs_author.asp?AUTHOR_ID=22322</link>
<copyright>Copyright (c) 2000-2004 by John Wiley & Sons, Inc. or related companies.
 All rights reserved.</copyright>
<language>en</language>
<image>
 <url>http://p2p.wrox.com/images/p2p/wrox_rss_logo.gif</url>
 <title>Wrox P2P Blogs - Andrew Watt</title>
 <link>http://p2p.wrox.com/blogs_author.asp?AUTHOR_ID=22322</link>
 <width>36</width>
 <height>31</height>
</image>
<item>
<title>Firefox 1.0 is available</title>
<description>Firefox 1.0 is available now for download from <a
href="http://www.mozilla.org" target="_blank"><a href="http://www.mozilla.org"
target="_blank">http://www.mozilla.org</a></a>.<br /><br />It downloaded quickly
for me, although that could change as the servers get busier, and it installed
smoothly. <br /><br />If you haven't already spotted the new functionality to add a
 live RSS or Atom feed to your Firefox bookmarks using the button at the extreme
bottom right of the Firefox window give it a go....</description>
<pubDate>Tue, 9 Nov 2004 12:01:11 GMT</pubDate>
<link>http://p2p.wrox.com/blog.asp?BLOG_ID=37</link>
<comments>http://p2p.wrox.com/blogs_comments.asp?BLOG_ID=37</comments>
</item>
</channel>
</rss>
```

The example document contains only one item and it does not use all of the many optional elements that the RSS 2.0 specification allows. Hopefully, it will give you an impression of what a simple RSS 2.0 document is like.

RSS 2.0 Extensions

The RSS 2.0 specification does not say much about extensions. All extension elements must be in a namespace (all RSS 2.0 elements are in no namespace). It is not clearly specified that extension elements can be inserted anywhere in an RSS 2.0 information feed document, but this seems to be the most likely meaning of the specification.

The blogChannel RSS Module

In the month following the release of the RSS 2.0 specification, Dave Winer issued a document relating to the `blogChannel` RSS module. The document is located at `http://backend.userland.com/blogChannelModule`. It is intended to relate to the context of a blog which has an associated information feed.

A typical namespace declaration for the `blogChannel` namespace is:

```
xmlns:blogChannel="http://backend.userland.com/blogChannelModule"
```

The following elements are in the `blogChannel` module:

- ❑ `blink`: This contains a URL that links to a blog that the author of the information feed wants to promote in some way.

- ❑ `blogRoll`: This contains a URL that specifies the location of an OPML (Outline Processor Markup Language) file containing the blogroll for the information feed.

- ❑ `changes`: This contains a URL that specifies the location of a `changes.xml` file. The idea behind the changes file is that bandwidth use may be reduced.

- ❑ `mySubscriptions`: This contains a URL that specifies the location of an OPML file containing the subscriptions of the blog author.

> **OPML, Outline Processor Markup Language, is an XML language that can express the structure of an outline. In the context of information feeds, an OPML document is often used to contain a list of information feeds to which a blogger subscribes, the so-called *blogroll*.**

Whether or not an extension module is supported can vary from one aggregator tool to another. A quasi-official list of RSS 2.0 extensions is maintained at `http://blogs.law.harvard.edu/tech/directory/5/specifications/rss20ModulesNamespaces`. Examples include Danny Ayer's Simple Semantic Resolution module and Joe Gregorio's Comment API.

Summary

RSS 2.0 adds the use of XML namespaces to the document structure of RSS 0.9x. It does not use the RDF. New elements add information about the software creating the feed, the author of the feed, and the location of a comments page for the information feed (a facility used primarily when the information feed relates to a blog).

In this chapter you learned that:

- ❑ RSS 2.0 uses XML namespaces.

- ❑ The document element of an RSS 2.0 document is the `rss` element.

- ❑ All information in an RSS 2.0 information feed is contained in the `channel` element.

- ❑ Information feed items are contained in `item` elements.

Looking Forward to Atom 1.0

At the time of writing the Atom 1.0 specification is under active development at the IETF. The RSS specifications all have some degree of ambiguity in the specification documents and they all attempt to be backwards compatible with their precursor formats. One of the intentions of the Atom effort is to improve the quality of the specification documents. Another is to create an information feed format free from a need to conform to earlier specifications. However, Atom 1.0 aims to go beyond simply creating a tidier, better specified feed format. It also includes the development of a protocol that can be used by blogging and similar software to update server-side resources in a standard way.

The aim of the information feed aspect of the Atom activity at IETF is to create a widely accepted Atom format that would be treated as a standard, perhaps the standard, in the information feed space. In that component of the Atom project, Atom 1.0 resembles RSS 2.0 and, to a smaller degree, RSS 1.0. The Atom 1.0 feed format, like Atom 0.3, is written in XML. The Atom 0.3 specification was a foundation for the development of Atom 1.0. At the time of writing some changes have been made from the document structure of the Atom 0.3 format, with further changes possible.

The Atom Protocol was designed to be a standard way for blogging-related software to communicate to a server edits made in content and in a corresponding information feed to the server from where the Web pages are requested and the information delivered.

In this chapter you learn:

- ❑ Motivations for an additional feed format specification
- ❑ What Atom 1.0 is
- ❑ What the document structure of the Atom 1.0 feed format may be
- ❑ About the other aspects of Atom 1.0

> **The description of the Atom 1.0 feed document structure described in this chapter is subject to change. The description in this chapter is based on the October 2004 draft of the Atom Syndication format located at** `http://atompub.org/2004/10/20/draft-ietf-atompub-format-03.html`**.**

Why Another Specification?

If you have been following the development of information feeds over the last four or five years or have read the descriptions in this book of the development of the various information feed formats, one question that may occur to you is, "Why another specification?" This section addresses that question.

Aiming for Clarity

One issue that has drawn the attention of some RSS tool implementers is that the specification documents are ambiguous in places. That is an assessment we can sympathize with, having had to work through the RSS specifications to write the preceding chapters. Because of these ambiguities, developers who write aggregators have to be permissive in the structure of markup they accept. Allowing for multiple formats and, possibly, errors in document formats means that aggregators are less easy to write and may be slower than might otherwise be necessary.

For the end user, the ambiguities in the specifications are unlikely to be an issue. The developers who create aggregators write the software so that it accepts almost any markup that reasonably resembles what the relevant specifications seem to say.

If Atom becomes *the* standard information feed format then, over time, aggregators might be slimmed down so that they only accept feeds expressed in one universal format — the Atom 1.0 format. At least that's what some hope. In practice, particularly in the short term, Atom is likely to add to the complexity caused by there being multiple information feed formats. Atom will simply add a little more complexity to the mix.

Archiving Feeds

One of the other areas where improvement is sought over RSS 0.9*x* and 2.0 relates to the issue of archiving information feeds and their contained items. The idea is that for some information it is important to archive the feed. If you archive a feed in what might possibly become a huge, global archive the need for a truly unique identifier for information feeds and their items becomes more of an issue. The vagueness of the RSS 2.0 specification regarding the guid element for example, becomes unacceptable, if you assume that uniqueness will need to be global and stretch over long periods of time, perhaps years or decades. The assumption that information feeds and their contents are of temporary interest only is a notion that some at the heart of Atom development reject.

The notion of archiving feeds is different from the idea of storing information discussed in Chapter 5. Atom 1.0 intends to archive information about the feed itself and the items in the information feed. Chapter 5 referred to storing information that was accessed from a feed. In that context the feed itself was seen as disposable but the information resources that you could, as a user, access from the feed might be of lasting interest.

The RDF Issue

One of the issues that, in my opinion, means that it is unlikely that Atom 1.0 will ever be the single information feed format is the likelihood that it won't use RDF. The use of RDF in the Atom 1.0 feed format has been discussed, but looks unlikely to happen because a significant proportion of those participating in developing the Atom feed format see RDF as not having a sufficiently advantageous complexity-to-benefit ratio.

The likely lack of RDF support in Atom 1.0 means that RSS 1.0 is the only viable option for a format for feed creators who want to make available the additional metadata that RDF can provide.

Perhaps, in time, Atom 1.0 and RSS 1.0 will be the dominant information feed formats. Atom 1.0 will be used by those who choose not to have the complexity and rich metadata of RDF; RSS 1.0 for those who choose to use RDF.

The Standards Body Aspect

None of the various versions of RSS have been developed under the auspices of a widely recognized standards body. That reality hasn't prevented the various versions of RSS from being widely adopted in information feeds. However, some in the information feed community believe that standard specifications shouldn't be in the hands of individuals. The decision to develop Atom 1.0 under the auspices of the IETF was, in part, influenced by that perception.

At the time of writing it remains uncertain how well Atom 1.0 will be received. A significant factor will be whether the authors of blogging software will adopt Atom 1.0. If the big hitters, such as Movable Type, all select Atom 1.0 (as it looks likely Movable Type will), then the number of Atom 1.0 feeds could increase rapidly. Blogging software and similar products now create most feeds automatically.

Whether the number of feeds using various versions of RSS will decrease is much less certain. If somebody produces an RSS 0.91 feed and it is processed correctly by many or all of the major aggregators, what incentive is there to change to Atom 1.0?

What Is Atom?

Atom 1.0 consists of both a feed format and a publishing protocol. In addition there are draft specifications for autodiscovery of Atom 1.0 feeds and for notification of updated feeds. Each of these aspects is discussed in the remainder of this chapter.

Further Information about Atom 1.0

Due to the stage of development of Atom 1.0 at the time that writing of this book is being completed, it is certain that at least some changes will be made in the specifications. The following resources are listed so you can have access to up-to-date information.

If you are interested in Atom 1.0 you will want to access online information that updates the material in this chapter. Currently, you can find links to some key Atom documents at `http://www.ietf.org/ids.by.wg/atompub.html`. Links from that page may be more up to date than those given here.

If the preceding URL returns a broken link at some future date, a likely way to find up-to-date Atom 1.0 information is to use the keyword search located at `http://search.ietf.org/` and search for "Atom."

The Atom 1.0 feed format document is, at the time of writing, located at `http://atompub.org/2004/10/20/draft-ietf-atompub-format-03.html`.

The Atom feed format mailing list is described at `www.imc.org/atom-syntax/index.html`. The Atom wiki is located at `www.intertwingly.net/wiki/pie/FrontPage`.

Atom 1.0 Document Structure

Atom 1.0 documents are written in XML. The Atom 1.0 draft of October 2004 on which the following description is based has many similarities to the Atom 0.3 specification described in Chapter 7.

XML digital signatures or encryption can be used with Atom 1.0 documents, when appropriate.

The following example is a simple Atom 1.0 document:

```xml
<?xml version="1.0" encoding="utf-8"?>
<feed version="draft-ietf-atompub-format-03: do not deploy"
 xmlns="http://purl.org/atom/ns#draft-ietf-atompub-format-03">
  <head>
    <title>An Example Information Feed</title>
    <link href="http://www.XMML.com/blog/"/>
    <updated>2004-12-15T18:30:02Z</updated>
    <author>
      <name>John Smith</name>
    </author>
  </head>
  <entry>
    <title>Atom 1.0 isn't ready yet.</title>
    <link href="http://www.XMML.com/blog/2004/12/15/atomslow.html"/>
    <id>http://www.XMML.com/blog/2004/12/15/atomslow.html</id>
    <updated>2004-12-15T18:30:02Z</updated>
  </entry>
</feed>
```

As you can see, the structure of an Atom 1.0 document is similar to that used in Atom 0.3.

The XML Declaration

It is recommended that Atom 1.0 documents have an XML declaration.

The feed Element

The `feed` element is the document element of an Atom 1.0 feed format document. It has a required `version` attribute. And it must have a namespace declaration specifying either the default namespace or associating a namespace prefix with the Atom 1.0 namespace. When the specification is complete, the allowed values of both the `version` attribute and the namespace URI for the Atom 1.0 namespace are likely to change.

```xml
<feed version="draft-ietf-atompub-format-03: do not deploy"
 xmlns="http://purl.org/atom/ns#draft-ietf-atompub-format-03">
```

> The namespace URI used in the October 2004 draft of Atom 1.0 is likely to be replaced later in the specification's development.

The child elements of the `feed` element are the `head` element, of which there can be only one, and one or more `entry` elements. The first child element of the `feed` element must be a `head` element.

The head Element

The `head` element is a container for metadata about the feed. The metadata is contained in several child elements of `head`, as follows:

- The `title` element contains a human readable title for the information feed. The `title` element has no attributes.

- The `link` element indicates a link to the source of the feed. At the time of writing the `link` element is not fully specified. It seems likely that the `link` element will have `rel`, `type`, and `href` attributes but the current draft does not make that clear. If a link is to an HTML or XHTML Web page then that page should implement the Atom Feed Autodiscovery mechanism, described later in this chapter.

- The `introspection` and `post` elements are service constructs. They are used in connection with the Atom Publishing Protocol described later in this chapter.

- The `author` and `contributor` elements are also child elements of the `head` element.

- The `tagline` element contains a human-readable description or tagline for the feed. The `id` element contains a unique identifier for the feed.

- The `generator` element indicates the software used to generate the feed. The `generator` element may, optionally, have a `uri` and a `version` attribute.

- The `copyright` element contains a human-readable statement of copyright for the feed. The `info` element contains a human-readable statement about the feed format. The `updated` element contains a date/time value that indicates the most recent time that the feed was updated.

The entry Element

The `entry` document can appear as a child element of the `feed` element (which is described in this section) or can be the document element of an Atom Entry document (which is described later in this chapter).

The `entry` element has the following child elements:

- The `title` element is required. It contains a human-readable title for the entry.

- The `link` element conveys a URI associated with the entry. At least one `link` element with a `rel` attribute with the value of `alternate` must be present on each entry.

- The `edit` element is used in association with the Atom Publishing Protocol. It represents a URI that can be used to retrieve the entry for editing.

- ❑ The `author` and `contributor` elements contain information about the principal author of an entry and about any other contributors to the content of an entry.

- ❑ The `id` element contains a unique identifier for an entry.

- ❑ The `updated` element contains a date/time value that specifies when the entry was most recently updated.

- ❑ The `published` element contains a date/time value; typically it would indicate when the entry was first published or made available for download.

- ❑ The `summary` element contains a brief summary of the entry or an extract from the entry.

- ❑ The `content` element may contain the text content of the entry or may be an empty element that references a URI from which the content can be retrieved. Optionally, the `content` element has a type and a `src` attribute.

- ❑ The `copyright` element contains a copyright statement about the entry. The `origin` element contains a URI reference to the original source of the entry.

Extending Atom 1.0 Documents

The mechanisms for extending an Atom 1.0 document had not been described in the draft specification used as the basis for this chapter. Because Atom 1.0 uses XML namespaces, it should be fairly straightforward to define a mechanism for extending Atom 1.0 feed documents.

Other Aspects of Atom 1.0

In addition to the feed format specification that has just been briefly described, Atom 1.0 includes the specification of a publishing protocol intended for editing blogs and similar online resources, as well as a notification protocol and an autodiscovery specification.

The Atom Publishing Protocol

The Atom Publishing Protocol defines a protocol used to edit and publish entries for information feeds. There are four uses to which URIs are put in the publishing protocol:

- ❑ `EditURI`: Specifies where to retrieve an entry for editing, and uses the PUT, GET and DELETE methods.

- ❑ `PostURI`: Used to create entries and uses the POST method.

- ❑ `FeedURI`: Used to retrieve an Atom feed document and uses the GET method.

- ❑ `ResourcePostURI`: Specifies how to add a new resource that's not an Atom entry. It uses the POST method.

> **The Atom Publishing Protocol documents appear likely to change significantly before the specification is finalized.**

The `introspection` element, which is a child element of the `head` element, specifies the location of an introspection file associated with the feed, using a URI.

The `post` element is a child element of the `head` element. It specifies a URI used to add content to a feed.

The `edit` element is a child element of the `entry` element. It specifies a URI used to retrieve an entry for editing.

The editURI

The `editURI` is used to edit a single entry. The `GET` method is used to retrieve the entry to the client for editing and the `PUT` method to put edited content on the server. The relevant `link` element may be written similar to the following markup:

```
<link rel="service.edit"
      type="application/atom+xml"
      href="URI for Editing goes here"
      title="A brief description of the entry" />
```

The postURI

The `postURI` is used to create entries. It can be used to create full entries or to allow comments to be added. The `postURI` can be determined from the `rel` attribute of a `link` element that has the value `service.post`.

The resourcePostURI

This is used to add a new resource that is not an Atom entry. The relevant `link` element would look similar to the following markup:

```
<link rel="resource.post"
 href="URI for the Resource to be POSTed to goes here"
 title="The name of the site.">
```

The feedURI

The `feedURI` is used to retrieve an Atom feed document. The relevant `link` element would look similar to the following markup:

```
<link rel="service.feed"
      type="application/atom+xml"
      href="URI for the feed goes here"
      title="The title of the site or feed." />
```

An Atom Entry Document

An Atom entry can exist as an XML document. In that case, the `entry` element from the Atom 1.0 namespace is the document element.

The Atom Notification Protocol

The Atom Notification Protocol is the newest part of Atom 1.0. It is intended to send notifications about new Atom feeds or entries. The first draft of the Notification Protocol was published just as this chapter was being written.

The Atom Notification Protocol is, at the time of writing, located at www.ietf.org/internet-drafts/ draft-snell-atompub-notification-00.txt. A link element might look like the following markup:

```
<link rel="service.notification"
    type="application/atom+xml"
    href="NotificationURI Goes Here"
    title="The Title of the feed, entry or web site." />
```

Atom Feed Autodiscovery

The Atom autodiscovery process is expected to use a link element similar to the following markup:

```
<link rel="alternate"
type="application/atom+xml"
  href="http://www.XMML.com/feeds/index.atom">
```

The Atom Feed Autodiscovery specification document is located at www.ietf.org/internet-drafts/ draft-ietf-atompub-autodiscovery-00.txt.

Summary

Atom 1.0 is an effort targeted at updating Atom 0.3 which was described in Chapter 7. It specifies a feed format, a publication protocol, a notification protocol, and a mechanism for autodiscovery of Atom feeds. All information presented is based on draft documents and is subject to change.

In this chapter you learned that:

❑ Atom 1.0 is currently being developed.

❑ Atom 1.0 aims to avoid limitations of RSS specifications in terms of creating an unambiguous specification document and facilitating archiving of information feeds.

❑ The document element of an Atom 1.0 feed document is the feed element in the Atom namespace.

❑ Atom 1.0 uses XML namespaces so it has potential for being extended, using elements in other namespaces.

Part III
The Tools

Feed Production Using Blogging Tools

The preceding chapters looked at the mechanics of how information feed documents are structured. Some information feeds will continue to be generated by custom software, as was the case with early tools in the field. We will look at several techniques to do that in later chapters. In reality, however, the majority of information feeds on the Web is likely to be produced automatically by blogging tools. The users of those tools need have no understanding of information feed technologies. They simply produce content and the blogging tool generates an information feed and often the HTML or XHTML Web pages too.

If you are a user you can view this chapter as a peek behind the scenes of what happens in a typical blogging tool when information feeds are created. If you are a developer thinking of creating a better blogging tool, look at the functionality the end user sees and think about how it can be improved on.

Blogging tools vary in terms of which information feed formats they support. In practice, because aggregators are generally very forgiving about the feeds they accept, the spectrum of supported feed formats is not an important factor in the choice of blogging tools by users.

In this chapter you learn about:

- ❑ Movable Type
- ❑ WordPress
- ❑ Blojsom

The tools described in this chapter illustrate the sort of functionality that you can expect to see in a typical blogging tool. The blogging tool field is huge; the inclusion of a particular blogging tool in this chapter is more a matter of familiarity. We do not mean to imply that tools that are included are better than those that are not.

Movable Type

Movable Type is the blogging tool that I use for my Reflecting on Microsoft blog located at www
.tfosorciM.org/blog/. Movable Type uses Perl server-side scripts and can be installed with a range
of database backends, including the MySQL relational database management system.

The current version of Movable Type at the time of writing is 3.14. General information about Movable
Type can be found at www.movabletype.org/. Documentation of Movable Type, including installation
instructions, is located at www.movabletype.org/help/. Installing Movable Type on a Web server is
both fairly straightforward (if you follow the installation instructions *carefully*) and fairly nerve-wracking,
particularly if you are unfamiliar with Perl. However, the installation and upgrade instructions provided
with Movable Type have always been well structured in my experience. For those who don't want to
fiddle with installing Movable Type, there is Web hosting with Movable Type preinstalled at www
.mediatemple.net/. Alternatively, Typepad (located at www.typepad.com/) provides an easier entry
into Movable Type blogging.

Movable Type uses templates behind the scenes. After logging in to Movable Type, you can navigate to
the Templates page shown in Figure 14-1 by choosing Manage Weblog and then choosing the Templates
option. The precise URL and user login are obscured in the figure, for security reasons.

Figure 14-1

You can edit the templates provided for RSS 2.0 for example, using the page shown in Figure 14-2. This can be useful if you want to add elements in an XML namespace that's not supported in the default version of the Movable Type RSS 2.0 template.

Figure 14-2

Movable Type allows you to assign posts to arbitrary categories. Figure 14-3 shows the creation of a new category, Visual Studio 2005, in my Reflecting on Microsoft blog.

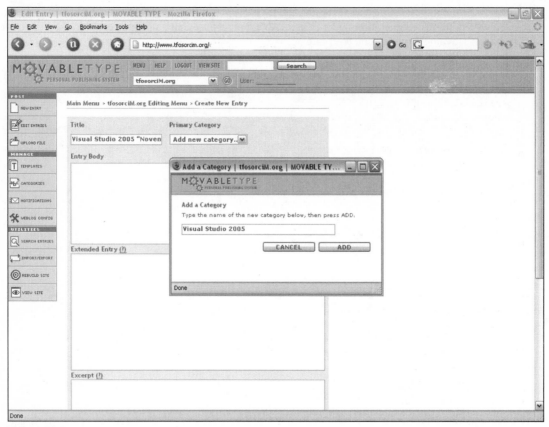

Figure 14-3

A new entry can include an excerpt, as shown in Figure 14-4.

Figure 14-4

When you edit an entry, you are editing plain text. You can add HTML code in that text. The text or HTML you create is then built into an XHTML Web page by Movable Type. After the Web page is built, sites that you specify are pinged about a change having been made in your weblog. Figure 14-5 shows the message you might see. The detail of the message will depend on the default choices in the version of Movable Type that you use and any others you may have added after install.

Figure 14-5

In Figure 14-4, you can see that we explicitly added an excerpt to the blog post. That excerpt is used in the RSS 1.0 feed created automatically by Movable Type.

```
<item rdf:about="http://www.tfosorcim.org/archives/000312.html">
<title>Visual Studio 2005 &quot;November&quot; CTP Released in December</title>
<link>http://www.tfosorcim.org/archives/000312.html</link>
<description><![CDATA[Microsoft has released a "November CTP" for Visual Studio
 2005, <a
href="http://blogs.msdn.com/Somasegar/archive/2004/12/13/284382.aspx">VS2005
November CTP (Standard Edition) now available!</a>.]]></description>
<dc:subject>Visual Studio 2005</dc:subject>
<dc:creator>Andrew Watt</dc:creator>
<dc:date>2004-12-19T16:07:29+00:00</dc:date>
</item>
```

The content of the excerpt area of the New Entry screen in Movable Type has been inserted into the description element of the RSS 1.0 feed document.

Different aggregators will handle the content of the description element differently. For example, Thunderbird ignores it and simply displays the whole Web page in the relevant pane of its interface (see Figure 14-6).

Others use the content of the description element as part of their display. For example, RSS Bandit displays the description element content, as shown in the lower-right pane in Figure 14-7.

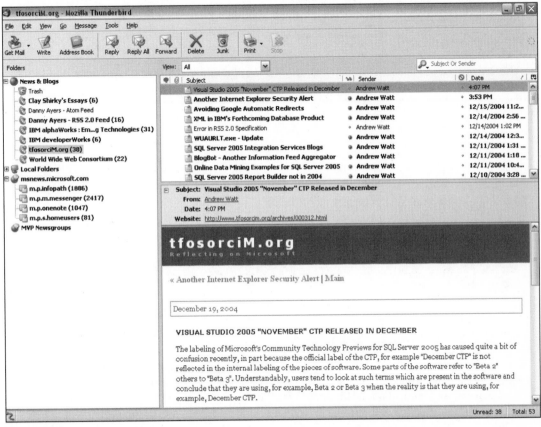

Figure 14-6

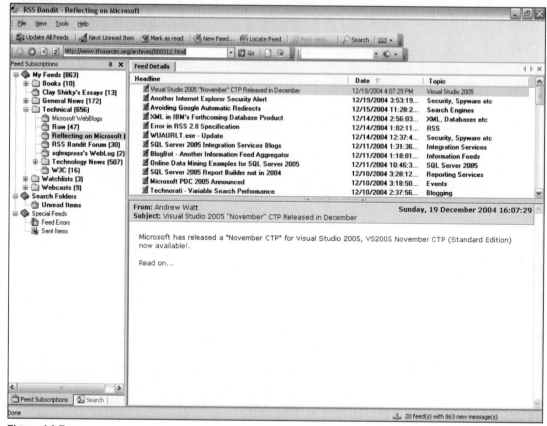

Figure 14-7

WordPress

WordPress is a blogging tool, similar to Movable Type. WordPress is used by Danny in his blog, www.dannyayers.com/. Full details about WordPress are available at http://wordpress.org/.

WordPress, like Movable Type, is a full-featured blogging tool. It is based on PHP whereas Movable Type is based on Perl. WordPress claims that it takes less disk space than Movable Type for similar size of blogs. Multiple authoring is supported. As with Movable Type, trackback and pingback is supported. Unlike Movable Type (which requires rebuilding of pages) changes made in WordPress do not require that static pages be rebuilt.

My impression is that on most Web hosts there is, at the time of writing, little to choose between WordPress and Movable Type. However, since both products are under ongoing development I suggest that you check the current information given at the respective URLs.

Detailed information about the features of WordPress is available at `http://wordpress.org/about/features/`. Screenshots that show functionality available in WordPress are located at `http://wordpress.org/about/screenshots/`.

WordPress provides several templates that allow you to customize the appearance of a blog created using WordPress. WordPress is based on PHP, and a full understanding of PHP is helpful if you want to customize beyond typical aspects such as displaying date and time of a blog post. Several PHP functions are used in templates and those are described at `http://wordpress.org/docs/template/`.

WordPress allows the use of plug-ins. Details of currently available plug-ins are described at `http://dev.wp-plugins.org/`.

Blojsom

Blojsom is a blogging package written in Java. It supports multiple blogs and multiple authors. The Blojsom project is based at Sourceforge and is located `http://sourceforge.net/projects/blojsom/`.

> **Blojsom is a Java application that is modeled on the Perl blogging tool Blosxom (pronounced blossom); see** `www.blosxom.com/`.

Blojsom can, for example, run on the Tomcat application server from the Apache Foundation. Further information on Tomcat, as well as a download which runs on just about any Java-enabled platform, can be found at `http://jakarta.apache.org/tomcat/index.html`. Tomcat is the servlet container used by the reference implementations of Java Servlet and JavaServer Page (JSP) technologies. At the time of writing, Tomcat 5.5 is the most recent version. Documentation for Tomcat 5.5, including installation and configuration information, is located at `http://jakarta.apache.org/tomcat/tomcat-5.5-doc/index.html`.

Assuming that you have successfully installed Tomcat, you should be able to access its home page on your server using a Web browser. Figure 14-8 shows the Tomcat home page, using version 5.0.18. If you have installed Tomcat on your local machine using its default port 8080, the URL `http://localhost:8080/` should bring up a page similar to the one you see in Figure 14-8.

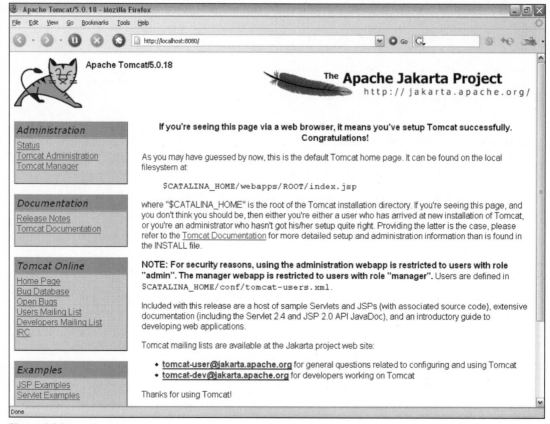

Figure 14-8

After you have successfully installed Tomcat you can download and install Blojsom. Blojsom is available from http://wiki.blojsom.com/wiki/display/blojsom/blojsom+Quickstart. The so-called Quickstart Bundle located at the preceding URL is a .war file which can be downloaded and installed in the $CATALINA_HOME/webapps directory. The CATALINA_HOME environment variable specifies the directory where you installed Tomcat. Depending on how you have the Tomcat server configured you might not need to stop and restart the Tomcat server before you can use Blojsom. If you have successfully installed the Blojsom war file, blojsom.war, you should see a page similar to Figure 14-9 when you enter the URL http://localhost:8080/blojsom/blog/default/ in a Web browser.

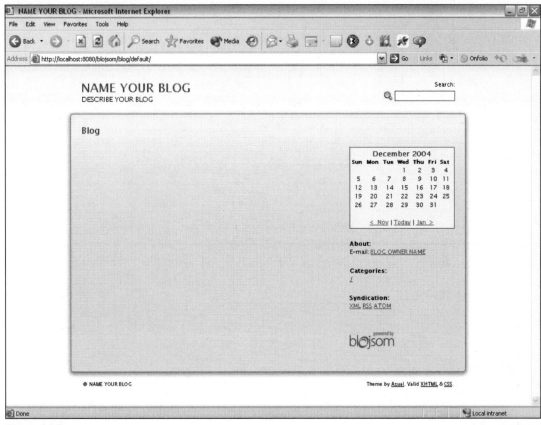

Figure 14-9

As you can see in Figure 14-9 there is some configuration to be done; for example, you have to give your blog a name and provide an e-mail address for contacting the blog author.

You need to log in to Blojsom at the URL `http://localhost:8080/blojsom/blog/default/` `?flavor=admin`. When Blojsom is first installed, the user name you use is `default` and the password is `123default456`; you will want to change those promptly after installation. Figure 14-10 shows the login screen.

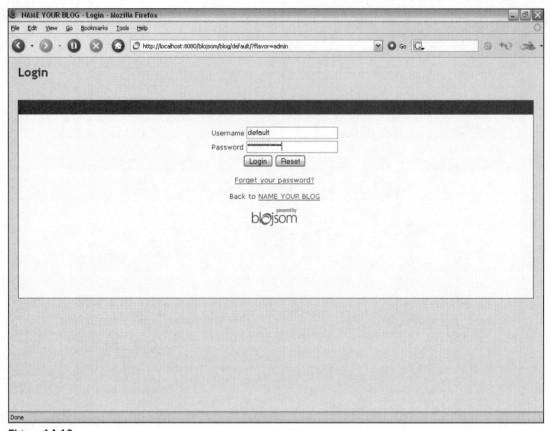

Figure 14-10

After you successfully log in, you can click the Weblog Settings tab to change the configuration of the blog, as shown in Figure 14-11. Farther down on the same settings page you can specify mappings for RSS and Atom information feed formats.

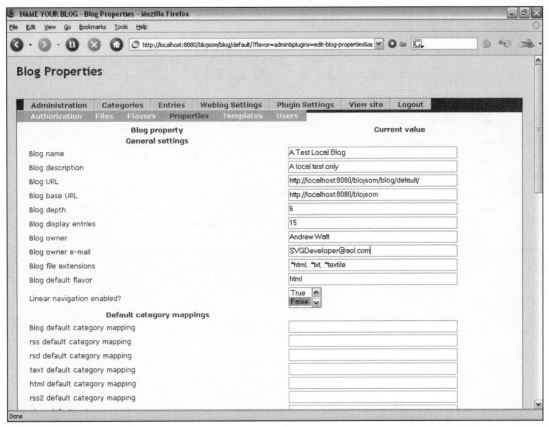

Figure 14-11

For example, you can subscribe to the Blojsom Atom 0.3 feed using Thunderbird by entering the URL `http://localhost:8080/blojsom/blog/default/?flavor=atom`. Figure 14-12 shows the appearance of the simple test feed in Thunderbird 1.0.

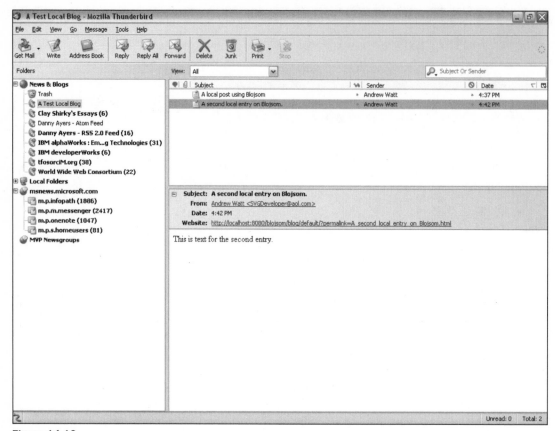

Figure 14-12

The RSS 1.0 feed produced by Blojsom is shown here. There seems to be a bug in the RSS 1.0 feed, since no `item` elements are created and the `rdf:Seq` element is empty. If you prefer to create an RSS 1.0 information feed using Blojsom then you will want to check carefully if the undesired behavior persists. If so, you may want to choose to use another information feed format when using Blojsom.

```
<?xml version="1.0" ?>
<!--   name="generator" content="blojsom v2.21"
  -->
<rdf:RDF xmlns:rdf="http://www.w3.org/1999/02/22-rdf-syntax-ns#"
  xmlns:dc="http://purl.org/dc/elements/1.1/"
  xmlns="http://purl.org/rss/1.0/">
<channel rdf:about="http://localhost:8080/blojsom/blog/default/">
<title>A Test Local Blog</title>
<link>http://localhost:8080/blojsom/blog/default/</link>
<description>A local test only</description>
<dc:publisher>Andrew Watt</dc:publisher>
<dc:creator>SVGDeveloper@aol.com</dc:creator>
<dc:date>2004-12-19T16:38:20+00:00</dc:date>
<dc:language>en</dc:language>
```

```
<items>
<rdf:Seq />
</items>
</channel>
</rdf:RDF>
```

The RSS 2.0 feed seems to be generated correctly. The structure of the RSS 2.0 document should be familiar if you worked through Chapter 12. If you are unfamiliar with the RSS 2.0 document structure we suggest you review Chapter 12.

```
<?xml version="1.0" ?>
<!-- name="generator" content="blojsom v2.21"
 -->
<rss version="2.0"
 xmlns:wfw="http://wellformedweb.org/CommentAPI/">
<channel>
  <title>A Test Local Blog</title>
  <link>http://localhost:8080/blojsom/blog/default/</link>
  <description>A local test only</description>
  <language>en</language>
  <image>
   <url>http://localhost:8080/blojsom/favicon.ico</url>
   <title>A Test Local Blog</title>
   <link>http://localhost:8080/blojsom/blog/default/</link>
  </image>
  <docs>http://blogs.law.harvard.edu/tech/rss</docs>
  <generator>blojsom v2.21</generator>
  <managingEditor>SVGDeveloper@aol.com</managingEditor>
  <webMaster>SVGDeveloper@aol.com</webMaster>
  <pubDate>Sun, 19 Dec 2004 16:42:03 +0000</pubDate>
  <item>
   <title>A second local entry on Blojsom.</title>
   <link>http://localhost:8080/blojsom
/blog/default/?permalink=A_second_local_entry_on
_Blojsom.html</link>
   <description>This is text for the second entry.</description>
   <guid>http://localhost:8080/blojsom
/blog/default/?permalink=A_second_local_entry_on
_Blojsom.html</guid>
   <pubDate>Sun, 19 Dec 2004 16:42:03 +0000</pubDate>
   <wfw:comment>http://localhost:8080/blojsom
/commentapi/default/?permalink=A_second_
local_entry_on_Blojsom.html</wfw:comment>
    <wfw:commentRss>http://localhost:8080/blojsom/blog/default/?permalink=A_second_
local_entry_on_Blojsom.html&page=comments&flavor=rss2</wfw:commentRss>
  </item>
  <item>
   <title>A local post using Blojsom</title>
   <link>http://localhost:8080/blojsom/blog/default/?permalink=A_local_
post_using_Blojsom.html</link>
   <description>This is a short post to demonstrate the use of
Blojsom.</description>
   <guid>http://localhost:8080/blojsom/blog/default/?permalink=A_local_post
```

```
_using_Blojsom.html</guid>
  <pubDate>Sun, 19 Dec 2004 16:37:09 +0000</pubDate>
  <wfw:comment>http://localhost:8080/blojsom/commentapi/default/
?permalink=A_local_post_using_Blojsom.html</wfw:comment>
  <wfw:commentRss>http://localhost:8080/blojsom/blog/default/
?permalink=A_local_post_using_Blojsom.html&page=comments&flavor=rss2</
wfw:commentRss>
  </item>
</channel>
</rss>
```

Your choice of a blogging tool is likely to be determined, at least in part, by the Web server or Web hosting service that you use. Not all Web hosts allow scripts to be run on the server. I suggest that you review the languages supported by your Web host in order to see which blogging tools might be supported.

Another factor that may influence your choice of blogging tool is the information feed format or formats which it supports. If you want to make use of RDF support (which is in RSS 1.0), then both Movable Type and WordPress are suitable. Blojsom also aims to support RSS 1.0 but as mentioned earlier there appears to be a bug in the version tested. Similarly if you want to use RSS 2.0 then either WordPress or Blojsom are suitable.

> **All bloggging tools are undergoing ongoing feature development. If you want to be certain of the features supported in the most recent version, check the documentation at the URLs given earlier in this chapter.**

Summary

Blogging tools allow blogging posts to be automatically converted into Web pages and information feeds without requiring any special knowledge on the part of users. Two blogging tools, Movable Type and Blojsom, were described in this chapter. There is a much wider range of blogging tools available than space permits to introduce here.

In this chapter you learned that...

❑   Movable Type is a blogging tool based on Perl.

❑   WordPress is a blogging tool based on PHP.

❑   Blojsom is a blogging tool based on Java.

❑   The Web host you use may determine which blogging tools are supported.

Aggregators and Similar Tools

RSS and Atom feeds automate the transmission of certain types of data through information feeds. However, the ultimate goal of these feeds is usually to present data from information feeds to human readers.

The term *aggregator* has been widely used to refer to the desktop and online tools that manage and display several information feeds. We use the term aggregator to refer to desktop tools. Online tools are described in Chapter 17. As you will see from the products described in this chapter there are many ways to present information to the human reader. Typical aggregators allow the feed subscription and display to be customized as well.

The software tools described here are sometimes called *news aggregators*. However, this term seems to be too narrow, because most aggregator tools can aggregate any information suitably presented in an RSS or Atom feed, not only news.

In this chapter you learn about:

- ❏ Some common characteristics of desktop aggregators
- ❏ Various desktop aggregators, their approach to information feeds, and some of their features

At the risk of stating the obvious, the RSS and Atom space is changing fast. The number of available aggregator tools is large and growing. Features in both desktop and online aggregators may be different when you read this book than they were when we wrote it. A number of URLs are given in this chapter so that you can check the latest available functionality.

Overview of Desktop Aggregators

Desktop aggregators are available in abundance. When we planned this chapter we hoped to be able to provide a comprehensive snapshot of the available desktop tools. In reality, there are simply too many aggregators and related tools to provide that kind of comprehensive overview.

> **The descriptions of the desktop applications here reflect their behaviors on Windows XP Pro using the version indicated in the product documentation. Because many of these tools are either betas or are otherwise under ongoing development, there may be significant changes in functionality or appearance compared to those described here. In particular, problems that I found when evaluating beta versions might have been remedied by the time you read this.**

Except where specifically stated, you can assume that all tools mentioned here are conventional aggregators that support the basic features of information feed subscription and feed update notification. The different tools support different default feed update frequencies, although most also support user-specified values for this.

Managing Subscriptions

Most aggregators enable you to subscribe to one or more feeds using a fairly intuitive interface. The tools differ in the interface provided to allow you to do this.

Updating Feeds

Aggregators enable you to update single feeds or all feeds together. Tools differ substantially in how convenient they make this basic functionality. Some tools update all feeds as soon as you start the software, whereas others enable you to specify when you want any onscreen display of feed items being updated.

Viewing Web Pages

Some aggregators, such as RSS Bandit, have a built-in browser. This enables you to view Web pages inside the RSS Bandit window (using tabbed browsing). Other aggregators, for example Habari Xenu, are built inside a Web browser. Habari Xenu is an extension for the Firefox browser that displays its information in its own tab. Right-clicking a link allows you open pages of interest in another tab.

Other tools, for example BlogBridge, have no built-in browser. Clicking on a link causes an external browser window to open.

Examples of these different approaches to browser integration are shown later in this chapter.

Individual Desktop Aggregators

The following sections describe several individual desktop aggregators. There are many other aggregators available. Inclusion in this chapter is, typically, more on the basis of familiarity of the authors with individual tools. Failure to include an aggregator does not imply that it fails to provide the core functionality that you would expect of an aggregator.

Abilon

I tested Abilon 2.5.1 from SisyphSoft. Abilon is a Windows-only aggregator. By default, it blocks popups that indicate that new items are present in feeds, and avoids making a sound every time a feed is updated. I find this approach much more pleasant than the approach of having everything turned on by default, which results in a minute of frenzied "pieces of toast" in the lower-right of the screen when you first open the aggregator or as each default feed is updated for the first time.

Program settings allow updating of feeds to be manual only (as shown in Figure 15-1) or at an interval set by the user.

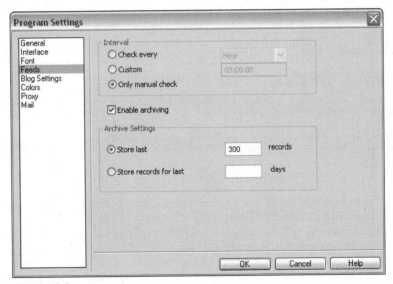

Figure 15-1

Abilon also has a nice facility to filter which feeds are displayed. Figure 15-2 shows a simple filter applied to the feed from www.tfosorciM.org/blog/. The filter selects for display only feed items that contain the terms XForms.

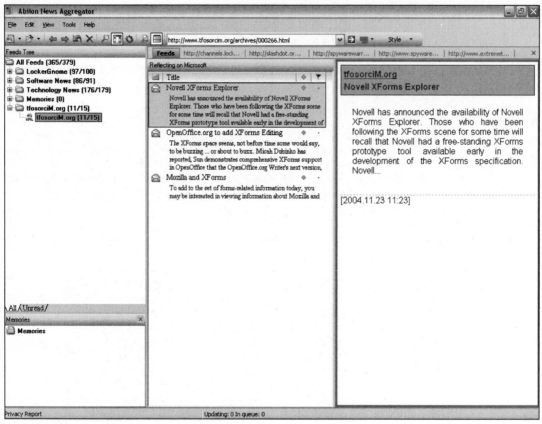

Figure 15-2

Notice in the Feeds Tree pane on the left that there are 15 items in the feed. I created a simple filter that specified that any item that contained the term XForms should be displayed (see Figure 15-3). By combining filters to include and exclude certain terms, you can express a very finely grained set of choices for each feed selected in the Feeds Tree pane.

Another use for Abilon filters is to stop display of advertisements. Lockergnome feeds, for example, use Google AdSense. In other words advertisements are feed items, not simply found in Web pages to which you choose to link. I find that approach intrusive, and having a tool that allows me to filter out ads is something I find very useful. Simply by adding the term AdSense to a filter you can stop advertisements of that type being displayed. Of course, the other option is to avoid subscribing to feeds that include advertisements. Figure 15-4 shows a filter that rejects feed items that contain the word AdSense. Filters are not case-sensitive.

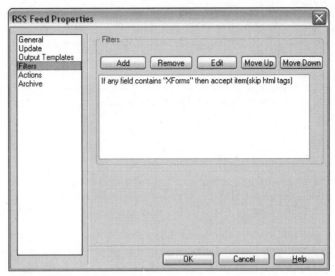

Figure 15-3

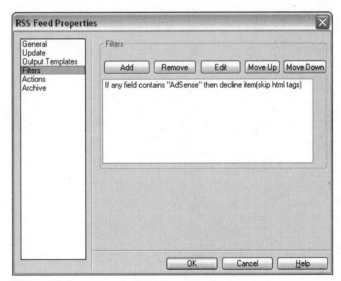

Figure 15-4

ActiveRefresh

SisyphSoft also makes a similar product, ActiveRefresh, which comes with very different defaults. I tested version 2.5.1. The first minute or so after opening ActiveRefresh about 30 percent of my screen real estate was covered with popups. Because the popups were significantly bigger on screen than those for several other aggregators I found this intrusive, messy, and unpleasant.

ActiveRefresh takes the idea of an aggregator a step further than Abilon. It also monitors Web sites that are of interest, and when they change the changed content is retrieved into ActiveRefresh. It uses the term *Web feed* for the updateable information derived from Web pages, rather than from traditional information feeds.

Both Abilon and ActiveRefresh allow a defined number of feed items to be retained. The term *archiving* is used but feed items are discarded on a first in, first out basis. So, it's not a true form of permanent archiving.

Aggreg8

Aggreg8 is a Mozilla-based aggregator that you can download from `www.aggreg8.net/`. It is an extension for Firefox. I tested a private build that was designed to work with Firefox 1.0. Aggreg8 loses some formatting in the extraction of a feed item. For example, in Figure 15-5 the link in the extract is not clickable.

If you want an aggregator that you can use inside the Firefox or Mozilla browsers you may want to check the current status of Aggreg8.

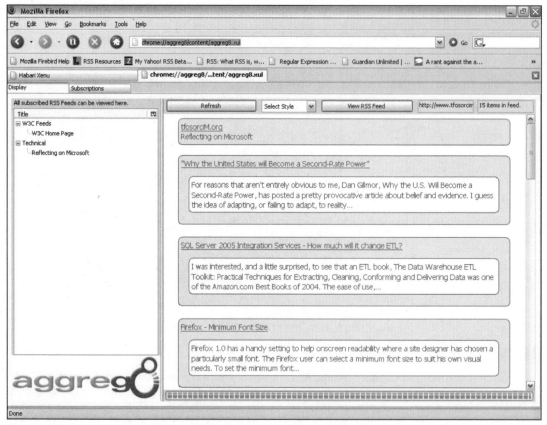

Figure 15-5

BlogBridge

BlogBridge is, at the time of writing, at version 0.6.4. It is a Java-based application that runs on Windows, Linux, and Mac OS X. The cross-platform targeting of BlogBridge means that it can't use Internet Explorer or any other individual browser internally in the way that Windows-specific aggregators such as RSS Bandit can. As a result an external browser is launched to view the Web pages associated with information feed items.

The BlogBridge layout has two panels on the left of the screen, one for Guides and one for Feeds. Guides are a way of grouping feeds; essentially they are folders of feeds. BlogBridge provides some preselected Guides. Figure 15-6 shows the appearance just after installing BlogBridge, with the default guides selected at install displayed.

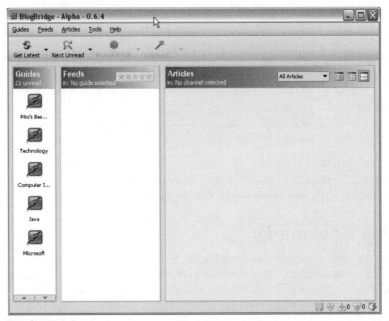

Figure 15-6

One of the most interesting features of BlogBridge is the BlogStarz feature. This is shown in Figure 15-7. It allows the users to select weightings for several aspects of the information feed. For example, if you are concerned with making choices based on keywords an important aspect of the weighting, you can drag the keywords slider to the right.

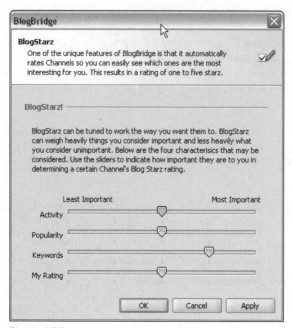

Figure 15-7

Discussions with Pito Salas have raised the possibility that the BlogStarz feature may be available in release 1.0 at the level of a feed rather than it is in the current version, applied equally across all feeds.

Firefox Live Bookmarks

Firefox 1.0 has limited aggregator-like functionality. If a Web page has a `link` element that links to an information feed, you can create a live bookmark. These look like typical Firefox bookmarks. To the best of our knowledge there is no way to configure feed subscriptions through live bookmarks in Firefox 1.0.

One advantage of Firefox Live Bookmarks is that you don't need to add a Firefox extension such as Aggreg8 or Habari Xenu. On the other hand, I find the Live Bookmarks interface clumsy relative to many dedicated aggregators such as RSS Bandit. The Firefox team is aware that the bookmarks interface needs to be improved, and improvement is planned for Firefox version 2.0.

Google News Alerts

One of the tools that is most useful for information aggregation across a large range of information sources is the Google News Alerts system, which is in beta at the time of writing. You might object that it doesn't use RSS or Atom, at least in the form that is presented to the end user, which is a fair objection. However, we don't reject information on paper because of a preference for the type of paper that it is printed on. Google News Alerts is a great way to monitor topics across the Web, rather than monitoring a single feed, which is what a more typical aggregator allows me to do.

Google makes it easy to subscribe and unsubscribe to Google News Alerts. Figure 15-8 shows the subscription page at www.google.com/alerts/. The unsubscription mechanism is easy. A single click in an e-mail and the news alert is cancelled. There is no need for logins and passwords; an elegant, efficient piece of usability in practice.

Figure 15-8

Habari Xenu

Habari Xenu is a Firefox 1.0 extension. When Habari Xenu is installed, you access it from the Tools menu in Firefox. It opens a separate tab in which you then carry out the usual actions associated with subscribing to and managing information feeds. Figure 15-9 shows Habari Xenu in Firefox 1.0.

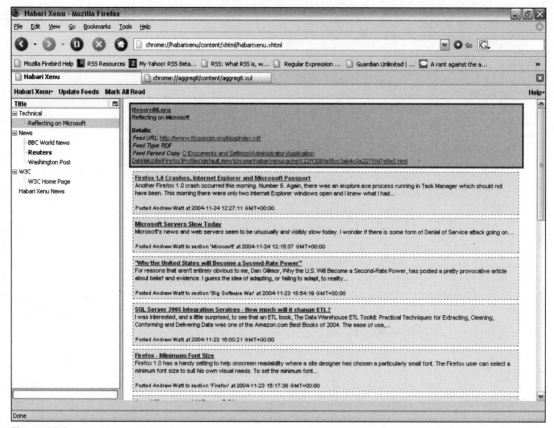

Figure 15-9

NewzCrawler

NewzCrawler is a full-featured aggregator. It is a standalone product. Figure 15-10 shows a post from my Reflecting on Microsoft blog. It also includes a blogging tool.

NewzCrawler needs some customization of its options to avoid multiple "pieces of toast" being displayed onscreen. After that is set then you will have an effective, feature-rich aggregator.

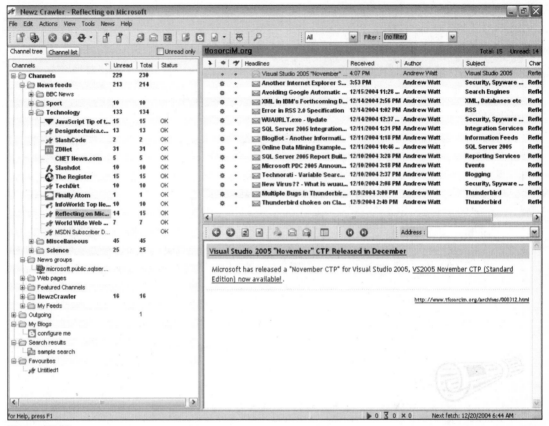

Figure 15-10

Newsgator

Newsgator is a Windows-only aggregator that's used inside Microsoft Outlook. Newsgator is currently at version 2.0. Figure 15-11 shows the appearance of Newsgator 2.0 in Outlook 2003.

If you use Outlook regularly you may find it convenient to use Newsgator so that you have e-mail and information feed items all available inside the Outlook interface. Since the Outlook interface is already fairly complex you may prefer to use a standalone aggregator to avoid added complexity.

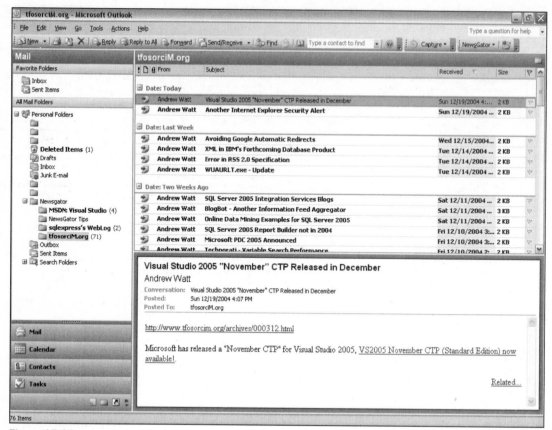

Figure 15-11

Omea

Omea is available in two editions: a free Omea Reader and the for-pay Omea Professional. Omea is termed an *integrated information environment*. It combines the functionality of a traditional aggregator with e-mail functionality from Outlook, as well as Outlook tasks and contacts, and newsgroup information. The interface works well despite the wide range of information that's contained in Omea Professional. We tested Omea Professional 1.0 Beta.

Omea has a feature that we don't recall seeing elsewhere, which is visually a bit surprising the first time it happens but works very well. Figure 15-12 shows a fairly typical three-pane view in Omea Professional. Notice the pointing hand over the link in the lower-right pane.

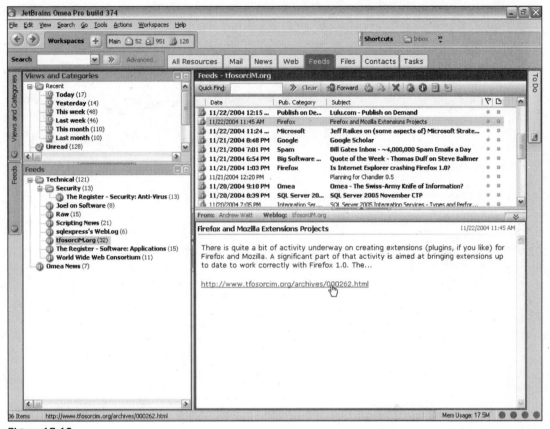

Figure 15-12

When you click the link, Omea automatically extends the display area for the linked Web page so that it fills most of the screen height, as shown in Figure 15-13. If you want to have almost all the screen area to display the Web page, click the vertical bar to the left of the Web page.

The functionality shown in the preceding two figures works very nicely. The increased screen area when viewing the Web page is quite nice. These features make Omea a strong candidate for one of our favorite aggregators.

There is one minor downside to Omea. It takes several seconds to start up, which is probably not surprising when you consider the range of information that it accesses and presents to the user. Likewise, there is a slight delay when you close down Omea. However, given the flexibility of what Omea does, you should be able to live with these delays.

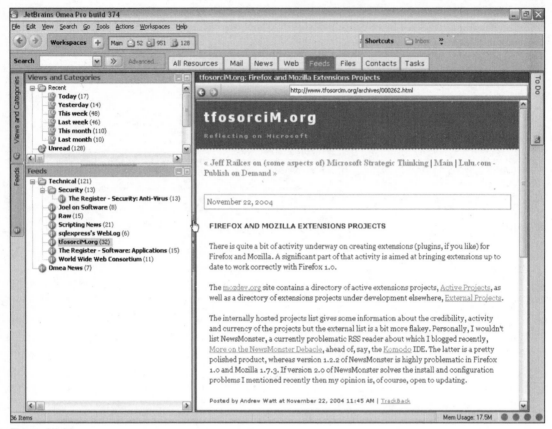

Figure 15-13

Onfolio

Onfolio version 1.0 worked only as an Internet Explorer add-on. However, the beta version of Onfolio 2.0 works in Firefox, and there is now an information feed facility added to Onfolio's long-term capability for long-term storage of Web information.

One nice touch when installing Onfolio 2.0 was that the range of preselected feeds is customizable. With some other information feed tools, up to several dozen feeds are dumped on the user. I liked the way that Onfolio allows categories of feeds or individual feeds to be deselected. As you can see in Figure 15-14, you can deselect categories or individual feeds. Much nicer, in my opinion, than having a raft of feeds installed which you then have to delete one by one.

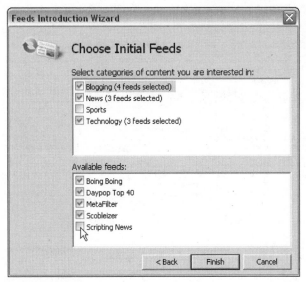

Figure 15-14

Autodiscovery of information feeds is supported and has a nice, simple interface. It is easy to add a new feed to any existing folder or create a new one. The same functionality is present in other aggregators but the Onfolio approach seems particularly elegant.

As mentioned in Chapter5, Onfolio also allows the long-term storage of Web pages, which can be accessed from feed items or in more traditional ways.

RSS Bandit

RSS Bandit is a widely used Windows-specific aggregator. In principle, you can use it on any platform that supports.NET Framework. For practical purposes that means Windows. We tested version 1.2.0.117 of RSS Bandit.

Figure 15-15 shows the Raw blog in RSS Bandit.

RSS Bandit, in general, works well, although, in our experience it occasionally somehow breaks the connection to information feeds. Not only did it bring its own connection down but it stopped other aggregators connecting too. Restarting Windows was sometimes necessary to fix the problem.

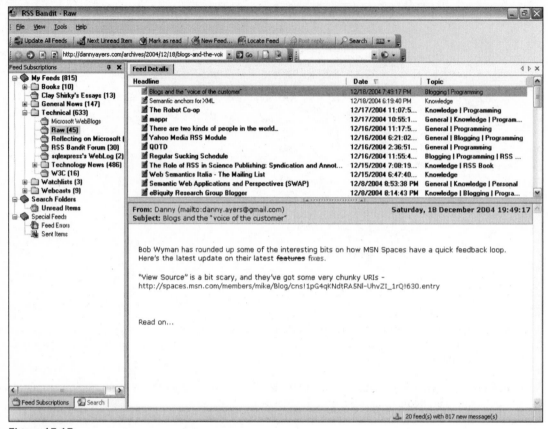

Figure 15-15

Thunderbird 1.0

Mozilla Thunderbird 1.0 provides a very simple information feed aggregator. It works well and is simple to use. If you want to have an aggregator that's also an e-mail client and that's free, Thunderbird is worth looking at. Figure 15-16 shows the Thunderbird interface.

As mentioned earlier in this chapter, you can choose from a huge number of aggregators. Two options that target the Apple Macintosh market are NetNewsWire (`http://ranchero.com/netnewswire`) and the Safari browser (`http://www.apple.com/macosx/tiger/safari.html`), which plans to add information feeds.

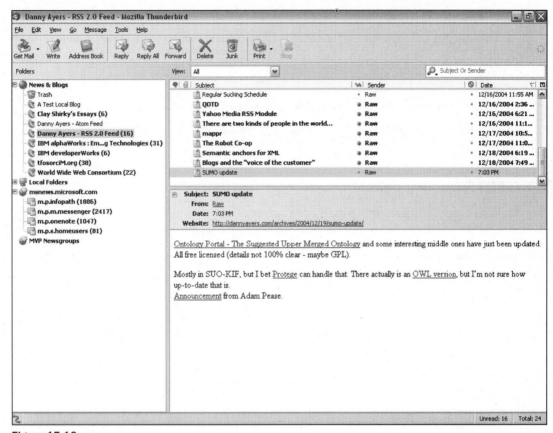

Figure 15-16

Summary

Users have access to a huge number of desktop aggregators. Some are standalone tools. Some are intended for use inside other applications. For example, Newsgator is used inside Microsoft Outlook. Most tools carry out the basic subscription management tasks well.

In this chapter you learned that...

❑ Many aggregators support the basic functionality for subscribing to feeds that any worthwhile aggregator requires.

❑ Abilon and ActiveRefresh support filtering of feeds.

❑ Aggreg8 and Habari Xenu are Firefox extensions.

❑ BlogBridge allows weighting of different factors, such as keywords, in processing feed items.

❑ NewsGator provides an information feed aggregator inside the Microsoft Outlook interface.

❑ RSS Bandit and NewzCrawler provide useful aggregators.

❑ Omea provides a nice user interface feature demonstrated in the text.

❑ Thunderbird provides a simple aggregator combined with an e-mail client.

Exercise

1. Visit the URLs given in this chapter for aggregators that sound likely to meet your needs and download the aggregators of your choice. Some aggregators are paid-for products and have free trial versions. Others are free.

Long-Term Storage of Information

If you take a narrow view of information feeds and look at them as being of only short-term interest, then long-term storage of information retrieved using RSS and Atom information feeds is a non-issue. However, that approach to the data in information feeds is for many uses a short-sighted one. At least some of the huge, and increasing, amounts of information that flow through information feeds is worth keeping for at least some users. So what's the most appropriate thing to do with it?

Consider what happens as you increase the number of items from the assortment of information feeds that you see each day. Let's assume that the majority of the items will be scanned as titles but never read. A minority of the items will be read. Of those items that are read, some will be potentially worth keeping, depending on your interests and intentions. So what do you do with those to facilitate easy and efficient retrieval of information?

The more information that you scan quickly, the more difficult it will become to recall where you saw it. If it's potentially important to your business project or field of study to know exactly what a Web page that you read contained you either need to be able to find the original material again (assuming the original Web site still exists and the page you are interested in hasn't been deleted) or to have stored the relevant information in some form of long-term storage.

Given the uncertainties about continued availability of any piece of information on the World Wide Web, it makes sense to plan for local storage of information that is of possible lasting value to you.

In this chapter you learn:

❑ How to choose an approach to long-term storage

❑ About the desirable characteristics of long-term storage

❑ About some possible software to support long-term storage

Choosing an Approach to Long-Term Storage

When you have decided that at least some information that you see in information feeds is possibly worth keeping, you need to think carefully about how to approach creating a long-term information store.

The Use Case for Long-Term Storage

One fundamental question when considering long-term storage is what you anticipate you will want to do with the information. The more important information from feeds is to your business, the more likely you will want to store it, review long-term trends, time patterns of activity, auditing of decisions and so on.

Storage Options

One of the simplest approaches to long-term storage of information derived from feeds is to use the bookmarks or favorites facility in your Web browser. Such an approach works well for fairly short-term storage of small amounts of data. However, bookmarks are vulnerable to the removal of individual Web pages or the disappearance of individual Web sites. In addition, bookmark functionality tends to become unwieldy when the number of items stored becomes large. Bookmarks just don't scale well.

The unavoidable weak point of bookmarks is that they depend on information of interest still being available at the original URL. One simple way around that problem is to save individual Web pages as separate files in the file system. This can work well on a small scale if the pages are saved in appropriately named folders. Search functionality can be provided using the Windows `findstr` utility or `grep`-like tools on Windows or Linux.

Some software, such as Onfolio and OneNote, allow information from Web pages to be stored long-term. They make capture of information fairly straightforward in different ways as well as allowing easier information retrieval, for example, by allowing searching of stored information. Individual products are discussed later in this chapter.

For storage that will scale, allow multiuser access, and support full backups of data, relational database management systems come fully into the picture.

Choosing Information to Store

Another fundamental question is what information you ought to store. How you answer that question will depend, at least in part, on whether the data store is a personal one or is intended for use by multiple people.

If you are storing information for your own use, because it's interesting or part of your work, you can make your own choices about what to store.

If you are a student, a writer, a journalist, a researcher, or other professional whose work depends on aggregating information in an intelligent way, the storage and retrieval of information is likely to be of crucial importance to you. Often when starting a piece of research you may have fragments of information that need to be consolidated to help you discern a pattern. So, in the early part of a project you may not be sure what information is relevant. In that setting you may well cast your net of information feeds wide and then, as the scope of the research and the information of highest relevance becomes clearer, you might narrow the feeds or topics significantly. The facility to be able to adjust the information to be stored could be useful as the project scope is clarified.

In a situation where information is being stored for corporate use the decision of what information ought to be stored is very likely going to be given careful thought. As corporations increasingly appreciate how information derived from feeds can help them get a handle on relevant news, business trends, and so on, it seems likely that they will pay serious attention to how it is collected.

Determining Who Will Access the Data

The issue of who will want to access stored data has already been briefly touched on. In a personal setting it may well be that only one person will ever need to browse or search the data. In a corporate setting the information needs of several or many individuals or departments may need to be considered. Deciding what information should be stored and who should be allowed to access it will depend on an understanding of your business and the activities of competitors. Also remember to include a process of review that allows you to update the stored information in the light of changing business circumstances.

Planning for multiuser access to the information can be a complex process. Informally or formally the information needs of teams or individuals need to be gathered. After that is done a system can be created that meets those needs or some prioritized subset of the needs.

If information stored from information feeds contains important data about your own business and that of competitors you will also need to consider how you prevent unauthorized access. If the storage system allows you and your colleagues to include comments on individual information items — for example, possible business tactics in the light of a report — you will want to ensure that only appropriately authorized staff have access to the information.

Ease of Storage

If you have spent time capturing significant amounts of information from feeds, you will already realize that the mechanical tasks of clicking, selecting text, and so on can become tedious and, particularly with large amounts of data, also time consuming. Software that makes it easy to capture information permanently is likely to be attractive to users who make heavy use of information feeds.

But why leave the choice of storage to manual actions by human beings at all? In some situations it will make sense to define characteristics of items to be stored, perhaps using keywords or other criteria, and then let software make choices of Web pages for long-term storage without involving users. For such an approach to work well there needs to be functionality to allow well-focused searches to be carried out; automatic archiving of Web pages is likely to lead very quickly to a data store size that would make browsing through it an inefficient process.

Choosing a Backup Strategy

Any data store that contains important information needs to be safeguarded. Even if you are storing data from information feeds only for personal use how inconvenient would it be if your hard disk crashed and the data couldn't be recovered? If the answer to that question suggests that it would be awkward or time consuming to attempt to replace your store of information, then you need to have some backup process in place. At a minimum, you should periodically back up the files to CD-ROM. If you have other backup arrangements for relational data, for example, consider including the data stored from information feeds in the backup process.

If the stored data is needed for corporate purposes, then the need for an appropriate backup strategy is even clearer. If data is stored in a relational database management system, then it makes sense to include the data in the routine daily or weekly backups.

Characteristics of Long-Term Storage

The characteristics of the needed long-term storage depend on what you or your company need the information for. Assuming that it is needed for business purposes, you will need to consider issues such as scalability and availability.

Scalability

The importance of scalability will depend on how many people need to access the information. Currently, many data stores for information from feeds are being created on an ad hoc personal basis. At the other end of the spectrum a few companies have custom written applications that handle very large amounts of information. It seems that the corporate need for information derived from feeds will grow substantially in the next couple of years. That means that the data stores need to be scalable, in order to allow department-wide, company-wide, or corporation-wide access to such information. As the need to achieve scalability becomes more important, the more likely it is that the back-end of the relevant applications will be built on a relational database management system. Because these applications are likely to use existing RDBMS systems, the issues of scalability for the company's needs should have already been assessed.

Availability

In some larger companies the issue of availability may also figure significantly. If there are several offices scattered around the globe then availability of a business intelligence resource may be of prime importance. Depending on the size of the information store it may be more convenient to replicate the data to branch offices rather than have a single central store that needs to be available 24/7.

Software to Support Long-Term Storage

Software for long-term storage of information derived from feeds can be seen as an emerging area of interest. Most tools, such as aggregators, currently limit their functionality to subscribing to feeds and displaying current information from the subscribed feeds.

From another point of view, suitable tools for data storage already exist. Relational database management systems can, for at least some Web pages, store all or part of the information on the page. However, issues of how best to store such information and later retrieve and display it are likely to be the focus of significant interest over the next few years.

The software mentioned in the remainder of this chapter provides solutions to some of the issues of long-term storage of information from information feeds, but there is certainly room for new tools to be added.

Onfolio

Onfolio 2.0 is currently in beta and was described in Chapter 15. Onfolio is used inside a Web browser. Version 2.0 can be used in both Internet Explorer and Firefox 1.0. Version 1.0 could be used only inside Internet Explorer.

Onfolio 1.0 allows Web pages to be saved, preserving page layout, images, and so on. Saving ("capturing" in Onfolio terminology) a Web page or Web site is straightforward. It is added to what Onfolio calls a *collection*.

Onfolio 2.0 adds fairly conventional functionality that allows subscribing to information feeds. However, from the same Onfolio interface, the user can save any Web pages that are of interest into a collection that they have created using the Collection tab.

The property tray, among other things, allows the user to add comments about a particular Web page, as you can see in Figure 16-1.

This ability to add annotations to saved Web pages illustrates another question about long-term storage. To what extent should the long-term storage be fixed and to what extent should it be a facility to allow information to be stored, aggregated, and used in projects relevant to an individual's research or a department's monitoring of selected competitor activity.

Onfolio has the best technique to preserve the original content and layout of a Web page that I am aware of in any currently available tool. If layout is important to you then Onfolio is well worth a look.

Onfolio 2.0 provides a search facility. As mentioned earlier, search functionality becomes increasingly important as the volume of stored data increases. Because Onfolio 2.0 has some stability limitations in the pre-beta version I tested I did not have the opportunity to explore how well the search functionality scales.

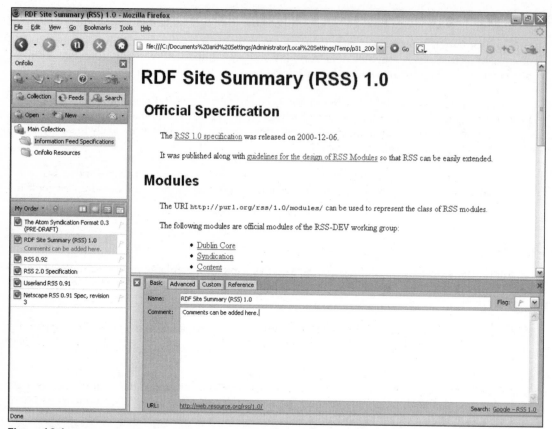

Figure 16-1

Microsoft OneNote

OneNote has different long-term storage strengths from those seen in Onfolio 2.0. It has no information feed functionality at all. In the context that we are considering it acts as a repository of selected information. That information can be user-written notes — for example, for a research project — together with content (which can include text and graphics) copied and pasted from selected Web pages. In itself, that content need not be associated in any way with information feeds but can be derived from them.

Unlike Onfolio, OneNote does not preserve the Web page layout precisely. It is the content that is preserved together with, optionally, a source URL and a date for the page into which the content is being copied. User notes on saved data are, given the nature of OneNote, well supported.

The OneNote metaphor is of pages and subpages which are contained in sections. Sections, in turn, are contained in folders. A section is a file with an .one file extension.

A folder can be created for a research project with individual topics assigned to sections. Pages and subpages within the folder can be used to collect thoughts about the project as well as information saved from selected Web pages. Figure 16-2 gives an indication of how OneNote can be used in a simple research project.

Microsoft SQL Server 2005

SQL Server 2005, currently in beta, is mentioned here as an example of the kind of functionality that a corporate user of stored information might need.

SQL Server 2005 is an enterprise grade relational database management system. It has scalability, availability, replication, backup, and other management tools likely to satisfy all but the most demanding user of the type of information store discussed in this chapter.

One of the questions about using any relational database management system is how the fairly disparate information can be processed and stored. SQL Server 2005 offers several ways to handle input XML data. For the remainder of this discussion we will assume that RSS and Atom documents are well-formed XML. Of course most, but not all, are well formed.

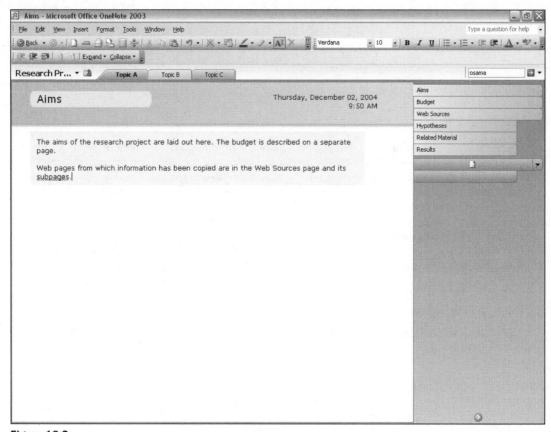

Figure 16-2

One approach is to use SQL XML on the middle tier and split XML data into a form that can be stored as relational columns.

An alternative approach is to make use of the xml datatype that is new in SQL Server 2005. The XML contained in such a column can be indexed and searches can be carried out using XPath and XQuery statements embedded inside Transact-SQL statements.

The SQL Server Integration Services functionality, which is new in SQL Server 2005, builds on Data Transformation Services that were present in SQL Server 2000. They allow various data sources to be used and transformed in a pipeline, with the data that result from one or several transformations being placed in suitable data stores, for example, tables in a SQL Server database. So data from an information feed can be accessed and then transformed in an arbitrary way to create SQL Server tables that store the needed data.

Integration Services allows errors that occur during transformations to be diverted to error outputs, processed using alternative (non-XML) transformations or handled in any other way which is appropriate to the circumstances in which the transformations are taking place. In the context of processing information feeds this could allow feeds that don't consist of well-formed XML to be identified and processed in some custom way.

Using the fairly basic regular expression functionality in the Transact-SQL LIKE keyword or the Full-text search capabilities of SQL Server a powerful, custom search facility could be relatively easily created.

Summary

Long-term storage of information that has been gathered from feeds is becoming increasingly important, both to individuals and to businesses. The approach you choose for long-term storage of such information will depend on your likely future needs to retrieve and search information. We also briefly discussed approaches ranging from bookmarks in Web browsers to fully featured relational database management systems.

In this chapter you learned that...

- ❏ Long-term storage can be important for some types of data accessed from information feeds.
- ❏ Controlling access to data is important.
- ❏ Backing up data is important.
- ❏ Tools such as Onfolio, OneNote, and SQL Server 2005 provide varied options for long-term data storage.

Online Tools

There are many online tools available with varying functionality that use RSS or Atom to provide options similar to those provided by the desktop aggregators described in Chapter 15, and, to some extent, provide functionality that might be available in personal or corporate long-term storage of the kinds described briefly in Chapter 16. Many online tools provide additional functionality, including providing a directory of feeds or ways to find similar feeds.

In this chapter you learn about:

- ❑ The pros and cons of online tools
- ❑ Several leading or long-established online tools

> **The information provided about online tools describes the observed functionality of the tools in late November 2004. Given the nature of any Web-based tool, the functionality described is subject to change at any time.**

Advantages and Disadvantages of Online Tools

With the range of functionality available in aggregators that you install on your desktop, a basic question arises: why is there any need for online information feed tools? Any tool that aggregates data from information feeds must have access to the Internet. But are such tools better hosted online or on your own desktop?

Personally, I am not as enthusiastic about online tools as I am about desktop tools. Desktop tools tend to fit better with my way of working although I appreciate that not everybody works that way. The following sections differentiate between online and desktop tools and make relevant comparisons.

Registration

One of the routine issues related to many of the online sites mentioned in this chapter is that, to have full access to the facilities offered, you must obtain a login name and password. The issue we have with this approach is having to manage a growing number of separate accounts. If the number of logins and passwords that a user needed was small then it might not be a significant issue. But, for many users, the need for different logins and passwords for many sites (for security reasons you ought not to use the same login name and password widely!) is a significant administrative burden. How do you store them? And how do you store them in a way that you can be sure is safe from prying (and therefore identity theft)? How do you ensure that all your logins are up to date and safely backed up so that, if your hard disk crashes, you don't lose all the information needed to log in to your favorite sites?

Interface Issues

One of the issues where both desktop and online tools pose a barrier to users is the sheer inconsistency of user interfaces. Given that many of the tools, particularly the online ones, attempt to differentiate themselves by their functionality it can be difficult to easily assimilate the range of functionality that any site offers. Similar issues arise with desktop tools. It would make the user's life easier if tools could clearly express their functionality.

Online Tools When Mobile

How useful an online tool is depends on how you want to use them and whether you have reliable Internet connectivity at the times when you do want to access them. If you have no Internet connectivity, then an online tool can't be used. Similar problems occur with many desktop tools. Onfolio 2.0, discussed in the previous chapter, can capture Web pages or other items linked from information feeds for offline use. Although that is not a reason that I would often use Onfolio, it does provide a way to download, for example, a range of items from information feeds so that they could be reviewed when offline and sitting, for example, in an airport lounge or on an aircraft.

Cost of Online Tools

Many online tools are currently free. Their business model, assuming that it has been fully thought out, does not depend on the user paying for access to the online tool. The fact that online tools are free is great in the short term for the user. However, since nothing is truly free in life, an online tool's site needs some kind of income to sustain it if it is not being run as a hobby. Although we're not sure whether there will be new versions of some free desktop tools, at least we know that we have the current version of a particular tool that we can continue to use for some time. If you go back to an online site where you have invested time into creating custom feeds and cannot log in because the site is no longer there, your time has, essentially, been wasted.

Stability of Access

One of our basic concerns about online aggregator tools and similar online facilities is that there is no guarantee that they will be there next year or next week. Of course, some sites are more stable than others. But there is no guarantee. For us, if we are going to invest effort into creating a custom set of feeds that suit our needs well, we want to be sure that that work isn't wasted.

In addition to our general background concern, some tools, such as Rollup, will delete your selections after periods of inactivity as short as 14 days. That would make us very cautious about using such a service. We find information feeds very useful, but we would hate to lose permanently our choices simply because for a short period we had chosen not to use them. These issues simply don't occur with desktop tools.

As with any site, access can be temporarily disrupted due to periods of site maintenance or heavy server or Internet load. Some tools mentioned later in this chapter load almost instantly on many occasions. At other times it can take many seconds even to load the home page of the site. This is not a huge inconvenience and doesn't occur often but it is less convenient than the consistency of performance of a desktop aggregator.

Performance

Many of the online sites enable you to search for recent posts of interest. However, the search isn't as consistent in terms of speed as a desktop search would be. Sometimes a search may take tens of seconds whereas the same search a short time later or the following day might take a second or two. To be sure, server loads may vary, but if we have stored data locally and search it locally it seems to us that search performance is both faster and more consistent in terms of time taken.

Notifications

A few sites enable users to download a utility that can be installed in some browsers. After the utility has been installed in the browser, if there are updates in subscribed feeds you can be notified of their occurrences. This functionality parallels the onscreen notifications that are supported by many desktop aggregators.

Cookies

If you decide to go online with only session cookies or with cookies turned off you may find that the functionality of some sites is reduced or absent. Again, this issue does not affect a desktop aggregator.

Using Multiple Machines

The primary advantage of using online tools becomes apparent if you use more than one computer. For example, you may have a desktop machine at work and another desktop machine at home. If you use an online tool, then the tool represents your current settings and also displays the relevant information feed items. There is no need to attempt to synchronize settings and to remember which feed items you have already seen.

When using two machines, it would be much less convenient to use a desktop aggregator on each machine. The installation on each machine would, when you connect it to the Internet, look for new feed items. However, it would recognize as "new" feed items that you may already have seen on your other machine. On average you would have to scan each feed item twice. The likely result is that you would waste time scanning information that you had already seen. This would be an inefficient use of time.

Making a Choice

In our opinion the key issue is whether you are using two machines. If you do, then an online tool offers the advantages of efficiency and having one central source of information derived from information feeds. This seems to outweigh the disadvantages discussed in earlier sections in this chapter. If you use one machine, the disadvantages of online tools seem to outweigh the benefits.

Choosing Between Individual Online Tools

The following sections briefly describe some aspects of a selection of online aggregators and similar tools. The sheer number of online sites that attempt to provide information feed–related functionality makes it difficult to know each site or tool equally well. Therefore any selection is, almost inevitably, an arbitrary one. There are many other tools that offer functionality with similarities to the functionality of the tools described in this chapter.

Bloglines

Bloglines (www.bloglines.com/) provides the opportunity to subscribe to a range of feeds. It also offers a way to browse through all the feeds that bloglines monitors. If you have a blog, you can see which Bloglines subscribers are subscribed to your feed—provided that they choose to allow their subscription to be made available to other Bloglines users.

Bloglines also has a Notifier utility that can be downloaded from www.bloglines.com/about/ notifier. This utility will notify registered users of Bloglines when new items are found on feeds to which the user has subscribed. Figure 17-1 shows the Bloglines home page.

Figure 17-1

Feedster

Feedster (www.feedster.com/) uses a minimalist Web page layout with some similarities to the simplicity of the Google.com site. Feedster functions as a search engine for information feeds. It claims to have more than 2,000,000 registered feeds with several thousand being added daily. You can search items from those feeds by single keyword, sorting by relevance or date. You can also find out if particular sites have an information feed, although a negative result in that search doesn't always correspond with the absence of a feed on the site of interest. It's easier using Firefox and allowing it to autodiscover the feeds when you visit the site of interest, provided that they are not already visible using the now traditional orange XML icon. Figure 17-2 shows the Feedster home page.

Figure 17-2

Furl

Furl (www.furl.net/) enables you to search for terms of interest. Our experiences with Furl have been patchy; for example, it can return results that are grossly out-of-date. For one search for XForms, in the first page of results one was from the year 2000 and wasn't particularly relevant to anyone who was interested in XForms. Furl's approach seems to target results from popular or big sites. Sometimes that works well, but at other times it returns inappropriate and outdated results. Not every page on a popular site is worth seeing.

Furl seems to offer functionality similar to Onfolio 2.0 on the desktop. You can create a personal archive of Web pages that you can browse or search, which is very useful. But one of my foundational concerns about online tools comes into play. What happens to the time and work that you invested to create the archive if you go back to the URL and find that Furl is no longer there? Figure 17-3 shows the Furl home page.

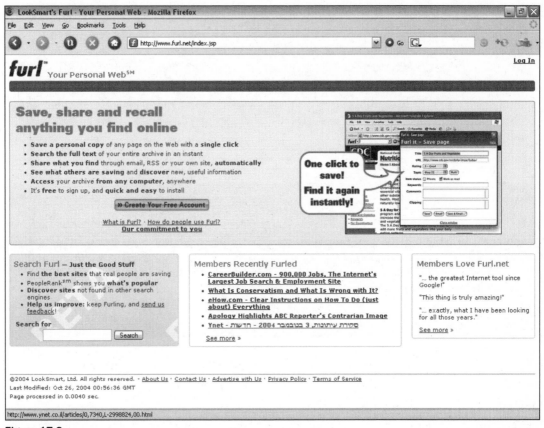

Figure 17-3

Google News Alerts

I mention Google News Alerts here because they do have an online component. The main description of Google News Alerts is in Chapter 15.

The signup process for Google News Alerts is simple. You go to www.google.com/alerts/ and fill in the form shown in Figure 17-4. You supply only four pieces of information, each of which is relevant to what you, the user, want to know. No extra information is gathered. You specify the subject of the alert. If you are fluent in Google search syntax you can create searches that are quite tightly filtered or targeted at a single Web site. No need to register or create yet another login.

Figure 17-4

Kinja

The Kinja aggregator is located at www.kinja.com/. At the time we tested it, it was in the beta stage. To use Kinja you must create an account with a login name and password. Once you have replied to an e-mail you are able to create an online aggregator. Figure 17-5 shows a simple selection of URLs for inclusion in the aggregator.

After Kinja confirms that the URLs that you entered are linked to what it deems are valid feeds then you can browse the favorites you chose.

Kinja did seem to work but, at least in the beta form that I tested, it didn't work as I expected. One slightly disturbing aspect is that Kinja sometimes seems to fail quietly. My blog at www.tfosorciM.org/blog/ was seemingly quietly ignored, without giving any indication that it had done so (see Figure 17-6). More confusing still, the W3C site is listed, but no feed items are found, possibly because Kinja again cannot handle RSS 1.0 feeds. However, later without me consciously changing anything Kinja would only display items from my blog and ignored items from the other two. Perhaps this was, in some way, by design. But I found it confusing.

Figure 17-5

Kinja allows a bookmarklet utility to be downloaded. When using Firefox the bookmarklet option in Kinja did not work. Altogether, I found the Kinja beta a disappointing experience. Hopefully, by the time you read this the teething problems will have been ironed out.

Figure 17-6

Newsgator Online

We describe the desktop version of Newsgator, which is a tool used inside Microsoft Outlook, in Chapter 15. The desktop version of Newsgator is a paid product. An online version of Newsgator (www.newsgator.com/ngs/default.aspx) is offered free of charge at the time of writing. Figure 17-7 shows the Newsgator home page.

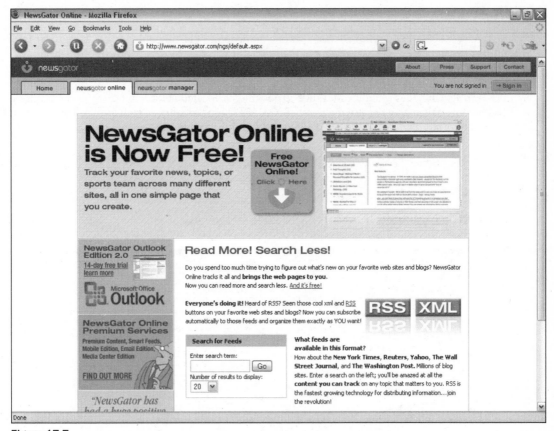

Figure 17-7

In addition to the Web-based version, the online version of NewsGator also includes editions for mobile devices, e-mail clients, and Windows Media Center. In addition, it supports per-post ratings of content and provides users the ability to automatically publish their blogroll on their site or even republish headlines from selected feeds.

Rollup.org

Rollup.org (www.rollup.org/rollup/) provided an aggregator for a range of feeds. However, during the period between the writing and final editing of this chapter the Rollup site closed. This illustrates the point I made earlier in the chapter about the possible lack of continuous availability of online tools.

Syndic8.com

Syndic8.com (`http://www.syndic8.com/`) is one of the longest lasting online tools. It registers information feeds based on human assessment of their activities. In that respect Syndic8.com is, arguably, more discerning than some other online tools.

Syndic8.com also includes a significant range of documents, located at `www.syndic8.com/documents/`, that include tutorials on how to use the Syndic8 XML-RPC functionality as well as many more general articles and tutorials. Figure 17-8 shows the Syndic8.com home page.

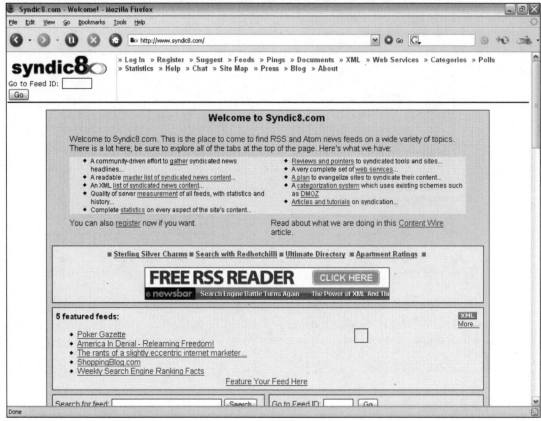

Figure 17-8

Technorati

Technorati (www.technorati.com/) requires that you create a login using a valid e-mail address. You can search a substantial number of information feeds for topics of interest. Search times for Technorati were surprisingly variable during our tests.

When using Technorati you can create watchlists that monitor topics or terms that are of interest to you.

One of the aspects of Technorati that we like is the ease with which you can drag a link to the Links toolbar, at least in Firefox 1.0, and when you highlight some text in a Web page, you can just click the Technorati favelet (called a bookmarklet in some other settings) to run a Technorati search for current information matching the search word or phrase. Figure 17-9 shows the Technorati home page.

The Technorati API is described at http://developers.technorati.com/wiki/TechnoratiApi.

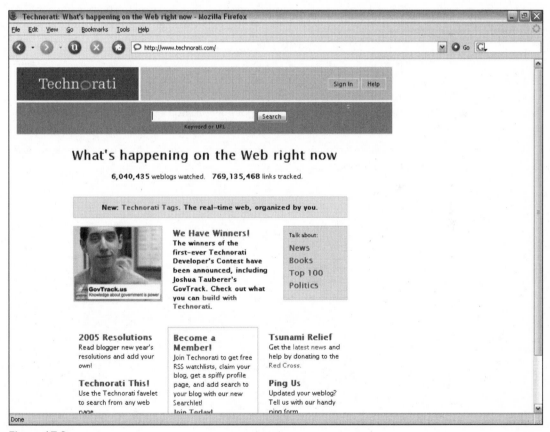

Figure 17-9

PubSub.com

PubSub.com (`www.pubsub.com`) enables you to create subscriptions to new information about chosen topics. Personally, I find it disconcerting that entering a term like XForms returns no results. We understand that the subscription may relate to "new" items, but we would find it more reassuring to be shown the results from, say, the last 24 hours or the last week or so on. It seems obvious that if you choose to subscribe to a topic, you would like at least the option to see recent results.

PubSub.com offers the PubSub sidebar which offers registered users updates from their chosen topics delivered to the PubSub sidebar in their Web browser.

Summary

Many online tools use RSS or Atom to provide functionality similar to a desktop aggregator. Online sites often offer a tool that you can download and install in your browser. These provide a range of functionality including notification of updates to subscribed feeds and searching the online site for matches for highlighted text in a Web page.

In this chapter you learned that...

❑   When you're using two machines an online tool may provide significant benefits of efficiency, because you can avoid double scanning information feeds, compared to a desktop aggregator.

❑   For users of one machine, online tools may be less responsive and may have question marks about long-term availability.

Language-Specific Developer Tools

From this chapter forward you will move from considering a range of general issues relating to information feeds and their use to specific development projects. At the risk of stating the obvious, to carry out development you need tools. This chapter briefly reviews a range of developer tools that are relevant to the manipulation of information derived from information feeds. We use many of these tools in the following chapters.

There are tools available in many languages for the creation or manipulation of information feeds. In this chapter you learn about:

- ❑ Python tools
- ❑ PHP tools
- ❑ Java tools
- ❑ XSLT tools
- ❑ Perl tools

Python Tools

Python, like Perl, has many tools available for processing XML and specifically for processing information feeds. If you don't already have a Python installation visit www.python.org/, where you can download the latest version of Python and also have access to the official documentation and a range of Python tutorials.

PyXML

PyXML is a collection of libraries to allow you to process XML using Python. PyXML can be downloaded from `http://pyxml.sourceforge.net/`. It includes a validating parser, xmlproc, and a nonvalidating parser, expat. It also includes PySAX to allow use of the Simple API for XML processing, SAX.

RSS.py

RSS.py is a Python tool created by Mark Nottingham. It can be downloaded from `www.mnot.net/python/RSS.py`. It requires that PyXML be installed.

Universal Feed Parser

The Universal Feed Parser, developed by Mark Pilgrim, is a Python module for downloading and parsing information feeds. It can handle RSS 0.9x, RSS 1.0, RSS 2.0, and Atom 0.3 feed formats. To make use of the Universal Feed Parser module you will need to have Python 2.1 or later installed.

The Universal Feed Parser is simple to use, because it only has one public function, `parse()`. When used with a single argument, the argument can be a URL or a file name in the local file system.

You can find full information on the Universal Feed Parser at `http://sourceforge.net/projects/feedparser/`.

xpath2rss

The xpath2rss module is an HTML to RSS tool. It works, in effect, by screen scraping the HTML and then identifying the information anticipated to be relevant parts of an RSS feed. Unlike some other similar tools it uses XPath, rather than regular expressions in the parsing.

You can download the xpath2rss module from `http://www.mnot.net/xpath2rss/`. At the time of writing the current version is 0.7.

Chumpologica

Chumpologica is an aggregator that uses Python. To run Chumpologica you will need to have installed Python 2.3 or later with XML libraries, HTML Tidy (`http://tidy.sourceforge.net/`), and the Python wrapper for the Redland RDF application framework (`http://librdf.org/`).

You can download version 1.0 of Chumpologica from `www.hackdiary.com/projects/chumpologica/Chumpologica-1.0.tar.gz`.

PHP Tools

Some PHP tools that are useful when processing XML and information feeds are briefly described here.

lastRSS

One PHP tool for information feed processing is lastRSS, which is a PHP class for parsing RSS. It can be used with RSS 0.9*x*, 1.0, and 2.0. Further information is located at `http://lastrss.webdot.cz/`. It has significantly less functionality than MagpieRSS but may be faster for some simple uses.

MagpieRSS

MagpieRSS is yet another Sourceforge project relevant to information feeds. Information about it is located at `http://magpierss.sourceforge.net/`. Features include parsing of RSS 0.9*x*, RSS 1.0, RSS 2.0, and Atom 0.3. Parsing in MagpieRSS depends on well-formed XML being presented for parsing. As mentioned earlier this typically does not cause problems since most feeds are now well-formed XML.

You can find information about projects using MagpieRSS and code snippets at `http://magpierss.sourceforge.net/links.php`.

Java Tools

There are several Java tools available for use with information feeds.

ROME

ROME is the abbreviation for RSS and atoM utilitiEs. At the time of writing the current version is 0.5. ROME supports the following information feed formats: RSS 0.9*x*, 1.0 and 2.0 and Atom 0.3. ROME absolutely requires well-formed XML in feeds, which it processes. If the feed is not well formed then ROME will fail.

The home page for the ROME project is `https://rome.dev.java.net/`. ROME can be downloaded from `http://wiki.java.net/bin/view/Javawsxml/Rome`. Documentation is available at the same URL.

To run ROME you will need to have Java 1.4+ installed and JDOM 1.0. A J2SE install can be downloaded from `http://java.sun.com/j2se/index.jsp`. JDOM can be downloaded from `www.jdom.org/`.

An interesting description of the internals of ROME is available at `www.rollerweblogger.org/page/roller/20040808#how_rome_works`. However, at the time of writing that URL contains a description of ROME 0.4, rather than the most recent version.

Jena

Jena is a Java framework that provides sophisticated, comprehensive, and specification-accurate support for RDF and other Semantic Web technologies. For more information go to `http://jena.sourceforge.net/`.

The Redland RDF Application Framework

The Redland RDF Application Framework has language bindings for Java and for several other languages, including Perl, PHP, and Python. For detailed information as well as the current information of the Redland RDF Application Framework go to `http://librdf.org/`.

You can use Redland with several packages when processing RDF.

The Raptor RDF Parser Toolkit is a parser and serialization package that allows the parsing of serialized RDF (most commonly RDF/XML) into RDF triples. Other components of the Raptor package can be used to serialize RDF triples in a desired format. Detailed information on Raptor is available at `http://librdf.org/raptor/`. Of particular interest in the context of this book is Raptor's full support for RSS 1.0, Atom and "Tag Soup" RSS 2.0 parsing and serialization.

The Rasqal RDF Query Library supports RDF query creation and execution using RDQL and SPARQL. Detailed information on the Rasqal RDF Query Library is available at `http://librdf.org/rasqal/`.

When using Redland with a language other than C you will also need the Redland RDF Language Bindings package, which you can download from `http://librdf.org/bindings/`.

XSLT Tools

XSLT processors depend absolutely on the source document being well-formed XML. An XSLT processor is, typically, built on top of an XML parser. The XML 1.0 specification indicates that if the document that is parsed is not well formed, an error should be raised and normal processing should stop. In the early days of information feeds you couldn't be confident that feeds were really well-formed XML so using XSLT was a potentially problematic choice. Now, most feeds are produced automatically from blogging tools and there has been time to iron out problems from other tools. Therefore the problems that can arise from feeds that are not well formed are likely to form a very small percentage of feeds. However, if you do choose to use XSLT and the feed appears broken to the user you may find that it is your aggregator that is blamed by the user rather than the malformed feed, since some other aggregator tools may be able to render the feed in the way that the user expects.

Perl Tools

Perl provides support for processing information feeds through a range of modules. If you don't already have a Perl installation, visit `www.perl.org/` to obtain the software suitable for your platform and copious accompanying documentation. If you intend to run Perl on Windows, you can download it from `www.activestate.com/Products/ActivePerl/`.

If you want to retrieve files from the Web you are likely to want to have modules such as LWP::Simple, `http://search.cpan.org/dist/libwww-perl/lib/LWP/Simple.pm`, which can retrieve and optionally store a file from a specified URL. The LWP::Simple module is a simplified version, as its name suggests, of the more powerful LWP::UserAgent module.

For full information on LWP, the WWW Library for Perl, visit `http://search.cpan.org/~gaas/libwww-perl-5.803/lib/LWP.pm`.

Other modules such as HTMLToke:Parser can be used to parse HTML files as a preparatory step to creating an RSS information feed using a module such as XML::RSS.

If you are processing an XML information feed, the XML::Simple module contains functionality to parse RSS 0.9x and RSS 1.0 and produces XHTML. One limitation of XML::Simple is that it can't process mixed content. Assuming that the RSS has been written according to the specification you shouldn't have problems. For more information on XML::Simple go to `http://search.cpan.org/dist/XML-Simple/lib/XML/Simple/FAQ.pod`. You can download the XML::Simple module from `ftp://ftp.cpan.org/pub/CPAN/authors/id/G/GR/GRANTM`.

There are many other, less simple than XML::Simple, Perl modules that can be used in XML processing. A good starting point for information is `http://perl-xml.sourceforge.net/faq/#cpan_modules`.

XML::RSS

XML::RSS is a Perl module that provides a framework for creating and maintaining RSS files. RSS versions 0.91, 0.92 and 1.0 are supported. At the time of writing neither RSS 2.0 nor any version of Atom is supported.

Full details on XML:RSS are located at `http://perl-rss.sourceforge.net/` and `http://search.cpan.org/~kellan/XML-RSS/lib/RSS.pm`.

Support for XSLT

There are several Perl modules for XSLT processing, if you choose to go down that route, such as XML::libXSLT and XML::Sablotron. Support is for XSLT 1.0 in the versions of XML::libXSLT and XML::Sablotron available at the time of writing.

You can download XML::libXSLT at `http://search.cpan.org/dist/XML-LibXSLT/`. To view the documentation go to `http://search.cpan.org/dist/XML-LibXSLT/LibXSLT.pm`.

XML::Sablotron is available for download from `http://search.cpan.org/dist/XML-Sablotron/`. You may also want to check `http://www.gingerall.org/charlie/ga/xml/d_sab.xml` for updates or patches.

The rss2html Module

The rss2html module is used to create an HTML representation of an RSS information feed. The rss2html module is best suited to RSS 0.9x.

The rss2html module can be downloaded from `http://freshmeat.net/projects/rss2html/`.

The Regular Expressions Approach

The Perl modules mentioned earlier in this section are intended for use with well-formed XML documents. If it's important to you to accept all feeds, whether or not the supposed XML is fully well-formed or not, then you can use regular expressions to process the information in the feed.

Using regular expressions means that you can avoid installing XML-related modules, if you choose. However, there is a definite downside in that the code is significantly more difficult to maintain than code intended to process XML. Chapter 23 discusses a PHP regular expression-based "Tag Soup" parser for handling feeds that aren't well-formed XML.

Miscellaneous Tools

Although not always strictly RSS/Atom tools, many applications will need to post new feed entries to a server using one of the XML-RPC protocols or Atom. Posting tools include:

- ❏ BlogEd (`https://bloged.dev.java.net/`)
- ❏ BlogClient (`http://rollerweblogger.org/page/roller/20050117#blogclient_1_0_an_atom`)
- ❏ IMHO (`http://sourceforge.net/projects/imho10`)

Weblog_Pinger (`www.cadenhead.org/workbench/weblog-pinger/`) is a PHP library for passing XML-RPC feed update notifications to services like Weblogs.Com, Blo.gs, Ping-o-Matic, and Technorati.

Useful Sources

New tools for working with syndication feeds are appearing all the time. Particularly good places to watch or search are:

- ❏ Sourceforge (`http://sourceforge.net`)
- ❏ The RSS Blog (`www.kbcafe.com/rss`)
- ❏ Atom Enabled (`www.atomenabled.org`)
- ❏ Finally Atom (`http://danja.typepad.com/fecho`)
- ❏ SWIG Scratchpad (`http://rdfig.xmlhack.com/`)

Summary

Many tools that can be used in the processing of XML and information feeds are available in languages such as Perl, Python, and PHP. This chapter introduced several tools, with brief descriptions of their functionality and where they can be downloaded. We are using many of these tools in the projects that are described in the following chapters. You learned about:

❑   Python tools

❑   PHP tools

❑   Java tools

❑   XSLT tools

❑   Perl tools

Part IV
The Tasks

Systematic Overview

This chapter looks at some of the workings of syndication systems, but stays at the system level. Virtually all the theory has been introduced in earlier chapters; here you have a reminder with practical anchors. You've seen very wide coverage in previous chapters from a variety of viewpoints. This chapter is here to refocus you on what's significant at a system level from a developer's perspective, and fill in some blanks about the practical side of HTTP.

Essentially the aim here is to provide a more technical description of feed systems and start moving towards the practical issues involved in handling RSS and Atom data. First of all you will see a recap of the underlying client-server paradigm that forms the basis of the Web. This is well known, but shouldn't be taken for granted as technical problems can be a direct result. Then you will see how the component systems of syndication can be viewed as operating on different layers of abstraction. At the bottom are the protocols that determine how the bits of data get distributed around the world, at the top is the user application. Commonly this application has a graphical user interface.

In this chapter you learn:

- ❏ A view of syndication applications as subsystems
- ❏ The basics of HTTP client-server communication
- ❏ How to implement simple clients and servers
- ❏ How RSS and Atom use a polling protocol

The component systems that send and receive RSS and Atom can very loosely be divided into four categories:

- ❏ Server Producer
- ❏ Client Consumer
- ❏ Client Producer
- ❏ Server Consumer

The first division made here is into those system components that usually run as a remote service (Server), and those that a user (Client) interacts with directly. The second division is made between those components that create or generate and send data (Producer) and those that receive and process or display data (Consumer).

In this categorization, the Server Producer is typically a content-management system such as a blogging tool that offers syndication feeds on a Web server. The Client Consumer is the user application, in other words the aggregator or newsreader. The Client Producer is the software used to create the individual posts, the authoring tool, blogging client, or device set up to pass photographs to a content-management system. The Server Consumer category actually covers two roles — receiving (and probably storing) data sent from a Client Producer and aggregating material delivered by Server Producer systems.

In practice, syndication applications often fulfill more than one of these roles, so that should be borne in mind as you read the overview of each of these components. Common to most systems is some kind of persistent data storage, which we cover in depth in later chapters.

Before You Start

This chapter includes some practical exercises. It isn't essential to work through the exercises to understand how things work; we will explain the code thoroughly. But we strongly recommended that you run the mini-applications and play around with the code yourself.

Web software, like off-the-shelf servers such as Apache and browsers that come with most operating systems, is generally built to work as if by magic. Much of the underlying operation of these systems is hidden. This is great for users, but can mean that the way in which these tools work tends to get shrouded in mystery, as if only experts can understand them. This isn't helped by the fact that web technologies are generally defined in technically worded specifications, so all in all it can seem very intimidating. As it happens, the techniques involved aren't difficult, although many can be confusing, and even experts regularly find surprises hidden in the piles of specifications. By working through the exercises in this book you will see that you don't have to be an expert to work web magic, and that things that appear confusing are usually built on simple principles. All you need are time and patience. Most programming languages include both low- and high-level support of Web protocols, so in practice you can choose the best level at which to work.

Python

The programming language used throughout this chapter, and in some later examples, is Python. There are two reasons for this choice. Firstly, it is close to being self-explanatory. We could have used human-readable pseudocode here, but Python code tends to be very readable and it *works*. Secondly, it's a powerful, modern language with excellent support for Web programming, and it is a *real* language in the sense that it is suitable for deployment in the enterprise. If you don't know Python, don't worry — you don't have to learn it to make sense of the examples here. After you've seen a few examples, you will probably feel like you know it already, it really is that straightforward.

Recommended Downloads

We use the GNU Wget tool as an example of a very useful but no-frills HTTP client. You can download it for free for all popular platforms at www.gnu.org/software/wget/wget.html.

The source code used is this chapter is in the Python language. Support for this on all major platforms is available as a complete package available at www.python.org.

The download includes everything you need—a Python interpreter, reference documentation, and tutorial—even a fairly sophisticated editor and development tool (IDLE). The package is enough to get you writing your own simple Python programs in a matter of minutes, and sophisticated software in a matter of hours.

Before getting onto some practical material, we begin with a brief look at the some of the theory surrounding Web architecture.

States and Messages: Exchanges Between Client and Server

Web architecture has evolved into something a step beyond what was previously found on computer networks. The software found on local and most wide area networks tended to be far more closely coupled than today's Web, with communication being far more oriented toward the specific tasks for which the software was designed. The Web on the other hand uses protocols based on message-passing, the actual systems and software being relatively loosely coupled. The distinction can be quite subtle, but it has a direct impact on the way the Web works.

In its minimal form, an interaction with the Web can be viewed as a process of exchange between a client computer that handles the user interface and a remote server computer that contains data of interest to the user. The Web can be viewed as a network of servers to which client machines are linked. But as far as software applications are concerned, the client-server view in itself isn't very meaningful or useful.

Resources and Representations

Conceptually, a *resource* is anything that can be identified. This can be a document, image, collection of other resources, or even something that can't be contained directly on the Web such as a person or his or her car. However, any of these items can be identified on the Web, and have useful representations on the Web such as a descriptive document.

When using a Web browser, for example, the resource could be someone's home page, and the representation the user sees will be the HTML version of the page rendered in the browser. However the home page may have other representations, such as a smaller WML (Wireless Markup Language) version for display on mobile devices or a plain text version aimed at voice readers. What's more, these representations may change over time—a home page might look completely different from one year to the next. What doesn't change is the conceptual resource, the home page is still the home page. This resource is known by its identifier, and on the Web that's the URI (Uniform Resource Identifier). Although the representations of a resource can change at the whim of the site owner, the conceptual resource and its identifier stay the same. As the inventor of the Web, Tim Berners-Lee, put it: "Cool URIs don't change" (www.w3.org/Provider/Style/URI).

To get to a particular page, a browser user will either enter the address of a Web site or click a link in another page. The address, entered directly or obtained through a link, will be the URI of the Web site.

States and Statelessness

So how does this fit in with the client and server? Generally the server sits, idle but listening, until a client initiates a transaction. Client software sends a request message, which first identifies the resources of interest on the network. These resources are then interpreted by the network to locate the resources. Subsequent parts of the request specify what operation is to be carried out on the identified resources; the simplest is to return a message containing a particular representation of the resource.

From the application and the user's point of view, the process of browsing the Web can be seen as moving along a series of different states. Initially, you're looking at a blank screen, or whatever you have configured for your starter page. By entering an address or clicking a link, you cause the browser to load the data found at that address. The state has changed from looking at the initial page to looking at this new one. The address entered will be a URI, that is, it will identify a resource. The data the browser obtains for you is a representation of that resource, which is transferred over HTTP from the server. This general architectural view of the Web was described by Roy T. Fielding in his doctoral thesis (www.ics.uci.edu/~fielding/pubs/dissertation/top.htm) as Representational State Transfer, or REST.

A key part of the REST architectural view is that all application state information should be maintained at the client. Representations of server-side resources can change, but this isn't tied to any particular application. This architecture does cover the most current use of the Web, but there are aspects of the existing Web that don't look good according to this view. Many commercial Web sites with shopping baskets store a reference client-side (in a *cookie*) to state information server-side. The shopping basket application thus breaks the REST rule. These applications do generally appear to work well, but it has been argued that not only does this introduce potential security risks, but also scalability issues.

However, as far as syndication applications are concerned, the different client and server components benefit from being loosely coupled, and there is no real need for the application state to be involved in client-server interactions.

RPC vs. Document-Oriented Messaging

Networks are all about passing data between systems, and some of that data can appear as commands. Pre-Web distributed computing usually treated remote systems as a simple extension of the local programming interface. In other words, remote procedure invocations looked very much like local procedure calls. The details of communicating with the remote system are hidden from the programmer, and the Remote Procedure Call (RPC) protocol transparently looks after the remote procedure or method execution. Post-Web, once XML appeared on the scene, it didn't take long for XML-RPC to emerge, essentially the same procedure calling protocol but wrapped in structured markup. The original XML-RPC is Pascal-like in its structure, and the SOAP protocol emerged as a more object-oriented revision. The RPC, XML-RPC, and early SOAP techniques focused on programming interfaces, which fairly directly involves the code that will handle the data. However, over the past few years there has been a shift of emphasis in the design of the protocols used on top of HTTP to determine how systems communicate with each other. Rather than looking at the programming interfaces, the focus has shifted to the data itself, the material that needs to be moved from one system to another. This is in the same environment that XML is used, so not surprisingly the data is usually formatted as XML. For example, imagine system A wants to tell system B that the price of a scarf is $3. Using an RPC style, the system A would contain a call in its code, something like `systemB.setPrice("scarf", 3)`, which would contain calls passed to a standard XML-RPC library. In the document-oriented style, system A would construct and deliver a message something like:

```
<price>
   <product>scarf</product>
   <cost>3</cost>
</price>
```

On receipt, system B would interpret this and make the appropriate changes to its local data.

On the face of it, the latter style involves a lot more work in constructing, sending, and interpreting the document. But under the hood of the first system a very similar process is happening. Assuming the systems were using XML-RPC, the `systemB.setPrice("scarf", 3)` method call would lead to the construction of an XML document that looked something like this:

```
<methodCall>
   <methodName>setPrice</methodName>
   <params>
     <param>
       <value>
         <string>scarf</string>
       </value>
     </param>
     <param>
       <value>
         <int>3</int>
       </value>
     </param>
   <params>
</methodCall>
```

This would be passed over the network to system B which would interpret it, presumably calling a local method something like `setPrice("scarf", 3)`. Okay, so the XML involved is a little more verbose, but isn't this outweighed by the convenience of those method calls?

Actually the convenience is illusory, as there's no reason why the software shouldn't wrap the document-construction code in similar method calls. All things being equal, the verbosity of the XML-RPC approach now looks a drawback. But perhaps the biggest problem with the XML-RPC is that it's tied to the software implementation at either end. Not in the sense that the same programming language must be used, but in the sense that the interface must have handling for the exact same set of values in the exact same order. Say you had extended your product range and wanted to add a little more description to the messages, to say what color each scarf was. With XML-RPC a whole new method would have to be built at both the producer and consumer ends to handle all three pieces of data. On the other hand, the document-oriented approach would only need to add one element:

```
<price>
   <product>scarf</product>
   <cost>3</cost>
   <color>red</color>
</price>
```

What's more, any system built to produce or consume the "color-less" messages could still use the "color-full" data without modification; they could simply ignore the new element.

The essence of this change in emphasis is moving from a procedural approach to data to a declarative approach. Rather than saying "do X, Y, and Z with this data," saying "here is some data with characteristics A, B, and C" and leaving the receiver to determine how it should act upon the data. The coupling between systems is looser, which in turn can make them more versatile, flexible, and scalable. What's more, the actual documents being passed around are much simpler and are comprehensible, so debugging isn't a nightmare.

The shift has little impact on traditional client-server delivery of Web pages (and syndication feeds), but is directly relevant to the way in which authoring tools communicate with server-side systems, and how services such as those involved in syndication relate to each other. When combined with a RESTful HTTP-based architecture, certain other advantages appear. One particular advantage seized by the Atom developers is that the same format or language can be used for communicating between authoring systems and syndication servers as that used for publication of the syndicated feeds. However, for systems to use the Web, somewhere along the line there will be an HTTP server and an HTTP client.

Communication Layers

A convenient way of looking at the operation of networked software is in terms of the languages and formats used in different parts of the system. The main actors in the drama of computing are the electronic machine and the human user, with application software somewhere in between. The machine is only really interested in bits of raw data, whereas humans prefer analogies that fit in with the rest of their world views. Again, application software falls somewhere in between. The data languages used reflect their position on this machine-human scale, and generally in layers, each layer providing a more human-friendly abstraction of the more machine-friendly layer below. The languages of the Web tend to be known by their acronyms, and syndication development involves a whole load of these.

Web Languages

The traditional Web has HTML (Hypertext Markup Language) on top, with browsers displaying this data in a form akin to that of books or magazines. For most users of the Web this layer is quite enough abstraction. But the HTML has to be moved from the server to the client, and to do this HTTP (Hypertext Transfer Protocol) is used.

The HTTP Client

The HTTP client we're all familiar with is the browser, whether we actually use Internet Explorer, Mozilla Firefox, Opera, or one of the many other alternatives. The visual sophistication of these applications hides much of the detail of what is going on behind the scenes. One HTTP client that enables you to know a little more about what's going on is Wget.

Wget is a free software package for retrieving files using HTTP, HTTPS, and FTP, the most widely used Internet protocols. The standard version is released by GNU for Unix-style operating systems, but there is a Windows version available. Downloads (and documentation) are available from www.gnu.org/software/wget/wget.html.

<hr>

Try It Out   **Client Requests**

   1.   Download and install Wget.

2. Open a command window and enter the following:

```
wget http://w3.org
```

After pressing Enter, you should see something like this:

```
C:\>wget http://www.w3.org
--11:43:29--  http://www.w3.org/
           => 'index.html'
Resolving www.w3.org... 18.7.14.127, 128.30.52.25, 128.30.52.24
Connecting to www.w3.org[18.7.14.127]:80... connected.
HTTP request sent, awaiting response... 200 OK
Length: 25,590 [text/html]

100%[====================================>] 25,590        7.72K/s    ETA 00:00

11:43:33 (7.72 KB/s) - 'index.html' saved [25590/25590]
```

3. Now, if you are running a MS Windows operating system, type:

```
type index.html
```

On Unix-style systems, a better command is:

```
head index.html
```

After pressing Enter, you should see the contents of this file, which will be text containing HTML markup.

4. Open the file in a Web browser.

You should now see the W3C home page.

How It Works

The command syntax for wget is straightforward:

```
wget [option]... [URI]...
```

By entering -h as the option you can get a list of the basic options; there are far too many to list here:

```
wget -h
```

The command used previously was:

```
C:\>wget http://www.w3.org
```

The default operation on a HTTP URI is to send a HTTP GET request and retrieve whatever the server offers:

```
--11:43:29--  http://www.w3.org/
           => 'index.html'
```

Here Wget has checked the URI and determined that it follows the URI scheme (http://) and that the address is at the root of the server. Because of this the data will be saved locally as a file called index.html. Next the client resolves the domain name to an IP (Internet Protocol) address and connects to that address:

```
Resolving www.w3.org... 18.7.14.127, 128.30.52.25, 128.30.52.24
Connecting to www.w3.org[18.7.14.127]:80... connected.
```

The address resolved to three alternate IP addresses, and Wget connected to the first of these. A detail to notice here is the :80. A HTTP URI includes an optional port, which is a value described in the TCP specification that usually corresponds to the required protocol. The default TCP port for HTTP when none is specified is 80, a value filled in by Wget. Once the connection has been made, a request message (GET) will be sent and Wget will wait for a response. In this case the HTTP response code 200 OK was returned, so everything went as it should. The next line contains some more information returned in the HTTP message, the length of the content in bytes and the MIME (Internet Media Type):

```
HTTP request sent, awaiting response... 200 OK
Length: 25,590 [text/html]
```

The tool displays a simple progress monitor, along with the download rate and the estimated time of arrival of the complete file:

```
100%[=====================================>] 25,590          7.72K/s     ETA 00:00
```

After less than a second, the whole file has been obtained:

```
11:43:33 (7.72 KB/s) - 'index.html' saved [25590/25590]
```

If you look in the current folder you will see a file called index.html has been added. The server declared the MIME type as text/html, so the general type here is text and the subtype html. Clearly this data was intended for viewing in a Web browser, and opening the file in a browser confirms this.

> *Wget is a very sophisticated tool. It's not immediately obvious because it runs from the command line, but it can be used for jobs like downloading a whole site (using the -r and -l options), or for checking links in a site (-spider).*

Server Response

Among its other functionality, Wget can be used to examine the HTTP header when a page is downloaded. This can be done be simply adding the -S (or --server-response) command-line option. Here is a listing of what happened when we applied this to the W3C home page URI:

```
 d:\>wget -S http://w3.org
--14:20:52--  http://w3.org/
           => 'index.html.4'
Resolving w3.org... 18.29.1.73
Connecting to w3.org[18.29.1.73]:80... connected.
HTTP request sent, awaiting response...
 1 HTTP/1.1 301 Moved Permanently
 2 Date: Sat, 07 Aug 2004 12:24:04 GMT
 3 Server: Apache/1.3.31 (Debian GNU/Linux)
 4 Location: http://www.w3.org/
 5 Connection: close
```

```
 6 Content-Type: text/html; charset=iso-8859-1
Location: http://www.w3.org/ [following]
--14:20:55--  http://www.w3.org/
          => 'index.html.4'
Resolving www.w3.org... 18.7.14.127, 128.30.52.24, 128.30.52.25
Connecting to www.w3.org[18.7.14.127]:80... connected.
HTTP request sent, awaiting response...
 1 HTTP/1.1 200 OK
 2 Date: Sat, 07 Aug 2004 12:24:05 GMT
 3 Server: Apache/1.3.28 (Unix) PHP/4.2.3
 4 P3P: policyref="http://www.w3.org/2001/05/P3P/p3p.xml"
 5 Cache-Control: max-age=600
 6 Expires: Sat, 07 Aug 2004 12:34:05 GMT
 7 Last-Modified: Fri, 06 Aug 2004 18:00:13 GMT
 8 ETag: "4113c72d"
 9 Accept-Ranges: bytes
10 Content-Length: 27145
11 Keep-Alive: timeout=4, max=100
12 Connection: Keep-Alive
13 Content-Type: text/html; charset=utf-8

100%[====================================>] 27,145        7.26K/s     ETA 00:00

14:20:59 (7.26 KB/s) - 'index.html.2' saved [27145/27145]
```

There are two blocks added to the previous console text, both of which are numbered lines (the line numbering isn't part of the HTTP protocol, it's just a convenience from Wget). The reason there are two blocks is explained by the first and fourth lines of response in the first block:

```
HTTP/1.1 301 Moved Permanently
...
Location: http://www.w3.org/
```

This tells the client that the page is now to be found at www.w3.org (rather than http://w3.org). The client then obediently fetches the data from its current location. The response there is:

```
HTTP/1.1 200 OK
```

If you were to visit the first address in a regular browser, all you would normally see is the address line magically change. Looking at what the server has responded gives a much clearer picture of what's actually going on.

Acronym City

Syndication is primarily based on HTML, XML (Extensible Markup Language), and HTTP. HTML and XML have a common origin in SGML (Standard Generalized Markup Language). XML includes in its definition reference to Unicode for its character handling as well as some language-related specifications. HTTP relies on other specifications such as MIME (Multipurpose Internet Mail Extensions) to define elements like content types and URIs (Uniform Resource Identifiers) for identifiers. HTTP is an Internet protocol, so it depends on the underlying Internet protocol TCP/IP. This in itself is one protocol layered on top of another: TCP (Transmission Control Protocol) looks after connections and allows hosts to exchange streams of data. IP (Internet Protocol) deals with routing packets of data around. On top of the numeric addressing used by IP, the Internet also uses DNS (Domain Name System) to allow naming of hosts.

Application Layers

Fortunately, you rarely have to juggle all these acronyms at once, no matter how sophisticated the system. Most syndication applications can be seen at a system level in terms of just three languages. Any content will usually be expressed as plain text, HTML, or XHTML. These are bundled together in Figure 19-1 as XHTML. This content is wrapped in a feed format, RSS or Atom, along with associated metadata like the title and date. All the leading formats are XML, and that's reflected in Figure 19-1. This wrapping envelope can be considered as a layer beneath the content. Below that is the layer responsible for moving the XML-wrapped data around, the HTTP protocol.

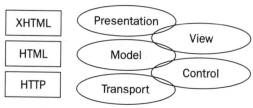

Figure 19-1

This view of three language layers, HTTP, XML, and XHTML, is a very coarse picture, but it corresponds reasonably well with typical subsystems found in a syndication application. There are the parts responsible for the data model, the transport subsystem that will look after sending or receiving of feed data, and the presentation subsystem that will look after user interaction. These subsystems in turn loosely correspond to the standard Model, View, and Control (MVC) software design elements. The MVC style of application architecture is used in examples in later chapters.

If you are writing software for syndication applications, the more you can learn about XHTML, XML, and HTTP and associated formats and protocols the better. Character encoding as used in (X)HTML and XML is particularly important, with Unicode being a complementary standard. Although Web developers are likely to have a basic familiarity with HTTP and MIME (Internet Media Types), the demands of syndication mean more detailed knowledge is highly desirable.

Server Producer: Producing Feeds

In the four-way categorization, Server Producers are the pieces of software that publish the feed data. In theory at least, these are the simplest parts of the whole syndication environment. All they have to do is take some existing data, wrap it up as XML, and serve it like any other Web page. In practice, as you probably guessed, there's a little more to it than that.

You will see in later chapters how data from the database of a weblog, content-management system, or other source can be converted into a form (in the RSS or Atom format) suitable for publication. What all syndication systems have in common is a web server to deliver the prepared XML.

The HTTP Server

The software used to serve RSS or Atom feeds will either be a general-purpose Web server such as Apache or Microsoft's IIS (Internet Information Services), a purpose-built system dedicated to the purpose or a combination of the two. The Wget HTTP client reveals some of the detail of the HTTP communication layer. Before looking at some simple server code, it's worth mentioning the layer on which these operate.

Sockets and Ports

There's more to the Internet than just the Web. As well as needing the low-level TCP/IP protocols, Internet applications need a mechanism for connecting over the wire (or wireless). The general approach to this is based on techniques developed for Berkeley Unix. The mechanism is known as *sockets*, and the analogy of telephone cables plugged into them is pretty good. Each socket will have associated with it a network address (the local IP address) and port number. Ports are separate logical channels. On the Internet there are standard communication protocols associated with each port; some of the more well-known ones appear in the following table.

Protocol	Port Number	Description
ftp	21	File Transfer Protocol
telnet	23	Telnet
smtp	25	Simple Mail Transport Protocol
http	80	HyperText Transfer Protocol
pop-3	110	Post Office Protocol
nntp	119	Network News Transfer Protocol (USENET)
ntp	123	Network Time Protocol
imap3	220	Interactive Mail Access Protocol
https	443	Secure HTTP

For a full list of standard port assignments go to www.iana.org/assignments/port-numbers.

By default HTTP servers and clients use port 80, and on Unix systems port numbers below 1024 are reserved for system (root) services. So for development work it's common practice to use ports above 1024 that will be easy to remember — 8080 and 8888 are used quite a lot.

An HTTP transaction will start with the client establishing a connection to the socket, and then making a request. The HTTP server has to interpret that request and respond appropriately. Python comes with suitable server classes already written, but for purposes of demonstration the following code (saved as InflexibleServer.py) takes one step back to make an HTTP server of less-than-average ability.

```python
# a single-minded HTTP server

import SocketServer
import BaseHTTPServer

PORT = 8008

DATA = \
"<rss version=\"2.0\">\n\
    <channel>\n\
        <title>My Channel</title>\n\
        <link>http://example.org/</link>\n\
        <description>A minimal feed</description>\n\
```

```
            <item>\n\
                <title>My First Item</title>\n\
                <description>This is the first post</description>\n\
            </item>\n\
            <item>\n\
                <title>My Second Item</title>\n\
                <description>This is the second post</description> \n\
            </item> \n\
            <item> \n\
                <title>My Third Item</title> \n\
                <description>This is the third post</description> \n\
            </item> \n\
        </channel> \n\
    </rss>"

class InflexibleServer(BaseHTTPServer.BaseHTTPRequestHandler):
    def do_HEAD(self):
        self.send_head()

    def do_GET(self):
        self.send_head()
        print "Request Header:"
        print self.headers
        print "---"
        self.wfile.write(DATA)

    def send_head(self):
        self.send_response(200)
        self.send_header("Content-Type", "application/rss+xml")
        self.end_headers()

httpd = SocketServer.ThreadingTCPServer(('', PORT), InflexibleServer)

print "serving at port", PORT
httpd.serve_forever()
```

Try It Out   Serving an RSS Feed

1. Enter the code listed above in a text editor and save it as a file called InflexibleServer.py (better still, download it from the book's Web site).

2. Open a command window in the folder containing InflexibleServer.py and type in the following:

```
python InflexibleServer.py
```

   If the code works correctly, when you press Enter, you will see the following response:

```
D:\rss-book\19\code>python InflexibleServer.py
serving at port 8008
```

3. Without closing the current window, open a command window in the folder where you saved Wget and type the following:

```
wget http://127.0.0.1:8008/
```

When you press Enter, you should see something like the following:

```
D:\rss-book\19\code>wget http://127.0.0.1:8008/
--19:18:59--  http://127.0.0.1:8008/
           => 'index.html'
Connecting to 127.0.0.1:8008... connected.
HTTP request sent, awaiting response... 200 OK
Length: unspecified [application/rss+xml]

    [ <=>                                       ] 553           --.--K/s

19:18:59 (5.27 MB/s) - 'index.html' saved [553]
```

If you look back to the first (server) command window, you should see something like this:

```
trotter - - [23/Jun/2004 19:45:24] "GET / HTTP/1.0" 200 -
Request Header:
User-Agent: Wget/1.9.1
Host: 127.0.0.1:8008
Accept: */*
Connection: Keep-Alive
```

This is the data contained in the header part of the request sent from the client. trotter here is the name of the host (set in the computer's system settings).

4.   Open the newly created file index.html in a text editor.

You should see the following:

```
<rss version="2.0">
    <channel>
        <title>My Channel</title>
        <link>http://example.org/</link>
        <description>A minimal feed</description>
        <item>
            <title>My First Item</title>
            <description>This is the first post</description>
        </item>
        <item>
            <title>My Second Item</title>
            <description>This is the second post</description>
        </item>
        <item>
            <title>My Third Item</title>
            <description>This is the third post</description>
        </item>
    </channel>
</rss>
```

You have served an RSS feed!

You might also like to try putting the address http://127.0.0.1:8008 into a Web browser like Internet Explorer or Firefox, just to confirm it really is being served like a regular Web page.

How It Works

Essentially the built-in classes are doing the hard work in setting up the server, and the source code here supplies the data to use in the HTTP messages.

The "Inflexible Server" uses some standard Python classes to set up a TCP socket server on port 8008 running on your local machine (such as 127.0.0.1). The specific way this server behaves is in part determined by the BaseHTTPServer and BaseHTTPRequestHandler classes, and by the way the code here extends the BaseHTTPRequestHandler to supply the feed data. The source begins by importing the required library classes, and then setting the value of the port to use. The body of the data that will be served is put in a string called DATA:

```
# a single-minded HTTP server

import SocketServer
import BaseHTTPServer

PORT = 8008

DATA = \
"<rss version=\"2.0\">\n\
    <channel>\n\
        <title>My Channel</title>\n\
        <link>http://example.org/</link>\n\
        <description>A minimal feed</description>\n\
        <item>\n\
            <title>My First Item</title>\n\
            <description>This is the first post</description>\n\
        </item>\n\
        <item>\n\
            <title>My Second Item</title>\n\
            <description>This is the second post</description> \n\
        </item> \n\
        <item> \n\
            <title>My Third Item</title> \n\
            <description>This is the third post</description> \n\
        </item> \n\
    </channel> \n\
</rss>"
```

The "\n" sequence is a stand-in for the newline character, which makes the served data a little easier to read. The "\" character at the end of the lines is for a different purpose; it's standard Python which simply means that the string continues on the next line.

The next line says that the InflexibleServer class should be a subclass of the BaseHTTPServer .BaseHTTPRequestHandler class. It inherits some basic functionality from that class to allow it to work as a simple HTTP-style message handler for a socket server:

```
class InflexibleServer(BaseHTTPServer.BaseHTTPRequestHandler):
```

The InflexibleServer class defines three new methods, two of which will look after the specific HTTP calls HEAD and GET, and the third method being a helper to put together the header material that is delivered in response to calls to either of these HTTP methods. In fact, all the do_HEAD method is call the send_head helper method, as you can see here:

```
def do_HEAD(self):
    self.send_head()
```

The Python method `do_GET` that will look after calls to the HTTP protocol's `GET` method is a little more interesting. It also calls the local `send_head` method to deliver the HTTP header information, and then prints some information to the command line. It prints whatever the calling client has sent in the header part of its request. This includes the host name of the client and so on — all the material you saw in the server command window. The next line here is most significant; it writes the `DATA` string to `wfile`, which is a member variable of the parent `BaseHTTPRequestHandler` class. This variable is actually the output stream for writing a response. Anything you write here is sent down to the client, which in the previous example was Wget. The last line of this method closes the output stream:

```python
def do_GET(self):
    self.send_head()
    print "Request Header:"
    print self.headers
    print "---"
    self.wfile.write(DATA)
    self.wfile.close()
```

The `send_head` method calls on three methods built into its parent request handler class. First of all it has an HTTP 200 OK response sent back to the client using the `send_response` method. The `send_header` method allows you to specify the name and value of a specific HTTP parameter, which will be wrapped up in the server message in a form that respects the HTTP protocol. The name of the parameter here is `Content-Type` and the value is `application/rss+xml`. If you look back to the window in which you ran Wget, you will see that this was indeed passed to the client. Specifically, this means that the Internet Media (MIME) Type of the payload (the feed data) is `application/rss+xml`.

After providing the value for the response code and the MIME type, a call to `end_headers` signals the end of this part of the response and prepares the client for any payload:

```python
def send_head(self):
    self.send_response(200)
    self.send_header("Content-Type", "application/rss+xml")
    self.end_headers()
```

The last lines of the code run this little application. If you're used to a compiled language like Java this probably seems strange. The Python interpreter allows you to mix class definitions like that of `InflexibleServer` alongside commands for immediate execution, like these. In this part of the code a server object called `httpd` is created, which will run on the address named `" "` and port number `PORT` (which is set to 8008). The server will use instances of the `InflexibleServer` class to handle requests. After the `httpd` server has been created, a message is printed to give you notification and then the server is told to serve forever, as you can see in the source here:

```python
httpd = SocketServer.ThreadingTCPServer(('', PORT), InflexibleServer)

print "serving at port", PORT
httpd.serve_forever()
```

Getting Flexible

The server created by this source code is only capable of serving up the contents of the `DATA` string, no matter what you ask for on the server. If you try a client request (using Wget or a browser) to:

```
http://127.0.0.1:8008/where-are-my-pages
```

or even:

```
http://127.0.0.1:8008/where-are-my-pages/anything/here
```

you will get exactly the same piece of XML as a response. The server wasn't called inflexible for nothing.

However, it's actually *easier* to write Python code that will serve up material in a more useful, hierarchical-path Web server fashion. The following is enough to run such a server:

```
import SocketServer
import SimpleHTTPServer

PORT = 8118

httpd = SocketServer.ThreadingTCPServer(('', PORT),
        SimpleHTTPServer.SimpleHTTPRequestHandler)

print "serving at port", PORT
httpd.serve_forever()
```

Note the different port value—this could have been 8008 again, but by using a different value here it will be possible for you to run this server alongside the InflexibleServer, if you would like to compare and contrast the behavior of the two.

Only one server can run on each port at a given IP address at any one time.

Try It Out   Improved Version with Python

1. Type the listing above into a text editor and save it as `TinyServer.py` in the same folder as `index.html` (generated by the Wget run in the previous *Try It Out*).

2. Open a command window in the same directory as `TinyServer.py`.

3. Type the following into the command window:

```
python TinyServer.py
```

4. Open a new command window and enter the following:

```
wget http://127.0.0.1:8118
```

You should see something like this:

```
D:\rss-book\19\code>wget http://127.0.0.1:8118
--21:23:49--  http://127.0.0.1:8118/
           => 'index.html.1'
Connecting to 127.0.0.1:8118... connected.
HTTP request sent, awaiting response... 200 OK
Length: 553 [text/html]

100%[====================================>] 553          --.--K/s

21:23:49 (5.27 MB/s) - 'index.html.1' saved [553/553]
```

How It Works

Instead of the home-baked, crude, and ineffective response methods of `InflexibleServer`, this improved version uses a class that comes with the standard Python distribution. The `SimpleHTTPServer` class contains pretty much everything needed to operate a standard Web server that will serve files found on the local file system. If you look in the Python distribution, in a directory called `Lib`, you should find a file named `SimpleHTTPServer.py`. Opening this file in a text editor will reveal a class called `SimpleHTTPRequestHandler`. If you look at the code for this class you will notice something slightly familiar, a method called `do_GET`. The version in `SimpleHTTPRequestHandler` looks like this:

```
def do_GET(self):
    """Serve a GET request."""
    f = self.send_head()
    if f:
        self.copyfile(f, self.wfile)
        f.close()
```

What's happening here is that a `send_head` method similar to that of the `InflexibleServer` class listed earlier is called to send the appropriate header back to the client. The `send_head` method has an additional function, which is to try to construct a file object based on the path and file name parts of the URI. This is put into the `f` variable in the `do_GET` method. If this object exists, the contents of the file on that path relative to the current directory will be served up.

In the run made here, there was a file called `index.html` in the directory in which the server was running, and this was recognized as an appropriate default file for the root path `/`. This was delivered to the client, Wget. For better or worse the Wget client was run in the very same directory as the server (not what is usually expected on the web!). Being a little smart Wget noticed the existing file `index.html` and rather than overwrite this with the file it had downloaded, saved the new file as `index.html.1`. If you open that in a text editor you can confirm that it is the same data.

In passing, there is something else of note here, if you look closely at the Wget messages:

```
...
HTTP request sent, awaiting response... 200 OK
Length: 553 [text/html]
...
```

The data has been served with the Internet Type `text/html`. The server determined this type by looking at the file name extension, in this case `.html`, and made the fairly reasonable assumption that this was old-fashioned (pre-XHTML) HTML, and set the type accordingly. If you try pointing a Web browser at the address you will see the contents of the file more or less rendered directly. But the data was in fact XML, specifically RSS, and `text/html` is wrong. More on that later.

Serving and Producing

As mentioned earlier, many syndication solutions will be using ready-made Web servers like Apache to deliver the feed data. You've just seen that it's relatively straightforward to write Python code to get a HTTP server to deliver a load of text data to Wget or a browser. It still might not be clear to you that the Web server is the syndication server, the Server Producer. Especially since the server code was running on your client machine. This is a situation you'll be seeing again pretty soon, since many aggregator clients include a Web server that will be running on your desktop.

But just so there's no mistake, you might like to fire up your favorite desktop aggregator or newsreader and run either of the little Web servers described here. If you add the address (including port) to the aggregator, then you should see something equivalent to Figure 19-2.

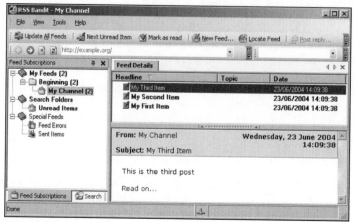

Figure 19-2

For this screenshot the address of a running `InflexibleServer` was added to the feed list of RSS Bandit, in a folder called Beginning. As you can see, the application has correctly obtained the name of the channel, My Channel, and is displaying the titles of the three items it found in the feed. It's interesting to note that RSS Bandit initially displays the items in the opposite order to that found in the feed data, or perhaps according to some other less obvious system. This is perfectly acceptable, and it's entirely up to the application developers how they want to interpret the order. The date of the individual items wasn't actually supplied, so it isn't even possible to use the blog convention of most-recent first. RSS Bandit is a fairly conventional Microsoft Windows application, so clicking the *Headline* column header will use that for the sort order, clicking again will use it in reverse order and so on with *Topic* and *Date*.

Client Consumer: Viewing Feeds

In our four-way categorization, the Client Consumer is the user tool that collects and displays information from feeds. These tools are commonly known as *RSS newsreaders* or *aggregators*. The level of sophistication varies widely between available products; some merely provide a simple display of each individual feed, whereas others combine several related feeds into a single view and allow categorization of feeds and items. Some aggregators help with information overload by hiding items that the viewer has already seen. As with most applications, the interface depends in part on data structures within the application (what information is available) and in part on conventions that determine the behavior and appearance (how it is presented). Few of the popular aggregator user interfaces hold any (interesting) surprises for a regular computer user.

You will see a lot more about the internals of aggregators in the chapters that follow, but at a high level they all have certain characteristics in common. Each will enable the user to create a *subscription list,* which is a list of the addresses of feeds that they want to monitor. The Client Consumer will periodically get fresh data from each of these feeds and usually store it locally. The manner in which the data is retrieved is different than the usual method of interaction with the Web through browsers. In a sense this is the defining characteristic of RSS and Atom applications, and can be seen as a common protocol, although this protocol doesn't have any single official specification.

The view presented to the user can take many forms, although most of today's aggregators have settled for either one of two alternatives: single page or three pane.

Single-Page View

The single-page view, sometimes known as a newspaper view, is a single list of items including their content, usually with the most recent item (from any feed) displayed at the top. A variation on this is to order the items by feed, so the items in the most recently updated feed are displayed first, followed by those of the second most recent and so on. An example can be seen in Figure 19-3. Note how entries from different sources have been interleaved. Some newsreaders provide all entries from one feed in a single block without interleaving; this approach seems a little less user-friendly.

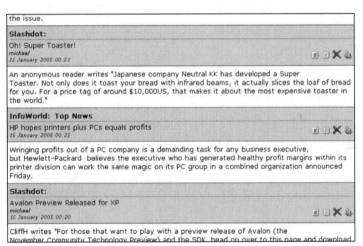

Figure 19-3

Three-Pane View

The three-pane view mimics the windowing system of e-mail applications like Microsoft Outlook and NNTP newsreaders. One window pane contains a list of subscribed feeds, another pane contains the titles of the most recent entries in the selected feed, and the third pane displays the content of the item corresponding to whichever title is selected (see Figure 19-4).

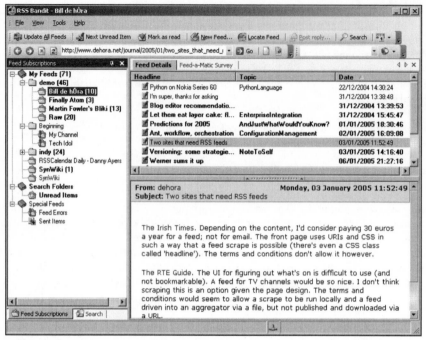

Figure 19-4

Some aggregators support multiple views. For example, Figure 19-3 was taken from Sauce Reader (`www.synop.com/Products/SauceReader/`), which generally appears as a three-pane display. Other display approaches include the use of a sidebar as a single-pane headline reader, with the full stories being provided in a regular browser window. It's interesting to note that the support for RSS/Atom built into the Firefox browser (Live Bookmarks) closely resembles that provided by Microsoft's ActiveChannels using the CDF format from many years ago. This displays the item titles group by feed in a sidebar; clicking an item displays the original weblog source content in the main window. In the future, it seems likely that the user will have a lot more say about which entries are displayed in what order and how they are rendered.

The "lite" nature of RSS and Atom feeds compared to regular Web pages makes them particularly suitable for use with devices such as mobile phones and personal organizers. Lack of space in this book means programming specifically for such devices won't be covered, but the general principles are the same. For an example of an aggregator like this, see Feeder Reader (`www.feederreader.com/`), which is written for Pocket PCs.

Syndication, the Protocol

Syndication applications are built around the notion of feeds of newslike information. Newslike, because the timeline is significant and the contents of the feed varies over time. This raises the question of how a client application knows when new data is available. It's certainly possible for a server on a network to notify clients when new information is available, broadcasting it as an event to any system that happens to be listening. But this event-driven approach doesn't fit very well with the HTTP Web, where the client initiates the communication. The server run by the publisher of the data is relatively inactive until a client comes along. So the approach employed by syndication clients is to determine periodically whether a particular information source has changed.

Polling

Often on startup or in response to a user request, an aggregator will immediately check a feed address for any changes. But it is easy to see that it would be inefficient to check continuously a long list of addresses, because the client would be devoting a lot of processor time and network bandwidth to checking feeds that might only change once a week. What's more, if a lot of people had their aggregators subscribed to a particular feed, then each of them would be checking a single Web address and the host of that feed would be under a barrage of requests. This would appear to the publisher as a huge demand for processor resources and network bandwidth, either leading to the publisher's service bills being astronomical, or more likely their system simply collapsing under the strain. Not only would this make the target site unusable, it's also rather impolite.

> *The effect of a flood of requests from multiple sources is exploited in the Distributed Denial of Service (DDoS) attack, a technique popular among virus authors and system crackers. Infected computers across the Internet make requests of a single host. This overload renders the service unobtainable for legitimate requests. The crippling effect of a DDoS attack has also been used historically to render systems vulnerable to other forms of attack.*

So to avoid DDoS-type hits, aggregators generally poll the addresses of interest only occasionally. There is a loose agreement among developers that the minimum time to wait between requests is one hour. Figure 19-5 shows how the polling mechanism is used on a single feed.

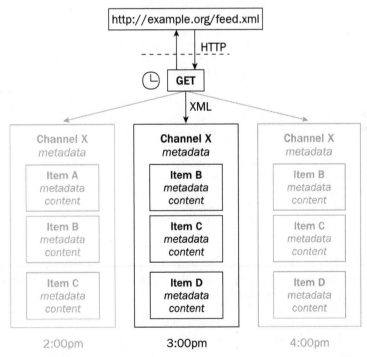

Figure 19-5

The aggregator or newsreader keeps track of the time elapsed since it last looked at the feed. In this example, the feed was last checked at 2:00 pm. Within the feed then were items A, B, and C. The delay has been set to an hour, so another HTTP GET request is sent to the publisher's host at 3:00pm. Now the feed contains items

225

B, C, and D. The aggregator will usually record the contents of the feed, in other words its data model will have a state corresponding to the XML data last time it was polled.

For simplicity's sake the scheduled times here are on the hour—in practice this should be avoided, because there may be a tendency for all clients to look at the feed at the same time. Choosing a fairly random point in the hour will break up any clustering, as will randomly adding or subtracting a few minutes between each check.

Note that in Figure 19-5, the items in the feed at 4:00 pm are no different from those at 3:00 pm. This situation is likely to happen a lot, and it wouldn't make much sense to download the whole feed again if nothing has changed.

Reducing the Load

Having a repeat time of at least an hour is a good start to keeping bandwidth requirements within reason; however, there are several other techniques that can be used to help keep this to a minimum. These all depend on the configuration being right at both client and server ends, and it is certain that not all of the systems with which you will be communicating will be set up for this. However, whether you are building a client or server application, whatever you implement to reduce bandwidth demands will give you an immediate improvement overall. Being able to consider yourself a good citizen of the Net is a nice side effect.

There are three primary techniques that can help reduce bandwidth: using data compression, using Conditional GET, and using hints in the feed data. You'll see the details of these techniques later, none of which is rocket science. The first two take advantage of features enabled by HTTP. Compression over HTTP works simply by zipping the file before sending and unzipping it on receipt. Most Web server software supports transparent compression of data using the gzip algorithm, and most programming languages provide simple library support. With Conditional GET, the client records certain details of the HTTP message when it last downloaded the file. When it comes time to check again, these details are provided in the HTTP request to the server. The server can then determine whether the file requested has altered since the last request. If it has, then the server responds with the requested data as usual. If it hasn't been changed, the server responds with a 304 Not Modified code, which tells the client that it has the most recent version.

The bandwidth saving provided by these methods depends very much on the nature of the data being published. Text files like those of XML feeds generally compress well, and the number of bytes in the compressed feed data is usually around a quarter to a half of the original. If the feed size is small, then there won't be much difference in the number of bytes moved around to signal that nothing's changed compared to getting a new copy of the file. But for feeds of average length, using Conditional GETs can easily lead to a tenfold reduction in bandwidth.

The third technique for bandwidth reduction that is immediately available uses elements in the syndication formats to provide hints about publication timing. These will suggest the likely frequency of the feed's publication, which makes it possible to optimize the polling frequency against the site update rate. Additionally, it is possible to specify that the feed won't be published at certain times or on certain days, so the client doesn't need to make any requests in those circumstances. Of the techniques for saving bandwidth this is probably the least effective—it's hard to be sure, but samples suggest that it isn't implemented very widely or consistently. However, implementing this approach almost certainly is likely to be worthwhile, because out of the numerous feeds consumed, some proportion of them are likely to support timing hints, meaning a net reduction in bandwidth demands.

> *Note the words zip and zipped are used loosely to refer to compression in general in the following text and code rather than to any specific algorithm.*

Try It Out   HTTP Client with gzip Compression

The following listing is a little HTTP client that's aware of gzip compression:

```python
import httplib
import urllib2
import StringIO
import gzip

URI = "http://thorne.id.au/feeds"

httplib.HTTPConnection.debuglevel = 1

request = urllib2.Request(URI)
request.add_header('Accept-Encoding', 'gzip')

opener = urllib2.build_opener()
message = opener.open(request)

print message.headers

if message.headers.get('Content-encoding') == 'gzip':
    print "ZIPPED!"
    zipped = message.read()
    fileObject = StringIO.StringIO(zipped)
    data = gzip.GzipFile(fileobj=fileObject).read()
else:
    data = message.read()

print data
```

1. Enter the code into a text editor, and save the file as `ZippyClient.py`.

2. Open a command window in the same directory as you saved `ZippyClient.py` and type the following:

```
python ZippyClient.py
```

   A header message should appear, closely followed by a lot of text content.

3. Modify the last line of the source code to read:

```
# print data
```

4. Again, open a command window in the same directory as you saved `ZippyClient.py` and type:

```
python ZippyClient.py
```

   Now that the printing of the data has been commented out, the header should be easier to read. It should look something like this:

```
D:\rss-book\19\code>python ZippyClient.py
connect: (thorne.id.au, 80)
send: 'GET /feeds HTTP/1.0\r\nHost: thorne.id.au\r\nUser-agent: Python-urllib/2.
1\r\nAccept-encoding: gzip\r\n\r\n'
reply: 'HTTP/1.0 200 OK\r\n'
header: Date: Thu, 24 Jun 2004 13:40:51 GMT
header: Content-length: 61411
header: Content-encoding: gzip
header: Content-type: text/html
header: Server: TwistedWeb/1.2.0
ZIPPED!
```

Note the values for `Content-length` (61411) and `Content-encoding` (gzip) returned by the server.

5. Now modify the source code again, this time to comment out this line by adding a # at the start:

```
# request.add_header('Accept-Encoding', 'gzip')
```

6. Again open a command window and type:

```
python ZippyClient.py
```

The result this time should be slightly different, something like this:

```
D:\rss-book\19\code>python ZippyClient.py
connect: (thorne.id.au, 80)
send: 'GET /feeds HTTP/1.0\r\nHost: thorne.id.au\r\nUser-agent: Python-urllib/2.
1\r\n\r\n'
reply: 'HTTP/1.0 200 OK\r\n'
header: Date: Thu, 24 Jun 2004 13:46:08 GMT
header: Content-length: 204733
header: Content-type: text/html
header: Server: TwistedWeb/1.2.0
```

Note the lack of gzip, and the considerably larger value of `Content-length`, 204733 bytes, which shows the gzip compression would save around three-fourths of the original bandwidth.

How It Works

The kind of data a client is prepared to accept is passed to the server in the header part of its request. When the server is told that the client *can* accept gzip compressed data, it *may* supply the material zipped. Note that this is all entirely optional. If the server does compress the feed data then the client will need to know so it can uncompress it. In this case the response header will have a value `gzip` in its `Content-Encoding` field. Figure 19-6 shows relevant parts of client-server HTTP dialog box where gzip is supported.

Most Web servers offer very good support for compression, and it's pretty straightforward to support it on the client side too.

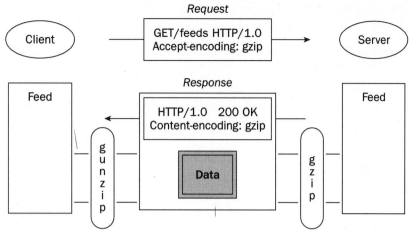

Figure 19-6

The source code for the client used here is relatively short and simple thanks again to the libraries that come with Python. The `httplib` and `urllib2` libraries are used to look after the communication side of things, with the `StringIO` and `gzip` libraries providing the classes needed to carry out the decompression of the data stream. These are all declared in the imports at the start of the source:

```
import httplib
import urllib2
import StringIO
import gzip
```

Of course for the system to work, there will have to be compression server-side. An address that's known to support gzip and serve fairly big feed files is placed in the string URI:

```
URI = "http://thorne.id.au/feeds"
```

Although it's possible to use print statements to show what data is being passed around, `HTTPConnection` has a convenient debug option, which will send messages to the console:

```
httplib.HTTPConnection.debuglevel = 1
```

Before the transaction can be initiated, the client has to prepare a request to pass to the server. The `urllib2` library has a class `Request` which makes this fairly easy. Here a `Request` object is created, and then the value of its 'Accept-Encoding' header is set to 'gzip':

```
request = urllib2.Request(URI)
request.add_header('Accept-Encoding', 'gzip')
```

Next a library function is used to create an `opener` object, which is then used to open the communication channel:

```
opener = urllib2.build_opener()
message = opener.open(request)
```

When opening the channel, the opener has passed the request to the server, and the message object contains the response headers and a pointer to the body of any data. The headers are checked to determine whether the `'Content-Encoding'` header has a value of `'gzip'`, and if it is an appropriate message is sent to the console:

```
if message.headers.get('Content-encoding') == 'gzip':
    print "ZIPPED!"
```

The zipped content is then read from the message into a buffer, which is then used to construct a file-like object on which the compression classes can operate. There are limits to the kinds of objects the compression code can work on, which is why the `StringIO` class is needed. It's not very elegant, but it works. A `GzipFile` object is created, and the `fileObject` reads through it, as you can see in the following lines:

```
zipped = message.read()
fileObject = StringIO.StringIO(zipped)
data = gzip.GzipFile(fileobj=fileObject).read()
```

The data that is read from the `GzipFile` object is decompressed back into its original form. However we are still in a block that runs only if the content encoding header says the data is zipped. If it isn't, the data can be read directly from the source. Finally the decompressed or as-delivered data is then printed to the console:

```
else:
    data = message.read()

print data
```

The Trade Off

In most circumstances the benefits of delivering or receiving compressed feed data far outweigh the costs. However, you should keep in mind that there are costs, not only for the additional code complexity but also for the processing required. For limited devices such as mobile phones it may make sense to avoid the computational load and always collect the uncompressed version of feeds.

Client Producer: Blogging APIs

The Client Producer part of a syndication system is the part the user employs to create the raw material for syndication. In other words, it's the authoring tool. Usually these are quite separate from the parts of the system that do the actual feed syndication. What the Client Producer produces is the content and metadata that corresponds to a weblog post, or perhaps to modify or delete an existing post. The data from the client is often sent back to the server and stored in a database, and only later is it converted into the RSS or Atom format. The fact that the authoring part of a system may be a separate component doesn't change the fact that the data it is dealing with is usually exactly the same kind of content and metadata that is published in feeds. All the same characteristics of content and metadata that are handled by the rest of a syndication system are produced by the Client Producer. But in current implementations at least, the Client Producer is the odd one out of these four categories. It may not involve any of the syndication format standards.

The Client Producer part of syndication systems may in effect be integrated with the backend, server-side of the system, with content being passed from an HTML form into the database using proprietary techniques. If the Client Producer is separate from the rest of the system, chances are it will use the Blogger API (unless it's a very recent piece of software). A Blogger API is a specification that uses the XML-RPC (Remote Procedure Call) protocol, introduced earlier in the chapter. More recent software might support the Atom API, which is based on a fundamentally different approach to Web communications.

There is a range of techniques that can be used when it comes to a piece of software either advertising what protocol(s) it supports or trying to discover what is supported by a service. In particular, the term *introspection* has been used for the advertising within Atom, and *autodiscovery* for the trick of pointing to service endpoint addresses. Although syndication is arguably the most widely deployed Web service, aside from autodiscovery of feeds from HTML pages there is no standard cross-system approach for discovering what is available.

The following sections should give you an overview of the protocol side of Client Producer subsystems, which are usually authoring applications. In Chapter 26, you will see some code that uses these protocols to post to weblogs.

XML-RPC

This protocol follows one traditional approach to client-server programming, in which program procedure calls are executed on a remote system rather than locally. XML is used to wrap the calls in a form that can be delivered over HTTP. The receiver of an XML-RPC message will unwrap the XML envelope to discover what parameters should be delivered to what programming procedures. XML-RPC is a predecessor of the SOAP protocol, which now plays a key role in Web services. Its adoption in the world of syndication began when Pyra Labs, the company that used to be behind the Blogger hosting service, released the Blogger API (Application Programming Interface) in 2001 as a specification for communicating between blogging clients (that is, Client Producers) and their server-side offerings. Although it was described as "experimental and alpha," developers quickly seized it to fill a gap in requirements. Unfortunately it didn't fill the gap too well (for example, entry titles were missing), and the Blogger spec was followed a few months later by the MetaWeblog API from UserLand, which added more structure to the messages echoing the components of an RSS item in procedure calls.

Implementations using the Blogger and MetaWeblog APIs generally use ready-made library code to enable the construction of the message at the producer and the interpretation of the message at the consumer. This is good news for developers, because the actual data sent in this fashion can be incredibly complex due to the way the data is built. For example, to specify the title of a new post, this has to be described in terms of a procedure call, giving its data type and value. These pieces of data will be wrapped in a `struct` structure corresponding to a parameter in the method call. A complete MetaWeblog API message is too long to include here, but the following listing contains the structural elements relating to the title:

```
<methodCall>
  <methodName>metaWeblog.newPost</methodName>
  <params>
    <param>
      <value>
        <struct>
```

```
          <member>
            <name>title</name>
            <value>
               <string>My Interesting Post</string>
            </value>
          </member>
        </struct>
      </value>
    </param>
  </params>
</methodCall>
```

The code does reuse the RSS element name `<title>`, and other components of a Really Simple Syndication item can be included in this way, but as you can see the end result isn't exactly simple.

RESTful Communications

The main reason XML-RPC is so verbose is that it describes all of the control interfaces required for the application as well as the data. With RSS, the data model is specified in terms of XML grammatical structures in the first place, what the Blogger and MetaWeblog APIs do is break these down and then reconstruct them on top of the description of the application interfaces. It's easier just to provide the structured data, and pass this using standard (HTTP) methods. Of course both the sender and receiver will need to have subsystems for mapping between the XML and their internal data models. But this can be done with respect to the form in which it's needed (that is, close to the heart of the application) rather than using a generic procedure mapping technique. This means that a whole layer of encoding can be avoided, along with its associated complexity and bug opportunities.

So in contrast to the Remote Procedure Call style of message passing, the REST-oriented way to communicate is to pass a whole document directly from one system to another. This is what happens when you point your browser at a Web page. The HTML markup is related to the document structure and layout, to make it look good to a human in a browser. But it isn't difficult to see that if the markup was XML, data could be passed around in this way as well. With a browser we are usually only using the HTTP GET method, but when we use an HTML form then the POST method can be used to pass data back to the server.

One of the aims of the Atom developers was to provide a more consistent approach to formats across the whole range of syndication applications. This led to the development of the Atom API as an alternative to the Blogger or MetaWeblog API. This reuses the basic Atom format for communicating between an authoring tool (Client Producer) and a server. Rather than using an RPC approach, the XML data is passed literally, using one of the standard HTTP methods. Atom messages are concise enough to be able to show one in full:

```
<entry xmlns="http://purl.org/atom/ns#">
  <title>Bonfire Night</title>
  <created>2004-11-05T20:30:00Z</created>
  <content type="application/xhtml+xml" xml:lang="en">
    <div xmlns="http://www.w3.org/1999/xhtml">
      <p>Light your fireworks!</p>
    </div>
  </content>
</entry>
```

This is almost identical to the way this entry would appear in a feed.

Rather than identifying the particular procedures within an application to which the individual data values should be passed, the RESTful approach is to pass the relevant data to the server using an HTTP method applied to specific URI. To create a new blog entry the message above could be passed to a server-side blogging tool's edit URI using the HTTP POST method.

Server Consumer

The job of a Server Consumer in this categorization depends a lot on the kind of setup. A straightforward Web-based blogging system is likely to use a simple form to pass data from the author to the server software for creating a new post or editing an existing one. In such a scenario, there isn't really a clean separation between Client Producer and Server Consumer. However, the tool that creates the content and the server-side system that consumes it can be separate. From an RSS point of view, a typical kind of Server Consumer would be the piece of software that receives blog post data (probably over XML-RPC) and passes it back to backend storage /or to the components of the system, which then look after generation of the blog pages. As it happens, many of the popular Web-based blogging systems support creation and editing of posts both by direct HTML form interfaces as well as calls from remote XML-RPC clients.

As well as the usual author-driven route to content creation, material can come from other sources. Strictly speaking these should perhaps be listed here as either Client or Server Producer, but as producers they aren't really systems in their own right. More to the point, it's the developer of the Server Consumer that deals with data from these sources.

Weblog Comments

Most content-management tools such as blogging systems support reader comments. In principle, the system requirements for this facility are identical to those needed for handling material from the original author. In practice, things can get more complicated when dealing with material submitted by third parties. An authentication system might be necessary, and if anonymous posters are allowed, there is a likelihood of receiving comments from automated systems designed for the purpose, such as comment spam.

Trackback

This technique is one of the more interesting innovations to come from the Weblogging world. Using trackback, if you refer to a post on someone else's blog on your own blog, and then a reference to your remarks can appear on that other person's blog. There is a standard way of implementing trackback based on the original specification, which was designed for the Movable Type blog authoring tool.

Systems that support trackback assign every published item a particular URI to which a trackback "ping" can be posted. Data posted to that URI in the correct format shows up alongside the comments made locally about the item.

The complication is that when you include a link in your blog post, your system has the URI of the entry itself, not the remote entry's trackback URI. However, systems that support trackback usually include a block of hidden markup as part of the entry, which contains machine-readable details of the entry, including its trackback URI. So when you link to someone's post, your blogging system visits that link, retrieves the trackback URI, and then posts an extract of your remarks to the other person's blog. We discuss trackback, and several other inter-system protocols, in greater depth in Chapter 31.

Architectural Approaches

The chapters that follow pick up on various aspects of RSS and Atom programming mentioned in the earlier sections of the book and those outlined in this chapter. Before moving on, be aware that there is a wide spectrum of approaches to development. Approaches range from the use of formal methodologies that demand significant up-front design, to more agile approaches that focus on continuous integration of new code into existing systems. This spectrum is reflected not only in the applications produced, but also to some extent in the design of Web formats and protocols. The Web is remarkably flexible in the way it can successfully support anything from the most rigid formal design to the most ill thought out five-minute hack. Most syndication development falls within these two extremes. In practice it's possible to apply virtually any developmental approach to any aspect of RSS and Atom programming. What you will see is plenty of "architecture by implication," where the code comes before the design, although a lot of the time any successes are due in part to the implied architecture corresponding directly with existing solid architecture.

Without some sense of an architecture, there can be hidden risks. On the other hand, you aren't likely to see much of the "architecture astronautics" found in some Web services development, nor are you likely to see many back-of-envelope doodles being adopted as specifications (at least until they've had some testing in the field). Because it builds more on existing languages you will tend to see more "big picture" architecture around RSS 1.0 and related specifications, and more "throw it against the wall and see what sticks" around RSS 2.0. Atom has steered a course somewhere in between. Whatever your own personal preferences, you should at least familiarize yourself with the best-practice recommendations in "Architecture of the World Wide Web" (www.w3.org/TR/webarch/).

Summary

In this chapter you learned...

❑ How most parts of syndication systems fall into one of four categories.

❑ The general nature of subsystems in each of those categories.

❑ The significance of state, resources, and representations on the Web.

❑ The basics of HTTP client-server communication.

❑ How syndication systems use a polling protocol.

In the chapters that follow you will see a lot more of the internals of the different parts of syndication systems, beginning with a high-level view of the data modeling needed for working with all kinds of feed data.

Exercise

1. The first example of HTTP server code in this chapter was `InflexibleServer.py`, which served up the same string whatever page was requested. You also saw `ZippyClient.py`, an HTTP client that knew how to manage data from a server that supported compression. Your task is to create a modified version of `InflexibleServer.py` to gzip its data before serving it, so `ZippyClient.py` can talk to it. To get you started, here is a method that will take a string and gzip it:

```
def compress(self, data):
    zipBuffer = StringIO.StringIO()
    zipFile = gzip.GzipFile(mode = 'wb',
        fileobj = zipBuffer, compresslevel = 6)
    zipFile.write(data)
    zipFile.close()
    zipped = zipBuffer.getvalue()
    zipBuffer.close()
    self.content_length = len(zipped)
    return zipped
```

Note that you will need to import the `StringIO` and `gzip` packages to use this method. It is trivial to add a call to this method on the data being served, but you also have to set up the code to check whether the client accepts gzipped data, and also return appropriate HTTP response codes—not so trivial. You need to add code to look for a header in the HTTP request that will look something like this:

```
Accept-Encoding: gzip
```

Before compressing and returning the data, the server should add a header that looks like this:

```
Content-Encoding: gzip
```

Don't be afraid to insert lots of `print` statements to see what's happening in both the client and server code.

Modeling Feed Data

A model is a way of looking at information a couple of steps removed from the details of specific pieces of data. The aim of creating a model is to enable you to organize data in a logical fashion. Once you have a model for your data and you have a means of managing the data consistently, everything should slot into place. Your software will somehow reflect the shape of the model, which in turn reflects the kind of material that your application is designed to handle. The model itself may just be specified in regular human language—what's found in most specifications. Alternatively the model can have a formal definition that enables it to be used alongside information expressed in other data languages. Certain modeling techniques can be used to automatically generate pieces of code for processing the data or storing it in a database. The specifications for Atom, RSS 1.0, and RSS 2.0 all imply models of one form or another into which the data fits. By acknowledging this and addressing the model up front, your software is likely to benefit from architectural consistency and there are less likely to be unwanted surprises further down the road.

This chapter uses a loose definition of model that also refers to the syntax and grammar, and describes the following:

- ❏ A conceptual model of a feed and its entries
- ❏ What that model looks like in XML
- ❏ How to model feeds in object-oriented languages
- ❏ How to map the model to a relational database
- ❏ What the model looks like in RDF

Model or Syntax?

What the model actually addresses is a whole other story. It may be a high-level object view, perhaps suitable for direct translation into a programming language. At another level it may be an abstraction of the meaning of the data in terms of formal logic. Another viewpoint that could also be (loosely) described as a model is how strings should be structured within a message, in other words the syntax and grammar.

Historically there has been considerable inconsistency in the design of syndication languages in terms of modeling. The original Netscape RSS (0.9) was based on the Resource Description Framework (RDF), which includes a formal, logical model. This carried through into RSS 1.0. Netscape's version of RSS 0.91 included a Document Type Definition (DTD), which described and constrained the syntax of the XML to be syndicated, but dropped the RDF model. The UserLand version of 0.91 dropped the DTD and that thread has backed away even further from constraining the language. Atom is primarily defined in terms of syntax, but the characteristics of Atom listed in the Working Group's charter begins with a conceptual model.

It has been argued convincingly that network integration takes place at the level of "bits-over-the-wire." Just as convincing is the argument that without some common interpretation of those bits at either end of the wire there can be no real communication. But whichever way you look at it, if you're writing software then you will need to work from some kind of data model, and if you want to interoperate with other systems then you need to make sure that your messages contain the appropriate bits. This is done with the use of modeling constraints.

One of the practical applications of modeling is to constrain the data to ensure that the syntax produced conforms to the appropriate specifications. At a high level this is about ensuring that the relationships between entities in the data model appear correctly, that information that must be present is present, and so on. At a lower level the concern is about ensuring that values are of the correct data type and within required ranges. If you are producing syndication data then your software should make sure that it fits with the data model and values only appear within valid ranges. However, if you are consuming syndication data then variation between the different formats and the messiness of data in the wild mean that it is generally unfeasible to maintain strict checking of the data. Although the basic structures have to be in place to do anything useful with the data, required elements are bound to be missing from a certain proportion of feeds and out-of-range values are to be expected.

The Conceptual Feed

When a publisher puts a feed on the Web, or an aggregator is used to read that data, the feed will appear as a file containing a bunch of XML. However, the terminology of syndication is a little misleading, because to call something a *feed* suggests the material is being pushed from server to client, which isn't strictly the case. The word *channel* is a little better, because the pattern isn't unlike that of radio or televisions channels to which your receiver can tune. However, the informal protocol of producer-publication/consumer-subscription does give the effect of something being piped from the server. Although in principle there would be nothing to prevent a single feed containing multiple channels, this kind of division doesn't appear in practice, and in fact isn't really catered for in the specifications. RSS 2.0 says its root <rss> element has a single subordinate <channel> element, so when someone talks about a channel or a feed they're talking about the same thing. But the way in which that channel or feed is considered can vary, and two different approaches predominate: the document- or feed-oriented model and the item-oriented model.

The Feed-Oriented Model

When you create a file in HTML and put it on the Web, the intention is usually to serve up some kind of document. It may well contain fancy formatting, images, hyperlinks, and even programs written in JavaScript. All the same, what users will see in their browsers is something not that different from a document printed on paper. The document is your content, what the HTML file provides is a fixed representation.

It's possible to view feeds in similar terms, with a syndication channel actually being a comparatively fixed representation of some data. The original RSS was RDF Site Summary, without any real content of its own, but designed to describe documents elsewhere on your site. This is still a perfectly good use for any of the syndication languages, but it's far more common for feeds to carry content inline and be essentially self-contained.

If the feed does contain content and you accept it as simply yet another kind of document, it follows that it should be possible to present this more or less directly to the user. It is not only possible but very straightforward, and you can even make the feed suitable for viewing in a regular browser. As you will see later in the chapter, there are a lot more interesting and useful ways of modeling a feed, but the document model is not without its uses.

> Here the term document model is used in a general sense, the Document Object Model as developed for HTML and XML does allow granular access to the contents of the document, as you will see later in this chapter.

Source or Styled?

It has been suggested that one of the main reasons the Web has been so successful is that HTML is so simple and straightforward, it's possible to make sense of it through just looking at the source code. With browsers that tolerate mistakes in the markup and self-explanatory element names, a reasonable-looking page can be created with a minimum of effort. This is a notion that crops up frequently in discussion of markup languages, and its supporters have been dubbed the *View Source Clan*. There's general agreement that access to source is a desirable characteristic of tools and legible source is a desirable feature for markup languages. Where disagreement can occur is when compromises are needed between machine-utility and human-readability.

The same point has been made about RSS — it should be simple to read, and there's certainly some truth in that a good code example can be worth more than a thousand words of explanation. However, a recent variation on this theme is when someone is surfing the Web and accidentally lands on an RSS feed (they're not uncommon in search results), the browser should show them raw code to let them know something's amiss. This is often the default browser behavior, so it's not hard to support. The counter-argument is that RSS data contains information, and even if a Web browser isn't really designed to render this material, it should at least present something useful. Well, you can decide for yourself whether or not this makes sense. Here is a fairly full example of an RSS 2.0 format feed that, to save paper, contains only 3 items (10 would be more typical):

```xml
<?xml version="1.0"?>
<?xml-stylesheet type="text/css" href="rss.css"?>

<!-- This is an RSS feed and is best viewed in an aggregator or newsreader -->

<rss version="2.0">
   <channel>
      <title>Tech Idol</title>
      <link>http://example.org/idol/</link>
      <description>The hottest performers on the Net!</description>
      <language>en-us</language>
      <pubDate>Tue, 10 Jun 2003 04:00:00 GMT</pubDate>
      <lastBuildDate>Tue, 10 Jun 2003 09:41:01 GMT</lastBuildDate>
      <docs>http://example.org/documentation</docs>
      <generator>Blinking Text</generator>
      <managingEditor>editor@example.org</managingEditor>
```

```
<webMaster>webmaster@example.org</webMaster>
<item>
    <title>Shelley</title>
    <link>http://example.org/idol/shelley</link>
    <description>Shelley first impressed the judges with
        her 3-line backup script, then trampled the opposition
        with her cover of "These Boots Were Made for Walking".
    </description>
    <pubDate>Thu, 01 Jul 2004 09:39:21 GMT</pubDate>
    <guid>http://example.org/idol/shelley</guid>
</item>
<item>
    <title>Sam</title>
    <link>http://example.org/idol/sam</link>
    <description>Test-driven development while plate-spinning?
        Sam's the man.
    </description>
    <pubDate>Thu, 01 Jul 2004  08:37:32 GMT</pubDate>
    <guid>http://example.org/idol/sam</guid>
</item>
<item>
    <title>Marc</title>
    <link>http://example.org/idol/marc</link>
    <description>Marc's multimedia presentation of "O Sole Mio"
        served him well, but perhaps he should have kept those
        knees covered!
    </description>
    <pubDate>Thu, 01 Jul 2004 08:56:02 GMT</pubDate>
    <guid>http://example.org/idol/marc</guid>
</item>
    </channel>
</rss>
```

Figure 20-1 shows the same data rendered in a browser.

Which looks best to you?

Ok, there was a little cheating involved there, in the form of a cascading style sheet (CSS). This isn't all that related to the modeling of feeds, but now is as good a time as any for you to see how it's done.

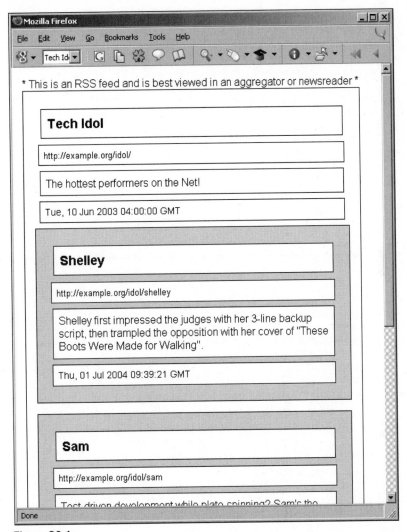

Figure 20-1

Here is the source code of the style sheet:

```
rss:before {
    content: "* This is an RSS feed and is best viewed in an
                    aggregator or newsreader *"
}

rss {
```

```
    display:block;
    margin:1em;
    font-family: Arial;
}

channel {
    display:block;
    border:1px solid #000;
    width: 30em;
    padding:1em;
    background-color:#fff;
}

item {
    display:block;
    margin-bottom:1em;
    border:1px solid #000;
    background-color:#ddd;
    padding:1em;
}

title {
    display: block;
    padding:0.5em;
    border:1px solid #000;
    font-size:120%;
    font-weight:bold;
    margin:0.5em;
    background-color:#fff;
}

description {
    display: block;
    padding:0.5em;
    border:1px solid #000;
    margin:0.5em;
    background-color:#fff;
}

pubDate {
    display: block;
    padding:0.5em;
    border:1px solid #000;
    margin:0.5em;
    font-size:90%;
    background-color:#fff;
}

link {
    display: block;
    padding:0.5em;
    border:1px solid #000;
    font-size:80%;
    margin:0.5em;
    background-color:#fff;
```

```
    }

    language, managingEditor, generator, image, guid, ttl, skipHours, skipDays,
    webMaster, lastBuildDate, updateBase, updateFrequency, updatePeriod, docs {
        display: none;
    }
```

Try It Out   RSS with CSS

1. Open a text editor and type the RSS 2.0 code listing (better still, download it).

2. Save that as `rss2sample.xml`.

3. Start a Web browser and open the file `rss2sample.xml` in it.

    Depending on your browser, you will see either the source code more or less as it appears in the previous listing, or as a single block of text (without the XML tags) or you will be asked whether you want to open or save the data. Whichever it is, close the browser again.

4. Open another text editor window and type the previous CSS code.

5. Save this in the same directory as `rss2sample.xml`, naming the file `rss.css`.

6. Again start up a Web browser and open the file `rss2sample.xml` in it.

    This time you should see something like the styled version in Figure 20-1.

How It Works

The technique is virtually identical to styling HTML with CSS, when the style sheet is a separate file. Here the source document is XML version 1.0, as declared in the first line. The line that follows is the most significant here, because it is an instruction to any processors of this data that there is a style sheet available in `rss.css` of type `text/css`. Processors designed for rendering documents, such as Web browsers, know how to interpret this instruction. Here are the first few lines of the RSS source again:

```
<?xml version="1.0"?>
<?xml-stylesheet type="text/css" href="rss.css"?>

<!-- This is an RSS feed and is best viewed in an aggregator or newsreader -->

<rss version="2.0">
  <channel>
     <title>Tech Idol</title>
...
```

The CSS code is made up of blocks each corresponding to an element name in the RSS format. For example, the following block of rendering instructions in the CSS will be applied to the `<title>` element:

```
title {
    display: block;
    padding:0.5em;
    border:1px solid #000;
    font-size:120%;
    font-weight:bold;
    margin:0.5em;
    background-color:#fff;
}
```

The result of this particular piece of content with styling looks like what you see in Figure 20-2.

Tech Idol

Figure 20-2

The content of the `<title>` element by default would be displayed inline, running across the page. Setting the `display` value to `block` overrides this, and enables the box features of border, padding, and margin to be used. The border is simply the thin (`1px`) black (`#000`) solid (`solid`) line around the box. Padding is spacing that goes between the content and the border, the margin is around the outside of the border. The values here are given in em units rather than pixels. An em unit is defined as the font size (originally an em was the width of an *m* character), which helps keep proportions right if the page as a whole is enlarged or reduced. The rest of the styling attributes are self-explanatory, and these and a lot more are defined at `www.w3.org/TR/REC-CSS2/`.

One thing to note here is that this piece of CSS doesn't discriminate between the `<title>` element found at the `<channel>` level and the `<title>` element found at the `<item>` level. However, you can apply different styling like this:

```
channel > title {

/* channel title-specific styling here */

}

item > title {

/* item title-specific styling here */

}
```

The > symbol here is used to select an element that is a direct child of another element (parent). However not all browsers support this functionality.

The CSS listing began with the following lines:

```
rss:before {
    content: "* This is an RSS feed and is best viewed in an
                    aggregator or newsreader *"
}
```

This is taking advantage of what the CSS specification calls a pseudo-element, `before`. The instruction is to render this message immediately before it renders the `<rss>` element (or any of its child elements). This is a convenient way of giving the browser user an appropriate message about the kind of data they're dealing with.

The styling code here follows the CSS 2 specification. Not all browsers offer support for all CSS 2 features. In particular Internet Explorer will ignore the :before pseudo-element, with the result that the explanatory line will be missed out of the display.

Another part of the CSS code that may not be obvious is this part:

```
language, managingEditor, generator, image, guid, ttl, skipHours, skipDays,
webMaster, lastBuildDate, updateBase, updateFrequency, updatePeriod, docs {
    display: none;
}
```

This again overrides the default display formatting (inline) for the listed elements, although this time rather than treating each as a block, the rendering style is none, and the instruction is not to render them at all. This is a handy way of dumping the more obscure elements that aren't likely to be of interest to the reader.

Note that the <link> value is displayed verbatim in the browser — you get the text of the URI but it isn't clickable. This specific fault is something that can be fixed by using XSLT style sheets, but it points toward a deeper problem.

Drawbacks of a Feed-Oriented Model

Treating syndication feeds as documents does suggest nifty tricks like CSS rendering, but this view overlooks some of the important characteristics of real feeds. As mentioned earlier, they don't necessarily have to include content. There may still be benefit in displaying a list of titles, links, even dates and the rest of the metadata, but this is stretching the idea of a document somewhat. A more significant drawback is that most syndication feeds are dynamic, changing every few days or perhaps even every hour.

The Dynamic Feed

The fact that a feed generally changes over time a lot more rapidly than a regular Web page is really only one consideration. In the example listing of "Tech Idol" it wasn't clear what the order of the items related to. If they were a kind of popularity chart, with the number one ranked Idol listed first, then the document-oriented approach is probably quite a good fit. Where the document model really goes awry is when the order of items in the feed is governed directly by time, such as in the reverse-chronological order of Weblogs and other news-like sources. Only a certain number of items can be realistically included in a feed, and the reverse-chrono order suggests new items got to the top of the feed. So what happens to the old items? Generally they drop off the bottom of the feed. This can be seen in Figure 20-3, which shows a feed that holds three items on two consecutive days. Here the numbering of the items corresponds to their creation order, so Item 1 was created first, 2 second, and so on. On Day 1 the newest item is Item 3, this is shown at the top of the feed. By Day 2 another item, Item 4 has been created. Being the newest, this now takes the position at the top of the feed. As this particular feed is designed to carry only three items at a time, the oldest item, Item 1, no longer appears on Day 2 (see Figure 20-3).

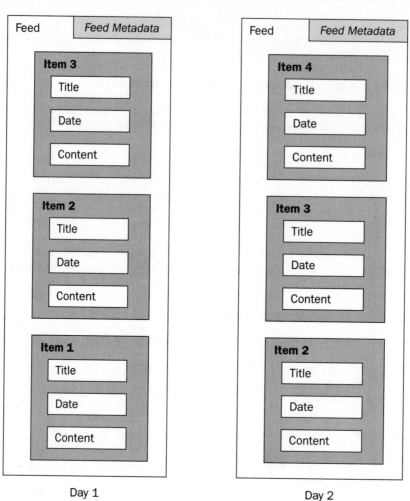

Day 1   Day 2

Figure 20-3

If you wanted your system to have a memory and keep track of the feed as it changed over time, the document-oriented model would suggest taking a snapshot of the document between every change. However, if you save what's in the feed on Day 1 and Day 2 as in Figure 20-3, then you'll have duplicate data corresponding to Item 2 and Item 3. In this little example that would mean a third of the item data (2/6 items) would be redundant. The data in feeds is usually text, and in these days of ever-cheaper storage this redundancy probably isn't a big deal.

The Opaque Feed

But there's a more significant problem. The information of interest on a given day is contained in the items that appear on that day. By wrapping up collections of items into documents, it makes it harder to see what's inside those items — what you see are daily feeds, not items. In effect the document-oriented approach makes the individual pieces of content and metadata opaque to systems that might want to index or search the items.

From the document-oriented view the redundancy and opacity could be seen as bugs in the system. However, if we turn things around into a different model, magically the bug becomes a feature and what was opaque becomes transparent.

Item-Oriented Models

The document-oriented view is a fairly direct analogy of the traditional paper publication. But rather than consider the feed as a package, if you think of it more like a source of continual information, it takes on some different characteristics.

Twenty-First Century Press Clippings

One of the less glamorous jobs in the old media of newspapers is clipping. For a very long time, certain publishers and press clipping services have offered a selective view of relevant media to their customers. Say your company is in the environment-friendly lawn mower business. You'll probably want to know what's going on elsewhere in the world of environment-friendly lawn mowers. You could read every newspaper and periodical in your area or even internationally, but that wouldn't leave much time for lawn mowers. So you could get some poor souls to do the reading for you, extracting any articles or advertisements of interest with a pair of scissors. At the end of every week you'd get a pile of individual clippings, all about lawn mowers. The material in such a system would be treated at the granularity level of the articles — of course you'd want to know the source of each clipping, but that information is auxiliary to the article itself.

A feed can be thought of as a kind of clipping service, except the clippings are available in real time, immediately after they appear. Your aggregator will visit each feed periodically to collect the clippings. Where this analogy is weak is in that current systems are rarely as specialized or personalized as a press clipping service. Such services do exist: PubSub.com will provide a feed based on the results of a custom search query. In fact, the following is the address of a feed of search results on the keywords "environment-friendly lawn mowers":

```
http://rss.pubsub.com/37/b5/3778cec38f25c9f8282681622a.xml
```

PubSub is ahead of most of the field in this respect, but in general the idea of treating individual clippings (that is, syndicated items) as standalone, self-contained pieces of information is very powerful.

Microcontent and Memes

Information can appear in many formats, and traditional print media tends to favor large chunks: books, magazines, and academic papers tend to be multipage collections of text that cover wide areas. However the tendency on the Web has been toward smaller pieces, and the newsflash or blog post represents the ultimate in granularity. Essentially you will have a single idea or meme, with a few lines of human-readable content backed by several pieces of machine-readable metadata. It is believed that this approach to information will offer better personalization (you only get the information you want) supported by more efficient search and organization of these small chunks of information.

The stereotype of this is of course the syndicated item. Being able to extract individual items from a feed enables the manipulation of information at this meme level. Which leads us to the entry or item-oriented model of feed data. Figure 20-4 shows the general idea. Items are detached from their originating feed, although they commonly will include a back reference to the source feed. The aggregator in its truest sense is a tool that aggregates items from a variety of sources.

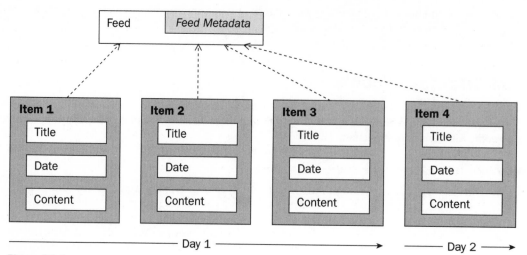

Figure 20-4

The most immediate advantage of the entry-oriented model is that it makes it possible for a user tool to group and sort items according to different criteria than the document order provided by a specific feed. The most likely criteria will be that of publication date and time, so that your aggregator displays the newest item first. The flow of items through your system might look something like what's shown in Figure 20-5.

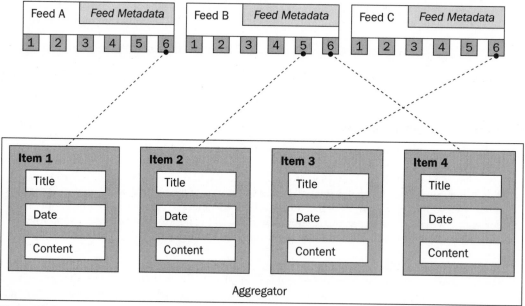

Figure 20-5

Here the aggregator is subscribed to three feeds: A, B, and C. The oldest item in each is number 1, the newest number 6. The aggregator is only looking at four items, which will have appeared in chronological order: 1, 2, 3, and 4. From the aggregator's point of view the oldest item of interest is Item 6 from Feed A and the newest is Item 6 from Feed B. The aggregator is in effect skimming off the most recent items from its subscribed feeds.

Another benefit of the item-oriented model is that it makes it possible to create composite or so-called *synthetic* feeds. An online system can aggregate content from various different sources and then republished the combined material as a whole new feed. This makes it possible to create a multiauthor feed on a particular topic, or (as PubSub.com) build a feed dynamically from search results.

In Figure 20-6, there is again an aggregator skimming off the most recent items from a number of feeds. The difference is that the aggregator here is building a composite feed from those items, which it publishes as an entirely separate feed, Feed D.

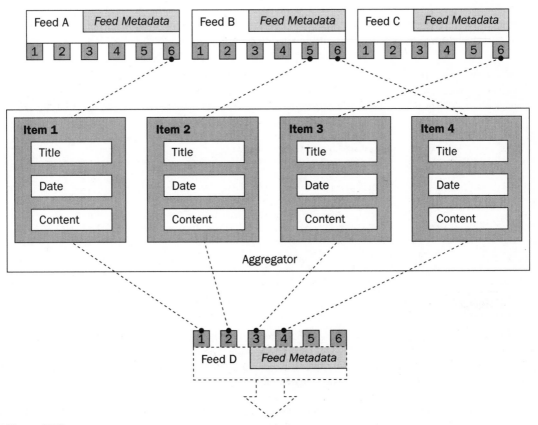

Figure 20-6

249

Including Item Provenance

In the document-oriented view, all the feed metadata of title and description and so on is present in the document. If an item is used outside of the original XML document in which it appeared then the feed metadata may be lost. In some circumstances this won't matter much, but then information such as the author of the items and copyright details may only be given at feed level. When items are extracted from a feed, such information can be attached directly to each individual item. Syndication technologies are still in their infancy, and the jury is still out on the best approach to take to this.

Here is an example of an item in one of the feeds from xml.com, published in RSS 0.91:

```
<item>
   <title>XML-Deviant: Something Useful This Way Comes</title>
   <link>http://www.xml.com/pub/a/2004/06/09/deviant.html</link>
   <description>The Semantic Web appears to be powering ahead:
    so why are there so many doubters in the XML world?</description>
</item>
```

The same item was aggregated and republished in a PubSub feed, which is RSS 2.0:

```
<item>
   <title><![CDATA[XML.com - XML-Deviant: Something Useful This Way Comes]]>
   </title>
   <link>http://www.xml.com/pub/a/2004/06/09/deviant.html</link>
   <pubDate>Mon, 05 Jul 2004 05:48:38 -0500</pubDate>

   <source>http://www.xml.com/</source>

   <description><![CDATA[Weblog:
       <a href='http://www.xml.com/'>XML.com</a><BR/>
       Source: <a href='http://www.xml.com/cs/xml/query/q/19'>
           XML-Deviant: Something Useful This Way Comes</a><BR/>
       Link: <a href='http://www.xml.com/pub/a/2004/06/09/deviant.html'>
           http://www.xml.com/pub/a/2004/06/09/deviant.html</a><BR/>
       <BR/>
       The <b style='background:#00ffff;'>Semantic Web</b> appears to be
       powering ahead: so why are there so many doubters in the XML world?]]>
   </description>
</item>
```

Some escaping of the content has taken place, presumably to help ensure well-formedness, but the interesting part is how PubSub provides item provenance information. The <source> element is used to point back to the host Web site from which the item came, here an aggregator is likely to display this as a link. The <link> element has been carried over exactly as it appeared in the original feed.

Although it makes full use of the item-oriented syndication model, PubSub also takes advantage of the document-oriented view and provides its feeds in an HTML browser-readable style (using XSL). The republished item appears in a browser, as shown in Figure 20-7.

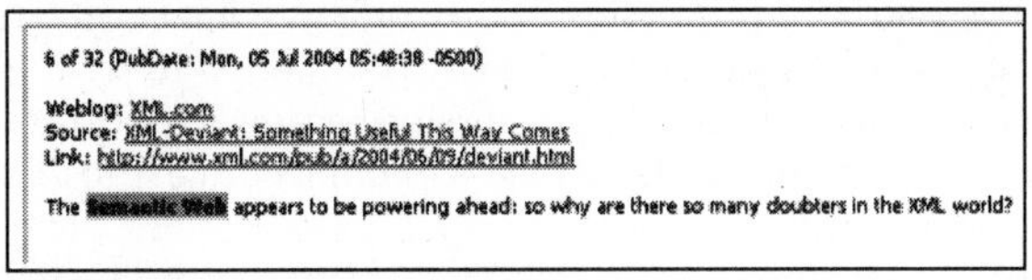

Figure 20-7

Where the `<source>` element is essentially machine-readable metadata, PubSub have also included details of the origin of the item inside the content `<description>` itself. In the browser this shows as links to the Weblog (host), the source RSS feed as well as the target of the `<link>` element.

The following is extracted from an original RSS 1.0 feed (the description content has been trimmed to take up less space):

```
<item rdf:about="http://jibbering.com/blog/index.php?p=134">
   <title>I found Phil Richards</title>
   <link>http://jibbering.com/blog/index.php?p=134</link>
   <dc:date>2004-07-05T01:29:06Z</dc:date>
   <dc:creator>site admin (mailto:)</dc:creator>
   <dc:subject>General</dc:subject>
   <description>When you know people just by reputation...</description>
</item>
```

RSS 1.0 doesn't include any provenance-related elements in its core, but what it does have is unlimited access to other RDF vocabularies through the use of namespaces. Here is how the Planet RDF composite feed (`http://planetrdf.com`) relays the item:

```
<item rdf:about="http://jibbering.com/blog/index.php?p=134">
   <title>I found Phil Richards</title>
   <description>
 When you know people just by reputation...
</description>
   <dc:creator>Jim Ley</dc:creator>
   <dc:date>2004-07-05T01:29:06Z</dc:date>
   <planet:content xmlns="http://www.w3.org/1999/xhtml" rdf:parseType="Literal">
<p>When you know people just by reputation...</p>
</planet:content>
   <link>http://jibbering.com/blog/index.php?p=134</link>
   <dc:source>Jibbering by Jim Ley</dc:source>
   <content:encoded
     rdf:datatype="http://www.w3.org/1999/02/22-rdf-syntax-ns#XMLLiteral">
<![CDATA[
<div xmlns='http://www.w3.org/1999/xhtml'>
<p>When you know people just by reputation...</p>
</div>]]></content:encoded>
   <dc:relation>http://jibbering.com/</dc:relation>
</item>
```

In this example, there has also been processing of the content which is given in three forms: the original RSS 1.0 plain text `<description>`, a custom `<planet:content>` XHTML-format version which has an added `<p>` element, and a `<content:encoded>` version escaped in a CDATA block. The provenance information appears in two machine-readable pieces of data, both expressed using the Dublin Core vocabulary (`http://dublincore.org/documents/dces/`). The first element is `dc:source`, which is defined as "A Reference to a resource from which the present resource is derived" and here contains the human-readable text name of the source Weblog. The `dc:relation` element, defined as "A reference to a related resource" provides the URI of the blog. Note also that the `<link>` element, which points to the HTML version of this item, has also been carried over verbatim. What's more the item is given exactly the same identifier URI in its `rdf:about` attribute, so any downstream aggregator will know that this is the conceptually the same item resource that appeared in the original feed.

As a general rule it's a good idea to include at least the URI of the feed from which an item was extracted. This way if the information is needed downstream then it can be obtained from the original feed later on. The drawback of this approach is that a lot more calls to the original feed may occur, coming from clients trying to reconstitute the provenance information. On the other hand, simply duplicating everything found at feed level with every item also has the potential to cause problems, as the amount of data being passed around will be significantly greater.

Element Order

Once freed from the confines of a particular feed, an item generally loses the position at which it appeared in the feed. Simple feeds such as RSS 2.0 have an order implied by the XML document order, which may be reflected in the way a client displays the items. RSS 1.0 makes an order explicit, but doesn't really say much about how that order is to be interpreted. It remains to be seen exactly how Atom will treat order but it is likely to be more clearly specified there than in the existing RSS specifications. For most purposes the loss of item order information won't be an issue, because a client can decide on the appropriate order itself according to the date of the item or some other piece of metadata. There isn't any reliable approach that will work for all systems when the order has some significance outside of the information expressed by core metadata. So if your plan is to publish the Top Ten X, whatever X may be, it may be advisable to provide some additional data in extension elements or as an additional part of the content to express the order.

Common Features Among Formats

So far in this chapter issues specific to the various formats (RSS 1.0, 2.0, and Atom) have largely been skirted — ideally that would continue to the end of the book, as it shouldn't really matter. There is only one basic domain model: the feed (and its metadata) and the items (and their content and metadata). But certain details of each format are different, there are minor conflicts, and to build systems that can reasonably handle all types of data some level of compromise is needed. To derive a common model something of a compare and contrast exercise is needed, but before you see the details you'll need to know what it is we're looking at.

Entities and Relationships

The kind of modeling techniques relevant to feed data are generally based around two basic sets of features found in the information to be modeled. One of these is the set of entities that the data is about, the *things*: documents, objects, concepts, people, places and so on. The other is the set of relationships between the things described by the data. For example a document (entity) will have been written by a person (entity), the relationship between these two entities will be something like *creator*. A common relationship is "is-a," as in *the author is a person*. This relationship crops up a lot in software where the entities are classes or type, and particular items are individual members of that class or have that type (in English you might say *my home page is a Web page*, for example). The entities themselves can be said to have *attributes*, a set of qualities of different types. For example, a person entity will probably have an attribute "name," so you could say (in English) the author's name is "Charles Dickens."

The entity-relationship way of looking at systems led to the development of specific set of techniques for modeling, and this approach is (not surprisingly) known as Entity-Relationship Modeling (E-R). Most CASE (Computer-Aided Software Engineering) tools allow you to describe systems in terms of entities and relationships one way or another because it's a fundamental way of developing a data model.

In the context of modeling feeds, it's not necessary to go the entire formal E-R route to take advantage of the basic ideas. For a particular kind of data, if you can select the entities, the attributes of those entities and the relationships between them, you have the essence of a data model.

Entities in Feeds

The entities in feeds roughly correspond to the elements in the XML format; there is the feed or channel itself, and the individual items. The feed has a set of attributes (`title`, `description`, and so on) as does each item. However, there is a slight snag in that some of the attributes could equally well be described as entities in their own right. The `<description>` part of an RSS 2.0 feed might contain a whole document, the text in the `<link>` element will be the URL of a document on the Web. Although in modeling you are looking at things at a conceptual level, what you decide should be entities and what should be attributes of those entities will be determined very much by what you want to do with them in practice. In the context of this book that means storing and manipulating feed data. The approaches covered in this chapter are XML-based, relational database-based, Object-Oriented and RDF-based, and as you will see the E-R models would look a little different in each case.

Relationships in Feeds

Starting at the top, the primary relationship between a feed and its items is one of containment. This can be seen as a variation of the document-oriented view that, at a given point in time, the document retrievable from a feed URL contains items [X, Y, Z]. A more useful view is that the conceptual feed (identified with the URI) contains every item ever published and every item that will ever be published from that address. This is a better fit for the item-oriented approach, although obviously some awareness of particular items will be needed — there's not a lot useful information associated with blog posts that haven't yet been written.

The relationship between an item and its associated elements is a little trickier to describe. On the one hand, the `<title>` and `<description>` are simply attributes of the item. On the other hand, in the RSS 2.0 case, if the `<description>` is a whole document, then it will make sense to consider this an entity in its own right.

Stepping back up to the feed level, there is to some extent the same dilemma. For example, do you model the managing editor of the feed as a simple attribute of the feed, or as an entity in its/his/her own right? You will see this general issue treated from several different angles later in the chapter.

One of the characteristics of entities in general is that they may be identified — you can distinguish one entity from others. On the Web this characteristic takes on special significance.

Identity

It's necessary to identify things before you can talk about them, no matter how abstract the things are. For humans, identification comes down to naming or labeling the things of interest. Similarly, from a computer's point of view, naming and labeling are the key. The Internet is a big place, and there's a potential risk of two different things being given the same name. There are ways of avoiding this, however, by providing Uniform Resource Identifiers (URIs).

Uniform and Unique

To avoid ambiguity it's desirable to give anything else you want to talk about on the Web a URI. It isn't essential, and some things aren't very amenable to this kind of identification—people, for example. But when the resources are on the Web anyhow, it can make life easier.

There are really two pieces to identification on the Web, URIs, and URI References (URIRefs). A URI is generally the absolute part, of the form http://example.org/thing. *A URIRef may be a URI, a relative reference, or have an additional fragment identifier like this:* http://example.org/thing#part. *These are rather evasive concepts that seem to behave differently at different times, whether they're used as identifiers (such as in RDF) or as locators (over HTTP). The whole issue of URIs and URIRefs has proved something of a nightmare for the W3C's Technical Architecture Group, though fortunately in practice rarely causes problems.*

Aside from the arcane details of URIs themselves, there's an identity issue specific to syndication formats. To locate and obtain a feed in the first place it's necessary to know its URI, but when it comes to identifying individual items, there are complications. It can be difficult to tell the relationship between an item URI, a link URI, and any inline content there may be. This issue has its roots in the use of RSS as pure metadata, without any content. The original RSS 0.9 included a link element like this:

```
<item>
    <link>http://www.example.org/stuff</link>
...
</item>
```

The item being described is the resource identified by that URI. Similarly, the RDF/XML-based RSS 1.0 give items an identifier like this:

```
<item rdf:about="http://www.example.org/stuff">
```

As the attribute name suggests, the properties of the item (title, description, and so on) will all be about the resource identified by that URI. But RSS 1.0 also adds a link for *"The item's URL."* This has generally been taken to mean the URI of an HTML version of the item, and will usually be the same URI:

```
<item rdf:about="http://www.example.org/stuff">
    <link>http://www.example.org/stuff</link>
    ...
</item>
```

The non-RDF thread of RSS also included a link element, which appeared in RSS 0.91 looking the same as in RSS 0.9:

```
<item>
   <link>http://www.example.org/stuff</link>
   ...
</item>
```

However, there followed a drift in the use of RSS as pure metadata about a resource to becoming a delivery mechanism for the resource itself. In other words, RSS got content. This gave the item something of a split personality, as demonstrated in this snippet of RSS 1.0:

```
<item rdf:about="http://www.example.org/one">
   <link>http://www.example.org/two</link>
   <content:encoded>Here is an item.</content:encoded>
   <description>This is an item</description>
   ...
</item>
```

By its unambiguous RDF/XML interpretation, the item the description property refers to is the resource identified in the rdf:about attribute. But what does it mean for the resource also to have a (different) <link> URI? What is the relationship between the content here and the identified resource? The most Web architecture–friendly interpretation would probably be that the inline content is a representation of the (rdf:about) identified resource, which may have other representations you can get over HTTP using the first URI. In these terms it's probably safest to think of the <link> as being a related resource. But the "true" interpretation only matters if people treat the material that way. The grassroots development of syndication has generally meant a shiny new feature stands a much better chance of adoption than any amount of theoretical spec-compliance.

GUID

Item identification became a problem for the simple XML-style formats because there was no reliable way of telling whether two items were the same. The result was that an item that had been published and later edited again could show up twice in newsreaders. This may sound obvious, but RSS 0.9x items already had fairly distinguishing features such as their title and pubDate (when the item was published). Except that pubDate was the official publication date, rather than any more dependable fixed point in time. The title could be changed at any time. So a new element was introduced: <guid>. Here is an example of how it might appear in a feed:

```
<guid isPermaLink="true">http://example.org/three.html</guid>
```

The optional isPermaLink attribute is an *http:* scheme URI that can be used to get a HTML representation of the item. Its default value is true, so most of the time the value of the <guid> element is equivalent to the RSS 1.0 rdf:about identifier. There is a caveat—the isPermaLink value might be false and the text of the <guid> element may not be a URI at all, it can be any string that the source of the feed has established as unique.

Crisis, What Crisis?

The bottom line is that the RSS formats are pragmatic solutions to the problems that were around when the specs were authored, much of which related to the behavior of existing aggregator tools. One of the aims of Atom is to sort out such muddles and build on what are considered best practices in terms of the overall architecture of the Web. However, Atom is also constrained by the real-world demands of developers. So although existing specifications are followed closely, and ambiguity avoided wherever possible, there is bound to be some degree of improvising to make things *work* in the fairly messy environment of the Web.

Parallel Elements

There are clear parallels between the entities supported by the different syndication formats — after all, they share the same historical roots and aim to fulfill more or less the same purpose. The following table lines up these formats against each other, with the Model column using the word that's most commonly used when talking about these entities.

Model	RSS 1.0	RSS 2.0	Atom
Feed	`rss:channel`	`channel`	`atom:feed`
Item	`rss:item`	`item`	`atom:entry`
Title	`dc:title`	`title`	`atom:title`
Date	`dc:date`	`pubDate`	`atom:issued`
Content	`dc:description,` `content:encoded`	`description,` `xhtml:body`	`atom:content`
Author	`dc:creator`	`author`	`atom:author`

There are various restrictions on the values that can appear in the elements and attributes in the RSS and Atom specifications. But as noted earlier, these aren't much for use as constraints, and for modeling purposes most can be reduced to simple strings. What causes a lot of work in practice is that the data appearing in the feeds is expressed in different ways, for example RSS 1.0 dates follow the W3CDTF (ISO 8601) format, whereas RSS 2.0 uses the RFC 822 format. But again this is a detail of the data, and doesn't really affect the overall models.

Groups of Feeds

Any application that uses data from multiple feeds will need to keep track of the feed addresses. In its simplest form, a subscription list could just be a set of feed URIs held in a text file. However, most applications will want to present the user with a little more information than this, such as the name of the feed, the author, and perhaps her e-mail address, and so on. A fairly common requirement is the ability to exchange lists of feeds or render them in a readable form. A few alternate approaches and formats have appeared for this purpose, and support for them in syndication tools varies. You will see examples of these later in the chapter.

Extending Structures

RSS and Atom systems are generally designed for syndication, aggregation, and viewing of "news-like" material. As a result the formats primarily cover the essentials for this job: title, description, and so on. However, the technologies can allow much richer material to be syndicated and aggregated. In terms of the formats, this means including terms from other XML or RDF vocabularies in the feed. In terms of the model, this can mean that completely arbitrary structures can appear. In practice there aren't yet a great deal of extensions currently in use, it's something of a chicken and egg situation with the publication and subscription tools.

An XML Model

The emphasis with syndication languages has often been down with the syntax—after all, their purpose is to deliver data from A to B, so the format of the data is significant. XML doesn't have a model in the formal sense, although its syntax structure is usually thought of as if it brought a data model to whatever it is used to represent. In general, the structure of XML documents is often used to represent lists or hierarchical data structures, and programming tools such as the Document Object Model (DOM) take advantage of the parent-child tree structure. In these terms RSS, particularly the plain-XML varieties, and Atom can be seen as having a hierarchical model. Figure 20-8 is a trimmed-down version of the RSS 2.0 example listed earlier, as displayed in the XMLmind XML editor (free, multiplatform: www.xmlmind.com).

Figure 20-8

The hierarchical structure of the elements is clear, and this can work as a starting point for an XML-oriented approach to modeling feeds. If you are interested in generating original feeds, then such an approach can offer a very quick solution.

However, there are drawbacks if you want to use data from other people's feeds, largely due to the not-quite-XML nature of many feeds. The RSS formats are unusual compared to most XML languages. The "Really Simple" versions are fairly loosely specified, and have lacked even a DTD since Netscape's version 0.91. The RDF-based versions are strictly defined by comparison. But again there's a problem with using DTDs and XML Schemas—valid RDF/XML extensions may break XML validity. However, if you assume that you are responsible for generating the data (or can suitably filter other people's data), DTDs or XML schemas can be used as the basis of a model.

A DTD for RSS 2.0 would look something like the following:

```
<!ELEMENT rss (channel)>
<!ATTLIST rss
```

```
   version  #REQUIRED>

<!ELEMENT channel (title,link,description,language,pubDate,
                   lastBuildDate,docs,generator,managingEditor,
                   webMaster,item+)>
<!ATTLIST channel>

<!ELEMENT language (#PCDATA)>
<!ATTLIST language>

<!ELEMENT lastBuildDate (#PCDATA)>
<!ATTLIST lastBuildDate>

<!ELEMENT docs (#PCDATA)>
<!ATTLIST docs>

<!ELEMENT generator (#PCDATA)>
<!ATTLIST generator>

<!ELEMENT managingEditor (#PCDATA)>
<!ATTLIST managingEditor>

<!ELEMENT webMaster (#PCDATA)>
<!ATTLIST webMaster>

<!ELEMENT item (title,link,description,pubDate,guid)>
<!ATTLIST item>

<!ELEMENT guid (#PCDATA)>
<!ATTLIST guid>

<!ELEMENT title (#PCDATA)>
<!ATTLIST title>

<!ELEMENT link (#PCDATA)>
<!ATTLIST link>

<!ELEMENT description (#PCDATA)>
<!ATTLIST description>

<!ELEMENT pubDate (#PCDATA)>
<!ATTLIST pubDate>
```

Most XML standard specifications ship with at least some form of schema, in fact the schema is usually created before any real data. But there isn't an official DTD for RSS 2.0, and truth be told no-one actually sat down and worked out the DTD listed previously. For relatively simple XML formats such as RSS 2.0 it's possible to take advantage of automatic tools to generate at least approximations to their schemas, which you can then hand-edit as needed. The tool used here was Trang, a free command-line Java application. Given a sample of an XML format it can generate a DTD, XML Schema, or RelaxNG schema corresponding to the format.

Try It Out   ## Reverse Engineering a Schema

You will need to have Java installed to run Trang, specifically a Java Runtime Environment (JRE) for the Java 2 Platform, Standard Edition (J2SE) version 1.4 or any later. This is a free download from `http://java.sun.com/j2se/downloads.html`.

Trang itself is available from `www.thaiopensource.com/relaxng/trang.html`. Once you have Java and Trang installed, follow these steps:

1. Copy the RSS 2.0 example file `rss2example.xml` into the directory into which you installed Trang.

2. Open a command window in that directory.

3. Enter the following command:

```
java -jar trang.jar rss2sample.xml rss2.rnc
```

> After pressing Return, the command prompt should reappear, hopefully without any error message. If you look in the current directory you should see a new file, `rss2.rnc`.

4. Open `rss2.rnc` in a text editor.

> You should see the following:

```
default namespace = ""

start =
  element rss {
    attribute version { xsd:decimal },
    element channel {
      title,
      link,
      description,
      element language { xsd:NCName },
      pubDate,
      element lastBuildDate { text },
      element docs { xsd:anyURI },
      element generator { text },
      element managingEditor { text },
      element webMaster { text },
      element item {
        title,
        link,
        description,
        pubDate,
        element guid { xsd:anyURI }
      }+
    }
  }
title = element title { text }
link = element link { xsd:anyURI }
description = element description { text }
pubDate = element pubDate { text }
```

This is a (compact) RelaxNG schema generated from the sample file.

You can use Trang to generate an XML Schema in exactly the same way, by giving the output file name the extension .xsd, for example:

```
java -jar trang.jar rss2sample.xml rss2.xsd
```

How It Works

The operation of Trang is well beyond the scope of this book, but essentially it operates by parsing the source data and building an object model. This internal model reflects the entities and relationships defined in Relax NG. Where conversion is required, the data is converted into an abstract language that is intermediate between Relax NG and XSD, and any necessary transformation applied before the data is serialized out. More information about Trang can be found at www.thaiopensource.com/relaxng/trang.html.

An Object-Oriented Model: XML to Java

There will be plenty of coverage of representing syndication data in object-oriented (OO) systems in later chapters, but by way of introduction there's a direct line that can be following from XML modeling into OO.

The Relaxer tool (available for free at www.relaxer.org) is a Relax NG–based schema tool similar to Trang, which offers certain additional facilities. These include generation of XSLT style sheets from schemas or instance data, and the facility of interest here, autogeneration of Java classes. The basic tool is another command-line application, and it couldn't be much easier to use. Once downloaded and installed, copy the rss2sample.xml file into the relaxer/bin directory. Then open a command window and type:

```
relaxer rss2sample.xml
```

If you look at the contents of the directory you will see the following files:

- ❑   Channel.java
- ❑   Item.java
- ❑   Rss.java
- ❑   RStack.java
- ❑   UJAXP.java
- ❑   URelaxer.java

These files represent a (Java language) object-oriented model of an RSS feed. The last three files are used internally by the first three and can generally be ignored. Figure 20-9 illustrates the object-oriented model.

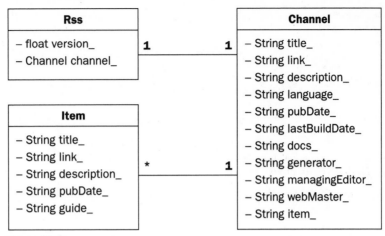

Figure 20-9

The fields shown here are the private member variables. These are all exposed through get or set methods such as setTitle(String title), or other accessors appropriate to the data type, for example Channel has an addItem(Item item) method.

Once generated, it's very simple to use the classes. For example, the following code will generate a fairly minimal RSS file:

```java
import java.text.SimpleDateFormat;
import java.util.Date;

/*
 * Creating a feed using Relaxer-generated RSS 2.0 classes
 */
public class Rss2Create {

    public static final SimpleDateFormat RFC822 =
        new SimpleDateFormat("EEE, d MMM yyyy HH:mm:ss z");

  public static void main(String[] args) {
    try {
      Rss rss = new Rss();
      rss.setVersion(2.0F);

      Channel channel = new Channel();
      channel.setTitle("A Demo Channel");
      rss.setChannel(channel);


      Item item = new Item();
      item.setTitle("One Item");

      String date = RFC822.format(new Date());
```

```
        item.setPubDate(date);
        channel.addItem(item);

        System.out.println(rss.makeTextDocument());
      } catch (Exception e) {
        e.printStackTrace();
      }


    }
  }
```

Try It Out   Creating a Feed

Assuming you have already downloaded Relaxer and run it on `rss2sample.xml`, the following steps
will generate some RSS:

1. Enter (or download) the previous code, saving it as `Rss2Create.java` in the same folder as the
Relaxer-generated files.

2. Open a command window in that folder and type the following:

```
javac -classpath . Rss2Create.java
```

This will compile `Rss2Create` along with the Relaxer-generated classes.

3. Now type the following:

```
java -classpath . Rss2Create
```

This will run the mini-application, and you should see something like this:

```
C:\relaxer\bin>java -classpath . Rss2Create
<rss version="2.0"><channel><title>A Demo Channel</title><link></link><descripti
on></description><language></language><pubDate></pubDate><lastBuildDate></lastBu
ildDate><docs></docs><generator></generator><managingEditor></managingEditor><we
bMaster></webMaster><item><title>One Item</title><link></link><description></des
cription><pubDate>Wed, 4 Aug 2004 12:13:00 CEST</pubDate><guid></guid></item></c
hannel></rss>
```

Reformatted, this is the same as:

```
<rss version="2.0">
  <channel>
    <title>A Demo Channel</title>
    <link/>
    <description/>
    <language/>
    <pubDate/>
    <lastBuildDate/>
    <docs/>
    <generator/>
    <managingEditor/>
    <webMaster/>
    <item>
      <title>One Item</title>
      <link/>
```

```
            <description/>
            <pubDate>Wed, 4 Aug 2004 12:13:00 CEST</pubDate>
            <guid/>
        </item>
    </channel>
</rss>
```

There are a lot of empty elements, but you can see you have the makings of a reasonable feed.

How It Works

The way Relaxer works internally is well beyond the scope of this book (it's quite well documented with the download, if you're interested) but the use of the files it generated is somewhat easier to explain. Essentially, a class has been generated for each of the higher-level elements found in the sample feed: Rss, Channel, Item. Each of these classes has been provided with appropriate get and set methods corresponding to each kind of material the XML elements can contain. To create a feed using these classes is as easy as can be, as you can see from the code example here. The code actually starts by setting up a date class to match the RSS 2.0 formatting:

```java
import java.text.SimpleDateFormat;
import java.util.Date;

public class Rss2Create {

    public static final SimpleDateFormat RFC822 =
        new SimpleDateFormat("EEE, d MMM yyyy HH:mm:ss z");
```

The code that will run is contained in this class's main method. It begins by creating a new instance of the Rss class. The version is set to 2.0 by a call to a method in that class which has been auto-generated by Relaxer:

```java
public static void main(String[] args) {
    try {
        Rss rss = new Rss();
        rss.setVersion(2.0F);
```

Every RSS 2.0 feed must have a channel element, and that's easy to provide here by creating a Channel object. Before assigning the channel to the Rss, its title is set:

```java
Channel channel = new Channel();
channel.setTitle("A Demo Channel");
rss.setChannel(channel);
```

The interesting parts of a feed are its items, and objects that model these can be created using the Item class. In this example, a single item is created and the value of a couple of its contained elements are set before the item is added to the channel:

```java
Item item = new Item();
item.setTitle("One Item");

String date = RFC822.format(new Date());
item.setPubDate(date);
channel.addItem(item);
```

Finally, for demonstration purposes a text representation of the feed is generated and printed to the console. In practice this would usually be passed over a HTTP connection. The Rss class has a convenience method for getting the text, makeTextDocument:

```
        System.out.println(rss.makeTextDocument());
    } catch (Exception e) {
        e.printStackTrace();
    }


    }
}
```

Reading a Feed

Reading a feed using the Relaxer-generated classes is no less straightforward. The following code is a little command-line application that will take a feed file name as an argument then print the title of the feed followed by the title of any items found in that feed:

```
/*
 * RSS 2.0 Feed Title Reader
 * uses Relaxer-generated classes
 */

public class Rss2Read {

    public static void main(String[] args) {

        try {
            Rss rss = new Rss(args[0]);
            Channel channel = rss.getChannel();
            String title = channel.getTitle();
            System.out.println(title);

            Item[] items = channel.getItem();

            for(int i=0;i<items.length;i++){
                title = items[i].getTitle();
                System.out.println(title);
            }
        } catch (Exception e) {
            e.printStackTrace();
        }
    }
}
```

Try It Out   A Demo Channel

1. Enter (or download) the previous code, saving it as Rss2Read.java in the same folder as the Relaxer-generated files.

2. Open a command window in that folder and type the following:

```
java -classpath . Rss2Create > test.xml
```

This will pass the feed data generated by `Rss2Create` into a file.

3. Now type the following:

```
javac -classpath . Rss2Read.java
```

This will compile the RSS file reading class along with the Relaxer-generated classes.

4. Now run this:

```
java -classpath . Rss2Read test.xml
```

In the console you should now see the following:

```
C:\relaxer\bin>java -classpath . Rss2Read test.xml
A Demo Channel
One Item
```

How It Works

Like `Rss2Create.java`, all the operating code is contained in the `main` method. It begins like this:

```
public class Rss2Read {

    public static void main(String[] args) {

        try {
```

Errors might occur while reading from file so the entire code is contained in a `try...catch` block. The first argument from the command line (`args[0]`) is used in the creation of an `Rss` class. This constructor, in the Relaxer-generated class, looks after reading the RSS data in from file and building an `Rss` object from it. Once created, the channel can be accessed from the `Rss` object, and from the channel its title can be read:

```
Rss rss = new Rss(args[0]);
Channel channel = rss.getChannel();
String title = channel.getTitle();
System.out.println(title);
```

The items contained in the data loaded from file can be accessed using the `getItem` method. This returns an array of the individual items. Here each item in the array is accessed in turn and its title obtained. The title string is then printed to the console:

```
Item[] items = channel.getItem();

for(int i=0;i<items.length;i++){
    title = items[i].getTitle();
    System.out.println(title);
}
```

The code finishes by closing the `try...catch` block and the brackets from the `main` method and `Rss2Read` class:

```
    } catch (Exception e) {
        e.printStackTrace();
    }
  }
}
```

Problems of Autogeneration

Clearly the Relaxer-generated classes can provide useful code. However, a recurring theme in syndication is that data, especially in the wild of the Web, doesn't conform to a single, simple model. If you want a quick way of generating RSS 2.0 feeds, Relaxer can do a lot of the work for you. But outside of a very controlled environment the reader wouldn't be much use due to variation in the RSS/Atom version (and quality) of feeds.

The same technique could be used to create RSS 1.0–generating code, though the handling of items would need care to ensure the individual items in the feed were consistent with there declaration in the channel's Seq element. Similarly, Atom classes could be automatically generated, although care would be needed to ensure that all the mandatory elements appear in their correct forms in the feed.

Certainly a multiformat toolkit could be built up by joining together individual auto-generated classes. However, there is a good case to be made for sharing common modeling classes for all formats, and separating this from classes that look after reading (parsing) and writing (serializing) the data.

Another possibility is to select a single object-oriented model, such as that of RSS 2.0 as demonstrated previously, but apply XSLT to the XML syntax it generates, to transform it to and from the other formats.

The RDF Models

Models are very important in RDF, to the extent that a set of RDF data is often described as a model. This can be rather confusing, especially since some of RDF's formal specifications are defined using a branch of logic called model theory. However, generally the basic idea of a model as "an abstraction that demonstrates how the parts of a system fit together" holds wherever the word crops up.

RDF can be seen in terms of two complementary abstractions. The first of these considers the information as a number of statements of the form subject-property-object. The subject of these statements is a resource, and from this perspective each statement can be looked at as an individual fact about a resource. The properties are defined in such a way as to enable logically complex pieces of information to be expressed while still allowing manipulation of the data at the level of subject-property-object triples. The other model is that of the node and arc graph. In this model resources are nodes and the properties appear as arcs in the graph.

The same information can be seen from either viewpoint, as a series of statements or as a graph. What's notable in the context of syndication is that either way the model is abstract, and XML data found in a feed is a representation of data in the model. The model itself isn't tied to any single representation and can be represented in other formats.

There Is No Syntax!

One source of confusion among XML developers when they first encounter RDF/XML is that the same pieces of information can be represented in very different ways. Take for example the following snippet of RDF/XML:

```
<item rdf:about="http://example.org/here">
  <title>The Title</title>
</item>
```

The same information could be expressed as follows:

```
<rdf:Description rdf:about="http://example.org/here">
    <rdf:type rdf:resource="http://purl.org/rss/1.0/item" />
    <rss:title>The Title</rss:title>
</rdf:Description>
```

This isn't RSS 1.0, as there are restrictions on that syntax, but like the RSS version it is valid RDF/XML, and the interpretation of RSS comes through RDF/XML. The two different versions meaning the same thing only really make sense when you approach RDF/XML from the point of view of the RDF model. Both of the previous snippets are XML serializations of a graph structure that looks like Figure 20-10.

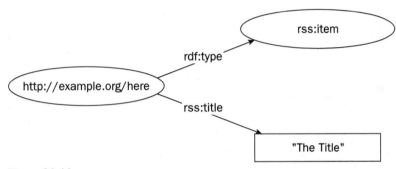

Figure 20-10

You can express this information in a form that can be serialized by treating each relationship as a three-part statement, the legendary RDF triple:

```
subject --property--> object
```

So you can break down the graph into individual statements like this:

```
http://example.org --rdf:type--> rss:item
http://example.org --rss:title--> "The Title"
```

When it comes to expressing this in XML you can do it directly, at the expense of a lot of verbosity:

```
<rdf:Description rdf:about="http://example.org/here">
    <rdf:type rdf:resource="http://purl.org/rss/1.0/item" />
</rdf:Description>

<rdf:Description rdf:about="http://example.org/here">
    <rss:title>The Title</rss:title>
</rdf:Description>
```

This is very similar to the previous version that uses `rdf:Description` as a placeholder element for the object of the triples, except in that version, the same `rdf:Description` is reused. Where the resource being described has a known type, RDF/XML provides another form of syntax that is convenient for a lot of data. The `rdf:Description` placeholder is replaced by the type of the resource being described, so in the first example `rss:item` is used instead of `rdf:Description` (the `rss:` prefix can be dropped when RSS is specified as the default namespace).

1. Open your Web browser at the W3C RDF Validator: `http://www.w3.org/RDF/Validator`.

2. Type the following into the edit box:

```
<rdf:RDF xmlns:rss="http://purl.org/rss/1.0/"
        xmlns:rdf="http://www.w3.org/1999/02/22-rdf-syntax-ns#">

  <rss:item rdf:about="http://example.org/here" rss:title="The Title" />

</rdf:RDF>
```

3. Under Display Result Options, select Triples and Graph.

4. Click the Parse RDF button.

The results page should look similar to Figure 20-11.

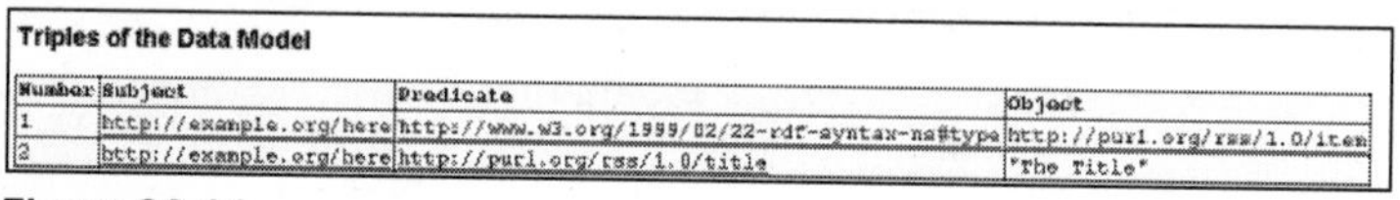

Triples of the Data Model

Number	Subject	Predicate	Object
1	http://example.org/here	http://www.w3.org/1999/02/22-rdf-syntax-ns#type	http://purl.org/rss/1.0/item
2	http://example.org/here	http://purl.org/rss/1.0/title	"The Title"

Figure 20-11

How It Works

As you may have guessed, the XML listing is simply one more possible way of expressing those two statements in RDF/XML. If you take the earlier examples and surround them with the `<rdf:RDF>` tags and namespace declarations you will find that they all mean the same thing.

Once more this chapter has drifted a little away from modeling as such, but there's a good reason for that. Because RSS 1.0 is defined as RDF/XML, it inherits the modeling language of RDF. That is to say, RSS 1.0 has a well-defined data model in RDF through which the entities and relationships found in a feed are expressed. A part of this model is inherent in the RDF/XML syntax, it unambiguously states some of the basic information: what is an entity, what is its type, what are the relationships. The type (class) and relationship names are all given as URIs using XML namespaces, so for example the `<title>` element found in an RSS 1.0 feed is actually the property with the URI `http://purl.org/rss/1.0/title`.

Most RDF vocabularies, RSS 1.0 included, are defined as more than just named classes and properties. This extra information pertaining to the model is provided in another set of RDF statements, usually available in an RDF/XML document on the Web at or near the namespace URI. This describes the classes and properties of a specific vocabulary generally using terms from another vocabulary, that of the RDF Schema.

RSS 1.0 RDF Schema

Schemas in RDF have a slightly different meaning and intention than those of XML. XML Schemas describe the way things should appear in the code, what can go where, and some more meaningful items such as the kind of data (type) that can appear. RDF Schemas on the other hand provide a way of talking about RDF data, by defining vocabularies. Where an XML Schema might say "book elements contain author elements which each contain a person element," an RDF Schema might say "an author of a book is a person."

The way the RDF Schema works for this particular example is by defining classes of things called book and person, and stating that there was a property of book called author, the value of which was fulfilled by members of the class person. In other words, in your instance data you would find triples with a subject of type book (it might be the URI of a best seller), property author and object person (which would somehow identify the person involved).

Turning to the RDF Schema for RSS 1.0, you will see that this is less complicated than it sounds. The schema is expressed in regular XML, though the root element <rdf:RDF> makes clear that this is an RDF document, and should be interpreted using the rules of RDF/XML. Two kinds of resources are described within the schema, classes and properties. The classes are channel, item, image, and textinput and the properties items, title, description, url, and name. You will see how each of these is defined in a moment, but here first is the schema in full:

```
<?xml version="1.0"?>
<!-- reformatted version of http://purl.org/rss/1.0/ -->

<rdf:RDF
    xmlns:rdf="http://www.w3.org/1999/02/22-rdf-syntax-ns#"
    xmlns:rdfs="http://www.w3.org/2000/01/rdf-schema#">

  <rdfs:Class rdf:about="http://purl.org/rss/1.0/channel">
    <rdfs:comment>An RSS information channel.</rdfs:comment>
    <rdfs:label>Channel</rdfs:label>
    <rdfs:isDefinedBy rdf:resource="http://purl.org/rss/1.0/"/>
  </rdfs:Class>

  <rdfs:Class rdf:about="http://purl.org/rss/1.0/item">
    <rdfs:comment>An RSS item.</rdfs:comment>
    <rdfs:label>Item</rdfs:label>
    <rdfs:isDefinedBy rdf:resource="http://purl.org/rss/1.0/"/>
  </rdfs:Class>

  <rdfs:Class rdf:about="http://purl.org/rss/1.0/image">
    <rdfs:comment>An RSS image.</rdfs:comment>
    <rdfs:label>Image</rdfs:label>
    <rdfs:isDefinedBy rdf:resource="http://purl.org/rss/1.0/"/>
  </rdfs:Class>

  <rdfs:Class rdf:about="http://purl.org/rss/1.0/textinput">
    <rdfs:comment>An RSS text input.</rdfs:comment>
    <rdfs:label>Text Input</rdfs:label>
    <rdfs:isDefinedBy rdf:resource="http://purl.org/rss/1.0/"/>
  </rdfs:Class>

  <rdf:Property rdf:about="http://purl.org/rss/1.0/items">
    <rdfs:comment>Points to a list of rss:item elements that are members
        of the subject channel.
    </rdfs:comment>
    <rdfs:label>Items</rdfs:label>
    <rdfs:isDefinedBy rdf:resource="http://purl.org/rss/1.0/"/>
  </rdf:Property>

  <rdf:Property rdf:about="http://purl.org/rss/1.0/title">
    <rdfs:subPropertyOf
```

```
            rdf:resource="http://purl.org/dc/elements/1.1/title"/>
        <rdfs:comment>A descriptive title for the channel.</rdfs:comment>
        <rdfs:label>Title</rdfs:label>
        <rdfs:isDefinedBy rdf:resource="http://purl.org/rss/1.0/"/>
    </rdf:Property>


    <rdf:Property rdf:about="http://purl.org/rss/1.0/description">
        <rdfs:subPropertyOf
            rdf:resource="http://purl.org/dc/elements/1.1/description"/>
        <rdfs:comment>A short text description of the subject.</rdfs:comment>
        <rdfs:label>Description</rdfs:label>
        <rdfs:isDefinedBy rdf:resource="http://purl.org/rss/1.0/"/>
    </rdf:Property>

    <rdf:Property rdf:about="http://purl.org/rss/1.0/link">
        <rdfs:subPropertyOf
            rdf:resource="http://purl.org/dc/elements/1.1/identifier"/>
        <rdfs:comment>The URL to which an HTML rendering of the subject
            will link.</rdfs:comment>
        <rdfs:label>Link</rdfs:label>
        <rdfs:isDefinedBy rdf:resource="http://purl.org/rss/1.0/"/>
    </rdf:Property>

    <rdf:Property rdf:about="http://purl.org/rss/1.0/url">
        <rdfs:subPropertyOf
            rdf:resource="http://purl.org/dc/elements/1.1/identifier"/>
        <rdfs:comment>The URL of the image to used in the 'src' attribute
            of the channel's image tag when rendered as HTML.
        </rdfs:comment>
        <rdfs:label>URL</rdfs:label>
        <rdfs:isDefinedBy rdf:resource="http://purl.org/rss/1.0/"/>
    </rdf:Property>

    <rdf:Property rdf:about="http://purl.org/rss/1.0/name">
        <rdfs:comment>The text input field's (variable) name.</rdfs:comment>
        <rdfs:label>Name</rdfs:label>
        <rdfs:isDefinedBy rdf:resource="http://purl.org/rss/1.0/"/>
    </rdf:Property>

</rdf:RDF>
```

The schema begins like most other XML documents by saying that it is XML:

```
<?xml version="1.0"?>
<!-- reformatted version of http://purl.org/rss/1.0/ -->
```

Next it makes it clear that it is specifically RDF/XML. Also in this root element the two key namespaces are declared, those of RDF and RDF Schema:

```
<rdf:RDF
    xmlns:rdf="http://www.w3.org/1999/02/22-rdf-syntax-ns#"
    xmlns:rdfs="http://www.w3.org/2000/01/rdf-schema#">
```

The outer <rdf:RDF> element is no longer a requirement of all RDF/XML documents, it is still common practice, and still a requirement of RSS 1.0. Even without <rdf:RDF>, you can expect to see at least a namespace declaration for the rdf: prefix, if not a considerable number of others. Typical of RDF Schemas, that of RSS is mostly comprised of class and property definitions. The pattern for each is essentially the same, you have a statement that the identified resource is a class (or property) and then a few pieces of extra information about that class (or property). The following is the first definition in the schema:

```
<rdfs:Class rdf:about="http://purl.org/rss/1.0/channel">
   <rdfs:comment>An RSS information channel.</rdfs:comment>
   <rdfs:label>Channel</rdfs:label>
   <rdfs:isDefinedBy rdf:resource="http://purl.org/rss/1.0/"/>
</rdfs:Class>
```

The first line says that http://purl.org/rss/1.0/channel is an rdfs:Class. This means that other resources (such as your RSS feed) can be members of this class, or, in other words, have the type rss:channel. The rdfs:comment and rdfs:label elements correspond to properties of the class, provided as human-readable description. The rdfs:isDefinedBy property points to the URI of the resource that defines this class, which in this case is the specification document:

```
<rdf:Property rdf:about="http://purl.org/rss/1.0/title">
   <rdfs:subPropertyOf
       rdf:resource="http://purl.org/dc/elements/1.1/title"/>
   <rdfs:comment>A descriptive title for the channel.</rdfs:comment>
   <rdfs:label>Title</rdfs:label>
   <rdfs:isDefinedBy rdf:resource="http://purl.org/rss/1.0/"/>
</rdf:Property>
```

The RSS 1.0 property definitions, in this example rss:title, are very similar to those of the classes. Several of the classes, however, do include an additional rdfs:subPropertyOf element, which itself corresponds to a property. The rdfs:subPropertyOf (and rdfs:subClassOf) properties can be very useful to RDF tools which support basic inference. Here the schema is saying that title as used by RSS has all the characteristics of Dublin Core's title property. So a system designed to be able to handle dc:title, displaying, for example, its value as a heading, once provided with this RDF Schema also knows something about how to handle values of rss:title — they can be displayed as headings too. The inheritance system of classes and properties in RDF Schemas isn't the same as object-oriented subclassing, though they do have a lot in common. Hierarchies can be built up, and the classes (or properties) at the bottom of the tree will be more specialized than those at the top. But this isn't the only kind of structure available, and subclass/subproperty relationships aren't constrained in quite the same way as in object-oriented (OO) programming. For example, every class is an rdfs:subClassOf itself, and it's perfectly reasonable to have a pair of classes being rdfs:subClassOf each other, the relationship going both ways. It can get confusing at times, and when it does it's usually helpful to completely forget about OO inheritance.

It would have been possible to define further aspects of the RSS vocabulary, in particular what types of resources can be the subject and object of a property (the sets of these types are known as the domain and range respectively). Presumably in the interests of keeping it brief, a lot of details like this were only expressed in the prose of the specification.

The RDF Schema then covers the basic terms used in RSS, which correspond to elements in the RDF/XML format. One of the major advantages RSS 1.0 has over the other formats is that different RDF vocabularies can be used meaningfully together with parts of RSS 1.0. This is demonstrated within RSS 1.0 itself by the use of Dublin Core terms. Here's a simple example:

```
<rdf:RDF
  xmlns:rdf="http://www.w3.org/1999/02/22-rdf-syntax-ns#"
  xmlns:dc="http://purl.org/dc/elements/1.1/"
  xmlns="http://purl.org/rss/1.0/"
>

<channel rdf:about="http://p2p.wrox.com/blogs_rss.asp?AUTHOR_ID=16108">
    <dc:publisher>Wrox</dc:publisher>
</channel>
```

This statement provides the name of the publisher of an RSS feed using the publisher property from the Dublin Core vocabulary, which is identified using XML namespaces as:

```
http://purl.org/dc/elements/1.1/publisher
```

It gets a lot more interesting for syndication purposes when you realize that other rich vocabularies are available, and that you can even write your own.

Groups of Feeds in RDF

An example of the blogroll format used by Planet RDF follows. The first thing you'll probably notice is its apparent complexity.

> *RDF/XML is notoriously hard on the eyes. You can find some historic notes on why it is the way it is at* www.w3.org/2001/sw/Europe/200407/swintro/syntaxdesign.html.

The extensive use of namespaces and URIs does make it quite hard to read. The RDF and RDFS vocabularies (rdf:nodeID, rdfs:seeAlso, and so on) are used for core terms and FOAF (Friend-of-a-Friend) is used for describing characteristics of the people involved (for example, foaf:weblog). The RSS vocabulary is used to point to each blog's RSS feed (rss:channel) and Dublin Core is used to give the title (dc:title) of the Weblog document. This example describes two blogs: one Journalblog and one named SchemaWeb. After the initial namespace declarations, you can see there are two blocks in the code.

```
<?xml version="1.0" encoding="UTF-8"?>

<rdf:RDF xmlns:rdf="http://www.w3.org/1999/02/22-rdf-syntax-ns#"
         xmlns:foaf="http://xmlns.com/foaf/0.1/"
         xmlns:rdfs="http://www.w3.org/2000/01/rdf-schema#"
         xmlns:rss="http://purl.org/rss/1.0/"
         xmlns:dc="http://purl.org/dc/elements/1.1/">

<foaf:Agent rdf:nodeID="id2246400">
    <foaf:name>Dave Beckett</foaf:name>
    <foaf:weblog>
        <foaf:Document rdf:about="http://journal.dajobe.org/journal/">
          <dc:title>Journalblog by Dave Beckett</dc:title>
          <rdfs:seeAlso>
            <rss:channel
        rdf:about="http://journal.dajobe.org/journal/comments.rdf">
                <foaf:maker rdf:nodeID="id2246400"/>
            </rss:channel>
```

```
            </rdfs:seeAlso>
            <foaf:interest rdf:resource="http://www.w3.org/2001/sw/"/>
            <foaf:interest rdf:resource="http://www.w3.org/RDF/"/>
          </foaf:Document>
      </foaf:weblog>
  </foaf:Agent>

  <foaf:Agent rdf:nodeID="id2245412">
      <foaf:name>SchemaWeb</foaf:name>
      <foaf:weblog>
          <foaf:Document rdf:about="http://www.schemaweb.info/">
            <dc:title>SchemaWeb</dc:title>
            <rdfs:seeAlso>
              <rss:channel
        rdf:about="http://www.schemaweb.info/blogrss.aspx?blogid=2">
                <foaf:maker rdf:nodeID="id2245412"/>
              </rss:channel>
            </rdfs:seeAlso>
            <foaf:interest rdf:resource="http://www.w3.org/2001/sw/"/>
            <foaf:interest rdf:resource="http://www.w3.org/RDF/"/>
          </foaf:Document>
      </foaf:weblog>
  </foaf:Agent>

</rdf:RDF>
```

Another contributory factor in this data's apparent complexity is that it does actually contain quite a lot of information. Part of the information about the first blog is laid out in Figure 20-12.

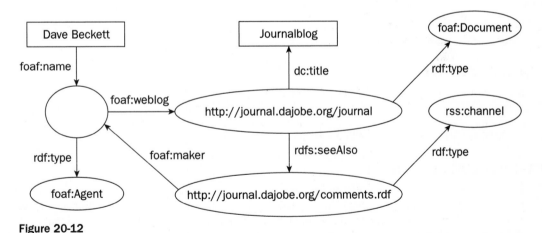

Figure 20-12

There are two primary entities here, the agent behind the blog and the blog itself. In this case the agent happens to be a person—it could have been an organization or anything else "that does stuff." The agent entity is modeled by the blank node on the left. Rather than having a URI, the agent has associated properties: the foaf:name provides a human-readable identifier, and the fact that this is an agent is expressed by the rdf:type foaf:Agent arrow. The other property associated with this agent is foaf:weblog, the value of which is the resource identified as http://journal.dajobe.org/journal. This is the blog in question, which is described as being a `foaf:Document`. It too has a human-readable name (`Journalblog`). However, where `foaf:name` is generally used to name people, `dc:title` is more appropriate for documents.

In Chapter 21, we continue our discussion of RDF and look at how RDF data can be stored.

A Relational Model

So far we've looked at modeling feed data through XML, object-oriented and RDF spectacles. This section looks at the data in terms of the relational model. Or to be more accurate, how feed data can be managed in a SQL (Structured Query Language) database. The true relational model is a formally defined mathematical system based on set theory originally proposed by E.F. Codd in 1970. SQL is a declarative language that can be used to manipulate data maintained in a relational form. Today's relational database management systems (RDBMSs) are usually a step or two removed from the original theory, with lots of convenience features bolted on. In practice developers usually deal with a system geared around the application of SQL queries to tables of data records. RDBMSs offer a fast and efficient way of storing data, a facility that has several uses within syndication.

Syndication Applications of Databases

A database is essentially a way of persisting data so that it can be managed easily. There are other kinds of databases than SQL ones, but their use in syndication is generally for one of the following purposes:

❑   Content storage

❑   Metadata management

❑   User tracking

❑   Indexing and search

Content Storage

Most producers of syndication feeds are content management systems of one form or another. The author will create articles or posts, the CMS will usually publish them on the Web in HTML and RSS/Atom form. Although it is not uncommon to use simple file system storage for articles and posts, an RDBMS back end is often used for storage of content data.

Metadata Management

To be able to do useful things with the data, it's essential to know something about the data, even if only the data type, string, date, or whatever. Syndicated data is very much associated with metadata, to the extent that often only a small part of feed data is the content, the rest is information *about* that content. When you start looking at tools like aggregators where many feeds need to be managed, the descriptive metadata becomes even more important. Metadata describes data and relationships between pieces of data. It is also data itself. Relational and other databases offer a systematic approach to managing the data and relationships.

User Tracking

For many applications it's desirable to keep track of the people involved. Typically, a blogging site may allow a certain list of people to post. In addition to looking after permissions and authentication through passwords for these first-class authors, it may also be desirable to record the authors of comments and even details of people behind material derived from other syndicated sources so that appropriate provenance information can be provided. For all these aspects, a database is a useful tool.

Query and Search

A search facility is one of the first requirements of any content management system. This crosses over somewhat into general data managements, where queries may be made at a metadata level, for example, showing all posts on a particular day. At a more granular level it's usually desirable to be able to find posts according to their textual content using keywords. These kinds of facilities depend on efficient storage and indexing, and databases are designed to provide exactly that kind of functionality.

Requirements for Storing Feed Data

A relational database may be used for management of content from which RSS/Atom feeds can be generated, and you'll be seeing this in action in later chapters. But in this chapter the focus is on modeling feed data, and a practical application of a database from this point of view would be in an aggregator. The structure of the database will be derived by the data model, determined is such a way as to take maximum advantage of the database's facilities. The scenario here is that the feeds and individual items have already been created, the job of the database is to store and manage these. This does introduce one or two requirements not found in a system dedicated to feed publishing, for example, to keep track of the items the user has read. However, most requirements will be common to both producer and consumer.

Storing Items

The most basic requirement is to store the information contained in items gathered from feeds. This is a combination of individually typed metadata properties and blocks of content, which is in text/XML form.

Feed Lists and State Management

As well as the individual items there will need to be a list of source feed addresses and metadata about those feeds, such as the site title. There is also a need to keep track of the state of the system, and it is appropriate to consider this alongside the feed lists as this information will generally apply at this level of granularity. The kind of items that need to be recorded are the times at which the feed data was last obtained and any problems encountered, for example, if the feed was unavailable when its address was last visited.

The Relational Model, Condensed

If you're reading this book then chances are you've encountered SQL databases before. The general idea is that the data is stored in rows or records in a number of tables. The columns of the tables correspond to different parts, or fields of the records. But before moving on with a practical viewpoint, it would be remiss not to mention the true model underlying relational databases, particularly as misconceptions are common.

Relations and Tables

A relation is a kind of connector between two (or more) objects, for example in arithmetic you might say 5 < 6. Clearly this relation doesn't only apply to the numbers 5 and 6; there is a huge set of values that could go in each position. The relation here, <, applies to two sets of values (sometimes known as domains) and is an example of a binary relation. The binary relation is used in RDF as properties relating one resource to another or to a literal value. The binary relation can also be expressed as an ordered pair of values $R(x, y)$. In the arithmetic example R would be the relationship "is less than" (the RDF triple is just a slight rearrangement: $x \, R \, y$).

But relations can be extended beyond pairs of values, so you might have R(w, x, y, z). For example, the first domain might be the set of human first names, the second domain the set of human surnames, the third possible ages (0...120?), and the fourth the set of genders (male, female). Values that fulfill this relation might be (John, Smith, 25, male). By fulfilling the relation we are stating that this ordered list (a tuple) of values exists, or is logically true. In this form, the order of the values is important, but the relational database modifies this to give each domain a label. This takes us to a view something like the following table.

Forename	Surname	Age	Gender
John	Smith	25	Male

It's easy enough to imagine filling a table like this with values from say, your address book. The table contains all values for which the relation holds in a given scope. To use a little logic jargon, the *intension* of the table is the relation, the *extension* is all the records (tuples or rows) over which the relation holds.

Before returning to more practical matters, it's worth noting that a table (or relation) like this is usually given a name, so one table (or relation) can be distinguished from another. Viewed directly in the relational database model, RDF statements look something like this:

subject	object
`http://p2p.wrox.com/blogs.rss`	"Wrox"

The representation of RDF (and hence RSS 1.0) in a relational database is discussed further in Chapter 21. But where the RDF model isn't required, it's convenient to make use of the multicolumn capability of relational databases.

Systems using relational databases generally follow the closed world assumption: all that cannot be proven true is considered false. Translated into practice this means that any piece of information that isn't in a table, or can be derived from the contents of the tables doesn't exist. On the other hand the RDF model follows the open world assumption, where anything that can't be proven is treated as unknown. This makes pragmatic sense in an environment like the Web where it's unfeasible to access every piece of data (and philosophical sense in that network is unlikely to know everything).

Tables, Take Two

Figure 20-13 shows a minimal representation of some RSS 2.0–style feed data in a table.

item #	title	guid	pub_date	description
1	My first post	http://example.org/blog/1	Thu, 01 Jul 2004	Woke up this morning feeling fine...
2	My secret post	http://example.org/blog/2	Fri, 02 Jul 2004	I've got something special on my mind...
...	...	...	...	...

Figure 20-13

There are two items, and as well as numbering the items the table contains four of the most important pieces of information about them. In database parlance the items here are records, and the column headers are the fields. Each of the records is actually a tuple, or set of values. The first value in the tuple is the number of the item, the second is its title, and so on. The order of the columns doesn't actually matter, the values in each column are associated with the name of the column (or attribute of the tuple, to be mathematical). The table is a set of tuples, and a set of tuples is also known as a relation, hence the name *relational* databases. A common misconception is that the name comes from the way relationships between tables are expressed in databases; this isn't the case, however, those relationships are a vital part of the utility of databases.

In a SQL database there is another important feature of the fields (columns): Each has a predefined datatype. It depends considerably on which particular database implementation you use, but the data you are likely to find in feeds can be expressed using two types that are found in practically all SQL databases: INTEGER for identification numbers, BOOL for boolean true/false values and TEXT for everything else. The layout of the tables and the types of each field can be expressed as a schema, and probably the clearest way of expressing this is in tabular form. Examining the table containing items you can see that the table structure, including datatypes, could be specified as Figure 20-14.

Name	Type
Item #	INTEGER
title	TEXT
guid	TEXT
pub_date	TEXT
description	TEXT

Figure 20-14

Please remember that the schemas described here (and practically all the code descriptions) are provided as examples. They demonstrate just one way of doing things. In practice your own schemas (and code) may vary widely from these examples depending on your own specific requirements and the tools you are using. The only fixed points in all this are the specifications (RSS, Atom, HTTP, XML, RDF). Whatever you are building, be sure to keep an eye on the specifications, one eye on each of them if you have enough eyes.

Tables, Take Three

The requirements for storing feed data in a database go a little beyond that contained in the simple table shown previously. As well as the items, it will be necessary to store information about the feeds and possibly the state management details (when a feed was last downloaded, and so on) as well. Going back to what we mentioned earlier in the chapter, a fairly general way of constructing data models is by identifying the entities and relationships. This applies quite comfortably to figuring out database construction as well. The main entities of interest each get a table of their own, and the relationships between them are generally expressed using *keys*. Figure 20-15 shows a graphical schema of two tables designed to accommodate feed and item data, designed for use in an aggregator.

Feeds			Items		
Name	*Type*		*Name*	*Type*	
id	INTEGER		id	INTEGER	
editor	TEXT		feed_id	INTEGER	
url	TEXT		author	TEXT	
title	TEXT		guid	TEXT	
description	TEXT		title	TEXT	
pub_date	TEXT		description	TEXT	
last_download_date	TEXT		pub_date	TEXT	
status	TEXT		item_read	BOOL	

Figure 20-15

On the right you can see the details are very like those of the first take. The item # field used before has been replaced by one called id, and several new fields have been introduced. The table on the left includes the most important pieces of information about a feed, including its state. Here is a list of what the fields of the Feeds table represent:

❑   id: An identification number for the feed

❑   editor: The managing editor of the feed, as described in RSS 2.0

❑   url: The URI which was used to download the feed

❑   title: The title of the feed

❑   description: The description of the feed

❑   pub_date: The publication date of the feed

❑   last_download_date: When the feed was last read into the database

❑   status: The HTTP status of the last download (for example, 200 OK)

Here is a list of what the fields of the Items table represent:

❑   id: An identification number for the item

❑   feed_id: The identification number of the feed from which this item came

❑   author: E-mail address of the author of the item

❑   guid: Globally unique identifier of the item

❑   title: Title of the item

❑   description: Description or content of the item

❑   pub_date: Publication date

❑   item_read: Whether or not the user has read the item

The purpose of these fields should be clear, most of them are derived directly from the RSS 2.0 specification. However, the id fields are artifacts of the database, and have special significance. Note that both tables contain an id field — there is no connection between these except that they are used for the purpose of identifying individual records. It's possible to distinguish between the two using *table.field* notation, so Feeds.id is not the same thing as Items.id.

Keys

The Feeds table has an INTEGER field called id (Feeds.id) and the Items table has an INTEGER field called feed_id (Items.feed_id). This makes it possible to cross-reference between the two tables, so if you wanted to get all items that have been published in a particular feed you could look up the value of id in the Feeds table for that feed, then select all the records in the Items table that have that value for their feed_id.

The database will be storing a long list of records relating to feeds table and potentially a very long list of records relating to items in that table. At first sight all the feeds and items should already each have their own unique identifiers: url in Feeds, guid in Items. However it's possible that these may not be entirely reliable — url *should* be ok, but guid is arbitrarily generated by the producer, so duplicates might easily appear. Another factor to bear in mind is that the same item may be received more than once, through different feeds. Whether you decide to throw away duplicates or make some kind of references to them depends on your application. So it makes sense to create identifiers local to the database that you can guarantee will be unique. These are the id fields in each table. As they are unique in the table, other tables can use them as keys to obtaining the full records. In database terms these are known as *primary keys*, and by declaring this when creating the tables the uniqueness of the id can be guaranteed.

The use of an INTEGER type is convenient in most SQL databases as they can provide autonumbering, so the first item will be item 1, the second item 2 and so on. Depending on the particular database, the use of this type may also bring efficiency gains.

The feed_id field in the Items table will contain references to a key (id) in the Feeds table, and a field that makes this kind of reference is known as a *foreign key*. Although each value of id in Feeds must appear only once, the same value can appear many times in feed_id in the Items table (many items can come from the same feed). So the relationship here is one-to-many between the id in Feeds and the feed_id in Items. One of the benefits of using a SQL databases is that they can look after the data in a more reliable way than, say, saving files to the regular file system. The general idea is that of *integrity constraints*, so for the data to be valid, some conditions must be fulfilled. For example, most SQL DBs have the built-in facility to guarantee the uniqueness of keys in a field. Additionally, for the reference between Items.feed_id and Feeds.id to work, every value found in the feed_id column of Items, the same value must be found in the id column of Feeds. More sophisticated databases will be able to ensure this kind of integrity is also maintained.

Extensibility in Databases

The information that needs to be maintained in terms of items and feed lists largely corresponds with features in the core of the RSS and Atom formats. However further information may be available either through extensions to those formats or other means. If the back-end infrastructure (the database) of your application doesn't support the extension, then there's not a lot you can do with it. One option is to design the back end so that it isn't tied to any specific domain model (like syndication), as you saw earlier this is the idea behind the RSS 1.0 RDF base. If you are aiming for the simplest thing that might possibly work, you may not be interested in providing for the RDF level of extensibility. The problem then becomes a tricky question of what specifically should you support. When it comes to planning ahead, there will always be some amount of guesswork involved, but it is possible to minimize this through care in modeling.

It's the early days in the deployment of large RDF stores, but there have already been reports of signifi-cant time/effort savings over XML or traditional RDBMSs in situations where up-front schema design is costly. Data merging in particular is an area where flexibility and agility are highly desirable.

Tables, Take Four

If you look through the fields listed in the Feeds and Items tables, you will see that several of them have the same name: `Feeds.title`/`Items.title`, `Feeds.description`/`Items.description`. What's not quite so obvious is that some of the fields are describing the same *kind* of thing: `Feeds.url` and `Items.guid` are both a kind of identification string; the value of `Feeds.editor`/`Items.author` will somehow identify a person. Returning to the entity-relationship notions again, what you need to do is consider whether any of these attribute/values are significant enough to raise them up to entities in their own right. Some systems may have use for a more granular representation of `title` and `description` elements, aspects like the (human) language of each being something worth covering in more details. This would lead to an entity called something like `TextInfo`, with attributes perhaps something like `infotype` ("title" or "description"), `content` ("My First Post") and `language` ("en-us"). After you have identified the entity and its attributes, it's a fairly direct step to make a table out of it.

For demonstration purposes, we pull out the `Feeds.editor`/`Items.author` as an entity in its own right. There's pretty good justification for this, such as when RSS 2.0 uses an e-mail address in its person-identifying elements.

```
<item>
    <guid>http://example.org/item</guid>
    <author>bruce@example.com</author>
    ...
</item>
```

Whereas RSS 1.0 generally uses the person's name as a Dublin Core *creator* property:

```
<item rdf:about="http://example.org/item">
    <dc:creator>Robert Bruce<dc:creator>
    ...
</item>
```

So what's the entity to be called? `Person` seems a reasonable choice. So each `Person` entity can have an `email` attribute or a `name` attribute (and if the information is available, both). From this analysis the structure of a corresponding database table can easily be determined. The table can be called `Persons`, with TEXT fields for `email` and `name`. Though an e-mail address is usually unique, especially when taken in combination with a name, it is convenient to use a locally unique `id` field to identify the pair, and act as a key in the table.

The next step is to consider the relationships this entity is involved in. Looking at the characteristic attributes of feeds and items, there is the `editor`/`creator` of the feed and `author`/`creator` of an item (to keep things simple we'll ignore RSS 2.0's `webMaster` element, which would be another `Person`). If the details of the people involved in creating feeds and items are stored in a `Persons` table with a unique `id`, all the Feeds and Items table need is a reference to that `id`. So `Feeds.editor` in the previous version of this table will be replaced by `Feeds.editor_id`, similarly `Items.author` will be replaced by `Items.author_id`, producing a new database structure that looks like Figure 20-16.

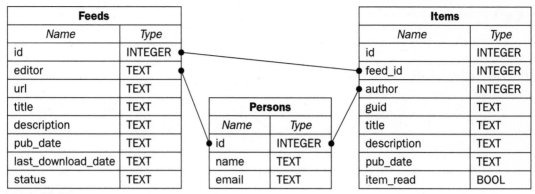

Figure 20-16

As before, the key fields are of type INTEGER. In passing it's worth mentioning another advantage of creating a separate table and using INTEGER keys like this. Say 1,000 items in the Items table have all been created by the same person. In the previous version then the name (or e-mail) of the person would have to be stored 1,000 times. That's a lot of characters even if the name is short. Using a separate table means that the full name (or e-mail) only has to be stored once, with the Items table instead holding 1,000 integer values, a low-cost data type.

Summary

In this chapter you have seen a broad view of the issues involved in data modeling within syndication:

❑ Model and syntax, the way in which feed data can be looked at from an abstract, structured point of view or as over-the-wire XML.

❑ The feed-oriented model is one possible approach; it can allow a feed to be styled for viewing in a browser. There are other advantages to treating feeds as opaque documents, but generally item-level granularity is more useful.

❑ Item-oriented modeling allows a useful abstraction, the notion of microcontent.

❑ The various feed formats have various features in common, and certain aspects, such as identification, can be problematic whatever format is used.

❑ An XML-oriented model can be used to view feed data as a tree. The XML (or Relax NG) Schema is an important part of this model.

❑ Feeds can be managed within an object-oriented model, and tools (like Relaxer) are available to autogenerate the necessary classes from XML data.

❑ RDF can be used not only to model feed data, but the way it can enable modeling of constructs (such as blogrolls) that aren't explicitly covered by the core of RSS 1.0.

❑ Practical relational database tables can be constructed to record various parts of the information needed by syndication applications.

Exercises

1. The following is an Atom 0.3 feed approximating the RSS 2.0 example:

```
<?xml version="1.0" encoding="UTF-8"?>
<?xml-stylesheet type="text/css" href="rss+atom.css"?>
<feed xmlns="http://purl.org/atom/ns#" version="0.3">
  <title>Tech Idol</title>
  <tagline>The hottest performers on the Net!</tagline>
  <link rel="alternate" type="text/html" href="http://example.org/idol/"/>
  <entry>
    <title>Shelley</title>
    <id>http://example.org/idol/shelley</id>
    <link rel="alternate" type="text/html"
            href="http://example.org/idol/shelley"/>
    <modified>2004-07-01T09:39:21Z</modified>
    <content type="text/html" mode="escaped">
            Shelley first impressed the judges with
            her 3-line backup script, then trampled the opposition
            with her cover of "These Boots Were Made for Walking".
        </content>
  </entry>
  <entry>
    <title>Sam</title>
    <id>http://example.org/idol/sam</id>
    <link rel="alternate" type="text/html" href="http://example.org/idol/sam"/>
    <modified>2004-07-01T 08:37:3Z</modified>
    <content type="text/html" mode="escaped">
            Test-driven development while plate-spinning?
            Sam's the man.
        </content>
  </entry>
  <entry>
    <title>Marc</title>
    <id>http://example.org/idol/marc</id>
    <link rel="alternate" type="text/html" href="http://example.org/idol/marc"/>
    <modified>2004-07-01T08:56:02Z</modified>
    <content type="text/html" mode="escaped">
          Marc's multimedia presentation of "O Sole Mio"
          served him well, but perhaps he should have kept those
          knees covered!
        </content>
  </entry>
</feed>
```

Modify the CSS rss.css to style this document in a similar fashion to the RSS document.

2. While discussing the RDF model, a simple node and arc diagram of a single item was shown. Later you saw a larger diagram of blogroll data. Of course it's possible to represent the data in a full RSS 1.0 feed in this fashion. Here is part of the sample feed data rewritten in RSS 1.0. See if you can sketch out the node and arc diagram for this data:

```
<rdf:RDF
    xmlns="http://purl.org/rss/1.0/"
    xmlns:rdf="http://www.w3.org/1999/02/22-rdf-syntax-ns#"
    xmlns:content="http://purl.org/rss/1.0/modules/content/">

    <channel rdf:about="http://example.org/idol.rdf">
        <title>Tech Idol</title>
        <items>
            <rdf:Seq>
                <rdf:li rdf:resource="http://example.org/idol/shelley"/>
            </rdf:Seq>
        </items>
    </channel>

    <item rdf:about="http://example.org/idol/shelley">
        <title>Shelley</title>
        <link >http://example.org/idol/shelley</link>
        <content:encoded>
                Shelley first impressed the judges with her 3-line backup script,
                then trampled the opposition with her cover of "These Boots Were
                Made for Walking".
        </content:encoded>
    </item>
</rdf:RDF>
```

Hint: The W3C's validator provides graphic views at `www.w3.org/RDF/Validator/`.

Storing Feed Data

In this chapter we extend and develop the ideas and techniques discussed regarding the modeling of feeds with an emphasis on building practical systems. In this chapter, you learn about:

❏ Simple DOM-based XML storage

❏ "Flat" relational database storage

❏ RDF-modeled data storage

There is another popular set of techniques for storing feed data based around native XML databases and the XPath standard for addressing their contents. These techniques tend to depend on the implementation details of the database being used, so coverage will be left to the practical example in Chapter 26.

The Document Object Model

In the previous chapter, we treated the modeling of a feed as a document rather dismissively. But the drawbacks we described didn't have anything to do with document modeling, but with treating the feed as an integral, fixed document. The Document Object Model (DOM) is a standard interface for working with documents that allows them to be created from or broken down into component parts. The DOM specifications can be found at www.w3.org/DOM/. DOM treats documents as tree structures comprising a root, branch, and leaf elements. DOM treats elements, attributes, and text as elements in a parent-child structure, and in a typical XML document the hierarchy is fairly clear, as you can see in Figure 21-1.

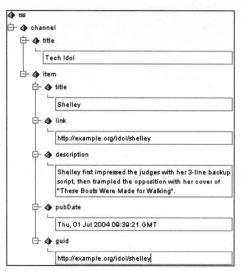

Figure 21-1

Here is part of the sample feed shown in the figure:

```
...
<rss version="2.0">
    <channel>
        <title>Tech Idol</title>
        <link>http://example.org/idol/</link>
...
    </channel>
</rss>
```

This data can be manipulated programmatically using the DOM, and it's very straightforward. In this extract, the <rss> element is the root of the tree, which is considered the only child of the document itself. <rss> has a single child, <channel>. That in turn has a set of child elements, <title>, <link> and so on. Each of these elements is considered a node, as is each block of text. There are a number of basic interfaces each of which has a number of methods. The following shows different parts of the RSS addressed using different methods:

```
doc->firstChild->nodeName = rss

doc->firstChild->nodeType = 1

doc->firstChild->attributes['version'] = 2.0

doc->firstChild->firstChild->nodeName = channel

doc->firstChild->firstChild->firstChild->nodeName = title

doc->firstChild->firstChild->firstChild->firstChild->nodeType = 3

doc->firstChild->firstChild->firstChild->firstChild->nodeValue = Tech Idol

doc->firstChild->firstChild->firstChild->nextSibling->nodeName = link
```

The names are fairly self-explanatory, `firstChild` refers to the first node in the next level of the document hierarchy, `nextSibling` refers to the next node in the current level of the hierarchy. Other methods include `parentNode`, `childNodes`, `lastChild`, and `previousSibling`. These particular methods are defined as part of DOM (Core) Level 1. There are also more recent levels 2 and 3, although support for the interfaces in programming languages lags a little behind the specifications. For that reason we will only use the interfaces and methods of DOM Level 1 in code here. In the DOM interface definition, the different types of nodes are associated with constants to help programming: elements are type 1, attributes type 2, text nodes type 3 — there are several more for other XML constructs. Although it depends on the language you're using, it isn't usually necessary to deal with these as numbers. They will be conveniently named; for example, the Java version of DOM has constants named `Node.TEXT_NODE` and so on.

The pointers to the different parts of the feed in the previous listing were generated using the following PHP code (`domecho.php`):

```php
<?php
    include('lib.xml.inc.php');
    error_reporting(E_ALL);
    $doc = new XML('rss2sample.xml');
?>
<html>
<head>
    <title>DOM</title>
</head>
<body>

<strong>doc->firstChild->nodeName = </strong>
<?php echo $doc->firstChild->nodeName; ?>

<br/><br/>
<strong>doc->firstChild->nodeType = </strong>
<?php echo $doc->firstChild->nodeType; ?>

<br/><br/>
<strong>doc->firstChild->attributes['version'] = </strong>
<?php echo $doc->firstChild->attributes['version']; ?>

<br/><br/>
<strong>doc->firstChild->firstChild->nodeName = </strong>
<?php echo $doc->firstChild->firstChild->nodeName; ?>

<br/><br/>
<strong>doc->firstChild->firstChild->firstChild->nodeName = </strong>
<?php echo $doc->firstChild->firstChild->firstChild->nodeName; ?>

<br/><br/>
<strong>
doc->firstChild->firstChild->firstChild->firstChild->nodeType =
</strong>
<?php echo $doc->firstChild->firstChild->firstChild->firstChild->nodeType; ?>

<br/><br/>
<strong>
doc->firstChild->firstChild->firstChild->firstChild->nodeValue =
</strong>
```

```
<?php echo $doc->firstChild->firstChild->firstChild->firstChild->nodeValue; ?>

<br/><br/>
<strong>
doc->firstChild->firstChild->firstChild->nextSibling->nodeName =
</strong>
<?php echo $doc->firstChild->firstChild->firstChild->nextSibling->nodeName; ?>
</body>
</html>
```

When placed on a suitably equipped Web server this will be delivered as an HTML page, viewable in a browser. The code begins by including a library file that provides DOM support. The error reporting is set to its most verbose level to help with debugging and a new XML object is created from an XML file and assigned to the variable $doc:

```
<?php
    include('lib.xml.inc.php');
    error_reporting(E_ALL);
    $doc = new XML('rss2sample.xml');
?>
```

Material wrapped in <?php ... ?> will be passed to the PHP interpreter, but everything else is published directly.

PHP only gained real support for XML DOM in version 5. However, most servers are still running version 4. The included library is a very basic implementation of DOM available from http://phpdomxml.webtweakers.com/, which will run on PHP 4.x. It is a limited implementation, several of the standard DOM facilities aren't available, but it provides enough to be very useful.

After initialization, there follows a block of HTML which will be delivered verbatim to a browser — not a lot is needed for demonstration purposes:

```
<html>
<head>
    <title>DOM</title>
</head>
<body>
```

In the body of the HTML there are a series of pieces of descriptive text (shown in a <strong> typeface), each followed by a little piece of PHP. Each of these lines of PHP contains a method call to address the document object that corresponds to the XML feed. Here is the first label and method call:

```
<strong>doc->firstChild->nodeName = </strong>
<?php echo $doc->firstChild->nodeName; ?>
```

The echo keyword passes the value of whatever follows out into the Web server's output stream, here filling in the values found by the method calls. As you can see, the labeling in the listing wasn't chosen arbitrarily. It is essentially the same as the PHP DOM code (dropping the variable's initial $ for appearance's sake). The rest of the listing is just a series of label or method calls following this same style, and finishing with the HTML closing tags.

This code simply pulls values out of the DOM structure of the XML file and displays them. Things get a lot more interesting when you start to manipulate the structure and values.

A (Forgetful) DOM-Based Weblog

To give you an idea of how the DOM can be a fairly easy route to building syndication tools, there now follows a little demonstration. The code is for a very simple Weblog system based around the RSS feed itself. The code is in PHP and designed to be runnable on a typical low-budget hosting setup. Figure 21-2 is a screenshot of the Weblog, as seen in a HTML browser.

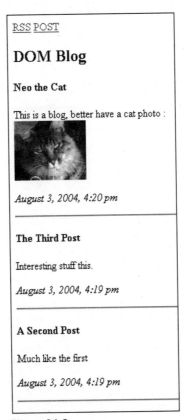

Figure 21-2

An RSS 2.0 file holds all the data, but a little bit of DOM manipulation is used to add new items and display an HTML rendition of the data. Like most feeds, this one only maintains a set number of items, newer posts appearing at the top and older posts dropping off the list. The result is that the blog only remembers the last three posts.

XML in PHP

Although there is a fair amount of support for XML in PHP, it varies considerably between distributions on different platforms. This is in part due to the fact that there is more than one standard XML library — expat and libxml being the most popular. PHP 5 was meant to sort everything out by settling on libxml2. Unfortunately, in the process namespace support was broken.

In practice this may mean PHP has to be recompiled or reinstalled if you need specific pieces of XML support (such as DOM), not an option with most hosting services. So the code presented in this chapter uses a basic DOM library written in PHP that will work with any setup using PHP 4.10 onwards. The library is phpdomxml, and is available from http://phpdomxml.webtweakers.com/.

The following list shows the required files for the application:

- ❏ domutils.inc.php: Some utilities to simplify DOM operations
- ❏ domblog.php: A template for viewing the blog in a Web page
- ❏ domblog.xml: The RSS 2.0 data
- ❏ domview.php: Reads the RSS, displays as HTML
- ❏ rss2shell.xml: Channel-level RSS 2.0 data
- ❏ dompost.php: Main functional code, adds data to feed
- ❏ lib.xml.inc.php: The phpdomxml library
- ❏ LICENSE: License for phpdomxml

A condition of the LGPL license of phpdomxml *is that the license be conspicuously available along with any code that uses the library, so keeping them together is good practice.*

Source Code

The phpdomxml library is rather limited, and as DOM interfaces are designed to be implementable across many programming languages, they do have something of a lowest-common-denominator nature. So the first of the source files wraps up phpdomxml methods into a form that is more convenient to use in the application. The first utility method is as follows (it appears in the file domutils.inc.php):

```php
<?php
function getFirstElementByTagName($parent, $name) {
  $maybeMatch = $parent->firstChild;

  while( ($maybeMatch->nodeName != $name) and !empty($maybeMatch) ){
    $maybeMatch = $maybeMatch->nextSibling;
  }
  return $maybeMatch;
}
```

Many operations on the DOM involve navigating between parent and child elements. The DOM 1 Core method getElementsByTagName returns all the children of the document or a given element that has a name matching the name given. This method is missing from phpdomxml. However, most RSS 2.0 has the pattern where a parent element only has one child of a given name, and to access this cases we wouldn't want a list of children, just a single child. So the getFirstElementByTagName method is given a parent element object and the name of the child of interest, and returns the first child element that matches. It works by loading a variable, $maybeMatch, with the first child of the supplied parent, then checking that and all the other sibling children that follow it to see if it has the required name. To avoid an infinite loop, a check is also made to make sure that the value of $maybeMatch isn't empty, and that there are no more child elements to examine. Say the document contained the following:

```
<a>
    <b>123</b>
    <c>456</c>
    <d>789</d>
</a>
```

A call on getFirstElementByTagName with the <a> element as the first argument and c the second would return the <c> element (or to be more precise, a pointer to it).

The next utility method, getFirstValueByTagName, is a simple extension of getFirstElementByTagName and looks like this:

```
function getFirstValueByTagName($parent, $name) {
  $maybeMatch = getFirstElementByTagName($parent, $name);
  if (!empty($maybeMatch)) {
    if (!empty($maybeMatch->firstChild)){
      return $maybeMatch->firstChild->nodeValue;
    }
  }
  return '';
}
```

After finding the first matching element, getFirstValueByTagName returns its value into $maybeMatch. However, there's a definite possibility that there isn't any such matching element, or if there is it doesn't have a value available (it isn't a text node). In either of those cases the value returned will be an empty string, which, unlike an empty PHP variable, is suitable for use as a value in the application.

Suppose the document contained the following:

```
<a>
    <b>123</b>
    <c>456</c>
    <d>789</d>
</a>
```

In that case, a call on getFirstValueByTagName with the <a> element as the first argument and c the second would return 456.

The next utility adds a named text node with its content as a child to a specified parent element:

```
function appendTextNode($document, $parent, $name, $text){
  $element = $document->createElement($name);
  $textNode = $document->createTextNode($text);
  $element->appendChild($textNode);
  $parent->appendChild($element);
  return $parent;
}
```

This wraps up a common sequence of DOM calls in which a named element is created along with a text node of the given value, and then the text node is attached to the element and the element attached to the specified parent node.

Using the same starter document again, a call on appendTextNode with a reference to this document as the first argument, the <a> element as the second and c the second, d as the third and ABC as the fourth would modify the document to look like this:

```
<a>
    <b>123</b>
    <c>456</c>
    <d>789</d>
    <e>ABC</e>
</a>
```

In the context of text-containing elements in RSS 2.0 you have certain issues to deal with. The RSS specification is vague on the type of markup that can appear in titles and descriptions, although the examples given escape any XML special characters (<, >, &, and so on). It would be possible to strip anything that looks like HTML, but more common practice is to escape anything that could potentially break the well-formed nature of the XML document. The PHP built-in method htmlentities can do this. Another potential source of problems in content are malicious scripts embedded in the HTML, which could be run when the blog's entries are displayed in a browser. To avoid this, you can use string replacement. Any blocks that look like this:

```
<script> //something nasty </script>
```

are replaced with:

```
<p style="color: red;"> // something nasty </p>
```

This will display any scripts in a red typeface, a little more entertaining than simply removing them.

Additionally, PHP itself tries to be helpful by escaping quotes, so the " character is replaced by \". To counteract this, the reverse replacement is carried out in the escape method, along with the entity encoding and script coloring:

```
function escape ($string){
    $string = str_replace ("<script", "<p style=\"color: red;\" ", $string);
    $string = str_replace ("</script>", "</p>", $string);
    $string = str_replace ("\\\"", "\"", $string);
    return htmlentities($string, ENT_QUOTES, 'utf-8');
}
```

For convenience, the escape method is combined with the appendTextNode method to make the following:

```
function appendCleanTextNode($document, $parent, $name, $text){
  $text = escape($text);
  return appendTextNode($document, $parent, $name, $text);
}
?>
```

The PHP file that will display the blog as HTML is a simple HTML template called `domblog.php`. It determines whether the `$postForm` variable has a value. If it doesn't, then a link to the `dompost.php` file is provided. The actual content (the items) of the blog is looked after by the inclusion of `domview.php`. The source of `domblog.php` is as follows:

```php
<?php
    error_reporting(E_ALL);

    include_once('lib.xml.inc.php');
    include_once('domutils.inc.php');
?>
<html>
<head>
    <title>A DOM-based RSS 2.0 Viewer</title>
</head>
<body>
<a href="domblog.xml">RSS</a>
<?php
if (empty($postForm)) {
   echo "<a href=\"dompost.php\">POST</a><br/>";
}
include('domview.php');
?>
</body>
</html>
```

This is probably as good a time as any to show you the RSS 2.0 feed file (`domblog.xml`), which contains the blog data. Here it contains three simple items:

```xml
<rss version="2.0">
  <channel>
    <title>DOM Blog</title>
    <link>http://example.org/domblog/</link>
    <description>A simple DOM-based RSS 2.0 Builder</description>
    <item>
      <title>Neo the Cat</title>
      <description>This is a blog, better have a cat photo : &lt;br/&gt;
      &lt;img src=&quot;http://dannyayers.com/neo-small.jpg&quot;
       /&gt;</description>
      <pubDate>August 3, 2004, 4:20 pm</pubDate>
    </item>
    <item>
      <title>The Third Post</title>
      <description>Interesting stuff this.</description>
      <pubDate>August 3, 2004, 4:19 pm</pubDate>
    </item>
    <item>
      <title>A Second Post</title>
      <description>Much like the first</description>
      <pubDate>August 3, 2004, 4:19 pm</pubDate>
    </item>
  </channel>
</rss>
```

The code that will display the blog content is contained in domview.php. This resembles the domecho.php file you saw earlier in that it opens an XML file then addresses parts of its content through the DOM. First it goes through the <channel> element to get hold of the channel's title, then finds the first <item> element. The code uses the utilities in domutils.inc.php to get the title, the description of the item, before obtaining the next item and looping. The source of domview.php looks like this:

```php
<?php

$doc = new XML('domblog.xml');

$channelElement = $doc->firstChild->firstChild;

$title = getFirstValueByTagName($channelElement, 'title');
echo '<h2>', $title, '</h2>';

$item = getFirstElementByTagName($channelElement, 'item');

while ($item) {

    $title = getFirstValueByTagName($item, 'title');
    $description = getFirstValueByTagName($item, 'description');
    $date = getFirstValueByTagName($item, 'pubDate');

    echo '<h4>', $title, '</h4>';
    echo '<p>', $description, '</p>';
    echo '<p><em>', $date, '</em></p>';
    echo '<hr/>';
    $item = $item->nextSibling;
}
?>
```

A browser pointed to domblog.php will display something like the next listing. The material up to the line with the header DOM Blog has come from domblog.php itself, there then follows the content from domblog.xml as interpreted by domview.php, and finally a little more of the markup in domblog.php closes the HTML document.

```html
<html>
    <head>
        <title>A DOM-based RSS 2.0 Viewer</title>
    </head>
    <body>
        <a href="domblog.xml">RSS</a>
        <a href="dompost.php">POST</a>
        <br/>
        <h2>DOM Blog</h2>
        <h4>Neo the Cat</h4>
        <p>This is a blog, better have a cat photo : <br/>
            <img src="http://dannyayers.com/neo-small.jpg"/>
        </p>
        <p>
            <em>August 3, 2004, 4:20 pm</em>
        </p>
        <hr/>
        <h4>The Third Post</h4>
        <p>Interesting stuff this.</p>
```

```
<p>
    <em>August 3, 2004, 4:19 pm</em>
</p>
<hr/>
<h4>A Second Post</h4>
<p>Much like the first</p>
<p>
    <em>August 3, 2004, 4:19 pm</em>
</p>
<hr/>
</body>
</html>
```

So far the code has been concerned with displaying the content of `domblog.xml`. The construction of this file happens in `dompost.php`, which you will see in a moment. The channel-level information for the feed remains the same effectively forever, so it is maintained in a static file called `rss2shell.xml`.

```
<rss version="2.0">
    <channel>
        <title>DOM Blog</title>
        <link>http://example.org/domblog/</link>
        <description>A simple DOM-based RSS 2.0 Builder</description>
    </channel>
</rss>
```

Content is added to the blog using a simple HTML form. When viewed in a browser it looks like Figure 21-3.

Figure 21-3

The text line at the top corresponds to the title of the blog post, the text area below it corresponds to the content (RSS 2.0's description). After something has been typed into these fields, clicking the Post button submits the data to `dompost.php`, which will look after adding it to the blog. The full source of `dompost.php` is as follows:

```php
<?php
$count = 3;
    header("Content-type: text/html; charset=utf-8");
    error_reporting(E_ALL);

    include_once('lib.xml.inc.php');
```

```php
    include_once('domutils.inc.php');

  if (array_key_exists('postTitle', $HTTP_POST_VARS)) {
    $postTitle = $HTTP_POST_VARS['postTitle'];
  }else{
    $postTitle = "";
  }
  if (array_key_exists('postDescription', $HTTP_POST_VARS)) {
    $postDescription = $HTTP_POST_VARS['postDescription'];
  }else{
    $postDescription = "";
  }
  $postForm = "Yes";
  ?>

<html>
<head>
   <title>A DOM-based RSS 2.0 Blog</title>
</head>
<body>
<form method="post" action="dompost.php">
  <input name="postTitle" type="text" cols="20"/>
  <br/>
  <textarea name="postDescription" rows="5" cols="20"></textarea>
  <br/>
  <input type="submit" value="Post" />
</form>
<a href="domblog.php">Return to blog</a>
<hr/>
<?php
if (($postTitle != "") and ($postDescription != "")) {

// load RSS 'shell'
$newdoc = new XML('rss2shell.xml');

$newChannel = $newdoc->firstChild->firstChild;

//// Add posted data
$itemElement = $newdoc->createElement('item');

$newChannel->appendChild($itemElement);

$itemElement = appendCleanTextNode($newdoc, $itemElement, 'title', $postTitle);

$itemElement = appendCleanTextNode($newdoc, $itemElement,
                                   'description', $postDescription);
$formattedDate = date("F j, Y, g:i a");
$itemElement = appendCleanTextNode($newdoc, $itemElement,
                                   'pubDate', $formattedDate);

// shouldn't be needed
```

```php
$newdoc->firstChild->firstChild = $newChannel;

//// Add existing data

$doc = new XML('domblog.xml');

$oldChannel = $doc->firstChild->firstChild;

$oldItem = getFirstElementByTagName($oldChannel, 'item');

// needed otherwise the pointers all go to the same item
$items = array();

for ($i = 0; $i < $count-1; $i++) {

  $title = getFirstValueByTagName($oldItem, 'title');

//  $title = escape($title);
//  $title = str_replace ("\\\"", "\"", $title);

  $description = getFirstValueByTagName($oldItem, 'description');

  // $description = escape($description);
  //   $description = str_replace ("\\\"", "\"", $description);
  $date = getFirstValueByTagName($oldItem, 'pubDate');

  $items[$i] = $newdoc->createElement('item');

  $items[$i] = appendCleanTextNode($newdoc, $items[$i], 'title', $title);
  $items[$i] =
   appendCleanTextNode($newdoc, $items[$i], 'description', $description);
  $items[$i] = appendCleanTextNode($newdoc, $items[$i], 'pubDate', $date);

  $newChannel->appendChild($items[$i]);

  $oldItem = $oldItem->nextSibling;

// shouldn't be needed
  $newdoc->firstChild->firstChild = $newChannel;
}

// dump to file
$filename = "domblog.xml";
$fp = fopen($filename, "w");
fwrite($fp, $newdoc->toString());
fclose($fp);

} // endif validity check

// view data
include('domview.php');
?>
</body>
</html>
```

The listing begins with some preparatory PHP code. The $count variable is set to the number of items that the feed should contain. Next, the mimetype of this document is set in the HTTP header, ready to be delivered to the client. Error reporting is switched on, and the files to which the code refers (the phpdomxml library and the utilities listed earlier) are included.

```php
<?php
$count = 3;
  header("Content-type: text/html; charset=utf-8");
  error_reporting(E_ALL);

  include_once('lib.xml.inc.php');
  include_once('domutils.inc.php');
```

Next, the code determines whether any values have been sent from an HTML form. Posted variables can be found in the PHP standard array $HTTP_POST_VARS. If the title and content boxes were filled in as shown in Figure 21-3, then after clicking post the $postTitle variable will get the value "A First Post" and $postDescription will get "This is the very first piece of content."

```php
if (array_key_exists('postTitle', $HTTP_POST_VARS)) {
  $postTitle = $HTTP_POST_VARS['postTitle'];
}else{
  $postTitle = "";
}
if (array_key_exists('postDescription', $HTTP_POST_VARS)) {
  $postDescription = $HTTP_POST_VARS['postDescription'];
}else{
  $postDescription = "";
}
$postForm = "Yes";
?>
```

The $postForm variable above is a simple flag used by domview.php to determine whether to display a link to this page. If $postForm isn't empty then no link is needed because the user will already be looking at this page.

The next block of source code is some basic HTML, including a form:

```html
<html>
<head>
  <title>A DOM-based RSS 2.0 Blog</title>
</head>
<body>
<form method="post" action="dompost.php">
  <input name="postTitle" type="text" cols="20"/>
  <br/>
  <textarea name="postDescription" rows="5" cols="20"></textarea>
  <br/>
  <input type="submit" value="Post" />
</form>
<a href="domblog.php">Return to blog</a>
<hr/>
```

The form has three significant elements: the input text line corresponding to the blog entry title, a `textarea` corresponding to the entry content, and a submit button labeled `Post`. The action when the button is clicked is determined by the attributes of the `form` element — here a HTTP POST request is made to the (relative) address `dompost.php`. In other words it will reload the current page, passing on whatever values have been entered in the form. If both form fields contain text, they are added as components of an RSS item in the feed using the following code:

```php
<?php
if (($postTitle != "") and ($postDescription != "")) {

// load RSS 'shell'
$newdoc = new XML('rss2shell.xml');

$newChannel = $newdoc->firstChild->firstChild;

//// Add posted data
$itemElement = $newdoc->createElement('item');

$newChannel->appendChild($itemElement);

$itemElement = appendCleanTextNode($newdoc, $itemElement, 'title', $postTitle);

$itemElement = appendCleanTextNode($newdoc, $itemElement,
                                   'description', $postDescription);
$formattedDate = date("F j, Y, g:i a");
$itemElement = appendCleanTextNode($newdoc, $itemElement,
                                   'pubDate', $formattedDate);

// shouldn't be needed
$newdoc->firstChild->firstChild = $newChannel;
```

After the outer elements of the feed have been loaded for `rss2shell.xml`, a new item is created and utility methods used to create and add appropriate `<title>` and `<description>` child elements. A date, formatted using PHP built-ins, is then added. It shouldn't be necessary according to the DOM specification, but in `phpdomxml` the document needs to be reminded that the channel is its first element.

The last block of source looked after loading the outer elements and adding the new `<item>` element. The next block takes care of the existing material on the blog, essentially by copying all but the last existing item (through the variable `$oldItem`) into the new DOM object. The individual items here are represented as separate objects in an array, otherwise the way pointers are used in `phpdomxml` leads to only a single item object. The item creation operations are essentially the same as those that created the entirely new item, with the exception that the text values, in this example, are read from the contents of the DOM representation of the XML file.

```php
//// Add existing data

$doc = new XML('domblog.xml');

$oldChannel = $doc->firstChild->firstChild;

$oldItem = getFirstElementByTagName($oldChannel, 'item');

// needed otherwise the pointers all go to the same item
```

```
$items = array();

for ($i = 0; $i < $count-1; $i++) {

  $title = getFirstValueByTagName($oldItem, 'title');

  $description = getFirstValueByTagName($oldItem, 'description');

  $date = getFirstValueByTagName($oldItem, 'pubDate');

  $items[$i] = $newdoc->createElement('item');

  $items[$i] = appendCleanTextNode($newdoc, $items[$i], 'title', $title);
  $items[$i] =
   appendCleanTextNode($newdoc, $items[$i], 'description', $description);
  $items[$i] = appendCleanTextNode($newdoc, $items[$i], 'pubDate', $date);

  $newChannel->appendChild($items[$i]);

  $oldItem = $oldItem->nextSibling;

// shouldn't be needed
  $newdoc->firstChild->firstChild = $newChannel;
}
```

The $newDoc variable now contains the root and channel elements, the newly posted item together with the more recent items currently in domblog.xml. In other words, it contains the latest state of the blog, ready to save to file. You can save to file using the standard PHP methods (note that the PHP process needs permission to write to the domblog.xml file).

```
// dump to file
$filename = "domblog.xml";
$fp = fopen($filename, "w");
fwrite($fp, $newdoc->toString());
fclose($fp);

} // endif validity check

// view data
include('domview.php');
?>
```

After the new version of the feed has been created and saved, dompost.php finishes by displaying the current view of the feed by including domview.php. Following what you see in Figure 21-3, after clicking post and dompost.php having done its work, the result displayed in the browser looks something like Figure 21-4.

The demonstration here used the file system as a simple storage mechanism; the data in the file is addressed through a DOM interface. There are several other ways of addressing XML files, most notably XPath, which, like DOM, also uses a hierarchical model of the data.

Figure 21-4

Representing Feed Lists in OPML

In the early days of aggregator development it became apparent that it would be desirable to pass around lists of feeds. This would allow the user to pass on a subscription list, for example a set of feeds on a particular topic, or simply to allow the list to be transferred from one tool to another. The UserLand Radio tool used the Outline Processor Markup Language for feed lists. and this also had the advantage of being hierarchical, so feeds could be grouped per topic or whatever. Before long, a lot of other tools supported this format for the import or export of feed lists. The following listing is an export from RSS Bandit of a feed list containing two feeds, which were filed in the category `Beginning`:

```
<?xml version="1.0" encoding="utf-8"?>
<opml version="1.0">
  <head />
  <body>
    <outline title="Beginning">
      <outline title="My Channel"
               xmlUrl="http://127.0.0.1:8008/"
               htmlUrl="http://example.org/"
               description="A minimal feed" />
      <outline title="Tech Idol"
               xmlUrl="http://127.0.0.1/temp/rss2sample.xml"
               htmlUrl="http://example.org/idol/"
               description="The hottest performers on the Net!" />
    </outline>
  </body>
</opml>
```

The format has a head-body structure like HTML, with the head being designed to carry information about the document (and the display of the document). The <head> element is mandatory, even when there isn't any useful information to put in it. Within the body the format consists of a series of <outline> elements, which may be nested. OPML can then be used to carry an index of RSS files.

Creating a SQL Database for Feeds

Modeling feed data is all very well, but feed diagrams on the printed page aren't much fun. When you have a model, implanting a database is straightforward. To create a database for feed data based on the tables above you will need a SQL database application. There are a great many to choose from, and you may already have one installed. The SQL used here and elsewhere is fairly generic, and should work directly with most databases. If necessary, check the database manual: minor changes at most will be needed.

The examples that follow work with a database through a SQL client tool. It would be possible to interact with the database like this in an user application; however, it is far more common for the interactions to take place through a purpose-built user interface. During development, a window onto the internals of the database is very useful. However, most people will see only the application's user interface.

Download Requirements

Here (and in later examples) we use the SQLite database—it's available for most platforms as a comparatively small download, and it is self-contained, fast, and reasonably powerful. It is also in the public domain. The database itself comes as a library file (or source code, if you prefer), so some form of client software is needed to work with it. There are graphic clients available for SQLite, as well as wrappers to enable the database to be used with most programming languages. However, there's a simple command-line client along with the database library on the SQLite site (www.sqlite.org).

> *At the time of writing, SQLite version 3.0 is available, but version 2.8 is best supported. If you want to use programming language wrappers or a GUI-based client such as SQLiteExplorer, it may be necessary to use version 2.8. Check the release notes.*

Try It Out Working with SQL

1. Download and unzip the database client to a convenient folder.

2. Open a command window in that folder.

3. Type the following:

```
sqlite simple.db
```

Your prompt should now look similar to the following:

```
C:\sqlite>sqlite simple.db
SQLite version 2.8.14
Enter ".help" for instructions
sqlite>
```

4. Type the following:

```
CREATE TABLE Persons (
    id INTEGER PRIMARY KEY,
    name TEXT,
    email TEXT
);
```

The prompts as you type this will look like this:

```
sqlite> CREATE TABLE Persons (
   ...>            id INTEGER PRIMARY KEY,
   ...>            name TEXT,
   ...>            email TEXT
   ...> );
sqlite>
```

You have created the Persons table. If you encounter any errors, type the following to delete the table and start again:

```
DROP TABLE Persons;
```

5. Type the following:

```
INSERT INTO Persons (name, email) VALUES ('Jane', 'jane@example.org');
INSERT INTO Persons (name, email) VALUES ('Joe', 'joe@example.org');
```

You should be returned to the sqlite> prompt.

6. Type the following:

```
SELECT * FROM Persons;
```

When you press Enter, you should see the following:

```
sqlite> SELECT * FROM Persons;
1|Jane|jane@example.org
2|Joe|joe@example.org
sqlite>
```

7. Type the following:

```
SELECT * FROM Persons WHERE name == 'Jane';
```

When you press Enter, you should see the following:

```
sqlite> SELECT * FROM Persons WHERE name == 'Jane';
1|Jane|jane@example.org
sqlite>
```

8. Type the following:

```
SELECT id FROM Persons WHERE name == 'Joe';
```

You should see the following:

```
sqlite> SELECT id FROM Persons WHERE name == 'Joe';
2
sqlite>
```

9. Now type the following:

```
CREATE TABLE Items (
    id INTEGER PRIMARY KEY,
    feed_id INTEGER,
    author_id INTEGER,
    guid TEXT,
    title TEXT,
    description TEXT,
    pub_date TEXT,
    item_read BOOL
);

INSERT INTO Items (title, author_id) VALUES ('A First Post', 1);
INSERT INTO Items (title, author_id) VALUES ('A Second Post', 2);
INSERT INTO Items (title, author_id) VALUES ('A Third Post', 1);

SELECT * FROM Items;
```

If you haven't mistyped anything, after you press Enter on that last line you should see the following:

```
1||1||A First Post|||
2||2||A Second Post|||
3||1||A Third Post|||
```

10. Now type:

```
SELECT Items.title, Persons.name
FROM Items, Persons
WHERE Persons.name == 'Jane'
AND Items.author_id == Persons.id;
```

This should produce:

```
A First Post|Jane
A Third Post|Jane
sqlite>
```

Typing the following will return you to the command prompt, and you can safely close the window (for now):

```
.exit
```

How It Works

Running the SQLite client at the command line followed by a file name either creates a database file of that name or it opens an existing database of that name. There are only a handful of basic commands in SQL, each with a few variations. You just used about half of the commands. The core of SQL is very simple, although you can build up very complex queries from the basic statements and expressions. The exact syntax does vary a little from database to database, and most have their own peculiar extensions, so it's worth keeping a command reference at hand. The SQL syntax reference for SQLite is online at www.sqlite.org/lang.html.

The SQL operations you just carried out began with creating and populating a Persons table using statements built around standard SQL keywords.

The CREATE TABLE statement gives the name of the required table (Persons), and then a list of the required field names and type. Note that the id field has been explicitly described as a primary key. The SQL looks like this:

```
CREATE TABLE Persons (
        id INTEGER PRIMARY KEY,
        name TEXT,
        email TEXT
 );
```

The semicolon at the end marks the end of the SQL statement. The next two statements add some data to the table, the SQL looks like this:

```
INSERT INTO Persons (name, email) VALUES ('Jane', 'jane@example.org');
INSERT INTO Persons (name, email) VALUES ('Joe', 'joe@example.org');
```

The INSERT INTO statements specify the table on which to operate, followed by the names of the individual fields into which the data should be inserted. After the VALUES keyword, the values that belong in the corresponding fields are then listed.

The first INSERT INTO statement says to put the value 'Jane' in the field name and the value 'jane@example.org' into the field email *of the same record*. SQLite has a special way of handling fields specified as INTEGER PRIMARY KEY. If no value is specified for this field when a record is being inserted, it will be given a value 1 greater than the largest value already used (other SQL dialects may require a keyword such as AUTO to do this). So although there's no reference to the id field in either INSERT statements, suitable (unique) values are automatically filled in.

The contents of the database can now be visualized as shown in Figure 21-5.

Persons		
id	name	email
1	Jane	jane@example.org
2	Joe	joe@example.org

Figure 21-5

You can see there are columns corresponding to the three feeds described in the CREATE TABLE statement, with an autonumbered id and the values specified in the INSERT INTO statements.

After you have some data in your database, you will usually want to work with it. The most common way of accessing data in SQL databases is through SELECT statements. The basic syntax is as follows:

```
SELECT result FROM tables WHERE expressions
```

The *result* value is a list of the required fields from the specified tables. The WHERE part enables you to specify a list of conditions that must apply to the records. A * may be used as a wildcard to specify all fields, and the WHERE part is optional. Next, you entered the following statement:

```
SELECT * FROM Persons;
```

```
1|Jane|jane@example.org
2|Joe|joe@example.org
```

The database responds to the SELECT command with a list of the records that fulfill the criteria you specified: you ask for every field from the Persons table without any conditions. The command-line tool makes a valiant effort at formatting the results in a table. By adding a WHERE clause you can narrow down the results, the next line of SQL you entered was:

```
SELECT * FROM Persons WHERE name == 'Jane';
```

The asterisk again means "give me data from all fields." However, here the records returned are restricted to those that satisfy the condition that the value of their name fields is 'Jane'. The client returns what it finds:

```
1|Jane|jane@example.org
```

The next line of SQL demonstrates limiting the returned results to a single field, here 'id':

```
SELECT id FROM Persons WHERE name == 'Joe';
```

If you look back at the table of the contents of the database, you can see that there's only a single record with a name field of 'Joe'. Because only the id field is specified in the results, that's all the client returns:

```
2
```

This is the ID corresponding to Joe's record in the table. The next block of SQL you entered creates the Items table:

```
CREATE TABLE Items (
        id INTEGER PRIMARY KEY,
        feed_id INTEGER,
        author_id INTEGER,
        guid TEXT,
        title TEXT,
        description TEXT,
        pub_date TEXT,
        item_read BOOL
);
```

Once again, the id field is specified as INTEGER PRIMARY KEY, so it will be unique within the table and autonumbered. There are a few more fields here, and in addition to the INTEGER and TEXT types there's a BOOL (boolean), which will contain true or false values. Next came another set of INSERT statements to put some data into the new Items table:

```
INSERT INTO Items (title, author_id) VALUES ('A First Post', 1);
INSERT INTO Items (title, author_id) VALUES ('A Second Post', 2);
INSERT INTO Items (title, author_id) VALUES ('A Third Post', 1);
```

In this example, there are only two of the fields (and their values) specified, title and author_id. The values entered for author_id correspond to those in the id column of the Persons table: 1 for Jane and 2 for Joe. Next you used a SELECT statement to display the contents of the new table:

```
SELECT * FROM Items;

1||1||A First Post|||
2||2||A Second Post|||
3||1||A Third Post|||
```

The first column of the results corresponds to the id of the record. The results have been autonumbered as before. Where values weren't specified in the INSERT statement, the database has entered a null value, so the first record returned here could be interpreted as:

```
id = 1, feed_id = null, author_id=1, guid=null,
title="A First Post", description=null, pub_date=null,
item_read=null
```

Null values in SQL databases don't fit well with relational database theory, but in practice they're fairly common. Before looking at the final query you ran, Figure 21-6 shows what the database currently looks like.

Items							
id	feed_id	author_id	guid	title	description	pub_date	item_read
1	–	1	–	A First Post	–	–	–
2	–	2	–	A Second Post	–	–	–
3	–	1	–	A Third Post	–	–	–

Persons		
id	name	email
1	Jane	jane@example.org
2	Joe	joe@example.org

Figure 21-6

The author_id field of Items refers to the id field of Persons, and that will allow meaningful queries across the tables.

> *SQLite doesn't actually know these fields are related, although it is possible with more sophisticated databases to state relationships like this. Some databases can also maintain what's known as referential integrity. For example, if a Person record was deleted when the value of Persons.id appears in an Items record as author_id, then an error may be flagged to say that this operation would like the data in an inconsistent form. It may be desirable to delete the corresponding Items record in these circumstances, although it certainly won't happen automatically in SQLite. This kind of occurrence is possible (using triggers) with SQLite. However, analyzing it is beyond the scope of this book.*

The final query looked like this:

```
SELECT Items.title, Persons.name
FROM Items, Persons
WHERE Persons.name == 'Jane'
AND Items.author_id == Persons.id;
```

This query is requesting values of the title field from the Items table along with values of the name field from the Persons table for the records in which the following conditions hold: the name field of Persons is 'Jane' and the id field in Persons is the same as the author_id field in Items. If you read through that slowly and compare with the table above, you will see that the results that fulfill this description have been returned by the database:

```
A First Post|Jane
A Third Post|Jane
```

If this last query sounds rather like very convoluted logic, don't be surprised. The relational model and SQL databases are (sometimes loosely) based around set theory and predicate logic. The data in a database can be thought of as a collection of facts, and the database structure and relationships between tables is a set of constraints that apply to those facts. When you do a SELECT query you request a subset of those facts that is consistent with the additional constraints in your query. It is possible to think of SQL databases as simple stores, although that view overlooks a lot of their potential as reasoning engines. Okay, they're not the smartest of reasoning engines (SQL implementations are notorious for dumbing down this aspect), but they're smarter than most file systems.

RDF in Relational Databases

From the point of view of the Semantic Web vision, the World Wide Web (with RDF and OWL extensions) *is* the database. Some developers see this vision as idealistic and misguided, but whether you like this vision or not, syndication is about data on the Web, and RDF was specifically designed to work with data on the Web. It wasn't a coincidence that both the RSS 0.9 and RSS 1.0 specification developers started with RDF. Whatever your viewpoint, there are practical considerations to take into account. For example, it is unfeasible to access all the data (or feeds) that may be of interest in real time directly from the Web. Even if you had extremely fast access and processing capability, there is also a problem specifically related to syndication technologies. The data provided in a feed is essentially short-lived, once an item passes out of an individual feed it may no longer be available. In most cases the information may still be available in the form of more permanent HTML-based pages, but how this appears will be specific to individual publishers. An aggregator application has to take advantage of conveniently packaged content with metadata in a feed while it's available.

A Minimal Triple Store

RDF data can be reduced to triples, simple three-part statements. This suggests an equally simple database schema, a database that could be created using the following SQL:

```
CREATE TABLE triples (
            subject TEXT,
            property TEXT,
            object TEXT,
            has_literal_object BOOL);
```

Say there was an item in an RSS 1.0 feed that looked like this:

```
<item rdf:about="http://example.org/post1">
  <title>This is the title of the item</title>
  <description>Everything you wanted to know</description>
  <dc:creator>Jane Doe</dc:creator>
  <dc:date>2004-07-12T08:23:25Z</dc:date>
  <link>http://example.org/post1</link>
</item>
```

The item would appear in the database as a set of records as shown in the following table.

Subject	Property	Object	has_literal_object
http://example.org/post1	rdf:type	rss:item	False
http://example.org/post1	rss:title	This is the title of theItem	True
http://example.org/post1	rss:description	Everything you wanted to know	True
http://example.org/post1	dc:creator	Jane Doe	True
http://example.org/post1	dc:date	2004-07-12T08:23:25Z	True
http://example.org/post1	rss:link	http://example.org/post1	True

The first statement is derived from the interpretation of RSS 1.0 as RDF/XML—the position of the `<item>` element says the post resource has type `rss:item`. The rest of the data, simple literal values for the characteristics of the item, map across directly.

An item on its own doesn't have a very interesting structure, but if we add a bit of context, the previous item probably came in a feed along with:

```
<channel rdf:about="http://example.org/">
    <items>
        <rdf:Seq>
            <rdf:li rdf:resource="http://example.org/post1"/>
        </rdf:Seq>
    </items>
</channel>
```

This will provide the triples shown in the following table.

Subject	Property	Object	has_literal_object
http://example.org/	rdf:type	rss:channel	False
_:0001	rdf:type	rdf:Seq	False
_:0001	rdf:_1	http://example.org/post1	False

Here the values that correspond to terms in the common vocabularies (RDF and RSS) have been abbreviated to their usual namespace-prefixed form, so `rdf:type` refers to `http://www.w3.org/1999/02/22-rdf-syntax-ns#type` and so on.

The subject listed here as _:0001 corresponds to the <rdf:Seq> element in the RDF/XML. This is a blank node, the Seq itself doesn't have a URI, so for the purposes of labeling a fairly arbitrary string is used. What the blank node provides here is support for the structure that connects the feed (http://example.org) with the item (http://example.org/post1). This node does have a type (rdf:Seq) which is useful information for RDF tools and user applications. The Seq and other RDF container classes (Bag, Alt) have some special properties that are used to associate the container with the content. In RSS the Seq uses rdf:li for this purpose, and an alternate (equivalent) form is used in the table, the property corresponding to rdf:li in the RDF/XML appearing as rdf:_1.

Filling the Store

In practice, getting RSS and Atom data into any kind of storage is not a simple task, thanks to the variation between the syntaxes and the less-than-perfect quality of syndication data on the Web. However, if you limit yourself to (mostly) valid RSS 1.0 data, it's a straightforward task. Practically every RDF toolkit (Redland, Jena, RAP, and so on) will let you load RDF/XML data from the Web.

RSS 1.0 Parser

RSS 1.0 conforms to the RDF/XML syntax, so any such RDF parser can be used to load a triple store. RDF/XML parsers are available for practically every programming language, many associated with a programming API and RDF store. For example, the Redland RDF Application Framework (www.redland .opensource.ac.uk/) includes a set of native libraries, with parser and storage facilities that can be used with C#, Java, Perl, PHP, Python, Ruby, and Tcl. However, if you want to use your own SQL database store, all you need is the parser. Perhaps the easiest to start using is the one found in the lightweight Python RDF toolkit, pyrple (http://infomesh.net/pyrple/).

The parser can be supplied with a class with a single method triple, which will be called whenever the parser encounters a triple in an RDF/XML document. This acts as a "sink" for these events, and is easier to demonstrate than describe. The following code will download and parse the W3C's RSS feed:

```
import rdfxml
import urllib

class ParserDemo:
    def triple(self, subject, property, object):
        print subject
        print property
        print object
        print

uri = "http://www.w3.org/2000/08/w3c-synd/home.rss"
doc = urllib.urlopen(uri).read()
print doc
demo = ParserDemo()
rdfxml.parseRDF(doc, sink=demo)
```

The source begins by importing the required libraries, in this case urllib, from the standard Python distribution, and rdfxml from the pyrple package.

```
import rdfxml
import urllib
```

Next comes the sink class. The name of the class doesn't matter, all that is important is that it implements a method called `triple` that takes three values. All that this method does is to print the values received to the console:

```
class ParserDemo:
    def triple(self, subject, property, object):
        print subject
        print property
        print object
```

An RDF/XML document is needed to give the parser something to parse, and Python's `urllib` makes it fairly trivial to get a document from the Web. An HTTP connection will be made using the given URI and data will be downloaded and read into the variable `doc`. This will then be printed to the console:

```
uri = "http://www.w3.org/2000/08/w3c-synd/home.rss"
doc = urllib.urlopen(uri).read()
print doc
```

To pass the data to the parser, an instance of the `ParserDemo` class is created. This instance and the RSS document are then passed to the `parseRDF` method contained in pyrple's `rdfxml` library.

```
demo = ParserDemo()
rdfxml.parseRDF(doc, sink=demo)
```

To run the code you will have to first download and unzip pyrple. We assume that pyrple's RDF/XML parser (`rdfxml.py`) will be available to Python, so save the source above to pyrple's `/parsers` folder. As always, you can run this from within an IDE such as Python's own IDLE, or from a command window. Quite a lot of output will appear, so if running from a command window, it's probably best to pipe the output into a file, so your command line would look something like:

```
C:\python\pyrple\parsers>python ParserDemo.py > output.txt
```

If you run this, and then open the newly created `output.txt` in a text editor, you should see a large block of XML (which we slightly reformatted here):

```
<?xml version="1.0" encoding="utf-8"?>
<?xml-stylesheet
    href="http://www.w3.org/2000/08/w3c-synd/style.css"
    type="text/css"?>

<rdf:RDF xmlns:dc="http://purl.org/dc/elements/1.1/"
        xmlns:h="http://www.w3.org/1999/xhtml"
        xmlns:hr="http://www.w3.org/2000/08/w3c-synd/#"
        xmlns:rdf="http://www.w3.org/1999/02/22-rdf-syntax-ns#"
        xmlns="http://purl.org/rss/1.0/">

<channel rdf:about="http://www.w3.org/2000/08/w3c-synd/home.rss">
    <title>World Wide Web Consortium</title>
...
```

If you scroll down through `output.txt` you should come to a slightly different-looking block of text, which will begin something like:

```
<http://www.w3.org/2000/08/w3c-synd/home.rss>
<http://www.w3.org/1999/02/22-rdf-syntax-ns#type>
<http://purl.org/rss/1.0/channel>

<http://www.w3.org/2000/08/w3c-synd/home.rss>
<http://purl.org/rss/1.0/title>
"World Wide Web Consortium"
...
```

These are the RDF triples the parser found in the RSS 1.0 feed. The two triples shown here correspond to the first two statements in the RSS document:

```
<channel rdf:about="http://www.w3.org/2000/08/w3c-synd/home.rss">
    <title>World Wide Web Consortium</title>
```

The specific formatting style of values by the pyrple parser is done for a reason. If you add a period (.) to the end of each triple as printed here, the format follows the NTriples RDF specification, a very simple syntax primarily used for testing purposes.

Whether you look at the NTriples or the XML, in English, these two statements are saying:

There is a resource of type `channel` *with URI* `http://www.w3.org/2000/08/w3c-synd/home.rss`*; this resource has a property called* `title`*, the value of which is the string of characters* "World Wide Web Consortium".

Connecting to a Database

Earlier you saw how it was possible to communicate with a SQL database using a command-line client. Most of the time you will want your application to do that for you, with code that talks to the database directly. There are code libraries available for many programming language and SQL database combinations to make this possible. For Python and the SQLite database such a library is PySQLite (`http://pysqlite.sourceforge.net/`).

If you follow the installation instructions you can then start communicating with databases programmatically. Again, this is easier to demonstrate than to describe.

Try It Out   Interfacing with a Database

1. Open a command window and start an interactive session Python by typing the following:

```
python
```

The interpreter should start up, responding with something like this:

```
D:\>python
Python 2.3.3 (#51, Dec 18 2003, 20:22:39) [MSC v.1200 32 bit (Intel)] on win32
Type "help", "copyright", "credits" or "license" for more information.
>>>
```

2. Type in the following lines (press the Enter key after each):

```
import sqlite

connection = sqlite.connect("data.db")
cursor = connection.cursor()

sql = "CREATE TABLE dictionary (english TEXT, italian TEXT)"
cursor.execute(sql)
connection.commit()

sql = "INSERT INTO dictionary (english, italian) VALUES ('dog','cane')"
cursor.execute(sql)

sql = "INSERT INTO dictionary (english, italian) VALUES ('cat','gatto')"
cursor.execute(sql)
connection.commit()
```

3. Now type in the following:

```
sql = "SELECT * FROM dictionary"
cursor.execute(sql)

results = cursor.fetchall()
for result in results:
    print result
```

The Python interpreter should respond as follows:

```
>>> for result in results:
...     print result
...
('dog', 'cane')
('cat', 'gatto')
>>>
```

4. Now try the following:

```
sql = "SELECT italian FROM dictionary WHERE english == 'cat'"
cursor.execute(sql)
results = cursor.fetchone()
print results[0]
```

The interpreter should return:

```
>>> print results[0]
gatto
>>>
```

How It Works

Programming interfaces to SQL databases tend to be very similar, with most operations executed through a *cursor*, which is a kind of marker in the database. In practice the cursor is an object through which statements and queries can be passed, and results retrieved. Until you need to consider tasks like optimizing your code for speed, you don't have to worry about any details of this, it just works.

The first few lines you entered make the `sqlite` library available, establish a connection to a database, and then obtain a cursor from the database:

```
import sqlite

connection = sqlite.connect("data.db")
cursor = connection.cursor()
```

The database is contained in a file called `data.db`. If this file doesn't already exist (it shouldn't), it will be created when the `connect` method is called.

The next part of the code creates a table in the database:

```
sql = "CREATE TABLE dictionary (english TEXT, italian TEXT)"
cursor.execute(sql)
connection.commit()
```

The command that will be passed to the database is contained in the `sql` string. It is an instruction to create a table called `dictionary` with two columns named `english` and `italian`, both of which will be storing text values. Calling the `execute` method with the `sql` string as a parameter, as you might expect, runs the SQL statement in the database. SQLite (and most other databases) support *transactions*, which are groups of statements that should be run together. Transactions can help optimize communication with the database. In PySQLite some support for transactions is provided transparently, which is convenient but means that if you want an instruction (or a set of instructions) to take effect, you must follow them with a call to `commit()`.

So having created a table in the database, you can start adding data to it. The following lines do just that:

```
sql = "INSERT INTO dictionary (english, italian) VALUES ('dog','cane')"
cursor.execute(sql)

sql = "INSERT INTO dictionary (english, italian) VALUES ('cat','gatto')"
cursor.execute(sql)
connection.commit()
```

Again the SQL statements are contained in a string called `sql`, which is passed to the cursor with an `execute` call. The first statement here inserts a new record in the table with the value `dog` in the `english` field and `cane` in the `italian` field. The other statement does the same for values `cat` and `gatto`. The two statements have been passed to the cursor, but for them to take effect a `commit()` method is needed.

So now you have a database containing a two-column table which in turn contains a couple of records. You can obtain the contents of the table in just the same way as at the command line using a SQL `SELECT *` statement, one of which is wrapped in Python code as follows:

```
sql = "SELECT * FROM dictionary"
cursor.execute(sql)
```

The cursor now has pointers to the results of this query, and they can be retrieved and listed to the console as follows:

```
results = cursor.fetchall()
for result in results:
    print result
```

Note that PySQLite is smart enough to figure out that when you want to fetch results, the statement should be committed, so no call to commit() is needed. Each individual value of result corresponds to a returned row (a tuple), and the printed results look like this:

```
('dog', 'cane')
('cat', 'gatto')
```

The fetchall() method will get every result. You can use an alternative fetchone() method when you only want the first record returned, as shown in the following query:

```
sql = "SELECT italian FROM dictionary WHERE english == 'cat'"
cursor.execute(sql)
results = cursor.fetchone()
print results[0]
```

The query here will only return a single record in results corresponding to the italian column. This will be returned as a tuple, so the value of interest is extracted by addressing the first element in the tuple with results[0]. The interpreter returns:

```
gatto
```

Now you have seen how triples can be extracted from an RDF/XML file using pyple's parser, and how you can address a SQL database programmatically. You will now see some code that hooks up a parser to a SQL database-backed RDF store.

Aggregating Triples

Earlier in this chapter, we explained how the triple-based RDF model could be implemented as a simple table in a SQL database. In the previous section we discussed how triples can be extracted from an RDF/XML file using pyrple's parser, and how a SQL database can be addressed programmatically. You will now see the code for a subsystem that will hook up a parser to a simple SQL database-backed RDF store. For want of a better name, the store setup will be called *Simpleton*. As presented here, the code is only really useful for experimental purposes, but with a little work could form the basis of an RDF-aware Python RSS aggregator, or for that matter any other application that needed to gather and store RDF.

Code Overview

To run the code that follows you will need to have a recent version of Python installed, along with the PySQLite library. You will also use the pyrple RDF/XML parser and the following directory layout:

❑   simpleton\parsers: The parsers directory copied from the pyrple distribution (contains rdfxml.py)

❑   simpleton\TripleStore.py: A Python wrapper around the database

❑   simpleton\create-triplestore.sql: SQL code to create tables and views

❑   simpleton\delete-triplestore.sql: SQL code to clear tables and views

❑   simpleton\Runner1.py: A simple demo of downloading an RSS document into the store

❑   simpleton\Runner2.py: A demo of basic feed aggregation

Store Wrapper

The core of this subsystem is `TripleStore.py`, which will act as an RDF-oriented interface to a SQLite database. This first version contains the generic RDF handling, some RSS-specific methods will be added later. The bulk of this file is a class `TripleStore`, which has the following methods:

- ❑ `connect()`: Connects to the SQLite database
- ❑ `commit()`: Commits a transaction to the database
- ❑ `getSQLStatus()`: Returns the status of the last interaction with the database
- ❑ `executeSQLFile(filename)`: Runs the SQL contained in a file
- ❑ `addStatement(subject, property, object, isLiteral)`: Adds the statement to the triple-store
- ❑ `triple(subject, property, object)`: Sink for pyrple RDF/XML parser

The first two methods contain direct calls to PySQLite for creating a connection and committing on that connection. The connection itself is maintained as a member variable, `connection`. Whenever some data is passed through to the database, there is the potential for an error to occur. The way the database is set up, some errors are purposefully ignored — duplicate inserts for example. In fact most errors can be safely ignored, so usually it would be overkill to stop the system operation on database errors. However during development and debugging there may be useful information in the error messages, so these are passed member variables, and their value is available through `getSQLStatus()`.

The `executeSQLFile(filename)` method is exceedingly useful — it takes the contents of the file and passes it to the database. This method will be used here to initialize the triple table and define some SQL views.

The `addStatement(subject, property, object, isLiteral)` adds a triple to the store, noting whether the object of the triple is a literal string (`isLiteral = "True"`) or a resource (`isLiteral = "False"`). The `triple(subject, property, object)` method is the target of the pyrple parser. When parsing this will be used alongside the `addStatement` method to populate the table, the `triple` method contains some simple type conversion code and what's needed to determine whether the object is a literal or not.

The full source listing looks like this:

```python
import sqlite
import re

# regular expressions
escapeQuotesA = re.compile("\"")
escapeQuotesB = re.compile("\'")

def escapeQuotes(string):
    """ Replaces quote marks in a string with Unicode escape values """
    string = escapeQuotesA.sub("\\u0022", string)
    return escapeQuotesB.sub("\\u0027", string)
class TripleStore:
    """ Wrapper around a SQL-based RDF store"""

    def __init__(self, storeName):
        self.storeName = storeName
```

```
        self.tripleCount = 0
        self.sqlStatus = "ok"

    def connect(self):
        """ Connects to the SQLite database """
        self.connection = sqlite.connect(self.storeName, encoding="utf-8")

    def commit(self):
        """ Commits a transaction to the database """
        self.connection.commit()

    def getSQLStatus(self):
        """ Returns the status of the last interaction with the database """
        return self.sqlStatus

    def executeSQLFile(self, filename):
        """ Runs the SQL contained in a file """
        f = open(filename, "r")
        sql = f.read()
        f.close()

        self.connect()
        cursor = self.connection.cursor()
        self.sqlStatus = "ok"
        try:
            cursor.execute(sql)
        except Exception, (strerror):
            self.sqlStatus = "Error:%s" % (strerror)
        self.connection.commit()
        self.connection.close()

    def addStatement(self, subject, property, object, isLiteral):
        """ adds the statement to the triplestore """
        cursor = self.connection.cursor()
        insert = "INSERT INTO triples \
                    (subject, property, object, has_literal_object) \
                  VALUES \
                  (\'" + subject \
                  + "\',\'" + property \
                  + "\',\'" + object \
                  + "\',\""+str(isLiteral)+"\")"
        cursor.execute(insert)

    def triple(self, subject, property, object):
        """ Callback listener (sink) for pyrple RDF/XML parser """
        self.tripleCount = self.tripleCount + 1
        print self.tripleCount

    # get the required strings from the triple data
        try:
            subjectString = subject.val
        except AttributeError:
            subjectString = subject
        try:
            propertyString = property.val
        except AttributeError:
```

```
            propertyString = property

    # check if the object is a literal
        if object[0] == "\"":
            isLiteral = True
            objectString = object[1:-1]
        else:
            isLiteral = False
            try:
                objectString = object.val
            except AttributeError: # is a bnode
                objectString = object

        self.addStatement(subjectString, propertyString,
                                objectString, isLiteral)
```

After imports to make the SQLite and (Python standard) regular expressions libraries available, the listing begins with some utility code. Python with PySQLite, in common with most SQL database interfaces does allow one or two different ways of passing statements and queries to the database. To avoid confusion, we took a non-idiomatic approach in the source listings here, simple strings are passed to the database. The strings will be constructed by patching together substrings containing the SQL keywords and data content as necessary. However, a side effect of this is that any quote marks or apostrophes in textual content would be interpreted as part of the SQL syntax, making a mess of any such statements or queries. To avoid this, strings are filtered before being added to SQL statements using regular expression methods to replace every quote mark and apostrophe with their Unicode-escaped equivalent (u0022 and u0027, respectively). So here is the start of the code with the `escapeQuotes` utility method:

```
import sqlite
import re

# regular expressions
escapeQuotesA = re.compile("\"")
escapeQuotesB = re.compile("\'")

def escapeQuotes(string):
    """ Replaces quote marks in a string with Unicode escape values """
    string = escapeQuotesA.sub("\\u0022", string)
    return escapeQuotesB.sub("\\u0027", string)
```

The tasty part of `TripleStore.py` is the `TripleStore` class. The listing begins with the initialization method `__init__`, which takes one value, the name of the file to use as a database. So to create a store held in file `my.db`, an instance of this class would be created using `TripleStore("my.db")`. Within this method the name of the store is passed to a local variable called `storeName`. A variable called `tripleCount` will keep tally of the number of triples added to the store, and this is initialized to zero, and the value of `sqlStatus` is initialized to `ok`. All three of these variables are prefixed with the keyword `self`, indicating that they are members variables of the `TripleStore` class.

```
class TripleStore:
    """ Wrapper around a SQL-based RDF store"""

    def __init__(self, storeName):
        self.storeName = storeName
        self.tripleCount = 0
        self.sqlStatus = "ok"
```

The connect method calls the connect method within the PySQLite library, passing the (file) name of the store and additionally encoding to use with the data. It makes sense to be as international as possible, so the common Unicode character encoding utf-8 is specified. The connection returned by PySQLite is put in a member variable connection for use by other methods in the class as needed:

```
def connect(self):
    """ Connects to the SQLite database """
    self.connection = sqlite.connect(self.storeName, encoding="utf-8")
```

The commit() method simply passes on a commit() call to the database connection, to ensure any SQL that has been passed to a cursor is pushed to the database:

```
def commit(self):
    """ Commits a transaction to the database """
    self.connection.commit()
```

The getSQLStatus method returns the value of sqlStatus that can be useful for debugging purposes:

```
def getSQLStatus(self):
    """ Returns the status of the last interaction with the database """
    return self.sqlStatus
```

The following method, executeSQLFile, begins by reading the data contained in the named file into the string sql. A connection is made to the database and a cursor obtained. The SQL statements or queries are then passed onto the database through the cursor.execute method. This is wrapped in a try...except block so that any errors are caught. The error handling here is simply to put any error message into the string sqlStatus and continue. Before the execution is attempted the value of this string is set to ok, so the success of the whole executeSQLFile operation can be checked by printing the status. The last two lines in the method commit whatever was in the sql string into the database, and then close the connection.

```
def executeSQLFile(self, filename):
    """ Runs the SQL contained in a file """
    f = open(filename, "r")
    sql = f.read()
    f.close()

    self.connect()
    cursor = self.connection.cursor()
    self.sqlStatus = "ok"

    try:
        cursor.execute(sql)
    except Exception, (strerror):
        self.sqlStatus = "Error:%s" % (strerror)

    self.connection.commit()
    self.connection.close()
```

The code so far has consisted of fairly generic convenience wrappers around the SQL database. The next method is more application oriented. The addStatement method takes three (string) values corresponding to an RDF statement's subject, property, and object, along with a value True or False to say whether or not the object is a literal. These strings are combined into a SQL statement using simple string concatenation, at the end of which the INSERT statement will look something like:

```
INSERT INTO triple (subject, property, object, has_literal_object)
VALUES ('http://subject/uri', 'http://property/uri', 'Some object', 'True')
```

Before building the SQL, the method puts each subject, property, and object string through the escapeQuotes filter to swap out any quotes that may confuse the SQL interpretation. Apostrophes are allowed in URIs though not double-quotes. However, there's no cost to being liberal in what is accepted here.

Once constructed, the insert statement is given to the cursor object to execute on the database. Note that unlike the executeSQLFile method, this doesn't end with a commit() method. The reason being that whereas the SQL loaded from file is likely to be a complete logical block, for example, one file is used to create the database, a statement is unlikely to be added in isolation. An RSS feed may contain several dozen individual triples. If a commit is done on a whole bunch of statements at once, less dialog is needed with the database and the overall operation can be done far more efficiently. So the commit() method is left for the calling code to look after:

```
def addStatement(self, subject, property, object, isLiteral):
    """ adds the statement to the triplestore """

# escape quote marks to avoid conflict when inserting in SQL statements
    subject = escapeQuotes(subject)
    property = escapeQuotes(property)
    object = escapeQuotes(object)

    cursor = self.connection.cursor()
    insert = "INSERT INTO triples \
            (subject, property, object, has_literal_object) \
            VALUES \
            (\'" + subject \
            + "\',\'" + property \
            + "\',\'" + object \
            + "\',\""+str(isLiteral)+"\")"
    cursor.execute(insert)
```

The next method is needed to interface with pyrple's parser. It will receive calls from the parser whenever a triple is encounter and converts pyrple's model of statements into that used in the database. As a crude progress marker, the tripleCount variable is incremented at each call and its value printed to the console. For the subject, property, and non-literal objects, where the value is a URI, the required string will be contained in subject.val, property.val, and object.val. To enable a little reuse of this method, if the values passes don't have a val attribute then the whole value of subject, property, or object is taken as the URI string. If the object string is enclosed in quotes then it is taken to be a literal (from the pyrple parser's NTriples approach).

```
def triple(self, subject, property, object):
    """ Callback listener (sink) for pyrple RDF/XML parser """
    self.tripleCount = self.tripleCount + 1
    print self.tripleCount

# get the required strings from the triple data
    try:
```

```
            subjectString = subject.val
        except AttributeError:
            subjectString = subject
        try:
            propertyString = property.val
        except AttributeError:
            propertyString = property

    # check if the object is a literal
        if object[0] == "\"":
            isLiteral = True
            objectString = object[1:-1]
        else:
            isLiteral = False
            try:
                objectString = object.val
            except AttributeError: # is a bnode
                objectString = object

        self.addStatement(subjectString,
            propertyString, objectString, isLiteral)
```

The `TripleStore` class looks after most of the functionality of the triplestore presented here, so now you can start to see how it works in practice.

Connecting Parser to Store

Assuming the other files referenced are in place, the following code (`Runner1.py`) will create a SQLite-backed triplestore and populate it with the data found in the W3C's RSS feed:

```
import sys
sys.path.append('parsers')
import rdfxml
import urllib

from TripleStore import TripleStore

store = TripleStore("triples-1.db")

store.executeSQLFile("delete-triplestore.sql")
store.executeSQLFile("create-triplestore.sql")

uri = "http://www.w3.org/2000/08/w3c-synd/home.rss"

doc = urllib.urlopen(uri).read()

store.connect()
rdfxml.parseRDF(doc, sink=store)
store.commit()
```

As you can see, there's not a lot to this. A `TripleStore` instance is created with its storage file called `triples-1.db`. Two calls to that class's `executeSQLFile` method are used to delete any existing store in that database and to create a new one. The document downloaded from the given URI is passed to the parser, along with the `TripleStore` instance that will act as the target for the parser.

Okay, so some of the functionality is hidden in `delete-triplestore.sql` and `create-triplestore.sql`, but not a lot. The `delete-triplestore.sql` looks like this:

```
DROP TABLE triples;
```

This simply deletes a table called `triple`, an index called `spo`, and a view called `items`. You've already encountered the `triples` table earlier in the chapter, in fact that is the table created with the `create-triplestore.sql` file, which begins like this:

```
CREATE TABLE triples (
            subject TEXT,
            property TEXT,
            object TEXT,
            has_literal_object BOOL);

CREATE INDEX spo ON triples (subject, property, object);
```

This is essentially the same table-creation SQL as described earlier, with an additional CREATE INDEX statement. The index significantly improves the speed of queries. Discussion of SQL indexes is beyond the scope of this book. Suffice it to say that during development, a typical query on the database containing 10,000 statements took around a minute without the index. With the index, this dropped down to a small fraction of a second.

The Joy of SQL VIEWs

The previous code will put RSS into a store in the form of individual RDF triples. This is fine in itself, but then comes the small matter of how to get something useful out of the store. Your application for the most part won't be interested in individual triples, rather the combination of these. Here another standard SQL facility can help considerably. SQL VIEWs are queries on the database that are prepared in advance. Though the capability varies from database to database (SQLite is actually quite limited in this respect), essentially these views can be treated as if they were tables in their own right. There's a brief example in `triplestore.sql`, which looks like this:

```
CREATE VIEW channel_uris AS
SELECT
Channels.subject
FROM
triples Channels
WHERE
Channels.property == "http://www.w3.org/1999/02/22-rdf-syntax-ns#type"
AND
Channels.object ==   "http://purl.org/rss/1.0/channel";
```

After the first line, this is a regular SELECT query. The CREATE VIEW line wraps up the contents of this, so that it's possible to run the SELECT just using the VIEW's name, `channel_uris`.

The actual SELECT statement uses a temporary name or alias, `Channels`, to refer to the `triples` table. In this listing this is a convenience to make the code more readable, but as you will see, sometimes this kind of aliasing is necessary. The result of this query will be the `subject` value of all the records in the `triples` table, which have the stated values for `property` and `object`. As far as the database is concerned the fact that the required values is irrelevant, they're just strings. However in terms of the RDF and RSS models that's quite an important piece of information. This query will return anything in the table that corresponds to RSS 1.0 of the form:

```
<channel rdf:about="http://example.org">
...
</channel>
```

The URI `http://example.org` is the subject, and assuming common namespace prefixes, the RDF/XML interpretation says that this resource has an `rdf:type` (property) `rss:channel` (object). So the previous query is in effect saying "fetch all channel URIs."

Try It Out   Using the Triplestore

For this exercise you will need to have Python, pyrple, and PySQLite installed, and have typed in or downloaded the source code for `TripleStore.py` and `Runner1.py`. If `sqlite.exe` (or the equivalent for your operating system) isn't on your system path, you should make it so (or just copy it to the `simpleton` directory). Assuming you're online, you can try the following:

1. Open a command window in the `simpleton\` directory.

2. Type:

```
python Runner1.py
```

There will be a short pause (somewhat longer if you're not online) and then you should see a list of numbers, counting up to around 50 or so.

3. Type:

```
sqlite triples-1.db
```

This will open the newly created database and start an interactive session with the SQLite client.

4. Type:

```
SELECT * FROM channel_uris;
```

You should see the following:

```
sqlite> SELECT * FROM channel_uris;
http://www.w3.org/2000/08/w3c-synd/home.rss
sqlite>
```

How It Works

As usual, the first few lines make the required libraries available, the `sys.path` line here putting the contents of the `simpleton\parsers` directory (the pyrple parsers) in reach:

```
import sys
sys.path.append('parsers')
import rdfxml
import urllib

from TripleStore import TripleStore
```

Next, an instance of the `TripleStore` class is created. This will use the file `triples-1.db` for its backing store. If the file doesn't exist, it will be created. This is done in a single line:

```
store = TripleStore("triples-1.db")
```

If a database file already exists, for the purposes of demonstration it will need to be wiped clean, so the SQL commands in `delete-triplestore.sql` are loaded and executed for this purpose. The simple database is then created afresh using the command in `create-triplestore.sql`:

```
store.executeSQLFile("delete-triplestore.sql")
store.executeSQLFile("create-triplestore.sql")
```

Next, a target URI is given, and then an HTTP GET done on that address; the data found there (an RSS document) is placed in `doc`. The Python code for this is remarkably concise:

```
uri = "http://www.w3.org/2000/08/w3c-synd/home.rss"

doc = urllib.urlopen(uri).read()
```

Now the `TripleStore` object is instructed to connect to the database:

```
store.connect()
```

The RSS document is then passed as the first argument to pyrple's RDF/XML parser, with the `TripleStore` instance as the second:

```
rdfxml.parseRDF(doc, sink=store)
```

Under the hood, the parser will read through the source document and whenever it encounters an RDF triple in the RDF/XML, it will call the `triple` method of `TripleStore`, which will in turn call its `addStatement` method to execute the SQL needed to pass the data into the `triples` table. When all the triples in the document have been read, it's time to ensure they have been passed to the database, so the listing ends with the line:

```
store.commit()
```

Customizing for RSS

The triplestore database is a very versatile way of managing data, although what you've seen so far has been general purpose. Time to get more syndication-oriented. To help with channel management, the following methods can be added to the `TripleStore` class (appended to `TripleStore.py`).

Utility Methods

The first method will simply run a SQL SELECT query on the predefined `channel_uris` VIEW, returning all the subjects that correspond to RSS channels. It looks like this:

```
def getChannelURIs(self):
    """ Returns all URIs of type rss:channel """
    cursor = self.connection.cursor()
    select = "SELECT * FROM channel_uris"
    try:
        cursor.execute(select)
    except Exception, (strerror):
        self.sqlStatus = "Error:%s" % (strerror)
    self.connection.commit()
    results = cursor.fetchall()
    return results
```

The other utility runs a SQL SELECT query of the form:

```
SELECT * FROM items LIMIT n
```

This will return the first *n* records in the items table. As you might have noticed, there isn't yet an items table in the triplestore database. In fact there won't be, items will be defined as another SQL VIEW of the triples table in a moment. But first, here is the utility method's source. As you can see it's essentially the same pattern as many of the preceding methods, it just constructs a string that is run as a query on the database:

```
def getRecentItems(self, count):
    """ Returns the most recent RSS items """
    cursor = self.connection.cursor()
    select = "\
        SELECT * FROM items \
        LIMIT " + str(count)
    try:
        cursor.execute(select)
    except Exception, (strerror):
        self.sqlStatus = "Error:%s" % (strerror)
    self.connection.commit()
    # print self.sqlStatus
    results = cursor.fetchall()
    return results
```

A View of Items

Earlier in the chapter you saw how feed data could be stored in a more direct form in a SQL database. The Items table contained a series of fields corresponding to the individual elements found within an RSS 2.0 <item> element. One for title, one for description and so on. In comparison the RDF-oriented RSS 1.0 store may seem a little convoluted — after all, most of the time your application is only going to need to address those title and description values directly. As it happens, you still can. Below is another listing of a SQL VIEW definition, which can also be placed in create-triplestore.sql to run when the database is initialized. The view will look to your application very much like the Items table, with the relevant values mapped out of the individual (triple) statements. Here we are looking at RSS 1.0 so the fields are a little different, instead of RSS 2.0's guid the URI (rdf:about attribute) of the item is returned. For the sake of saving space, we consider only four fields here.

The values returned (Items.subject, Titles.object, Descriptions.object, Dates.object) correspond to the values found in an individual RSS 1.0 item. In the FROM clause, four aliases are created corresponding to each aspect of the item a query will be made on. The WHERE clause is a list of conditions that the results must fulfill. If you compare this with the table of triples shown earlier, you should be able to see what records each condition is intended to line up against.

```
CREATE VIEW items AS
SELECT DISTINCT
Items.subject,
Titles.object,
Descriptions.object,
Dates.object
FROM
triples Items,
triples Titles,
triples Descriptions,
```

```
triples Dates
WHERE
Items.has_literal_object == "False"
AND
Items.property == "http://www.w3.org/1999/02/22-rdf-syntax-ns#type"
AND
Items.object == "http://purl.org/rss/1.0/item"

AND
Titles.subject ==  Items.subject
AND
Titles.property == "http://purl.org/rss/1.0/title"

AND
Descriptions.subject ==  Items.subject
AND
Descriptions.property == "http://purl.org/rss/1.0/description"

AND
Dates.subject ==  Items.subject
AND
(Dates.property == "http://purl.org/dc/elements/1.1/date"
OR
Dates.property == "http://purl.org/dc/terms/created"
OR
Dates.property == "http://purl.org/dc/terms/modified")

ORDER BY Dates.object DESC;
```

In addition to the multiple matching that's going on in the query, the last line adds a little garnish. The records returned by queries using this view will appear in descending order of their dc:date property. When the query built in the Python code is run, such as

```
SELECT * FROM items LIMIT n
```

The results will thus contain the most recent *n* items, in reverse chronological order.

Starting with a Blogroll

The next listing (Runner2.py) begins essentially the same as Runner1.py. However, rather than directly loading a single feed, it first reads in a list of channels expressed in RDF/XML, stores this data in the triplestore database, and then reads each feed in turn. Here's the listing:

```
import sys
sys.path.append('parsers')
import rdfxml
import urllib
from TripleStore import TripleStore

store = TripleStore("triples-2.db")

store.executeSQLFile("delete-triplestore.sql")
```

```
store.executeSQLFile("create-triplestore.sql")

uri = "http://journal.dajobe.org/journal/2003/07/semblogs/bloggers.rdf"
print "Reading "+uri

doc = urllib.urlopen(uri).read()

store.connect()
rdfxml.parseRDF(doc, sink=store)

store.commit()
print store.tripleCount

channels = store.getChannelURIs()

for channel in channels:
    try:
        print "Reading "+str(channel[0])
        doc = urllib.urlopen(channel[0]).read()

        rdfxml.parseRDF(doc, sink=store)
        store.commit()
        print store.tripleCount
    except Exception, (strerror):
        print "Error:%s" % (strerror)

items = store.getRecentItems(10)
for item in items:
    print item[1]
```

Try It Out　　**Aggregating with a Triple Store**

1. Open a command window in the simpleton directory.

2. Type the following:

```
python Runner2.py
```

That's it!

In the command window you should see something that looks like this:

```
D:\rss-book\python\simpleton>python Runner2.py
Reading http://journal.dajobe.org/journal/2003/07/semblogs/bloggers.rdf
370
Reading http://blog.asemantics.com/index.rdf
ok
500
Reading http://www.techquila.com/blog/index.rdf
ok
630
...
many more similar lines
...
Reading http://norman.walsh.name/index.rss
```

```
ok
4725
Redland Porting Hints
IronPython released as open source
Parsing 8G of RDF/XML
Triple Store Bake-Off
HEML & RDF iCal
At OSCON
Pepys-Map: 27th July 1661
Latest DOAP article at IBM developerWorks
OWL-S 1.1 Beta Release
Principles of Boundaries in...

D:\rss-book\python\simpleton>
```

The run has started by getting the blogroll, the first URI in the output. The number on the line that follows (370) is the count of triples added to the store so far. The other URIs are extracted from the blogroll, and then each of these is visited in turn. The number after each is the cumulative total of the triples loaded. After every feed has been visited (and 4725 triples accumulated), you get your results — the titles of the most recent 10 items posted by the bloggers in the Planet RDF blogroll.

How It Works

The initial part of the code works in exactly the same way as that of `Runner1.py` above. An RDF/XML file is retrieved and parsed, and the triples it describes are loaded into the store. The difference is that rather than being a regular RSS 1.0 feed file, this is a blogroll expressed in RDF/XML. No matter, it contains wholesome RDF. Only a small amount of the data contained in the blogroll is actually used by this mini-application, the statements that identify channels:

```
<rss:channel rdf:about="http://journal.dajobe.org/journal/comments.rdf">
```

After the blogroll has been loaded into the database, the code continues:

```
channels = store.getChannelURIs()
```

The `getChannelURIs` method executes a *select all* query on the `channel_uris` view, obtaining a list of objects corresponding to the channel URIs. The objects are actually tuples, and it's the first (and only) element in each tuples that contains the URI itself. Indexing starts at zero, so it's the value `[0]` that's of interest. It's then straightforward to run through the same data-loading sequence with each of the URIs:

```
for channel in channels:
    try:
        print "Reading "+str(channel[0])
        doc = urllib.urlopen(channel[0]).read()

        rdfxml.parseRDF(doc, sink=store)
        store.commit()
        print store.tripleCount
    except Exception, (strerror):
        print "Error:%s" % (strerror)
```

The steps carried out here are again to download the RDF/XML into a string and run the parser on it with the triplestore as the sink for data found in the file (these steps should probably be wrapped in a method themselves, as they appear quite a few times — that exercise is left for the reader...).

Once the table in the database has been populated with the data of interest, an RSS-oriented query can be run against it. The utility method `getRecentItems` is called to request 10 row tuples from the `items` view. These are then stepped through and the second value in each is printed to the console:

```
items = store.getRecentItems(10)
for item in items:
    print item[1]
```

Looking back at the SQL that comprises the `items` view used by `getRecentItems`, you can see the significance of printing `item[1]` from the row:

```
CREATE VIEW items AS
SELECT DISTINCT
Items.subject,
Titles.object,
...
FROM
triples Items,
triples Titles,
...
WHERE
...
Titles.subject ==  Items.subject
AND
Titles.property == "http://purl.org/rss/1.0/title"
...
```

The value of this particular element in the tuple is obtained from the object of triples that have the URI of the `rss:item` as the subject and the property `rss:title`. This view sorts the items by descending date; the `getRecentItems` method uses a query that only returns the top values. The net result is that the titles of the 10 most recent items are printed to the console.

Pros and Cons of Using an RDF Store

Most RSS stores use either file-based, possibly using XML facilities, or fairly flat database structures like those seen earlier in the chapter. In some respects these are much easier approaches than building an RDF-oriented store. If you build a store from scratch, there's a lot more work involved in setting up appropriate methods of inserting and querying data. However, there are libraries and code freely available for practical programming language and platform, so there is no need to build it from scratch. The ideas and techniques behind RDF can be very confusing, especially coming from the point of view of XML or object-oriented programming. RDF is related to these technologies, but there are fundamental differences that can trip up the unwary. But the core ideas are relatively simple, and from that viewpoint no harder to implement than any other data system.

The primary benefit of using an RDF-based store in RSS systems is probably that of extensibility. You saw how a blogroll format could be read transparently and understood by the same system as the RSS 1.0 data. The same applies for any vocabulary based on RDF, you will see a demo of this in the exercises. What's more, there are many techniques beyond using RDF's model as a simple data model. Logical inference is directly supported, a simple application of this would be to determine how to display unrecognized data based on class relationships. RDF (with RDF Schemas) has basic inferencing capability, but the OWL Web Ontology Language builds on this, allowing fairly sophisticated knowledge representation.

*Note that the store demonstrated here was built on top of a SQL database, but it is certainly possible to build RDF software using a more direct approach to data storage. For example, several open source RDF toolkits allow the use of the (non-XML) Berkeley DB, a lower-level data manager. One or two projects have gone further, for example the Kowari toolkit (*http://kowari.sourceforge.net/*) features an optimized, highly scalable store. Parts of this code base are actually used in an enterprise-class commercial product, Tucana Knowledge Server.*

There's a useful report on mapping between regular relational databases and RDF data at www.w3.org/ 2001/sw/Europe/reports/scalable_rdbms_mapping_report/.

Summary

In this chapter you saw examples of some of the techniques that can be used for storing feed data and accessing that stored data. They included:

❑ File-based storage with DOM access

❑ A SQL database used with RSS-specific tables

❑ A general purpose RDF store customized for RSS use

Each approach has various advantages and disadvantages. Using the XML of the feed documents as the primary storage mechanism, whether using the DOM and file system as described in this chapter or using a native XML database is a simple approach, but does mean you are largely tied to the hierarchical XML model. The SQL database approach lets a standard, very well known subsystem look after data storage and allows more direct modeling of the domain (feeds, entries, and so on). However, it is more complex. Additionally there has to be some up-front commitment to the modeling, as it's difficult to modify database structure later on. By using the RDF model there is considerably less commitment needed in terms of the kinds of data that can be managed, meaning the system will be easier to extend. The disadvantage is that setting up a suitable RDF store in the first place can be time consuming.

Exercises

1. You have seen the SQL needed to create the Items and Persons tables. Your task is to work out the SQL needed to create a table to hold feed-related data. Refer to one or more of the format specification (RSS 1.0, RSS 2.0, or Atom) and choose the fields that you think you're likely to need. Your solution will fill in the blank here:

```
CREATE TABLE Feeds (
 ...
 );
```

2. There's a demonstration of an RDF query language (Squish) at www.ilrt.bris.ac.uk/ discovery/2000/11/rss-query/.

   The demo uses an RDF vocabulary for talking about jobs alongside RSS 1.0 — job advertisements appear in feeds. Here is an example:

```
<item rdf:about="http://example.com/job1.html">
    <title>Digging a Big Hole</title>
        <link>http://example.com/job3.html</link>
        <description>
            The job involves going out into a busy road with a spade and
            digging for several years.
        </description>

        <job:advertises>
            <wn:Job job:title="Hole Digger"
                    job:salary="10000"
                    job:currency="GBP">
                <job:orgHomepage rdf:resource="http://example.com/"/>
            </wn:Job>
        </job:advertises>

</item>
```

The exercise is to use the Runner1.py code to load some of this data into the triplestore (for
example, from www.ilrt.bris.ac.uk/discovery/2000/11/rss-query/jobs-rss.rdf),
and then write a SQL view that will return a list of job titles and salaries from the data.

Consuming Feeds

RSS and Atom syndication are about the publishing of information feeds and subscribing to those feeds. In other words one system will be producing data and another consuming it. A system that consumes feeds may operate as an end-user tool like a newsreader or aggregator, running on the desktop or on a Web site. The consumer might be part of a larger system to collect and redistribute feed data. However it is deployed, there is a set of tasks common to most subsystems designed to consume feed data. This chapter gives you a general description of these tasks and examples of some of the practical techniques that can be used. A feed consumer generally does the following:

❑ Discover feeds — Given a Web site, find the associated feed

❑ Read feed data — *Conditionally* obtain the raw data from the feed

❑ Parse feed data — Determine the structure of the data

❑ Interpret feed data — Work out the significance of the various parts of data within the structure

❑ Process or store feed data — Do something useful with the interpreted data

In this chapter you learn:

❑ The stages that are generally used in consuming feed data

❑ The general approaches to reading, parsing and interpreting feed data

❑ What are the key problems associated with consuming feed data

Consumer Strategies

The most common interaction with the Web is getting a HTML page and displaying it in a browser, as shown in Figure 22-1.

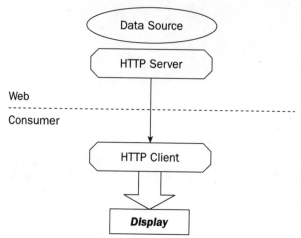

Figure 22-1

Following a client request, a single page is generated or loaded from file (the data source), passed to an HTTP server, and delivered to the client. This page is then displayed. The HTML browser contains both the HTTP client that will get the data from the Web as well as the rendering system needed to present it to the user. Both the HTTP client and display parts of Figure 22-1 are composed of various subsystems. The HTTP client may have to follow redirects, negotiate a suitable encoding, decompress zipped data, and so on. The display will have to interpret the delivered markup in order to render it on screen.

Nowadays it is common for there to be (at least) two sets of data delivered by the server for each Web page: the document data itself as well as CSS styling. The functionality needed to load the style sheet is hidden from the user, but the extra work is needed under the hood to display the page as intended.

The syndication equivalent of Figure 22-1 is shown in Figure 22-2.

Above the dotted line is the World Wide Web, on which can be found many RSS and Atom syndication feeds. Three of these are shown in Figure 22-2. The data from one of these feeds is collected by an HTTP client and delivered through a parser to the feed application. As well as having some kind of internal model of a feed, the application also maintains a list of subscribed feeds and will visit these in turn. Parsers have been mentioned earlier in the book, but as a key part of the feed consumer they deserve some detailed attention in this chapter.

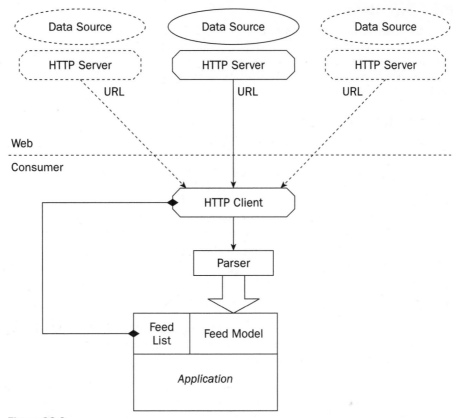

Figure 22-2

Parsing Data

A key feature in the pipeline from HTTP client to display is the parsing of the received data. Parsing is the term used to cover the analysis and low-level interpretation of markup languages such as HTML and XML. The word is borrowed from the field of human language grammar, and strictly speaking it refers to a specific part of the interpretation process. In the context of markup, however, it's used loosely to refer to the whole process of breaking down a marked-up document into its constituent parts. There are generally three different stages to the process, often rolled into one in markup systems: scanning, parsing, and interpretation.

Scanning for Tokens

The interpretation process first involves reading the document as a stream of characters and identifying groups of characters known as *tokens*. In a human language the tokens would be the words. A practical language has a syntax, defined by its grammar, which describes the sequences of characters that make up the tokens. The scanning is known by the linguists (human or computer) as *lexical analysis*.

Parsing for Structure

The syntax also determines which tokens can appear where in relation to each other. In a human language this would be the definition of phrase and sentence structure built from nouns and verbs and so on. After scanning into tokens, the sequence of tokens is analyzed to determine the structure of the specific piece of data, based on the grammar. The resulting structured view of the data can then be interpreted to determine its meaning.

Interpretation for Semantics

The structured data obtained from parsing can be analyzed at a more abstract level to determine the semantics or meaning of the document. The notion of semantics is generally a little confusing, as what is thought of as meaning by humans is considerably different from what may be considered meaning in a mathematical sense. Although artificial intelligence research tries to get closer to the human level, the bottom line is that computers are mathematical tools and their semantics reflect that. Generally with XML data, the semantics are the logical statements encoded in the markup taken in the context of the domain model. For example, if you were to use the XML for a commercial application, you might get something like this:

```
<product>
    <name>Flea Collar</name>
    <price>25</price>
</product>
```

The statements being made here could be that there is a product called *Flea Collar* that has a price of $25. These semantics would likely be provided by this instance data in combination with an XML Schema (to provide data typing) and a prose specification.

Unlike most XML languages, those of the Semantic Web initiative (RDF and OWL) and certain others such as Topic Maps aren't tied to any single application domain model but are based around general-purpose constructions derived from mathematical logic. As such they can be used as higher-level languages to describe domain-specific models.

Looking at HTML, some of the tokens can be considered semantic: p, href, em; and others purely presentational: br, font, i. In most browsers <i>this</i>, this will appear exactly the same. But where the first describes the visual details, that is, display in italics, the second gives more meaningful information, that the content should be emphasized. The difference is rather subtle, until you consider how the material would be delivered by a speech browser. You know without thinking how to say a word with emphasis, but how do you *speak* italics? If there's still any doubt about the difference between semantic and presentation markup, the lesser-known HTML <var> element should help. The markup <var>this</var> will again be rendered in italics in most browsers, but actually means that the text is an instance of a variable or program argument.

XML Parsing

Fortunately for developers, most of the work involved in writing parsers for XML (and to a lesser HTML) has already been done. Tools are available for virtually every language and platform, many wrapped up in standardized libraries. The most common is SAX, the Simple API for XML. Often this is also used under the hood to provide direct construction of a DOM model, which can then be accessed programmatically. SAX is simple in design, but is relatively low-level and can be hard to use in implementations. It originated from developer discussions on the xml-dev mailing list. DOM came from the W3C and is fairly simple conceptually (it's a tree). In practice, however, it has been described as a typical result of design-by-committee, trying to generalize across programming languages. Like SAX, it isn't very user-friendly and can also be hard to use. Although SAX and DOM are the most common interfaces, there are many more, often customized in a specific programming language, usually with the aim of making the developer's life easier. With a couple of exceptions, the code in this book will use the less language-specific tools, so porting is more straightforward. In the next chapter, you will see SAX in action.

Semantics in Feeds

It's worth noting in passing a difference in emphasis between the syndication formats when it comes to semantics. The basic elements of all syndication languages are essentially semantic: title, description, and so on. However, material outside of this core vocabulary may appear as part of the content (presentation) or as additional extension elements.

Both RSS 1.0 and 2.0 can support extensions. Generally speaking, however, RSS 2.0 is oriented more toward presentation and RSS 1.0 more toward semantics. If a series of blog posts were, for example, about cities, the name of the city would likely appear as the title in both types of feed. Both might also include the map reference (latitude and longitude) of the city as well. Chances are this information would appear as part of the <description> element in RSS 2.0, aimed at the human reader. On the other hand, such information might be hidden from the human in an RSS 1.0 feed, appearing within the item similar to the following:

```
<p:cityName>Lucca</p:cityName>
<geo:lat>43.50</geo:lat>
<geo:long>10.29</geo:long>
```

If the client tool understood this vocabulary, then the user could be shown the geographic location of the city as a dot on a map. The same basic terms could also be used to describe the geographic location of *anything*. Imagine you were to replace the p:cityName element with the following:

```
<seismo:quake>epicenter</seismo:quake>
```

Now the item is being used to describe a geological event. An application that understood the detailed significance of this might notify emergency services personnel in the area. But an application that didn't know that could still draw a dot on a map thanks to the coordinates.

This *could* be done with RSS 2.0. However, agreement between the producer, consumer, and mapping tool would be needed on the details of how the extension data is expressed. The RDF base of RSS 1.0 provides quite a significant level of agreement making the addition of new semantics a lot easier.

A very similar technique has been used in a WordPress plug-in to provide data about the countries blog-gers have visited in their (RDF/XML) FOAF Personal Profile Document. This data appears as a map in FOAF Explorer (see www.wasab.dk/morten/blog/archives/2004/07/05/wordpress-plugin-semantic-visits *and* http://xml.mfd-consult.dk/foaf/explorer/). *For more information about geographic applications of RDF go to* http://esw.w3.org/topic/GeoInfo.

A More Practical Consumer

Country and Western might cover both kinds of music, but there's a lot more variety in syndicated XML. There are the numerous format variations. However, as we suggested before, it's reasonable to narrow these down to three: RSS 1.0, RSS 2.0, and Atom. There is still another complication—not all feeds are well-formed XML, and that should be taken into consideration in application design. This will be covered in more detail in Chapter 23. Most syndication applications are likely to treat the material in RSS 2.0 and Atom feeds in a simi-lar fashion, following the same kind of model of an entry or item. For good-quality (that is, well-formed

XML) feeds this means a standard XML parser can be used. For basic news-reading applications the same can apply for RSS 1.0. If your application uses an RDF store or you want to read information from RDF extensions to RSS 1.0, then a separate RDF/XML parser is one option.

All Kinds of XML

Assuming you want your application to consume a wide range of the data available from syndication feeds, a more realistic input section for the consumer will cover RSS 2.0, Atom, RDF/XML, and ill-formed XML. Figure 22-3 shows one possible setup for dealing with these.

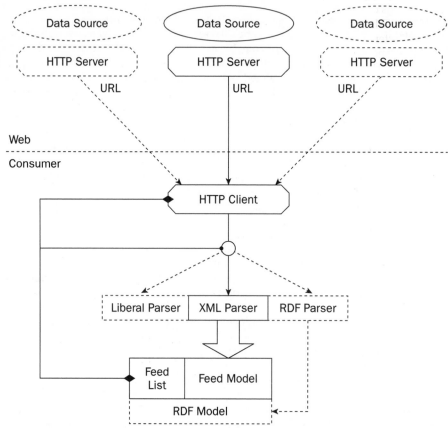

Figure 22-3

The core of the application at the bottom will retain a list of the subscribed feed URIs, which will be passed to the HTTP client as needed for it to obtain the individual feed documents. These may be in a syndication-specific XML format like RSS 2.0 or Atom, in which case a standard XML parser can be used. This same parser could also be used for RSS 1.0. However, if support for arbitrary extensions is required, then you may want to use a dedicated RDF/XML parser. Remember that a lot of the syndication data on the Web isn't well-formed XML, so consumer applications that want to use this data will have to include some means of reading such data. You can provide this functionality using a third parser subsystem, shown as the Liberal Parser in Figure 22-3. Note that these three different parsers could be built from the same basic code. One technique (as used in the BottomFeeder aggregator, written in Smalltalk) is to override the default error handling of a true XML parser, so that the application handles such events in a more lenient fashion than that defined for XML alone. You will see an example of how a liberal parser can be constructed in Chapter 23.

Markup in Content

Another issue to bear in mind when designing a feed consumer is that the content of the feed may be markup itself. This can appear as an island of non-syndication language XML within an RSS or Atom feed, such as XHTML. More commonly at present such content appears as HTML escaped using either individual character replacement (< for < and so on) or as CDATA blocks. To the XML parser these are equivalent. Depending on subsequent systems it may be necessary to process the content, for example to extract links from a post. This would require the introduction of an additional, post-XML parser as shown in Figure 22-4.

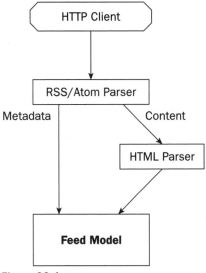

Figure 22-4

Other Approaches

There are other ways of dealing with the multiplicity of formats found in the wild. One in particular, XSLT normalization, offers a great deal of versatility at the possible cost of intricate programming. In this scenario the raw data first is cleaned up to make the XML well-formed, and then an XSLT (XML Stylesheet Language Transformation) can be applied to turn RSS 1.0, RSS 2.0, Atom or any other data into a form that the application can read. Various different style sheets are already available on the Web, in particular for converting any format into RDF/XML. Figure 22-5 shows the pipeline for a system that takes this approach.

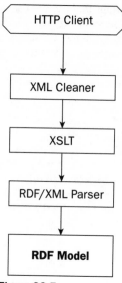

Figure 22-5

The XSLT transformation process is based on extracting the pieces of data of interest from an XML document using XPath expressions. The same basic technique can be applied programmatically to the feed using one of the many XPath-capable XML toolkits. This is essentially the same as using DOM calls to get at the data according to where it sits in the XML tree. Following an XML-oriented approach, a sophisticated system can be constructed relatively simply by using an XML database, as shown in Figure 22-6.

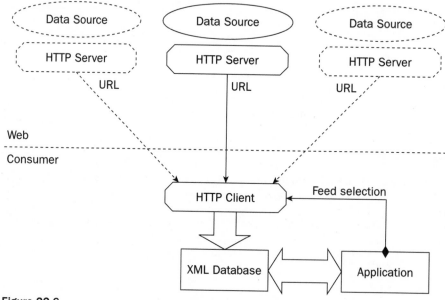

Figure 22-6

Such a system isn't tied to any single format or model, but some domain-specific processing or rendering would be needed to do useful things with syndication feed data. In Figure 22-6, the assumption is made that all data is good (XML) data. This can be achieved by preprocessing to clean up ill-formed documents. The same basic setup could be used substituting in an RDF database, with the assumption that everything that goes in will be valid RDF/XML. Again you can achieve this using preprocessing. However, in addition some form of mapping to the RDF model is needed, which brings us back to Figure 22-5 and using XSLT.

Reading Feed Data

Syndication feed data is published on the Web, and getting hold of data from the Web is generally carried out by one operation, the HTTP GET method. You have seen some description of this method in earlier chapters, and in Chapter 26, you will see some of the other HTTP methods (POST, PUT, and so on) to give you a better idea of the "big picture" of the Web. The GET method is very simple conceptually: you supply a resource identifier (URI), do a GET, and the server gives you a representation of that resource (for example, the Web page, XML data, or RSS feed). In the context of syndication, this simple idea gets a little complicated. This is in part thanks to the requirements of XML when delivered over HTTP. Another complication is the additional demand made by feed consumers when they poll servers for data. The Web is robust enough that it can deal with a very large number of reasonably well-behaved HTML browsers. Extra care is needed in syndication, and aggregators and the like should always be on their best behavior in public.

The Polite Client

The content of a particular Web page, say that of a blog, may change two or three times a day. Ideally someone who is interested in the page would like to know right away when new material is available. If you visited that site two or three times a day with a regular browser it would be a matter of luck whether you happen to see the pages before or after their last update. One aim of syndication is to minimize that element of luck, so you receive new material as soon as possible after it has been published. Another is to reduce the manual effort involved to get that news. These aims are all about potential benefits for the subscriber (client), but they can only be realized in a form that will scale to Web proportions if some consideration is given to the publisher (server).

Push and Pull

Getting information absolutely up-to-date is possible with the "push" approach to syndication, where the server directly notifies clients. However, with the possible exception of e-mail newsletters, this predecessor of today's syndication hasn't really caught on. The approach to syndication used with RSS and Atom is *pull-based*. The client has to go and find out for itself whether content has changed. A syndication consumer operates by periodically visiting servers hosting the user's subscribed feeds and downloading the RSS or Atom file. This approach brings with it certain problems. The automated client acts like a visitor to the site coming back at regular intervals. The convenience of aggregators means that providing an RSS or Atom feed is bound to increase traffic to a site, if only to read the feed. Increased traffic is considered by most publishers to be a good thing. However, without careful design, over a given period a syndication client can use bandwidth considerably greater than a handful of regular browser visitors to HTML pages. Given that a particular site can easily have thousands of feed subscribers it is essential that client developers do whatever they can to minimize their demands on servers.

The *polite client* respects the server and doesn't make unnecessary demands.

HTTP Status Codes

Another aspect to respecting the server is responding appropriately to HTTP response codes. The options are to get the data from the current address; get the data from another address (redirect); unsubscribe; try again later. Whatever happens, the client must not keep trying to get feed data if it's not available right away. There are quite a lot of alternative response codes, most of which are rarely seen. The definitive reference is the HTTP specification (www.ietf.org/rfc/rfc2616.txt), which should be read by anyone writing client software (yes, it is hard work!). Unfortunately in many cases it isn't obvious how an ideal aggregator client should behave. If data isn't immediately available and the appropriate action isn't certain, then a rule of thumb is to try again later. If failure continues more than a handful of times it probably makes sense to either unsubscribe from the feed or at least stop attempting to obtain the feed and notify the user. If possible, when there is an error or uncertainty about the status of the server, the client should "throttle back." If an aggregator normally makes a request every hour, then it should increase this period significantly (maybe double it) until either successful communications start again or it's clear the feed really is unavailable.

The 200 OK is the normal response, which will be handled by any client interested in the data. The 3xx codes relate to redirection indicating that the client should extract the Location field in the HTTP header and make a request at that address to get the data. The appropriate action is clear with some of the 4xx codes, such as 410 Gone, where the server is clearly stating that the resource isn't available and never will be again. The appropriate action for an aggregator here (and with some of the other 4xx codes) is to remove the URI from its subscription list. The 5xx codes relate to server errors, and it isn't unreasonable to assume that these are temporary even if the server is suggesting otherwise. Some justification is needed for that statement: the client will have obtained the URI from somewhere on the understanding that it identifies a syndication feed. So getting a 501 Not Implemented, for example, will come as a surprise. If this is the true status, then there's no real harm in getting confirmation by trying again later — maybe three or four times over a period of several hours or days. It may be that this is the true status, but it may just be a symptom of an error condition. If the same response appears repeatedly over an extended period, it would be appropriate to unsubscribe or notify the user. But the condition could be a temporary one, and the server reverts to giving the expected response.

This approach is also reasonable for several of the 4xx codes that cover client errors. A 404 Not Found is the result of the client trying to access a resource that isn't on the Web, although the reason the resource isn't on the Web may be that the server is temporarily down. Trying again a while later is reasonable. Trying again immediately, frequently or indefinitely isn't.

Suggested actions for a client are listed in the following table. These actions are by no means the last word on the subject. Your client may be able to provide a better response, for instance asking for a different media type if a 415 Unsupported Media Type is encountered. If in doubt consult RFC 2616. The actions marked with an asterisk (*) are of particular relevance to syndication clients and should be supported wherever possible. The default application behavior for unexpected server responses should be to record the fact that data wasn't available and to unsubscribe (or notify the user) if this condition continues for any length of time.

Status Code	Reason Phrase	Appropriate Action
100	Continue	Record; if persistent, unsubscribe
101	Switching Protocols	Record; if persistent, unsubscribe
200	OK	* Read data
201	Created	Record; if persistent, unsubscribe
202	Accepted	Record; if persistent, unsubscribe
203	Non-Authoritative Information	Record; if persistent, unsubscribe
204	No Content	Record; if persistent, unsubscribe
205	Reset Content	Record; if persistent, unsubscribe
206	Partial Content	Record; if persistent, unsubscribe
300	Multiple Choices	* Follow redirection (keep current URI)
301	Moved Permanently	* Follow redirection, replace URI
302	Found (Temporary Redirect)	* Follow redirection (keep current URI)
303	See Other	* Follow redirection (keep current URI)
304	Not Modified	* Use current cache
305	Use Proxy	* Follow redirection (keep current URI)
307	Temporary Redirect	* Follow redirection (keep current URI)
400	Bad Request	Record; if persistent, unsubscribe
401	Unauthorized	* Unsubscribe
402	Payment Required	* Unsubscribe
403	Forbidden	* Unsubscribe
404	Not Found	* Record; if persistent, unsubscribe
405	Method Not Allowed	Record; if persistent, unsubscribe
406	Not Acceptable	Record; if persistent, unsubscribe
407	Proxy Authentication Required	Record; if persistent, unsubscribe
408	Request Time-out	Record; if persistent, unsubscribe
409	Conflict	Record; if persistent, unsubscribe
410	Gone	* Unsubscribe
411	Length Required	Record; if persistent, unsubscribe
412	Precondition Failed	Record; if persistent, unsubscribe
413	Request Entity Too Large	Record; if persistent, unsubscribe
414	Request-URI Too Large	Record; if persistent, unsubscribe

Table continued on following page

Status Code	Reason Phrase	Appropriate Action
415	Unsupported Media Type	Record; if persistent, unsubscribe
416	Requested range not satisfiable	Record; if persistent, unsubscribe
417	Expectation Failed	Record; if persistent, unsubscribe
500	Internal Server Error	Record; if persistent, unsubscribe
501	Not Implemented	Record; if persistent, unsubscribe
502	Bad Gateway	Record; if persistent, unsubscribe
503	Service Unavailable	Record; if persistent, unsubscribe
504	Gateway Time-out	Record; if persistent, unsubscribe
505	HTTP Version not supported	Record; if persistent, unsubscribe

Timing Issues

The "push" approach has production and consumption (or at least notification) in sync, as soon as something new is served, the client knows about it. This is the ideal for news delivery systems, but there are many disadvantages associated with push, including that it isn't widely implemented. The polling-based "pull" approach on the other hand involves a looser link between server and client (and is arguably better suited to the Web environment), but can only approximate the ideal of data synchronization. If polling the feeds for changes only occurs once a week, and new material appears once a minute then either the new material will reach the user in a big clump or much of it will be out-of-date. More likely a lot of material will have been missed. At the other extreme, if the material changes only once a week and client polling takes place every minute, the user will see it when it's very fresh, but a lot of unnecessary calls to the server are taking place, bandwidth is wasted, and both client and server are wasting processing cycles.

The rough consensus of the syndication community is that under most circumstances (that is, without prior arrangement) a consumer shouldn't attempt to get feed data from a given address more often than once an hour. Where there have been errors at the HTTP (and possibly the XML level) it's good to increase this period until the problem is resolved one way or the other.

However, even by making the interval between polls an hour or greater, problems can still arise. If clients poll every hour on the hour, then the server will receive all the requests within a short space of time. If there are thousands of clients this may appear as an overload, equivalent to the distributed denial of service (DDoS) attack popular amongst crackers. It's possible to minimize the effects server-side by reducing the net demand by implementing conditional GET and compression mechanisms. It's also advantageous when a feed has moved for the server to use HTTP 301 Moved Permanently rather than the temporary redirects 302 and 307. But this is treating symptoms, not the cause. The only real answer to top-of-the-hour overload is for the clients to avoid using that as the polling time, by setting the polling time to a randomly chosen number of minutes plus seconds past the hour, or varying the polling period a little at random.

XML-Level Timing Hints

The RSS 2.0 specification includes the <ttl> (time to live) feed-level element, which is the number of minutes a channel can be cached before refreshing from the source. Additionally, there are the <skipHours> and <skipDays> elements to indicate times of the day or days of the week where the client may not read the feed. The RSS 1.0 specification allows the use of the syndication module (http://purl.org/rss/1.0/modules/

syndication/), which offers `<updatePeriod>`, `<updateFrequency>`, and `<updateBase>`. These elements can provide details of the feed update schedule. For example, it can be said that updates will occur three times (frequency) daily (period) starting at midnight on New Years Eve 2005 (base).

These elements look good on paper, but are less useful in practice. For example, there's only so much a feed publisher can determine in advance — a company feed may skip out-of-office hours. Support for these features is patchy at best in current aggregators and authoring tools. Because of this, there's not much motivation for tool builders to provide support.

The Atom project's approach to timing hints reflects the experience of RSS (as well as the study of the HTTP specification). There is a proposal in Atom for an optional `<refreshRate>` element, but a note in the proposal asks for an explanation of what this offers over HTTP-level caching — at the time of writing, none has been forthcoming. There is an `Expires` HTTP header field (that can be used to give the date/time at which the current data is stale), as well as `Cache-Control` and various other mechanisms that can be used for more sophisticated handling of the timing. As it says in the `<refreshRate>` proposal, the XML-level information is only really suitable for use as a fallback when HTTP-level mechanisms can't be used.

The bottom line is that the benefits offered by XML-level hints are likely to be minimal compared to using an hourly refresh rate (at a random hour) along with the bandwidth reduction mechanisms of HTTP compression and conditional `GET`. It's not a bad thing for syndication clients to support feed hints, but they should be considered less of a priority than supporting the basic HTTP techniques.

If a more frequent update is required then XML hints are an option, although in these circumstances lower-level HTTP options should also be considered as they may offer considerably more efficient throughput.

HTTP Compression

The topic of compressed feeds is discussed in Chapter 19. Essentially the text content of a feed can be transparently compressed at the server and decompressed at the client. The `Accept` field in the HTTP request header contains details of the kinds of compression the client can deal with. If the server supports one of these, it can compress the data before sending it and let it be known in the `Content-Encoding` field of the response header. Given that this can reduce the bandwidth requirements down to a third or a quarter of those of uncompressed data, this is something that should be looked at by anyone developing a syndication feed consumer.

Conditional GET

HTTP may be a simple protocol, but its developers included a few neat tricks. When requesting data from a server, it's possible to find out if the data at a particular location has changed since the last visit to the location. Although the syndication client may download a feed every hour, unless it has changed from one hour to the next, the feed data is of no interest, and a full download isn't needed. This can make the difference between having to download a couple of hundred bytes (for the header) or some tens of kilobytes (for header and content).

There are two mechanisms for doing this, using different fields in the HTTP response header: `Last-Modified` and `ETag`. A polite client, after making a regular (successful) request should keep hold of whatever values were found in the `Last-Modified` and `ETag` fields. Next time a request is made at that particular URI, the previous value from `Last-Modified` should be put in a field called `If-Modified-Since` and the value obtained for `Etag` placed in the `If-None-Match` field. In response to a HTTP `GET`, the server normally returns a `200 OK` response code, followed by the data in the body of the message. However, if the server matches either the modification date or `ETag` value to its *own* values, then it will return a `304 Not Modified` response code and an empty body.

The date-based technique for conditional GET operations comes from HTTP 1.0, and is used with the request header fields If-Modified-Since *and* If-Unmodified-Since. *These do provide most of what is needed for efficient caching of data, but there are problems with this approach. For example, it's not always easy to generate a value for last-modified from a database. A more versatile system, using entity tags, was introduced in HTTP 1.1. These are strings generated by the server. They have no significance to the client except in comparisons. They are used alongside* If-Match *and* If-None-Match *and* If-Range *(for partial updates) request fields. The process is very similar; however, the complication of dealing with dates between different hosts is taken out of the picture, the construction of the marker tag being entirely up to the server.*

A Reasonably Polite Client

The following example shows the complete Java source code for an HTTP client that will support compression and a conditional GET operation. It can be used to download feed (or any other) files. It's described as only *reasonably* polite, as it assumes other code will be used to determine the update rate, when to unsubscribe from a feed and so on. We provide a detailed description of the following example after you have had a chance to try out the code for yourself.

```java
package org.urss.io;

import java.io.File;
import java.io.FileWriter;
import java.io.IOException;
import java.io.InputStream;
import java.net.HttpURLConnection;
import java.net.MalformedURLException;
import java.net.URL;
import java.util.zip.GZIPInputStream;
import java.util.zip.Inflater;
import java.util.zip.InflaterInputStream;

/**
 * HTTP connection handler designed primarily for syndication feeds supports
 * Conditional GET and gzip encoding
 */
public class HttpConnector {

    private URL url = null;

    private int responseCode = -1;

    private String eTag = null;

    private String previousETag = null;

    private String lastModified = null;

    private String previousLastModified = null;

    private String contentType = null;

    private String encoding = null;
```

```
    private InputStream inputStream = null;

    private boolean dead = false;

    static {
        HttpURLConnection.setFollowRedirects(true);
    }

    public HttpConnector(String uri) {
        try {
            url = new URL(uri);
        } catch (MalformedURLException e) {
            e.printStackTrace();
        }
    }

    /**
     * Carries out everything needed to obtain an input stream if one is needed
     * by the feed. Returns true on success Any problems, or the feed is already
     * up-to-date returns false.
     */
    public boolean load() {
        HttpURLConnection connection = null;
        responseCode = -1;
        dead = true;
        try {
            connection = connect();
        } catch (IOException e) {
            //  e.printStackTrace();
            dead = true;
            return false;
        }
        try {
            responseCode = connection.getResponseCode();
        } catch (IOException e1) {
            // e1.printStackTrace();
            dead = false;
            return false;
        }
        if (responseCode == HttpURLConnection.HTTP_NOT_MODIFIED) {
            connection.disconnect();
            dead = false;
            return false;
        }
        InputStream inputStream = null;
        try {
            inputStream = getInputStream(connection);
        } catch (IOException e2) {
            dead = true;
            //  e2.printStackTrace();
            return false;
        }
dead = false;
        return true;
```

```
        }

    public HttpURLConnection connect() throws IOException {

        HttpURLConnection connection = (HttpURLConnection) url.openConnection();

        connection.setRequestProperty("Accept-Encoding", "gzip, deflate");

        if (previousETag != null) {
            connection.addRequestProperty("If-None-Match", previousETag);
        }

        if (previousLastModified != null) {
            connection.addRequestProperty("If-Modified-Since",
                    previousLastModified);
        }
        connection.connect();
        return connection;
    }

    public InputStream getInputStream(HttpURLConnection connection)
            throws IOException {

        lastModified = connection.getHeaderField("Last-Modified");
        previousLastModified = lastModified;
        eTag = connection.getHeaderField("ETag");
        previousETag = eTag;

        encoding = connection.getContentEncoding();
        contentType = connection.getContentType();

        if (encoding != null && encoding.equalsIgnoreCase("gzip")) {
            inputStream = new GZIPInputStream(connection.getInputStream());
        } else if (encoding != null && encoding.equalsIgnoreCase("deflate")) {
            inputStream = new InflaterInputStream(connection.getInputStream(),
                    new Inflater(true));
        } else {
            inputStream = connection.getInputStream();
        }
        return inputStream;
    }

    public void downloadToFile(String filename) {
        InputStream in = getInputStream();
        FileWriter out;
        int character;
        try {
            out = new FileWriter(new File(filename));
            while ((character = in.read()) != -1) {
                out.write(character);
            }
            in.close();
            out.close();
        } catch (IOException e) {
            e.printStackTrace();
        }
```

```
    }

    public String getStatus() {
        StringBuffer buffer = new StringBuffer();
        buffer.append("\n\nFeed:" + url);
        buffer.append("\nresponse code:" + getResponseCode());
        buffer.append("\nencoding:" + getContentEncoding());
        buffer.append("\ncontent-type:" + getContentType());
        buffer.append("\nlast-modified:" + getLastModified());
        buffer.append("\nisDead:" + isDead());
        return buffer.toString();
    }

    public void setPreviousETag(String previousETag) {
        this.previousETag = previousETag;
    }

    public void setPreviousLastModified(String previousLastModified) {
        this.previousLastModified = previousLastModified;
    }

    public String getETag() {
        return eTag;
    }

    public String getLastModified() {
        return lastModified;
    }

    public String getContentEncoding() {
        return encoding;
    }

    public String getContentType() {
        return contentType;
    }

    public InputStream getInputStream() {
        return inputStream;
    }

    public boolean isDead() {
        return dead;
    }

    public int getResponseCode() {
        return responseCode;
    }

    public static void main(String[] args) {
        HttpConnector connector = new HttpConnector(args[0]);
        boolean isOk = connector.load();
```

```
        if (isOk) {
            connector.downloadToFile("C:/test.xml");
        }
        System.out.println(connector.getStatus());
    }
}
```

In this code example (and in several other places in the book) file names are hard-coded for use on Microsoft Windows systems in the interest of simple code. In practice, certainly if you're working on different platforms, you may need to change these to something like: `System.getProperty` `("user.dir") + File.separatorChar + "test.xml"`.

Try It Out   Downloading a Feed

The `HttpConnector` class contains a `main` method set up to provide a simple demonstration. To use it, you will need to have the J2SE SDK (`http://java.sun.com/`) installed. You will also need to be online for the demos to work.

1.   Type and save `HttpConnector.java` to a convenient folder, with the directory structure:

```
[anywhere]\org\urss\io\HttpConnector.java
```

For example:

```
C:\source\org\urss\io\HttpConnector.java
```

2.   Open a command window in the `[anywhere]` directory, and type:

```
javac -classpath . org/urss/io/HttpConnector.java
```

That should compile the Java class.

3.   Now type the following (without line breaks):

```
java -classpath . org.urss.io.HttpConnector http://martinfowler.com/bliki/bliki.rss
```

You should now see something like this:

```
C:\source>javac -classpath . org/urss/io/HttpConnector.java
C:\source>java -classpath . org.urss.io.HttpConnector
                    http://martinfowler.com/bliki/bliki.rss
SAVING:C:/test.xml

Feed:http://martinfowler.com/bliki/bliki.rss
response code:200
encoding:null
content-type:text/xml
last-modified:Fri, 13 Aug 2004 19:20:46 GMT
isDead:false
```

4.   Now try the following:

```
java -classpath . org.urss.io.HttpConnector http://example.org/nothing.xml
```

You should see the following:

```
C:\source>java -classpath . org.urss.io.HttpConnector
          http://example.org/nothing.xml

Feed:http://example.org/nothing.xml
response code:404
encoding:null
content-type:text/html; charset=iso-8859-1
last-modified:null
isDead:false
```

5. Disconnect from the Internet, and do the same again. You should now see the following:

```
C:\source>java -classpath . org.urss.io.HttpConnector
          http://example.org/nothing.xml

Feed:http://example.org/nothing.xml
response code:-1
encoding:null
content-type:null
last-modified:null
isDead:true
```

How It Works

The list of imported classes provides a lot of explanation:

```
package org.urss.io;

import java.io.File;
import java.io.FileWriter;
import java.io.IOException;
import java.io.InputStream;
import java.net.HttpURLConnection;
import java.net.MalformedURLException;
import java.net.URL;
import java.util.zip.GZIPInputStream;
import java.util.zip.Inflater;
import java.util.zip.InflaterInputStream;
```

`File` and `FileWriter` look after saving data to a local file. `IOException` is needed to catch errors in practically all data-transport operations. `InputStream` is the form in which the data will come from the Web. `HttpURLConnection` does the low-level protocol stuff necessary to get the stream. `URL` and `MalformedURLExcception` are used in the mutation of the feed URI (identifier) into a URL (locater, that is, a URI plus HTTP transport). `GZipInputStream`, `Inflater`, and `InflaterInputStream` are standard library classes that handle decompression of the data when HTTP compression is used. (Inflate is another common compression algorithm or tool used for Web data, in fact it is used inside GZip.)

The class definition sets up a number of member variables that will be available through accessor methods:

```
public class HttpConnector {

    private URL url = null;

    private int responseCode = -1;

    private String eTag = null;

    private String previousETag = null;

    private String lastModified = null;

    private String previousLastModified = null;

    private String contentType = null;

    private String encoding = null;

    private InputStream inputStream = null;

    private boolean dead = false;
```

The URI from which data will be obtained is wrapped in url. The HTTP response code number (for example, 200 for Ok, 404 for Not Found) is initialized to a value way outside the standard range (-1) so it's clear from its value when communication has taken place. To avoid confusion, two variables are used for ETag and Last-Modified values, one pair for the values found in the current response (eTag, lastModified) and one pair that will carry the values in the response of the last GET operation (previousETag, previousLastModified). The contentType string will hold a value returned by the server in the corresponding HTTP header, something like application/xml. If one of the supported kinds of compression has been used, then encoding will receive a value from the server of gzip or deflate. The inputStream variable will be used to carry the stream of data containing the body of the HTTP message, in syndication applications this will be the feed itself. The dead flag will indicate when the GET operation has failed for some reason.

The next method effectively delegates handling of redirect response codes (3xx) to the HttpURLConnection class. This feature is actually true by default, but the method is included as a starting point in case custom redirect handling is required later.

```
    static {
        HttpURLConnection.setFollowRedirects(true);
    }
```

The HttpConnector class has a simple constructor which takes the target URI and from that constructs a URL:

```
    public HttpConnector(String uri) {
        try {
            url = new URL(uri);
        } catch (MalformedURLException e) {
            e.printStackTrace();
        }
    }
```

Most of the time `HttpConnector` objects will be used to carry out the same sequence of operations: connect to the server; check if there's new material; if there is new material, get hold of it. The `load()` method can be used to call methods to carry out each operation in turn. This method returns `true` if some new data is available for downloading, `false` otherwise. If any exceptions are thrown by the IO classes then `dead` will be set to `true`. The check for new material is done by looking at the response code — the server will have been passed a modification date and `ETag` from which it can tell whether there has been any change. If there hasn't, it will respond with "Not Modified," which can be recognized by comparing the response code value with the built-in constant `HttpURLConnection.HTTP_NOT_MODIFIED`. The last `try...catch` block merely obtains a reference to the `inputStream`, it doesn't actually do any downloading. In most cases it will be convenient to pipe this stream to other parts of the application.

```
public boolean load() {
    HttpURLConnection connection = null;
    responseCode = -1;
    try {
        connection = connect();
    } catch (IOException e) {
        //  e.printStackTrace();
        dead = true;
        return false;
    }
    try {
        responseCode = connection.getResponseCode();
    } catch (IOException e1) {
        //  e1.printStackTrace();
        dead = true;
        return false;
    }
    if (responseCode == HttpURLConnection.HTTP_NOT_MODIFIED) {
        connection.disconnect();
        dead = false;
        return false;
    }
    InputStream inputStream = null;
    try {
        inputStream = getInputStream(connection);
    } catch (IOException e2) {
        dead = true;
        //  e2.printStackTrace();
        return false;
    }
    dead = false;
    return true;
}
```

The `connect()` method opens a connection through the URL object, and adds several properties that will be used by the `HttpURLConnection` to construct the HTTP request header. The first property signals that this client is prepared to accept compressed data (in `gzip` or `deflate` formats). The next passes along the value of the `ETag` found the last time this URI was accessed with the instruction to only return the body of the data if the server doesn't have a matching tag associated with this resource. The third property allows the server to make date-based comparison, based on the previous value of the `Last-Modified` header.

```
public HttpURLConnection connect() throws IOException {

    HttpURLConnection connection = (HttpURLConnection) url.openConnection();

    connection.setRequestProperty("Accept-Encoding", "gzip, deflate");

    if (previousETag != null) {
        connection.addRequestProperty("If-None-Match", previousETag);
    }

    if (previousLastModified != null) {
        connection.addRequestProperty("If-Modified-Since",
                previousLastModified);
    }
    connection.connect();
    return connection;
}
```

If there is new data and your application wants to get it, the getInputStream method should be called. Because new data will be downloaded, the ETag and Last-Modified values need updating and passing along to be recorded as the "previous" values when another update is required. The encoding and contentType values are then obtained from the HTTP header using methods of HTTPURLConnection. The encoding value is then checked to see if it matches one of the supported compression formats. If it does, one of the library classes is used to pipeline the stream through decompression processing. The returned InputStream will be directly usable, whether or not it has been compressed in transit will be irrelevant to the rest of the application. The source for getInputStream is as follows:

```
public InputStream getInputStream(HttpURLConnection connection)
        throws IOException {

    lastModified = connection.getHeaderField("Last-Modified");
    previousLastModified = lastModified;
    eTag = connection.getHeaderField("ETag");
    previousETag = eTag;

    encoding = connection.getContentEncoding();
    contentType = connection.getContentType();

    if (encoding != null && encoding.equalsIgnoreCase("gzip")) {
        inputStream = new GZIPInputStream(connection.getInputStream());
    } else if (encoding != null && encoding.equalsIgnoreCase("deflate")) {
        inputStream = new InflaterInputStream(connection.getInputStream(),
                new Inflater(true));
    } else {
        inputStream = connection.getInputStream();
    }
    return inputStream;
}
```

The downloadToFile method is provided as a convenience for when some data on the Web needs to be copied to a local file. It should only be called after connect (or better still, load) and getInputStream have been called to set up the data stream. It creates a FileWriter based on the supplied file name and then reads the stream data from the Web, character by character, passing the values to the FileWriter and then to a file. The code looks like this:

```
public void downloadToFile(String filename) {
    System.out.println("SAVING:" + filename);
    InputStream in = getInputStream();
    FileWriter out;
    int character;
    try {
        out = new FileWriter(new File(filename));
        while ((character = in.read()) != -1) {
            out.write(character);
        }
        in.close();
        out.close();
    } catch (IOException e) {
        e.printStackTrace();
    }
}
```

The following methods are simple set and get methods on the `HttpConnector` class's private member variables:

```
public void setPreviousETag(String previousETag) {
    this.previousETag = previousETag;
}

public void setPreviousLastModified(String previousLastModified) {
    this.previousLastModified = previousLastModified;
}

public String getETag() {
    return eTag;
}

public String getLastModified() {
    return lastModified;
}

public String getContentEncoding() {
    return encoding;
}

public String getContentType() {
    return contentType;
}

public InputStream getInputStream() {
    return inputStream;
}

public boolean isDead() {
    return dead;
}

public int getResponseCode() {
    return responseCode;
}
```

It's useful to know how an operation went, and `getStatus` is provided for this purpose. It simply builds up a string containing the values of the various member variables together with labels for each. String concatenation (`stringX + stringY`) is notoriously inefficient in Java, so as a tiny bit of optimization a `StringBuffer` is used (there's concatenation within the individual appends, but optimizing those would have made the code marginally less readable).

```
public String getStatus() {
    StringBuffer buffer = new StringBuffer();
    buffer.append("\n\nFeed:" + url);
    buffer.append("\nresponse code:" + getResponseCode());
    buffer.append("\nencoding:" + getContentEncoding());
    buffer.append("\ncontent-type:" + getContentType());
    buffer.append("\nlast-modified:" + getLastModified());
    buffer.append("\nisDead:" + isDead());
    return buffer.toString();
}
```

The final method is `main`, which can be used as a simple test of the class, and it is the entry point taken in the previous Try It Out. An instance of `HttpConnector` is created and a `load()` called on it. If some fresh data is available it's downloaded using the `downloadToFile` method. A dump of the status is then printed to the console.

```
public static void main(String[] args) {
    HttpConnector connector = new HttpConnector(args[0]);
    boolean isOk = connector.load();
    if (isOk) {
        connector.downloadToFile("C:/test.xml");
    }
    System.out.println(connector.getStatus());
}
}
```

Note that when using the `main` method, the `ETag` values needed for conditional `GET` aren't recorded, and so a new download will be made every time (assuming there's data available).

Parsing XML with SAX

SAX defines an application programming interface (API) for parsing XML documents. Originally written for Java, the same functional interface is now available for most languages. The current version is known as SAX2, and operates in the same fashion as the original, but there were various (incompatible) changes. Details, including its genesis, can be found at www.saxproject.org.

SAX presents the developer with a lower-level interface than DOM. You point a DOM API at an XML source and get a populated data structure (the DOM tree). SAX on the other hand reads the data serially from the source, and in the process calls various standard methods to say when it encounters particular structural features in the source. You use the method calls to build up your own objects depending on what you want to do with the data. The parts of the XML document recognized include the start and end of a document, the start and end of elements (that is, the opening and closing tags) and any blocks of characters found between the elements that would appear as text nodes in DOM. Architecturally, SAX is event-driven, the events occurring when the parser identifies features in the stream of input data. Your listener implementation will depend on what information you want from the XML; all SAX does is call methods in series as elements and so on are encountered in the source syntax. For example, if you wanted to build a tree structure like DOM you would have to keep track of element nesting yourself.

XML has strictly defined syntax rules, that is, all opening tags should be closed in the right place and certain characters are disallowed. SAX includes syntax checking and will throw exceptions when the XML rules are broken. On top of this, most SAX parsers also support validation against DTD or XML Schemas. If this feature is turned on then you can also check that the data matches your own language definition.

There are several implementations of SAX in Java each with minor differences, but generally speaking the developer will be working with two objects: the parser itself and the listener which will receive the events. To demonstrate a SAX parser in action, you will now see some code that will read a list of feed URIs from an XML file. The format of the file will be a little variation on RSS 1.0, actually RSS 1.0 cut down to the barest minimum that can list channel URIs and still be valid RDF/XML, as shown in the following example (`feedlist.rdf`):

```
<rdf:RDF
  xmlns="http://purl.org/rss/1.0/"
  xmlns:rdf = "http://www.w3.org/1999/02/22-rdf-syntax-ns#"
>

<channel rdf:about="http://dannyayers.com/feed/rss2" />
<channel rdf:about="http://martinfowler.com/bliki/bliki.rss" />
<channel rdf:about="http://www.dehora.net/journal/index.rdf" />
<channel rdf:about="http://danja.typepad.com/fecho/atom.xml" />

</rdf:RDF>
```

This format uses terms from the RSS and RDF namespaces, so these are declared in the outer `rdf:RDF` element. As in RSS 1.0, the channel resource is identified by a URI which is the value of the `rdf:about` attribute. Unlike RSS 1.0, there is no further information about the channel—no title or description, or even any items. Structurally this is a small, stubby tree, with the root (`rdf:RDF`) containing a handful of minimal branches (`channel`), each of which has only one leaf (`rdf:about`). But SAX itself does not see that structure. It is entirely up to the application developer to handle the events, and build whatever structures they like. The structure built by this example is a `Set` collection containing all the URI strings listed in the file.

The channel list file uses namespaces, and SAX2 contains complete namespace support, so for convenience the namespace strings used are placed in constants in a separate class. This class also contains three feed format-related constants. Here is the definition of those constants (`FeedConstants.java`):

```
package org.urss.feeds;

public class FeedConstants {

    public static final String RDF_NS =
                "http://www.w3.org/1999/02/22-rdf-syntax-ns#";

    public static final String RSS_NS =
                "http://purl.org/rss/1.0/";
```

```
        public static final char UNKNOWN = 0;

        public static final char RSS1 = 1;

        public static final char RSS2 = 2;

        public static final char ATOM = 3;
    }
```

The code to read the channel list file is as follows (`ChannelSetReader.java`):

```java
package org.urss.io;

import java.io.File;
import java.io.FileInputStream;
import java.io.InputStream;
import java.util.HashSet;
import java.util.Iterator;
import java.util.Set;

import org.xml.sax.Attributes;
import org.xml.sax.InputSource;
import org.xml.sax.XMLReader;
import org.xml.sax.helpers.DefaultHandler;
import org.xml.sax.helpers.XMLReaderFactory;

import javax.xml.parsers.SAXParserFactory;

public class ChannelSetReader extends DefaultHandler {

    private Set feedURIs;

    private static final String channelTerm = FeedConstants.RSS_NS + "channel";

    private static final String rdfAboutTerm = FeedConstants.RDF_NS + "about";

    public Set load(String storeFilename) {
        feedURIs = new HashSet();
        try {
            SAXParserFactory parserFactory = SAXParserFactory.newInstance();
            parserFactory.setNamespaceAware(true);
            XMLReader xmlReader = parserFactory.newSAXParser().getXMLReader();
            xmlReader.setContentHandler(this);
            InputStream inputStream = new FileInputStream(new File(
                    storeFilename));
            InputSource inputSource = new InputSource(inputStream);
            xmlReader.parse(inputSource);
        } catch (Exception e) {
            e.printStackTrace();
        }
        return feedURIs;
    }

    public void startElement(String namespaceURI, String localName,
```

```
                            String qName, Attributes attributes) {

            if (namespaceURI.equals(FeedConstants.RSS_NS)
                    && localName.equals("channel")) {

                String uriString = attributes.getValue(FeedConstants.RDF_NS,
                        "about");
                feedURIs.add(uriString);
            }
        }
    }

    public static void main(String[] args){
        ChannelSetReader reader = new ChannelSetReader();
        Set channelSet = reader.load(args[0]);
        Iterator channelIterator = channelSet.iterator();
        while(channelIterator.hasNext()){
            System.out.println(channelIterator.next());
        }
    }
}
```

Try It Out   **Reading an RDF/XML Channel List**

1.   Type the previous listings into a text editor (or download them) and save them as:

```
[anywhere]\feedlist.rdf
[anywhere]\org\urss\feeds\FeedConstants.java
[anywhere]\org\urss\io\ChannelSetReader.java
```

2.   Open a command window in the root [anywhere] directory and enter:

```
javac -classpath . org\urss\io\ChannelSetReader.java
```

This will compile the classes.

3.   Now enter:

```
java -classpath . org\urss\io\ChannelSetReader feedlist.rdf
```

You should now see something like this:

```
C:\source>javac -classpath . org\urss\io\ChannelSetReader.java
C:\source>
C:\source>java -classpath . org.urss.io.ChannelSetReader feedlist.rdf

http://danja.typepad.com/fecho/atom.xml
http://dannyayers.com/feed/rss2
http://martinfowler.com/bliki/bliki.rss
http://www.dehora.net/journal/index.rdf
```

How It Works

As an event-driven system, SAX has one part to generate the events (the parser itself) and another to act as a listener to receive notification of events. In the ChannelSetReader demonstration, an object that implements the XMLReader interface looks after the parser functionality. The object is obtained from a built-in factory class (SAXParserFactory), which hides the specific implementation of the parser. Ask nicely and it will give you a working parser.

The source data is read from file and passed to this reader with a call to the `parse` method of the `XMLReader`. A SAX2 listener implements the `org.xml.sax.ContentHandler` interface, which defines methods including `startDocument`, `startElement`, `endElement`, and so on.

When you have a parser, the most important thing to do is attach a listener to it, using the `setContentHandler` method. The listener will implement the methods defined in `ContentHandler`.

There are a lot of these methods, so for convenience an implementation class `DefaultHandler` is provided in the `org.xml.sax.helpers` package. This contains dummy (do nothing) methods that can be overridden as needed to give useful (do *something*) implementations. The number of these methods you need to implement depends on the complexity of the objects you want to build from the XML data.

All that is required from the channel list data are the URIs, which in `ChannelSetReader` will be placed in a `Set`. These values all appear as attributes of the `channel` elements, so the only `ContentHandler` method needed is `startElement`, which gets passed the attributes of the element. Given this small requirement, rather than writing a separate class to implement `ContentHandler` it's easier just to make the class that creates the parser and initiates the parsing also act as the listener. By making `ChannelSetReader` extend `DefaultHandler`, you make provisions for the required `ContentHandler` method implementations. All your custom listener code needs is a suitable `startElement` method to recognize the channel elements and from them extract the value of the `rdf:about` attribute. In fact, `ChannelSetReader` only has three methods. The `load` method loads the data from file, creates a parser, and sets it on the data. The class itself acts as a listener, all the calls to `ContentReader` are handled by the `ChannelSetReader` parent class (`DefaultHandler`) with the exception of one class, `startElement`, which is implemented locally. A `main` method is provided to run the demonstration.

`ChannelSetReader` uses some standard Java I/O classes, some of the Collections classes (for containing the URIs obtained from the feed list file) and of particular interest here, some classes from the `org.xml.sax` and `org.xml.sax.helpers` packages. The parser factory is in `javax.xml.parsers`, outside of the core XML classes. If you choose to use a SAX library different from the one that comes with Java, then you will probably have to obtain a parser through another means, although the core interface definitions of `org.xml.sax` will remain the same. The import list looks like this:

```
package org.urss.io;

import java.io.File;
import java.io.FileInputStream;
import java.io.InputStream;
import java.util.HashSet;
import java.util.Iterator;
import java.util.Set;

import javax.xml.parsers.SAXParserFactory;

import org.xml.sax.Attributes;
import org.xml.sax.InputSource;
import org.xml.sax.XMLReader;
import org.xml.sax.helpers.DefaultHandler;
```

The class itself has a single member variable, SET, into which the URIs are placed (`feedURIs`):

```
public class ChannelSetReader extends DefaultHandler {

    private Set feedURIs;
```

The `load` method looks like this:

```
public Set load(String storeFilename) {
    feedURIs = new HashSet();
    try {
        SAXParserFactory parserFactory = SAXParserFactory.newInstance();
        parserFactory.setNamespaceAware(true);
        XMLReader xmlReader = parserFactory.newSAXParser().getXMLReader();
        xmlReader.setContentHandler(this);
        InputStream inputStream = new FileInputStream(new File(
                storeFilename));
        InputSource inputSource = new InputSource(inputStream);
        xmlReader.parse(inputSource);
    } catch (Exception e) {
        e.printStackTrace();
    }
    return feedURIs;
}
```

This method receives the name of the file containing the XML data, and begins by initializing the `feedURIs` to an instance of `HashSet`, a simple collection suitable for holding a set of objects without duplicates. The rest of the method is enclosed in a `try...catch` block, as there are various I/O and parser exceptions that may be thrown. A `static` method of `SAXParserFactory` is used to obtain an instance of the factory, and that factory is set to be namespace aware. A chain of methods is used on the factory to get a `SAXParser` instance and from that obtain the `XMLReader`, which will do the data reading and effectively provide the parsing functionality. The architecture around the `SAXParser` is quite convoluted but you generally don't have to worry about it, just use the boilerplate code for whichever SAX library you're using. After the current instance of `ChannelSetReader` has been passed to the `XMLReader` to act as a listener, I/O code needed to pass the data from file through the parser follows. This creates a `File` object based on the file name and uses that in the constructor of a `FileInputStream`. This `InputStream` isn't passed directly to the parser; rather it is used to construct an `InputSource` object. This is one of several places where versatility in the architecture of the SAX implementation calls for an extra level of indirection between the objects. Once constructed, the `InputSource` is passed to the `XMLReader` to parse.

The parser will then scan through the source data and whenever it encounters the opening tag of an XML element the `startElement` method will be called. That method appears as follows:

```
public void startElement(String namespaceURI, String localName,
        String qName, Attributes attributes) {

    if (namespaceURI.equals(FeedConstants.RSS_NS)
            && localName.equals("channel")) {

        String uriString = attributes.getValue(FeedConstants.RDF_NS,
                "about");
        feedURIs.add(uriString);
    }

}
```

The list of parameters of startElement shows the characteristics of a namespace-qualified XML element. For example, when the parser encounters the opening tag of the <rdf:RDF> element in the source data, the startElement method will be called with the following values:

```
namespaceURI: "http://www.w3.org/1999/02/22-rdf-syntax-ns#"
localName: "RDF"
qName: "rdf:RDF"
```

The details of this particular element, and most of the other information supplied by the parser about the data, is irrelevant to getting the URI values. The only information of interest is associated with the name channel in the namespace http://purl.org/rss/1.0. So the method has an if statement to check for matching values. If such an element is encountered, the Attributes object is queried to obtain the value for the about attribute in the RDF namespace. This value will be the required URI string, which is then added to the set.

The main method was used as the entry point into the demonstration run, and looks like this:

```java
public static void main(String[] args){
    ChannelSetReader reader = new ChannelSetReader();
    Set channelSet = reader.load(args[0]);
    Iterator channelIterator = channelSet.iterator();
    while(channelIterator.hasNext()){
        System.out.println(channelIterator.next());
    }
}
} // end of class
```

This method simply creates an instance of the ChannelSetReader class, and calls its load method on the first of the command-line arguments (feedlist.rdf). The return value will be a Set containing the URIs found in the named file, which are then printed in turn to the console.

Feed/Connection Management Subsystem

The code listed so far in this chapter has been for reading a list of URIs from an XML file and using HTTP to get data from the Web. Neither of these operations is necessarily tied to syndication operations. If you glance back at Figures 22-1 through 22-4, data from the HTTP client will be passed through a parser to interpret it within the syndication feed model. You will see feed parser implementations based on the SAX design in the next chapter. But different feeds will need different parsers, and some management of the feed URIs will be needed. You will now see code that will look after some of this functionality, providing a simple framework for managing the components of a consumer subsystem and keeping local feed data up-to-date.

An overview of the code that follows is shown in Figure 22-7. The Runner class, shown in the center, contains the main method that will get the consumer running, and does the top-level needed to work with the other classes.

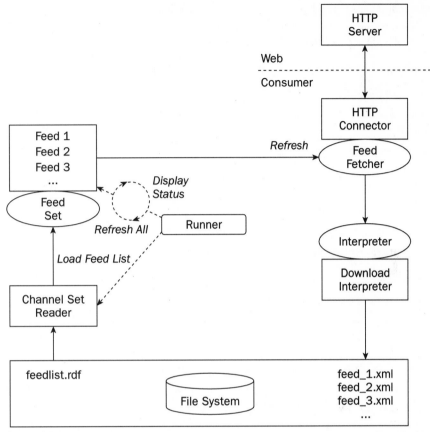

Figure 22-7

Starting from top-right, the HTTPConnector class you've already seen is used to get the data from the Web. This fairly general-purpose client is accessed through a more syndication-oriented interface, FeedFetcher. Every individual feed will have its own HTTPConnector, FeedFetcher, and an Interpreter. It may seem a little excessive having all these separate objects per feed rather than sharing them somehow. However, the objects themselves are relatively lightweight, mostly consisting of various flags that describe the current state of operations. Their purpose is more to simplify communications rather than carry data themselves.

When new data is fetched from the Web, a FeedFetcher interface will pass it to its Interpreter object to parse or otherwise process. In the listing here all the Interpreter implementation (DownloadInterpreter) does is to save the feed data as a file. At the bottom left of Figure 22-7, is the ChannelSetReader class. An instance of that class will be used to load a list of feed URIs from file. The FeedSet interface defines a simple wrapper for a collection of feeds, or rather in this setup FeedFetcher interfaces. The FeedSet interface has a method refreshAll(), and this will be used to call each FeedFetcher interface in turn to ask them to refresh themselves. Whereupon the FeedFetcher interface will get data from the Web using an HttpConnector class.

The interfaces and classes used in this subsystem are as follows.

In `org.urss.io`, the following classes and interfaces are used:

- ❑ `ChannelSetReader`: Reads the subscription list of channel URIs
- ❑ `Interpreter`: Interface that determines how feed data should be handled
- ❑ `DownloadInterpreter`: Implementation of `Interpreter`, saves the data from individual feeds locally
- ❑ `HttpConnector`: Handles HTTP communications

In `org.urss.feeds`, the following classes and interfaces are used:

- ❑ `FeedConstants`: Application constants, listed earlier
- ❑ `FeedEntity`: Interface to characteristics common to several components of a feed
- ❑ `FeedEntityBase`: Implementation of `FeedEntity`
- ❑ `FeedFetcher`: Syndication-oriented access to HTTP operations
- ❑ `FeedFetcherImpl`: Implementation of `FeedFetcher`
- ❑ `FeedSet`: Models a set of feeds or connections
- ❑ `FeedSetImpl`: Implementation of `FeedSet`
- ❑ `Runner`: Command-line demonstration of consumer classes

A Fetcher That Fetches the Feeds

Having said that `FeedFetcher` objects are lightweight, there is one set of data they carry, a set of member variables corresponding to feed-level elements in syndication feeds. As we discuss in Chapter 20, these variables are very similar to those of individual feed items, with names such as title, description, link, and date. What's more they are essentially the same across the different formats (RSS 1.0, 2.0, and Atom). So to allow reuse later, the get and set methods to access these variables are defined in a separate interface (`FeedEntity`) and a basic implementation is provided (`FeedEntityBase`). All the variables are defined as strings (as they are found in feeds) and the source code for both interface and base implementation is fairly trivial. Note the methods to get or set `URIString` — this refers to the URI of the feed itself.

The interface looks like this:

```
package org.urss.feeds;

public interface FeedEntity {

    public void setURIString(String uri);

    public String getURIString();

    public void setTitle(String title);
```

```
    public String getTitle();

    public void setDescription(String description);

    public String getDescription();

    public void setLink(String link);

    public String getLink();

    public void setDate(String date);

    public String getDate();
}
```

The class that provides a basic implementation of the FeedEntity interface looks like this:

```
package org.urss.feeds;

/**
 * Characteritics common to several components of a feed
 */
public class FeedEntityBase implements FeedEntity {

    private String uriString = "";

    private String description = "";

    private String title = "";

    private String link = "";

    private String date = "";

    public FeedEntityBase() {
    }

    public FeedEntityBase(String uriString) {
        this.uriString = uriString;
    }

    public void setURIString(String uriString) {
        this.uriString = uriString;
    }

    public String getURIString() {
        return uriString;
    }

    public void setTitle(String title) {
        this.title = title;
    }

    public String getTitle() {
        return title;
```

```
    }

    public void setDescription(String description) {
        this.description = description;

    }

    public String getDescription() {
        return description;
    }

    public void setLink(String link) {
        this.link = link;

    }

    public String getLink() {
        return link;
    }

    public void setDate(String date) {
        this.date = date;

    }

    public String getDate() {
        return date;
    }
}
```

The `HttpConnector` class described earlier hides a lot of the detail of connecting and obtaining data from the Web, and the `FeedFetcher` interface takes this a step further by providing a more feed-oriented view. This interface (and its implementation `FeedFetcherImpl`) doesn't do a great deal itself. Rather it brings together the top-level characteristics of feed data (by extending `FeedEntity`), provides access to Web data (through `HttpConnector`), and allows the association of an `Interpreter` with the feed data to make sense of what is found. Again the interface (and its implementation) is relatively simple, but the choice of methods shows a lot about the architectural approach taken here, so here it is piece by piece:

```
package org.urss.feeds;

import java.io.InputStream;

import org.urss.io.Interpreter;

public interface FeedFetcher extends FeedEntity {
```

The first methods are a `get`/`set` pair. The value passed here is a `char` that will correspond to one of those listed in `FeedConstants` earlier. Possible values are (currently) `FeedConstants.UNKNOWN`, `FeedConstants.RSS1`, `FeedConstants.RSS2`, and `FeedConstants.ATOM`. They name what is provisionally assumed to be the format of the feed. This choice may not be correct, or the data may be invalid in some way, hence the `hint` part.

```
    public void setFormatHint(char hint);

    public char getFormatHint();
```

The `refresh` method will bring the data associated with this feed up-to-date. This may involve getting it from the Web again, but only if the feed is due for an update according to its refresh period. This period is given as a number of milliseconds and is held in a long integer. Until the time since the last update is greater than this value, the feed data is considered current and the refresh method won't have any effect. After that it will be up to the HTTP client part of the code (`HttpConnector`) to decide whether or not the feed data needs to be updated according to the response it gets from the server.

```
    public boolean refresh();

    public void setRefreshPeriod(long refreshPeriod);
```

The next three methods will be used by an application to find out what's happening with the data and determine what kind of operations should take place on the feed data. If `FeedFetcher` responds true to `isNew`, then there is new data available, and usually the application will want to fetch it. If `FeedFetcher` responds true to `isDead`, then the last attempt at getting data from the feed URI ended in failure. The application may need to indicate this to the end user or whatever. Implementations of `FeedFetcher` can have some logic built in to decide locally whether a subscription really isn't worth continuing. The `shouldExpire` method tells the caller that it would be appropriate to stop trying to get data from this feed.

```
    public boolean isNew();

    public boolean isDead();

    public boolean shouldExpire();
```

The next three methods correspond directly to HTTP header information, returning values found the last time the feed URI was visited. If new data is available, the `getInputStream` method will provide a means of accessing it.

```
    public String getETag();

    public String getLastModified();

    public String getContentEncoding();

    public InputStream getInputStream();
```

The `getStatus` method will return a human-readable message describing the current status of the feed. As you might expect, `downloadToFile` will get the feed data (assuming some is available) and save it to disk. The `setInterpreter` method will pass the object responsible for extracting useful information from the raw data found in the feed.

```
    public String getStatus();

    public void downloadToFile(String filename);

    public void setInterpreter(Interpreter interpreter);
}
```

Before looking at the implementation of FeedFetcher, a look at the Interpreter interface should help you get an idea where all this is leading. The Interpreter interface is pretty minimal, in itself it only defines a single method, interpret, which will be passed the FeedFetcher object that needs to be interpreted. However, the interface does extend the SAX2 ContentHandler interface, so all implementations will be expected to handle SAX method calls (startElement and so on). The reason for this is that on paper at least, all syndication feeds are XML and so should be parseable using SAX. This is hopelessly inaccurate in practice, but the assumption does provide a useful starting point.

```
package org.urss.io;

import org.urss.feeds.FeedFetcher;
import org.xml.sax.ContentHandler;

public interface Interpreter extends ContentHandler {

    public void interpret(FeedFetcher feed);

}
```

The next listing is the FeedFetcher implementation, which is mostly a more convenient way of dealing with an HttpConnector object (one of its member variables). It also looks after the refresh period logic. By extending FeedEntityBase the class implements FeedEntity, and most of the FeedFetcher methods are handled by delegating method calls to its HttpConnector object. The code begins as follows:

```
package org.urss.feeds;

import java.io.InputStream;
import java.util.Date;

import org.urss.io.HttpConnector;
import org.urss.io.Interpreter;

public class FeedFetcherImpl extends FeedEntityBase implements FeedFetcher,
        FeedEntity {
```

The refresh period handling is looked with the help of the lastRefresh and refreshPeriod variables and a constant called ditherFactor. The value of lastRefresh will be the time at which the last refresh occurred, measured in milliseconds since Java's Date baseline, the January 1, 1970. As mentioned earlier, it's desirable to avoid any rigidly timed updates to avoid overloading servers at the top of the hour. The time of the first download of feed data will depend on when the consumer subsystem is first used. But just in case any of the application code attempts to follow overly regular timekeeping a randomly varying number of milliseconds is added to the period whenever a check is made to see if a download is due. The maximum value of the random number is determined by the dither factor, which here is set at 0.1, corresponding to 10 percent of whatever value the period has been set to.

```
    private long lastRefresh;

    private long refreshPeriod;

    private static final double ditherFactor = 0.1D;
```

This class contains an example of how feeds that don't appear to be working can be dealt with. The algorithm is simply to assign a feed three lives, and every time an attempt to update the feed fails a life is lost. At the same time the period between downloads is doubled, to allow time for the server to recover if the problem is temporary.

```java
private int MAX_LIVES = 3;

private int lives = MAX_LIVES;
```

The remaining member variables are here declared and, if appropriate, given initial values:

```java
private char hint = FeedConstants.UNKNOWN;

private boolean isNew = false;

private HttpConnector httpConnector = null;

private Interpreter interpreter;
```

The only constructor of `FeedFetcher` objects takes the URI of the feed. This is passed onto the parent `FeedEntityBase` class where it will be maintained, being accessible through that class's `getURIString()` method.

```java
public FeedFetcherImpl(String uri) {
    super(uri);
}
```

The most interesting method of this class is `refresh`. This will return `true` if some new feed data is available. It begins by checking whether a refresh period (plus a random amount) has passed. If the current time is before the next due update, the method returns right away. The source is as follows:

```java
public boolean refresh() {
    if (now() < lastRefresh + refreshPeriod + getPeriodDither()) {
        return false;
    }
    if (httpConnector == null) {
        httpConnector = new HttpConnector(getURIString());
    }
    isNew = httpConnector.load();

    if (isNew) {
        System.out.println("Connected, interpreting...");
        interpreter.interpret(this);
        lives = MAX_LIVES;
    } else {
        if (httpConnector.isDead()) {
            System.out.println("Error, feed life lost.");
            lives--;
            refreshPeriod = refreshPeriod*2;
        }
    }
    lastRefresh = now();
    return isNew;
}
```

An instance of the `HttpConnector` class is created if one doesn't already exist, and then its `load` method is called to see if any new data is available. If there is, this `FeedFetcher` object is passed to the `Interpreter` for it to obtain and process the new data. Note that the number of lives is also reset to its maximum here as the server is behaving as hoped. If there isn't any new data available, that doesn't necessarily mean there's a problem. It may just be that the conditional GET functionality of `HttpConnector` has determined that the feed hasn't changed. If there has been some kind of error, then `httpConnector.isDead()` will return `true`, and the feed expiry mechanism kicks in, removing a life.

The mechanism given here is only provided for demonstration purposes, there are serious problems with this simple error handling. Not least that if your connection to the Internet is lost then all the feeds will start to lose lives, and you could end up with an empty subscription list. Also note that the period stays at its extended value even after the server has been found to be working again.

The next two methods are local utilities, `now` returns the current time (expressed as milliseconds since January 1, 1970), and `getPeriodDither` returns a random number based on the `refreshPeriod` and the `ditherFactor` constant.

```
private long now() {
    return (new Date()).getTime();
}

private long getPeriodDither() {
    return (long) (Math.random() * ditherFactor * refreshPeriod);
}
```

The `shouldExpire` method (declared in the `FeedFetcher` interface) simply checks to see if all lives have been lost. If so, the caller is told it should drop this feed.

```
public boolean shouldExpire() {
    return lives < 1;
}
```

The remaining methods in `FeedFetcherImpl` all either get or set local member variables or delegate calls to the `HttpConnector` object:

```
public void setFormatHint(char hint) {
    this.hint = hint;
}

public char getFormatHint() {
    return hint;
}

public Interpreter getInterpreter() {
    return interpreter;
}

public boolean isNew() {
    return isNew;
}

public boolean isDead() {
```

```
            return httpConnector.isDead();
        }

    public String getETag() {
            return httpConnector.getETag();
        }

    public String getLastModified() {
            return httpConnector.getLastModified();
        }

    public String getContentEncoding() {
            return httpConnector.getContentEncoding();
        }

    public String getContentType() {
            return httpConnector.getContentType();
        }

    public InputStream getInputStream() {
            return httpConnector.getInputStream();
        }

    public String getStatus() {
            return httpConnector.getStatus();
        }

    public void downloadToFile(String filename) {
            httpConnector.downloadToFile(filename);
        }

    public void setInterpreter(Interpreter interpreter) {
            this.interpreter = interpreter;
        }

    public long getRefreshPeriod() {
            return refreshPeriod;
        }

    public void setRefreshPeriod(long refreshPeriod) {
            this.refreshPeriod = refreshPeriod;
        }

    public long getLastRefresh() {
            return lastRefresh;
        }
}
```

When a FeedFetcherImpl object discovers that its connection can supply new data, it will pass a reference to that data onto an implementation of Interpreter. That object will usually parse and interpret the feed XML, but for demonstration purposes the only implementation here will save the data to file. Here is the source to DownloadInterpreter:

```
package org.urss.io;

import org.urss.feeds.FeedFetcher;
import org.xml.sax.helpers.DefaultHandler;

public class DownloadInterpreter extends DefaultHandler implements Interpreter{

    private String  downloadDir;

    public DownloadInterpreter(String downloadDir){
        this.downloadDir = downloadDir;
    }

    public void interpret(FeedFetcher feed) {
        String filename = feed.getTitle() + ".xml";
        System.out.println("SAVING:" + feed.getURIString()+"\n=>"+filename);
        feed.downloadToFile(downloadDir+filename);
    }
}
```

This class gets around `Interpreter`'s need to implement all the SAX `ContentHandler` methods by extending the SAX helper class `DefaultHandler`, which contains dummies. The constructor of `DownloadInterpreter` receives the path to the directory into which feed data files will be downloaded. The `interpret` method itself creates a file name from the title of the feed, prints a message to the console, and then uses the `HttpConnector downloadToFile` utility method to save the data.

So far you've seen how the various parts of the consumer mini-framework fit together at the feed level. Next comes the code that looks after the set of feeds in the subscription list. `FeedSet` is the interface and `FeedSetImpl` the implementation. The interface looks like this:

```
package org.urss.feeds;

import java.util.Collection;

public interface FeedSet{

    public void addFeed(String uriString);

    public void addFeed(String uriString, char formatHint);

    public void addFeed(FeedFetcher feed);

    public void addFeeds(FeedSet feeds);

    public Collection getFeedCollection();

    public FeedFetcher createFeed(String uri);

    public FeedFetcher getNext();

    public void refreshAll();
}
```

The methods declared here are self-explanatory, most of them being obvious collection-oriented operations. The implementation will in fact wrap a class from Java's `Collection` framework. The `refreshAll` method will update all the feeds contained in the collection, with the details of how this is done hidden from the caller. Most of the methods in the implementation are collection oriented, too, as you can see in this listing of `FeedSetImpl`:

```
package org.urss.feeds;

import java.util.Collection;
import java.util.HashSet;
import java.util.Iterator;
import java.util.LinkedList;
import java.util.Set;

public class FeedSetImpl implements FeedSet {

    private final int SLEEP_PERIOD = 1000;
```

The `SLEEP_PERIOD` constant corresponds to an arbitrary pause after each feed in the collection is updated, to spread out this class's demands on system resources a little, especially when all feeds are up-to-date and refreshing is of little use.

The collection of feeds is contained in a `LinkedList` method. This type of Java collection has been chosen as it can form a simple first-in, last-out queue or a first-in, first-out stack as required. A new instance of the class is created in the constructor of `FeedSetImpl` in the following block:

```
    private LinkedList feedQueue;

    public FeedSetImpl() {
        feedQueue = new LinkedList();
    }
```

To hide a little more of the implementation setup, this class has a factory method `createFeed` to make a new instance of the `FeedFetcherImpl` class:

```
    public FeedFetcher createFeed(String uri) {
        return new FeedFetcherImpl(uri);
    }
```

The next block of methods provides various differing ways of creating, accessing, and manipulating the `FeedFetcher` objects in the collection:

```
    public void addFeed(String uriString) {
        addFeed(uriString, FeedConstants.UNKNOWN);
    }

    public void addFeed(FeedFetcher feed) {
        feedQueue.addFirst(feed); // it's shiny new and interesting
    }

    public void addFeed(String uriString, char formatHint) {
```

```
        FeedFetcher feed = createFeed(uriString);
        feed.setFormatHint(formatHint);
        addFeed(feed);
    }

    public void addFeeds(FeedSet feeds) {
        feedQueue.addAll(feeds.getFeedCollection());
    }

    public Collection getFeedCollection() {
        return feedQueue;
    }

    public FeedFetcher getNext() {
        FeedFetcher next = (FeedFetcher) feedQueue.removeFirst();
        feedQueue.addLast(next);
        return next;
    }
```

The primary operation of the refreshAll method is to tell each of the FeedFetcher instances in the collection to refresh itself. An iterator will step through each in turn. No action may be needed, so to stop the metaphorical wheels from spinning a brief pause is inserted into the loop. However, there is a possibility that there is an incurable problem with the feed and it has been marked for expiration. So any feeds that return true on their shouldExpire method are added to a Set method. After each of the FeedFetcher objects has been handled, each of the problem feeds is then removed from the main collection. The use of a separate collection is necessary to avoid concurrency problems that could be caused by deleting items when iterating through the collection.

```
    public void refreshAll() {
        Set expiring = new HashSet();
        Iterator iterator = feedQueue.iterator();
        FeedFetcher feed;
        while (iterator.hasNext()) {
            feed = (FeedFetcher) iterator.next();
            System.out.println("Checking: " + feed.getURIString());
            feed.refresh();
            if(feed.shouldExpire()){
                expiring.add(feed);
            }
            try {
                Thread.sleep(SLEEP_PERIOD);
            } catch (InterruptedException e) {
                e.printStackTrace();
            }
        }
        iterator = expiring.iterator();
        while (iterator.hasNext()) {
            feed = (FeedFetcher) iterator.next();
            System.out.println("Unsubscribing from "+feed.getURIString());
            feedQueue.remove(feed);
        }
    }
}
```

The final class in this consumer subsystem is `Runner`, a little demo class to set everything else in action. The complete source code looks like this:

```
package org.urss.feeds;

import java.util.Iterator;
import java.util.Set;

import org.urss.io.ChannelSetReader;
import org.urss.io.DownloadInterpreter;

public class Runner {

    static int REFRESH_PERIOD = 10000; // milliseconds

    public static void main(String[] args) {

        ChannelSetReader channelSetReader = new ChannelSetReader();
        Set feedlistURIs = channelSetReader.load(args[0]);
        FeedSet feeds = new FeedSetImpl();

        Iterator feedIterator = feedlistURIs.iterator();
        FeedFetcher feed;
        int nameCounter = 1;
        while (feedIterator.hasNext()) {
            feed = new FeedFetcherImpl((String) feedIterator.next());
            feed.setTitle("feed_" + Integer.toString(nameCounter++));
            feed.setInterpreter(new DownloadInterpreter(args[1]));
            feed.setRefreshPeriod(REFRESH_PERIOD);
            feeds.addFeed(feed);
        }

        while (true) {
            feeds.refreshAll();
            displayStatus(feeds);
        }
    }

    private static void displayStatus(FeedSet feeds) {
        Iterator feedIterator = feeds.getFeedCollection().iterator();
        while (feedIterator.hasNext()) {
            System.out.println(((FeedFetcher) feedIterator.next()).getStatus());
        }
        System.out.println("---------------");
    }
}
```

Try It Out   ## Running the Consumer

After you've downloaded the source code from the Wrox Web site and unzipped it into a convenient directory, you need to compile the classes before running the demo. You also need to be online.

1. Open the file `feedlist.rdf` and, following the existing format (listed earlier in the chapter), add references to any feed addresses you would like to examine. Be sure and include at least one address that doesn't point to a feed, for example:

```
<channel rdf:about="http://example.org/this/is/not/a/feed" />
```

2.   Open a command window in the root of the source directory, and type:

```
javac -classpath . org/urss/feeds/Runner.java
```

That should compile the Java class.

3.   Now type:

```
java -classpath . org.urss.feeds.Runner c:\source\feedlist.rdf C:\data
```

The consumer subsystem will now start collecting data from the feeds listed in feedlist.rdf, and will continue until you tell it to stop. It will save the feeds it finds in C:\data—after receiving a few messages on the command line you may want to check this, and confirm that the feeds sent with gzip compression have been decompressed into plain text. Note that the time intervals in the demo source are set to very short periods, so it would be impolite to run it for long, a minute or so should be enough to produce an interesting trace of events.

The following output was taken from a trace obtained by using the feedlist.rdf listed earlier, with the dud URI added. It begins by checking each feed in turn and finding data at each (except for the dud) saves the data to disk.

```
Checking: http://www.dehora.net/journal/index.rdf
Connected, interpreting...
SAVING:http://www.dehora.net/journal/index.rdf
=>feed_5.xml
Checking: http://example.org/this/is/not/a/feed
Error, feed life lost.
Checking: http://martinfowler.com/bliki/bliki.rss
Connected, interpreting...
SAVING:http://martinfowler.com/bliki/bliki.rss
=>feed_3.xml
Checking: http://dannyayers.com/feed/rss2
Connected, interpreting...
SAVING:http://dannyayers.com/feed/rss2
=>feed_2.xml
Checking: http://danja.typepad.com/fecho/atom.xml
Connected, interpreting...
SAVING:http://danja.typepad.com/fecho/atom.xml
=>feed_1.xml
```

The runner will then print the status of each feed in turn:

```
Feed:http://www.dehora.net/journal/index.rdf
response code:200
encoding:null
content-type:application/rdf+xml
last-modified:Fri, 20 Aug 2004 23:37:08 GMT
isDead:false


Feed:http://example.org/this/is/not/a/feed
response code:404
```

```
encoding:null
content-type:text/html; charset=iso-8859-1
last-modified:null
isDead:true
...
```

For most subsequent loops, no fresh data will be available when the feed is checked, so each refresh loop will pass through quite quickly:

```
Checking: http://www.dehora.net/journal/index.rdf
Checking: http://example.org/this/is/not/a/feed
Error, feed life lost.
Checking: http://martinfowler.com/bliki/bliki.rss
Checking: http://dannyayers.com/feed/rss2
Checking: http://danja.typepad.com/fecho/atom.xml
```

However, when conditions are right (the refresh period for a feed has been exceeded and fresh data is available), a download will take place, overwriting the previous saved version of the feed data. If you look ahead quite a ways through the trace you will see a line like this for each dud feed you added:

```
Unsubscribing from http://example.org/this/is/not/a/feed
```

The subsequent checking phase will include one feed less:

```
Checking: http://www.dehora.net/journal/index.rdf
Checking: http://martinfowler.com/bliki/bliki.rss
Checking: http://dannyayers.com/feed/rss2
Checking: http://danja.typepad.com/fecho/atom.xml
```

How It Works

By now you may have forgotten the overall view of the consumer subsystem built from the previous source. So before looking at the source of Runner.java (and a description of the top-level operation of the classes it controls), you should refer back to Figure 22-7.

There's nothing fancy in the imports of the runner, a couple of Collections classes and the ChannelSetReader (to read the list of feeds) and DownloadInterpreter (to write individual feeds to file). These correspond to the bottom left and bottom right of Figure 22-7, the file system I/O. The source begins like this:

```
package org.urss.feeds;

import java.util.Iterator;
import java.util.Set;

import org.urss.io.ChannelSetReader;
import org.urss.io.DownloadInterpreter;

public class Runner {

    static int REFRESH_PERIOD = 10000; // milliseconds
```

The basic time between refresh attempts (REFRESH_PERIOD) is set at 10 seconds so you can see what's happening at the command line without waiting too long. However, in a practical implementation this should be set to a figure of 3600000 milliseconds (one hour) or more.

The main method is the entry point when the Runner application is run, with the command-line arguments being passed into the string array args. After a ChannelSetReader object has been created, it is given the value of the first command-line argument as the name of the file to load. An instance of the FeedSetImpl class is then created. This contains the FeedFetcher objects corresponding to each of the channels in the list. The source of main looks like this:

```
public static void main(String[] args) {

    ChannelSetReader channelSetReader = new ChannelSetReader();
    Set feedlistURIs = channelSetReader.load(args[0]);
    FeedSet feeds = new FeedSetImpl();
```

The next block of code initializes the FeedFetcher objects that will manage each individual feed. Create an iterator to step through the channel URIs found in the feed list file, and create a FeedFetcherImpl object from each. Each of those objects is given a title of the form *feed_x*. That will be used to form the file name for the data saved to disk (if you integrate this subsystem into an application then you may want to change the naming, for example to extract the title from within the feed data to serve as the basis of the file name). The interpreter for each feed is a DownloadInterpreter created from the second command-line argument (the storage directory path). The refresh period of each FeedFetcher is then set to the constant defined previously, and then each initialized FeedFetcher is added to the FeedSet container.

```
    Iterator feedIterator = feedlistURIs.iterator();
    FeedFetcher feed;
    int nameCounter = 1;
    while (feedIterator.hasNext()) {
        feed = new FeedFetcherImpl((String) feedIterator.next());
        feed.setTitle("feed_" + Integer.toString(nameCounter++));
        feed.setInterpreter(new DownloadInterpreter(args[1]));
        feed.setRefreshPeriod(REFRESH_PERIOD);
        feeds.addFeed(feed);
    }
```

After the FeedSet container is loaded with the initialize FeedFetchers, it is used to keep local data up-to-date by calling the refreshAll method again and again in an infinite loop. The individual FeedFetcher objects handle the timing of when each individual feed is downloaded. After all have been refreshed, the local displayStatus method is called. This method will print the status of each FeedFetcher to the console in turn. As all the real work is delegated through the FeedSet to the individual FeedFetcher objects (and from there to HttpConnector objects), very little actual running code is needed, as you can see:

```
    while (true) {
        feeds.refreshAll();
        displayStatus(feeds);
    }
}
```

The method that displays the status simply iterates through all the FeedFetcher objects and calls their getStatus method to obtain this information, which is output to the console. The Runner.java source thus finishes like this:

```
        private static void displayStatus(FeedSet feeds) {
            Iterator feedIterator = feeds.getFeedCollection().iterator();
            while (feedIterator.hasNext()) {
                System.out.println(((FeedFetcher) feedIterator.next()).getStatus());
            }
            System.out.println("---------------");
        }
    }
```

Implementation Notes

The code presented here isn't intended as a finished package, in practice you may need to make quite a lot of adjustments to use it in an application. The algorithm for determining when a feed has expired is weak, and much of the support for HTTP is entirely left to Java's HTTP client (`HttpURLConnection` in `HttpConnector`). The application should include some custom handling of response codes, such as `301 Moved Permanently`, which signals that the URI should be replaced.

The code all operates essentially in a single thread and through a single (blocking) HTTP connection. Neither of these should present any major problems. Multiple non-blocking connections such as those offered by Java's `java.nio` classes could be used in a pool, but for most syndication applications this will be unnecessary as individual feeds change very slowly compared to the time it takes to visit each. The consumer subsystem could run in a separate thread from the rest of the application, as long as no attempts are made to write to the objects in the consumer. If more two-way communication is needed with the consumer then the affected methods will probably need declaring as synchronized, and the collection within `FeedSet` modifying to take a synchronized form.

So there are a lot of caveats about this code, but it demonstrates many of the ideas involved in consuming feed data and is suitable as a starting point for development. In the next chapter you will see some more interesting implementations of the `Interpreter` interface, to actually look at material within the feed. However the download-to-file interpretation is far from useless, and several aggregators follow a similar approach. The feed files saved locally can be used as the *database* or handed to a local Web server so they can be displayed (after a little styling) in a browser.

Summary

In this chapter you explored many different possible strategies for consuming syndication feeds. A key part of all of them is the process of parsing raw data to obtain a meaningful interpretation, even if the end result is a simple display of the data.

In this chapter, you learned...

❑   That compression and conditional GET could minimize bandwidth wastage.

❑   How an application can look after timing of feed refreshes.

❑   That XML-level hints can help with efficiency.

❑   How SAX works, and can be used to read channel lists.

❑   How a set of feeds can be managed.

The next chapter looks deeper inside the consumer, and you learn what next to do with feed data obtained from the Web.

Exercises

1. Make a copy of `ChannelSetReader.java` and modify it to read URIs from OPML subscription lists.

Here is an example of source data (`feedlist.opml`):

```
<opml version="1.0">
    <head>
        <ownerName>John Doe</ownerName>
        <ownerEmail>jd@example.org</ownerEmail>
    </head>
    <body>
            <outline text="Bill de hÓra" type="rss"
                    xmlUrl="http://www.dehora.net/journal/index.rdf"/>
            <outline text="Martin Fowler's Bliki" type="rss"
                    xmlUrl="http://martinfowler.com/bliki/bliki.rss"/>
            <outline text="Finally Atom" type="rss"
                    xmlUrl="http://dannyayers.com/feed/rss2"/>
            <outline text="Raw" type="rss"
                    xmlUrl="http://danja.typepad.com/fecho/atom.xml"/>
    </body>
</opml>
```

Note: The guidelines suggest using `type="rss"` for every kind of syndication feed.

Hint: OPML doesn't use namespaces. This means that an element type can be identified by its local name alone. You can examine the data sent to `startElement` when parsing a document by replacing that method with something like this:

```
public void startElement(String namespaceURI, String localName,
                         String qName, Attributes attributes) {

    System.out.println("\nnamespaceURI:" + namespaceURI);
    System.out.println("localName:" + localName);
    System.out.println("qName:" + qName);

    for(int i=0;i<attributes.getLength();i++){
        System.out.println("    attribute "+
                attributes.getLocalName(i)+
                " = "+
                attributes.getValue(i));
    }
}
```

Also note that the `Attributes` class includes a method `attributes.getValue` that takes as a single (string) parameter the local name of the attribute and returns the value.

2. See if you can come up with a good strategy for keeping track of feeds that aren't providing data as they should. For example, the consumer code in this chapter managed errors in feeds by deducting a "life" every time something went wrong, and unsubscribing when a `FeedFetcher` had no lives left. A big drawback of this approach is that a subscription list will fairly rapidly get emptied if the connection to the Internet is lost. Can you think of a better approach? There is no single solution to this problem, and it will depend to some extent on how you intend your application to interact with end users.

Parsing Feeds

Chapter 22 looks at consumer systems from a relatively high level, and then went into detail about the practice of getting data over HTTP. We also discuss parsers in that chapter and provide a simple SAX parser (for feed lists). This chapter continues the discussion of feed consumption, looking more closely at the issues involved in parsing feed data.

Parsing is about extracting useful information from a series of characters, and the aim in this chapter is to take feed data and use it to populate a data structure.

If you're planning on consuming feeds, then one of the first obstacles you need to get past is poor-quality data. If you're building a newsreader-style system to view the contents of feeds then you'll have to deal with material that won't display as the publisher intended. If you're building a system to aggregate and republish feed data in one form or another, you're going to have to make sure that the material you receive makes sense.

If you're planning on publishing feeds, you should be aware of the kind of pitfalls that lie in wait for the unwary developer. Even if you are just looking to set up a feed on your personal Weblog, the issue of bad data is something you're bound to encounter one way or another. Most probably you'll encounter it when one of your subscribers informs you that it's unreadable. Even if you're not the consumer, it's useful to know what the syndication environment looks like from the subscriber's point of view.

In this chapter, you will learn about:

- ❏ Extracting data from XML feeds
- ❏ Problems commonly encountered with XML
- ❏ Strict XML parsing (with demonstration code)
- ❏ Parsing "tag soup" markup (with demonstration code)
- ❏ Issues specific to XML over HTTP
- ❏ Integrating the parsing code with the consumer code from the previous chapter

A Target Model

Earlier in the book you saw various different ways in which feed data could be modeled. The parsing code presented in this chapter is designed with a specific target in mind, an object-oriented data model of syndicated items. This is in a sense an arbitrary target, in that you might want your data to go directly into a database of some form, or into some strange and wonderful processing pipeline for subsequent republishing. But within the application environment a data model that reflects the domain model is likely to be the most versatile starting point from which to build.

In Chapter 20 we discuss how Relaxer could be used to generate a set of classes to contain feed data. The code that follows is very similar, albeit somewhat simplified to make it easier for you to see what's going on. The following interfaces and classes will hold the data:

❑   `Entry`: An OO mapping of an RSS item or Atom entry

❑   `EntryImpl`: A simple implementation of `Entry`

❑   `EntryList`: Defines a container for an ordered series of `Entry` objects

❑   `EntryListImpl`: A simple implementation of `EntryList`

In Chapter 22 we list an interface, `FeedEntity`, and a class, `FeedEntityImpl`. These provide simple set or get access to a set of strings corresponding to elements commonly found at feed level: a URI, the title, description, link, and date. In that chapter, we also suggest that these could be reused, because they are essentially the same named elements found inside individual items or entries within a feed. A feed has a title, so do each of the items it carries, likewise for the other elements. Most of the required functionality for `Entry`/`EntryImpl` can be provided by simply inheriting that of `FeedEntity`/`FeedEntityImpl`. However, there are variations between formats to take into consideration, most notably the variation in the meaning of the <description> element between RSS 1.0 and 2.0. In the former the description is what it says, a description of the resource identified by the item. In the latter the <description> element is used to carry the item content itself. To allow the different usage, `Entry` objects will hold an additional value called `content`.

The source code for `Entry.java` is as follows:

```
package org.urss.feeds;

public interface Entry extends FeedEntity {

    public void setContent(String content);

    public String getContent();
}
```

As you can see, there isn't much to it. The source code of `EntryImpl.java` is also fairly minimal:

```
package org.urss.feeds;

public class EntryImpl extends FeedEntityBase implements Entry {

    private String content = "";

    public EntryImpl() {
```

```
            super();
    }

    public EntryImpl(String uriString) {
        super(uriString);
    }

    public void setContent(String content) {
        this.content = content;
    }

    public String getContent() {
        return content;
    }

    public String toString() {
        return toHTML();
    }

    public String toHTML() {
        return "<div class=\"entry\">" + super.toHTML() + "<p>" + getContent()
               + "</p>" + "</div>";
    }
}
```

There are a couple of things to note in this listing. Both zero parameter and single (`uriString`) parameter–based constructors are provided, with the latter passing the string value up to the parent class directly through the call to `super`. A custom `toString` method has been included, which in turn calls a `toHTML` method. This constructs a little snippet of XHTML based on the content of carried by this class (in content) and whatever is returned from a call to the parent class's `toHTML` method. The fact that this data has come from an entry is made clear by surrounding the snippet with `<div class="entry">`...`</div>`. The main reason for returning XHTML is that it can be used to provide a formatted view of the data.

The `FeedEntityBase` listing earlier didn't actually contain a `toHTML` method, so before going any further, here is what needs to be inserted into `FeedEntityBase.java`:

```
    ...
    public String getDate() {
        return date;
    }

    public String toHTML() {
        StringBuffer html = new StringBuffer();
        html.append("<a href=\"" + getLink() + "\">");
        html.append(getTitle());
        html.append("</a>");
        if (getDescription().trim().length() > 0) {
            html.append("\n<p>" + getDescription() + "</p>");
        }
        if (getDate().trim().length() > 0) {
            html.append("\n<p>" + getDate() + "</p>\n");
        }
        return html.toString();
    }
}
```

A `StringBuffer` is used to build up the XHTML representation of the object modeled by this class (and its descendents). The title and link elements are combined to provide a hyperlink, along the lines of this:

```
<a href="http://example.org">The Title</a>
```

Checks are made on the description and date variables to make sure that they contain something worth displaying. This is achieved by first using `trim` to remove leading and trailing whitespace and then testing the length of the result. If there is something interesting in either of these variables it is wrapped in a `<p>` element before being added to the HTML representation.

You may be wondering how these classes fit in with the feed-level classes in Chapter 22. In short, the earlier classes were designed to address the needs of the transport, whereas the classes here are designed to handle the actual data transported. Toward the end of this chapter you will see how these two complimentary aspects can be joined and later, in Chapter 27, we will extend the combined system.

Parsing Feeds as XML

All the major feed formats are based on the W3C's XML 1.0 specification. It's generally agreed that this is a good idea. The standard is widely adopted, and relatively straightforward to support. A multitude of tools are available off the shelf for generating and reading XML. That syndication feeds are based on XML suggests an application that consumes this kind of data will want an XML parser in its input stages. That's reasonable in itself, but not the whole story. Before venturing into the morass that is the real world of syndicated data, there now follows an example of how things might work, in an ideal world. We use the following two Java classes for this example:

❑   `Rss2ParserDemo`: Creates and runs a standard SAX parser

❑   `Rss2Handler`: Handles SAX events, creating `Entry` objects

The `ChannelSetReader` class described in Chapter 22 operates by running an event-driven SAX parser on some XML data, and by listening to those events itself. The code in `Rss2ParserDemo` is very similar to the part of the `ChannelSetReader` code that creates and runs a parser, but this time the listener is defined as a separate class. `Rss2ParserDemo.java` contains just two methods, one to create the parser (`readFeed`) and apply it to an RSS 2.0 file, and the other is the `main` method, which is the application entry point. All the `main` method does is pass the file name from the command line to `readFeed`, and then display the objects the handler has created at the command line.

Here is the code for `Rss2ParserDemo.java`:

```
package org.urss.parsers;

import java.io.File;
import java.io.FileInputStream;
import java.io.InputStream;

import javax.xml.parsers.SAXParserFactory;

import org.urss.feeds.EntryList;
import org.urss.feeds.EntryListImpl;

import org.xml.sax.InputSource;
```

```
import org.xml.sax.XMLReader;

public class Rss2ParserDemo {

    public EntryList readFeed(String feedFilename) {
        EntryList entries = new EntryListImpl();
        try {
            SAXParserFactory parserFactory = SAXParserFactory.newInstance();
            parserFactory.setNamespaceAware(true);
            XMLReader xmlReader = parserFactory.newSAXParser().getXMLReader();

            Rss2Handler handler = new Rss2Handler();
            handler.setEntryList(entries);

            xmlReader.setContentHandler(handler);
            InputStream inputStream = new FileInputStream(
                    new File(feedFilename));
            InputSource inputSource = new InputSource(inputStream);
            xmlReader.parse(inputSource);

        } catch (Exception e) {
            e.printStackTrace();
        }
        return entries;
    }

    public static void main(String[] args) {
        Rss2ParserDemo reader = new Rss2ParserDemo();
        EntryList entries = reader.readFeed(args[0]);
        for (int i = 0; i < entries.size(); i++) {
            System.out.println(entries.getEntry(i));
        }
    }
}
```

ChannelSetReader only needed to implement one of the SAX listener methods (startElement) to be able to extract the required information from the simple channel list file format. RSS 2.0 constructs need more complex handling to get at the text data within elements. They require three methods: startElement, characters, and endElement. These are used in combination to create Entry objects and load a container EntryList with them, based on what's found in the XML. The source code of Rss2Handler.java looks like this:

```
package org.urss.parsers;

import org.urss.feeds.Entry;
import org.urss.feeds.EntryImpl;
import org.urss.feeds.EntryList;
import org.xml.sax.Attributes;
import org.xml.sax.helpers.DefaultHandler;
public class Rss2Handler extends DefaultHandler {

    private StringBuffer textBuffer;

    private final static char IN_NOTHING = 0;

    private final static char IN_CHANNEL = 1;
```

```
    private final static char IN_ITEM = 2;

    private char state = IN_NOTHING;

    private Entry entry;

    private EntryList entries;

    public Rss2Handler() {
        textBuffer = new StringBuffer();
    }

    public void setEntryList(EntryList entries) {
        this.entries = entries;
    }

    public void startElement(String namespaceURI, String localName,
            String qName, Attributes attributes) {
        switch (state) {
        case IN_NOTHING:
            if ("channel".equals(localName)) {
                state = IN_CHANNEL;
            }
            return;

        case IN_CHANNEL:
            if ("item".equals(localName)) {
                state = IN_ITEM;
                entry = new EntryImpl();
            }
            return;

        case IN_ITEM:
            textBuffer = new StringBuffer();
            return;

        default:
            return;
        }
    }

    public void characters(char[] ch, int start, int length) {
        textBuffer.append(ch, start, length);
    }

    public void endElement(String namespaceURI,
                            String localName, String qName) {

        switch (state) {

        case IN_NOTHING:
            return;

        case IN_CHANNEL: // switch down
            if ("channel".equals(localName)) {
```

```
                    state = IN_NOTHING;
            }
            return;

        case IN_ITEM:
            if ("item".equals(localName)) {
                state = IN_CHANNEL;
                entries.addEntry(entry);
                return;
            }
            if ("title".equals(localName)) {
                entry.setTitle(textBuffer.toString());
                return;
            }
            if ("link".equals(localName)) {
                entry.setLink(textBuffer.toString());
                return;
            }
            if ("description".equals(localName)) {
                entry.setContent(textBuffer.toString());
                return;
            }
            textBuffer.append(localName);
            return;

        default:
            return;
        }
    }
}
```

Try It Out   Parsing RSS with SAX

1. Save the files `Entry.java`, `EntryImpl.java`, `Rss2ParserDemo.java`, and `Rss2Handler.java` into a folder in a directory structure that looks like this:

```
[anywhere]\org\urss\parsers\Rss2ParserDemo.java
[anywhere]\org\urss\parsers\Rss2Handler.java
```

For example:

```
C:\source\org\urss\parsers\Rss2ParserDemo.java
C:\source\org\urss\parsers\Rss2Handler.java
```

2. Save or copy an RSS 2.0 file into the `[anywhere]` directory (for example `rss2sample.xml` listed in Chapter 20).

3. Open a command window in `[anywhere]` and enter:

```
javac -classpath . org\urss\parsers\*.java
```

This will compile the source files.

4. Now enter the following, but substitute the name of your RSS 2.0 file if necessary:

```
java -classpath . org.urss.parsers.Rss2ParserDemo rss2sample.xml
```

You should now see something that begins like this:

```
java -classpath . org.urss.parsers.Rss2ParserDemo rss2sample.xml
<div class="entry"><a href="http://example.org/idol/shelley">Shelley</a><p>Shell
ey first impressed the judges with her 3-line backup script, then trampled the
 opposition with her cover of "These Boots Were Made for Walking".</p></div>
...
```

How It Works

The Rss2ParserDemo code appears quite complex, mostly due to what's needed to set up the parser. The core operation can be seen in the following lines, extracted from the earlier listing. First an EntryList object is created to receive any Entry objects that are created:

```
EntryList entries = new EntryListImpl();
```

A handler (listener) for the SAX parsing events is created:

```
Rss2Handler handler = new Rss2Handler();
```

The EntryList container is passed to the handler:

```
handler.setEntryList(entries);
```

The handler is attached to the parser:

```
xmlReader.setContentHandler(handler);
```

The XML document is parsed:

```
xmlReader.parse(inputSource);
```

As the document is parsed, methods in the handler are called. These methods are called sequentially according to what is encountered in the XML — startElement (an element's opening tag), characters (text within an element), or endElement (an element's closing tag). However, if you imagine that occurring on a piece of feed XML, a series of calls won't make much sense unless you remember something of the document structure. Here is a snippet of RSS 2.0, and as you can see there is indeed quite a lot of structure:

```
<rss version="2.0">
   <channel>
      <title>Tech Idol</title>
      <item>
         <title>Shelley</title>
         <link>http://example.org/idol/shelley</link>
         <description>Shelley first impressed the judges with her 3-line
            backup script, then trampled the opposition with her cover of
            "These Boots Were Made for Walking".</description>
         <pubDate>Thu, 01 Jul 2004 09:39:21 GMT</pubDate>
         <guid>http://example.org/idol/shelley</guid>
      </item>
      <item>
         <title>Sam</title>
         <link>http://example.org/idol/sam</link>
         <description>Test-driven development while plate-spinning?
```

```
            Sam's the man.</description>
        <pubDate>Thu, 01 Jul 2004  08:37:32 GMT</pubDate>
        <guid>http://example.org/idol/sam</guid>
      </item>
    </channel>
  </rss>
```

When reading this document, the parser will call the `startElement` method for the `<rss>` tag, then the `<channel>` tag, and then the `<title>` tag. The `characters` method will be called, with a pointer to the text `Tech Idol`, then the `endElement` method will be called with the details of `</title>`. This is something of a simplification, with the XML above the `characters` method will also be called to signal the whitespace characters between the first line and the second, and so on. What's more, the `characters` method may be called once for each chunk of character data, but the SAX definition allows for an implementation to call the method several times, passing the data as smaller chunks. This is fairly straightforward to deal with. All the handler has to do is to add all the material passed to `characters` between a `startElement` call and an `endElement` call. The `textBuffer` variable is used to retain the text between these calls.

Although it's certainly possible to record practically everything about the document structure (as DOM does), when you know in advance what kind of structure to expect in your XML, you can concentrate on mapping the data to your application model. As the parser steps through different substructures in the XML, the handler can create objects corresponding to those structures. From a high-level viewpoint, the RSS 2.0 feed is a document that contains one large structure (the `<channel>`), which contains several smaller structures (the `<item>` elements). Each of these structures has a set of text data contained in elements with a common name: `<title>`, `<description>`, and so on. So it is necessary to remember how far the parser has reached when it encounters the opening tag of one of these data elements, to know which object the data should be associated with. A simple member variable `state` is used in the code to track this, and the values it can take correspond to different positions in the RSS documents structure. You can see the variable and its possible values early in the source:

```
private final static char IN_NOTHING = 0;

private final static char IN_CHANNEL = 1;

private final static char IN_ITEM = 2;

private char state = IN_NOTHING;
```

The first value `IN_NOTHING` signifies that the parser is outside of any interesting parts of the document. What's considered interesting in this sample code are the channel and the items it contains, and these substructures are flagged using `IN_CHANNEL` and `IN_ITEM`. The value of state is initialized to `IN_NOTHING`.

The handler also has a member variable for an `Entry` and `EntryList` to hold the object representations of the content of the RSS. When an opening `<item>` element is encountered, a new entry object will be created. The state will shift to `IN_ITEM` and all handler method calls in that state will be interpreted as relating to that entry. When the next `</item>` tag is encountered that is interpreted as the end of that entry, and the entry will be added to the `EntryList`.

The `startElement` method is called whenever an element's opening tag is encountered by the parser. The key to its operation is a switch based on the current value of `state`. The method starts like this:

```
public void startElement(String namespaceURI, String localName,
        String qName, Attributes attributes) {
    switch (state) {
    case IN_NOTHING:
        if ("channel".equals(localName)) {
            state = IN_CHANNEL;
        }
        return;
```

The first `state` case checked for is `IN_NOTHING`. If the handler is in this state (that is, the parser isn't within any interesting parts of the XML), then a check is made to see whether the `localName` passed to the method has the value `channel`, to see if the current element is `<channel>`. If it is, then the state is switched to `IN_CHANNEL` and the method returns.

> *Note that the namespace-aware feature of the SAX parser is turned on, even though RSS 2.0 doesn't use namespaces. This is in the interest of consistency, because the* `startElement` *parameters will be different when namespace functionality is turned off. In this example, the local name passed to this method will still be* `channel` *whether or not the* `<channel>` *element is namespace-qualified.*

The next case is when the system is already inside a `<channel>` but not an `<item>`. If the tag that has been encountered is an `<item>`, the state is switched to reflect this, and a new `entry` object is created, ready to receive data. The code looks like this:

```
case IN_CHANNEL:
    if ("item".equals(localName)) {
        state = IN_ITEM;
        entry = new EntryImpl();
    }
    return;
```

If the parser is actually inside an `<item>...</item>` block, what is expected are text-containing elements such as `<title>`. The call to this method signals such an element has been encountered. However, the text hasn't been read yet, so there isn't much to do apart from creating a new buffer ready to receive that text. So the `startElement` method ends like this:

```
case IN_ITEM:
    textBuffer = new StringBuffer();
    return;

default:
    return;
    }
}
```

The `characters` method adds whatever text data has been encountered to the current text buffer:

```
public void characters(char[] ch, int start, int length) {
    textBuffer.append(ch, start, length);
}
```

Note the parameters of the method call. It is passed a reference to a character array corresponding to the characters of the whole XML document, together with a start index pointing to the start of the chunk of text and a figure for its length. By referring to the text chunk in terms of its place in the source document this method provides a lot of information, although for the purposes of parsing RSS it's only necessary to get the chunk of text referred to and append it to the text buffer.

Although a reference to a character array is given, SAX specifies that the application must not attempt to read from the array outside of the specified range. There's a reason for this: In practice the array will usually be characters coming in from a stream, so the application doesn't yet know what the rest of the array contains.

The handler here will only be making use of the contents of items, and much of the work is done by the `endElement` method, the source of which begins like this:

```
public void endElement(String namespaceURI,
                       String localName, String qName) {
```

The namespace-capable SAX `endElement` method receives the namespace and local name of the element, together with the prefixed version that appears in the XML, the `QName`. Again, as RSS 2.0 doesn't have a namespace, the code will only look at the local name. Like the `startElement` method, `endElement` consists of a conditional switch based on the state variable. If `endElement` is called when the current state is `IN_NOTHING`, which will occur when the `</rss>` tag is encountered, there's nothing to do and the method returns. If the current state is `IN_CHANNEL` and the `</channel>` tag is encountered, the handler returns to the `IN_NOTHING` state, as you can see in the second case here:

```
switch (state) {

case IN_NOTHING:
    return;

case IN_CHANNEL: // switch down
    if ("channel".equals(localName)) {
        state = IN_NOTHING;
    }
    return;
```

If the handler is in the `IN_ITEM` state and `endElement` has been called, then the first check is to see if the tag encountered is an `</item>` tag. If it is, the state is dropped back down to `IN_CHANNEL` and the entry object (created when `startElement` hits the `<item>` tag) is added to `EntryList`:

```
case IN_ITEM:
    if ("item".equals(localName)) {
        state = IN_CHANNEL;
        entries.addEntry(entry);
        return;
    }
```

However, most of the time encountering an `endElement` item in the `IN_ITEM` state will mean that the reader has reached the end of an element like `<title>...</title>`. So a check is made on each of the possible values that are of interest. If the local name matches, the contents of `textBuffer` (put there by `characters`) are passed to the current entry object. There are several possible child elements of `<item>`; this simple handler deals with the most common ones in core RSS 2.0: `<title>`, `<link>`, and `<description>`. The value checks look like this:

```
if ("title".equals(localName)) {
    entry.setTitle(textBuffer.toString());
    return;
```

```
        }
        if ("link".equals(localName)) {
            entry.setLink(textBuffer.toString());
            return;
        }
        if ("description".equals(localName)) {
            entry.setContent(textBuffer.toString());
            return;
        }
```

There is another piece of handling here. The RSS 2.0 specification doesn't rule out there being other XML or (X)HTML elements inside the core elements, but is quiet on how these should be handled. Rather than ignore or throw away what may be useful information, the local name of any such elements is passed to the current text buffer as another piece of plain content, using an append method as you can see here:

```
        textBuffer.append(localName);
        return;

    default:
        return;
    }
```

The method source ends with the default behavior of the case statement, which is to do nothing and return.

The Trouble with Feeds

The vast majority of feeds are generated automatically by software. Where there is software there are bugs. Syndication is a relatively young technology, so the products available are comparatively new, and new software is likely to have more bugs. In a standalone application it's usually clear when it has a fault—if you bought a word processor and your screen goes blue when you run it, you might go looking for a refund. In distributed systems things aren't quite so simple. Fortunately the Web environment is quite robust, so most of the time reliable communication is possible between client and server. But the result of that separation of client and server means that many bugs in the system won't cause problems at the server end but at the client end. Server-side software is only half the system; it's dependent on what's on the client side. There are dozens of client applications to choose from, and for the server-side developer these are moving targets. All the developer can rely on are the standards that (hopefully) those client applications will be following.

Syndication formats can be described as simple, and certainly the syntax when viewing the source code can look completely straightforward. But if you consider any Web format in the context of the specifications on which it is based, and the protocols on which its distribution depends, the simplicity soon evaporates. You have to take a lot into consideration, and naturally things sometimes get overlooked.

There are millions of feeds from which you can choose your subscriptions, which will be produced by hundreds of publication systems. Given these factors, it's not surprising that some of them will not be up to scratch. Estimates on the proportion of bad feeds found in the wild are generally within the 10 percent range.

The Syndication Stack

Whichever syndication format is appropriate for a particular task, there is a dependency on other systems. The Web is built on generally accepted standards that describe how data should be expressed and communicated. As we point out in Chapter 19, these standards are more or less layered one on top of the other, each providing an abstraction of the layer underneath. This allows humans working at the top of the stack to think in terms of more sophisticated concepts and forget the mechanics of networking and low-level data representation. But whether we like it or not, the dependencies are there.

Most of the time it is possible to look at applications in terms of the top of the stack. Unfortunately, abstractions are never perfect and symptoms that appear at the top layer may have been caused by problems further down the stack. When it comes to syndication, most of the problems can be found close to the top, as XML errors.

The Postel Paradox

In RFC 793, which defines the Transmission Control Protocol, Internet pioneer Jon Postel made the following statement: "TCP implementations will follow a general principle of robustness: be conservative in what you do, be liberal in what you accept from others."

This is generally accepted as a good design principle, applicable in any communication system and popularly known as *Postel's Law*. However, the XML specification defines certain kinds of errors as *fatal*, and once a fatal error is detected, the processor must not continue normal processing. Of particular significance to syndication systems are the well-formedness constraints, which are classified as fatal errors.

So what happens when an RSS feed contains ill-formed markup? Take this for example:

```
<title><Shelley></title>
```

The author of this data may simply have wanted to use the angle brackets as a little bit of emphasis. But to the XML processor this is broken syntax. The processor should report an error and stop in its tracks. The author has broken the first part of Postel's Law by not being conservative and getting the markup wrong. But isn't the XML processor breaking the second part of the law by not being liberal and getting what it can from the markup?

This apparent conflict can be resolved by reading between the lines. For example, Postel described a principle of robustness. A robust system is one that can recover gracefully from a wide range of error conditions. But XML isn't designed that way. The error handling is harsh, described by its developers as *Draconian* (Draco was the first lawgiver of ancient Athens, his laws gave the death penalty for even minor crimes). This is entirely reasonable if you consider some of the potential applications of XML. For example, suppose you're involved in an electronic transaction with your bank and an error on the line causes the data to be corrupted. Would you prefer the bank made its best guess of your intentions or cancelled the whole transaction and started again?

So an XML processor isn't designed to be robust, and hence Postel's principle of robustness doesn't apply. However, that isn't the end of the story. The XML specification distinguishes between the XML processor and the application using that processor. So although an XML processor must behave in a Draconian fashion, the application as a whole can use Postel-friendly recovery mechanisms.

In the context of syndication this means that there are various alternatives to parsing feed data. The first is to insist on the strict behavior the XML specification demands, without any attempt to handle bad data. This may be feasible within a closed environment, but if the data is coming from arbitrary RSS feeds on the Web, then the proportion of ill-formed XML feeds pretty well precludes this. Atom is being designed in a way that should make good data more probable, but the specification isn't yet ready, there's no true deployment and it's too early to tell whether a Draconian policy would be a realistic choice for a consumer application.

A second approach to parsing is to work around the Draconian rules. In other words, don't treat the source data as XML, but as a format with liberal rules that just happens to look like XML. This can be achieved either using a purpose-built liberal parser, or by overriding the behavior of a conformant parser and implementing alternate error handling. A third alternative is to use separate parsers for data that is known to be good quality and that is discovered to be flawed. In terms of implementation effort there isn't a great deal to choose between any of these alternatives, though using separate parsers can enable a more modular approach.

The Bozo Bit

Experts in the field have suggested that it takes a fool to generate an ill-formed syndication feed. Early in the discussion of whether XML should be Draconian, the term *bozo* was used for this kind of fool. Elsewhere in the software development community the pattern of "setting the bozo bit" emerged, as a way of flagging that the opinions of a particular person should always be ignored. (It is now considered an antipattern, largely because of the bad feeling it engenders.) Aside from showing that software developers are not immune to arrogance, against this background has condensed a useful term and technique for ill-formed feed data. If a feed is ill-formed, its bozo bit will be set to true. This can help hide much of the internal implementation of a consumer subsystem. There's no need to know exactly which parser was used to extract the data, the value of the bozo bit will tell you whether the feed data passed XML's well-formedness rules. This is the approach taken by the Python Universal Feed Parser (`http://feedparser.org/`), which was formally known as the "Ultra-Liberal Feed Parser" and still supports liberal parsing. However it features bozo bit indication that the source data may not be true XML, making it suitable for use by even the most Draconian developer.

Note that obvious markup errors like the inserted characters in the previous example aren't the only cause of ill-formedness. There is a whole range of situations related to the encoding of the document and its MIME type, which can result in non-conformant XML.

Try It Out   Draconian Parsing

This demonstration uses the same setup as the XML parsing in the previous Try It Out.

1. Open your RSS 2.0 sample in a text editor and make the following modification.

Before:

```
...
<item>
        <title>Shelley</title>
...
```

After:

```
...
<item>
        <title><Shelley></title>
...
```

2. Save this file as `rss2sample-broken.xml`.

3. In a command window in your working directory, enter the following:

```
java -classpath . org.urss.parsers.Rss2ParserDemo rss2sample-broken.xml
```

You should see something like:

```
C:\source>java -classpath . org.urss.parsers.Rss2ParserDemo rss2sample-broke.xml
org.xml.sax.SAXParseException: Expected "</Shelley>" to terminate element starti
ng on line 19.
        at org.apache.crimson.parser.Parser2.fatal(Parser2.java:3339)
        at org.apache.crimson.parser.Parser2.fatal(Parser2.java:3333)
        at org.apache.crimson.parser.Parser2.maybeElement(Parser2.java:1660)
...
```

How It Works

The error message explains what's happened. The parser has encountered the character sequence `<Shelley>` and assumed this is the opening tag of an XML element. But for the XML to be well-formed, there should have been a closing `</Shelley>` tag. An XML processor must treat breakage of the well-formedness constraint as a fatal error, and so the exception is thrown and the parsing comes to a halt.

Tag Soup

This piece of charming terminology is employed, usually with implied criticism, to describe markup in which anything can appear anywhere. The phrase emerged in the context of HTML and the use of tags as presentation instructions, without much regard for their descriptive or structural potential. Nowadays it's a good term for material found in many RSS feeds. Either the feed as a whole isn't well-formed XML thanks to clumsy construction, or the content of `<description>` and other elements is a mess of HTML-like content. The phrase is handy to avoid the contradiction inherent in *liberal* XML parsing. Non-XML parsing in the Python Universal Feed Parser is achieved using an extension of Python's classes for handling HTML to deal with ill-formed feed data. There is a parser for Java available called *TagSoup* (`http://mercury.ccil.org/~cowan/XML/tagsoup/`), although at the time of writing this only includes support for (soupy) HTML. It would be possible to modify some of Java's HTML parsing classes to handle feed data, but instead the code that follows is a fairly simple general-purpose parser that can be applied to any XML-like data.

> *This code, like the rest of the code in this book, is aimed at demonstrating a specific technique rather than being a copy-and-paste solution. It has only undergone minimal testing. If any bugs are discovered post-publication, fixed code will be made available online.*

Soup Parser

Before looking at the parser code itself, the following listing is an interface which the `SoupParser` class will implement. Its purpose is to wrap features of different parsers in a way that will enable their use with the `FeedFetcher` code presented in Chapter 22. The `setContentHandler` method takes a standard SAX `ContentHandler` as its argument that will act as a listener to parser events. The parse method will apply the parser to the `InputStream` supplied.

```
package org.urss.parsers;

import java.io.InputStream;

import org.urss.feeds.FeedFetcher;
```

```
import org.xml.sax.ContentHandler;

public interface FeedParser {

    public void setContentHandler(ContentHandler contentHandler);

    public void parse(InputStream inputStream);
}
```

Now onto the parser itself. SoupParser is based on SAX's event-driven design. It is primarily built to deal with one of the more common faults encountered within bad feeds, tags that break well-formedness. Every opening tag should be followed by a corresponding closing tag at the same level of nesting. So the parser pushes the name of every opening tag onto a stack, and under normal circumstances, when the appropriate closing tag is encountered, the name is removed from the stack. As the parser moves through the source document, startElement and endElement calls will be made as required. However, if an incorrectly nested closing tag is encountered, then the last name on the stack is pulled out and an extra endElement call made, simulating the missing tag. Note this code only approximates what a SAX parser can do, for example it can't handle nested default namespace declarations. What's more, it would be impossible to write a parser that correctly interprets arbitrarily bad XML; there will always be some amount of guessing involved in figuring out what the producer intended. The code here does an acceptable job with some errors, while behaving like a correct parser for most correct XML.

There's quite a lot of code, so here it's broken into chunks, which we will describe in turn. Here is the source code:

```
package org.urss.parsers;

import java.io.File;
import java.io.FileInputStream;
import java.io.IOException;
import java.io.InputStream;
import java.util.HashMap;
import java.util.Map;
import java.util.Stack;
import java.util.regex.Matcher;
import java.util.regex.Pattern;

import org.urss.feeds.FeedFetcher;
import org.urss.io.FeedParser;
import org.xml.sax.Attributes;
import org.xml.sax.ContentHandler;
import org.xml.sax.Locator;
import org.xml.sax.SAXException;
import org.xml.sax.helpers.AttributesImpl;

public class SoupParser implements FeedParser, ContentHandler {
```

Most of the imports are from core Java packages. Various I/O classes are used for reading and writing data, and the HashMap, Map, and Stack classes from the Collections framework are used as object containers. Java's relatively recent support for regular expressions is used to simplify the recognition of markup in the source data.

The `SoupParser` class implements the `FeedParser` interface as well as SAX's `ContentHandler`, the latter to provide a default parser event listener to help with debugging.

The regular expressions used are defined in static variables as follows:

```java
private static Pattern attributeSplitRe = Pattern
        .compile("\\S+?\\s*=\\s*[\"|\'].+?[\"|\']");

private static Pattern whitespaceRe = Pattern.compile("\\s+");

private static Pattern commentRe = Pattern.compile("^!--.+?-->",
        Pattern.DOTALL);

private static Pattern piRe = Pattern
        .compile("^<\\?.+?\\?>", Pattern.DOTALL);

private static Pattern cdataRe = Pattern.compile("^!\\[CDATA\\[.+?\\]\\]>",
        Pattern.DOTALL);
```

You should consult Java's documentation for details of the regular expression syntax, although you should be reasonably familiar with it if you've used regexps in other languages. Most of the expressions are geared to testing a chunk of text that begins with the < character, the usual indicator of significant markup in XML. That character will actually be omitted from the text to which the regexp is applied, so you can read the ^ symbol that points to the start of the data in the regexp as pointing to the next character after <.

The first of the regular expression patterns, `attributeSplitRe`, will be used to recognize the structure of XML/HTML attributes, `name = "value"`. The next, `whitespaceRe`, simply recognizes whitespace, including newline characters. `commentRe` recognizes the structure of XML comments: `<!-- like this -->`. `piRe` will match XML processing instructions `<? like this ?>`. The `cdataRe` pattern is designed to match blocks in the source XML code `<[CDATA[ like this ]]>`.

In the listing of `Rss2Handler.java` earlier in the chapter, a variable called `state` was used to remember the position in the source data of the parser. The same technique is used here, except in this case the source data will be read in a more finely grained fashion, down at the char-by-char and tag level, so the values the state variable can take are at this level. Here are the relevant variables:

```java
private static char NOT_TAG = 0;

private static char START_TAG = 1;   GALWAY COUNTY LIBRARIES

private static char END_TAG = 2;

private char state = NOT_TAG;
```

The value of `state` will be `START_TAG` when the parser's position in the source data is within the opening tag of an element, that is, one of the Xs in `<XXX>`. Similarly, the state will be `END_TAG` when the parser's position in the source data is within the closing tag of an element, that is, one of the Xs in `</XXX>`. `NOT_TAG` will be the state the rest of the time.

The next block of code lists the rest of the member variables. Each variable name reflects its purpose, which will be described when the variable is used.

```
        private ContentHandler contentHandler;

        private Map prefixMap;

        private String defaultNS = "";

        private String qname;

        private String name;

        private AttributesImpl attributes;

        private Stack openTags;

        private int charIndex;

        private String data;

        private String cdata;

        private String block;

        boolean firstInTag = false;

        private FeedFetcher feed;

        private boolean unescape;
```

The constructor for most SAX parsers can throw an exception. It's not likely to happen here, but to make this class appear like other parsers the constructor here also declares that it may throw an exception. The constructor initializes prefixMap, which will contain the prefix/namespace mappings declared by the document. For example, if there's an initial declaration xmlns:dc="http://purl.org/dc/elements/1.1/" in the XML, calling prefixMap.get("dc") later will return "http://purl.org/dc/elements/1.1/". Also in the constructor the default namespace is set to the empty string and the default content handler (event listener) is set to the current object. The source code is as follows:

```
    public SoupParser() throws SAXException {
        this.prefixMap = new HashMap();
        this.defaultNS = "";
        setContentHandler(this);
    }
```

The setContentHandler method simply passes the SAX content handler specified to a member variable:

```
    public void setContentHandler(ContentHandler contentHandler) {
        this.contentHandler = contentHandler;
    }
```

The qnameSplit method is a utility to take a string of the form prefix:localname and convert it into a two-item array, the first item being the namespace corresponding to the prefix and the second item the local name part. If the string is of the form localname, then the second item in the array will be the default namespace. Here's the method source code:

```
public String[] qnameSplit(String qname) {
    String[] namePair = new String[2];
    String[] prefixSplit = qname.split(":");
    if (prefixSplit.length == 1) {
        namePair[0] = this.defaultNS;
        namePair[1] = qname;
        return namePair;
    }

    String prefix = prefixSplit[0];
    String localname = prefixSplit[1];

    String namespace = (String) this.prefixMap.get(prefix);
    namePair[0] = namespace;
    namePair[1] = localname;
    return namePair;
}
```

When this parser encounters an end tag, all it sees is the QName, a string of the form `"prefix:localname"`. The end method will be called and given that string. The method obtains the appropriate information to make a call to the SAX `endElement` method of whatever object has been set as the content handler of this parser. Here's the method:

```
public void end(String qname) {
    String[] namePair = qnameSplit(qname);
    try {
        contentHandler.endElement(namePair[0], namePair[1], qname);
    } catch (SAXException e) {
        e.printStackTrace();
    }
}
```

The start method carries out a similar function to end, except rather than just being passed a QName it receives the whole of the string found within an opening tag, including any attributes. The first few lines of the method normalize the whitespace so there's just a single space between different series of characters. The QName of the element is obtained by getting the first chunk of non-whitespace text. The `attributeSplitRe` regular expression is then applied using an instance of `java.util.regex.Matcher` to produce a series of attribute expressions of the form `name = "value"`. These are passed in turn to the local `extractAttribute` method. The QName of the element is then passed for processing. Note that this takes place *after* the attributes have been dealt with, as the namespace prefix mapping for this element might be contained within the list of attributes. The code to the `start` method is as follows:

```
public void start(String tag) {
    this.qname = "";
    Matcher m = whitespaceRe.matcher(tag);
    tag = m.replaceAll(" "); //# normalize whitespace

    this.qname = tag.split(" ")[0]; // first chunk before space

    Matcher ma = attributeSplitRe.matcher(tag);
    this.attributes = new AttributesImpl();
    while (ma.find()) {
        this.extractAttribute(ma.group());
    }
```

```
            this.doName(qname);

            if (tag.charAt(tag.length() - 1) == '/') {// ugly
                this.end(qname);
            }
        }
```

The last part of the start method is a quick-and-dirty hack to deal with empty elements, that is, of the form <something/>. If the last section of the opening tag ends with a / then the end method is called. Although a quick-and-dirty hack, in practice it actually works rather well, but it would be dishonest to suggest that we planned it that way...

The doName method is called after the attributes in an opening tag have been dealt with, and it receives the QName of the element. After resolving the prefixed name into namespace and localname it calls the SAX startElement method. At this point the member variable attributes will contain a SAX Attributes object. You will see how that object is created next, after the source code of doName which looks like this:

```
    public void doName(String qname) {
        String[] namePair = this.qnameSplit(qname);
        try {
            this.contentHandler.startElement(namePair[0], namePair[1], qname,
                    attributes);
        } catch (SAXException e) {
            e.printStackTrace();
        }
    }
```

A new SAX Attributes object (class AttributesImpl) was created in the start method prior to a regular expression being used to obtain all the expressions in the start tag of the form name = "value". Those individual expressions were passed to the extractAttribute method. This method splits the string into name and value, and after a little trimming adds the values associated with this attribute to the SAX Attributes object which is passed in a startElement call. That is unless the expression is recognized as a namespace declaration, in which case it will have custom handling through the doNamespace method, which follows. The source code of extractAttribute looks like this:

```
    public void extractAttribute(String rawAttribute) {

        int index = rawAttribute.indexOf("=");
        String qname = rawAttribute.substring(0, index);
        String value = rawAttribute.substring(index + 1);
        qname = qname.trim(); // remove spaces
        value = value.trim();
        value = value.substring(1, value.length() - 1); // remove quotes

        if (qname.split(":")[0] == "xmlns") {
            this.doNamespace(qname, value);
            return;
        }
        String[] namePair = this.qnameSplit(qname);
        attributes
                .addAttribute(namePair[0], namePair[1], qname, "CDATA", value);
    }
```

The doNamespace method does a bit of simple string manipulation of expressions of the form xmlns:spam=
"http://eggs.com", putting the prefix and namespace string into the prefixMap. The code looks like this:

```
public void doNamespace(String qname, String value) {
    String[] qnameParts = qname.split(":");
    if (qnameParts.length == 1) { // "xmlns"
        this.defaultNS = value;
        return;
    }

    String prefix = qnameParts[1];
    this.prefixMap.put(prefix, value);
}
```

The next two methods are placeholders; they aren't needed immediately but are provided to simplify
coding later.

```
public boolean isProcessingInstruction() {
    return false;
}

public boolean isComment() {
    return false;
}
```

The isCDATA method is called to test whether a block of text in the input XML is a CDATA section. The
test is a regular expression, which is applied to a string containing the section of the XML document from
the parser's current position (charIndex) to the end. If there is a match, the CDATA block is returned
after a little trimming by the cdata method, which follows. The method looks like this:

```
public String isCDATA() {
    Matcher match = cdataRe.matcher(this.data.substring(this.charIndex));

    if (match.find()) {
        int start = this.charIndex - 1; //?
        this.charIndex = this.charIndex + match.end();
        this.cdata(match.group());
        String cdata = "<" + match.group();
        return cdata;
    }
    return null;
}
public void cdata(String raw) {
    this.cdata = raw.substring(8, raw.length() - 3);
}
```

The most important method in SoupParser is parseData, which takes as its string argument the whole
of the XML document to parse. This method starts with a block of code, which converts the XML
escaped entities back into their corresponding characters. As you can see, this code isn't exactly elegant,
but seems to work in practice:

```
    public void parseData(String data) {

        if (unescape) {
            if ((data.length() > 12) && data.startsWith("<![CDATA[")) { // ugh!!
                data = data.substring(8, data.length() - 3);
            } else {
                data.replaceAll("&amp;", "&");
                data.replaceAll("&lt;", "<");
                data.replaceAll("&gt;", ">");
            }
        }
    }
```

After unescaping, the local string data is passed to a member variable of the same name. That happens in the following section, where the characters in the string are also placed in an array, dataChars:

```
    this.data = data;
    char[] dataChars = new char[data.length()];
    data.getChars(0, data.length(), dataChars, 0);
```

The next section of the parseData method is where things really happen. First of all, a Stack data structure is created. As element opening tags are encountered, they will be pushed onto the stack. The characters will be stepped through using the charIndex integer indexing the dataChars array in the for... loop as the following snippet demonstrates:

```
    this.openTags = new Stack();
    block = "";
    char character;
    for(charIndex = 0;charIndex<dataChars.length; charIndex++){
        character = dataChars[charIndex];
```

The parser has to figure out what is going on at the current point in the document based on the characters it encounters and its current state. If a < character is encountered, then it will be recognized as significant and various tests made against the material that follows using helper methods. This character may signal the start of a processing instruction or a comment (those methods aren't yet implemented) or it may indicate the start of a CDATA section. Otherwise it will be interpreted as an element's opening tag, and the state variable set appropriately. If that is the case, then the character data that preceded this < is sent to the SAX characters method, using the call in the last part of this code block:

```
        if (character == '<') {
            if (this.isProcessingInstruction()) {
                continue;
            }
            if (this.isComment()) {
                continue;
            }
            cdata = this.isCDATA();
            if (cdata != null) {
                block = block + cdata;
                continue;
            }
            state = START_TAG;
            firstInTag = true;
            if (block != "") {
                try {
```

```
                contentHandler.characters(dataChars,
                charIndex - block.length(), block.length());
            } catch (SAXException e) {
                e.printStackTrace();
            }
        }
    block = "";
    continue;
}
```

Another character that is likely to have significance to the parser is the forward slash. If this is the first character after the opening < in a tag, then the firstInTag flag will have the value true. This combination causes the state to switch to END_TAG, as the parser is likely to be seeing the start of a structure like </this>. The handling is here:

```
if (character == '/') {
    if (firstInTag) {
        state = END_TAG;
        firstInTag = false;
        continue;
    }
}
```

The > character can indicate a few different things, depending on its position in the source data. Some of these circumstances should have been dealt with by the helper methods, isCDATA and so on. If it is encountered while the START_TAG flag is true, then it signals the closing bracket of an opening tag. If so the material contained in block (whatever was between the angle brackets in the opening tag) is pushed onto the stack. It may be signaling the closing bracket of an element-closing tag. In that case a test is made to see if the openTags stack has any content, in other words whether this is occurring as part of a nested structure or is simply the last closing tag of a document. If it is part of a nested structure then the corresponding opening tag is popped from the top of the stack. If the contents of block don't match the popped tag then a loop steps back down until a match *is* found. The match should be the current (closing) tag, and a call to end will be made to cause a SAX-endElement call. If there isn't a match, with every step down the stack an endElement call will be produced, corresponding to the closing tag(s) that are missing. You can see the (rather convoluted) logic in the following code:

```
if (character == '>') {
    if (state == START_TAG) {
        this.start(block);
        openTags.push(this.qname);
    }
    if (state == END_TAG) {
        if (openTags.size() == 0) {
            continue;
        }
        String lastOpen = (String) openTags.pop();
        while (!lastOpen.equals(block)) {
            this.end(lastOpen);
            if (openTags.size() > 0) {
                lastOpen = (String) openTags.pop();
            } else {
                break;
```

```
                        }
                }
                this.end(block);
            }
            state = NOT_TAG;
            block = "";
            continue;
        }
```

If none of the special character checks has identified the markup, the current character is simply added to the block string, and the flag to say, this was the first character after a <, is set to false (it may have had that value already). The `parseData` method finishes like this:

```
            block = block + character;
            firstInTag = false;
        }
        while(openTags.size()>0){
            this.end((String) openTags.pop());
        }
    }
```

That last `while...` loop is another part of the error correction. If the parser arrives at the end of a document and there are still unclosed element tags, they will each be closed in turn, at least virtually, by delivering calls through the `end` method to the `endElement` method of the SAX handler. In other words, if the source document looks like this:

```
<rss><channel><item><title>
```

the parser will behave as if it looked like this:

```
<rss><channel><item><title/></item></channel></rss>
```

The next block of code features some simple implementations of the SAX `ContentHandler` methods, which will be called when the parser is used as its own listener for debugging purposes. Note that many of these methods aren't implemented in the parser, in which cases the handler has a do-nothing method.

```
public void startDocument() throws SAXException {
    System.out.println("Start Document");
}

public void endDocument() throws SAXException {
    System.out.println("End Document");
}

public void startElement(String namespaceURI, String localName,
        String qName, Attributes atts) throws SAXException {
    System.out.println("\nstartElement- \nns:" + namespaceURI + "\nname:"
            + localName + "\nqname:" + qName + "\natts:");
    for (int i = 0; i < atts.getLength(); i++) {
        System.out.println("   " + atts.getLocalName(i) + " "
                + atts.getValue(i));
    }
}
```

```
        }

        public void endElement(String namespaceURI, String localName, String qName)
                throws SAXException {
            System.out.println("\nendElement- \nns:" + namespaceURI + "\nname:"
                    + localName + "\nqname:" + qName);

        }

        public void characters(char[] ch, int start, int length)
                throws SAXException {
            StringBuffer buffer = new StringBuffer();

            buffer.append(ch, start, length);
            System.out.println("characters: " + buffer);
        }

        public void processingInstruction(String arg0, String arg1)
                throws SAXException {
            // not implemented
        }

        public void ignorableWhitespace(char[] ch, int start, int length)
                throws SAXException {
            // not implemented
        }

        public void endPrefixMapping(String prefix) throws SAXException {
            // not implemented
        }

        public void skippedEntity(String name) throws SAXException {
            // not implemented
        }

        public void setDocumentLocator(Locator locator) {
            // not implemented
        }

        public void startPrefixMapping(String prefix, String uri)
                throws SAXException {
            // not implemented
        }
```

You may have noticed that the SoupParser takes its data in the form of a string, where the true SAX parser shown earlier took a stream (actually wrapped with an InputSource interface). However, a method is provided to read such a stream into a string for subsequent parsing. The parse method is listed here:

```
        public void parse(InputStream inputStream) {
            StringBuffer buffer = new StringBuffer();
            int character;
            try {
                while ((character = inputStream.read()) != -1) {
                    buffer.append((char) character);
```

```
            }
        } catch (IOException e) {
            e.printStackTrace();
        }
        parseData(buffer.toString());
    }
```

Yes, this process will be inefficient compared with the streaming parsing supported by the SAX parser. But addressing a string allowed code simplifications (like having the array ready for characters calls), the memory needed isn't excessive and the extra time taken is unlikely to affect the overall feed-handling time too much, given that the source data has to be retrieved from the Internet.

The next two methods are simple setters, implementing parts of the `FeedParser` interface:

```
    public void setFeed(FeedFetcher feed) {
        this.feed = feed;

    }

    public void setUnescape(boolean unescape) {
        this.unescape = unescape;
    }
```

To make testing a little easier, a simple `main` method is provided. This method will take data from a file and run it through the parser, using the local content handler methods:

```
    public static void main(String[] args) {
        File inputFile = new File(args[0]);
        StringBuffer buffer = new StringBuffer();
        try {
            FileInputStream in = new FileInputStream(inputFile);
            SoupParser parser = new SoupParser();
            parser.parse(in);
            in.close();

        } catch (Exception e) {
            e.printStackTrace();
        }
    }
```

Different Parser, Same Handler

The `SoupParser` is designed to have behavior reasonably close to that of a SAX parser for one very good reason: so it can be used as a direct replacement. The current version isn't as close to SAX as it could be, but it's near enough for practical purposes as you will see.

The following code is that of `SoupParserDemo.java`, which is a modified version of `Rss2ParserDemo.java` we use earlier in this chapter. The significant changes are shown in bold:

```
package org.urss.parsers;

import java.io.File;
```

```
import java.io.FileInputStream;
import java.io.InputStream;

import org.urss.feeds.EntryList;
import org.urss.feeds.EntryListImpl;
import org.xml.sax.helpers.DefaultHandler;

public class SoupParserDemo extends DefaultHandler {


    public EntryList readFeed(String feedFilename) {
        EntryList entries = new EntryListImpl();
        try {
//          SAXParserFactory parserFactory = SAXParserFactory.newInstance();
//          parserFactory.setNamespaceAware(true);
//          XMLReader xmlReader = parserFactory.newSAXParser().getXMLReader();
            SoupParser parser = new SoupParser(); //+
            Rss2Handler handler = new Rss2Handler();
            handler.setEntryList(entries);

            parser.setContentHandler(handler); //+
            InputStream inputStream = new FileInputStream(
                    new File(feedFilename));
//          InputSource inputSource = new InputSource(inputStream);
//          xmlReader.parse(inputSource);
            parser.parse(inputStream);//+

        } catch (Exception e) {
            e.printStackTrace();
        }
        return entries;
    }

    public static void main(String[] args) {
        SoupParserDemo reader = new SoupParserDemo();
        EntryList entries = reader.readFeed(args[0]);
        for (int i = 0; i < entries.size(); i++) {
            System.out.println(entries.getEntry(i));
        }
    }
}
```

The most significant part of this listing is the following:

```
Rss2Handler handler = new Rss2Handler();
handler.setEntryList(entries);
```

These lines are exactly the same as those used with the true SAX parser. Although there's a lot of difference in the way the parser is constructed, it is given the very same handler. The methods of SoupParser can call the methods of the Rss2Handler. When given an ill-formed feed to parse this can provide an approximation of the behavior that might be expected if the source data was correct XML and a true XML parser was used.

Try It Out   **Parsing Tag Soup**

1. Save the previous file into a folder alongside the parser code described earlier:

```
[anywhere]\org\urss\parsers\SoupParserDemo.java
```

For example:

```
C:\source\org\urss\parsers\SoupParserDemo.java
```

2. Save or copy an RSS 2.0 file into the `[anywhere]` directory (for example, `rss2sample.xml` listed in Chapter 20).

3. Open a command window in `[anywhere]` and enter:

```
javac -classpath . org\urss\parsers\*.java
```

This will compile the source files.

4. Open your RSS 2.0 sample in a text editor and make the following modification.

Before:

```
...
<item>
        <title>Shelley</title>
...
```

After:

```
...
<item>
        <title><Shelley></title>
...
```

Does that look familiar? Yes, the aim here is to see the behavior of `SoupParser` on the data earlier rejected by the conformant XML processor.

5. Save this file as `rss2sample-broken.xml`, if you didn't already

6. In a command window in your working directory, enter the following:

```
java -classpath . org.urss.parsers.SoupParserDemo rss2sample-broken.xml
```

You should now see something like the following:

```
C:\source>java -classpath . org.urss.parsers.SoupParserDemo rss2sample-broke.xml
<div class="entry"><a href="http://example.org/idol/shelley">Shelley</a><p>Shelley
first impressed the
 judges with her 3-line backup script, then trampled the opposition with her
cover of "These Boots Were Made for Walking".</p></div>
...
```

If you look back to the first Try It Out in this chapter, you will see that this is the same as the output produced by the correct XML parser on the original well-formed data.

How It Works

Here is the bad XML again:

```
<title><Shelley></title>
```

When the SoupParser encountered this part of the data, just like the SAX parser it interpreted `<Shelley>` as an XML element. Internally it pushed this tag on the top of the openTags stack. When the conformant XML parser discovered that there wasn't a closing tag for the element, it considered this ill-formedness as a fatal error (as it should, according to the XML specification).

When the SoupParser encountered a closing tag (`</title>`) it popped the top tag name off its stack (`Shelley`) and sent a corresponding call to the endElement handler method. However, the top tag wasn't title as expected in XML, but Shelley. So the next candidate for a closing tag match was popped from the stack, title, and an endElement call made for that. This did match the expected closing tag name, so from there regular char-by-char parsing of the source data resumed. The series of method calls was thus: startElement (element name = title), startElement (name = Shelley), endElement (name = Shelley), endElement (name = title).

In other words, the parser behaved as if it were a proper XML parser encountering:

```
<title><Shelley></Shelley></title>
```

You may now be wondering how something like that ended up being interpreted in exactly the same way as the correct example. If you look back to the source code of Rss2Handler, toward the end of endElement, but still within the IN_ITEM case, you will see the following lines:

```
. . .
            textBuffer.append(localName);
            return;
. . .
```

This appeared after the tests for expected values of the element's local name (item, title, link, and description). The aim was to offer useful treatment of unrecognized child elements of an `<item>`, by simply adding the element name to the buffer, which accumulates any text content.

This example is a little contrived, because we knew in advance how the SoupParser would handle the kind of breakage that was introduced into the XML. However, if you play with the source data a little, you will find that most of the time more useful data is obtained than you would get had the parser halted at the first error, as XML requires of its processors.

HTTP, MIME, and Encoding

You have just seen how it was possible to work around the rules of XML to get useful information out of ill-formed feeds. But the true XML parser and SoupParser were demonstrated using data loaded from file. The data a syndication consumer will receive comes from the Web, over HTTP, and that introduces a certain complication.

Encoding Declaration in XML

To be able to read the character data found in an XML document, you must first know how those characters are encoded in the document. There are many different ways of interpreting the values of bits and bytes of raw data as characters. The US-ASCII character set has been used for many years, unfortunately it is limited to the characters common in English text so can't handle the requirements of an international Web. XML is defined in terms of Unicode, which allows any character in any language to be expressed in a standard way. But even then XML tools have to be able to handle two byte/character encodings, known as UTF-8 and UTF-16. They generally support a range of other commonly encountered encodings too. The encoding used can be stated in the XML declaration of a document, for example:

```
<?xml version="1.0" encoding="iso-8859-1" ?>
```

If no encoding is stated, the default is UTF-8. Typically there is a complication even with this — if the processor doesn't know the encoding, how can it read the characters that state the encoding? A good start is that any document that doesn't make its encoding known in another way must begin with the characters sequence "<?xml". Appendix F of the XML specification includes tables of how the first few bytes of a piece of XML data will look in different baseline encodings. This isn't enough to give the exact encoding, but it makes it possible to read as far enough to find out what it actually is. Fortunately, most of the time you can ignore details like this, just let the XML processor figure it out.

The behavior of the XML processor from then on is to some extent determined by the encoding. If character values appear in the data that aren't defined in that encoding, then the processor won't know how to handle them. Being a Draconian creature, it should signal a fatal error and stop what it's doing. When working with local file data problems of this kind are relatively rare, you aren't likely to see a mismatch between the encoding declared in the XML and the true encoding. However, there is another place where data can come from, and another place the encoding can be declared.

Encoding Declaration in HTTP

The main job of HTTP is to shift data from server to client. For the client to be able to do anything useful with that data, the server has to tell the client how it is encoded for transmission. This is done using the Content-Type header, which will look something like this:

```
Content-Type: application/xml; charset="utf-8"
```

The first part gives the MIME (Internet Media) type, the second part gives the character set. If the MIME type is a text type, for example, text/html, according to the HTTP 1.1 specification the default encoding is ISO-8859-1. If it's not a text type, then the encoding must be labeled with an appropriate encoding value.

As you've probably guessed, there's plenty of room for conflict between what HTTP says the encoding of a document is and what the document itself says it is. It may seem a little counter-intuitive, but if you think of XML as just one of many formats that use the HTTP protocol it makes sense that in general, whatever HTTP says takes precedence.

The details of how the encoding should be worked out in XML over HTTP are described in RFC 3023, XML Media Types. This defines types such as text/xml and application/xml and provides a framework in which other types can be defined. There are some changes to rules found in other specifications. For example if the MIME type is a text type, for example, text/xml, then the default encoding is us-ascii and HTTP's default is overridden.

The Bad News

To cut a very confusing story short, XML processors should decide the encoding of a document according to what HTTP says. If the encoding is wrong, the XML processor should signal a fatal error and stop what it's doing. So publishers of XML documents, for their data to work with spec-conformant XML consumers, should be aware of the rules contained in RFC 3023. So the theory goes.

It is straightforward to explicitly set the MIME type and `charset` when generating syndication feeds dynamically. Similarly it's usually simple to set the encoding within an XML file to be consistent with this. However many blogging and similar syndication systems create static RSS/Atom files which are served by a regular Web server such as Apache or IIS. Most servers determine the MIME type of the file they're serving by looking at the file name extension. Without intervention, most HTTP servers will deliver a file with the extension `.xml` with the MIME type `text/xml` and no `charset`. RFC 3023 states that XML documents served this way should be interpreted with the encoding `us-ascii`. Remember that the default encoding for XML documents is UTF-8, so to conform to what the server is saying these documents must include the line:

```
<?xml version="1.0" encoding="us-ascii" ?>
```

More significantly they should only contain characters allowed by `us-ascii`. Blogging or authoring tools with this kind of restriction are in the minority. The net result of all this is that a large proportion of feeds are served with the incorrect encoding, and therefore aren't valid XML. But it gets worse. For many servers, if the file name extension isn't recognized (often the case with `.rss`), then the data will be served as `text/plain`, which isn't an XML type and so will also be invalid.

The Good News

The developers of the popular servers have been notified of the problems highlighted in syndication and are very much willing to act (for example, new releases of Apache and IIS will deliver `.atom` files as `application/atom+xml`). This bodes well for the future. But still there is the question of how to handle the large number of syndication feeds that are delivered as ill-formed XML. Fortunately for the feed consumer developer, few if any of the leading XML parsers correctly support RFC 3023. It may be a total nightmare for specification fans to discover that all these tools from Microsoft, Sun Microsystems, IBM, and the Open Source community are technically broken. But it does mean that in general, no special action is needed to deal with feeds that are ill-formed due to incorrect encoding, as most of the parsers will ignore or work around this class of error already.

Gluing Together the Consumer

In Chapter 22, we provide figures of possible architectures for a feed consumer, and an implementation of a subsystem to fetch feed data from the Web. Earlier in this chapter, we explain how parsers can be used to populate a simple object representation of items in a feed. The first parser is a true, spec-conformant XML parser, the second is designed to deal with tag soup. The code that follows will show that you can glue parsers into the feed-fetching code. To save paper, we will present only the new code. You may have to skip back and remind yourself of how the sections already listed work.

In short, the code in Chapter 22 could systematically (and relatively politely) obtain feed data from the Web. Each individual feed has an associated `FeedFetcher` object which looks after checking for new data. When new data is found, the `FeedFetcher` responsible will pass the payload details onto an `Interpreter`, which in the demonstration simply downloads the data to file.

To do more useful things with the data within the feeds, it's necessary to extract the items from them, which is what the parsers in this chapter do. So what the code that follows will do is define a different kind of `Interpreter`, one that will wrap the functionality of the parser into a form that only needs a very simple interface (in fact all the feed-fetching part of the subsystem sees is the `interpret` method). The overall operation is shown in Figure 23-1.

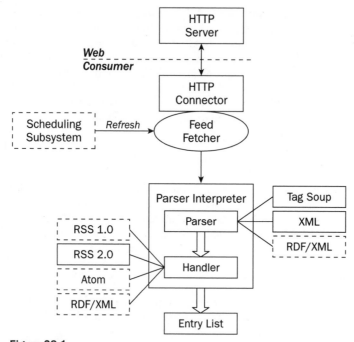

Figure 23-1

The general idea is to plug in different parsers or content handlers according to the format of the feed. The parser/handler combination will be selected according to the format, and will create objects from the raw data. The code listed has been for RSS 2.0, but by swapping in a different handler the same system could just as easily deal with Atom or RSS 1.0. As it stands it would be treating RSS 1.0 data as just a simple XML format, which may be adequate for many applications. However, if you want to support a wide range of extensions, or your application is RDF-based, then it may be desirable to implement a general RDF/XML parser, and a handler to interpret the RDF structures found in the data. Then again, you may want to slot in an altogether different `Interpreter` implementation, and perhaps rather than producing `Entry` objects provide your application with another representation of the information found in feeds.

The code that follows will integrate the XML and Tag Soup (`SoupParser`) parsers and the RSS 2.0 handler with the `FeedFetcher` subsystem. The new code is contained in the following classes:

❑ `ParserInterpreter`: Acts as a connector between the feed fetching classes and the parsers and content handlers

❑ `XMLReaderParser`: A simple wrapper around SAX parser construction code

- ❑ `FeedConstants`: A new feed type constant will be added
- ❑ `InterpreterFactory`: Creates interpreters suitable for different feed types
- ❑ `Runner2`: Demonstration of the glued-together system

A true XML parser will be contained in the `XMLReaderParser` class, and the `SoupParser` code will be used as-is (the necessary interface implementation has already been slipped in). The only handler described so far receives events from one or the other of these parsers and uses it to create objects based on the structure and content of RSS 2.0 feeds. So the system as described here is able to cater for true XML RSS 2.0 feeds (the constant `FeedConstants.RSS2` is used to flag this) and ill-formed, bozo RSS 2.0 feeds (`FeedConstants.RSS2_BOZO`). Adding further formats is a matter of providing a handler class (like `Rss2Handler`) to turn SAX events into items.

The key to joining the pieces together is the `ParserInterpreter` class. This wraps `FeedParser` objects and implements `Interpreter`. The source code is as follows:

```
package org.urss.parsers;

import org.urss.feeds.FeedFetcher;
import org.urss.io.Interpreter;
import org.xml.sax.ContentHandler;
import org.xml.sax.helpers.DefaultHandler;

public class ParserInterpreter implements Interpreter {

    private FeedParser feedParser;

    private ContentHandler contentHandler;

    public ParserInterpreter(FeedParser feedParser) {
        super();
        this.feedParser = feedParser;
    }

    public void setContentHandler(ContentHandler contentHandler) {
        feedParser.setContentHandler(contentHandler);
    }

    public void interpret(FeedFetcher feed) {
        feedParser.parse(feed.getInputStream());
    }
}
```

The `ParserInterprer` class doesn't actually do very much itself; it's more of a junction box. The constructor takes a `FeedParser` object (the source for `FeedParser.java` was listed earlier in the chapter), which offers a simple interface for running a parser. The `setContentHandler` method passes whatever implementation of SAX's `ContentHandler` interface is specified onto the parser. The interpret method takes a `FeedFetcher` object and runs the parser on the data it supplies.

The `FeedParser` interface is used to provide a simple wrapper for the creation and running of a parser. The `SoupParser` listed already implements this; here `XMLReaderParser` wraps the standard SAX parser in an implementation. The source to `XMLReaderParser` looks like this:

```
package org.urss.parsers;

import java.io.IOException;
import java.io.InputStream;

import org.urss.feeds.FeedFetcher;
import org.urss_.io.Constants;
import org.xml.sax.ContentHandler;
import org.xml.sax.InputSource;
import org.xml.sax.SAXException;
import org.xml.sax.XMLReader;
import org.xml.sax.helpers.XMLReaderFactory;

public class XMLReaderParser implements FeedParser {

    private XMLReader reader = null;

    private FeedFetcher feed;

    private boolean unescape;

    public XMLReaderParser() {
        try {
            reader = XMLReaderFactory
                .createXMLReader(Constants.DEFAULT_PARSER_NAME);
        } catch (SAXException e) {
            e.printStackTrace();
        }
    }

    public void setContentHandler(ContentHandler contentHandler) {
        reader.setContentHandler(contentHandler);
    }

    public void parse(InputStream inputStream) {
        InputSource inputSource = new InputSource(inputStream);
        try {
            reader.parse(inputSource);
        } catch (IOException e) {
            e.printStackTrace();
        } catch (SAXException e) {
            e.printStackTrace();
        }
    }

}
```

The constructor of XMLReaderParser creates a SAX parser. The setContentHandler passes on the ContentHandler to the parser. The parse method makes an InputSource object for the SAX parser from the InputStream supplied as an argument. You could call it a thin wrapper. Again it doesn't actually do very much itself, it delegates all the work to the SAX parser.

The following code supports XML-correct RSS 2.0 as well as its ill-formed variation. A constant is used for identification of this variant, so in org.urss.feeds.FeedConstants you will need to add the line:

```
...
    public static final char RSS2 = 2;
    public static final char RSS2_BOZO = 4;
...
```

(The number doesn't actually matter, as long as it doesn't conflict with any of the others.)

The `Interpreter` objects are all of a very similar shape, so it's convenient to use a factory to create them, and initialize each type as appropriate. This is where the selection of a particular parser/handler combination takes place. The code looks like this:

```
package org.urss.parsers;

import org.urss.feeds.EntryList;
import org.urss.feeds.FeedConstants;
import org.urss.io.Interpreter;

public class InterpreterFactory {

    public static Interpreter createInterpreter(char formatHint,
            EntryList entries) {
        Interpreter interpreter = null;
        FeedParser feedParser = null;
        Rss2Handler rss2handler = null;

        switch (formatHint) {
        case FeedConstants.RSS2:
            System.out.println("RSS2: Using Rss2Interpreter, XMLReaderParser");
            feedParser = new XMLReaderParser();
            interpreter = new ParserInterpreter(feedParser);
            rss2handler = new Rss2Handler();
            rss2handler.setEntryList(entries);
            feedParser.setContentHandler(rss2handler);
            return interpreter;

        case FeedConstants.RSS2_BOZO:
            System.out.println("RSS2_BOZO: Using Rss2Interpreter, SoupParser");
            feedParser = new SoupParser();
            interpreter = new ParserInterpreter(feedParser);
            rss2handler = new Rss2Handler();
            rss2handler.setEntryList(entries);
            feedParser.setContentHandler(rss2handler);
            return interpreter;

        default:
            return null;
        }

    }
}
```

The `createInterpreter` method takes as its first argument a `char`, which will be one of the constants corresponding to feed type. At present only `FeedConstants.RSS2` and `FeedConstants.RSS2_BOZO` are supported. The other argument taken by `createInterpreter` is an `EntryList`, which will act as a container for entry objects created by the parser/handler combination. The method creates and initializes an

`Interpreter` implementation with the parser/handler combination determined by the kind of feed to be parsed. The choice is made using a switch statement, and the two cases here are actually very similar, only differing in the parser selected. You can see how the use of (relatively trivial) wrappers and interfaces has made the selection process very simple.

The last of the new classes here is one to demonstrate the joined-up system in action. It's essentially the same as the code used to demonstrate the `FeedFetcher` setup in Chapter 22, except that now the feed type has to be specified, rather than loading a list of feeds from file a couple of feeds are named (and typed) explicitly. In a practical system the feed type is likely to be partly determined by what's found at the address on the first visit, then possibly varied if the quality of the data varies. A feed may be well-formed XML most days, just occasionally including inappropriate characters. It's debatable where the decisions on parser/handler selections should take place, in the consumer subsystem or elsewhere in an application. It's also closely related to decisions like when an apparently dead feed should be dropped from the subscription list. But in the interests of a simple demonstration, the feed type is stated explicitly here.

The source to `Runner2.java` is as follows, the lines that differ significantly from the previous chapter's `Runner.java` are highlighted in bold (channel list reading has been removed):

```
package org.urss.feeds;

import java.util.Iterator;
import java.util.Set;

import org.urss.io.Interpreter;
import org.urss.parsers.InterpreterFactory;

public class Runner2 {

    static int REFRESH_PERIOD = 10000; // milliseconds

    static EntryList entries = new EntryListImpl();

    public static void main(String[] args) {

        FeedSet feeds = new FeedSetImpl();

        FeedFetcher feed1 = new FeedFetcherImpl(
                "http://martinfowler.com/bliki/bliki.rss");
        feed1.setTitle("feed_1");
        Interpreter interpreter1 = InterpreterFactory.createInterpreter(
                FeedConstants.RSS2, entries);
        feed1.setInterpreter(interpreter1); // ++
        feed1.setRefreshPeriod(REFRESH_PERIOD);
        feeds.addFeed(feed1);

        FeedFetcher feed2 = new FeedFetcherImpl(
                "http://dannyayers.com/feed/rss2");
        feed2.setTitle("feed_2");
        Interpreter interpreter2 = InterpreterFactory.createInterpreter(
                FeedConstants.RSS2_BOZO, entries);
        feed2.setInterpreter(interpreter2); // ++
        feed2.setRefreshPeriod(REFRESH_PERIOD);
```

```
        feeds.addFeed(feed2);

        while (true) {
            feeds.refreshAll();
            displayStatus(feeds);
        }
    }

    private static void displayStatus(FeedSet feeds) {
        Iterator feedIterator = feeds.getFeedCollection().iterator();
        while (feedIterator.hasNext()) {
            System.out.println(((FeedFetcher) feedIterator.next()).getStatus());
        }
        System.out.println("---------------");
        for (int i = 0; i < entries.size(); i++) {
            System.out.println(entries.getEntry(i));
        }
    }
}
```

Try It Out   A Consumer Subsystem

1. Enter the previous listings and save them in your source tree. The new or modified files are:

```
[anywhere]\org\urss\parsers\ParserInterpreter.java
[anywhere]\org\urss\parsers\XMLReaderParser.java
[anywhere]\org\urss\feeds\FeedConstants.java
[anywhere]\org\urss\parsers\InterpreterFactory.java
[anywhere]\org\urss\feeds\Runner2.java
```

2. Open a command window in the root of the source directory, and type:

```
javac -classpath . org/urss/feeds/*.java
```

then:

```
javac -classpath . org/urss/parsers/*.java
```

That should (re)compile the Java classes.

3. Now check you are online then type:

```
java -classpath . org.urss.feeds.Runner2
```

Almost immediately you should see:

```
C:\source>java -classpath . org.urss.feeds.Runner2
RSS2: Using Rss2Interpreter, XMLReaderParser
RSS2_BOZO: Using Rss2Interpreter, SoupParser
```

A moment or two later you should see:

```
Checking: http://dannyayers.com/feed/rss2
Connected, interpreting...
Checking: http://martinfowler.com/bliki/bliki.rss
Connected, interpreting...
```

Another moment later, things should get more interesting, something like the following appearing at the console:

417

```
Feed:http://dannyayers.com/feed/rss2
response code:200
encoding:gzip
content-type:text/xml
last-modified:null
isDead:false

Feed:http://martinfowler.com/bliki/bliki.rss
response code:200
encoding:null
content-type:text/xml
last-modified:Wed, 25 Aug 2004 20:29:31 GMT
isDead:false
---------------
<div class="entry"><a href="http://dannyayers.com/archives/2004/09/01/foaf-in-ga
lway/">FOAF in Galway: Now!</a><p>The workshop is on today and tomorrow, and is
...
```

This is followed by a lot more marked-up content, extracted from the feed.

How It Works

`Runner2.java` begins by creating an `EntryList` to act as a container for `Entry` objects created during parsing:

```
static EntryList entries = new EntryListImpl();
```

The `main` method creates a `FeedSet` to contain `FeedFetchers`:

```
public static void main(String[] args) {

    FeedSet feeds = new FeedSetImpl();
```

Where the earlier code read the feed URIs from file, here a `FeedFetcher` object is created directly from a hardcoded URI, and given a hardcoded title:

```
FeedFetcher feed1 = new FeedFetcherImpl(
        "http://martinfowler.com/bliki/bliki.rss");
feed1.setTitle("feed_1");
```

An `Interpreter` is now created for this feed, the `InterpreterFactory` is requested for one suitable to deal with RSS 2.0 feeds. A reference to the target `EntryList` is also passed into the factory method. The `Interpreter` is then passed to the `FeedFetcher` instance, which has its refresh period set before being added to the `FeedSet`. The system to handle this feed is completed in this block of source code:

```
Interpreter interpreter1 = InterpreterFactory.createInterpreter(
        FeedConstants.RSS2, entries);
feed1.setInterpreter(interpreter1);
feed1.setRefreshPeriod(REFRESH_PERIOD);
feeds.addFeed(feed1);
```

The necessary feed-handling objects are created in the same fashion for another address, only this time the factory is asked for an Interpreter suitable for ill-formed RSS 2.0 using the `RSS2_BOZO` constant you see in this code:

```
FeedFetcher feed2 = new FeedFetcherImpl(
        "http://dannyayers.com/feed/rss2");
feed2.setTitle("feed_2");
Interpreter interpreter2 = InterpreterFactory.createInterpreter(
        FeedConstants.RSS2_BOZO, entries);
feed2.setInterpreter(interpreter2); // ++
feed2.setRefreshPeriod(REFRESH_PERIOD);
feeds.addFeed(feed2);
```

The demonstration runner uses the same infinite loop as before, getting the `FeedSet` object to keep all of the feed data fresh before calling a local method to display the status of the feeds:

```
while (true) {
    feeds.refreshAll();
    displayStatus(feeds);
}
}
```

Where previously the feed data was simply dumped to file, this time it's used to create `Entry` objects, which will be placed in the `EntryList` entries. So the extra lines you see here step through each entry object getting it to print itself to console:

```
private static void displayStatus(FeedSet feeds) {
    Iterator feedIterator = feeds.getFeedCollection().iterator();
    while (feedIterator.hasNext()) {
        System.out.println(((FeedFetcher) feedIterator.next()).getStatus());
    }
    System.out.println("---------------");
    for (int i = 0; i < entries.size(); i++) {
        System.out.println(entries.getEntry(i));
    }
}
}
```

The management of the entries found in feeds is as minimal as it could be here. They are placed in a container by the interpreters and then printed out every loop. It is hoped that any application that uses this code will do something considerably more useful than that with them.

One More Thing...

If you examine the material produced at the console by `Runner2`, chances are you will see evidence that a little more processing of feed data may be needed. The following was pasted from the console:

```
<div class="entry"><a href="http://martinfowler.com/bliki/
JunitNewInstance.html">JunitNewInstance</a>
<p>
<table>
<tr>
...
```

The `<div..` at the start is HTML wrapped around the content of an item by `EntryImpl` to prepare it for display. The content was extracted from a `<description>` element in the feed. However, as you can see, that content is already HTML. How your application handles content depends largely on what you intend doing with it. If you're only interested in simple text display, then you might want to strip all markup from content. If you want to use the formatting provided as HTML you will have to consider the possibility of malicious script elements, and if you have a renderer that is fussy about the quality of the HTML it receives, then you may have to do some cleaning (the SoupParser could form a basis for this).

A Universal Feed Consumer?

It would seem a reasonable hope that a single set of code would be able to handle every kind of feed. This certainly isn't a simple task, as you've probably gathered by now. Not only would there be the requirement to handle all formats, at least RSS 1.0, RSS 2.0, and Atom, but also the need to deal with ill-formed XML versions of these. The code listed in this and the previous chapter should make a good starting point for such a system in Java, although there is still work to do in creating a handler for Atom and RSS 1.0 data. Of the course, the approach taken here isn't the only one, and a good alternative would be to normalize the data before parsing into the application's model. The SoupParser here could be used to create a preprocessor to correct XML errors, followed by XSLT transformation of data from the various formats into a single application-oriented format.

> Whatever language you're working in, it's worth searching the Web to find existing work in your preferred language. A lot of libraries are available with unrestrictive licenses. At this point in time the most versatile consumer library is the Python Universal Feed Parser (http://feedparser.org/), which can handle data in all the major formats (including tag soup) and make it available through a simple program-ming interface. This kit is designed to be polite to servers, and includes a vast num-ber of test cases to ensure it conforms to specifications wherever possible.

It's worth mentioning in passing that universality in this context is only relative, in that syndication feed data is only a subset of the wide range of machine-readable data available on the Web that could be useful for a client. Not only can the formats have arbitrary extensions, support for other sources such as the RDF/XML of FOAF (Friend-of-a-Friend) profiles could be used to enhance the functionality of a client application. Then again, if the application's core functionality isn't syndication related, it might be possible to use client code with far less functionality than that described here.

Summary

In this chapter you saw how good-quality feed data can be parsed and how problems associated with poor quality data can be worked around. You also saw some of the colorful terminology that has appeared in the development community, and you discovered the dark secret of XML processors — they are virtually all broken according to RFC 3023.

In this chapter, you learned how to...

- ❑ Parse feeds as XML.
- ❑ Use SAX to parse well-formed XML feeds.
- ❑ Parse "tag soup" markup.
- ❑ Discretely ignore certain issues related to XML over HTTP.
- ❑ Build on the code from Chapter 22.

Exercises

1. Modify the `SoupParser` to provide support for XML comments.

The `SoupParser` as listed was missing various bits of functionality that could be useful in syndication applications, among these are support for comments and processing instructions. A typical XML comment looks like this:

```
<!-- Some text -->
```

There isn't a standard SAX handler for these, but (regrettably) they are sometimes used to contain useful information. A case in point is Trackback, the inter-Weblog notification mechanism that uses blocks of RDF/XML hidden in comments on the (X)HTML page.

The `SoupParser` code already includes a suitable regular expression; this is it (early on in the source):

```
private static Pattern commentRe = Pattern.compile("^<!--.+?-->",
Pattern.DOTALL);
```

The `isComment` method is already being called at appropriate times; all your code needs to do is recognize the comment syntax and print the contents to the console.

Hint: The code for `isComment` will be like the existing `isCDATA` method, but quite a lot simpler.

2. Modify the `SoupParser` to provide support for XML Processing Instructions.

XML can use Processing Instructions to associate a CSS (cascading style sheet) or XSL (XML Stylesheet Language) with the document. This may be needed for re-rendering an XHTML page or transforming an XML document. The following is a typical example:

```
<?xml-stylesheet href="lurid.css" type="text/css"?>
```

The SAX2 specification includes a listener in the `ContentHandler` interface:

```
void processingInstruction(String target, String data)
```

The target part of the PI is the first text chunk after `<?`, in the previous example `xml-stylesheet`. The data part is the rest of the material up to the closing `?>`. Note that although `xml-stylesheet` and some other common PIs use what appear to be attributes, these have no individual meaning for SAX and are usually referred to as pseudo-attributes. The data string is just the whole chunk of text.

The source of `SoupParser` already contains a suitable regular expression pattern for recognizing PIs, it looks like this:

```
private static Pattern piRe = Pattern.compile("^<\\?.+?\\?>", Pattern.DOTALL);
```

Note that the pattern misses the starting `<`; it has a start-of-string marker `^` instead, as the test will be made immediately after the parser has encountered a `<`.

What your code has to do is to implement the `isProcessingInstruction` method so that it checks to see whether the data at this point is a PI, and if it is, you should make a call to the SAX method passing the appropriate arguments, for example:

```
this.contentHandler.processingInstruction( target, data);
```

Hint: The code for `isProcessingInstruction` will be similar to the existing `isCDATA` method.

Producing Feeds

The production of feed data is important to publishers. If you have a lot of data, how do you publish it through information feeds? The key to answering this question is the manner in which you are already managing that data. Nine times out of 10 the material in your system to be published is something that can be loosely characterized as *content*. Your system will be managing this content. Syndication with RSS and Atom has its roots in content management, and the technologies involved are still intimately linked. In this chapter, you see how to produce information feeds from a simple content management system (CMS). Much of this chapter is devoted to the code for a very basic CMS. This in itself might not seem directly relevant to producing feeds. However, most CMSs are very similar, and adding syndication support requires some knowledge of what is going on under the hood of these systems. After going over the core CMS code, you will see how syndication support can be a smooth extension of such a system.

Before moving on to the practical side of feed production, it's worth looking at existing systems through syndication-tinted spectacles to get an idea of the circumstances in which it might be useful for you to produce feeds. In this chapter you get:

❑   A high-level view of content management systems

❑   A sample approach to content management (a Wiki)

❑   The code to such a system

❑   A Weblog view of a CMS

❑   An understanding of how this view can lead directly into producing RSS feeds

The core practical technologies used in this chapter are server-side PHP programming and SQL database access, with a few side journeys to visit regular expressions, HTTP rewriting, and other such related techniques.

Content Management Systems

A CMS is a system for managing content, usually on the Web. Content here can loosely be defined as human-readable material — articles, news stories, technical information like bug tracking, and so on. Early Web sites were built around file system–based storage behind Web servers. This is still a perfectly reasonable approach in many circumstances. The hierarchical store on the file system is easily mapped by URI syntax, and the use of static files to store the content enables delivery optimization by the server. However, as sites grew larger it became clear that ad hoc file management could be a poor way of maintaining the content. The growth of Weblogs has also created demand for CMSs that can handle the submission of short news-like pieces of information, and will display them in a reverse-chronological order.

Content and Other Animals

Much of the material handled by a site will share the same structure, so it makes sense to take advantage of this not only in storage but also to allow consistent presentation. One of the first steps in enabling the management of large quantities of information is the separation of content from presentation.

Metadata

Following the separation of content into presentation, follows the separation of human-readable content from machine-readable information about that content, otherwise known as metadata. This enables the CMS to deal with the content in a more fine-grained fashion, so that the manner of presentation of the information can be derived from business rules applied to the metadata. Syndication technologies have been blazing a trail here, with information feeds being comprised of both content and metadata. A simple example of how the metadata can be used is the order of displayed items — you might want to see items in the familiar reverse-chronological order (sorted by date) or you may want to see them displayed in alphabetical order by author. By providing the metadata in the feed such choices are completely decoupled from the publisher's end and left to the client system.

Applications and Services

There has also been a growth in Web applications and services, notably in search engines and e-commerce. Today, these more active server-side systems are to some extent disjoint from the pure content-oriented systems, although the gap is narrowing. It's interesting from the syndicator's point of view that one of the most useful tools to system integration is metadata and corresponding data that describes services and applications. There are already several online services that derive much of their functionality from the use of RSS and Atom, and the utility of these formats (and others such as general-purpose RDF/XML) in system-to-system communication is beginning to show significant benefits. In many respects syndication is at the cutting edge of Web services. The Atom project has been surveying the field, and developing techniques that will cover the maximum range of scenarios with the minimum complexity.

Accessibility

It's a basic premise of the Web that its utility derives from its universality. To be universal it's essential that no one should be denied access to the information and services it can provide because of disability. The W3C's Web Accessibility Initiative has condensed the requirements for accessibility down to four major principles: Systems should be perceivable, operable, understandable, and robust. As their Web Content Accessibility Guidelines document (http://www.w3.org/TR/WCAG20/) puts it:

- ❏ Content must be perceivable.

- ❏ Interface elements in the content must be operable.

- ❏ Content and controls must be understandable.

- ❏ Content must be robust enough to work with current and future technologies.

furthermore specifically, the material and systems must not only *work*, they must work for *everyone*. In practice the separation of content, metadata, and presentation is an enormous aid to developing accessible systems. As is typical in young technologies, few syndication tools are built with accessibility high on their priority lists. Fortunately the formats are inherently well-suited for maximizing usability. The emphasis is generally on textual content rather than fancy graphics, and among other things this makes it potentially ideal for screen-reading audio devices.

Device Independence

Closely associated with the idea of Web systems being available to all people is support for a wide range of devices. Devices in this context are the tools with which users interact with the Web, the hardware and software needed to access and generate information. In recent years there has been an explosion in the use of Web-enabled mobile devices such as phones and more novel hardware (like browser-equipped microwave ovens) is becoming available. The key techniques relating to device independence describe the characteristics of devices in such a way as to enable delivery of appropriate formats by servers, and to create sites and applications that are suitable for a wide range of devices. Again the W3C are on the case in general, with a Device Independence Working Group (www.w3.org/2001/di/). As with accessibility, syndication technologies have a head start, especially in this case because the content they deliver can be extremely lightweight, with low demands on bandwidth and user interface sophistication. Bear in mind that this isn't a given—a badly designed syndication system could be far worse on both counts than a traditional HTTP/HTML browser setup.

Personalization

Whether it's in the commercial or academic domain, all content is supposed to be consumed by humans. To be more user friendly, systems should have some awareness of the individual user, allowing the presentation to be configured to meet the user's personal requirements. This may take the form of active involvement of the user through some form of login-based membership, or may be entirely transparent, based on what can be deduced from a user's behavior using automatic (or stealth) client-tracking techniques. The whole syndication setup of voluntary subscription by the user means that there's a high level of personalization built into syndication from the start. The sheer volume of syndicated data means that some form of personal filtering is essential, and tools like the excellent search-subscription service provided by PubSub.com indicate there are interesting solutions available if a little creativity is applied.

The Friend-of-a-Friend (FOAF) project is concerned with being able to describe people, their relationships and interests. This is in a manner largely compatible with syndication formats and therefore offers a path to integrating personal information with Web content information.

Security

Security is obviously very important in commercial systems where money is involved. In general, the integrity of server-side systems needs to be maintained in an environment that has its share of hostile elements. So any CMS must have controls to ensure the integrity of the system. In some respects security is orthogonal to syndication, as the majority of feeds are designed to be publicly accessible. But the capability to create material is a prerequisite of a CMS, so there is some overlap, and systems like the Blogger authoring API, and more recently the Atom Protocol, have to be deployed with security in mind.

Inter-System Communication

The Web is a distributed system, and many individual subsystems such as CMSs need to be able to exchange information internally, between their components, and externally with other systems. Standardization on formats and domain models are key here, and the syndication formats offer an excellent solution as a basic communication medium.

Legacy Integration

One characteristic of most modern systems is that they somehow replace existing, less modern systems. One CMS may need to be replaced by another because of commercial or technical demands. Syndication formats are simple enough that it's usually straightforward to map data from legacy systems onto them, and it's not difficult for new systems to consume and integrate information presented in these formats. As such transitions from old to new systems can be seen as a special case of inter-system communication. Additionally, syndication formats can make a good basis for data archiving, assuming that comparatively standardized XML-based formats will be relatively easy to read by any system in the foreseeable future.

Managing Content: Many Tiers

Although practical CMSs can include varying support for the different aspects described previously, a simplification that is useful from the point of view of syndication is shown in the schematic of Figure 24-1.

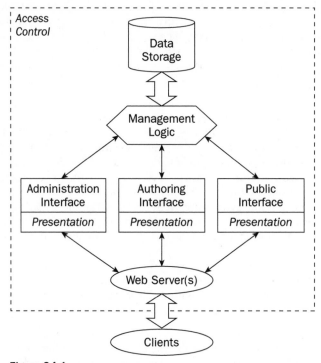

Figure 24-1

In a typical CMS, the data store will be a SQL database with management logic built in using a standard programming language. There will be three primary interfaces, one for the system administrators, another for content providers, and a third for the target audience. The interface for each user will commonly be built around the HTTP protocol, so most interaction will be through Web servers. Traditional CMS clients are regular HTML Web browsers, but with syndication you can use blogging tools as authoring clients (using syndication protocols) and viewers such as aggregators. This simplification ignores all the potential inter-system communications. However, from the CMS's point of view it doesn't really matter how the client is implemented if standard protocols and formats are used.

Early Web systems tended to be two-tier, with little separation of data, presentation, and business logic functionality at the server side. Many CMSs are now built as three-tiered systems with a data store, an application layer, and interfaces. However, there is an ongoing shift toward more modular systems, and the components of those systems are becoming commodities in their own right. Less of the business logic is hard-wired into the application, more of it will be expressed declaratively. General-purpose application servers are used rather than being coded from scratch per application. To some extent current systems are tied to individual programming languages or platforms, although systems are becoming increasingly abstracted from the platform thanks to environments such as Java and Microsoft .NET. The Semantic Web technologies of RDF and OWL take things a step further, where the data languages used are not dependent on any domain-specific interpretation. The stored data is made available as logical statements and the business logic can be managed by a generic inference engine. Similarly, toward the front end there is increased pluggable, declarative control of the material in preparation for delivery. This will typically involve templates or style sheet technologies. A CMS architecture may be geared toward a particular content type: fixed-format material (like magazine articles, news articles, or most blogs), or it may take a more unstructured approach, maybe allowing for *microcontent* of arbitrary types. If you're looking at any of those system from afar, however, they all look remarkably similar. So by looking at one in detail in this chapter, you should be able to understand other systems you may come across in the future.

> *Web scientist and commentator Nova Spivack offers this definition of microcontent: "It is a finite collection of metadata and data that has at least one unique identity and at least one unique address on the network, and that encapsulates no more than a small number of central ideas, where the number of central ideas encapsulated is usually 1"* (`http://novaspivack.typepad.com/nova_spivacks_weblog/2003/12/defining_microc.html`).

SynWiki: A Minimal CMS

To demonstrate how feeds can be generated from an existing CMS, we give you a description and the code for a bare-bones CMS. It's a basic Wiki clone, modeled on the WikiWikiWeb (`http://c2.com/cgi/wiki?WikiWikiWeb`). Such sites allow *anyone* to edit any page, the *wiki* of the name is Hawaiian for *fast*. They are very easy to use, and they have become a popular tool for collaborative projects. Two notable projects that use Wikis are the Wikipedia (`http://en.wikipedia.org`), a free encyclopedia with more than one million entries in 50 languages, and the Atom syndication system (`www.intertwingly.net/wiki/pie/FrontPage`). For want of a better name, the Wiki we describe here is called *SynWiki*. The code is written in PHP.

What Is PHP?

PHP (Hypertext Preprocessor) is probably the leading platform for CMSs. It's a scripting language that generally takes a template-based approach; your code is embedded in HTML.

Installing PHP

To run PHP applications, you need to install a Web server and add PHP support. If you're on Microsoft Windows, then you might already have PWS or IIS for the server. On Linux platforms you may already have the Apache server (which is also available for Windows). Installing PHP is straightforward. There's an installer for Windows that will incorporate it into your existing setup. For Apache it's usually a matter of adding a few lines to the `httpd.conf` configuration file.

To run the demos and the SynWiki application described in this chapter, you will need to have a Web server (such as Apache) with PHP support available, along with an installation of MySQL. You can download all of the required software for free at the following sites:

❑   Apache: `www.apache.org/`

❑   PHP: `www.php.net/`

❑   MySQL: `www.mysql.com/`

All three are well documented online. Installation instructions will vary depending on which operating system you are using.

Open Web

Each page of our sample system appears as a regular HTML Web page. It also has an Edit This Page button or link. Clicking that link takes the user to an editable text area containing the content of the page. The user adds or modifies the content, and then clicks another link or button to go back to the regular page view. The editable content can include simple formatting instructions that are magically converted into HTML when the page is viewed. A cunning trick is used to create new pages. All the user has to do is include a WikiWord in the content; this is a series of joined-up words beginning with an initial uppercase letter. When the edited page has been saved, the WikiWord will be rendered as a hyperlink. Clicking the link takes the user to an editor page for the new link, or if the page already exists to a rendered view of the existing page.

Basic Operation

Most Wikis support a wide range of features, but the system described here only contains the bare minimum to create and view content. Figure 24-2 shows what the initial page of the system looks like.

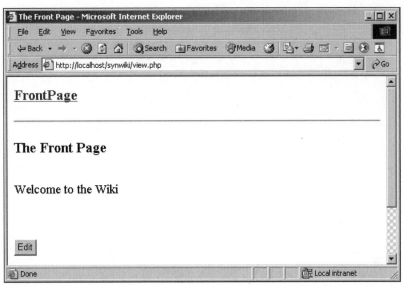

Figure 24-2

When the Edit button is clicked, the user is presented with a view similar to the one in Figure 24-3.

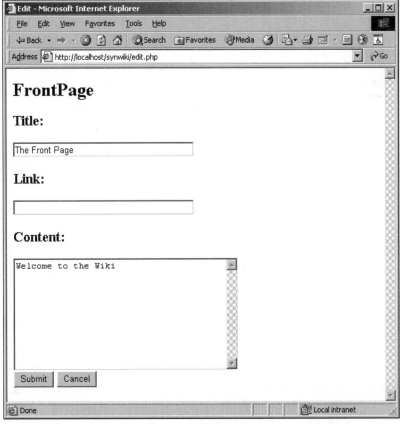

Figure 24-3

This is a little unusual in having fields for a title and link. We have added them to make it appear a little closer to a Weblogging system. The content can be freely modified, as shown in Figure 24-4.

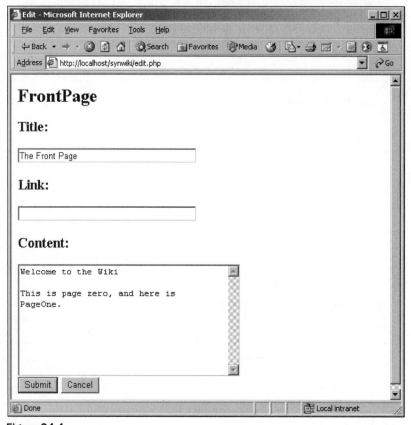

Figure 24-4

Pressing the Cancel button will return to the initial view, but pressing Submit will give the result shown in Figure 24-5.

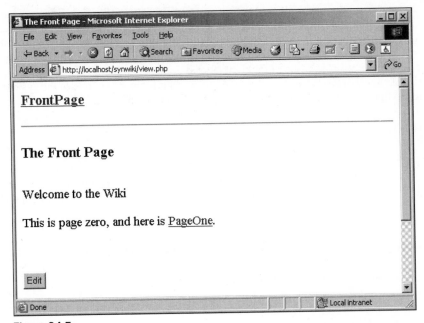

Figure 24-5

As you can see, the text PageOne has been recognized as a WikiWord and turned into a hyperlink. Clicking this link would take you to the edit screen as in Figure 24-4, but for this new page.

System Operation

The diagram in Figure 24-6 shows the role of the main files in the SynWiki code.

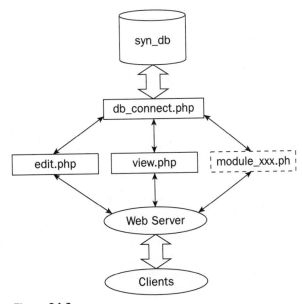

Figure 24-6

As you can see the structure is like that of the generic CMS in Figure 24-1. Key differences are that there is no administrative interface, and no access control system. The content management logic has been rolled into the code of the authoring interface (edit.php) and the public interface (view.php). Each of these will present unstyled HTML to the user, so the presentation layer has in effect been pushed into these files as well. One addition here is the block on the right labeled module_xxx.php. The templating nature of PHP lends itself well to modularization of delivery. When you study the basic code of the system, you'll see three little modules, including the one that will deliver RSS from the system.

System Requirements

Probably the most popular setup for CMSs is LAMP: Linux, Apache, MySQL, and Perl/PHP/Python. The system described here will be suitable for such an environment, although you could easily substitute Windows for Linux, IIS for Apache, and SQL Server for MySQL. The code is in PHP, but it isn't especially complicated, and it wouldn't be difficult to rework it for another template-oriented language like ASP.

Files

The code that goes to make up SynWiki can be found in the following files:

- ❏ edit.php: Editing/authoring interface
- ❏ view.php: Page view
- ❏ dbconnect.php: Database interface
- ❏ config.php: System configuration constants
- ❏ create.sql: SQL commands to the create the database
- ❏ init.php: Initializes the system
- ❏ http_headers.php: Shared HTTP header settings
- ❏ util.php: Various utilities
- ❏ module_backlinks.php: Lists pages linking to a Wiki page
- ❏ module_blog.php: Provides a blog-like view of the data
- ❏ module_rss1.php: Provides an RSS 1.0 feed
- ❏ module_rss2.php: Provides an RSS 2.0 feed
- ❏ .htaccess: Optional redirection script

All the files with the exception of create.sql will be placed in the same directory on a PHP-enabled Web server. You will need to prepare the config.php file to match your setup.

Data Store

The data storage of SynWiki is based on a single MySQL database containing a single table. To keep things simple it contains five TEXT type fields, each corresponding to an aspect of a piece of content. Although it's not declared as such, the first of these, entry_id, will be used as the primary key to the records. In this application it will contain the URI of an individual Wiki page. There's a title field for the title of the page. Wiki pages generally use the page's WikiWord as the title, but having a separate title field is useful for blog-like use of the application. Similarly a link field is provided which may be the same as the URI of the page, although it might potentially contain the address of a page outside of the system. The content of the Wiki page will be stored in the content field, and the date/time at which a page was last modified will be stored in the date field.

The SQL commands that give a user (the PHP system) permission to access the database and to create this table are as follows (create.sql):

```
CREATE DATABASE syn_db;

GRANT ALL PRIVILEGES ON syn_db.* TO 'syn_user'@'localhost'
IDENTIFIED BY 'syn_pass' WITH GRANT OPTION;

USE syn_db;

CREATE TABLE syn_content(
        entry_id    TEXT,
        title       TEXT,
        link        TEXT,
        content     TEXT,
        date        TEXT
);
```

We assume that the MySQL database is running on the local machine, and that you have sufficient rights to create a new database (called syn_db). If this isn't the case, these settings are easy enough to change. The login and other details needed to provide access to the database are included in config.php:

```php
<?php
    $DB_HOST = 'localhost';    // Database host name or IP address
    $DB_NAME = 'syn_db';       // Database name
    $DB_USER = 'syn_user';     // Database user account to use
    $DB_PASSWORD = 'syn_pass';    // Password for user account

    $URI_BASE = "http://localhost/synwiki/"; // web-visible root location
?>
```

Functions in the file db_connect.php interface with the database. As is, this file only does the minimum work necessary with the database. For live deployment it would be desirable to add proper handling of errors and to ensure the connection with the database is closed after use. But it does enough for demonstration purposes. The db_connect.php file begins with the function dbConnect, which will make a connection to the database:

```php
<?php
    function dbConnect(){
        global $dbConnection;
        include("config.php");

    if (!$dbConnection) {
        $dbConnection = mysql_connect($DB_HOST,$DB_USER ,$DB_PASSWORD);
        if (!$dbConnection) {
        print "<h3>could not connect to database</h3>\n";
        exit;
        }
            mysql_select_db($DB_NAME);
    }
    }
```

This function uses a global variable to keep track of whether a connection has already been made. If it hasn't, then the library `mysql_connect` function is called to make a connection, using the details supplied in the included `config.php` data.

After a connection has been established, getting information from the database encompasses preparing suitable SQL query strings and then passing them to library functions. The next function in `dbconnect.php` does this to look up all records in the `syn_content` table that match the supplied `$entry_id` value:

```
function getPageData($entry_id){
    dbConnect();
    $query = "SELECT * FROM syn_content WHERE entry_id = '".$entry_id."'";
    $result = mysql_query($query);
    if($result){
        $row = mysql_fetch_array($result);
          mysql_free_result($result);
        return $row;
    }
    return NULL;
}
```

The `getPageData` data function begins by calling `dbConnect` to make sure the database is accessible, and then it builds a SQL query based on the value of `$entry_id`. This is passed to the database through `mysql_query`, which will return the top row in the results (there should only be one) in an array that's returned.

The next function in `dbconnect.php` adds a new record into the table based on values supplied for each field using a SQL `INSERT INTO...VALUES` instruction. This substitutes values in the query string as needed:

```
function createEntry($entry_id, $title, $link, $content, $date) {
    dbConnect();
    $query = "INSERT INTO syn_content "
            ." (entry_id, title, link, content, date) VALUES "
            ."('$entry_id', '$title', '$link', '$content', '$date')";
    mysql_query($query);
}
```

If a record has been modified, that is, a Wiki page has been edited, then the data needs to be updated to reflect the changes. This is done using a SQL `UPDATE` statement in the `updateEntry` function. Again the required values are inserted programmatically into the query string before being passed to the `mysql_query` function:

```
function updateEntry($entry_id, $title, $link, $content, $date) {
    dbConnect();
    $query = "UPDATE syn_content "
            ."SET title ='$title',"
            ."link ='$link',"
            ."content = '$content',"
            ."date = '$date'"
            ." WHERE entry_id = '$entry_id'";
    mysql_query($query);
}
?>
```

For the Wiki to work it needs at least a single page, corresponding to one entry in the database table. It would be possible to do this using the command-line MySQL interface, but for convenience here it's wrapped in a little PHP in init.php:

```php
<?php
include("dbconnect.php");

    $query = "INSERT INTO syn_content "
            ." (entry_id, title, link, content, date) VALUES "
            ."('FrontPage', 'Front Page', 'FrontPage',
                'Welcome to the Wiki', '1970-01-01T00:00')";
    mysql_query($query);

    print "Front Page Initialized <br />";
    print "<a href=\"view.php\">View</a>";
?>
```

Opening the page init.php in a browser will add a record for the FrontPage Wiki page. Note that this only need to be called once, and since there is no maintenance of pages as unique entries (via entry_id), subsequent calls would only add additional junk records. So after installation it's probably a good idea to delete this file.

Try It Out   Interacting with the Database

This exercise assumes that you have a suitable Web server with PHP running on your local machine, and the files listed so far saved in a directory called synwiki in the root of the Web server. It also assumes that you have MySQL installed in the C:\mysql directory.

If you run into problems, Apache, PHP, and MySQL are all well documented on the Web; see in particular the troubleshooting section in the PHP manual:
http://dev.mysql.com/doc/mysql/en/Starting_server.html.

1. Open a command window and navigate to C:\mysql\bin.

2. Type the following:

```
mysql -u=root
```

This will start the MySQL client as user root, and you should then see something like this:

```
C:\mysql\bin>mysql -u=root
Welcome to the MySQL monitor.  Commands end with ; or \g.
Your MySQL connection id is 15 to server version: 4.0.16-nt

Type 'help;' or '\h' for help. Type '\c' to clear the buffer.

mysql>
```

3. Now enter the following:

```
CREATE DATABASE syn_db;
```

This will create the database. You should see something like this:

```
mysql> CREATE DATABASE syn_db;
Query OK, 1 row affected (0.03 sec)

mysql>
```

4. Now enter (on one line, or pressing Enter after each line, it doesn't matter) the following:

```
GRANT ALL PRIVILEGES ON syn_db.* TO 'syn_user'@'localhost'
IDENTIFIED BY 'syn_pass' WITH GRANT OPTION;
```

You should now see the following:

```
mysql> GRANT ALL PRIVILEGES ON syn_db.* TO 'syn_user'@'localhost'
    -> IDENTIFIED BY 'syn_pass' WITH GRANT OPTION;
Query OK, 0 rows affected (0.13 sec)

mysql>
```

5. Now enter the following:

```
USE syn_db;
```

You should now see this:

```
mysql> USE syn_db;
Database changed
mysql>
```

6. Now type the following:

```
CREATE TABLE syn_content(
    entry_id    TEXT,
    title       TEXT,
    link        TEXT,
    content     TEXT,
    date        TEXT
);
```

The client should respond with a line beginning `Query OK`.

7. Now launch a Web browser and point it at the following address:

```
http://localhost/synwiki/init.php
```

You should see something like the screenshot in Figure 24-7.

Figure 24-7

If you click the View link you can confirm that the FrontPage has been created.

8. Go back to the MySQL command-line client and enter the following:

```
select * from syn_content;
```

The client should respond with the following:

```
mysql> select * from syn_content;
+-----------+------------+-----------+--------------------+------------------+
| entry_id  | title      | link      | content            | date             |
+-----------+------------+-----------+--------------------+------------------+
| FrontPage | Front Page | FrontPage | Welcome to the Wiki | 1970-01-01T00:00 |
+-----------+------------+-----------+--------------------+------------------+
1 row in set (0.00 sec)

mysql>
```

9. At the client type the following:

```
INSERT INTO syn_content(entry_id, title, link, content, date)
VALUES ('PageOne','A title', 'The Link',
'This is page one.','2004-09-25T15:45:21+02:00');
```

The client should give a Query OK message.

10. Now enter the following again:

```
select * from syn_content;
```

You should now see this:

```
mysql> select * from syn_content;
+-----------+------------+-----------+--------------------+------------------+
| entry_id  | title      | link      | content            | date             |
+-----------+------------+-----------+--------------------+------------------+
| FrontPage | Front Page | FrontPage | Welcome to the Wiki | 1970-01-01T00:00 |
| PageOne   | A title    | The Link  | This is page one.  | 2004-09-25T15:45 |
+-----------+------------+-----------+--------------------+------------------+
2 rows in set (0.00 sec)

mysql>
```

11. Now go back to the browser and change the address line to read:

```
http://localhost/synwiki/view.php?page=PageOne
```

After pressing Enter you should see something like the screenshot in Figure 24-8.

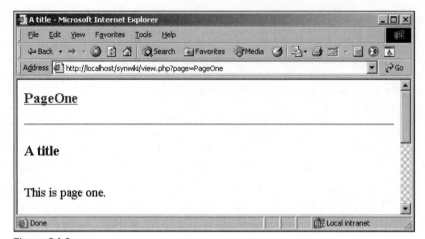

Figure 24-8

How It Works

The following SQL statement created a new database called syn_db:

```
CREATE DATABASE syn_db;
```

The following SQL statement is needed with MySQL to give a user named syn_user with the password syn_pass full rights to do what they like with everything in the syn_db database:

```
GRANT ALL PRIVILEGES ON syn_db.* TO 'syn_user'@'localhost'
IDENTIFIED BY 'syn_pass' WITH GRANT OPTION;
```

These are the same settings as in config.php, which PHP will use to access the database.

This statement informs the MySQL client that the statements that follow are to be applied to the syn_db database:

```
USE syn_db;
```

This statement created a table in syn_db called syn_content with fields (table columns) named entry_id, title, link, content, and date, all defined to hold data of type TEXT:

```
CREATE TABLE syn_content(
        entry_id    TEXT,
        title       TEXT,
        link        TEXT,
        content     TEXT,
        date        TEXT
);
```

When the page init.php is called up in your browser, that page acts as a MySQL client connecting through db_connect.php and running the query:

```
INSERT INTO syn_content (entry_id, title, link, content, date)
VALUES ('FrontPage', 'Front Page', 'FrontPage',
        'Welcome to the Wiki', '1970-01-01T00:00')
```

The SELECT queries show the content of the table, and after init.php has been visited a new record is present. Compare this with the INSERT statement you ran from the command-line client:

```
INSERT INTO syn_content(entry_id, title, link, content, date)
VALUES ('PageOne','A title', 'The Link',
'This is page one.','2004-09-25T15:45:21+02:00');
```

This too added another record, although it came from another source.

Clients Are Clients

The hidden agenda behind that last exercise was to demonstrate what the PHP code is doing: It acts as a client to the SQL database, sends queries, and receives results much like the MySQL client. The idea that it doesn't matter what the client is, as long as it addresses the server according to the required protocol is one that crops up throughout syndication and Web programming in general. Here the server was the database, but the principle is exactly the same for other kinds of servers.

A practical consequence in the context of content management systems is that if you have access to the database, then you can build your own (sub)systems to address the same data as the rest of the CMS. Care is most definitely needed if you plan to add material to the database or modify existing content in this fashion. It depends on the way in which the database has been set up, but you may inadvertently break internal references and potentially damage the integrity of the database as a whole, in a very-difficult-to-mend fashion. However, if all you want to do is generate an RSS or Atom feed based on existing content in the database, your system will only need to read from the database, so in most circumstances it will be secure. If the tables are simple, then it will be simple to generate the feeds. Even if the database has a complex structure, the code required should still be relatively straightforward.

If concurrent operations are likely to cause problems with database integrity or data synchronization, then it may be necessary to schedule queries when the system is otherwise silent. Better still, take advantage of whatever transaction support the database offers. However, databases are designed to look after data safely, so problems caused by reading data should be rare.

Before moving onto the real functional part of the code, the following is the contents of util.php, a series of utility functions called by the main operation code. These rely a lot on PHP-specific constructs, so don't worry too much about understanding how these functions work, you can just consider them black boxes.

Utilities

The utilities begin with a function that isn't actually used in normal operation, but is useful for debugging. When PHP pages are called from an HTTP client (such as a browser) the so-called super global variables $_GET and $_POST will receive the values passed in the call, depending, of course, on which HTTP method was used.

For example, if http://localhost/synwiki/view.php?page=PageOne was used in the address line of a browser the $_GET variable would contain a single key-value, which would be displayed by showArrays as "page = PageOne". Here is the source to showArrays (in util.php):

```php
<?php
// only used for debugging
    function showArrays($arrays) {
        $keys = array_keys($arrays);
        foreach ($keys as &$key) {
            print $key." = ".$arrays[$key]."<br />";
        }
    }
```

The next utility function returns the current date/time expressed in the ISO 8601 (W3CDTF) format used by RSS 1.0 (for example, `2004-09-25T15:45:21+0200`):

```php
function getDateString(){
    return isoDate(time());
}
```

`getDateString` simply calls `isoDate` to convert the format of the current time given by the built-in `time` function. The conversion function reads as follows:

```php
function isoDate($time) {
    $timezone = date('O',$time);
    $timezone = substr(chunk_split($timezone, 3, ':'),0,6);
    $date = date('Y-m-d\TH:i:s', $time) . $timezone;
    return $date;
}
```

The `date` function enables you to format the date/time values. It's used twice here to give correct handling of the time zone part of the string (for more information on dates and times in PHP go to `http://php.net/date`). The date will be stored in the database as the W3CDTF/ISO 8601 value (as text). However, for display purposes the RFC 2822 format (for example, `Sat, 25 Sep 2004 15:45:21 +0200`) is more suitable. The next function converts the W3C date format into the RFC 2822 format:

```php
function convertDateW3CtoRFC2822($dateW3C) {
    //   print "Date:$dateW3C";
return date('r',strtotime(str_replace("+"," +",str_replace("T",
" ",ereg_replace("([+].*):","\\1",$dateW3C)))));
}
```

The application will need to include HTML as content in XML, so the following function replaces disallowed characters with their XML-escaped equivalents using Perl-style regular expressions:

```php
function escapeChars($content) {
    $content = preg_replace("/&/", "&amp;", $content);
    $content = preg_replace("/</", "&lt;", $content);
    $content = preg_replace("/>/", "&gt;", $content);
    return $content;
}
```

Wikis rely on simple text editing, which is formatted to HTML for rendering. The following function in `util.php` uses regular expressions to replace certain strings found in the content with an HTML version. Here's the source of the `replaceExpression` function:

```php
function replaceExpressions($content) {
    $content = preg_replace("/</", "&lt;", $content);
    $content = preg_replace("/>/", "&gt;", $content);

    $content = preg_replace("/\n/", "<br />", $content);
    $content = preg_replace("/-{4,}/", "<hr />", $content);
    $content = preg_replace("/(\*)(.*?)(\*)/",
                                "<strong>\\2</strong>", $content);

    $WikiWordPattern="/([A-Z][a-z]+[A-Z][A-Za-z]*)/";
    $content = preg_replace($WikiWordPattern,
                "<a href=\"view.php?page=\\0\">\\0</a>", $content);
    return $content;
}
?>
```

The first two replacements escape the < and > symbols, again to prevent them from getting tangled with other markup in the page. Line breaks will occur in the text box as newline characters (or newline/carriage return pairs) so the next replacement changes \n to <br />, its XHTML equivalent. The fourth swap will replace ---- with <hr /> to create a horizontal line, a piece of syntax commonly used in Wikis. As one more example of Wiki formatting, the next replacement will take any blocks of text in the content that is highlighted with asterisks *like this* and replace them with a suitable HTML version, like this. The \\2 sent to the preg_replace function inserts the second token (the quoted text) from the source into the output. This isn't standard Wiki syntax; usually a sequence of three apostrophes is used to make text render in a bold typeface.

The final regular expression is the crucial one that will replace expressions in the content text such as WikiWord with hyperlinks that will refer to other Wiki pages:

```
<a href="view.php?page=WikiWord">WikiWord</a>
```

You can find discussion of formatting syntax and corresponding regular expressions on the original Wiki at http://c2.com/cgi/wiki?TextFormattingRegularExpressions.

> *Unfortunately PHP brings with it complications (while trying to help) when it comes to the handling of apostrophes and quotes. These issues are sidestepped here. For more information see the "Magic Quotes" section of the PHP manual at* www.php.net/manual/en/security.magicquotes.php.

The Wiki allows you to edit pages online, but this may cause problems with proxy servers and browser caches, returning you to a cached, unedited version of the required page. To help avoid this, the http_headers.php contains a series of statements that will be passed in the HTTP header of the pages in which it is included to override any caching behavior.

```php
<?php
    header("Cache-Control: no-store, no-cache, must-revalidate");  // HTTP 1.1
    header("Cache-Control: post-check=0, pre-check=0", false);
    header("Pragma: no-cache");                                     // HTTP 1.0
    header("Content-Type: text/html;charset=utf-8");
?>
```

The `Content-Type` header is used to make sure the view and edit pages are served with a suitable mime type and encoding. The HTML used in this application is non-strict XHTML and the `text/html` mime type is likely to work in most browser. It's usually a good idea to favor the UTF-8 character encoding because it supports all languages.

There is a more subtle reason for being explicit about the encoding here. When data is passed from HTML forms, the encoding of the data can be inappropriate for the system that receives it. By default the form data will be submitted using the encoding of the page that contains the form. So making explicit that this page should be treated as UTF-8 reduces the chances of problems later on. Additionally the following line will be included in the HTML, just to ensure that the encoding is under control:

```
<meta http-equiv="Content-Type" content="text/html; charset=utf-8" />
```

Authoring Page

Now that the helper files have been covered it's time to move on to the core application files. The first of these is `edit.php`, which is rendered as shown in Figures 24-3 and 24-4. This file and `view.php` (the viewer) share the same overall structure:

❑   Initialization and includes

❑   Handling of the HTTP GET method

❑   Handling of the HTTP POST method

❑   A little variable shuffling

❑   An HTML-based template for display

The source code begins by including the files containing the database connection and utility functions. The code in `http_header.php` isn't expressed in a function, so this will be executed inline, providing appropriate headers for this page when it gets passed to the client. The variable `$entry_id` is initialized with the ID of the default page. So the source of `edit.php` begins like this:

```php
<?php
include("dbconnect.php");
include("util.php");
include ("http_headers.php");

$entry_id = "FrontPage";
```

The next block is a conditional to check whether this page has been called by a client using the HTTP POST method. If it has, then the super global variable `$_POST` can be used as a dictionary to look up whatever has been passed (from an HTML form) for the value of `entry_id.`, which will be the `entry_id` of the page to edit:

```php
if ($_POST) { // coming from view Edit button
    // showArrays($_POST);
    $entry_id = $_POST["entry_id"];
}
```

`edit.php` will also be called (under normal circumstances), when a link has been clicked to a WikiWord named `page`, but that page doesn't exist yet in the database. Under these circumstances the address used will look something like `http://localhost/synwiki/view.php?page=PageOne`. The name of the page is obtained and passed to the `$entry_id` variable. The code for this looks like this:

```
if($_GET) {  // coming from a WikiLink where no page exists
  // showArrays($_GET);
  $entry_id = $_GET["page"];
}
```

Now that the page that is to be edited has been identified, the next thing to do is to obtain the database record for that page. A call to `getPageData` (included in `db_connect.php`) may provide that:

```
$pageData = getPageData($entry_id);
```

However, if that page doesn't exist, then it will have to be created. The following block of code will first create a new entry with some default values and the current date. The `getPageData` function is then called again. Now there is some data available for this page/entry.

```
if(!$pageData) {
    createEntry($entry_id, "Title", "Link", "Enter Content", getDateString());
    $pageData = getPageData($entry_id);
}
?>
```

That's the end of the "pure PHP" code in this file. The rest is HTML-based, acting as a template for values obtained from the database. It starts like this:

```
<html>
  <head>
    <title>Edit</title>
    <meta http-equiv="Content-Type" content="text/html; charset=utf-8" />
  </head>

  <body>
```

The value of the variable `$entry_id` is echoed as a medium-sized heading:

```
<h2><?php echo $entry_id; ?></h2>
```

This file is provided to edit the data, so the bulk of the rendered page will be a form. The `form` method is declared as HTTP POST (values in the database will be changed, so GET wouldn't be appropriate). When actions (button clicks) occur in the form, then the data in the form will be passed in an HTTP request to `view.php` (this is addressed relatively; in the demonstration code it will be the page `http://localhost/synwiki/view.php`).

```
<form method="post" action="view.php">
```

The user will be presented with two single-line text boxes entitled `Title:` and `Link:` followed by a larger editable text area labeled `Content:` (see Figures 24-3 and 24-4). These will be prefilled with data loaded from the database by setting the value attribute in the `input` elements to the corresponding named field in the data returned earlier from the `getPageData` function. Whatever values appear here will be passed to the server within the POST request. The code for these elements is as follows:

```
                <h3>Title:</h3>
                <input type="text" size="40" name="title"
                       value="<?php echo $pageData['title']; ?>"/>
                <br />

                <h3>Link:</h3>
                <input type="text" size="40" name="link"
                       value="<?php echo $pageData['link']; ?>" />
                <br />

                <h3>Content:</h3>
                <textarea name="content" cols="40" rows="10"
                wrap="virtual"><?php echo $pageData['content']; ?>
                </textarea>
                <br />
```

The form is provided with two buttons, labeled Submit and Cancel. There is an additional no-visible field that will be used to pass the `entry_id` for the page that has been modified or created.

```
                <input type="submit" name="submit" value="Submit" />
                <input type="submit" name="cancel" value="Cancel" />
                <input type="hidden" name="entry_id" value="<?php echo $entry_id; ?>" />
            </form>
        </body>
    </html>
```

Viewing Page

The structure of the PHP file that will render the Wiki pages for viewing has the same overall structure as `edit.php`:

❑ Initialization and includes

❑ Handling of the HTTP GET method

❑ Handling of the HTTP POST method

❑ A little variable shuffling

❑ An HTML-based template for display

Included are the database connection and utility functions, along with the HTTP header setters that will be called inline. The values of the `$entry_id` and `$content` variables are initialized to potentially usable default values. The source to `edit.php` begins as follows:

```
<?php
include("dbconnect.php");
include("util.php");
include ("http_headers.php");

$entry_id = "FrontPage";
$content = "<a href=\"view.php?page=FrontPage\">FrontPage</a>";
```

If the `view.php` page has been accessed using a HTTP GET, then it will have a query part in the URI pointing to the required page, for example, `http://localhost/synwiki/view.php?page=FrontPage`. If available, the value in the query part is extracted. This provides the `entry_id` for the required page, which is used to obtain the rest of the data from the database using the getPageData function (listed previously in db_connection.php). If no data is available for the identified page, then there will be an immediate redirect to edit.php with the name of the missing page as the value of the page parameter in the query part of that URI. The GET-specific section is as follows:

```
if ($_GET) { // normally coming from view
    showArrays($_GET);
    $entry_id = $_GET["page"];
    $pageData = getPageData($entry_id);
    if(!$pageData) {
        header("Location: edit.php?page=$entry_id");
    }
}
```

Calling the header function with a Location: value has the effect of sending an immediate HTTP 302 Found redirect code back to the client, causing it to move to the target page.

The HTTP POST method will (under normal circumstances) only be encountered after one of the buttons in the form on the edit.php page has been clicked. The entry_id (page name) is made available as a hidden form variable that is passed from the super global $_POST into the variable $entry_id. The isset function is used to check whether the Submit field in the form has been given a value. This will only have occurred if the Submit button was clicked. If that's what happened then the other values that were placed in the form — that is, the title, content and so on — are taken from $_POST and used to update the database with the new page data.

```
if ($_POST) { // coming from edit
    //showArrays($_POST);
    $entry_id = $_POST["entry_id"];

    if (isset($_POST["submit"])){
        $title   = $_POST["title"];
        $link = $_POST["link"];
        $content = $_POST["content"];
        $date = getDateString();
        updateEntry($entry_id, $title, $link, $content, $date);
    }
}
```

In whatever manner the page was approached, by this point $entry_id should contain the identifier of a database record corresponding to the required page. So the data is obtained, and the new few lines pass the various field contents into individually named variables that will be used when it comes to displaying the data. The following lines also contain a little bit of default value-passing into fields that have no content, in the interests of giving a reasonably consistent page appearance.

```
$pageData = getPageData($entry_id);
$title   = $pageData['title'];

if($title == ""){
    $title = $entry_id;
}

$link = $pageData['link'];

if($link == ""){
```

```
    $link = $entry_id;
}

$date = $pageData['date'];
$content = $pageData['content'];
```

The next line contains a vital operation—making the text substitutions needed to convert text-oriented Wiki-format content (perhaps containing WikiWords) into HTML. The `replaceExpressions` function is the one with the regular expressions in `util.php`, listed previously. The date stored in the database will be in the ISO 8601/W3CDTF format, so a conversion is made to the more human-friendly RFC 2822 (e-mail) format.

```
$content = replaceExpressions($content);
$displayDate = convertDateW3CtoRFC2822($date);
?>
```

So once again the end of the PHP proper has been reached, and what follows in `view.php` is the HTML-based page template. Various variables defined in the PHP code have their values echoed in the HTML page. The template part of the code is as follows:

```
<html><head><title><?php echo $title; ?></title>
<meta http-equiv="Content-Type" content="text/html; charset=utf-8" />
</head>
<body>
```

The following line creates a link of the following form:

```
<a
href="http://localhost/synwiki/module_backlinks.php?page=WikiPage">WikiPage</a>
```

More on that in the section entitled "URL Rewriting." Meantime, the source to `view.php` continues:

```
<?php
print "<h3><a href=\"module_backlinks.php?page=$entry_id\">$entry_id</a></h3>";
?>
<hr />
<h3><?php echo $title; ?></h3>
<br />
<?php echo $content; ?>
<br /><br />
<br /><br />
```

The form on the `view.php` page displays a single Edit button to the user. Clicking that button will take the user to the `edit.php` page. This form also uses the POST method (as it *may* change things server-side). The value of the `$entry_id` variable is passed along with the POST method to instruct which page should be edited. The form code is as follows:

```
    <form method="POST" action="edit.php">
        <input type="submit" name="submit" value="Edit"  />
        <input type="hidden" name="entry_id" value="<?php echo $entry_id; ?>" />
    </form>
```

The code for `view.php` finishes with a nicely formatted date along with several links, the targets of which we will discuss next:

```
<br />
<em>Last edited: <?php echo $displayDate; ?></em>
<br /><br />
<a href="module_blog.php">Blog</a>
<br />
<a href="module_rss1.php">RSS 1.0</a>
<br />
<a href="module_rss2.php">RSS 2.0</a>
 </body>
</html>
```

Making Modules

Most CMSs support the construction of modules to extend core functionality in one way or another. The SynWiki code will use an ultra-simple approach, by defining PHP files that directly access the underlying database. This approach should be available in most database-backed CMSs whatever other module support is provided. The following module will list the pages that contain the supplied string. The main purpose of this module is to provide a list of other pages that link to a particular page, although it could just as easily be used as a simple general-purpose word search facility. The key to its operation is the SQL LIKE operator, which is supported by most databases. Here is an example of the syntax:

```
SELECT * FROM syn_content WHERE content LIKE '%WikiPage%'
```

The % symbols act as wildcards, so the WHERE clause will look for any occurrences of the string WikiPage in the content field of the syn_content table. The SELECT clause uses * so all the fields of records in the table that match this criterion will be returned. The full source to `module_backlinks.php` is as follows:

```
<html><head><title>BackLinks</title></head>
<body>
<?php
include("dbconnect.php");

$entry_id = $_GET["page"];

print "<a href=\"view.php?page=$entry_id\">$entry_id</a>";
print "<br />";

dbConnect();
$query = "SELECT * FROM syn_content WHERE content LIKE '%".$entry_id."%'";
$result = mysql_query($query);
if ($result) {
    while ($row = mysql_fetch_array($result)) {
        $page = $row["entry_id"];
        print "<a href=\"view.php?page=$page\">$page</a>";
        print "<br />";
    }
}
print "<a href=\"view.php?page=FrontPage\">FrontPage</a>";
?>
</body>
</html>
```

So basically a module in this system just runs some kind of SQL query and formats the result into an HTML page. This particular example isn't particularly relevant to syndication beyond showing how CMS data can be displayed selectively, so detailed description of the code will be skipped. However, in a moment you'll see another example, `module_blog.php`, which is very relevant to syndication. First another issue is worth mention in passing.

URL Rewriting

A common situation when generating content dynamically is that the URIs needed to get at the data are inconveniently complex. To view pages with this Wiki, it's necessary to provide a URI of the following form:

```
http://localhost/view.php?page=WikiPage
```

This is difficult to remember if you want to type an address directly, and it isn't very neat for including in hyperlinks in the code. In the code of `view.php` a redirect from one addressed URI was made to another programmatically using:

```
header("Location: edit.php?page=$entry_id");
```

However this isn't very good as a general solution as you want the URI of the page containing this code to be simple, and every target page is likely to need one of these simple-URI pages. A much better approach to simpler URI syntax can be used if the Web server you're using supports URL rewriting. Most do, but you may need to check the manual in case it's not enabled. On Apache, (assuming it's enabled) you can use URL rewriting by placing a file named `.htaccess` in the directory in which you want the rewriting to take place (or any parent directory if the paths are modified accordingly). Here's an example:

```
RewriteEngine on
RewriteRule ^([A-Z][a-z]+[A-Z][A-Za-z]*) view.php?page=$1
```

The first line switches the rewriting functionality on (this may not be needed). The second line defines the rewriting rule. The left-hand side of this is a regular expression that is designed to match the URIs you want to rewrite. The ^ here will match the path up to the current directory, the rest is designed to match the WikiWord syntax. The right-hand side of the rule describes what is wanted as a replacement. The net result of this rewrite rule (placed in the `synwiki` directory) is that it will match addresses of the form:

```
http://localhost/synwiki/WikiPage
```

And then automatically change these to the form:

```
http://localhost/synwiki/view.php?page=WikiPage
```

This allows a far neater syntax to be used wherever URIs are required.

Blog Module

Now back to the Wiki code, and `module_blog.php`. Here's the full source code:

```php
<?php
include("config.php");
include("dbconnect.php");
```

```
include("util.php");

header("Content-type: text/html;charset=utf-8");

dbConnect();
$query = "SELECT * FROM syn_content ORDER BY date DESC LIMIT 3";
$result = mysql_query($query);
?>

<html><head><title>SynWiki Blog</title>
<meta http-equiv="Content-Type" content="text/html; charset=utf-8" />
</head>
<body>
      <h2>SynWiki Blog</h2>
<?php
if ($result) {
    while ($row = mysql_fetch_array($result)) {
        $displayDate = convertDateW3CtoRFC2822($row["date"]);
        $content = $row["content"];
        $content = replaceExpressions($content);
        $title = $row["title"];
        $url = $URI_BASE."view.php?".$row["entry_id"];
?>
    <h3><a href="<?php echo $url; ?>"><?php echo $title; ?></a></h3>
    <p><?php echo $content; ?></p>
    <p><em><?php echo $displayDate; ?></em></p>
    <hr />
<?php
    }
}
?>
<br />
<a href="view.php?page=FrontPage">FrontPage</a>
<br />
<a href="module_rss1.php">RSS 1.0</a>
<br />
<a href="module_rss2.php">RSS 2.0</a>
 </body>
</html>
```

Figure 24-9 shows what this will look like when displayed in a browser.

In passing it's interesting to note that in one sense Weblogs and Wikis are very similar — they provide user-friendly ways of editing Web content. Both can be built on essentially the same code base. However, from the user's point of view they can be very different, particularly in terms of site structure and access control.

Figure 24-9

Reverse-Chrono Here We Go

If you look closely at the dates in Figure 24-9 you will see the items are displayed with the most recent first. This blog-like reverse chronological view of the data is fairly straightforward to achieve by using a SQL query based on the date:

```
SELECT * FROM syn_content ORDER BY date DESC LIMIT 3
```

All fields are obtained from the table for the first three records when the records are taken in descending order of their date fields. The source to module_blog.php begins with the common includes and sets the HTTP header to give a suitable MIME type for the page, then runs this query, as you can see here:

```
<?php
include("config.php");
```

```
include("dbconnect.php");
include("util.php");

header("Content-type: text/html;charset=utf-8");

dbConnect();
$query = "SELECT * FROM syn_content ORDER BY date DESC LIMIT 3";
$result = mysql_query($query);
%>
```

An HTML template shell is then started:

```
<html><head><title>SynWiki Blog</title>
<meta http-equiv="Content-Type" content="text/html; charset=utf-8" />
</head>
<body>
      <h2>SynWiki Blog</h2>
```

Inside this shell, there is a loop that is run through for each entry returned by the query:

```
<?php
if ($result) {
    while ($row = mysql_fetch_array($result)) {
```

Suitable values for presentation are taken from the query results:

```
        $displayDate = convertDateW3CtoRFC2822($row["date"]);
        $content = $row["content"];
        $content = replaceExpressions($content);
        $title = $row["title"];
        $url = $URI_BASE."view.php?".$row["entry_id"];
?>
```

Note that the same expression-replacement used for the Wiki page view is applied to each block of content; the HTML rendition is what's required. The values are then mixed into HTML formatting elements, and the loop is closed:

```
    <h3><a href="<?php echo $url; ?>"><?php echo $title; ?></a></h3>
    <p><?php echo $content; ?></p>
    <p><em><?php echo $displayDate; ?></em></p>
    <hr />
<?php
    }
}
?>
```

There are then links to the Wiki front page and two other modules before the HTML shell is completed:

```
<br />
<a href="view.php?page=FrontPage">FrontPage</a>
<br />
<a href="module_rss1.php">RSS 1.0</a>
<br />
<a href="module_rss2.php">RSS 2.0</a>
 </body>
</html>
```

Producing RSS 1.0

From the reverse chronological blog view it's a fairly small step to produce feed data. Here is an example of the kind of feed data that is required:

```
<rdf:RDF
  xmlns="http://purl.org/rss/1.0/"
  xmlns:rdf="http://www.w3.org/1999/02/22-rdf-syntax-ns#"
  xmlns:dc="http://purl.org/dc/elements/1.1/"
  xmlns:content="http://purl.org/rss/1.0/modules/content/">

  <channel rdf:about="http://localhost/synwiki/module_rss1.php">
    <title>SynWiki</title>
    <link>http://localhost/synwiki/</link>
    <description>New Material on the SynWiki</description>
    <dc:date>2004-09-27T12:01:17+02:00</dc:date>
    <items>
      <rdf:Seq>
      <rdf:li rdf:resource="http://localhost/synwiki/view.php?PageTwo" />
      <rdf:li rdf:resource="http://localhost/synwiki/view.php?PageOne" />
      </rdf:Seq>
    </items>
  </channel>

  <item rdf:about="http://localhost/synwiki/view.php?PageTwo">
   <title>Page two</title>
    <link>http://localhost/synwiki/view.php?PageTwo</link>
    <content:encoded>this is page two     </content:encoded>
    <dc:date>2004-09-26T20:31:35+02:00</dc:date>
  </item>

  <item rdf:about="http://localhost/synwiki/view.php?PageOne">
    <title>A title</title>
    <link>http://localhost/synwiki/view.php?PageOne</link>
    <content:encoded>This is page one.</content:encoded>
    <dc:date>2004-09-25T15:45</dc:date>
  </item>

</rdf:RDF>
```

Only two items are shown here, in practice you most likely will want to include 10 to 20 items in the feed. The main part of the feed contains the most recent items, the very same data used in the blog view. There is a minor complication with RSS 1.0 feeds as the channel element contains a list of all the items (in reverse-chronological order) before the individual items are listed. The values used in the rdf:resource attributes are the URIs of the individual Wiki pages. It would be possible to first get all the result fields, display only the URIs in this block and retain the data for subsequent display inside the individual items. The approach taken here is less elegant, but demonstrates a query giving more limited results:

```
SELECT entry_id FROM syn_content ORDER BY date DESC LIMIT 3
```

This will return only the values for the entry_id for each of the records, but in the required reverse-chronological order.

The RSS 1.0 feed has quite a bit of namespace and channel-level information, which needs to be presented first. Here it appears early in the PHP file, as you can see in the start of the source to module_rss1.php:

```php
<?php
include("config.php");
include("dbconnect.php");
include("util.php");

header("Content-type: application/rdf+xml;charset=utf-8");
?>

<rdf:RDF
  xmlns="http://purl.org/rss/1.0/"
  xmlns:rdf="http://www.w3.org/1999/02/22-rdf-syntax-ns#"
  xmlns:dc="http://purl.org/dc/elements/1.1/"
  xmlns:content="http://purl.org/rss/1.0/modules/content/">

  <channel rdf:about="<?php echo $URI_BASE."module_rss1.php" ?>">
    <title>SynWiki</title>
    <link><?php echo $URI_BASE ?></link>
    <description>New Material on the SynWiki</description>
    <dc:date><?php echo isoDate(time()) ?></dc:date>
```

Note that the MIME type has been set to `application/rdf+xml`, as RSS 1.0 is RDF/XML. The channel URI is that of this module, which is constructed from the `$URI_BASE` constant (declared in `config.php`) with `module_rss1.php` appended. The channel-level `dc:date` value needs to be the date at which this feed was generated, so the current date and time is obtained using the built-in time function which is formatted with `isoDate` (in `util.php`).

The next section of `module_rss1.php` uses the `entry_id`-only query to fill in the item URI values:

```php
    <items>
      <rdf:Seq>
<?php
dbConnect();

$query = "SELECT entry_id FROM syn_content ORDER BY date DESC LIMIT 3";
$result = mysql_query($query);

$date = isoDate(time());

if ($result) {
    while ($row = mysql_fetch_array($result)) {
?>
    <rdf:li rdf:resource=
          "<?php echo $URI_BASE."view.php?".$row["entry_id"]; ?>" />
<?php
    }
}
?>
      </rdf:Seq>
    </items>
  </channel>
```

The URIs for individual items will be of the following form:

```
http://localhost/synwiki/view.php?page=WikiPage
```

The next section of `module_rss1.php` applies the same query as `module_blog.php` and then runs through each record and formats each into an `<item>` block:

```php
<?php
$query = "SELECT * FROM syn_content ORDER BY date DESC LIMIT 3";
$result = mysql_query($query);

if ($result) {
    while ($row = mysql_fetch_array($result)) {
        $content = $row["content"];
        $content = replaceExpressions($content);
        $content = escapeChars($content);
        $link = $URI_BASE."view.php?".$row["entry_id"];
?>
  <item rdf:about="<?php echo $link; ?>">
    <title><?php echo $row["title"]; ?></title>
    <link><?php echo $link; ?></link>
    <content:encoded><?php echo $content; ?></content:encoded>
    <dc:date><?php echo $row["date"]; ?></dc:date>
  </item>
<?php
    }
}
?>
```

Finally the RSS 1.0 XML data is terminated with a closing tag:

```
</rdf:RDF>
```

The resulting feed can be loaded into a newsreader, as shown in Figure 24-10.

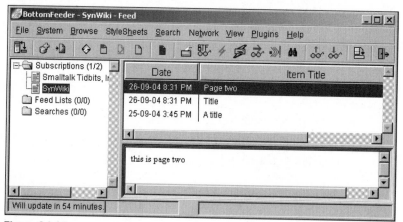

Figure 24-10

The BottomFeeder aggregator shown in Figure 24-10 also provides a useful channel properties view. The SynWiki feed in this view is shown in Figure 24-11.

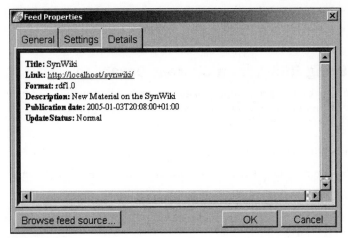

Figure 24-11

Alternative Techniques

Although the setup described in this chapter was similar to that found in many CMSs, you should bear in mind that many different CMS architectures are possible, and there are many other ways of generating feeds from them. The CMS was a simple one, and because all the data was in a single table, we only needed very simple SQL queries.

Your storage system may be RDF- or XML-oriented, in which case you wouldn't be using SQL queries but XPath/XQuery or one of the RDF query languages. The data may be stored on the file system, in which case you may be able to use a similar feed generation subsystem to that described here but would have to create an alternative to the database access code to get at the raw data. Under such circumstances you may have to write a lot more code to get at the data programmatically rather than simply employing a query language.

The approach taken in this chapter treated the material to be output as string data, pushing XML out in an unstructured fashion. This is a reasonable pragmatic way of working with CMSs that use similar techniques to serialize their content as (X)HTML. However, if the system to which you want to add feed-generation capabilities is already using some other form of XML management, it would make sense to reuse that instead. For example, the system may be passing around DOM (Document Object Model) objects, in which case those could be used to build up the feed XML, and their associated serialization code can be used to generate the feed data itself. If the system you're using doesn't have any existing subsystem that might lend itself to RSS production, then your best bet is to employ a dedicated RSS serialization library such as the PHP RSS Writer class (www.phpclasses.org/rsswriter). Failing that a purpose-built XML serializer such as Genx (www.tbray.org/ongoing/When/200x/2004/02/20/GenxStatus) can save a lot of effort while minimizing the chances of your feeds being ill-formed or invalid.

If you have no control over the content management code then you may be forced to use a screen-scraping technique, for example, converting the site's XHTML to RSS with XSLT. This is likely to be brittle, if the XHTML format changes, then the feed may break. The templating approach that we use in this chapter can be sensitive to character encoding, for example, if the content for publication is pasted from another application. The use of a dedicated XML generation library rather than string construction can help avoid such issues.

Whatever approach you take, before you go live with your system you should check your feeds with a variety of content on the Feed Validator (http://feedvalidator.org/). It's also good practice to check your feeds periodically after they are live.

Steps in Producing RSS from a Content Database

You've now seen how a simple content management can be put together, and how the database can be accessed directly to produce an RSS feed. This approach will essentially be the same whatever system you want to generate feeds from. The steps are as follows:

1. Understand the data storage system.

2. If possible, find existing data formatting that resembles the feed structure (ideally using XML).

3. Create suitable queries to extract the necessary data.

4. Format the results as XML as demanded by the target feed format, using a dedicated XML library if necessary.

5. Check the feed in the Feed Validator.

Much of the material in the rest of the book will be relevant to these steps, but the CMS example should give you an idea of one way in which they can fit together.

Summary

In this chapter you learned...

❑ About the general shape of content management systems.

❑ How to construct a simple database-backed system.

❑ How Weblogs and syndication use a reverse-chronological view.

❑ How modular templating can make for a versatile system.

❑ How to produce feeds using templates.

Exercise

1. Create a module for SynWiki called module_rss2.php to deliver RSS 2.0 formatted data. The data you're aiming for will look something like this:

```
<rss version="2.0">
   <channel>
      <title>Wiki News</title>
      <link>http://localhost/synwiki/</link>
      <description>New stuff on the Wiki</description>
      <language>en-us</language>
      <pubDate>Mon, 27 Sep 2004 12:45:38 +0200</pubDate>
      <lastBuildDate>Mon, 27 Sep 2004 12:45:38 +0200</lastBuildDate>
      <docs>http://example.org/docs</docs>
```

```
        <generator>SynWiki</generator>
        <managingEditor>synwiki@example.org</managingEditor>
        <webMaster>webmaster@example.org</webMaster>

    <item>
        <guid>http://localhost/synwiki/view.php?PageTwo</guid>
        <title>Page two</title>
        <description>this is page two</description>
        <pubDate>Sun, 26 Sep 2004 20:31:35 +0200</pubDate>
    </item>

    <item>
        <guid>http://localhost/synwiki/view.php?PageOne</guid>
        <title>A title</title>
        <description>This is page one.</description>
        <pubDate>Sat, 25 Sep 2004 15:45:00 +0200</pubDate>
    </item>

    </channel>
</rss>
```

Queries and Transformations

This chapter introduces the following technologies with practical examples relating to syndication:

- ❑ XPath
- ❑ XQuery
- ❑ XSLT (Extensible Stylesheet Language Transformations)

The leading syndication formats are based on XML, so standard XML tools can be useful. In previous chapters you have seen how different data models can be used to make sense of XML data. A tree-based data model, very much like that of the Document Object Model (DOM), lies behind the XPath, XSLT, and XQuery technologies. XPath is used for navigating XML documents and locating items of interest. Although it can be used in isolation, both XSLT and XQuery derive much of their functionality from XPath. XSLT is a true programming language, although in practice it is primarily used to transform one XML format to another, using templates. XQuery is like an XML version of SQL (Structured Query Language), allowing you to select parts of documents according to your query rules. Each of these can be applied in different ways to Web data for use in syndication, to extract information from existing feeds, translate between formats, or generate feed data from other kinds of markup. All three systems are described in W3C specifications and are reasonably mature. This chapter gives a brief introduction to these three technologies and then provides some simple examples of how they may be used in the context of RSS and Atom.

In the section "Graphic Display: SVG in a Very Small Nutshell" later in this chapter, we will introduce another XML technology, SVG (Scalable Vector Graphics), and we demonstrate how you can use XSLT to produce graphic representations of syndication feeds.

Paths and Queries

XPath isn't expressed in XML itself. It is used to locate parts of an XML document, and the (abbreviated) syntax usually used is very similar to that of file system paths. As an example, the following is an XML document (book.xml) that could be used to describe a set of articles (the elements used are a tiny subset of the popular DocBook format, http://docbook.org):

```
<book lang="en">
    <bookinfo>
        <title>A Book of Articles</title>
    </bookinfo>
    <article>
        <articleinfo>
            <title>The First Article</title>
        </articleinfo>
        <para>The contents of the first article.</para>
    </article>
    <article>
        <articleinfo>
            <title>A Second Article</title>
        </articleinfo>
        <para>The contents of the second article.</para>
    </article>
</book>
```

To address the document root, the / is used. To step up to elements from there, the name of the element is added, so in the previous example /book is the path to the root element, /book/bookinfo to the next element. Unlike most file systems, it's not uncommon to have several elements of the same name at the same level in the hierarchy. So to refer to the first <article> element here you would have to say /book/article[1] and the second /book/article[2]. But often you will want to apply the same processing to all elements of the same name, so in this case to operate on all the <article> elements you could use the location selector /book/article.

As well as this kind of *absolute* location path, referenced from the root (/), it's also possible to use relative references. When working in a command shell there is the idea of the current working directory, and the parallel in XPath is known as the context node. From the context node an XPath tool can make relative references, very much as with a file system. So if the context node was the element <bookinfo>, then the XPath locator title would point to its only child element. Again like file systems, to refer to the current context node you can use the expression . and .. will refer to the parent of the context node.

Most programming languages have XPath libraries that allow these kinds of locators to be used alongside regular code. But their utility is magnified considerably when they are used within one of the XML-oriented languages such as XSLT or XQuery. In the section "Introducing XSLT" later in the chapter, you will see how they fit in with XSLT. First, however, we'll give you a quick demonstration of what you can do with XQuery.

XQuery Runner

A fairly straightforward tool for experimenting with XQuery (and XPath) is XQEngine, a Java toolkit that you can download at http://sourceforge.net/projects/xqengine/. This is actually a full-text search engine, but it is designed to enable XQuery expressions to be run against its data. XQEngine is designed to be used within a Java program, so to get at its functionality some kind of user interface is needed. The two code listings that follow provide a simple command-line interface to the toolkit.

Source Code

The first listing, LineInterpreter.java, provides basic console reading and writing. The source looks like this:

```
import java.io.BufferedReader;
import java.io.IOException;
import java.io.InputStreamReader;

public class LineInterpreter {

    private BufferedReader reader;

    public LineInterpreter() {
        InputStreamReader streamReader = new InputStreamReader(System.in);
        reader = new BufferedReader(streamReader);
    }

    public void start() {
        String input = null;
        String output = null;
        try {
            while ((input = reader.readLine()) != null) {
                output = process(input);
                System.out.println(output);
            }
        } catch (IOException e) {
            e.printStackTrace();
        }
    }

    public String process(String input) {
        if(input.equals("quit")){
            System.exit(0);
        }
        return input;
    }

    public static void main(String[] args) {
        new LineInterpreter().start();
    }
}
```

This is standard Java I/O. The `LineInterpreter` constructor creates a reader to get data from the command line. The `start` method includes a loop that uses the reader to take data from the console one line at a time and pass it to the `process` method. Whatever the `process` method returns will be sent back to the console. All the `process` method does here is to check whether the string it has been passed (from the console) is `quit`, in which case it halts the program. Otherwise the value it has been passed is simply passed back, and will be echoed back to the console. The `main` method creates a new instance of the `LineInterpreter` class and calls its `start` method to set it running. The `main` and `process` methods here aren't necessary for running the XQuery engine, they are just a convenience so that this class can be built and run on its own if any problem is encountered later. This provides an easy way to check I/O is working as it should.

The `XQ` class is a subclass of the simple console interpreter that overrides the process method to pass queries to, and retrieve results from the XQuery engine. The `XQ.java` source looks like this:

```
import javax.xml.parsers.SAXParser;
import javax.xml.parsers.SAXParserFactory;

import org.xml.sax.XMLReader;

import com.fatdog.xmlEngine.ResultList;
import com.fatdog.xmlEngine.XQEngine;

public class XQ extends LineInterpreter {

    private XQEngine engine;

    public XQ() {
        engine = new XQEngine();
        installXMLReader();
        engine.setUseLexicalPrefixes(true);
    }

    private void installXMLReader() {
        SAXParserFactory parserFactory = SAXParserFactory.newInstance();
        try {
            SAXParser parser = parserFactory.newSAXParser();
            XMLReader xmlReader = parser.getXMLReader();
            engine.setXMLReader(xmlReader);
        } catch (Exception e) {
            e.printStackTrace();
        }
    }

    public String process(String input) {
        if (input.startsWith("quit")) {
            System.exit(0);
        }
        if (input.startsWith("data")) {
            load(input.substring(5));
            return input.substring(5) + " loaded.";
        }
        if (input.startsWith("load")) {
            loadQueryFile(input.substring(5));
            return loadQueryFile(input.substring(5));
        }
        return query(input);
    }

    private String query(String input) {
        String output = "";
        System.out.println("'" + input + "' = ");
        try {
            ResultList results = engine.setQuery(input);
            output = results.emitXml();
        } catch (Exception e) {
            e.printStackTrace();
        }
        return output;
```

```
        }

        private String loadQueryFile(String filename) {
            String output = "";
            try {
                ResultList results = engine.setQueryFromFile(filename);
                output = results.emitXml();
            } catch (Exception e) {
                e.printStackTrace();
            }
            return output;
        }

        private void load(String filename) {
            try {
                engine.setDocument(filename);
            } catch (Exception e) {
                e.printStackTrace();
            }
        }

        public static void main(String[] args) {
            new XQ().start();
        }
    }
```

This code is tied in with the operation of the XQuery engine, so it's worth looking at how it works in a little more detail. The class begins with imports for the SAX parser used by the query engine, along with those for the XQEngine classes themselves:

```
import javax.xml.parsers.SAXParser;
import javax.xml.parsers.SAXParserFactory;

import org.xml.sax.XMLReader;

import com.fatdog.xmlEngine.ResultList;
import com.fatdog.xmlEngine.XQEngine;
```

Reading and writing from the console is looked after by LineInterpreter, which this class extends. A member variable is used to hold the XQuery engine, which will be an instance of the XQEngine class:

```
public class XQ extends LineInterpreter {

    private XQEngine engine;
```

The constructor creates the instance of XQEngine and calls a local method to initialize the parser the engine will use. To keep things simple the "use lexical prefixes" option is switched on, so namespaced elements and attributes can be addressed using their prefix:localname combination. The constructor is as follows:

```
    public XQ() {
        engine = new XQEngine();
        installXMLReader();
        engine.setUseLexicalPrefixes(true);
    }
```

The XQuery engine is going to work on XML data, and uses a SAX parser to read that data. A little boilerplate code is used to get hold of an XMLReader from the classes that come bundled with Java 2. This is created and passed to the XQuery engine in the installXMLReader method which looks like this:

```
private void installXMLReader() {
    SAXParserFactory parserFactory = SAXParserFactory.newInstance();
    try {
        SAXParser parser = parserFactory.newSAXParser();
        XMLReader xmlReader = parser.getXMLReader();
        engine.setXMLReader(xmlReader);
    } catch (Exception e) {
        e.printStackTrace();
    }
}
```

The process method is called by this class's superclass when a line of input has been typed at the console. The input string, which will be the line of data, is first checked to see if the quit command has been entered. If not, it then checks to see if a line beginning with data has been entered. This will be the command to tell the application to load an XML file from disk or the Web. What follows the data keyword will be the required file, and this name part is passed to the local load method before a simple confirmation message is displayed.

Similarly, if the input line begins with load then this will be an instruction to load an XQuery file and apply it to the previously loaded XML document. The file name is passed to the loadQueryFile method. The process method returns any output that results when the query is run.

The final possibility (aside from errors) is that a single-line query expression has been entered. This is passed to the query method and whatever that returns is passed back from the process method.

```
public String process(String input) {
    if (input.startsWith("quit")) {
        System.exit(0);
    }
    if (input.startsWith("data")) {
        load(input.substring(5));
        return input.substring(5) + " loaded.";
    }
    if (input.startsWith("load")) {
        loadQueryFile(input.substring(5));
        return loadQueryFile(input.substring(5));
    }
    return query(input);
}
```

The query method forwards the input string it has received to the XQuery engine using its setQuery method. This will return a ResultList object. There are other ways of dealing with such an object, but for demonstration purposes here an XML string representation of the object is obtained by calling emitXml. The query method looks like this:

```
private String query(String input) {
    String output = "";
    System.out.println("'" + input + "' = ");
    try {
        ResultList results = engine.setQuery(input);
```

```
        output = results.emitXml();
    } catch (Exception e) {
        e.printStackTrace();
    }
    return output;
}
```

To be able to deal with something a little more interesting than a single-line query, the `loadQueryFile` method is used. The work is done by the XQuery engine, which is passed the name of the query file (or URL) through the `setQueryFromFilename` method. Like `query`, the results are obtained in an XML string and returned. The method is as follows:

```
private String loadQueryFile(String filename) {
    String output = "";
    try {
        ResultList results = engine.setQueryFromFile(filename);
        output = results.emitXml();
    } catch (Exception e) {
        e.printStackTrace();
    }
    return output;
}
```

Loading an XML data file from disk or the Web is simply a matter of passing the file name or URL to the engine in its `setDocument` method, as you can see here:

```
private void load(String filename) {
    try {
        engine.setDocument(filename);
    } catch (Exception e) {
        e.printStackTrace();
    }
}
```

Finally a `main` method creates a new instance of the `XQ` class and sets it running, so it will listen for input from the console:

```
public static void main(String[] args) {
    new XQ().start();
}
```

Try It Out   XPath Queries

To run the code you will need to have Java installed, and have downloaded and unzipped the XQEngine distribution. The files you need are the two previous listings (`LineInterpreter.java` and `XQ.java`), the sample XML (`book.xml`), and `XQEngine.jar`. It's easiest if you place all three in the same folder, for example, `C:\xqengine`.

1.   Open a command window in the directory containing the files.

2.   Enter the following:

```
javac -classpath XQEngine.jar *.java
```

This will compile the source files.

3. Enter the following:

```
java -classpath .;XQEngine.jar XQ
```

The cursor should now be on a blank line; the interpreter is ready for your input.

4. Type the following and press Enter:

```
data book.xml
```

You should now see:

```
C:\xqengine>java -classpath .;XQEngine.jar XQ
data book.xml
book.xml loaded.
```

5. Now type the following and press Enter:

```
/book/bookinfo/title
```

You should now see:

```
/book/bookinfo/title
'/book/bookinfo/title' =
<title>A Book of Articles</title>
```

6. Now type the following:

```
/book/article/articleinfo/title/text()
```

You should now see:

```
/book/article/articleinfo/title/text()
'/book/article/articleinfo/title/text()' =
The First ArticleA Second Article
```

7. Now try:

```
/book/@lang
```

You should see:

```
/book/@lang
'/book/@lang' =
@lang="en"
```

8. Finally, try:

```
count(/book/article)
```

You should see:

```
count(/book/article)
'count(/book/article)' =
2
```

Typing quit will exit the application, although you may want to leave it available for some more demonstrations that follow shortly.

How It Works

In step 4, the source XML data is loaded into the XQuery engine. The commands you subsequently typed act as XPath locators on the XML. As it happens these are also valid XQuery expressions, and the results were those returned by the XQuery engine.

The first expression, in step 5, is a simple path that only matches one piece of data:

```
'/book/bookinfo/title' =
<title>A Book of Articles</title>
```

In step 6, a new piece of syntax is introduced:

```
'/book/article/articleinfo/title/text()' =
The First ArticleA Second Article
```

The `text()` part is an XPath function call. As a query it returns the text content of the node(s) addressed by the path expression that precedes it. In this case the path matched the two `<title>` elements, so the XQuery brought back the text content of those.

Step 7 demonstrates one way in which XML attributes can be accessed. The corresponding XML looks like this:

```
<book lang="en">
```

This is the query again:

```
'/book/@lang' =
@lang="en"
```

The path part locates the nodes immediately under the book node, and then the @ symbol refers to the attribute found there, the name of the required attribute following the symbol.

Step 8 demonstrates another built-in function:

```
'count(/book/article)' =
2
```

The function operates on the path expression `/book/article`, returning the number of nodes that the expression matches.

XQuery and Syndication Formats

Given that all the major syndication formats are XML, as long as the feed is well-formed data you can extract parts of interest. You can either apply an XQuery tool to local files, or even to query live feeds without making a local copy. This is straightforward with the little XQ interpreter, as the following Try It Out shows.

Try It Out   Querying Live Feeds

Repeat steps 1 and 3 of the previous Try It Out if you've closed the application, and ensure you are online.

1. Enter the following:

```
data http://www.w3.org/2000/08/w3c-synd/home.rss
```

You should see:

```
data http://www.w3.org/2000/08/w3c-synd/home.rss
http://www.w3.org/2000/08/w3c-synd/home.rss loaded.
```

2. Now enter this:

```
/rdf:RDF/item/title
```

You should now see something like this:

```
/rdf:RDF/item/title
'/rdf:RDF/item/title' =
<title>Speech Synthesis Markup Language Is a W3C Recommendation</title><title>SV
G's XML Binding Language (sXBL)</title><title>EMMA Working Draft Updated</title>
<title>Upcoming W3C Talks</title><title>XForms 1.1 Requirements Updated</title><
title>Working Drafts: Quality Assurance</title><title>XML Activity Chartered Thr
ough June 2006</title>
```

These are all the titles of news items in the W3C's feed.

How It Works

This time, the source XML data came from the Web; it's the World Wide Web Consortium's RSS news feed. That feed is RSS 1.0, and if you care to point a browser at

```
http://www.w3.org/2000/08/w3c-synd/home.rss
```

you will see the RDF/XML structure, which (trimmed heavily) looks like this:

```
<rdf:RDF xmlns="http://purl.org/rss/1.0/"
    xmlns:dc="http://purl.org/dc/elements/1.1/"
    xmlns:rdf="http://www.w3.org/1999/02/22-rdf-syntax-ns#">

...channel data...
...items sequence...

<item rdf:about="http://www.w3.org/News/2004#item145">
    <title>Speech Synthesis Markup Language Is a W3C Recommendation</title>
    <description>The World Wide Web Consortium today...</description>
    <link>http://www.w3.org/News/2004#item145</link>
    <dc:date>2004-09-08</dc:date>
</item>

<item rdf:about="http://www.w3.org/News/2004#item141">
    <title>SVG's XML Binding Language (sXBL)</title>
    <description>Through joint efforts...</description>
    <link>http://www.w3.org/News/2004#item141</link>
    <dc:date>2004-09-01</dc:date>
</item>

...more items...

</rdf:RDF>
```

If you look again at the query `/rdf:RDF/item/title`, you should see how this matches the individual item `<title>` elements within the feed. Note this time that a `text()` wasn't used, and so containing element tags were also returned.

As noted earlier, the XQEngine is set to treat namespace prefixes and local names as simple strings, so `rdf:RDF` *addresses the root here and* `item` *the items without need for true qualification. The current release of XQEngine only has limited namespace support. In practice full namespace support is to be preferred, if it's a viable option, although it may make your code less pleasing to the eye.*

XQuery Is More Than XPath

So far all the query examples have been XPath expressions. There is quite a bit more to XPath than you've seen so far, but you should now have the general idea. There is also another *big* layer to XQuery. A common analogy is that XQuery is like SQL for XML. Where the database language uses quite a wide variety of terms in its expressions (starting with SELECT...WHERE), XQuery has a small number of terms that can be combined in many and varied ways. These terms are FOR, LET, WHERE, and RETURN, giving the acronym FLWR (pronounced *flower*).

As a simple example of an XQuery expression, take the following:

```
let $title :=  /rdf:RDF/channel/title
return
  $title
```

Here `$title` is used as a variable that is assigned a value based on an XPath expression using `let`, and its value is then returned (using `return`). Executing this query will produce the same results as the XPath expression on its own would have done. On the W3C feed it returns:

```
<title>World Wide Web Consortium</title>
```

However, there is one important thing to note — the variable is passed a set of nodes, so if the XPath expression had matched more than that single node, the whole lot would have been returned. To demonstrate, here is another useful piece of XPath syntax: `//`. When used as a replacement for the single path slash, this will act as a kind of structural wildcard. For example, the XPath expression `/rdf:RDF//title` will match all `<title>` elements inside the root `rdf:RDF` element.

Here's another XQuery expression:

```
let $uris :=  //rdf:li/@rdf:resource
return
  $uris
```

This time the node set returned will contain each `rdf:resource` attribute of all `<rdf:li>` elements in the document. Running this on the W3C feed will produce something like this:

```
@rdf:resource="http://www.w3.org/News/2004#item145"
@rdf:resource="http://www.w3.org/News/2004#item141"
@rdf:resource="http://www.w3.org/News/2004#item140"
...
```

The query is in effect addressing the following structure within the RSS 1.0 feed:

```
<rdf:RDF>
    <channel>
        <items>
            <rdf:Seq>
                <rdf:li rdf:resource="http://www.w3.org/News/2004#item145"/>
                <rdf:li rdf:resource="http://www.w3.org/News/2004#item141"/>
                <rdf:li rdf:resource="http://www.w3.org/News/2004#item140"/>
...
            </rdf:Seq>
        </items>
    </channel>
</rdf:RDF>
```

Another way of getting the same results would be to use an expression based on FOR, for example:

```
for $uri in  //rdf:li/@rdf:resource
return
   $uri
```

Getting Selective

You may have guessed from the FLWR terms (FOR, LET, WHERE and RETURN) that more complex programming language-like expressions are possible. This is true enough, but despite using keywords found in the prehistoric (in Internet time) procedural language BASIC, XQuery operates much more like the declarative approach of SQL. It's beyond the scope of this book to go much further, but as a final example here is a piece of XQuery designed to extract items that appeared on a particular day from the W3C feed, and format the results (titles and content) in such a way that they can be inserted in an HTML Web page.

Here's the XQuery (query.txt):

```
for    $item in /rdf:RDF/item
where  $item/dc:date = "2004-09-01"
return
   <div class="entry">
      <h1>
        { $item/title/text() }
      </h1>
      <p>
        { $item/description/text() }
      </p>
   </div>
```

Try It Out   A Selective XQuery

1. Type the previous listing into a text editor (or download it).

2. Open the W3C's RSS feed in a Web browser:

    `http://www.w3.org/2000/08/w3c-synd/home.rss`

    Incidentally, this is styled using CSS.

3. Pick a date that is associated with one or more of the items, and modify the date value in the XQuery listing to match.

4. Save `query.txt` in the same directory as the interpreter code listed earlier.

5. Open a command window in that directory.

6. Enter the following:

```
java -classpath .;XQEngine.jar XQ
```

The cursor should now be on a blank line, the interpreter is ready for your input.

7. Enter the following:

```
data http://www.w3.org/2000/08/w3c-synd/home.rss
```

You should see:

```
data http://www.w3.org/2000/08/w3c-synd/home.rss
http://www.w3.org/2000/08/w3c-synd/home.rss loaded.
```

8. Now enter this:

```
load query.txt
```

You should now see something like this:

```
C:\xqengine>java -classpath .;XQEngine.jar XQ
data http://www.w3.org/2000/08/w3c-synd/home.rss
http://www.w3.org/2000/08/w3c-synd/home.rss loaded.
load query.txt
<div class="entry">
    <h1>SVG's XML Binding Language (sXBL)</h1>
    <p>2004-09-01: Through joint efforts, the Scalable Vector Graphics (SVG)
        Working Group...
    </p>
</div>
<div class="entry">
    <h1>EMMA Working Draft Updated</h1>
    <p>2004-09-01: The Multimodal Interaction Working Group has released
        an updated Working Draft of EMMA...
    </p>
</div>
<div class="entry">
    <h1>Upcoming W3C Talks</h1>
    <p>2004-09-01: Browse upcoming W3C appearances and events...
    </p>
</div>
```

The output has been reformatted and trimmed a little for clarity, but when you run this you should be able to see that only items with the date you used have been returned. A `<div>` block has been produced for each item, with the titles of the item going into a `<h1>` element and the description into a `<p>` element. You may like to copy and paste this into a text editor, save it as `something.html`, and then open it in a browser. If you do, you should see a (fairly crudely) formatted representation of the items.

How It Works

Here is the XQuery again:

```
for     $item in /rdf:RDF/item
where   $item/dc:date = "2004-09-01"
```

471

```
return
  <div class="entry">
    <h1>
      { $item/title/text() }
    </h1>
    <p>
      { $item/description/text() }
    </p>
  </div>
```

This uses a FOR...IN subexpression to step through items in the node set matched by the XPath expression /rdf:RDF/item. A WHERE subexpression is used to narrow down the selected items by means of a simple comparison. Without this, variable $item would contain all the item nodes found in the RSS 1.0 document. The WHERE uses an XPath-based expression itself ($item/dc:date) to test the text content of the <dc:date> element inside the node currently pointed to by $item.

The RETURN section behaves in quite an interesting fashion. The subexpressions in that block, like everything else below FOR, get evaluated for each value $item takes. The results of those evaluations are added to previous results, and the whole lot is returned in one go. The expressions used in this example are essentially more XPath-based locators based on the value of $item, in this case getting the title and description text from inside each item. Those titles and descriptions are wrapped, template-fashion, by the little bits of inline HTML—<div>, <h1>, and <p>.

Although the XQuery 1.0 specification has been around for quite a while, it still isn't a W3C Recommendation, and this is one factor for its relatively low deployment and implementation. Perhaps a larger factor is that another technology from the same source, XSLT, has been around a while longer (its already on version 2.0), and it provides much of the same functionality.

Introducing XSLT

XSLT (Extensible Stylesheet Language Transformations) is one part of what started life as XSL, the other being XSL-FO (XSL Formatting Objects). XSLT can be used very like cascading style sheets (CSS), using a style sheet to generate nicely formatted Web pages. However, it operates in a different way and lends itself to a broader range of applications, many unrelated to display. Basically you give an XSLT processor some source XML data along with an XSLT document (which also happens to be XML) and as an output get a predictably modified version of the input (which may or may not be XML). Like XQuery, XSLT makes use of XPath locators, but the processing model is rather different.

Templates

By way of demonstration, here's the source document we used at the beginning of this chapter (book.xml):

```
<book lang="en">
    <bookinfo>
        <title>A Book of Articles</title>
    </bookinfo>
    <article>
        <articleinfo>
            <title>The First Article</title>
        </articleinfo>
        <para>The contents of the first article.</para>
    </article>
```

```
      <article>
        <articleinfo>
           <title>A Second Article</title>
        </articleinfo>
        <para>The contents of the second article.</para>
      </article>
</book>
```

The first XPath/XQuery you ran on this was:

```
/book/bookinfo/title
```

The following is one way in which this locator could be used within an XSLT style sheet (minimal.xslt):

```
<xsl:stylesheet version="1.0" xmlns:xsl="http://www.w3.org/1999/XSL/Transform">

    <xsl:template match="/book/bookinfo/title">
        <xsl:copy-of select="."/>
    </xsl:template>

    <xsl:template match="text()"/>
</xsl:stylesheet>
```

The output from applying this to the source document (book.xml) is as follows:

```
<?xml version="1.0" encoding="UTF-8"?><title>A Book of Articles</title>
```

Breaking down the style sheet, it starts with the opening tag of the root element:

```
<xsl:stylesheet version="1.0" xmlns:xsl="http://www.w3.org/1999/XSL/Transform">
```

All XSLT style sheets have <xsl:stylesheet> as their root element, and at present most use XSLT 1.0, which is expressed in the version attribute here. The convention is to explicitly declare the xsl prefix, mapping it to the XSLT namespace http://www.w3.org/1999/XSL/Transform. It's very common to find multiple namespaces used with XSLT transformations, many source documents may have no namespace (which parsers may report as the empty string: ""), so the use of the prefix helps to avoid conflict. A key mechanism in XSLT is the template, as in this example:

```
<xsl:template match="/book/bookinfo/title">
    <xsl:copy-of select="."/>
</xsl:template>
```

Generally a template has the form:

```
match something in the source XML
    do something with what's been matched
```

This template is set up to match the XPath expression /book/bookinfo/title. What this template does with parts of the source that match this construction is to copy them to the output document. The xsl:value-of element is used to select a piece of the input, in this case ., out of what's been matched by the template itself. As developers would say, the template match has provided the context node, and the locators used inside the template are applied relative to the context node. Using the same source data we used here (but not necessarily any other document), you could achieve exactly the same effect with the following:

```
<xsl:template match="/book/bookinfo">
    <xsl:copy-of select="title"/>
</xsl:template>
```

The next line in the source is another template:

```
<xsl:template match="text()"/>
```

This is needed because in addition to the template rules occurring in the style sheet, an XSLT processor will apply a handful of very simple default rules, one of which is to pass any text content onto the output. The template here will match all such text, and take priority over the default rules. There isn't anything inside the template, so the net effect is to strip out the text that would otherwise appear in the output. As the style sheet is XML itself, it ends with the root element's closing tag:

```
</xsl:stylesheet>
```

More Templates

Things start to get more interesting when you have a few more templates. First, here's a template that uses the XPath locators you tried with XQuery:

```
    <xsl:template match="/">
Title = <xsl:value-of select="/book/bookinfo/title"/>
Language = <xsl:value-of select="/book/@lang"/>
Number of articles = <xsl:value-of select="count(/book/article)"/>
        <xsl:apply-templates select="/book/*"/>
    </xsl:template>
```

This template will match /, the document root. The first three lines within the template element begin with some text and then have an `xsl:value-of` element. `xsl:value-of` is used to write the string value of whatever has been selected to the output. The output generated by the first three lines when applied to `book.xml` will be:

```
Title = A Book of Articles
Language = en
Number of articles =    2
```

Although the XML syntax is rather confusing, the functionality for this part is pretty clear — the content of elements or attributes that match the locators are output.

When the style sheet initially runs, the templates are looking at the very base of the document, so / matches the document root here and the previous template example matches `/book/bookinfo/title`. The selections within the template are relative to whatever the template has matched. The next line in the template is rather interesting:

```
<xsl:apply-templates select="/book/*"/>
```

What this does is ask the processor to try matching the templates relative to the selected node or nodes (don't forget that the XPath locators may have multiple matches). Here another new piece of XPath syntax is introduced, * is a wildcard that will match any element node. Knowing the expected document structure, it's possible to catch the article elements matched by this selector with another template:

```
<xsl:template match="article">
Article : <xsl:apply-templates/>
</xsl:template>
```

Whenever this template is matched, the text `Article :` will be passed to the output and then the templates will be tried again, relative to the node or nodes matched here. Again, knowing the expected structure you can create an appropriate template:

```
<xsl:template match="articleinfo/title">
    <xsl:value-of select="text()"/>
</xsl:template>
```

This will match any structure that begins with the elements `<articleinfo><title>`. So far there has been a call to try the templates beginning at the base of the document, at `/book/*` and at `article` (from the `xsl:apply-templates` in the previous template). It is possible for a source node to match more than one template rule, but the precedence rules of XSLT determine which is acted upon. These rules are a little convoluted, but usually boil down to the more specific template having the higher priority. In this case the `article` match is chosen instead of `/book/*`.

Another template can be provided to handle the paragraph content of the articles:

```
<xsl:template match="para">
Content : <xsl:value-of select="text()"/>
</xsl:template>
```

This is very similar to the template used to match the titles of the articles. The `<para>` elements are only a step above the `<article>` elements, so the test to match is a little shorter, and the output passed by `xsl:value` this time will be preceded by the string `"Content : "`.

Here is the entire style sheet (`minimal2.xslt`):

```
<?xml version="1.0" encoding="UTF-8"?>
<xsl:stylesheet version="1.0" xmlns:xsl="http://www.w3.org/1999/XSL/Transform">

    <xsl:template match="/">
Title = <xsl:value-of select="/book/bookinfo/title"/>
Language = <xsl:value-of select="/book/@lang"/>
Number of articles =    <xsl:value-of select="count(/book/article)"/>
        <xsl:apply-templates select="book/article"/>
    </xsl:template>

    <xsl:template match="article">
    Article : <xsl:apply-templates/>
    </xsl:template>

    <xsl:template match="articleinfo/title">
        <xsl:value-of select="text()"/>
    </xsl:template>

    <xsl:template match="para">
Content : <xsl:value-of select="text()"/>
```

```
        </xsl:template>

        <xsl:template match="text()"/>

    </xsl:stylesheet>
```

Note the use again of an empty template to eat any stray text that might otherwise be output by the default rules.

XSLT Processors

XSLT is useful enough and has been around long enough that there are plenty of engines and toolkits available and practically every programming language has support of some kind available. Most modern browsers such as Internet Explorer and Mozilla Firefox have built-in support for XSLT, which (as you will see shortly) can be employed to reformat material client-side. It is also possible to use the browser XSLT engine from client-side Javascript/ECMAScript within HTML, but cross-browser support problems mean this is of limited use.

Outside of the browser, it's usually just a matter of using an XSLT library from within your preferred programming environment. Whether you are programming for a client or server, the basic series of operations is essentially the same:

1. Obtain XML data.

2. Obtain XSLT transform.

3. Apply transform to XML data.

4. Do something with result.

The details of each step will vary according to the libraries you are using; often the XML and XSLT documents will be loaded into XML DOM objects prior to processing. As an example, the following is a utility script for applying XSLT transforms at the command line on Microsoft Windows (transform.wsf):

```
<package>
 <job id="transform">
  <script language="JScript">

     var msXmlImpl = "Microsoft.XMLDOM";
     var fsImpl = "Scripting.FileSystemObject";

     if (WScript.Arguments.length == 0) {
        WScript.Echo(
     "Usage : transform input.xml stylesheet.xsl [output.txt]");
        WScript.Quit();
     }
     var xmlFilename = WScript.Arguments(0);
     var xsltFilename = WScript.Arguments(1);

     var xml = WScript.CreateObject(msXmlImpl);
     xml.validateOnParse = false;
     xml.async = false;
     xml.load(xmlFilename);
     if (xml.parseError.errorCode != 0){
        WScript.Echo ("Error parsing XML: "
```

```
                                    + xml.parseError.reason);
        }

        var xslt = WScript.CreateObject(msXmlImpl);
        xslt.async = false;
        xslt.load(xsltFilename);

        if (xslt.parseError.errorCode != 0){
            WScript.Echo ("Error parsing XSLT: "
                            + xslt.parseError.reason);
            WScript.Quit();
        }

        var outputString = "";
        try{
            outputString = xml.transformNode(xslt.documentElement);
            WScript.Echo(outputString);
        } catch(err) {
            WScript.Echo("Error during transformation : "
                            + err. number + "*" + err.description);
            WScript.Quit();
        }

        if (WScript.Arguments.length == 3) {
            var outputFilename = WScript.Arguments(2);
            try {
                var outputFile =
    WScript.CreateObject(fsImpl).CreateTextFile(outputFilename, true);
                outputFile.Write (outputString);
                outputFile.Close();
            }catch(err){
                WScript.Echo("Error writing output : "
                                + err. number + "*" + err.description);
                WScript.Quit();
            }
        }
    </script>
  </job>
</package>
```

The code is essentially a dialect of ECMAScript (JScript) wrapped up to run on Windows Script Host, a facility found in Microsoft operating systems since Windows 98. The wrapping is just the XML at the start and end. DOM object creation and various other parts of this script use the WScript object that comes with WSH, but most parts could be replaced directly using ActiveX or other Microsoft equivalents. The actual script code begins with the names of two of the object types that will be used:

```
var msXmlImpl = "Microsoft.XMLDOM";
var fsImpl = "Scripting.FileSystemObject";
```

This approach to object construction makes it easier to swap out the implementations; some systems may require the DOM object to be `Msxml2.DOMDocument`. You can find documentation and downloads for the "traditional" XML support (MSXML), the latest .NET support, and scripting facilities at `http://msdn.microsoft.com`.

The utility runs from the command line, and the next few lines echo back a help message if the script is run without arguments and exit, or obtain the values provided for the XML and XSLT file names:

```
if (WScript.Arguments.length == 0) {
   WScript.Echo(
"Usage : transform input.xml stylesheet.xsl [output.txt]");
   WScript.Quit();
}
var xmlFilename = WScript.Arguments(0);
var xsltFilename = WScript.Arguments(1);
```

Next the DOM object that will contain the original XML data is created and the data loaded into the object. If the XML isn't well-formed or there are any file system–related errors this will fail, so a little error handling code follows to provide a message and exit:

```
var xml = WScript.CreateObject(msXmlImpl);
xml.validateOnParse = false;
xml.async = false;
xml.load(xmlFilename);
if (xml.parseError.errorCode != 0){
   WScript.Echo ("Error parsing XML: "
                   + xml.parseError.reason);
   WScript.Quit();
}
```

Next, the XSLT transformation itself is loaded in exactly the same fashion. The XSLT is also XML, and it is also accessed through a DOM object:

```
var xslt = WScript.CreateObject(msXmlImpl);
xslt.async = false;
xslt.load(xsltFilename);

if (xslt.parseError.errorCode != 0){
   WScript.Echo ("Error parsing XSLT: "
                   + xslt.parseError.reason);
   WScript.Quit();
}
```

A string that holds the transformed data will now be prepared. The XSLT transformation is then applied by passing the document element of the DOM representation of the XSLT to the DOM representation of the original data. This is done through the transformNode method. (This utility only needs the output as a string, although the DOM object also supports a transformNodeToObject method if you want to experiment; refer to the MSDN documentation.) After the transformation has been applied, the resulting string is sent to a popup box:

```
var outputString = "";
try{
   outputString = xml.transformNode(xslt.documentElement);
   WScript.Echo(outputString);
} catch(err) {
   WScript.Echo("Error during transformation : "
                   + err. number + "*" + err.description);
   WScript.Quit();
}
```

Having the result in a popup box is a useful quick test, but in case you want to do things with the output it is also saved to file using the next block of code:

```
if (WScript.Arguments.length == 3) {
    var outputFilename = WScript.Arguments(2);
    try {
        var outputFile =
WScript.CreateObject(fsImpl).CreateTextFile(outputFilename, true);
        outputFile.Write (outputString);
        outputFile.Close();
    }catch(err){
        WScript.Echo("Error writing output : "
                    + err. number + "*" + err.description);
        WScript.Quit();
    }
}
```

Of course this script is useful only if you're running a Microsoft operating system, unless perhaps you have one of the Linux .NET environments like Mono (and plenty of time to figure out how to do it). A simple alternative is to use a different set of tools, such as the Java-based XT, which you can download for free at www.jclark.com/xml/xt.html (this will also run on Windows). It includes a batch file (demo\xt.bat or demo/xt.sh depending on your platform) that will also allow command-line transformation.

Try It Out   Transforming XML to Text

1. Type or download a copy of the previous script (transform.wsf), the sample data (book.xml), and the demo style sheet (minimal2.xslt). Save these to the same directory.

Alternatively, download and unzip XT, and copy the XML and XSLT files to the directory xt\demo.

2. Open a command window in that directory and type:

```
transform book.xml minimal2.xslt output.txt
```

Or if you are using XT, type:

```
xt book.xml minimal2.xslt output.txt
```

If you're using the script, you should see the popup in Figure 25-1.

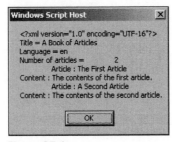

Figure 25-1

3. Click OK in the popup.

4. Now open the newly created file `output.txt` in a text editor. You should see:

```
<?xml version="1.0" encoding="UTF-16"?>
Title = A Book of Articles
Language = en
Number of articles =    2
     Article : The First Article
Content : The contents of the first article.
     Article : A Second Article
Content : The contents of the second article.
```

What's wrong with this output? The first line declares it as XML when clearly it is intended as plain text. The solution is an extra line in the style sheet:

```
<xsl:stylesheet version="1.0" xmlns:xsl="http://www.w3.org/1999/XSL/Transform">
<xsl:output method="text" />
     <xsl:template match="/">
...
```

5. Open `minimal2.xslt` in a text editor and insert the new line.

6. Again run:

```
transform book.xml minimal2.xslt output.txt
```

Or if you are using XT, type:

```
xt book.xml minimal2.xslt output.txt
```

7. Click OK in the popup.

8. Reopen `output.txt` in the text editor. You should see the following:

```
Title = A Book of Articles
Language = en
Number of articles =    2
     Article : The First Article
Content : The contents of the first article.
     Article : A Second Article
Content : The contents of the second article.
```

How It Works

The data in an XSLT system flows as shown in Figure 25-2.

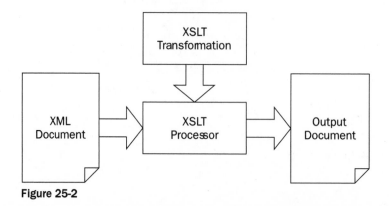

Figure 25-2

The XSLT processor essentially works by running through the XML document trying to match a series of XPath locators (one per template) against the data. Where there is a match, whatever the template specifies is then passed to the output. This particular example uses a very common XSLT pattern, that of recursive descent—that is, it tries to match the top-level element first, and then tries matches on child elements, then on children of those, and so on to the leaf (text) nodes of the document. Each time it is calling its own set of templates, hence the recursion, as shown in Figure 25-2.

Output Format

A modification is needed to the original XSLT to stop the output producing the XML declaration. So we added the following line:

```
<xsl:output method="text" />
```

The xsl:output element is a top-level instruction that controls the overall formatting of the output. Without one of these elements the processor defaults to XML output, hence the unwanted XML declaration. The method attribute usually has a value that is xml, html, or text. The xsl:output element also supports other attributes that allow more fine-grained control of the output, for example, to indent XML output to make it easier to read, or to set the media type and encoding.

XSLT in Syndication

So now you've seen the general idea behind XSLT, it's time to see how it can be used in syndication. XSLT can be applied to any XML, so there are two primary applications available—transforming non-syndication data to RSS or Atom, or transforming syndication XML into another format for display or further processing.

Transforming to RSS

If you look back to the DocBook-like XML example we've been using in the examples so far (book.xml), you will notice that you can easily map to RSS 2.0, as shown in the following listing (article-rss.xml):

```
<?xml version="1.0" encoding="UTF-8"?>
<rss version="2.0">
    <channel>
        <language>en</language>
        <title>A Book of Articles</title>
        <item>
            <title>The First Article</title>
            <description>The contents of the first article.</description>
        </item>
        <item>
            <title>A Second Article</title>
            <description>The contents of the second article.</description>
        </item>
    </channel>
</rss>
```

The template you used in the Try It Out is fairly close to what you need to produce this output. Here's a style sheet (book2rss.xslt) that will take the format of book.xml and transform it to the format of article-rss.xml:

```
<?xml version="1.0" encoding="UTF-8"?>
<xsl:stylesheet version="1.0" xmlns:xsl="http://www.w3.org/1999/XSL/Transform">
    <xsl:output method="xml" indent="yes"/>

    <xsl:template match="/">
        <xsl:apply-templates/>
    </xsl:template>

    <xsl:template match="book">
        <rss version="2.0">
            <channel>
                <language>
                    <xsl:value-of select="@lang"/>
                </language>
                <xsl:apply-templates/>
            </channel>
        </rss>
    </xsl:template>

    <xsl:template match="bookinfo">
        <xsl:apply-templates/>
    </xsl:template>

    <xsl:template match="title">
        <title>
            <xsl:value-of select="."/>
        </title>
    </xsl:template>

    <xsl:template match="article">
        <item>
            <xsl:apply-templates/>
        </item>
    </xsl:template>

    <xsl:template match="para">
        <description>
            <xsl:value-of select="."/>
        </description>
    </xsl:template>

</xsl:stylesheet>
```

This style sheet uses the recursive-descent approach in a very direct fashion, if you look at the XPath expressions in the template match attributes, you can see how they correspond to the elements found in the XML document. There's a minor structural change here over the previous style sheet (minimal2.xslt), in that the same template is used to match the <title> element whether it occurs inside book/bookinfo or article/articleinfo, the recursion stepping through the <articleinfo> element. Note that xsl:output is set to indented XML. Most of the RSS/XML is constructed directly within the templates for passing to the output; this is most obvious where the book element is matched:

```
<xsl:template match="book">
    <rss version="2.0">
        <channel>
            <language>
```

```
                <xsl:value-of select="@lang"/>
            </language>
            <xsl:apply-templates/>
        </channel>
    </rss>
</xsl:template>
```

All the RSS elements here will be passed directly to the output, although you must remember that XSLT is defined in XML itself, so whatever goes in to act as output must be consistent with the whole document being well-formed. It is possible to construct XML structures for the output using XSLT terms (notably xsl:element and xsl:attribute). However, when they will be fixed no matter what appears in the input document, entering them as you want to see them at the output is a more straightforward and concise approach.

Note here that the value of the lang attribute from <book lang="en"> is extracted and placed in an element, <language>en</language>. This kind of manipulation is quite common when converting from one XML format to another. After that particular piece of output has been built, there is an <xsl:apply-templates/> instruction. This will carry out this particular part of the document descent, attempting to match the templates against what is found below the <book> element. The position of <xsl:apply-templates/> is significant in another way—whatever is output by the template matched at this point will appear in the output at this position in the document. In this case that will mean nested inside the <rss><channel> structure, exactly the position you want for RSS 2.0 <item> elements.

You can run this style sheet in exactly the same way as the one in the previous Try It Out, using the following command:

```
transform book.xml book2rss.xslt book-rss.xml
```

or

```
xt book.xml book2rss.xslt book-rss.xml
```

Transforming from RSS

The next example turns things around. Say you feature news articles on the front page of your site. One thing you might want to do is provide a less fancy version of the headlines on other pages on another page, for example, for mobile devices. If your content management system already provides an RSS feed this is fairly easy to do with XSLT. Say the site feed looks like this (book-rss.xml):

```
<?xml version="1.0" encoding="UTF-8"?>
<rss version="2.0">
    <channel>
        <language>en</language>
        <title>A Book of Articles</title>
        <item>
            <title>The First Article</title>
            <description>The contents of the first article.</description>
        </item>
        <item>
            <title>A Second Article</title>
            <description>The contents of the second article.</description>
        </item>
    </channel>
</rss>
```

Yes, that should look familiar, but the data generated earlier will do nicely for this demonstration.

The most straightforward approach is to transform this RSS into HTML. The following is the kind of HTML you might be aiming for (book.xhtml):

```
<?xml version="1.0" encoding="UTF-8"?>
    <!DOCTYPE html PUBLIC "-//W3C//DTD XHTML 1.0 Strict//EN"
"http://www.w3.org/TR/xhtml1/DTD/xhtml1-strict.dtd">
  <html xmlns="http://www.w3.org/1999/xhtml">
  <head>
    <title>A Book of Articles</title>
  </head>
  <body xml:lang="en" lang="en">
    <div class="item">
      <h1>The First Article</h1>
      <p>The contents of the first article.</p>
    </div>
    <div class="item">
      <h1>A Second Article</h1>
      <p>The contents of the second article.</p>
    </div>
  </body>
</html>
```

This is XHTML, but that isn't particularly significant in this context as the output of the XSLT can be pretty much whatever format you like, although sticking with an XML format makes life easier all around. A suitable XSLT style would be this (rss2html.xslt):

```
<xsl:stylesheet version="1.0"
    xmlns:xsl="http://www.w3.org/1999/XSL/Transform"
    xmlns="http://www.w3.org/1999/xhtml">

<xsl:output method="xml" indent="yes"/>

<xsl:template match="rss">
  <xsl:text disable-output-escaping="yes">
    &lt;!DOCTYPE html PUBLIC "-//W3C//DTD XHTML 1.0 Strict//EN"
        "http://www.w3.org/TR/xhtml1/DTD/xhtml1-strict.dtd"&gt;
  </xsl:text>
  <html>
    <xsl:apply-templates />
  </html>
</xsl:template>

<xsl:template match="channel">
  <head>
    <title>
      <xsl:value-of select="title" />
    </title>
  </head>
  <body xml:lang="{language}" lang="{language}">
    <xsl:apply-templates />
  </body>
```

```
    </xsl:template>

    <xsl:template match="item">
    <div class="item">
      <h1><xsl:value-of select="title" /></h1>
      <p><xsl:value-of select="description" /></p>
    </div>
    </xsl:template>

    <xsl:template match="text()" />

</xsl:stylesheet>
```

If you look through this you should recognize this as another recursive-descent style sheet, first attempting to match the outer element (<rss> in this case), and then to apply the templates to whatever's found inside. Where book2rss.xslt wraps material extracted from the source document in RSS 2.0 XML elements, this style sheet wraps material from the RSS source in XHTML elements. You may like to try this with the transform script (or XT) using the following command:

```
transform book-rss.xml rss2html.xslt book.xhtml
```

You may find that this produces an error, saying that the encoding isn't supported. During tests we found that the Microsoft XSLT engine stubbornly insists on the output encoding declaration being UTF-16, no matter what is declared in the style sheet. A crude but effective workaround is to modify the xsl:output element in book2rss.xslt to read as follows:

```
    <xsl:output method="xml" indent="yes" omit-xml-declaration="yes" />
```

This prevents the line: <?xml...?> from appearing.

Going Live

If you're running a 24/7 Web site, you don't want to spend your time running data transformations at the command line. So the following is a little PHP that will run the transformation online (file-transform.php):

```php
<?php

$xml = file_get_contents ('book-rss.xml') ;
$xsl = file_get_contents ('rss2html.xslt') ;

$arguments = array(
    '/_xml' => $xml,
    '/_xsl' => $xsl
);

// create a new XSLT processor
$processor = xslt_create();

// transform
// returns the result to $output
```

485

```
$output = xslt_process($processor, 'arg:/_xml', 'arg:/_xsl', NULL, $arguments);

echo $output;

// clean up
xslt_free($processor);
?>
```

This follows the same basic pattern as the Windows Scripting Host transformer, loading the data and XSLT files and then running the processor on them. As it appears here you will need the data and transformation files in the same directory on the server, although you can simply change the file names in the first two lines in the body of the code.

The script is written for PHP version 4 using the Sablotron processor that comes with the distribution, but should work with other versions. However, there have been changes in XSLT support from versions 4 to 5. Go to www.php.net/ *if you run into problems.*

Figure 25-3 shows the result of pointing a browser at `file-transform.php` on a live Web site.

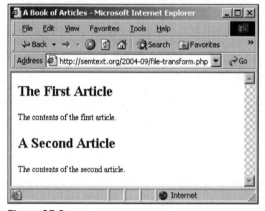

Figure 25-3

If you do run this live, be sure to view the source on the result to confirm that it is in fact the XHTML as listed earlier. And don't forget that you can apply CSS styling to HTML to get an even prettier rendering.

Graphic Display: SVG in a Very Small Nutshell

The previous example took some RSS 2.0 data and transformed it into XHTML. This is only scratching the surface of the kind of things that are possible — XSLT can transform the feed data into whatever you like. As a taste of something a little more interesting, you will now see how you can use Scalable Vector Graphics (SVG) to provide a graphic representation of feed data.

SVG is a specification from the W3C that describes an XML language designed for 2D graphics on the Web. It can be used as a simple means of getting a graphic display, although it does support scripting and animation, and is generally rather sophisticated. It has two features in particular that make it suitable for a demonstration here: it's XML and it's very easy to get started. In general it is eminently suitable for use in syndication applications, given that it is Web-oriented and (repeat after us) XML.

To view SVG graphics you'll need either a task-specific viewer such as the one provided with the (Java) SVG toolkit Batik, or a Web browser plug-in. The screenshots shown here were taken from Adobe's free plug-in for Internet Explorer (www.adobe.com/svg/). To create SVG files you can either use purpose-built design tools, or anything that can work with XML. A text editor is plenty to get started. So here is a first example (text-box.svg):

```
<?xml version="1.0" encoding="UTF-8"?>
<svg width="100%" height="100%">
    <rect x="20" y="20" width="260" height="70" fill="white"
                                stroke="green" stroke-width="2"/>
    <text x="50" y="60" font-size="30">Text in a box</text>
</svg>
```

This will display in a suitable viewer as shown in Figure 25-4.

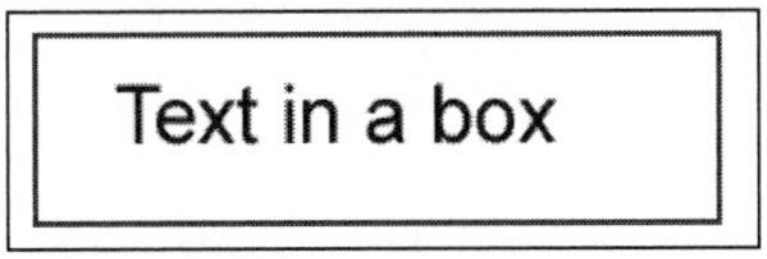

Figure 25-4

Now a breakdown of the source:

```
<?xml version="1.0" encoding="UTF-8"?>
```

It's XML.

```
<svg width="100%" height="100%">
```

The outer element of an SVG document is <svg>. Here the width and height are declared to use all the space available in the browser:

```
<rect x="20" y="20" width="260" height="70" fill="white"
                            stroke="green" stroke-width="2"/>
```

This element describes a rectangle. The x and y attributes give the position of the top left-hand corner of the rectangle, relative to the top left-hand corner of the viewing area. These coordinates and the dimensions that follow are in pixels. The space inside the rectangle will be filled with the color white. The perimeter of the rectangle will be drawn in green, the width of the perimeter line is 2 pixels. SVG defines a handful of basic shapes (line, rect, circle, ellipse, polyline, and polygon) that are used to construct most graphics. If you ignore the XML syntax, their description is fairly intuitive. To keep things simple in this chapter, we use only the rect shape. To display text in SVG you can use the text element, as follows:

```
<text x="50" y="60" font-size="30">Text in a box</text>
```

Again the x and y attributes refer to the position at which the text will appear relative to the top left-hand corner of the viewing area, so this text will be displayed 60 pixels down and 50 to the right.

Finally, because SVG is XML, the document ends with the closing tag of the root svg element:

```
</svg>
```

One thing you need to know about SVG rendering is that it follows what's known as the *Painter's Model*. Things that appear earlier in the document are painted earlier, so if something follows in the same position then this may obscure the earlier object. If you reversed the order of the <rect> and <text> elements in this first example, the white fill of the rectangle would obliterate the text. However, XML nesting is used to good effect, so the painting order generally applies between things at the same level of nesting within the document. The next code example shows one way in which nesting can be helpful (text-box2.svg):

```
<?xml version="1.0" encoding="UTF-8"?>
<svg xmlns:xlink="http://www.w3.org/1999/xlink" width="100%" height="100%">
   <a xlink:href="http://www.w3.org/">
      <g transform="rotate(90, 100,100)">
         <rect x="20" y="20" width="260" height="70"
               fill="white" stroke="green" stroke-width="2"/>
         <text x="50" y="60" font-size="30">Text in a box</text>
      </g>
   </a>
</svg>
```

The inner text and rect elements appear just as in the previous example. Now, however, they are enclosed in a <g> element. This is used to group together elements that will share the same styling or, as in this case, share the same transform. Transforms in SVG enable you to shift, scale, stretch, rotate, and generally distort graphic elements. The transform applied here is rotate(90, 100, 100), which defines a 90-degree rotation around the point 100, 100. Everything inside the <g> element with be distorted in this way, leading to the result in Figure 25-5.

Figure 25-5

The <g> element is itself enclosed by an <a> element. This has an href attribute, defined in the XLink namespace. As the name suggests, this is a link and the construct as a whole corresponds more or less to HTML's link construct, for example <a href="http://example.org"></a> . It doesn't change the color of what it contains or underline it, but does have the effect of making the contents a clickable hyperlink. If you save the source to file and then open it in an SVG viewer (such as IE with the Adobe plug-in) then move your mouse pointer over the rectangle, you should see the mouse pointer change to a pointing finger icon, and clinking the rectangle should take you to the linked Web page.

Graphic RSS

Although there's nothing to stop an RSS or Atom feed carrying SVG as a payload, the demonstration here is to use XSLT to convert RSS to SVG to provide a graphic representation of the data. As SVG is a W3C technology, it seems appropriate to use their RSS feed in the demonstration. Here is a snippet from `www.w3.org/2000/08/w3c-synd/home.rss`:

```
<rdf:RDF xmlns:rdf="http://www.w3.org/1999/02/22-rdf-syntax-ns#"
         xmlns="http://purl.org/rss/1.0/">

<channel rdf:about="http://www.w3.org/2000/08/w3c-synd/home.rss">
    <title>World Wide Web Consortium</title>
    <items>
        <rdf:Seq>
            <rdf:li rdf:resource="http://www.w3.org/News/2004#item145"/>
...
        </rdf:Seq>
    </items>
</channel>

<item rdf:about="http://www.w3.org/News/2004#item145">
    <title>Speech Synthesis Markup Language Is a W3C Recommendation</title>
    <description>The World Wide Web Consortium today released the Speech
    Synthesis Markup Language (SSML) Version 1.0 as a W3C Recommendation.
    </description>
    <link>http://www.w3.org/News/2004#item145</link>
</item>
...
</rdf:RDF>
```

As you can see, it's RSS 1.0. There is a general problem with applying XSLT to arbitrary RDF/XML, as the same data may be expressed in many different ways, which means templates have to handle all the possibilities. However the core RSS 1.0 format only uses a single XML structural representation, which means it is well-suited for XSLT transformation. In fact the template matching for RSS 2.0 demonstrated earlier isn't very far from what's required for matching, only minor changes will be necessary to accommodate the RSS 1.0 structure. Unfortunately there is a complication on the SVG side.

Handling Text Blocks

The current version of SVG (1.1) makes life difficult when it comes to displaying blocks of text. There is no direct way of displaying the text so that it flows, line by line, wrapping onto the next line at an appropriate place. One way text blocks can be displayed is to split them into individual lines, and then offsetting each line on the y-axis to place each new line beneath the previous line. Take for example the following piece of XML, which contains a single `<description>` element (`stuff.xml`):

```
<?xml version="1.0" encoding="UTF-8"?>
<description>
The World Wide Web Consortium today released the Speech Synthesis Markup
 Language (SSML) Version 1.0 as a W3C Recommendation. With the XML-based SSML
 language, content authors can generate synthetic speech on the Web, controlling
 pronunciation, volume, pitch and rate.
</description>
```

This text can be rendered in SVG as a block with separate lines as follows:

```
<?xml version="1.0" encoding="UTF-8"?>
<g>
    <text y="20" font-size="6">The World Wide Web Consortium today released
the Speech Synthesis Markup Language</text>
    <text y="26" font-size="6">(SSML) Version 1.0 as a W3C Recommendation.
With the XML-based SSML language, content</text>
    <text y="32" font-size="6">authors can generate synthetic speech on the
Web, controlling pronunciation, volume, pitch and rate.</text>
</g>
```

The block as a whole is now contained within a `<g>` element, and each line is in its own `<text>` element, with a steadily increasing value for the y attribute. Note that the lines are all slightly different lengths as they have been split at spaces rather than in the middle of words. It's this human-friendly splitting that is the real complication.

Using a divide-and-conquer approach, it's possible to split off the code that will do the line splitting into a separate style sheet. For this it will be necessary to introduce a few more XSLT elements. This next listing (`split-stuff.xslt`) will take XML such as `stuff.xml` and process it using a separate style sheet, `line-split.xslt`. The code is as follows:

```
<?xml version="1.0" encoding="UTF-8"?>
<xsl:stylesheet version="1.0" xmlns:xsl="http://www.w3.org/1999/XSL/Transform">
    <xsl:import href="line-split.xslt"/>
    <xsl:output method="xml" version="1.0" encoding="UTF-8" indent="yes"/>
    <xsl:template match="/">
        <xsl:variable name="raw" select="description"/>
        <g>
            <xsl:call-template name="lineSplit">
                <xsl:with-param name="content"
                        select="normalize-space($raw)"/>
                <xsl:with-param name="blockOffset" select="20"/>
                <xsl:with-param name="lineCount" select="0"/>
            </xsl:call-template>
        </g>
    </xsl:template>
</xsl:stylesheet>
```

Note first of all the `xsl:import` element. This element effectively adds the templates defined in that separate file with those of this file. The technique used to apply the template that will do the line splitting is essentially that of a procedure call. The data of interest in the original XML is extracted using an XPath locator, and that data is placed in a variable called `raw`. This happens in the following two lines:

```
<xsl:template match="/">
    <xsl:variable name="raw" select="description"/>
```

There is a difference from most programming languages, in that once an XSLT variable has been given a value, that value can't be changed. It isn't an issue here, but something to bear in mind if you're experimenting.

The results of the line splitting go in a `<g>` block, so this is included verbatim in the style sheet, wrapping around the lines of code that call the template which does the splitting. The call itself looks like this:

```
<xsl:call-template name="lineSplit">
    <xsl:with-param name="content"
            select="normalize-space($raw)"/>
    <xsl:with-param name="blockOffset" select="20"/>
    <xsl:with-param name="lineCount" select="0"/>
</xsl:call-template>
```

The name of the template which will be called is given in the first line, this is followed by three elements that describe named values that will be passed to the template as parameters, like a procedure or method call in an object-oriented language. Before being passed as the content parameter, the data in the variable raw undergoes a little preprocessing. The standard XSLT function normalize-space trims any leading or trailing whitespace, and replaces any blocks of whitespace within the data with a single space character. This means the line splitting that follows is more likely to produce something neatly formatted. The blockOffset parameter is a value that will be added to the y-coordinate of every text line produced by the called template. The lineCount parameter will be used within the called template to keep track of the number of text lines generated from the original data.

The template that does the splitting is called lineSplit and is contained in the file line-split.xslt. The code syntax may be unfamiliar, but the processing is very straightforward and will be explained in a moment. The contents of line-split.xslt are as follows:

```xml
<?xml version="1.0" encoding="UTF-8"?>
<xsl:stylesheet version="1.0" xmlns:xsl="http://www.w3.org/1999/XSL/Transform">
    <xsl:output method="xml" indent="yes"/>

    <xsl:variable name="fontSize">6</xsl:variable>
    <xsl:variable name="lineSpace">6</xsl:variable>
    <xsl:variable name="minLength">80</xsl:variable>
    <xsl:variable name="maxLength">100</xsl:variable>
    <xsl:variable name="sliceLength">20</xsl:variable>

    <xsl:template name="lineSplit">

        <xsl:param name="content"/>
        <xsl:param name="blockOffset"/>
        <xsl:param name="lineCount"/>

        <xsl:variable name="start" select="substring($content,1, $minLength)"/>
        <xsl:variable name="slice"
            select="substring($content,$minLength+1, $sliceLength)"/>
        <xsl:variable name="end" select="substring($content,$maxLength+1)"/>

        <xsl:variable name="preSpace" select="substring-before($slice,' ')"/>
        <xsl:variable name="postSpace" select="substring-after($slice,' ')"/>

        <text y="{$blockOffset+$lineSpace*$lineCount}" font-size="{$fontSize}">

            <xsl:choose>
                <xsl:when test="contains($slice, ' ')">
                    <xsl:value-of select="concat($start, $preSpace)"/>
                </xsl:when>
                <xsl:otherwise>
                    <xsl:value-of select="concat($start, $slice)"/>
```

```
            </xsl:otherwise>
        </xsl:choose>

    </text>

    <xsl:variable name="remainder" select="concat($postSpace,$end)"/>

    <xsl:choose>
        <xsl:when test="string-length($remainder)>$maxLength+1">
            <xsl:call-template name="lineSplit">
    <xsl:with-param name="content" select="$remainder"/>
    <xsl:with-param name="lineCount" select="$lineCount+1"/>
    <xsl:with-param name="blockOffset" select="$blockOffset"/>
            </xsl:call-template>
        </xsl:when>
        <xsl:otherwise>
            <text
    y="{$blockOffset+$lineSpace*$lineCount+$lineSpace}"
    font-size="{$fontSize}">
                <xsl:value-of select="$remainder"/>
            </text>
        </xsl:otherwise>
    </xsl:choose>
    </xsl:template>
</xsl:stylesheet>
```

A simple algorithm is used to split the lines, which depends on two indexes within the source text. The template includes three variables that identify a section of this text: minLength, maxLength, and sliceLength. The values of these variables are set in the xsl:variable elements early in the listing. minLength is the minimum required line length for the output, maxLength the maximum line length, and sliceLength is the difference between these (this third variable is stated explicitly rather than being calculated to make it easier to see what's going on).

The text starts as follows:

```
The World Wide Web Consortium today released the Speech Synthesis Markup
  Language (SSML) Version 1.0 as a W3C Recommendation. With the XML-based SSML
  language, content authors...
```

The code divides this text into three sections: start, end, and slice. Each section is held in a variable. The start variable is the block of text before the index of minLength, end is the block after maxLength, and slice is the section in between. The slice section is underlined in the previous text. The value of each of these variables is created using the standard XSLT substring function, which takes two parameters, the start index and the length of the required substring. The required values are given based on the values of minLength, sliceLength, and maxLength. This part of the splitting occurs in the following lines:

```
<xsl:variable name="start"
            select="substring($content, 1, $minLength)"/>
<xsl:variable name="slice"
            select="substring($content, $minLength+1, $sliceLength)"/>
<xsl:variable name="end"
                select="substring($content, $maxLength+1)"/>
```

Note that when variables are referred to, their name is preceded with a $.

Next, the content of the slice variable is split into two sections, the string before the first space and the string after the first space:

```
<xsl:variable name="preSpace" select="substring-before($slice,' ')"/>
<xsl:variable name="postSpace" select="substring-after($slice,' ')"/>
```

From the initial slice underlined previously, this would yield preSpace= "ge" and postSpace= "(SSML) Version 1.". Although its position isn't particularly significant, there now follows the line that will provide the start tag of the text element in the output:

```
<text y="{$blockOffset+$lineSpace*$lineCount}" font-size="{$fontSize}">
```

Again the variables are referred to with a $ prefix, and there's an additional XSLT abbreviation here, the curly brackets. When used inside the quotes of an attribute in this way, they are interpreted as meaning *the value of*. So the required y coordinate is calculated from various variables and the font-size value simply inserted. No x coordinate is necessary, because the default 0 is what is required for the text to left-justify. Next, the code returns to string juggling. What's needed in the example is to append the characters that appear before the next space (ge) to the start of the line (The World Wide Web Consortium today released the Speech Synthesis Markup Langua). This is all well and good, but there is the distinct possibility that the slice of text won't contain a space character, and this eventuality needs to be handled in some way. This situation is tested for using one of XSLT's conditional constructs, choose...when...otherwise, which roughly corresponds to the if...then...else statement of other languages, although there may be multiple when clauses. Here the conditional test uses another built-in function, contains, to see if there's a space in the slice. If there is, then the material before the space in slice is concatenated to the start of the line using another built-in, concat. The result of this will be passed to the output thanks to the xsl:value-of element. If there isn't a space then the start of the line is concatenated with the whole of the slice, and the result of that sent to the output. This, under most circumstances, will conclude the construction of the text content, so the conditional block is followed by the closing tag of the text element, which will be passed to the output. The code for this block is as follows:

```
<xsl:choose>
    <xsl:when test="contains($slice, ' ')">
<xsl:value-of select="concat($start, $preSpace)"/>
    </xsl:when>
    <xsl:otherwise>
        <xsl:value-of select="concat($start, $slice)"/>
    </xsl:otherwise>
</xsl:choose>

</text>
```

Now that the first line of text has been output, it's time to look at what's left. The text that remains in the content after this line is the material after the space in the slice (if there was one) together with the material in the end variable. This is now concatenated to form the remainder variable:

```
<xsl:variable name="remainder" select="concat($postSpace,$end)"/>
```

Now either there is more than a line's worth of text left, or there isn't. Another conditional is used to test this. If there is, then this very same template will be applied again to the remaining text, with the line counter incremented and the `blockOffset` value passed again with the same value. You can see this part of the conditional here:

```
<xsl:choose>
    <xsl:when test="string-length($remainder)>$maxLength+1">
        <xsl:call-template name="lineSplit">
<xsl:with-param name="content" select="$remainder"/>
<xsl:with-param name="lineCount" select="$lineCount+1"/>
<xsl:with-param name="blockOffset" select="$blockOffset"/>
        </xsl:call-template>
    </xsl:when>
```

However, if there was less than a full line's worth left, this trailing part will need to go to the output as an additional line. The default part of the conditional handles this as follows:

```
<xsl:otherwise>
    <text
y="{$blockOffset+$lineSpace*$lineCount+$lineSpace}"
font-size="{$fontSize}">
        <xsl:value-of select="$remainder"/>
    </text>
</xsl:otherwise>
</xsl:choose>
```

There is now code available to break up long `<description>` elements, so now it's time to return to the top-level handling of the RSS data.

Note that the XSLT here uses two important programming constructs: the conditional and recursion. Its support of these constructs is the key to making XSLT "Turing complete," in other words it can run any program you'd like to throw at it. For more details, refer to `http://en.wikipedia.org/wiki/Turing-complete`.

Multiformat Handling

Here is the snippet of source code from `www.w3.org/2000/08/w3c-synd/home.rss` again:

```
<rdf:RDF xmlns:rdf="http://www.w3.org/1999/02/22-rdf-syntax-ns#"
        xmlns="http://purl.org/rss/1.0/">

<channel rdf:about="http://www.w3.org/2000/08/w3c-synd/home.rss">
    <title>World Wide Web Consortium</title>
    <items>
        <rdf:Seq>
            <rdf:li rdf:resource="http://www.w3.org/News/2004#item145"/>
...
        </rdf:Seq>
    </items>
</channel>

<item rdf:about="http://www.w3.org/News/2004#item145">
    <title>Speech Synthesis Markup Language Is a W3C Recommendation</title>
    <description>The World Wide Web Consortium today released the Speech
```

```
      Synthesis Markup Language (SSML) Version 1.0 as a W3C Recommendation.
      </description>
      <link>http://www.w3.org/News/2004#item145</link>
  </item>
  ...
  </rdf:RDF>
```

The material the style sheet will be looking at is found along the following XPaths (note the use of namespace prefixes, the reason for that will become clear in a moment):

```
/rdf:RDF/rss:item/rss:description
/rdf:RDF/rss:item/rss:title
```

These will appear in pairs with `rss:item` elements. In this light, you might think that it would be straightforward to write templates to match these parts and (after line-split processing) output the data as required. Not so fast. The XSLT listings so far have demonstrated how it's possible to step down into the structure of an XML document through the levels of nesting. The different levels covered here are:

```
/
rdf:RDF
rss:item
rss:description
rss:title
rss:link
```

Although the structure is a little different, each of these can be mapped against corresponding RSS 2.0 substructures:

```
/ = /
rdf:RDF = rss/channel
rss:item = item
rss:description = description
rss:title = title
rss:link = link
```

XSLT is namespace aware, so that is reflected here. RSS 1.0 elements are in a namespace and so have different names (their local names are preceded by the namespace URI, here abbreviated to the usual prefix).

The fact that such a mapping is possible means that it's possible to convert between formats using XSLT. The code needed to do this doesn't really need any more than the techniques shown in this chapter, however there is a lot of code required. Morten Frederickson has made available a style sheet that will convert virtually any syndication format (including Atom, RSS 1.0, and RSS 2.0) to RSS 1.0:

```
http://purl.org/net/syndication/subscribe/feed-rss1.0.xsl
```

Sjoerd Visscher has a similar offering:

```
http://w3future.com/weblog/2002/09/09.xml
```

Note that sometimes these conversions may be lossy, especially if the source data contains material beyond its core format. Incidentally, if you look inside these, it's an eye-opener to see how much code is needed to convert between date formats compared to other aspects of the transformation.

To give you an idea of why this mapping might be useful, here is the W3C news snippet reformatted as RSS 2.0:

```
<rss version="2.0">
  <channel>
    <title>World Wide Web Consortium</title>
...
    <item>
      <title>Speech Synthesis Markup Language Is a W3C Recommendation</title>
      <description>The World Wide Web Consortium today released the Speech
      Synthesis Markup Language (SSML) Version 1.0 as a W3C Recommendation.
      </description>
      <link>http://www.w3.org/News/2004#item145</link>
    </item>
...
  </channel>
</rss>
```

XSLT is designed to handle the RSS 1.0 format; there's a direct mapping to the RSS 2.0 format, so is it possible to handle both formats with the same style sheet? The answer is yes, and it's remarkably easy. But before moving on to the details of the style sheet, you need to have an idea of what the target output will look like.

SVG Output

Here is a two-item sample of SVG that has been generated by passing the W3C's feed through an XSLT style sheet (output.svg):

```
?xml version="1.0" encoding="UTF-8"?>
<svg xmlns:rdf="http://www.w3.org/1999/02/22-rdf-syntax-ns#"
    xmlns:rss="http://purl.org/rss/1.0/"
    xmlns:xlink="http://www.w3.org/1999/xlink"
    width="100%" height="100%">
  <g transform="scale(0.285714285714286)">
  <g transform="translate(10,20)">
    <a xlink:href="http://www.w3.org/News/2004#item136">
      <rect width="280" height="70"
         fill="white" stroke="green" stroke-width="2"/>
      <g transform="translate(10,0)">
      <text y="20" font-size="6">2004-08-26: W3C is pleased to announce the
relaunch of the Extensible Markup Language</text>
      <text y="26" font-size="6">(XML) Activity. The Activity's Working,
Interest and Coordination Groups given below</text>
      <text y="32" font-size="6">have been chartered through 30 June 2006. New
in March, the XML Binary Characterization</text>
      <text y="38" font-size="6">Working Group is chartered through March
2005. Participation is open to W3C Members.</text>
      <text y="44" font-size="6">Learn about XML in 10 Points and visit the
XML home page. (News archive)</text>
      <text x="10" y="10" fill="red" font-size="8">XML Activity Chartered
Through June 2006</text>
      </g>
    </a>
  </g>
  </g>
```

```
     <g transform="scale(0.571428571428571)">
       <g transform="translate(20,40)">
         <a xlink:href="http://www.w3.org/News/2004#item137">
           <rect width="280" height="70"
                 fill="white" stroke="green" stroke-width="2"/>
           <g transform="translate(10,0)">
             <text y="20" font-size="6">2004-08-30: The Quality Assurance (QA)
Working Group has published three Working</text>
             <text y="26" font-size="6">Drafts. Written for W3C Working Group
Chairs and Team Contacts, The QA Handbook provides</text>
             <text y="32" font-size="6">techniques, tools, and templates for
test suites and specifications. QA Framework:</text>
             <text y="38" font-size="6">Specification Guidelines are designed
to help make technical reports easy to interpret</text>
             <text y="44" font-size="6">without ambiguity, and explain how to
define and specify conformance. Variability</text>
             <text y="50" font-size="6">in Specifications is a First Public
Working Draft. Formerly part of the Specification</text>
             <text y="56" font-size="6">Guidelines, the document contains
advanced design considerations and conformance-related</text>
             <text y="62" font-size="6">techniques. Read about QA at W3C. (News
archive)</text>
             <text x="10" y="10" fill="red" font-size="8">Working Drafts:
Quality Assurance</text>
           </g>
         </a>
       </g>
     </g>
</svg>
```

This code uses techniques described so far, although two new kinds of transform have been introduced: scale, which will multiply the dimensions of an object by whatever is provided as a scale factor, and translate, which will shift an object down and to the right by the values given. Note the nesting—the transform that does the translation will be applied first, followed by the scale transform specified in the parent <g> element.

Figure 25-6 shows what this looks like when displayed in a viewer (here containing seven items).

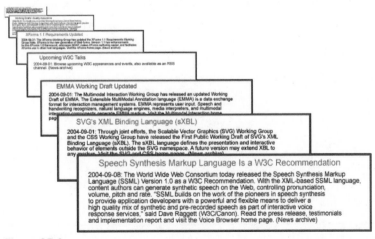

Figure 25-6

The top-level XSLT code is as follows (rss2svg.xslt):

```
<xsl:stylesheet version="1.0"
    xmlns:xsl="http://www.w3.org/1999/XSL/Transform"
    xmlns:rdf="http://www.w3.org/1999/02/22-rdf-syntax-ns#"
    xmlns:rss="http://purl.org/rss/1.0/"
    xmlns:xlink="http://www.w3.org/1999/xlink">

  <xsl:import href="line-split.xslt"/>

  <xsl:output method="xml" indent="yes"/>

  <xsl:template match="/">
      <svg width="100%" height="100%">
          <xsl:apply-templates/>
      </svg>
  </xsl:template>

  <xsl:template match="rss/channel | rdf:RDF">
      <xsl:for-each select="item | rss:item">
          <xsl:sort select="position()" order="descending"/>
          <xsl:call-template name="itemBox">
    <xsl:with-param name="itemPosition" select="position()"/>
          </xsl:call-template>
      </xsl:for-each>
  </xsl:template>

  <xsl:template name="itemBox">
      <xsl:variable name="raw" select="description | rss:description"/>
      <xsl:param name="itemPosition"/>
      <xsl:variable name="itemCount"
                    select="count(../item | ../rss:item)"/>
      <xsl:variable name="scaleFactor"
                    select="2*$itemPosition div $itemCount "/>
      <g>
<xsl:attribute name="transform">scale(<xsl:value-of
 select="$scaleFactor"/>)</xsl:attribute>
          <g>

    <xsl:attribute name="transform">translate(<xsl:value-of
select="10*$itemPosition"/>,<xsl:value-of
select="20*$itemPosition"/>)</xsl:attribute>

              <a xlink:href="{link|rss:link}">

                  <rect width="280" height="70" fill="white"
                            stroke="green" stroke-width="2"/>
                  <g>
    <xsl:attribute name="transform">translate(10,0)</xsl:attribute>
        <xsl:call-template name="lineSplit">
            <xsl:with-param name="content" select="normalize-space($raw)"/>
          <xsl:with-param name="blockOffset" select="20"/>
    <xsl:with-param name="lineCount" select="0"/>
  </xsl:call-template>
  <text x="10" y="10" fill="red" font-size="8">
  <xsl:value-of select="title | rss:title"/>
```

```
                    </text>
                </g>
            </a>
        </g>
    </g>
</xsl:template>

<xsl:template match="text()"/>

</xsl:stylesheet>
```

Once again, you've already encountered most of the techniques used here. A first new thing is the way the match attribute of the template elements is set up to match either RSS 2.0 (no namespace) or RSS 1.0 (namespace-qualified) elements in the source feed. The syntax uses a vertical bar to express a logical OR, as follows:

```
<xsl:template match="rss/channel | rdf:RDF">
```

The xsl:for-each element operates a loop, iterating through the nodes that match the select expression. This is often used as an alternative to using other templates directly, and here it makes the program flow a little clearer by calling another template directly in each iteration:

```
<xsl:for-each select="item | rss:item">
    <xsl:sort select="position()" order="descending"/>
    <xsl:call-template name="itemBox">
    <xsl:with-param name="itemPosition" select="position()"/>
    </xsl:call-template>
</xsl:for-each>
</xsl:template>
```

The xsl:sort element is used to reverse the order of the items within the data. This is needed for the following reason: If the sequence of items in the SVG followed the reverse-chronological order of the source feed, then the SVG painter's model would cover the newer items with older ones. The position function gives the position of this element amongst its peers, so in this case it would give the item number: 1, 2, 3...

The template that is called for each item begins by obtaining the content of this item's description element and putting it in a variable named raw, as follows:

```
<xsl:template name="itemBox">
    <xsl:variable name="raw" select="description | rss:description"/>
```

If you refer back to Figure 25-6, you can see both the position and the scale of each item is determined by its position in the feed. The next few lines use the position function along with the count function (which counts the nodes that match its XPath expression) to calculate suitable scale and translate values for each item. These values are placed inside the attributes of the <g> elements. The XSLT source looks dreadful at this point, although it is functionally fairly simple. It helps to compare the XSLT with an example of the SVG it produces (in output.svg). The code section is as follows:

```
<xsl:param name="itemPosition"/>
<xsl:variable name="itemCount"
              select="count(../item | ../rss:item)"/>
<xsl:variable name="scaleFactor"
              select="2*$itemPosition div $itemCount "/>
<g>
<xsl:attribute name="transform">scale(<xsl:value-of
```

```
select="$scaleFactor"/>)</xsl:attribute>

            <g>
    <xsl:attribute name="transform">translate(<xsl:value-of
select="10*$itemPosition"/>,<xsl:value-of
select="20*$itemPosition"/>)</xsl:attribute>

            <a xlink:href="{link|rss:link}">

            <rect width="280" height="70" fill="white"
                        stroke="green" stroke-width="2"/>
            <g>
    <xsl:attribute name="transform">translate(10,0)</xsl:attribute>
```

Here is a snippet of the SVG generated by that last section:

```
<g transform="scale(0.5)">
  <g transform="translate(20,40)">
    <a xlink:href="http://www.w3.org/News/2004#item137">
      <rect width="280" height="70"
            fill="white" stroke="green" stroke-width="2"/>
      <g transform="translate(10,0)">
```

The next piece of code is the call to the (imported) line splitter template:

```
            <xsl:call-template name="lineSplit">
        <xsl:with-param name="content" select="normalize-space($raw)"/>
        <xsl:with-param name="blockOffset" select="20"/>
    <xsl:with-param name="lineCount" select="0"/>
</xsl:call-template>
```

This template finishes by pulling out the title of the item, for display in the color red, and then closing all the XML elements constructed in this template.

```
<text x="10" y="10" fill="red" font-size="8">
<xsl:value-of select="title | rss:title"/>
            </text>
        </g>
    </a>
</g>
</xsl:template>
```

Now you have all the code needed to produce the graphic representation of a live feed. You could save the current contents of the W3C's newsfeed to disk and run the XSLT from the command line, for example:

```
transform home.rss rss2svg.xslt output.svg
```

You could then open the output in a standalone viewer or a browser equipped with an SVG plug-in. This is all Web material, so you may prefer to try it live. The following is a variation of the PHP listed earlier, which will load XML data from anywhere on the Web, before applying a (local) XSLT style sheet:

```php
<?php
// Uses the PEAR HTTP Request utility
// which also depends on the PEAR Net package.

require_once "Request.php";

// source file
$req =& new HTTP_Request("http://www.w3.org/2000/08/w3c-synd/home.rss");
$req->sendRequest();

// Check for HTTP 200
if ( $req->getResponseCode() != '200' ) {
    die ( "Request failed: ".$req->getResponseCode() );
}

$xml = $req->getResponseBody();

// XSLT file
$xsl = file_get_contents ('rss2svg.xslt') ;

$arguments = array(
    '/_xml' => $xml,
    '/_xsl' => $xsl
);


// create a new XSLT processor
$processor = xslt_create();

// transform
$output = xslt_process($processor, 'arg:/_xml', 'arg:/_xsl', NULL, $arguments);

if ($result) {
        // set mime type
        header("Content-Type: image/svg+xml");
    // print it
    echo $output;
}

// clean up
xslt_free($processor);
?>
```

This code uses the PEAR HTTP_Request utility, which in turn uses Net_URL. These are available from http://pear.php.net. They are PHP files themselves, so installation is just a matter of making the files available on PHP's path. The easiest way to run the previous code is to copy Request.php (from PEAR) to the same directory as rss2svg.xslt and transform.php, with a subdirectory called Net containing URL.php.

Summary

We covered a lot of ground in this chapter, but you should now have some idea of how XPath, Xquery, XSLT, and SVG work. More specifically, you've seen how...

❑   XPath is used as a location mechanism with XML.

❑   XQuery is a query language like SQL but geared toward XML.

❑   XSLT is used to transform XML documents into other formats.

❑   XPath, XQuery, XSLT, and SVG all have useful applications within syndication.

Exercise

1.   In the examples in the text you saw how the DocBook-like format of book.xml could be transformed into RSS 2.0. Later, the resulting RSS was converted into XHTML. See whether you can shorten this sequence by creating a single book2html.xslt style sheet, which will take book.xml as input and output an XHTML representation like that listed in the text.

The Blogging Client

In the practical chapters so far you've seen how feed data can be modeled and stored and various other aspects of content management systems (CMSs). In the Wiki code you saw a simple user interface for authoring content. This chapter focuses on how content gets from the authoring tool to the back end, and the protocols that enable remote control of CMSs. The sites most associated with feeds are Weblogs due to their episodic nature and use of ongoing updates. So it's not surprising that the most popular protocols are to be found in the world of blogs. In this chapter you will learn about:

❑ General approaches to communication from client to CMS

❑ Remote procedure calling with XML-RPC

❑ The Blogger API

❑ How a SOAP-based transport can be built using WSDL

❑ Richer HTTP communication and the Atom protocol

Talking to the Server with a Variety of Clients

For a system to be able to generate feeds it must have a source of data to use in the feeds. Usually a CMS will be the immediate source of that data, but that doesn't answer the question of where the material originated. As mentioned in Chapter 24, a CMS typically will have three user interfaces: the administration interface, the authoring interface (usually with restricted access), and the public interface (usually view-only). All three of these interfaces will be connected in some form or other to the client side, and information will somehow be passed between user interface software and the server-side CMS. The user interface of the public view feeds will usually be the aggregator or newsreader, and communication will take place using XML over HTTP. Both the administration and authoring interfaces can use the same kind of transport, but before looking at specific techniques it will be worth looking at the big picture, or rather, a series of small diagrams.

Figure 26-1 gives you an idea of the kind of interface provided by many CMSs.

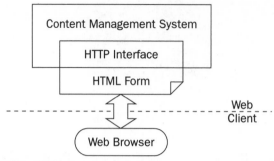

Figure 26-1

The CMS itself provides HTML forms through which the user can author material. This is essentially the same as the authoring interface of the Wiki in Chapter 24. This interface is highly appropriate where system-specific tasks need to be carried out such as in administration, although the interface can offer a simple solution for authoring purposes as well. Note that the separation of HTML Form and Web browser in Figure 26-1 is a little artificial; the form will actually appear in the browser at the client side. The reason this is placed server-side here is to distinguish it from the architecture in which the form window is actually created client-side.

The form itself is used to collect content or other data from the user that will be passed back to the server-side system using the HTTP POST method supported by HTML forms. Normally this happens when you click a Submit button.

Browser Scripts

A common practice with Weblog systems is to provide a Blog This! link or browser button, so users can quickly make a post referring to whatever material they happen to be looking at in their browsers. The link or button may be relatively passive, acting just like a regular hyperlink. This would lead to the kind of interface in Figure 26-1. However, more often than not the browser button will actually contain some active code, in the form of a brief snippet of JavaScript. This will run in the client, creating a popup window and then (usually) calling the server-side side to populate the form with appropriate controls and editing areas. This general idea is shown in Figure 26-2.

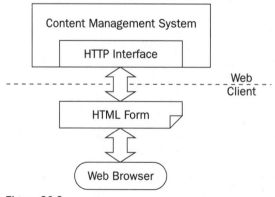

Figure 26-2

When the server is actually providing the HTML for the form, the distinction between these approaches is subtle (and not particularly significant). However, it is possible for the entire content submission form to be built client-side, thus, communication with the server occurs after a button or link in the submission form is pressed.

The Fat Client

The Web browser can offer rich functionality as a client, but the limitations of HTML forms tend to mean it generally gets used where a lightweight user interface is needed. Where more complex user interaction is required, or in circumstances where a browser may not be available, a custom-built client may be constructed. What's more the client is no longer restricted to the HTTP protocol used by browsers. These lead to the general situation shown in Figure 26-3.

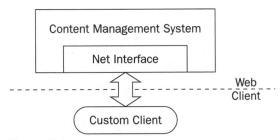

Figure 26-3

This is of course just a simplification or generalization of the browser-based client setup. The common protocols you will see discussed shortly fit into this general pattern, although they aren't that far removed from the browser-oriented setup. HTTP is the primary protocol of the Web, and XML-based formats are used for the communication, although there are divergent transport architectures. Space limitations mean this book can only cover so much of the wide range of the different practices found on the (syndication) Web. That in turn is only a small fraction of what is possible in this developing field. But before looking once more at HTTP, the architecture of Figure 26-4 is worth mentioning in passing.

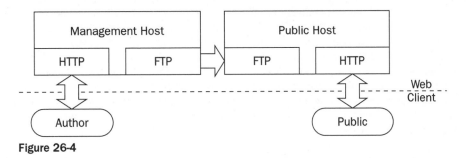

Figure 26-4

Figure 26-4 shows a separation server-side between the part of the system that manages the content and the part that serves the material as a public Web site. The author/administrator part interacts over HTTP with the CMS part, which in turn passes the content as required to the hosting server over FTP (File Transfer Protocol). This is a good option when the user already has space on a Web server, but lacks the ability or inclination to host the CMS him- or herself. Aside from being a useful architecture in practical terms, it's also interesting in the way the Web can enable further componentization and distribution of different parts of a system.

The Language of HTTP

The Web is a communication medium, and that communication takes place first and foremost between pieces of software. The primary protocol of the Web is HTTP. An analogy can be made between HTTP communication and human language. To say things, humans use sentences, and the main components of those sentences are nouns and verbs. The nouns name the things being talked about; the verbs describe actions or relationships between the things. The nouns of the Web are URIs, identifiers of resources, and there are an unlimited number of them. The verbs are the methods of HTTP, of which there are just eight: GET, HEAD, POST, PUT, DELETE, OPTIONS, TRACE, and CONNECT (see the following table). There are other verbs available, including the WebDAV (Web-based Distributed Authoring and Versioning) specification, and a PATCH method has been proposed for partial document changes. But today's Web is largely built with HTML and HTML browsers in mind, and the capabilities of servers and services reflect this.

Method	Purpose
OPTIONS	Requests information about the communication options available
GET	Retrieves information identified by the URI
HEAD	Returns same metadata headers as GET, without the message body
POST	Asks server to accept enclosed data and process as appropriate
PUT	Asks server to place enclosed data at the request URI
DELETE	Requests deletion of the resource identified by the request URI
TRACE	Loops back request message, for testing purposes
CONNECT	Reserved for use with proxies

HTML's Legacy

When interacting with a service through a browser, usually an HTML form is used, and HTML forms only support the HTTP GET and POST methods. The GET method enables you to retrieve data from the server, the POST method enables you to send data to the server (and get data back). The same result as the other verbs like PUT (which uploads a whole file to the server to appear at the given URI) and DELETE (which deletes the identified resource) can be mimicked using POST alone. As the essential operations for dialog are covered in GET and POST, many other software systems like J2ME and Macromedia Flash only support those two verbs (and sometimes HEAD, which returns header information without the body of the page or document). On the face of it this appears to be a desirable simplification. However, when it comes to reliable communication between systems, verbs like PUT and DELETE can make life a lot easier (imagine you didn't have a Delete key on your keyboard—you could still get rid of files, but it would take several, potentially error-prone steps).

In the past, syndication applications followed the same line as the language-limited browser, with POST being used to pass material from client to server to publish it and GET to retrieve it (as a feed). All the interesting operations are wrapped up in the (XML) documents that are passed around. Similarly, in the wider world of Web services the tendency was, until recently at least, toward using a narrow range of HTTP methods with material like processing instructions packaged into the content of XML documents. SOAP (Simple Object Access Protocol) is the leading standard for Web services of this type. An early fork of SOAP, XML-RPC (Remote Procedure Calling) is a simpler but limited protocol that has considerable deployment in blogging systems. However, the inflexibility of XML-RPC and the relative complexity of SOAP have led to reexamination of what HTTP itself has to offer, especially when used in combination with XML. The more HTTP-oriented approaches to Web services are generally bundled under the banner of REST (Representation State Architecture). Purists of either camp may suggest otherwise, but generally the same activities can be carried out using either "RESTful" or "SOAPy" techniques. Which approach is more appropriate depends on individual circumstances.

In principle, the XML-RPC, SOAP, and REST-based protocols have the same basic shape. Whatever the architectural principles, the goals are generally the same: to make it possible to communicate between applications running on different operating systems, with different technologies and programming languages. They share similar handshaking strategies. But as you get closer to the wire along which they travel, significant differences emerge. In particular, XML-RPC/SOAP tends to use a small number of service location URIs and usually just the HTTP POST method. Details of the actions are contained within the XML message. REST tends to use a larger number of URIs (to identify different actions) and a wider range of the HTTP methods.

All these approaches (when used on the Web) pass XML messages over HTTP. In all cases the XML will usually contain data that needs to be conveyed from sender to receiver. However, there is a difference in the way the receiver is told what to do with the data. Where SOAP and SOAP derivatives describe the verb-like target procedural calls in the XML, the REST approach uses the nouns and verbs of the Web (URIs and HTTP methods) to describe the processing, with the XML as pure payload. This may sound like a high-level, philosophical difference, but it's worth remembering that on the wire the differences aren't exactly substantial. All HTTP messages are comprised by a start-line, followed by (optional) headers, an empty line, and an (optional) body. The headers are text-based, XML is text based. So the main practical difference between the two approaches is which side of the blank line the verbs are found.

Authentication

Before looking at specific approaches to authentication, it may be useful to clarify some of the jargon. In practice, different operations may form part of the authentication process, although they are so closely associated they are often thought of together. These operations usually fall into one of three categories: the authentication itself, authorization, and access control.

Authentication is the part of the process in which your identity is verified. It corresponds to an action like showing your passport at a border control. This differs from *authorization,* which is the part of the process by which a check is made to see whether an identified individual has permission to, for example, access the resource. This corresponds roughly to operations like checking you are on the passenger list of an airplane. *Access control* is about checking more than site-specific characteristics; in the real world this might be something like whether you are considered legally old enough to fly unaccompanied.

A key aspect of security, authentication is how a system verifies people are who they say they are. The most common way this is done is through a user name and password combination, the assumption being that users keep their passwords secret and that it can't easily be guessed. There are many ways this can be implemented, but conveniently for syndication the HTTP protocol already includes a framework with support for two authentication techniques, and it's not difficult to devise others. The HTTP techniques are known as Basic and Digest Access Authentication, and are specified in RFC 2617 (www.ietf.org/rfc/rfc2617.txt). Both methods follow essentially the same challenge-response handshaking pattern. The client will try to access a restricted zone or realm, the server responds with code, 401 Unauthorized, along with a header field, WWW-Authenticate, with details of what it requires before the client will be allowed to access the restricted areas. Although Basic Authentication is relatively simple to implement it offers no real security as the password is sent over the wire in a form that is easy for third parties to read (using the so-called man-in-the-middle approach).

HTTP Basic Authentication

When a client tries to access a URI where the resource has been protected with Basic Authentication, the server will send a response code of `401 Unauthorized`. On receiving this status code, assuming the client has support for authentication, it will send another message to the server, typically including a user name and password for authentication. You will undoubtedly have encountered this challenge-response dialog as it presents itself in a browser, typically as a popup box with fields for the entry of a user name and password.

Usually the server will protect an area of the site rather than a specific page. This area is known as the authentication name or realm. The message including the `401` will usually include other information for the client's benefit such as this realm name.

After the user has entered a name and password, the client will then call on the server again but this time include an `Authorization` header, with the word `Basic` and a string that is the base64-encoded version of `username:password`. The server will base64-decode this and compare the user name and password with local records, and if there's a match the server will deliver the requested page/data to the client.

Note that although Base64 encoding makes the authentication credentials unreadable to the human eye, it's not really encrypted, because decoding is just a matter of pushing the data directly through a decoder. If a third party intercepts the message, it will be a trivial matter for them to obtain your ID and password. It is possible to use a one-way encryption technique like SHA1 hashing to make it extremely difficult for a cracker to get the password. In this scenario the client would encrypt the user name and password before posting, and the server would compare these to a locally encrypted version of the credentials. Unfortunately this approach is still insecure, because if a third party can intercept the encrypted credentials they can use that as a key into the server by simply replaying it.

Because the HTTP protocol is stateless, every time a protected resource is requested from the server the client will have to supply authentication credentials again in order to receive access to the resource, even though the request is coming from the same client. Your browser will usually look after this detail for you, and it's not difficult to include password caching in your own client applications, although care is advisable about their controlling their visibility.

HTTP Digest

A more secure approach to authentication also described in RFC 2617 is known as HTTP Digest Authentication. This avoids passing anything over the wire that would be useful to any cracker (like everything else around computers, this approach isn't 100 percent secure, but it does make it generally unfeasible for most malicious agents to get in).

The trick to this is a protocol where a new piece of data is thrown into the mix, a challenge that must be processed correctly by the client for it to gain access.

The client will initially request a protected resource on the server, without passing any credentials. The server will reject this initial request but respond with a uniquely generated message, the *challenge* (also called a nonce value). The client will now use its password as part of a digest function (often MD5) on the received challenge. Then it will try to access the resource on the server again but this time sending the digest of the challenge, the *response*. A valid response is a digest of the challenge, the password, the user name, the HTTP method, and the URI. Now the server will look up the user name and retrieve the corresponding password. It will then apply the same digest function as the client did to the original challenge, which should produce the same result if the user name and password are valid. The matching digest values demonstrate that the client knows the secret and thus is who it says it is.

HTTPS

HTTPS is a variant of HTTP. It adds a Secure Sockets Layer (SSL) underneath the standard connection protocol (by default port 443 is used). Basically, anything that can be passed over HTTP can be given this extra level of security, although both client and server must understand SSL for it to work. Most Web servers include HTTPS support, as do numerous client tools, including several aggregators.

There are certain terms that, although not specific to security, crop up frequently in the context of authentication, so some basic definitions might be useful.

Base64 Encoding

This a format using 64 ASCII characters to encode 6-bit binary data. It's used for things like the MIME standard for e-mail attachments. It also sometimes appears as a means of encoding binary objects for inclusion in XML documents, as all 64 characters used (ABCDEFGHIJKLMNOPQRSTUVWXYZ abcdefghijklmnopqrstuvwxyz0123456789+/) are legal in XML. It offers no security in itself, as it can simply be decoded. It is used in authentication as a way of encoding passwords or other potentially non-text secrets for exchange between client and server.

Hashes and Digests

Hashing or digest algorithms take a message of arbitrary length and from it produce a near-unique *fingerprint* or *message digest*, usually of fixed length. These can be used for indexing in data stores (hence hashtables), but certain algorithms are found in the field of cryptography. When used for security purposes the algorithms are one-way processes, so it is impossible or at least unfeasible to decode the message from its hash. Two algorithms in particular are in widespread use: MD5 (Message Digest 5), specified in RFC 1321, and SHA1 (Secure Hash Algorithm 1"), specified in FIPS 180.

Nonces

The rather antiquated word *nonce* refers to the present occasion. In secure communications it is a value sent during an exchange that is short lived, that is to say the value will only appear once and is never reused. These nonce values can help prevent replay attacks, in which the cracker records the authentication credentials of a trusted client and replays them to gain access. A nonce is usually generated from a random number or the current time, or a combination of the two.

Please don't interpret the minimal coverage of security in this book to mean that security isn't important in syndication — for many applications it's absolutely crucial. But it's a huge field, and security techniques that work on the Web will generally also work just the same for syndication applications.

Protocols for Blogging

If you have a client tool for writing content on the desktop and a CMS on a server capable of organizing and delivering that material to the reader, you also need some way of getting that content from the client to the server. HTTP is enough to carry data, but how do you communicate what it is that you want the server to do with the data? This is the primary role of the blogging APIs.

The Blogger API and XML-RPC

The first remote-posting protocol to gain wide adoption was the Blogger API. This was initially introduced as an experimental prototype specification but is currently supported by a large number of syndication tools, both client applications and server-side CMSs. It's based on XML-RPC (Remote Procedure Calls). Normally when your code includes procedure, function, or method calls, all the work is done in the local runtime system. With RPC the local system will call upon a remote system to do the work. Like its local counterpart, a remote procedure is called by name, and will often be passed one or more parameter values. With XML-RPC the details of the procedure call are wrapped up (marshaled) in an XML document, which is passed over HTTP to the remote system. The remote system will then unwrap the document to find the procedure name and parameters, call the requested procedure, and return any results (again marshaled as XML) back to the calling system. The basic idea is shown in Figure 26-5, although to keep things simple the path of any results from the procedure call isn't shown. The results go through a pipeline essentially the same as the forward path, with any return values from the procedure encoded in XML and passed back in the HTTP response body. This is then decoded and the actual values passed to the calling code. As far as the programmer is concerned, the XML-RPC calls behave as if they were local methods. The XML-RPC specification can be found at www.xmlrpc.com/spec.

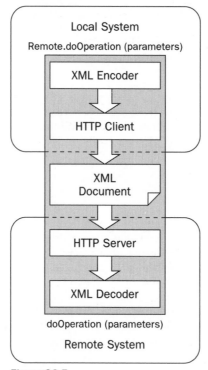

Figure 26-5

The Blogger API defines a set of XML-RPC interfaced procedures that a server can support to allow clients to modify their blogs using any client that supports those procedures. The Blogger API specification describes the available methods as follows:

❑   blogger.getUserInfo: Authenticates a user and returns basic user info (name, e-mail, userid, and so on).

- ❑ `blogger.newPost`: Makes a new post to a designated blog. Optionally, will publish the blog after making the post.

- ❑ `blogger.editPost`: Edits a given post. Optionally, will publish the blog after making the edit.

- ❑ `blogger.getUsersBlogs`: Returns information on all the blogs of which a given user is a member.

- ❑ `blogger.getTemplate`: Returns the main or archive index template of a given blog.

- ❑ `blogger.setTemplate`: Edits the main or archive index template of a given blog.

For an example of how the Blogger API and XML-RPC work, you will now see the kind of data that gets passed backward and forward when using the `blogger.getUserInfo` method. It will depend on the particular implementation, but from the point of view of calling code the method will look something like this:

```
struct blogger.getUserInfo(string appKey, string userName, string password)
```

The `appKey` is an identifier associated with the application making the call. The `userName` and `password` strings identify and provide authentication for the user at the target site. The return values will be a structure containing information about the user's accounts.

If you use a library that supports the Blogger API then you may be able to use a method like the previous one. If you use an XML-RPC library, it isn't much more difficult, you will have to provide the server details and then the types and values of each method parameter in turn. You will see code that will carry out this kind of encoding shortly, but first here is a sample of a method call encoded in XML:

```xml
<?xml version="1.0"?>
<methodCall>
  <methodName>blogger.getUsersBlogs</methodName>
  <params>
    <param>
      <value>
        <string>7367ffffffabffffff92</string>
      </value>
    </param>
    <param>
      <value>
        <string>jlambda</string>
      </value>
    </param>
    <param>
      <value>
        <string>fido</string>
      </value>
    </param>
  </params>
</methodCall>
```

The first thing of note (it's hard to miss) is that this is rather verbose compared to the one-line method call it represents. But terseness is of minimal importance in XML. What is generally considered important is that any structure in the data is made explicit in the XML document. Here the data is the method call, and it is clearly broken down into its structural parts in the XML. Note that order is significant in the method call, as the parameters aren't named. After the XML has been passed over HTTP, the XML document returned will look something like this:

```
<methodResponse>
  <params>
    <param>
      <value>
        <struct>
          <member>
            <name>nickname</name>
            <value>monad</value>
          </member>
          <member>
            <name>userid</name>
            <value>185155</value>
          </member>
          <member>
            <name>email</name>
            <value>joe.lambda@gmail.com</value>
          </member>
          <member>
            <name>url</name>
            <value>http://joelambda.com</value>
          </member>
          <member>
            <name>lastname</name>
            <value>Lambda</value>
          </member>
          <member>
            <name>firstname</name>
            <value>Joe</value>
          </member>
        </struct>
      </value>
    </param>
  </params>
</methodResponse>
```

The result has a root element of `methodResponse` and in it a list of (unnamed) parameters, like the method call. There is only one parameter here, the value of which is a more complex type, expressed as `<struct>` element. The `struct` here resembles the data structure of that name found in Pascal and other languages. It contains a series of name-value pairs, each pair being wrapped in a `<member>` element.

Although XML-RPC works well when everything works, errors can occur. There are quite a lot of places where errors may occur along the path of calling code to remote application and then back again. However, if the XML-RPC infrastructure is working correctly, then errors occurring at the remote end will be reported back to the client in much the same way that successful calls can return values. Here is an example of an error message:

```
<methodResponse>
  <fault>
    <value>
      <struct>
        <member>
          <name>faultString</name>
          <value>com.pyra.blogger.api.UserNotAuthorizedException:
                We're sorry but the Username/Password combination you've
```

```
                          entered is either invalid or you don't have permission to
                          access this Blog.
               </value>
            </member>
            <member>
              <name>faultCode</name>
              <value>
                 <int>0</int>
              </value>
            </member>
         </struct>
      </value>
   </fault>
</methodResponse>
```

This was returned after a call was made to blogger.com using the wrong password. The fact that it is a fault report is clear from the first inner element, <fault>. In addition to an (system-specific) error code, a helpful (and polite) human-readable message has also been provided, as you can see.

Command-Line Tool

The code that follows demonstrates client-side programming of a couple of basic functions using some of the leading Weblog protocols. For reasons of space the server side will not be covered in these listings. For the most part server components will be a direct reflection of the code here, attached to an HTTP server rather than a client.

Some of the source code will be modified after it's first presented — if you're working from a downloaded copy of the code, then be prepared to insert or remove comments as necessary. The code described here is contained in the following files:

- ❑   Account.cs: Holds user account details
- ❑   account.xml: Holds user account data
- ❑   Main.cs: Application entry point (various versions)
- ❑   BloggerClient.cs: Partial implementation of Blogger API
- ❑   MethodCall.cs: XML-RPC helper for Blogger API
- ❑   XmlRpcStruct.cs: XML-RPC helper for Blogger API
- ❑   AtomProtocol.cs: Implements the Atom newPost method
- ❑   AtomAPI.cs: Full implementation of the Atom API
- ❑   AtomAPI.cs: Ditto; see the following note
- ❑   BlogClient.exe: Compiled client (various versions)

Some of the code here is designed to work with pre-existing systems. There is a naming clash between the AtomAPI.cs source file used inside the Atomizer library and a file of the same name generated by the .NET wsdl.exe tool. Both include classes to implement the Atom Protocol, the Atomizer version covering the REST approach and the WSDL-generated version covering the SOAP approach. The classes described in these files are in separate .NET namespaces (packages) but it's easy to get the files mixed up, especially since the demonstration code here is all in the default namespace. You'll probably want something better structured when you're producing code for deployment, but for experimentation it's probably easiest to create two entirely separate folders, one for Atom/SOAP and one for Atom/REST.

You will now see some C# code that can retrieve information about a Weblog system user's account, which will then be extended to make it possible to post content to the blog. About a third of the code is devoted to what's needed for a minimal command-line application interface, another third is concerned with building the XML document describing the method call and the other third to the HTTP client functionality needed to pass the document over the wire. The code implements just enough XML-RPC functionality to provide basic Blogger API support.

The XML construction code listed in this chapter is generally built around DOM. There are other library classes for working with XML in C# that could have been used (notably XmlTextReader/ XmlTextWriter*). However DOM programming is very similar across languages, which means the code should be easier to port (and understand) without knowledge of any language-specific libraries.*

The following is the command-line interface part of the source, featuring the Main method that will act as the entry point into the application (Main.cs):

```
using System;
using System.Collections;

namespace DefaultNamespace {

    class MainClass {

        public static void Main(string[] args) {
            Account account = new Account();
            account.loadFromFile("account.xml");

            BloggerClient client = new BloggerClient();
            client.setTargetURI(account.postURI);

            Hashtable info =
        client.getUserInfo(account.appKey, account.userName, account.password);
            displayHashtable(info);
        }

        public static void displayHashtable(Hashtable hashtable){
            IDictionaryEnumerator enumerator = hashtable.GetEnumerator();

            while (enumerator.MoveNext()){
        Console.WriteLine("\t{0}:\t{1}", enumerator.Key, enumerator.Value);
            Console.WriteLine();
            }
        }
    }
}
```

The key part of this code is contained in the Main method, as follows:

```
            Account account = new Account();
            account.loadFromFile("account.xml");

            BloggerClient client = new BloggerClient();
```

```
        client.setTargetURI(account.postURI);

        Hashtable info =
    client.getUserInfo(account.appKey, account.userName, account.password);
        displayHashtable(info);
```

The `Account` object is used to contain basic details of the user's account. These will be loaded from a local file. The Blogger API interface is addressed through an instance of the `BloggerClient` class. The URI to which the data will be POSTed is passed to the client object, and then the method corresponding to `blogger.getUserInfo` is called. The returned values are placed in a `Hashtable`. Although C# does have a `struct` class, to support the XML-RPC construction it was convenient to generalize the returned results to a `Hashtable`, so it isn't necessary to know the names of individual fields in advance. The `displayHashtable` method does what its name suggests, listing the name-value pairs found in the `Hashtable`.

Handling Account Details

The most obvious, and in most circumstances probably the best way of representing user accounts, is as objects containing all the necessary information. Rather than hardcode user account details here, they will be loaded from a simple XML file. The `Account` class will include a facility to do this loading. The account data file will look something like this (`account.xml`):

```xml
<struct>
  <member>
    <name>postURI</name>
    <value>http://www.blogger.com/api/RPC2</value>
  </member>
  <member>
    <name>appKey</name>
    <value>7367ffffffabffffff92</value>
  </member>
  <member>
    <name>blogID</name>
    <value>8539727</value>
  </member>
  <member>
    <name>userName</name>
    <value>joelambda</value>
  </member>
  <member>
    <name>password</name>
    <value>epsilon</value>
  </member>
</struct>
```

Yes, the syntax is just like that of part of the XML-RPC format. It could have been done as a text file or better still an encrypted binary. But as code will be needed to make sense of this kind of XML-RPC construct anyway, that code might as well be reused.

So the code for handling these `<struct>` constructs can be found in `XmlRpcStruct.cs`. To build up a `<struct>`, regular DOM methods are used. To extract data from an existing `<struct>`, XPath-based queries are used. The approach to each is largely the same as you've seen in previous chapters, and in other languages such as PHP in Chapter 21. However, there may be multiple `<struct>` elements within a single XML-RPC document, and they appear in different places depending on the role of the document. So the position of a

<struct> block within a document will be determined elsewhere. Within this code the struct is built as an XmlDocumentFragment, which although associated with a particular document has no fixed position until it's given one. Here is the entire source code of XmlRpcStruct.cs:

```csharp
using System;
using System.Xml;
using System.Text;
using System.Net;
using System.IO;
using System.Collections;

namespace DefaultNamespace {

  public class XmlRpcStruct{

    private XmlDocumentFragment structFragment;
    private XmlDocument document;
    private XmlElement structElement;

    public XmlRpcStruct(XmlDocument document){
      this.document = document;
      this.structFragment = document.CreateDocumentFragment();
      structElement = document.CreateElement("struct");
      structFragment.AppendChild(structElement);
    }

    public override string ToString(){
      return structFragment.OuterXml.ToString();
    }

    public void addMember(string name, string type, string value){

      XmlElement memberElement = document.CreateElement("member");
      structElement.AppendChild(memberElement);

      XmlElement valueElement = document.CreateElement("value");

      memberElement.AppendChild(valueElement);
      XmlElement typeElement = document.CreateElement(type);
      valueElement.AppendChild(typeElement);

      typeElement.AppendChild(document.CreateTextNode(value));
    }

    public void setInnerXml(string xml){
      structFragment.InnerXml = xml;
    }

    public XmlDocumentFragment getFragment(){
      return structFragment;
    }

    public string getValue(string name){
      XmlNode named = structFragment.SelectSingleNode("//name[text()='"+name+"']");
      return getMemberValue(named);
```

```
      }

    public Hashtable getValues(){
      Hashtable hashtable = new Hashtable();
      string memberName;
      string memberValue;
      XmlNodeList namedNodes = structFragment.SelectNodes("//name");

      for (int i=0; i < namedNodes.Count; i++){
        memberName = namedNodes[i].InnerText;
       // uncomment for debugging
       // Console.WriteLine(memberName);
        memberValue = getMemberValue(namedNodes[i]);
        hashtable.Add(memberName, memberValue);
      }
      return hashtable;
    }


    public string getMemberValue(XmlNode named){
      XmlNode valueNode = named.NextSibling;
      XmlNode typeNode = valueNode.SelectSingleNode("*");
      string memberValue = "";
      if(typeNode != null){
        memberValue = typeNode.InnerText;
      }else{
        memberValue = valueNode.InnerText;
      }
      return memberValue;
    }
  }
}
```

The account data is managed using the following class (`Account.cs`):

```
using System;
using System.Xml;
using System.Text;
using System.Net;
using System.IO;

namespace DefaultNamespace {

  public class Account {
    public string postURI;
    public string appKey;
    public string blogID;
    public string userName;
    public string password;

    public Account(){
      postURI = "";
      appKey = "";
      blogID = "";
      userName = "";
```

```
      password = "";
    }

    public void loadFromFile(string filename){
      XmlDocument document = new XmlDocument();
      document.Load(filename);
      XmlRpcStruct accountStruct = new XmlRpcStruct(document);
      accountStruct.setInnerXml(document.SelectSingleNode("//struct").InnerXml);
      postURI = accountStruct.getValue("postURI");
      appKey = accountStruct.getValue("appKey");
      blogID = accountStruct.getValue("blogID");
      userName = accountStruct.getValue("userName");
      password = accountStruct.getValue("password");
    }
  }
}
```

Minimal XML-RPC Client

The encoding required here will take the method parameters and from them construct an XML document with <methodCall> as its root element. This will then be send (using POST) over HTTP to the appropriate endpoint address. The code that does this is as follows (MethodCall.cs):

```
using System;
using System.Xml;
using System.Text;
using System.Net;
using System.IO;

namespace DefaultNamespace {

  public class MethodCall {

    private XmlDocument document;
    private XmlElement paramsElement;

    public MethodCall(string name){
      document  = new XmlDocument();
      XmlElement root = document.CreateElement("methodCall");
      document.AppendChild(root);

      XmlElement methodNameElement = document.CreateElement("methodName");
      methodNameElement.AppendChild(document.CreateTextNode(name));
      root.AppendChild(methodNameElement);

      paramsElement = document.CreateElement("params");
      root.AppendChild(paramsElement);
    }

    public void addParam(string type, string value){
      XmlElement paramElement = document.CreateElement("param");
      paramsElement.AppendChild(paramElement);
```

```
        XmlElement valueElement = document.CreateElement("value");

        paramElement.AppendChild(valueElement);
        XmlElement typeElement = document.CreateElement(type);
        valueElement.AppendChild(typeElement);

        typeElement.AppendChild(document.CreateTextNode(value));
    }

    public Stream call(string uri){

        HttpWebRequest request =
          (HttpWebRequest)WebRequest.Create(uri);

        request.Method = "POST";
        byte [] bytes = null;

        bytes = System.Text.Encoding.UTF8.GetBytes (ToString());
        request.ContentLength = bytes.Length;

        Stream outputStream = request.GetRequestStream ();
        outputStream.Write (bytes, 0, bytes.Length);
        outputStream.Close ();

        WebResponse response = request.GetResponse();
        return response.GetResponseStream();
    }

    public override string ToString(){
        return document.DocumentElement.OuterXml.ToString();
    }
  }
}
```

Although the `XmlRpcStruct` and `MethodCall` hide much of the ugly details of XML-RPC implementation, they are still a step beyond the kind of simple method call that will be convenient to work with. So the following listing will bridge that gap, in the shape of the `BloggerClient` class:

```
using System;
using System.Xml;
using System.Text;
using System.Net;
using System.IO;
using System.Collections;


namespace DefaultNamespace{

  public class BloggerClient{
    string targetURI;

    public BloggerClient(){
    }

    public void setTargetURI(string targetURI){
```

```
        this.targetURI = targetURI;
    }

    public Hashtable getUserInfo(string appKey, string userName,
                                    string password){
        MethodCall call = new MethodCall("blogger.getUserInfo");
        call.addParam("string", appKey);
        call.addParam("string", userName);
        call.addParam("string", password);

        Stream responseStream = call.call(targetURI);

        XmlDocument responseDocument = new XmlDocument();

        responseDocument.Load(responseStream);

    // uncomment for debugging:
    //   Console.WriteLine(responseDocument.DocumentElement.OuterXml);

        responseStream.Close();

        XmlNode structNode =
responseDocument.SelectSingleNode("/methodResponse/params/param/value/struct");

        XmlRpcStruct infoStruct = new XmlRpcStruct(responseDocument);
        infoStruct.setInnerXml(structNode.InnerXml);

        return infoStruct.getValues();
    }

    private Hashtable extractStructValues(XmlDocument document){
        XmlNode structNode = document.SelectSingleNode("//struct");
        XmlRpcStruct xmlRpcStruct = new XmlRpcStruct(document);
        xmlRpcStruct.setInnerXml(structNode.InnerXml);
        return xmlRpcStruct.getValues();
    }


    }
}
```

Try It Out　　**Running the Blogger Client**

To try out this code you'll need to have Microsoft .NET SDK (or an equivalent such as Mono) installed. You will also need access to a server-side content management system that supports the Blogger API. This could be your own installation of one of the many available blogging systems such as WordPress or Movable Type, either local or on the Web. The company that gave the Blogger API its name offers free accounts that are very easy to set up and which follow the API specification (see www.blogger.com). Whatever you use for a test system, you will need to make a note of your user name and password.

If you create a Blogger account, you should also obtain your own application key to use with Blogger's servers; there's a simple form at:

```
http://www.blogger.com/developers/api/1_docs/register.html
```

If you use the code that follows with a different CMS, be sure and check the system's documentation for any deviation from the Blogger API specification. There are incompatible extensions in the wild.

1. Put the files containing the previous listings into the same folder and open a command prompt in that folder. To check everything's in place, enter the following:

```
dir /b
```

You should see this list:

```
Account.cs
account.xml
BloggerClient.cs
Main.cs
MethodCall.cs
XmlRpcStruct.cs
```

2. Now enter the following:

```
csc /out:BloggerClient.exe *.cs
```

This will compile the application code. You should see a response similar to the following:

```
C:\blogs\blogger>csc /out:BloggerClient.exe *.cs
Microsoft (R) Visual C# .NET Compiler version 7.10.3052.4
for Microsoft (R) .NET Framework version 1.1.4322
Copyright (C) Microsoft Corporation 2001-2002. All rights reserved.
C:\blogs\blogger>
```

If you do a dir, you should now see BloggerClient.exe listed.

3. Now open the file account.xml in a text editor. Replace the contents of the <value> elements corresponding to appKey, userName, and password with your own values.

Don't worry about the value for blogID; you'll see where that value comes from shortly. If you're not using Blogger to test the code then you will need to consult your system's documentation to find what it expects for appKey — an arbitrary value may be enough.

4. Enter the following command:

```
BloggerClient
```

You should see something like:

```
C:\blogs\blogger>BloggerClient

          url:     http://joelambda.blogspot.com/

          email:   joe.lambda@gmail.com

          userid:  4857681

          nickname:       monad

          firstname:      Joe

          lastname:       Lambda

C:\blogs\blogger>
```

These should correspond to the profile details you entered when creating the Blogger account.

Make a note of the value returned for userid; you'll need it later.

How It Works

The `Main` method in `Main.cs` was the entry point from the command-line execution. It begins by creating an instance of the `Account` class, and then loading the details from file:

```
Account account = new Account();
account.loadFromFile("account.xml");
```

The `Account` class firsts loads the `account.xml` file from disk into an instance of `XmlDocument` (in `Account.cs`):

```
XmlDocument document = new XmlDocument();
document.Load(filename);
```

The extraction of data as name/value pairs from the document is delegated to the `XmlRpcStruct` class, which is prepared by setting its internal reference to the a `<struct>` with the value returned from an XPath query on the XML document (in `Account.cs`):

```
XmlRpcStruct accountStruct = new XmlRpcStruct(document);
accountStruct.setInnerXml(document.SelectSingleNode("//struct").InnerXml);
```

Once the `XmlRpcStruct` instance has been lined up to the right place in the document, it's easy to get the required values (in `Account.cs`):

```
postURI = accountStruct.getValue("postURI");
appKey = accountStruct.getValue("appKey");
blogID = accountStruct.getValue("blogID");
userName = accountStruct.getValue("userName");
password = accountStruct.getValue("password");
```

So now the `Account` instance is ready with your account details. The member variables in `Account` are all public, so they can be accessed directly using, for example, `account.userName`. This and the rest of the account data will be used by an instance of `BloggerClient`, which is created next (in `Main.cs`):

```
BloggerClient client = new BloggerClient();
```

The URI for use in HTTP communications is handled separately from the other account details, and is passed to the client object to prepare it for operation (in `Main.cs`):

```
client.setTargetURI(account.postURI);
```

Now the client is ready to receive method calls, a call is made to its `getUserInfo` method, which implements the method of the same name in the Blogger API (in `Main.cs`):

```
Hashtable info =
    client.getUserInfo(account.appKey, account.userName, account.password);
```

The operations carried out by `BloggerClient` to get the info are in several stages. First of all an instance of the `MethodCall` class is created and loaded with suitable values. Internally the `MethodCall` class uses DOM to build up an XML document, but the methods it exposes directly relate to parts of the XML-RPC message (in `BloggerClient.cs`):

```
MethodCall call = new MethodCall("blogger.getUserInfo");
call.addParam("string", appKey);
call.addParam("string", userName);
call.addParam("string", password);
```

Once the XML-RPC document has been constructed within `MethodCall`, another method call can be used to pass the data to the server. Internally the `MethodCall` class uses an `HttpWebRequest` object to pass the request to the server, and a `WebResponse` object to handle the data returned over HTTP. This is all hidden in a single method call in `BloggerClient.cs`:

```
Stream responseStream = call.call(targetURI);
```

The body of the data returned from the server should be XML, so an `XmlDocument` instance is created to receive this, and the data streamed into it (in `BloggerClient.cs`):

```
XmlDocument responseDocument = new XmlDocument();

responseDocument.Load(responseStream);
responseStream.Close();
```

The XML-RPC data returned from a `blogger.getUserInfo` call will resemble that shown in the listing in the section "The Blogger API and XML-RPC" earlier this chapter, with a `<methodResponse>` element as root. If you refer back to that listing you will see the information of interest is contained within a `<struct>` element, so the work of extracting values is delegated to an `XmlRpcStruct` (the element being pointed to using an XPath expression), and finally the client returns those values as a `Hashtable` (in `BloggerClient.cs`):

```
XmlNode structNode =
responseDocument.SelectSingleNode("/methodResponse/params/param/value/struct");

XmlRpcStruct infoStruct = new XmlRpcStruct(responseDocument);
infoStruct.setInnerXml(structNode.InnerXml);

return infoStruct.getValues();
```

In `Main.cs` the `Hashtable` of name/value pairs returned is passed to a local method for console display:

```
displayHashtable(info);
```

Adding Post Support

Although the BloggerClient application demonstrated the XML-RPC call/answer sequence, it didn't really do anything very interesting. The next listing is a method that implements the `blogger.newPost` method, allowing you do post to a Blogger API-capable system from the command line. The source is as follows:

```
public Hashtable newPost(string appKey, string blogID,
        string userName, string password, string entryText, string publish){

    MethodCall call = new MethodCall("blogger.newPost");

    call.addParam("string", appKey);
    call.addParam("string", blogID);
    call.addParam("string", userName);
    call.addParam("string", password);
```

```
        call.addParam("string", entryText);
        call.addParam("boolean", publish);

        Stream responseStream = call.call(targetURI);
        XmlDocument responseDocument = new XmlDocument();
        responseDocument.Load(responseStream);

        Hashtable results;
        XmlNode fault = responseDocument.SelectSingleNode("//fault");

        if(fault != null){
    results = extractStructValues(responseDocument);
        } else {
    Console.WriteLine(responseDocument.DocumentElement.OuterXml);
    results = new Hashtable();
    string responseValue =
        responseDocument.SelectSingleNode("//value").InnerText;
    results.Add("value", responseValue);
        }
        return results;
    }
}
```

This is operationally the same as `blogger.getUserInfo`, except this method passes two more string parameters to the server: `entryText` and `publish`. The first will be the content of the blog post, and the second will have the (string) value `"true"` if the content should be published on the Web right away. The response data may signal a fault condition, if so this will be recognized using the `//fault` XPath expression and the whole XML document dumped to the console.

To run this extended client you will need to modify the `Main` method a little too. The following is a suitable approach:

```
...
client.setTargetURI(account.postURI);

if(args.Length == 0){
    Hashtable info = client.getUserInfo(account.appKey,
                            account.userName, account.password);
    displayHashtable(info);
}
if(args.Length == 1){
    Hashtable results = client.newPost(account.appKey, account.blogID,
        account.userName, account.password,
                                args[0], "1");
    displayHashtable(results);
}
```

To run the new mini-application you will first have to copy the appropriate `blogID` value into `account.xml`, recompile (as in the Try It Out section "Running the Blogger Client") and execute a command like this:

```
BloggerClient "Here is a new post"
```

Assuming there aren't any problems, after a moment the system should return with a single (long) number at the command line, the Blogger system ID for this new post. If you visit the blog on the Web you should see the content of your new post has been added to the site.

We encountered problems during code testing with the `getUserInfo` *derived* `blogID` *value with blogger.com—it didn't work. Check out the following blog on the Web:*

`www.blogger.com/app/blog.pyra?blogID=86125888`

MetaWeblog and other APIs

Many common tasks, such as giving posts a title, can't be done with the Blogger API. In response to this shortfall, MetaWeblog API (`www.xmlrpc.com/metaWeblogApi`) was released. This also uses XML-RPC and was designed to enhance the Blogger API. It has seen a moderate amount of adoption, and provides the following methods:

```
metaWeblog.newPost (blogid, username, password, struct, publish)
metaWeblog.editPost (postid, username, password, struct, publish)
metaWeblog.getPost (postid, username, password)
metaWeblog.newMediaObject (blogid, username, password, struct)
```

The methods are similar to those of the Blogger API, but allow for a more complex content payload to be delivered by passing it as a `struct` rather than a `string`. The `struct` will contain name/value pairs corresponding to those of the child elements of RSS 2.0's `<item>`, so, for example, including a `<title>` becomes possible. The `appkey` parameter has been dropped, which is a problem for server-side systems that rely on it for access control, notably Blogger.

There have been various extensions and variations of the XML-RPC approach to client posting, for example Movable Type have a set of methods of their own. A Blogger API 2.0 was slated, and then withdrawn as community development began on the Atom API (officially the Atom Publishing Protocol).

XML-RPC proved itself generally adequate for simple posting applications, but brought with it certain problems that were exacerbated when more sophisticated client-server interaction was required. The message going over the wire becomes significantly more complex and difficult to manage. The mapping between RSS 2.0 elements and the expression of its data in XML-RPC is convoluted, especially as the feed format can contain XML attributes and potentially namespace-qualified data from other vocabularies.

An additional downside to XML-RPC based APIs is their lack of security. Although security can be introduced by other means such as HTTPS, in their basic operation these transports deliver user credentials as plain text. This leaves an open door to password interception.

Atom Protocol

The IETF Atom Working Group Charter includes in its requirements an editing protocol. This is clearly aimed at overcoming the problems of its predecessors and encouraging greater standardization. As a group with open membership a wide range of preferences have been expressed. These include reusing or otherwise building on the XML-RPC techniques, using more industrial-strength Web Service tools such as SOAP and employing other relatively mature techniques such as WebDAV. However the greatest consensus has been around using more direct, REST-oriented HTTP techniques. The primary specification follows this technique, with allowance for the use of SOAP as required. The SOAP definition bears most similarity to the XML-RPC approach you've already seen, so that will be covered next.

Note that the WSDL-based technique described in the following section doesn't currently work with Blogger's services, or probably any other service. The underlying reason is that at the time of writing Atom isn't finished (it should be by March/April 2005). The blog hosting companies are likely to implement services that comply with the specification very soon after the specifications are stable. The code here generally describes how Atom 0.3 should work, and will need revision to work with Atom 1.0.

Atom Protocol, SOAP and WSDL

SOAP is similar to XML-RPC in that it enables communication between systems or services by wrapping instructions in an XML envelope. The request envelope is passed from one system to another (usually over HTTP) and a response is returned in a similar envelope. Again like XML-RPC, it is common to abstract the details of the transport itself into a programming API. But a key difference is that the definition of a service won't just be in human-readable prose, perhaps with syntax examples, but in a machine-readable form. The language used for this is WSDL, the Web Service Definition Language.

Here's a small snippet to give you a taste:

```
<operation name="POST">
  <soap:operation
        soapAction="http://schemas.xmlsoap.org/wsdl/http/POST" style="document" />
  <input>
<soap:body use="literal" />
<soap:header message="http:POSTSecurity" part="Security" use="literal" />
  </input>
  <output>
<soap:body use="literal" />
  </output>
</operation>
```

This particular snippet describes one small part of one particular operation, giving the data type of the input and output. WSDL and SOAP make widespread use of other XML technologies, notably namespaces and XML Schemas. Namespaces offer the versatility of vocabulary mixing while XML Schemas make it possible to tie down exactly what should be sent over the wire and how the receiver should interpret it at the level of datatypes.

After the service is defined in an unambiguous, machine-readable way, it makes it possible to auto-generate tools that can generate and read the format, as well as send and receive the message over the chosen transport. This means it is possible to create communication systems of fairly arbitrary complexity that will behave in a predictable fashion, including controlled error handling.

This elegantly sidesteps one of the critical problems of XML-RPC: the explosion in complexity of the transport format for even relatively minor extensions. You no longer care about the details of the transport format, rather you concentrate on the definition of the service and let tools do the work.

The details of the Atom API are in flux, and its WSDL/SOAP implementation is based on standard Web Service techniques that extend well beyond the scope of this book. But to get started in practice, there isn't all that much you need to know. The .NET SDK includes a WSDL tool. So get hold of the latest version of the Atom Protocol WSDL file and place it in a convenient directory. (You can find the latest Atom Protocol WSDL file at www.intertwingly.net/wiki/pie/FrontPage or by searching Randy Charles Morin's Weblog at www.kbcafe.com/iBLOGthere4iM/?search=atom+wsdl.) Open a command window in that directory and enter the following:

```
wsdl /out:AtomAPI.cs AtomAPI.wsdl
```

This will generate a C# file called AtomAPI.cs. This file provides classes in a similar vein to that of the XML-RPC classes for the Blogger API you saw previously, but with support for a much wider range of functionality. To simplify access to the protocol, it's possible again to hide much of the internal detail. The listing that follows (adapted from one of Sam Ruby's) just exposes a method, newPost, to operate in a similar manner to that of BloggerClient.cs.

The source for `AtomSoapClient.cs` is as follows:

```csharp
using System;
using System.Net;
using System.Security.Cryptography;
using System.Text;
using System.Web.Services.Protocols;
using System.Xml;
using System.Collections;

public class AtomSoapClient {
    string targetURI;

    public void setTargetURI(string targetURI){
        this.targetURI = targetURI;
    }

    public Hashtable newPost(string userName, string password,
                    string title, string entryText){

        // Create a blog entry
        entryType blog = new entryType();
        blog.issued = DateTime.Now;
        blog.title = title;

        // Author
        blog.author = new authorType();
        blog.author.name = "The Author";
        blog.author.url = "http://www.example.org/";

        // Generator
        blog.generator = new generatorType();
        blog.generator.url = "http://www.example.org";
        blog.generator.Value = "WSDL C# Client";

        // Fill in the content
        XmlDocument d = new XmlDocument();
        d.InnerXml = "<div xmlns='http://www.w3.org/1999/xhtml'>"+entryText+"</div>";
        blog.content = new contentType[1];
        blog.content[0] = new contentType();
        blog.content[0].mode = contentTypeMode.xml;
        blog.content[0].type = "application/xhtml+xml";
        blog.content[0].Any = new XmlNode[1];
        blog.content[0].Any[0] = d.DocumentElement;

        // Create an 'atom' authorization header
        Security auth = new Security();
        UsernameToken unt = new UsernameToken();
        auth.UsernameToken = new UsernameToken();
        auth.UsernameToken.Nonce = new Random().Next().ToString();
        auth.UsernameToken.Username=userName;
        auth.UsernameToken.Created=DateTime.Now.ToString("u").Replace(' ','T');

        // Fill in the password
```

```
        SHA1 md = new SHA1CryptoServiceProvider();
        string v = auth.UsernameToken.Nonce + auth.UsernameToken.Created + password;
        byte[] digest = md.ComputeHash(Encoding.Default.GetBytes(v));
        auth.UsernameToken.Password=new passwordType();
        auth.UsernameToken.Password.Value=Convert.ToBase64String(digest);
        auth.UsernameToken.Password.Type="wsse:PasswordDigest";
        auth.UsernameToken.Password.AnyAttr=new XmlAttribute[1];
        auth.UsernameToken.Password.AnyAttr[0]=d.CreateAttribute("wsse:placeholder",
           "http://schemas.xmlsoap.org/ws/2002/07/secext");
        Hashtable results = new Hashtable();
      try {
        // Post the request
        AtomAPI api = new AtomAPI();
        api.SecurityValue = auth;
        api.Url = targetURI;
        api.POST(ref blog);
      } catch (SoapException fault) {
        System.Console.WriteLine(fault.Message);
      } catch (WebException httpStatus) {
        System.Console.WriteLine(httpStatus.Message);
      }
      return results;
      }
    }
```

To run this client you'll need another adaptation of the `BloggerClient.cs` file, this time looking like this:

```
    public static void Main(string[] args) {
       Account account = new Account();
       account.loadFromFile("account.xml");

       AtomSoapClient client = new AtomSoapClient();
       Console.WriteLine(account.postURI);
       Console.WriteLine(account.userName);
       Console.WriteLine(account.password);
       client.setTargetURI(account.postURI);
       Hashtable results = client.newPost(account.userName, account.password,
                                    args[0], args[1]);

    }
```

You will need to save `AtomAPI.cs` and `Main.cs`, together with the WSDL-generated `AtomAPI.cs` in the same directory. In addition, the `Account` class is again used to look after user details, so you will also need `Account.cs` and appropriate source data in `account.xml`. To compile the classes, in a command window type:

```
   csc /out:BlogClient.exe *.cs
```

To run the mini-application, type:

```
   BlogClient "This has a Title" "Here is some content"
```

But as noted at the start of the section, until the services are implemented, this approach is very unlikely to work.

Atom Protocol — RESTful HTTP

The approach to Web services that meshes best with the REST architectural view of the Web is illustrated in a minimal form in Figure 26-6.

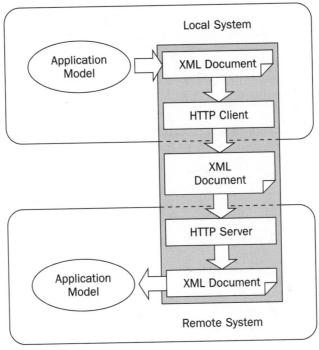

Figure 26-6

Here the format of the data passed over the wire is determined by the application itself. If, for example, you wanted to pass an OpenOffice Word Processor document from A to B, the format would be OpenOffice's own XML. If you look at the box labels here, you will see there is a clear simplification over the XML-RPC (and SOAP) approach — the XML corresponds directly to the application model, there is no encoding or decoding of the data to go over the wire. But what is missing here are the instructions to the receiver telling it what to do with the data. In the XML-RPC and SOAP versions this is all wrapped up inside the message. However those protocols are usually limited to HTTP POST operations, whereas in the more RESTful approach, the HTTP protocol does more of the work and a greater number of its verbs (GET, POST, PUT, DELETE, and so on) are employed. Figure 26-7 conveys this aspect of the RESTful approach. The small arrow between the Application Model and the HTTP Client/Server are really behavior related, suggested by server-side updates and client-side polling, which may be independent of the XML documents that are passed around.

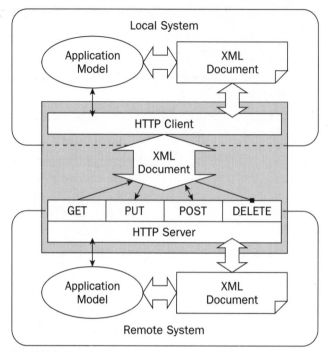

Figure 26-7

What Figure 26-7 doesn't show is that multiple URIs will be used in the communication, each corresponding (in combination with the HTTP method) to the required operation.

The following snippet of code uses the Atomizer library to create RESTful Atom Protocol calls:

```
using Atomizer;
...
class MainClass {
      public static void Main(string[] args) {
          Account account = new Account();
          account.loadFromFile("account.xml");

            generatorType generator = new generatorType();
          generator.url = "http://www.winisp.net/dstewartms/atomizer";
          generator.Value = "AtomizerSample";
          generator.version = "1.7";

          Atom atom =
                        Atom.Create(new Uri(account.postURI),
                        generator, account.userName, account.password);
              service[] services = atom.GetServices();
              foreach (service serviceObject in services) {
              Console.WriteLine(serviceObject);
              Console.WriteLine(serviceObject.srvType);
              Console.WriteLine(serviceObject.postURL);
          }
      }
}
```

The result from running this code is a list of services; the one of particular interest here will look something like:

```
AtomTestBlog
post
http://www.typepad.com/t/atom/weblog/blog_id=64253
```

The URI is the endpoint for POST operations:

```
c:\BlogClient>BlogClient "Title of My Post" "Content of My Post"

alternate:
http://danja.typepad.com/atomtestblog/2004/10/title_of_my_pos.html

service.edit:
    http://www.typepad.com/t/atom/weblog/blog_id=64253/entry_id=2298145
```

Building Your Own Atomic Device

We can't go into every detail of the Atom Protocol or its implementation in Atomizer in this book. However, the basic principles are relatively straightforward.

The message looks like this:

```
<atom:entry atom:version="0.3" xmlns:atom="http://purl.org/atom/ns#">
  <atom:generator
atom:version="0.01">http://example.org#TestAtomClient</atom:generator>
  <atom:title>Titlley</atom:title>
  <atom:issued>2004-10-04T10:58:18Z</atom:issued>
  <atom:content atom:mode="escaped" type="text/html">Connnntentet</atom:content>
</atom:entry>
```

The response looks like this:

```
<?xml version="1.0"?>
<entry xmlns="http://purl.org/atom/ns#">
  <title>Titlley</title>
  <summary/>
  <content mode="xml">
    <div xmlns="http://www.w3.org/1999/xhtml">Connnntentet</div>
  </content>
  <issued>2004-10-04T03:58:18Z</issued>
  <link type="text/html" rel="alternate"
href="http://danja.typepad.com/atomtestblog/2004/10/titlley_
21.html" title=""/>
  <id>tag:typepad.com,2003:post-2298094</id>
  <link type="application/x.atom+xml" rel="service.edit"
 href="http://www.typepad.com/t/atom/weblog/blog_id=64253/entry_id=2298094"
 title="Titlley"/>
</entry>
```

The code of `Main.cs` will need to be modified yet again to include something like this:

```
AtomProtocolClient client = new AtomProtocolClient();
client.setTargetURI(account.postURI);
Hashtable results = client.newPost(account.userName, account.password,
                                   args[0], args[1]);
displayHashtable(results);
```

The source of `AtomProtocolClient.cs`, which describes the `AtomProtocolClient` class, is as follows:

```
using System;
using System.Xml;
using System.IO;
using System.Text;
using System.Security.Cryptography;
using System.Net;
using System.Collections;
using System.Globalization;


namespace DefaultNamespace {

  public class AtomProtocolClient {

    string targetURI;
    string ATOM_NS = "http://purl.org/atom/ns#";
    string NS_PREFIX = "atom";

    string GENERATOR_URI = "http://example.org#TestAtomClient";
    string GENERATOR_VERSION = "0.01";

    public void setTargetURI(string targetURI){
      this.targetURI = targetURI;
    }

    public AtomProtocolClient(){
    }

    public Hashtable newPost(string userName, string password,
                             string title, string content){
      Hashtable results = new Hashtable();
      HttpWebRequest request = (HttpWebRequest)HttpWebRequest.Create(targetURI);

      // headers
      request.UserAgent     = GENERATOR_URI;

      request.ContentType   = "application/xml";
      request.Method        = "POST";

      //set up the password encryption
      string xwsse = getXWSSEHeader(userName, password);
      request.Headers.Add("X-WSSE", xwsse);

      Stream newStream = request.GetRequestStream();

      XmlDocument entryDoc = CreateAtomDOM(title, content);
```

```
    entryDoc.Save(newStream);

    newStream.Flush();
    newStream.Close();

    HttpWebResponse response = (HttpWebResponse)request.GetResponse();

    if (response.StatusCode != HttpStatusCode.Created){
      response.Close();
      throw(new WebException(response.StatusDescription));
    }
    XmlDocument responseDoc = new XmlDocument();

    responseDoc.Load(response.GetResponseStream());

    response.Close();

    XmlNamespaceManager xmlnsManager =
            new XmlNamespaceManager(responseDoc.NameTable);
    xmlnsManager.AddNamespace("atom", ATOM_NS);

    XmlNodeList links =
      responseDoc.SelectNodes("/atom:entry/atom:link", xmlnsManager);

    foreach (XmlElement linkElement in links){
      results.Add(linkElement.GetAttribute("rel"),
                  linkElement.GetAttribute("href"));
    }
    return results;
}

private XmlDocument CreateAtomDOM(string title, string content) {
    XmlDocument document  = new XmlDocument();
    // Create an XML declaration.

    XmlElement root = document.CreateElement(NS_PREFIX, "entry", ATOM_NS);
    document.AppendChild(root);

    XmlDeclaration xmldecl = document.CreateXmlDeclaration("1.0", null, null);
    xmldecl.Encoding="UTF-8";
    document.InsertBefore(xmldecl, root);

    root.SetAttribute("version", ATOM_NS, "0.3");

    XmlElement generator =
            document.CreateElement(NS_PREFIX, "generator", ATOM_NS);
    root.AppendChild(generator);
    generator.SetAttribute("version", ATOM_NS,  GENERATOR_VERSION);
    generator.AppendChild(document.CreateTextNode(GENERATOR_URI));

    XmlElement titleElement =
            document.CreateElement(NS_PREFIX, "title", ATOM_NS);
    root.AppendChild(titleElement);
    titleElement.AppendChild(document.CreateTextNode(title));

    XmlElement issuedElement =
```

```
            document.CreateElement(NS_PREFIX, "issued", ATOM_NS);
        root.AppendChild(issuedElement);
        issuedElement.AppendChild(document.CreateTextNode(getDateTimeString()));

        XmlElement contentElement =
                document.CreateElement(NS_PREFIX, "content", ATOM_NS);
        root.AppendChild(contentElement);
        contentElement.SetAttribute("mode", ATOM_NS, "escaped");
        contentElement.SetAttribute("type", "text/html"); //??
        contentElement.AppendChild(document.CreateTextNode(content));
        return document;
    }

    public string getXWSSEHeader(string username, string password) {
        string nonce = new Random().Next().ToString(CultureInfo.InvariantCulture);
        string created = getDateTimeString();

        // Fill in the password
        SHA1 sha1 = new SHA1CryptoServiceProvider();
        string raw = nonce + created + password;
        byte[] digest = sha1.ComputeHash(Encoding.Default.GetBytes(raw));
        string password64 = Convert.ToBase64String(digest);
        string nonce64 = Convert.ToBase64String(Encoding.Default.GetBytes(nonce));

        return "UsernameToken Username=\""+
            username+"\", "+
            "PasswordDigest=\""+
            password64+"\", "+
            "Nonce=\""+
            nonce64+"\", "+
            "Created=\""+
            created+"\"";

    }

    public string getDateTimeString(){
        return DateTime.UtcNow.ToString("u",CultureInfo.InvariantCulture)
                        .Replace(' ','T');
    }
  }
}
```

If you compile and run this code as a command-line application (as in the Try It Out section: "Running the Blogger Client"), and then load your target blog in a browser, you should see something like Figure 26-8.

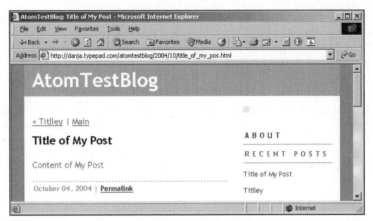

Figure 26-8

Other Formats, Transports, and Protocols

The Blogger API, the MetaWeblog API, and a handful of proprietary methods and extensions are currently supported by quite a range of blogging-oriented CMSs. Another protocol in this domain is the LiveJournal API, which is a simple non-XML text-based protocol that uses HTTP in a direct fashion. A growing number of systems are supporting the Atom Protocol, even before it's finished. It seems likely that when this specification is finalized it will become the standard for communication with Weblogs, and probably also for a wider range of systems that require a relatively simple but well-defined protocol for content transmission and editing.

There are quite a number of formats, transports, and protocols near to the Weblog/HTTP domain that are also worth a mention, especially as they have all contributed to a greater or lesser extent to the development of Atom.

Jabber/XMPP

Jabber (www.jabber.org) is the popular name for systems based around the IETF-developed XMPP (Extensible Messaging and Presence Protocol) and related protocols. The primary application of this is in instant messaging, along the lines of the AIM, ICQ, MSN, and Yahoo! systems. There are certain key differences from the other IM protocols — the specifications are free, open, and based on (streaming) XML. Aside from there being general overlap with syndication technologies, there is already direct crossover in the form of virtual real-time syndication. The technique is described in an IETF draft entitled "Transporting Atom Syndication Data over the XMPP PubSub Extension" (www.xmpp.org). This is implemented by PubSub.com and supported by their plug-in for Internet Explorer/Firefox as well as in the Gush aggregator (www.2entwine.com/).

WebDAV

WebDAV stands for Web-based Distributed Authoring and Versioning (www.webdav.org). It is specified in a series of RFCs. Basically it is a set of extensions to the HTTP protocol that enables users to collaboratively edit and manage files on remote Web servers. The extensions primarily take the form of a dozen or so new methods to be used alongside GET, POST, and so on. These systematically allow handling of the details of pages (properties), sets of documents (collections), prevention of concurrent-editing problems using locking and various namespace operations. Although its use is far from ubiquitous, WebDAV is mature and in widespread use. DeltaV is an associated protocol that adds versioning capabilities that provide greater control of site changes.

Annotea

Annotea is a W3C project aiming to enhance collaboration on the Web using annotations and bookmarks (`www.w3.org/2001/Annotea/`). The techniques used make it possible to associate private or public notes to any Web pages without having to edit the pages themselves. The protocol is based around HTTP, XML, and RDF and has a lot in common with the blogging protocols. Although not widely deployed, a mature server implementation is available and the W3C's testbed Web browser Amaya implements client capabilities.

InterWiki

InterWiki (`http://c2.com/cgi/wiki?InterWiki`) is the idea of having one unified Wiki system distributed across many servers. In practice this remains something of a dream, thanks to the diversity of Wikis (and WikiSyntax). However there has been a practical side to discussions about standard protocols for communication between systems. The Atom Protocol is one avenue of research. Another is the use of a metadata-enriched profile of XHTML (`www.altheim.com/specs/iwml/`).

Usenet, E-mail, and Friends

Last, but hardly least, it's worth remembering that there are various other fully specified systems that were well deployed long before RSS or even the Web saw the light of day. E-mail systems, in particular subscription-based mailing lists and newsletters, can also fulfill much of the same requirements as RSS and Atom syndication. The rise of spam has in some cases had a crippling effect on the practicality of these systems. Another drawback is the fact that these systems are built around transports other than HTTP, which means that interoperability with other Web systems requires some form of bridging mechanism. There have been claims that RSS will replace e-mail — that seems extremely unlikely, although the e-mail newsletter at least for now has very strong competition. Perhaps a better way of viewing the situation is that syndication languages make it possible, often easy, to create new systems that can do things that would be difficult or even inconceivable with previous technologies.

Summary

In this chapter you saw an overview of various techniques for posting data from a client to a syndication-friendly server. You saw descriptions of the following:

❏ General client-server architectures for editing

❏ HTTP's role in editing protocols

❏ XML-RPC and the Blogger API

❏ The Atom Protocol in its SOAP and RESTful forms

❏ A quick overview of related protocols

Exercise

1. Add code to `BlogClient.cs` that will implement the `blogger.editPost` method.

Building Your Own Planet

This chapter is tied to one of the core notions of syndication, aggregation. The word's dictionary definition in this context suggests collection and accumulation of data from information feeds. This is still a useful definition, but to date the primary job of the tools known as aggregators has been to collect and display feed data; accumulation of that data is a secondary consideration. The feed-fed desktop personal knowledgebase is still a ways off, but tools such as blog-oriented search engines are making use of longer-term persistence of feed data. A different kind of online application that comes under the umbrella has emerged: software that will automatically collect feed data from a set of sources and republish it as a new feed or Weblog in its own right. This chapter provides a brief discussion of the role of these systems, followed by the implementation of such a system that builds on the code of Chapters 22 and 23.

In this chapter, you learn:

- ❏   Why server-side aggregation is useful
- ❏   About an overview of the Planet style of aggregator
- ❏   About code for such an aggregator
- ❏   About source-related requirements for such an aggregator

Why Aggregate?

This may seem like a redundant question in this book, but it's worth asking. Syndication technologies are making major changes in not only the way people use the Web, but also how they perceive it. Much of the early Web was static in the sense that the contents of sites changed little. Although news-oriented sites have been around since the early days, blogs and other rapidly changing sites now form a significant proportion of the Web as a whole. Syndication lies somewhere in between old-fashioned semi-static home pages and instant messaging. For at least some users of the Web this aspect is the most significant, with the Weblog medium being the Internet's democratized answer to television soap operas. However, like television the content that is distributed can be entertaining, educational, and informative. The users have access to a huge amount of data. But the vast majority of the data will not be of interest to them. Random feed subscription is like drinking from a very big fire hose; somehow the pipe has to be narrowed and the pressure reduced.

Planet Core

The essential operations of a Planet-style aggregator can be summarized as follows:

- ❑ Get feeds
- ❑ Extract and accumulate items
- ❑ Select recent items
- ❑ Format and write output

It's worth looking at existing implementations to see how other people have approached the task. Here are three open-source examples:

- ❑ Planet Planet, the application behind Planet Gnome and Planet Debian, uses the (Python) Universal Feed Parser (`http://sourceforge.net/projects/feedparser/`) to get and parse feeds using the file system as a cache. It uses the htmltmpl: templating engine (`http://htmltmpl.sourceforge.net/`) for output.

- ❑ The Chumpologica aggregator (`www.hackdiary.com/projects/chumpologica`), used by Planet XMLHack and Planet RDF, is built with Python and uses the Redland RDF toolkit, with XSLT output styling. It also uses the Universal Feed Parser followed by HTML Tidy for cleaning item content.

- ❑ Urchin (`http://urchin.sourceforge.net`) is used by the Nature Publishing Group for aggregation of its own scientific publication data alongside that found in the wild. It's built around standard Perl modules and can use XSL transformations or HTML::Template on its output. It also features a long-term data store using MySQL. The Mindswap group (`www.mindswap.org/`) has built a variation that replaces MySQL with the Kowari RDF store as a queryable knowledgebase.

Since construction of the original Planets, Redland (specifically Raptor, the parser toolkit it uses [`http://librdf.org/raptor/`]) gained support for Atom and "tag soup" RSS 2.0 parsing. This should significantly simplify the construction of any future Planets, as well as offering potential as a feed normalizer (to RSS 1.0) subsystem.

Figure 27-1 shows the key parts of a Planet style aggregate-republish system. The shaded block on the left may look familiar — this is essentially the same feed aggregation system described in Chapters 22 and 23.

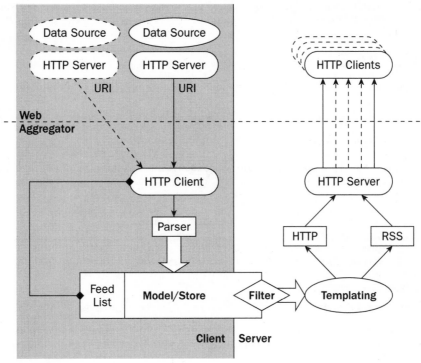

Figure 27-1

Implementing a Planet

You've already seen most of the code needed to obtain feed data for a Planet aggregator in Chapters 22 and 23. However, the feed-fetching code we discuss in those chapters only goes as far as getting minimal information out of the source data; we skipped certain aspects essential for a Planet aggregator.

During our discussion of the modeling of feed data in Chapter 20, we highlight the item-oriented approach as the key to aggregation. One function this allows is the removal of items that may be considered duplicates. The item-oriented approach also enables the subscribe-republish aggregator to sort items or entries by date so that only the most recent are shown, irrespective of the time of the last feed-level update. This functionality calls for the feed parsing subsystem to extract item identifiers and dates. To display the aggregated data, references back to the sites from which the items came is also desirable. This information is provided at the feed-level in the XML.

The code we develop in Chapters 22 and 23 simply dumps items in a list without any consideration for redundant or out-of-date information as items are extracted from feeds. More control is needed over the items, and this needs extra work on the existing code, addressing the areas corresponding to Model/Store and Filter in Figure 27-1.

After the left (client, consumer) side of the system has been assembled, templating will be provided in the form of XSLT style sheets and a class that will apply those style sheets and serialize the data to file.

Extending the Entry

The additional information that will be extracted from feeds is highlighted in bold in the following listing:

```
<rss version="2.0">
    <channel>
        <title>Jane's News</title>
        <language>en</language>
        <link>http://example.org/lambda/index.html</link>
        <author>Jane Lambda</author>
        <item>
            <title>Puss in Boots</title>
            <link>http://example.org/lambda/puss.html</link>
            <description>Today our cat got some new shoes.</description>
            <pubDate>Tue, 03 Jun 2004 09:39:21 GMT</pubDate>
            <guid>http://example.org/lambda/puss.html</guid>
        </item>
    </channel>
</rss>
```

The first step in adding this support is at model level. Individual items are managed using `Entry` objects. The interface that defines these items needs to be extended. Here is the source of `Entry.java` with the necessary additions:

```
package org.urss.feeds;

public interface Entry extends FeedEntity {

    public void setContent(String content);

    public String getContent();

    // added for Planet
    public void setSourceTitle(String feedTitle);

    public String getSourceTitle();

    public void setSourceLink(String feedLink);

    public String getSourceLink();

    public void setAuthor(String author);

    public String getAuthor();
}
```

The values will come from the source feed of each particular entry. The `Entry` implementation is fairly trivial, and the additions called for to support the interface are three member variables with GET/SET methods. Here is the new material for `EntryImpl.java`:

```
package org.urss.feeds;

public class EntryImpl extends FeedEntityBase implements Entry {

... existing code

    // added for Planet

    private String sourceTitle;

    private String sourceLink;

    private String author;

    public void setSourceTitle(String sourceTitle) {
        this.sourceTitle = sourceTitle;
    }

    public String getSourceTitle() {
        return sourceTitle;
    }

    public void setSourceLink(String sourceLink) {
        this.sourceLink = sourceLink;
    }

    public String getSourceLink() {
        return sourceLink;
    }

    public void setAuthor(String author) {
      this.author = author;
    }

    public String getAuthor() {
        return author;
    }
}
```

The entries will again be accumulated in a list, but with a few enhancements (to EntryList and EntryListImpl).

This Planet implementation will reuse the interpreter and parser architecture you saw in Chapter 23. To keep things simple, for the purposes of demonstration this code will use the SoupParser and Rss2Handler configuration. Modifications are needed to the Rss2Handler class to pick up the extra feed data to spot duplicate items and to sort by date. Those pieces of data will be retained in member variables, which are declared at the start of Rss2Handler.java.

```
public class Rss2Handler extends DefaultHandler {
    // added for Planet
    private String sourceURI = "";

    private String sourceTitle = "";
```

```
      private String author = "";

... existing code
```

The modified methods with `Rss2Handler` are as follows:

```
      public void startElement(String namespaceURI, String localName,
              String qName, Attributes attributes) {

... existing code

          case IN_CHANNEL:
//            added for Planet
              textBuffer = new StringBuffer();
              if ("item".equals(localName)) {
                  state = IN_ITEM;
                  entry = new EntryImpl();
//                added for Planet
                  entry.setAuthor(author);
                  entry.setSourceTitle(feedTitle);
                  entry.setSourceLink(feedLink);
              }
              return;

... existing code
      }
```

The `startElement` method is called when the parser encounters an opening tag in the feed XML. The differences are that the buffer that will contain the text within elements is now reinitialized for every element found inside the channel level, and certain values are pushed to any newly created entry that appears within the channel. Those values are extracted in the `endElement` method, which also includes extra conditionals to recognize and extract additional data found at the item level:

```
      public void endElement(String namespaceURI, String localName, String qName) {

          switch (state) {

          case IN_NOTHING:
              return;

          case IN_CHANNEL: // switch down
              if ("channel".equals(localName)) {
                  state = IN_NOTHING;
              }

              // added for Planet
              if ("title".equals(localName)) {
                  feedTitle = textBuffer.toString();
                  return;
              }
              if ("author".equals(localName)) {
                  author = textBuffer.toString();
                  return;
              }
```

```
        if ("link".equals(localName)) {
            feedLink = textBuffer.toString();
            return;
        }
        return;

    case IN_ITEM:
        if ("item".equals(localName)) {
            state = IN_CHANNEL;
            entries.addEntry(entry);
            return;
        }
        if ("title".equals(localName)) {
            entry.setTitle(textBuffer.toString());
            return;
        }
        if ("description".equals(localName)) {
            entry.setContent(textBuffer.toString());
            return;
        }
        // added for Planet
        if ("guid".equals(localName)) {
            entry.setURIString(textBuffer.toString());
            return;
        }
        if ("pubDate".equals(localName)) {
            entry.setDate(textBuffer.toString());
            return;
        }

        if ("link".equals(localName)) {
            entry.setLink(textBuffer.toString());
            return;
        }
        textBuffer.append(localName);
        return;

    default:
        return;
    }
}
```

Note that each `Entry` object will get its `uriString` value set with the value contained in `<guid>` elements. This is less than ideal, as that value may not actually be a URI. The code that will use this value only uses it as an identifier for local data, and doesn't actually care if it's a URI or not, so this isn't such a terrible approximation.

Entry Collection

The class that will accumulate the entries implements the `EntryList` interface. The requirements for the Planet application are fairly generic and likely to be reused, so it's not unreasonable to extend the interface a little. The extra method here is `trimList`, which will reduce the list of items down to the required number required for display. The full source of `EntryList.java` is as follows:

```
package org.urss.feeds;

public interface EntryList {

    public void addEntry(Entry entry);

    public int size();

    public Entry getEntry(int i);

    // added for Planet
    public void trimList(int trimSize);
}
```

The revised implementation of EntryList includes two helper methods as well as trimList, the full source looking like this (in EntryListImpl.java):

```
package org.urss.feeds;

import java.util.ArrayList;
import java.util.HashSet;
import java.util.List;
import java.util.Set;

import org.urss.planet.EntryDateSorter;

public class EntryListImpl implements EntryList {

    private List entries;

    public EntryListImpl() {
        entries = new ArrayList();
    }

    public void addEntry(Entry entry) {
        entries.add(entry);
    }

    public int size() {
        return entries.size();
    }

    public Entry getEntry(int i) {
        return (Entry) entries.get(i);
    }

    // added for Planet
    public void trimList(int trimSize) {
        removeDuplicates();
        sort();
        if (trimSize > size()) {
            return;
        }
        entries.subList(trimSize - 1, size() - 1).clear();
```

```
        }

    public void removeDuplicates() {
        Set entryIDs = new HashSet();
        String id;
        for (int i = entries.size()-1; i == 0; i--) {
            id = ((Entry) entries.get(i)).getURIString();
            if (entryIDs.contains(id)) {
                entries.remove(i);
            }
            entryIDs.add(id);
        }
    }

    public void sort() {
        EntryDateSorter.sort(entries);
    }
}
```

The `trimList` method initially calls `removeDuplicates`, which steps through the items, extracting each `uriString` value and adding it to a `Set`. If a value is already found in the `Set` then the corresponding item will be removed from the accumulated list of entries. Note that this checking is done in reverse order, as the most recent (and hence required) items will appear later in the list. A bonus is that this also avoids reindexing remaining parts of the list as items are deleted.

The `sort` method delegates to a utility class that you will see in a moment. After duplicates have been removed and the list sorted according to reverse-chronological order, the list is cropped using the handy idiom of clearing the latter part of the list with `entries.subList().clear()`.

To sort the items by date it is necessary to look inside each item to read its date. This demonstration only deals with the "Simple" RSS family of formats, which gives each item a `<pubDate>` element, the value of which is expressed as an RFC 822 date format, for example, `Tue, 15 Jun 2004 02:02:03 GMT`. These values can't be compared directly (string sorting won't work), but Java provides the `SimpleDateFormat` class that can be used to parse these dates into `Date` objects that can be compared. Badly formatted dates aren't uncommon in the wild, so if a parsing error occurs, then the date for a particular item is defaulted back to the date a week (or 604,800,000 milliseconds) ago. Java has the facility to sort lists according to implementations of the `Comparator` class, which requires the single compare method. The `EntryDateSorter` class implements this, and uses a singleton instance of itself in the static `sort` method, which delegates to Java's sorting mechanism in `Collection.sort`.

The source for `EntryDateSorter` is as follows:

```
package org.urss.planet;

import java.text.SimpleDateFormat;
import java.util.Collections;
import java.util.Comparator;
import java.util.Date;
```

```
import java.util.List;

import org.urss.feeds.Entry;

public class EntryDateSorter implements Comparator {

    private final SimpleDateFormat RFC822 = new SimpleDateFormat(
            "EEE, d MMM yyyy HH:mm:ss z");

    private Date fallbackDate = new Date(System.currentTimeMillis() - 604800000);

    private static EntryDateSorter dateComparator = new EntryDateSorter();

    public static void sort(List unsorted) {
        Collections.sort(unsorted, dateComparator);
    }

    public int compare(Object objectA, Object objectB) {
        String dateStringA = ((Entry) objectA).getDate();
        String dateStringB = ((Entry) objectB).getDate();
        Date dateA;
        Date dateB;
        try {
            dateA = RFC822.parse(dateStringA);
        } catch (Exception eA) {
            dateA = fallbackDate;
            eA.printStackTrace();
        }
        try {
            dateB = RFC822.parse(dateStringB);
        } catch (Exception eB) {
            dateB = fallbackDate;
            eB.printStackTrace();
        }
        return dateB.compareTo(dateA); // reverse-chrono
    }
}
```

Top-Level Runner

The listing so far, on top of the code described in Chapters 22 and 23, is enough to build a trimmed, reverse-chronological list of item objects downloaded and extracted from a given set of feeds. This is what's required of the left side in Figure 27-1. You will shortly see the code that will look after the right side of Figure 27-1, serializing and formatting those items according to templates. However, before looking at that code, you may want to look at the class that binds the application together, Planet.java, for a better understanding of what's going on here. This is essentially a modified and extended variation of the Runner.java and Runner2.java listings that appear in Chapters 22 and 23. Some explanation will follow, but here is the full source of Planet.java:

```
package org.urss.planet;

import java.util.Iterator;
import java.util.Set;

import org.urss.feeds.EntryList;
```

```
import org.urss.feeds.EntryListImpl;
import org.urss.feeds.FeedConstants;
import org.urss.feeds.FeedFetcher;
import org.urss.feeds.FeedFetcherImpl;
import org.urss.feeds.FeedSet;
import org.urss.feeds.FeedSetImpl;
import org.urss.io.OpmlSetReader;
import org.urss.io.Interpreter;
import org.urss.parsers.InterpreterFactory;

public class Planet {

    static int REFRESH_PERIOD = 10000; // milliseconds

    static int MAX_ITEMS = 5;

    static EntryList entries = new EntryListImpl(); //++

    public static void main(String[] args) {
        Planet planet = new Planet();
        Set channelURIs = planet.loadChannelList("input/feedlist.opml");
        FeedSet feeds = planet.initFeeds(channelURIs);
        FileEntrySerializer serializer = new FileEntrySerializer();
        serializer.loadDocumentShell("input/shell.xml");

        while (true) {
            feeds.refreshAll();
            //    displayStatus(feeds);

            entries.trimList(MAX_ITEMS);

          serializer.clearEntries();

            for (int i = 0; i < entries.size(); i++) {
                serializer.addEntry(entries.getEntry(i));
            }
            System.out.println("Writing RSS 2.0...");
            serializer.write("output/rss.xml");
            System.out.println("Writing HTML...");
            serializer.transformWrite("output/index.html",
                    "templates/rss2html.xslt");
            System.out.println("Writing RSS 1.0...");
            serializer.transformWrite("output/feed.rdf",
                    "templates/feed-rss1.0.xsl");
        }
    }

    public Set loadChannelList(String filename) {
        OpmlSetReader reader = new OpmlSetReader();
        return reader.load(filename);
    }

    public FeedSet initFeeds(Set channelURIs) {
        FeedSet feeds = new FeedSetImpl();
        Iterator channelIterator = channelURIs.iterator();
        FeedFetcher feedFetcher;
```

```
            Interpreter interpreter;
            String uriString;
            while (channelIterator.hasNext()) {
                uriString = (String) channelIterator.next();
                feedFetcher = new FeedFetcherImpl(uriString);
                interpreter = InterpreterFactory.createInterpreter(
                        FeedConstants.RSS2_BOZO, entries);
                feedFetcher.setInterpreter(interpreter); // ++
                feedFetcher.setRefreshPeriod(REFRESH_PERIOD);
                feeds.addFeed(feedFetcher);
            }
            return feeds;
        }

    private static void displayStatus(FeedSet feeds) {
        Iterator feedIterator = feeds.getFeedCollection().iterator();
        while (feedIterator.hasNext()) {
            System.out.println(((FeedFetcher) feedIterator.next()).getStatus());
        }
        System.out.println("----------------");
        for (int i = 0; i < entries.size(); i++) {
            System.out.println(entries.getEntry(i));
        }
    }
}
}
```

The class begins with a couple of constants, one of which dictates the period between feed refreshes. For demonstration purposes this has been set artificially low — for live use this must be increased to a value of 3600000 seconds (1 hour) or greater, unless you really want to make yourself unpopular with feed publishers.

MAX_ITEMS is the number of individual items that should be retained for publication or display from the combined feeds. In practice, a figure of around 15 to 30 is probably more desirable, but 5 is large enough to check everything works. As in the previous Runner code, the entries will be placed in an EntryList, one of which is created here:

```
public class Planet {

    static int REFRESH_PERIOD = 10000; // milliseconds

    static int MAX_ITEMS = 5;

    static EntryList entries = new EntryListImpl();
```

The main method is the application starter and ties everything together. It begins by making an instance of the Planet class. Next a Set of URIs is loaded from file with the help of the loadChannelList method (listed next). These are the addresses of the source feeds. Another local method, initFeeds, is then called to set up the FeedFetcher object that will be responsible for obtaining the feed data, along with the interpreters that will extract the data from the feeds.

```
public static void main(String[] args) {
    Planet planet = new Planet();
    Set channelURIs = planet.loadChannelList("input/feedlist.opml");
    FeedSet feeds = planet.initFeeds(channelURIs);
```

The output of the application will be looked after by an instance of the `FileEntrySerializer` class. The approach taken to serialization and templating here is to initially build up an RSS 2.0 representation of the items, which can be serialized directly for a combined feed or fed through XSLT transformation for styling to other formats such as HTML. The feed and channel-level elements of the output will always be the same whatever happens at entry level, so a *shell* RSS 2.0 document is loaded from file to act as a container. So the next two lines create the serializer and load the shell document from file:

```
FileEntrySerializer serializer = new FileEntrySerializer();
serializer.loadDocumentShell("input/shell.xml");
```

The next block of code is very like that found in the earlier runners, in that it loops forever, calling on the `FeedList` object to update all the data from the Web and then to do something useful with what it has loaded in the `EntryList`. The earlier runners dumped a display of what was found to the command line; this code passes the entries (after trimming) to the serializer. So the loop begins as follows:

```
while (true) {
    feeds.refreshAll();
    //    displayStatus(feeds);

    entries.trimList(MAX_ITEMS);

    serializer.clearEntries();

    for (int i = 0; i < entries.size(); i++) {
        serializer.addEntry(entries.getEntry(i));
    }
```

Now the serializer has had the individual items added to its original shell, the code proceeds to call upon the serializer to write the RSS 2.0 data to file, after giving the user command-line notification:

```
System.out.println("Writing RSS 2.0...");
serializer.write("output/rss.xml");
```

The next few lines cause similar writing to file to take place, except now the RSS 2.0 data held by the serializer will be passed through XSLT transformation, first a style sheet that will produce an HTML output, and then one which will produce RSS 1.0:

```
        System.out.println("Writing HTML...");
        serializer.transformWrite("output/index.html",
                "templates/rss2html.xslt");
        System.out.println("Writing RSS 1.0...");
        serializer.transformWrite("output/feed.rdf",
                "templates/feed-rss1.0.xsl");
    }
}
```

The initial list of URIs is loaded from an OPML file using the `ChannelSetReader` presented in Chapter 22, with the modification (the solution of Exercise 1 in Chapter 22) needed to make it load OPML, the modified class is named `OpmlSetReader`:

```
public Set loadChannelList(String filename) {
    OpmlSetReader reader = new OpmlSetReader();
    return reader.load(filename);
}
```

The `FeedFetcher` objects, parser, and interpreters are initialized in essentially the same way as in the earlier Runner examples. This time, however, every feed found in the OPML file is treated as *Bozo* (possibly ill-formed) format. This takes place in the `initFeeds` method:

```
public FeedSet initFeeds(Set channelURIs) {
    FeedSet feeds = new FeedSetImpl();
    Iterator channelIterator = channelURIs.iterator();
    FeedFetcher feedFetcher;
    Interpreter interpreter;
    String uriString;
    while (channelIterator.hasNext()) {
        uriString = (String) channelIterator.next();
        feedFetcher = new FeedFetcherImpl(uriString);
        interpreter = InterpreterFactory.createInterpreter(
                FeedConstants.RSS2_BOZO, entries);
        feedFetcher.setInterpreter(interpreter); // ++
        feedFetcher.setRefreshPeriod(REFRESH_PERIOD);
        feeds.addFeed(feedFetcher);
    }
    return feeds;
}
```

Serializing Output

The output section of the application is handled by the `FileEntrySerializer` class, which writes its output to file. When used live, that file should be written to a Web server's document directory. The class could be modified to serialize directly over HTTP as a servlet, but the file output approach has the advantage that the result will effectively be cached on the server, and what's more, makes this description a whole lot easier.

Description of the more interesting methods will follow, but first here is the full source code of `FileEntrySerializer.java`:

```
package org.urss.planet;

import java.io.File;
import java.io.FileInputStream;
import java.util.ArrayList;
import java.util.List;

import javax.xml.parsers.DocumentBuilderFactory;
import javax.xml.transform.Result;
import javax.xml.transform.Source;
import javax.xml.transform.Templates;
import javax.xml.transform.Transformer;
import javax.xml.transform.TransformerFactory;
import javax.xml.transform.dom.DOMSource;
import javax.xml.transform.stream.StreamResult;
import javax.xml.transform.stream.StreamSource;

import org.urss.feeds.Entry;
import org.w3c.dom.Document;
import org.w3c.dom.Element;
```

```java
import org.w3c.dom.NodeList;

public class FileEntrySerializer {

    private Document doc;

    private Element channelElement;

    private static TransformerFactory transformerFactory = TransformerFactory
            .newInstance();

    private static DocumentBuilderFactory factory = DocumentBuilderFactory
            .newInstance();

    public void loadDocumentShell(String filename) {
        doc = loadXml(filename);
        channelElement = getChannelElement();
    }

    public Element getChannelElement() {
        NodeList top = doc.getDocumentElement().getElementsByTagName("channel");
        return (Element) top.item(0);
    }

    public void addEntry(Entry entry) {
        Element item = doc.createElement("item");
        item.appendChild(simpleElement("guid", entry.getURIString()));
        item.appendChild(simpleElement("title", entry.getTitle()));
        item.appendChild(simpleElement("description", unescape(entry
                .getContent())));
        item.appendChild(simpleElement("link", entry.getLink()));
        item.appendChild(simpleElement("pubDate", entry.getDate()));
        String sourceTitle = entry.getAuthor();
        if(sourceTitle.equals("")){
            sourceTitle = entry.getSourceTitle();
        }
        Element sourceElement = simpleElement("source", sourceTitle);
        sourceElement.setAttribute("url", entry.getSourceLink());
        item.appendChild(sourceElement);
        channelElement.appendChild(item);
    }

    public String unescape(String content) {
        content = content.replaceAll("&amp;", "&");
        content = content.replaceAll("&apos;", "'");
        content = content.replaceAll("&quot;", "\"");
        content = content.replaceAll("&lt;.+?&gt;", "");
        return content;
    }

    private Element simpleElement(String name, String value) {
        Element element = doc.createElement(name);
        element.appendChild(doc.createTextNode(value));
        return element;
```

```
    }

    public static Document loadXml(String filename) {
        Document doc = null;
        try {
            doc = factory.newDocumentBuilder().parse(new File(filename));
        } catch (Exception e) {
            e.printStackTrace();
        }
        return doc;
    }

    public static void writeXmlFile(Document doc, String outputFilename,
            String xslFilename) {
        try {
            Source source = new DOMSource(doc);

            Result result = new StreamResult(new File(outputFilename));

            Transformer transformer = getTransformer(xslFilename);

            transformer.transform(source, result);

        } catch (Exception e) {
            e.printStackTrace();
        }
    }

    public void transformWrite(String outputFilename, String xslFilename) {
        writeXmlFile(doc, outputFilename, xslFilename);
    }

    public void write(String outputFilename) {
        writeXmlFile(doc, outputFilename, null);
    }

    public static Transformer getTransformer(String xslFilename) {
        Transformer transformer = null;
        try {
            if (xslFilename == null) {
                return transformerFactory.newTransformer();
            }
            Source xslSource = new StreamSource(
                    new FileInputStream(xslFilename));

            Templates template = transformerFactory.newTemplates(xslSource);
            transformer = template.newTransformer();
        } catch (Exception e) {
            e.printStackTrace();
        }
        return transformer;
    }

    public void clearEntries() {
        NodeList items = channelElement.getElementsByTagName("item");
```

```
            List itemList = new ArrayList();
            for (int i = 0; i < items.getLength(); i++) {
                itemList.add(items.item(i));
            }
            for (int i = 0; i < items.getLength(); i++) {
                channelElement.removeChild((Element) itemList.get(i));
            }
            System.out.println(itemList.size());
    }
}
```

This serializer uses a DOM representation of the RSS 2.0 data. It is initialized by using the loadXml method to read the outer elements of an RSS 2.0 document from file. The shell will look something like this (shell.xml):

```
<rss version="2.0">
    <channel>
        <language>en</language>
        <title>Planet RSS</title>
    </channel>
</rss>
```

When adding the items it will be necessary to address the DOM tree at the channel level, so a helper method is used to obtain a reference to the channel element. Loading the shell and getting that element is carried out by the following two methods:

```
public void loadDocumentShell(String filename) {
    doc = loadXml(filename);
    channelElement = getChannelElement();
}

public Element getChannelElement() {
    NodeList top = doc.getDocumentElement().getElementsByTagName("channel");
    return (Element) top.item(0);
}
```

Entry data is added to the shell using standard DOM calls, although as most elements follow the same pattern of creating an element and adding a text node to it, <name>value</name>, a little utility method makes the code a little less long-winded:

```
private Element simpleElement(String name, String value) {
    Element element = doc.createElement(name);
    element.appendChild(doc.createTextNode(value));
    return element;
}
```

Each entry's representation in RSS 2.0/DOM is built up in the addEntry method. Most of this just uses the simpleElement helper to transfer the values inside Entry to the DOM directly. The entry content is unescaped prior to being placed in the <description> element to counteract it gaining an extra escape level on being fed into DOM. If the entry had been given a value for author, then this value is used as the value for the content of the source element, which is a nice fit for the Planet kind of display. Otherwise the feed title is passed for this value. This element will also have an attribute containing the source URI. The result looks like this:

```
<source url="http://example.org/blog/index.html">Jane Lambda</source>
```

The DOM construction method looks like this:

```
public void addEntry(Entry entry) {
    Element item = doc.createElement("item");
    item.appendChild(simpleElement("guid", entry.getURIString()));
    item.appendChild(simpleElement("title", entry.getTitle()));
    item.appendChild(simpleElement("description", unescape(entry
            .getContent())));
    item.appendChild(simpleElement("link", entry.getLink()));
    item.appendChild(simpleElement("pubDate", entry.getDate()));
    String sourceTitle = entry.getAuthor();
    if(sourceTitle.equals("")){
        sourceTitle = entry.getSourceTitle();
    }
    Element sourceElement = simpleElement("source", sourceTitle);
    sourceElement.setAttribute("url", entry.getSourceLink());
    item.appendChild(sourceElement);
    channelElement.appendChild(item);
}
```

Writing to file is carried out by the `writeXmlFile` method. This is based around the XSLT functionality that now comes as standard with Java. The key operation here is `transformer.transform(source, result)`. This applies the XSLT styling loaded into `transformer` to the XML data loaded into `source` to push the output into `result`, which leads through a stream to a file.

```
public static void writeXmlFile(Document doc, String outputFilename,
        String xslFilename) {
    try {
        Source source = new DOMSource(doc);

        Result result = new StreamResult(new File(outputFilename));

        Transformer transformer = getTransformer(xslFilename);

        transformer.transform(source, result);

    } catch (Exception e) {
        e.printStackTrace();
    }
}
```

If no XSLT file is provided (the file name is `null`), the transformer will be what is provided by `transformerFactory.newTransformer`, which will apply an identity transformation (that is, change nothing). The result is passed to file in `writeXmlFile`. If a style sheet is provided, it will be streamed into the `TransformerFactory` to create a `Template` object, from which a `Transformer` can be created. This all happens in `getTransformer`:

```
public static Transformer getTransformer(String xslFilename) {
    Transformer transformer = null;
    try {
        if (xslFilename == null) {
            return transformerFactory.newTransformer();
```

```
        }
        Source xslSource = new StreamSource(
                new FileInputStream(xslFilename));

        Templates template = transformerFactory.newTemplates(xslSource);
        transformer = template.newTransformer();
    } catch (Exception e) {
        e.printStackTrace();
    }
    return transformer;
}
```

The code looks very convoluted, but all that is happening is that the constructed DOM object will be passed to file directly as RSS 2.0, or is used as source data for an XSLT transform to produce other formats.

The `clearEntries` method wipes any `<item>` elements found in the DOM below the `<channel>` element, so the shell can be reused. To decouple the listing of the items from their removal, they're passed to an `ArrayList` in between operations on the DOM. That method is as follows:

```
public void clearEntries() {
    NodeList items = channelElement.getElementsByTagName("item");
    List itemList = new ArrayList();
    for (int i = 0; i < items.getLength(); i++) {
        itemList.add(items.item(i));
    }
    for (int i = 0; i < items.getLength(); i++) {
        channelElement.removeChild((Element) itemList.get(i));
    }
}
```

Templates

The use of one format as a baseline representation and then applying XSLT to produce other formats gives a straightforward solution for templating the output. The final representation is decoupled from any internal representation by use of the style sheet, and the output can be modified without delving into the program core. Generally speaking RSS 2.0 is probably not the best format choice for handling extension material, but the format is used here in part as an intermediary, so any extensions could potentially appear in the internal representation but be filtered out for the RSS 2.0 serialization.

We use two XSLT style sheets in this demonstration — one to produce HTML from RSS 2.0, the other to produce RSS 1.0. The latter is Morten Frederikson's any-format-to-RSS 1.0 style sheet, available at `http://purl.org/net/syndication/subscribe/feed-rss1.0.xsl`.

The RSS to HTML style sheet is an extension of the one described in Chapter 25.

```
<xsl:stylesheet version="1.0"
    xmlns:xsl="http://www.w3.org/1999/XSL/Transform"
    xmlns="http://www.w3.org/1999/xhtml">


<xsl:output method="xml" indent="yes"/>


<xsl:template match="rss">
  <xsl:text disable-output-escaping="yes">
```

```
      &lt;!DOCTYPE html PUBLIC "-//W3C//DTD XHTML 1.0 Strict//EN"
    "http://www.w3.org/TR/xhtml1/DTD/xhtml1-strict.dtd"&gt;
    </xsl:text>
    <html>
      <xsl:apply-templates />
    </html>
  </xsl:template>

  <xsl:template match="channel">
    <head>
      <title>
        <xsl:value-of select="title" />
      </title>
    </head>
    <body xml:lang="{language}" lang="{language}">
      <xsl:apply-templates />
    </body>
  </xsl:template>

  <!-- new for Planet -->
  <xsl:template match="item">
  <div class="item">
    <h3>
        <xsl:element name="a">
          <xsl:attribute name="href">
             <xsl:value-of select="link" />
          </xsl:attribute>
          <xsl:value-of select="title" />
      </xsl:element>
    </h3>
    <p><xsl:value-of select="description" /></p>
    <p>
        <xsl:element name="a">
          <xsl:attribute name="href">
             <xsl:value-of select="source/@url" />
          </xsl:attribute>
          <xsl:value-of select="source" />
      </xsl:element>
  <br/>
      <xsl:value-of select="pubDate" /></p>
  </div>

  </xsl:template>

  <xsl:template match="text()" />

  </xsl:stylesheet>
```

Running the Planet

To run the Planet application you'll need Java installed (J2SE SDK 1.4 or later). The code and associated files need to be organized together in a common directory, for example, C:\planet. You'll need the source code from Chapters 22 and 23, modified as described in this chapter.

```
C:\planet\org\urss\feeds
C:\planet\org\urss\io
C:\planet\org\urss\parsers
```

The new Java source files listed in this chapter should be in the following locations:

```
C:\planet\org\urss\planet\EntryDateSorter.java
C:\planet\org\urss\planet\FileEntrySerializer.java
C:\planet\org\urss\planet\Planet.java
```

As starting data for the application you will need the shell of an RSS 2.0 file, along with an OPML feed list. This should be placed in a directory called `input`:

```
C:\planet\input\feedlist.opml
C:\planet\input\shell.xml
```

The following code is the content of the OPML file used in the following run (`feedlist.opml`):

```xml
<opml version="1.0">
    <head>
        <ownerName>John Doe</ownerName>
        <ownerEmail>jd@example.org</ownerEmail>
    </head>
    <body>
            <outline text="Clarissa" type="rss"
                xmlUrl="http://www.livejournal.com/users/sogn/data/rss"/>
            <outline text="Knom" type="rss"
                xmlUrl="http://unreasonables.org/?q=node/feed"/>
            <outline text="Chuck" type="rss"
                xmlUrl="http://chuck.mahost.org/weblog/wp-rss2.php"/>
    </body>
</opml>
```

The style sheet from Chapter 25, modified as described in this chapter, and the any-feed-to-RSS 1.0 style sheet should go in a directory called `templates`:

```
C:\planet\templates\feed-rss1.0.xsl
C:\planet\templates\rss2html.xslt
```

You also have to create a directory called output to receive the files produced by the application:

```
C:\planet\output
```

Try It Out   Aggregating the Planet

1. Open a command window in the directory below those listed previously (that is, `C:\planet`), and enter the following:

```
javac -classpath . org/urss/planet/Planet.java
```

That should compile the source files.

2. Enter the following:

```
java -classpath . org.urss.planet.Planet
```

You should now see something like this:

```
C:\planet>java -classpath . org.urss.planet.Planet
RSS2_BOZO: Using Rss2Handler, SoupParser
RSS2_BOZO: Using Rss2Handler, SoupParser
RSS2_BOZO: Using Rss2Handler, SoupParser
Checking: http://unreasonables.org/?q=node/feed
Connected, interpreting...
Checking: http://chuck.mahost.org/weblog/wp-rss2.php
Connected, interpreting...
Checking: http://www.livejournal.com/users/sogn/data/rss
Connected, interpreting...
Writing RSS 2.0...
Writing HTML...
Writing RSS 1.0...
Checking: http://unreasonables.org/?q=node/feed
Connected, interpreting...
...
```

Don't let this run for long — the REFRESH_PERIOD *value in* Planet.java *is set extremely low, and should be increased (to around 3600000) before using the application for anything other than quick tests.*

3. Open C:\planet\output\rss.xml in a text editor. You should see the shell.xml top-level with data from the feeds inserted at item level.

4. Open C:\planet\output\feed.rdf in a text editor. You should see an RSS 1.0 representation of the same data.

5. Open C:\planet\output\index.html in a browser. Your output should resemble Figure 27-2.

Figure 27-2

How It Works

Most of the operation of this application has already been described in Chapters 22, 23, and 25, as well as alongside the code listing in this chapter. However, you may be wondering about the actual XML/HTML output delivered by the application.

If one of the feeds in the application's list contained the RSS 2.0 sample listed earlier in this chapter, after being picked up by the Planet, the result in `output\rss.xml` will look like this (ignoring any other items):

```
<?xml version="1.0" encoding="UTF-8"?>
<rss version="2.0">
  <channel>
    <language>en</language>
    <title>Planet RSS</title>
    <item>
      <guid>http://example.org/lambda/puss.html</guid>
      <title>Puss in Boots</title>
      <description>Today our cat got some new shoes.</description>
      <link>http://example.org/lambda/puss.html</link>
      <pubDate>Fri, 29 Oct 2004 09:39:21 GMT</pubDate>
      <source url="http://example.org/lambda/index.html">Jane Lambda</source>
    </item>
  </channel>
</rss>
```

You can confirm this result if you have a Web server available (perhaps running locally); simply copy the RSS sample onto the server and add its URI to the OPML listing. After being passed through the HTML style sheet (`templates\rss2html.xslt`), the result (`output\index.html`) looks like this:

```
<?xml version="1.0" encoding="UTF-8"?>
    <!DOCTYPE html PUBLIC "-//W3C//DTD XHTML 1.0 Strict//EN"
  "http://www.w3.org/TR/xhtml1/DTD/xhtml1-strict.dtd">
    <html xmlns="http://www.w3.org/1999/xhtml">
    <head>
        <title>Jane's News</title>
    </head>
    <body xml:lang="en" lang="en">
        <div class="item">
            <h3>
                <a href="http://example.org/lambda/puss.html">Puss in Boots</a>
            </h3>
            <p>Today our cat got some new shoes.</p>
            <p>
                <a href="http://example.org/lambda/index.html">Jane Lambda</a>
                <br/>Tue, 03 Jun 2004 09:39:21 GMT</p>
        </div>
    </body>
</html>
```

The first `href` link (on the title) came from the item's `<link>` element in the original feed, which also went to an item-level `<link>` in the combined RSS 2.0. The second `href` link came from the feed-level `<link>` element in the original feed, which was passed on as the `url` attribute of the `<source>` element in the RSS 2.0. The text of this link started inside a feed-level `<author>` element and was passed as the text in the `<source>` element. Had there been no `<author>` element in the original feed, then the value would have been taken from the feed-level `<title>` element.

You can check the transformations using Saxon, as described in Chapter 25. Assuming you had the source and style sheet in the same directory, the command for this is:

```
java -jar saxon7.jar -o output.html rss.xml rss2html.xslt
```

The output of the second XSLT transformation looks like this (after a little reformatting for clarity):

```
<rdf:RDF
    xmlns:rdf="http://www.w3.org/1999/02/22-rdf-syntax-ns#"
    xmlns:dcterms="http://purl.org/dc/terms/"
    xmlns:dc="http://purl.org/dc/elements/1.1/"
    xmlns:rss="http://purl.org/rss/1.0/">

<rss:channel rss:about="">
  <dc:language>en</dc:language>
  <rss:title>Planet RSS</rss:title>

  <rss:items>
    <rdf:Seq>
      <rdf:li rdf:resource="http://example.org/lambda/puss.html"/>
    </rdf:Seq>
  </rss:items>

</rss:channel>

<rss:item rdf:about="http://example.org/lambda/puss.html">
  <rss:title>Puss in Boots</rss:title>
  <rss:description>Today our cat got some new shoes.</rss:description>
  <rss:link>http://example.org/lambda/puss.html</rss:link>
  <dcterms:created>2004-10-29T09:39:21Z</dcterms:created>
</rss:item>

</rdf:RDF>
```

Note that although this output is perfectly valid RSS 1.0, it uses a prefix for the RSS namespace that may confuse namespace-unaware tools. We'll have a word with Morten about tweaking the XSLT to take pity on the poor things.

Summary

In this chapter, you saw...

❑ The architecture of a Planet-style application.

❑ How the feed fetcher code could be extended to include references to the feed source.

❑ How items could be selected and filtered by date.

❑ How multiple output formats could be supported using XSLT.

The next two chapters continue exploring the potential of aggregation from different viewpoints.

Building a Desktop Aggregator

There are a great many desktop newsreaders/aggregators on the market, many of them free and open source. It wouldn't be possible to list all of the code for anything approaching the sophistication on many of these in the space available here. Instead, the purpose of this chapter is to give you a general picture of the kind of issues you are likely to run into if you decide to write a desktop aggregator yourself.

In this chapter you learn:

❏ How an object-oriented model of feeds can be constructed

❏ How inter-class communication can be implemented using events

❏ How to build a minimal three-pane user interface

❏ How the data in the feeds can be extracted using DOM

❏ How an RDF-based data model can be used as an alternative to the DOM

The application that is described here really is just a first pass at implementing a desktop aggregator in C#. If you want to dig deeper you should have a look at the source of RSS Bandit, which uses XPath, XSLT, XML Schema, the DOM, and XML Serialization in the .NET Framework to build a very user-friendly application. The reason this particular project is highlighted is because it is comparatively well documented on the RSS Bandit site itself (www.rssbandit.org/), as well as through at least two articles at http://msdn.microsoft.com/ (search for "rss"). The approach taken in RSS Bandit is only one of many, and notably lacks the benefits of an RDF model, but as far as application architecture and implementation of the most common functionality is concerned it's very well put together.

Of course, C# may not be your language of choice. Google will almost certainly find you an existing open-source desktop RSS application coded in that language. Whatever, the listing and description here should still make sense if you are moderately familiar with any object-oriented language.

Desktop Aggregator Overview

The application here will give a three-pane view of a set of RSS feeds. The user is initially presented with empty panes, and has to load either an OPML or RDF/XML format list of feeds from file. Once loaded, the left column of the application will contain a list of the feeds (by name). When the user clicks on one of these, the application will retrieve the data from the Web and then display a list of entry titles in the top-right pane. If the user clicks one of these titles, the contents of that entry will be displayed in the bottom-right area.

Figure 28-1 shows what the application looks like in use.

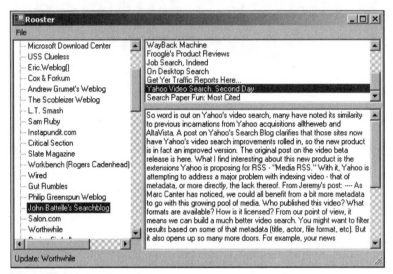

Figure 28-1

Note that the application doesn't have any data persistence itself, and no real attempt is made to clean up the content of entries ready for display or deal with ill-formed feed data. In a couple of places where there is a clear development path, minimal skeleton code has been put in place to suggest where the next steps may be. For example, the component used to list the feed titles is actually a `TreeView`. This could be modified to allow hierarchical organization of the feeds.

The source code to this little application was developed using the open source (GPL) SharpDevelop IDE (www.icsharpcode.net/). This has a graphic UI builder that is a great time saver; much of the main form was auto-generated this way.

To make the code structure a little clearer, the source files each contain a single class or interface, which has the same name as the file name (as in Java). The application has the working title "Rooster" (not brilliant, but no worse than most aggregator names), so all classes are in the `Rooster` namespace.

The source files are as follows:

❑ `MainForm.cs`: Application entry point and GUI

❑ `IFeed.cs`: Interface modeling a feed

- ❑ `IFeedStore.cs`: Interface modeling a set of feeds
- ❑ `Item.cs`: A struct representing an individual entry in a feed
- ❑ `FeedBase.cs`: Partial implementation of `IFeed`
- ❑ `FeedStoreBase.cs`: Partial implementation of `IFeedStore`
- ❑ `FeedEventTrigger.cs`: Used for event notification between classes
- ❑ `FeedEventArgs.cs`: Contains data relating to feed events
- ❑ `Utils.cs`: Utility methods
- ❑ `DomFeed.cs`: Extends `FeedBase` to fully implement `IFeed` based on an XML DOM model
- ❑ `DomFeedStore.cs`: Implements `IFeedStore` for the `DomFeed` implementation

System Construction

The Rooster application generally follows the well-known object-oriented architecture of Model, View, and Control. The model core is constructed around a couple of interfaces (`IFeed`, `IFeedStore`) and a struct (`Item`). The view is all built around a single form (`MainForm`), which will provide a window having three panes to display the list of subscribed channels, a list of item titles, and the content of the selected item. The control aspect is defined partially by these user interface components and top-level construction in the `MainForm` class, and partially by event-driven message passing between the classes. The following sections describe these different aspects of the application alongside the source code.

Feed Data Model

The domain model used by this application is the obvious one, suggested by the structure of syndication feeds. It is defined by two interfaces and one `struct`. The interfaces are `IFeed` and `IfeedStore`; the struct is `Item`. The reason for using interfaces for the former is to make it easier to plug in different concrete implementations. A feed entry is modeled by `Item`, this is implemented as a concrete `struct` as it is unlikely that an application will need to change much at this level of granularity. So starting at the bottom, here is the source to `Item.cs`:

```csharp
using System;

namespace Rooster
{

    public struct Item
    {
        private string uri;
        private string title;
        private string content;

        public Item(string uri, string title, string content)
        {
            this.uri = uri;
            this.title = title;
```

```
            this.content = content;
        }

        public string URI {
            get { return this.uri; }
            set { this.uri = value; }
        }

        public string Title {
            get { return this.title; }
            set { this.title = value; }
        }

        public string Content {
            get { return this.content; }
            set { this.content = value; }
        }


        public override string ToString(){
            return title;
        }
    }
}
```

As you can see, the `Item` struct is really just a trivial set of properties with accessors (a Java equivalent would consist of a simple class with the three member variables and get/set methods for each).

A syndication feed consists of a set of entries and some common metadata. In this application this is modeled by the `IFeed` interface, the source of which looks like this:

```
using System;
using System.Collections;

namespace  Rooster
{
    public interface IFeed
    {
        string Name {
            get;
            set;
        }

        string URI {
            get;
            set;
        }

        ArrayList Items {
            get;
            set;
        }
```

```
        IFeedStore Store {
            get;
            set;
        }

        void loadData();
        void update();

        void updateEvent(object ob, System.Timers.ElapsedEventArgs arg);
    }
}
```

This is also fairly straightforward, defining properties for the URI and a user-friendly name for the feed. The entries contained in the feed will be made available as a standard `ArrayList` collection. The object representing a feed will also have a pointer to the store to which it belongs (an object that supports the `IFeedStore` interface), which will also be available through get/set accessors. A `loadData` and `update` method are defined; the architectural idea here is that `loadData` will be an immediate call to get the feed from the Web and `update` will be a polite call to the implementing object to update itself, which it will generally do using its implementation of the `loadData` method but not necessarily immediately. The `updateEvent` method is provided as a way of receiving automated requests from a `Timer` object — this functionality won't actually be implemented here, but there will be a skeleton of code to suggest how you might implement it.

The next listing is for `IFeedStore`, the interface that will model the set of feeds that the application knows about. Here is the source:

```
using System.Collections ;

namespace  Rooster
{
    public interface IFeedStore
    {
        event MainForm.FeedEventHandler feedEventHandler;

        void loadChannelsList(string filename);
        IFeed selectNamedFeed(string title);
        IDictionaryEnumerator GetFeedEnumerator();
        void updateFeeds();
        void OnFeedEvent(string statusString);
        IFeed createFeed(string name, string uri);

        Hashtable FeedTable {
            get;
            set;
        }
    }
}
```

The `feedEventHandler` given here will be used as part of the inter-object feed event notification chain; we will explain its use shortly. This interface as a whole is only intended to act as a starting point, there's a fair amount of redundancy in the access to the set of feeds that might well be smoothed out in subsequent development cycles. The method functionalities are given in their names — again their use will be clearer when you see the implementations.

The next two listings are base implementations of the two interfaces listed previously. FeedBase provides functionality that is expected to be common to all full implementations of the IFeed interface, and similarly FeedStoreBase implements methods that are likely to be the same whatever is used for an underlying store.

Here is the code in FeedBase.cs:

```
using System;
using System.Collections ;
using System.Threading;
using System.Timers;

namespace  Rooster
{
    public abstract class FeedBase: FeedEventTrigger, IFeed
    {
        public abstract void loadData();

        public abstract ArrayList Items {
            get;
            set;
        }

        private IFeedStore store;

        private string uri;
        private string name;

        public FeedBase(IFeedStore store, string name, string uri) {
            this.store = store;
            this.name = name;
            this.uri = uri;
        }

        public string Name {
            get{ return name;}
            set{ this.name = value; }
        }

        public string URI {
            get { return uri;}
            set { this.uri = value; }
        }

        public IFeedStore Store {
            get { return store;}
            set { this.store = value;}
        }

        public void update(){
            updateThread = new Thread(new ThreadStart(this.loadData));
            updateThread.Start();
        }
    }
}
```

The abstract `FeedBase` class begins with abstract definitions for the `loadData` method and `Items` property; these will be implemented by concrete subclasses. The `Name`, `URI`, and `Store` properties (for the Java developer that's member variables with get/set methods) are trivially implemented with accessors to private members. The `update` method implementation creates a new thread in which the `loadData` method is run. The aim here is to isolate any slow-moving feed download operation from the fast-moving user interface thread. How this download (or other data acquisition operation) occurs is left to subclasses.

Here's the base implementation of the `IFeedStore` interface, found in `FeedStoreBase.cs`:

```csharp
using System;
using System.Collections;

namespace Rooster
{
    public abstract class FeedStoreBase: FeedEventTrigger, IFeedStore
    {
        private Hashtable feedTable = new Hashtable();

        public FeedStoreBase()
        {
        }

        public abstract void loadChannelsList(string filename);
        public abstract IFeed createFeed(string name, string uri);

        public Hashtable FeedTable {
            get { return feedTable;}
            set { this.feedTable = value;
            }
        }

        public IDictionaryEnumerator GetFeedEnumerator(){
            return FeedTable.GetEnumerator();
        }

        public IFeed selectNamedFeed(string feedName){
            return (IFeed)FeedTable[feedName];
        }

        public void updateFeeds(){
            IDictionaryEnumerator enumerator  = GetFeedEnumerator();
            while(enumerator.MoveNext()){
                IFeed feed = (IFeed)enumerator.Value;
                feed.update();
            }
        }
    }
}
```

This source is largely self-explanatory, except for the `feedTable` part. This is a `Hashtable`, which will contain a mapping between feed names (keys) and feed objects (values). Architecturally this approach is a little clunky, and might be expected to be refactored out fairly soon were this application to be taken further. But for a first pass it does make it easy to access feeds by name. The `updateFeeds` method simply steps through each of the feeds contained in this store and calls their own `update` method.

Event Notification

One aspect of development of an application like this that can be problematic is keeping the linkage between objects loose enough that you don't end up with a tangle of spaghetti code. A common programming language tool is *event-driven communication,* which enables a separation with certain objects generating events and listeners set up to receive them. C# offers a very flexible approach to this in the form of delegates. The delegate used here is actually defined with the `MainForm` class that you will see shortly. However, there are two classes that are used directly for event-driven communication between the objects in the application. This is probably a good point to say what those events will be, and what the desired actions are. The assumption is made here that it will be useful to communicate state changes in the feed-level processing to the user. That means when something significant happens in one of the feed (or related) objects, an event is triggered. In fact the events that will be monitored are simply the actions of starting to download and having downloaded feed data. The end user notification will simply be a message on the application's status bar. The same basic wiring can be built upon to handle more elaborate messages, but here only the passing of a status string is implemented.

The class that will wrap up the message data is `FeedEventArgs`, the source of which looks like this:

```
using System;

namespace Rooster
{

    public class FeedEventArgs: EventArgs

    {
        private readonly string statusString = "Here";

        public FeedEventArgs(string statusString) {
            this.statusString = statusString;
        }

        public string Status { get {return statusString;} }
    }
}
```

The following class is a superclass of those classes that may trigger feed event notifications — the implementations of `IFeed` and `IFeedStore`. The definition of the `FeedEventHandler` you will see shortly (in `MainForm`), but all the class does here is take a `string`, wrap it in a `FeedEventArgs` object, and then pass it to one of these `FeedEventHandler` things, triggering an event that will be picked up by any listeners registered on that handler. The source of `FeedEventTrigger.cs` looks like this:

```
using System;

namespace Rooster
{

    public class FeedEventTrigger
```

```
        {
            public event MainForm.FeedEventHandler feedEventHandler;

            public virtual void OnFeedEvent(string statusString){
                if (feedEventHandler != null){
                    feedEventHandler(this, new FeedEventArgs(statusString));
                }
            }
        }
    }
}
```

Before seeing the code for the implementation of the feed and feed stores themselves, it should help for you to see how the top-level application code combines the user interface with those constructs.

User Interface

The application front end and basic structure is built in `MainForm.cs`. The following listing shows the source code. However, since it's a long listing, we include explanations inline. So here is `MainForm.cs`:

```
using System;
using System.Windows.Forms;
using System.Timers;
using System.Collections;

namespace  Rooster
{
    public class MainForm : System.Windows.Forms.Form
    {
        private System.Windows.Forms.TextBox contentTextBox;
        private System.Windows.Forms.RichTextBox richTextBox1;
        private System.Windows.Forms.MainMenu mainMenu;
        private System.Windows.Forms.Splitter horizontalSplitter;
        private System.Windows.Forms.Panel feedsPanel;
        private System.Windows.Forms.StatusBar statusBar;
        private System.Windows.Forms.Panel contentPanel;
        private System.Windows.Forms.ListBox titlesListBox;
        private System.Windows.Forms.Panel titlesPanel;
        private System.Windows.Forms.Splitter verticalSplitter;
        private System.Windows.Forms.TreeView feedTreeView;
```

The user interface form components are all taken from the standard WinForms library, and the variables corresponding to these appear previously. These components are used in a standard fashion, actually dictated here by SharpDevelop's visual builder, and aren't really worthy of comment. If you refer back to Figure 28-1, you should be able to identify the parts that correspond to the components described in the code.

The next little block is more interesting. It has the member variable that will hold the applications single feed store object. This is followed by the delegate definition that will act as the communication channel for event-driven message passing between the application objects. This `MainForm` class holds the GUI and so is also the receiver of the feed events, which will appear as calls to the `OnFeedEvent` method here. When this is called, the value of interest (the status `string`) is unwrapped from the `FeedEventArgs` object and passed onto the status bar component, which is refreshed to ensure rapid display of its new value.

```
private IFeedStore store;

public delegate void FeedEventHandler(object sender, FeedEventArgs e);

public void OnFeedEvent(object sender,
                        FeedEventArgs e) {
    this.statusBar.Text = e.Status;
    this.statusBar.Refresh();
}
```

The `MainForm` constructor that will be called on application startup comes next. The code begins with two calls to methods that will look after most of the GUI construction. The next statement attaches an event handler to the `feedTreeView` component, so that when the user clicks on a node (a feed title) in the tree, the local `treeSelect` method is called. The same kind of listening is also hooked to the `titlesListBox` in the statement that follows, so a user who clicks on that will generate a call to the `listSelect` method. The constructor code looks like this:

```
public MainForm(){

    InitializeComponent();
    CreateMainMenu();

    this.feedTreeView.AfterSelect
                += new TreeViewEventHandler(this.treeSelect);

    this.titlesListBox.SelectedIndexChanged
                    += new EventHandler(this.listSelect);
}
```

When the user clicks on a named feed in the list (held by the tree component) the `treeSelect` method will be called, a `TreeViewEventArgs` object carrying the details of the action. The information used here is the text of the node in the tree, which will be the name of the feed. This `string` is used to obtain the corresponding feed object from the store. That feed is updated immediately using its `loadData` method. In a subsequent development iteration, this call should either be shifted to `update` or perhaps cause the display of an hourglass. For now, however, the current version works well enough for demonstration purposes. Once the data has been obtained, the local `placeTitles` method is called to do the layout of titles extracted from the feed in question. The method finishes by updating the status bar with an appropriate message. Here is the method source code:

```
public void treeSelect(object sender, TreeViewEventArgs e){

    IFeed selectedFeed = store.selectNamedFeed(e.Node.Text);
    if(selectedFeed == null){
        return;
    }
    selectedFeed.loadData();
    placeTitles(selectedFeed, titlesListBox);
    contentTextBox.Clear();
```

```
        this.statusBar.Text = e.Node.Text+" : "+selectedFeed.URI;
        this.statusBar.Refresh();
    }
```

As you saw in the Item.cs listing, these objects have an overridden ToString method that returns the title of the feed. This makes the placing of titles relatively simple, because they can be added as items to the data structure behind the ListBox component, and when the component is displayed the title strings will appear.

```
    public void placeTitles(IFeed feed, ListBox titlesListBox){
        titlesListBox.Items.Clear();
        if(feed == null){
            return;
        }
        foreach(Item item in feed.Items){
            titlesListBox.Items.Add(item);
        }
        titlesListBox.Refresh();
    }
```

When a title is selected from the titlesListBox, the listSelect method will be called. This obtains the ListBox Item of interest from the arguments passed by the caller, which also happens to be a (feed) Item object. The content of this feed entry is accessed and placed in the user interface's content area. The listSelect method looks like this:

```
    public void listSelect(object sender, EventArgs e){
        contentTextBox.Clear();
        object selectedItem = ((ListBox)sender).SelectedItem;
        string content =    ((Item)selectedItem).Content;
        contentTextBox.AppendText(content);
    }
```

The entry point to the application, the Main method simply creates and runs a MainForm:

```
    public static void Main(string[] args)
    {
        Application.Run(new MainForm());
    }
```

The code used to create the menu is pretty standard; an event handler is used to attach the importMenuItemClick method to respond to the user's action:

```
    public void CreateMainMenu()
    {
        MenuItem fileMenuItem = new MenuItem();
        fileMenuItem.Text = "File";
        mainMenu.MenuItems.Add(fileMenuItem);

        MenuItem importMenuItem = new MenuItem();
        importMenuItem.Text = "Import";
        fileMenuItem.MenuItems.Add(importMenuItem);
        importMenuItem.Click
                += new System.EventHandler(this.importMenuItemClick);
    }
```

The menu click handler pops up a standard open file dialog box and obtains the user's choice of file. If the file name ends with .rdf, then a CarpFeedStore implementation will be used; otherwise a DomFeedStore implementation will be created. Whichever implementation is selected, the object is passed the name of the file containing the list of syndication feeds and the local initFeedView method called to refresh the user interface with this new data.

```
void importMenuItemClick(object sender, System.EventArgs e)
{
    OpenFileDialog openDialog = new OpenFileDialog();
    openDialog.Filter =
            "feedlist files (*.rdf)|*.opml|All files (*.*)|*.*" ;
    openDialog.FilterIndex = 2 ;
    openDialog.RestoreDirectory = true ;
    openDialog.InitialDirectory = ".";

    if(openDialog.ShowDialog() == DialogResult.OK)
    {
        if(openDialog.FileName.EndsWith(".rdf")){
            store = new CarpFeedStore();
        }else{
            store = new DomFeedStore();
        }
        store.loadChannelsList(openDialog.FileName);
        initFeedView();
    }
}
```

The feed view is initialized by stepping through the feeds in the store and adding their names to the tree component. At this point a feedEventHandler is also attached to each feed to enable the event-driven communication discussed earlier.

```
public void initFeedView(){
    feedTreeView.Nodes.Clear();
    IDictionaryEnumerator enumerator = store.GetFeedEnumerator();

    while(enumerator.MoveNext()){
        string name = (string)enumerator.Key;
        IFeed feed = (IFeed)enumerator.Value;

        feedTreeView.Nodes.Add(new TreeNode(name));
        ((FeedEventTrigger)feed).feedEventHandler
                    += new FeedEventHandler(OnFeedEvent);
    }

}
```

The final block of code in MainForm.cs is the IDE-generated material that sets up the application form:

```
private void InitializeComponent() {
    this.feedTreeView = new System.Windows.Forms.TreeView();
    this.verticalSplitter = new System.Windows.Forms.Splitter();
    this.titlesPanel = new System.Windows.Forms.Panel();
    this.titlesListBox = new System.Windows.Forms.ListBox();
```

```
this.contentPanel = new System.Windows.Forms.Panel();
this.statusBar = new System.Windows.Forms.StatusBar();
this.feedsPanel = new System.Windows.Forms.Panel();
this.horizontalSplitter = new System.Windows.Forms.Splitter();
this.mainMenu = new System.Windows.Forms.MainMenu();
this.richTextBox1 = new System.Windows.Forms.RichTextBox();
this.contentTextBox = new System.Windows.Forms.TextBox();
this.titlesPanel.SuspendLayout();
this.contentPanel.SuspendLayout();
this.feedsPanel.SuspendLayout();
this.SuspendLayout();
//
// feedTreeView
//
this.feedTreeView.Anchor =
    ((System.Windows.Forms.AnchorStyles)
    (((System.Windows.Forms.AnchorStyles.Top |
                System.Windows.Forms.AnchorStyles.Bottom)
      | System.Windows.Forms.AnchorStyles.Left)));

this.feedTreeView.ImageIndex = -1;
this.feedTreeView.Location = new System.Drawing.Point(0, 0);
this.feedTreeView.Name = "feedTreeView";
this.feedTreeView.SelectedImageIndex = -1;
this.feedTreeView.Size = new System.Drawing.Size(200, 512);
this.feedTreeView.TabIndex = 1;
//
// verticalSplitter
//
this.verticalSplitter.Location =
                        new System.Drawing.Point(200, 0);
this.verticalSplitter.Name = "verticalSplitter";
this.verticalSplitter.Size = new System.Drawing.Size(3, 511);
this.verticalSplitter.TabIndex = 1;
this.verticalSplitter.TabStop = false;
//
// titlesPanel
//
this.titlesPanel.Controls.Add(this.titlesListBox);
this.titlesPanel.Dock = System.Windows.Forms.DockStyle.Top;
this.titlesPanel.Location = new System.Drawing.Point(203, 0);
this.titlesPanel.Name = "titlesPanel";
this.titlesPanel.Size = new System.Drawing.Size(597, 100);
this.titlesPanel.TabIndex = 2;
//
// titlesListBox
//
this.titlesListBox.Dock = System.Windows.Forms.DockStyle.Fill;
this.titlesListBox.Location = new System.Drawing.Point(0, 0);
this.titlesListBox.Name = "titlesListBox";
this.titlesListBox.Size = new System.Drawing.Size(597, 100);
this.titlesListBox.TabIndex = 0;
//
```

```
        // contentPanel
        //
        this.contentPanel.Controls.Add(this.contentTextBox);
        this.contentPanel.Dock = System.Windows.Forms.DockStyle.Fill;
        this.contentPanel.Location = new System.Drawing.Point(203, 103);
        this.contentPanel.Name = "contentPanel";
        this.contentPanel.Size = new System.Drawing.Size(597, 408);
        this.contentPanel.TabIndex = 4;
        //
        // statusBar
        //
        this.statusBar.Location = new System.Drawing.Point(0, 511);
        this.statusBar.Name = "statusBar";
        this.statusBar.Size = new System.Drawing.Size(800, 22);
        this.statusBar.TabIndex = 2;
        this.statusBar.Text = "OK";
        //
        // feedsPanel
        //
        this.feedsPanel.Controls.Add(this.feedTreeView);
        this.feedsPanel.Dock = System.Windows.Forms.DockStyle.Left;
        this.feedsPanel.Location = new System.Drawing.Point(0, 0);
        this.feedsPanel.Name = "feedsPanel";
        this.feedsPanel.Size = new System.Drawing.Size(200, 511);
        this.feedsPanel.TabIndex = 0;
        //
        // horizontalSplitter
        //
        this.horizontalSplitter.Dock =
                    System.Windows.Forms.DockStyle.Top;
        this.horizontalSplitter.Location =
new System.Drawing.Point(203, 100);
        this.horizontalSplitter.Name = "horizontalSplitter";
        this.horizontalSplitter.Size = new System.Drawing.Size(597, 3);
        this.horizontalSplitter.TabIndex = 3;
        this.horizontalSplitter.TabStop = false;
        //
        // richTextBox1
        //
        this.richTextBox1.AutoSize = true;
        this.richTextBox1.Dock = System.Windows.Forms.DockStyle.Fill;
        this.richTextBox1.Location = new System.Drawing.Point(0, 0);
        this.richTextBox1.Name = "richTextBox1";
        this.richTextBox1.Size = new System.Drawing.Size(792, 443);
        this.richTextBox1.TabIndex = 0;
        this.richTextBox1.Text = "";
        //
        // contentTextBox
        //
        this.contentTextBox.Dock = System.Windows.Forms.DockStyle.Fill;
        this.contentTextBox.Location = new System.Drawing.Point(0, 0);
        this.contentTextBox.Multiline = true;
        this.contentTextBox.Name = "contentTextBox";
```

```
            this.contentTextBox.ScrollBars =
                System.Windows.Forms.ScrollBars.Vertical;
            this.contentTextBox.Size = new System.Drawing.Size(597, 408);
            this.contentTextBox.TabIndex = 0;
            this.contentTextBox.Text = "";
            //
            // MainForm
            //
            this.AutoScaleBaseSize = new System.Drawing.Size(5, 13);
            this.ClientSize = new System.Drawing.Size(800, 533);
            this.Controls.Add(this.contentPanel);
            this.Controls.Add(this.horizontalSplitter);
            this.Controls.Add(this.titlesPanel);
            this.Controls.Add(this.verticalSplitter);
            this.Controls.Add(this.feedsPanel);
            this.Controls.Add(this.statusBar);
            this.Location = new System.Drawing.Point(4, 22);
            this.Menu = this.mainMenu;
            this.Name = "MainForm";
            this.Text = "Rooster";
            this.titlesPanel.ResumeLayout(false);
            this.contentPanel.ResumeLayout(false);
            this.feedsPanel.ResumeLayout(false);
            this.ResumeLayout(false);
        }
        #endregion
    }
}
```

So far you've seen the application infrastructure as a model described in terms of interfaces and base implementations, the user interface visual components and the event-handling code, which deals with interactions, and the top-level application code, which glues it all together. Now you will see a simple implementation of the interfaces based on DOM.

DOM-Based Implementation

As suggested in earlier chapters, for simple aggregation/newsreading the XML DOM can make a reasonable model of feeds. This is demonstrated here in the following classes, DomFeed, which will implement IFeed, and DomFeedStore, which will implement IFeedStore.

Here's the source to DomFeed.cs:

```
using System;
using System.Collections;
using System.Xml;

namespace Rooster
{

    public class DomFeed: FeedBase
    {
        string RDF_NS = "http://www.w3.org/1999/02/22-rdf-syntax-ns#";
```

```csharp
string RSS_NS = "http://purl.org/rss/1.0/";
string ATOM_NS = "http://purl.org/atom/ns#";

XmlDocument    doc;
XmlNamespaceManager nsManager;

private  ArrayList items = null;


public DomFeed(IFeedStore store, string name, string uri):
    base(store, name, uri){
    doc    =    new XmlDocument();
    initNSManager();
}

private void initNSManager(){
    nsManager = new XmlNamespaceManager(doc.NameTable);
    nsManager.AddNamespace("rss", RSS_NS);
    nsManager.AddNamespace("rdf", RDF_NS);
    nsManager.AddNamespace("atom", ATOM_NS);
}

public override void loadData(){
    string title = getFeedTitle();
    try{
       OnFeedEvent("Loading: "+URI);
       doc.Load(URI);
       readItems();
       OnFeedEvent("Loaded: "+URI);
    }catch(Exception exception){
       OnFeedEvent("Error: "+exception);
       return;
    }
}


public override ArrayList Items {
    get{ return items; }
    set{ this.items = value; }
}

// /rdf:RDF//rss:item/rss:title/text()
private void readItems(){
    items = new ArrayList();
    XmlElement root = doc.DocumentElement;
    XmlNodeList itemNodes =
                   root.SelectNodes("//item|rss:item|atom:entry", nsManager);
    foreach(XmlNode itemNode in itemNodes){
        string uri = "";
        XmlNode linkNode = itemNode.SelectSingleNode("link");
        if(linkNode == null){
           linkNode = itemNode.SelectSingleNode("@rdf:about",
                                      nsManager);
```

```
            }
            if(linkNode == null){
                linkNode = itemNode.SelectSingleNode("guid");
            }
            if(linkNode != null){
                uri = linkNode.InnerText;
            }
            string title = "";
            XmlNode titleNode = itemNode.SelectSingleNode("title");
            if(titleNode != null){
                title = titleNode.InnerText;
            }
            string content = "";
            XmlNode contentNode =
                            itemNode.SelectSingleNode("description");
            if(contentNode != null){
                content = contentNode.InnerText;
            }
            Item   item = new Item(uri,title,content);
            items.Add(item);
        }
    }


    public string getFeedTitle(){
        XmlElement root = doc.DocumentElement;
        if(root == null){
            return null;
        }
        XmlNode title = root.SelectSingleNode("/rss/channel/title",
                    nsManager);
        if(title != null){
            return title.InnerText;
        }
        title = root.SelectSingleNode("/rdf:RDF/rss:channel/rss:title",
                        nsManager);
        if(title != null){
            return title.InnerText;
        }
        title = root.SelectSingleNode("/atom:feed/atom:title", nsManager);
        if(title != null){
            return title.InnerText;
        }
        return "untitled";
    }
  }
 }
```

The previous listing is very similar to the DOM code that has appeared previously in the book. The DomFeed implementation works essentially by applying XPath selections onto a DOM document, and checking these against what is to be expected in feeds. The only unusual part perhaps is the way a namespace manager has to be used in the .NET XML libraries to look after the prefix bindings. This is all well documented at http://msdn.com.

The `DomFeedStore` class will look after the list of feeds for the application. This list will initially obtain from an OPML-format feed list. The source is as follows:

```csharp
using System;
using System.Xml;
using System.Collections ;
using System.IO;

namespace Rooster
{
    public class DomFeedStore: FeedStoreBase
    {
        private XmlDocument channelsList;

        public DomFeedStore()
        {
        }


        public override void loadChannelsList(string filename){
            channelsList = new XmlDocument();
            channelsList.Load(filename);
            XmlNodeList elements =
                        channelsList.GetElementsByTagName("outline");

            foreach (XmlElement element in elements){
                if(element.GetAttribute("type") == "rss"){
                    string name = element.GetAttribute("title");
                    string uri = element.GetAttribute("xmlUrl");
                    IFeed feed = createFeed(name, uri);
                    if(!FeedTable.ContainsKey(name)){
                        FeedTable.Add(name, feed);
                    }
                }
            }
        }

        public override IFeed createFeed(string name, string uri){
            IFeed feed = new DomFeed(this, name, uri);
            return feed;
        }
    }
}
```

The application makes use of the following utility class to clean up the content a little. The `Replace` method simply replaces all occurrences of one `string` in a piece of text with another `string`. Here is the source code:

```csharp
using System;

namespace Rooster
{
    public class Utils
    {
```

```
        public static String Replace(String text, String oldString,
                                      String newString){
    int position = text.IndexOf(oldString);
    String newText = "";
    while(position != -1){
       newText += text.Substring(0,position) + newString;
       text = text.Substring(position + oldString.Length);
       position = text.IndexOf(oldString);
    }
    if(text.Length > 0){
       newText += text;
    }
    return newText;
  }
 }
}
```

Using an RDF Model

Although the DOM-based model can lead you to a useful application, there's also a lot of additional potential available by using an RDF model behind the scenes. The following is a fairly naive first pass implementation of such a model. The reason this can be described as naive is because it treats the feed data in the same way that the DOM modeling did—one structure for the feed list, another separate structure for each of the individual feeds. This does work, and there can be advantages to this approach, for example, as a first step when additional provenance information needs to be added. However, it should be noted that the same kind of functionality offered here could be achieved by storing all the feed list and individual feed data in a single (RDF) model. Taking things further, it would be possible to replace parts of the domain model code (such as the Item struct) with direct references to corresponding representations in the RDF model. But as a first step in such a refactoring, a straight swap is made here from DOM to RDF.

The RDF libraries used here are RdfLib and Carp (http://www.semanticplanet.com). As you will see in the listings, coding using these libraries is straightforward, the classes and methods are put together in a fairly intuitive fashion. To run the application you'll need to have the .dll library binaries somewhere in your path.

So here is the source code of CarpFeed.cs:

```
using System;
using System.Collections;
using SemPlan.Carp.Core;
using SemPlan.Carp.Vocabularies;

namespace Rooster
{

    public class CarpFeed: FeedBase
    {
        private  ArrayList items = new ArrayList();

        public CarpFeed(IFeedStore store, string name, string uri):
            base(store, name, uri)
```

```
        {
        }

    public override ArrayList Items {
        get{
            items = getItems();
            return items;}
        set{ this.items = value;
        }
    }

    public override void loadData(){
        OnFeedEvent("Loading: "+URI);
        KnowledgeBase feedKB = ((CarpFeedStore)Store).getFeedKB(this);
        feedKB.include(URI);
        OnFeedEvent("Loaded: "+URI);
    }

    public ArrayList getItems(){
        KnowledgeBase feedKB = ((CarpFeedStore)Store).getFeedKB(this);
        Rss.Item itemPattern = new Rss.Item();
        ArrayList items = new ArrayList();
        foreach (Rss.Item rssItem in itemPattern.findAllMatching(feedKB) )
                {
            string uri = rssItem.ToString();
            string title = rssItem.title.ToString();
            string content = rssItem.description.ToString();
            Item item = new Item(uri, title, content);

            items.Add(item);
        }
        return items;
    }
    }
}
```

Here is the source code of `CarpFeedStore.cs`:

```
using System;
using System.Collections;
using SemPlan.Carp.Core;
using SemPlan.Carp.Vocabularies;
using System.IO;
using SemPlan.RdfLib.XsltParser;
namespace  Rooster {
    public class CarpFeedStore: FeedStoreBase {
        public static XsltParserFactory ParserFactory = new XsltParserFactory();
        KnowledgeBase channelsKB;
        Hashtable feedKBs;
        public CarpFeedStore() {
            channelsKB = new KnowledgeBase(ParserFactory);
            feedKBs = new Hashtable();
```

```
        }

        public KnowledgeBase getFeedKB(IFeed feed){
            return (KnowledgeBase)feedKBs[feed];
        }

        public override void loadChannelsList(string filename){
            try {
                OnFeedEvent("Reading: "+filename);
                channelsKB.include(new StreamReader(filename), "");
            } catch (Exception e) {
                Console.WriteLine(e);
            }
            initFeedTable();
        }

        public override IFeed createFeed(string name, string uri){
            IFeed feed = new CarpFeed(this, name, uri);
            feed.Name = name;
            feed.URI = uri;
            return feed;
        }

        private void initFeedTable(){
            FeedTable = new Hashtable();
            Foaf.Agent pattern = new Foaf.Agent();

            foreach (Foaf.Agent agent in pattern.findAllMatching(channelsKB) ) {
                string name = agent[Foaf.name].ToString();
                foreach (Foaf.Document doc in agent.weblog) {
                    try {
                        string uri = doc[Rdfs.seeAlso][0].ToString();
                        IFeed feed =   createFeed(name, uri);
                        FeedTable.Add(name, feed);
                        feedKBs.Add(feed,
                                                new KnowledgeBase(ParserFactory));
                    } catch (Exception e) {
                        Console.WriteLine( e );
                    }
                }
            }
        }
    }
}
```

Automating Updates

The application as it stands is very basic; probably the crudest aspect is the lack of a local persistent store to retain feed data in between views. This would be relatively straightforward to set up for either the DOM- or RDF-based versions. However, a related shortcoming is that the application updates the feeds from the Web in response to the user clicking on the feed's title in the list. In practice it would be better for the updates to happen independently so the user didn't have to wait. This would allow the update operation to take place politely, according to a schedule that didn't unreasonably snatch bandwidth. To

see how this kind of facility might be implemented, you can add the following source code to
FeedBase.cs; this code employs a Timer instance that provides hourly updates.

```
public void updateEvent(object ob, System.Timers.ElapsedEventArgs arg){
    OnFeedEvent("Update: "+Name);
}

int UPDATE_PERIOD = 3600000;
private Thread updateThread;
private  System.Timers.Timer updateTimer;

private void startTimerThread(){
    this.updateTimer = new System.Timers.Timer();
    this.updateTimer.Interval = UPDATE_PERIOD;
    this.updateTimer.Elapsed +=
                new ElapsedEventHandler(updateEvent);
    this.updateTimer.Enabled = true;
}
```

The update event will be called automatically every hour. As it stands all this will do is to display the
message on the status bar. However, depending on how exactly you wanted things to happen, you can
add the appropriate method calls in the updateEvent method.

Summary

In this chapter you saw how you might approach the first steps in creating a desktop aggregator. You
learned that...

❑   Different data models can be used for handling RSS.

❑   Object-oriented coding techniques make it possible to separate blocks of functionality.

❑   A simple desktop aggregator can be constructed from relatively simple code.

The following chapter revisits the client side of syndication systems and explores how other forms of
data can be used alongside the core Atom/RSS material.

Social Syndication

In this chapter, we briefly discuss various roles social relationships can play in the Web environment, before we describe how FOAF (Friend-of-a-Friend) data relating to human relationships can be used alongside RSS/Atom.

In this chapter you will learn:

- ❑ About the general notion of "social software"
- ❑ How FOAF data can introduce a social angle to syndication
- ❑ How to interact with an RDF store using a query language
- ❑ How normalized RSS and FOAF data can be held in the same store
- ❑ How to start building your own personal knowledgebase

What Is Society on the Web?

Technology has removed many of the traditional limitations on social activity such as geography, authority hierarchies, and, to some extent, language. The Web goes further than the telephone in various ways: It enables the sharing of information, acting as a huge multidimensional whiteboard. Simple authoring facilities like Weblogs encourage contact between people. New modes of communication have appeared, like instant messaging (IM) and Wikis. The ideas of augmenting human capabilities with computers on a social as well as an individual level date back at least to the work of Doug Englebart 30 years ago. His ideas of developing collaborative, knowledge management applications are at least showing promise of fruition on today's Web. Tim Berners-Lee's work that led to the development of the Web was all about facilitating sharing of information amongst researchers.

Ideas around "Social Software" have gained a lot of attention in recent years. One notable result has been the flourishing of loosely organized groups, from the blogging-oriented, such as Many2Many (`www.corante.com/many/`), through online tool development, for example, Blue Oxen Associates (`www.blueoxen.org/`), right out into philosophical activism like that of Minciu

Sodas (www.ms.lt/). But these are only the groups associated with group-forming—starting from the poster child of the group blog, Slashdot (http://slashdot.org/), these things are ubiquitous. Whatever the angle, in the Web environment, all software is social software.

Social Software and Syndication

So if everything on the Web is in some way social, how does that relate to syndication? Feeds are all about moving information around, and the "blogosphere" can be seen as a fairly fluid emergent social network joining together millions of people, shifting enormous quantities of information. The social angle can appear as topic-oriented blogs of the Planet variety, or the focus may be on the individual people themselves, such as in closed networking systems such as Friendster and Orkut. Systems which combine these qualities have started appearing, such as Rojo (http://rojo.com). No doubt some of the bigger players in the market (Microsoft, Google, and Yahoo!) will become increasingly visible in this space. More grassroots initiatives like Broadband Mechanics' Open Source Infrastructure project aim to make the Web more useful through development of tools such as the "Digital Lifestyle Aggregator" (http://marc.blogs.it/). The exact nature of next-generation syndication software isn't clear yet, but there's no doubt it will include a strong social element.

Avoiding Overload

The limit of what can be done with social software and syndication isn't really technological, it's more a matter of imagination. So rather than vainly attempting to fulfill the need for imagination, this chapter will focus on a single, relatively simple crossover between social software and syndication. The issue of information overload is ever-present in syndication. One of the big challenges of both syndication and social software is to be selective about this information, so that the right information finds its way to the people, who want or need it.

Counting Atoms

Putting the social parts aside for a moment, it may be helpful to try and put figures on what your syndication systems need to handle. To get useful figures, some kind of measurable units are needed.

Viewing the traditional Web as a universe, the atoms of that universe would be around the size of a Weblog post. Add the physics of syndication to that universe and the atoms are RSS items or Atom entries. The naming isn't a coincidence in the latter case, it's at least a handy analogy. At a quantum level these microcontent atoms may have greater or lesser amounts of metadata associated with them. But the addition and subsequent interpretation of metadata often makes the consumption of the content easier (imagine picking up and reading a book without knowing the title, author, or genre). So how much of this stuff do you want?

Predictably there isn't a single answer. The number of items you're likely to want to handle varies according to several factors. You may want to read the Weblogs of a handful of colleagues every day, or even check every few hours. Similarly many people like to keep an eye on the kind of content found in newspapers, be it current events, the affairs of celebrities, or special interest material.

Friends as Filters

To recap, a recurring theme on the Web is information overload. The problems associated with this are rarely as evident as in the field of syndication, where the aim is to produce and consume a flow of data. But the availability of vast amounts of information isn't a problem in itself; the problem is really our inability to effectively cope with the flood. But, as the saying goes, a problem shared is a problem halved. If you pick a few feeds yourself, and rely on the judgment of a few people you trust, then you each should be able to obtain a selection of feeds with a high degree of relevance to your own interests: high signal, low noise.

A Personal Knowledgebase

As a demonstration of how to leverage social relationships to help deal with information overload, we will use a FOAF profile as the starting point in aggregating feeds. In this way there should be greater relevance of the items retrieved to the person whose profile was used. In the process you will also see how a query language can be used with an RDF store to deal with quite a mixture of source data.

Kowari RDF Store

Kowari (`www.kowari.org`) is an open-source, massively scalable, transaction-safe database for storing and retrieving metadata.

RDF Queries

The query language used here is iTQL, originally developed by Tucana Technologies. There are several different RDF query languages in circulation, but not long ago a W3C Task Force was set up to survey existing languages and develop a single, unified query language. This language already has a name, SPARQL (SPARQL Protocol and RDF Query Language), which clearly shows significant progress has been made. This language isn't finished (progressing well), but Kowari's iTQL has many features that are likely to appear in SPARQL, and it is very easy to use (and demonstrate in a book).

If you want to try SPARQL, a good toolkit with advanced implementation is the open-source Redland RDF Application Framework (`http://librdf.org/`). This is a set of native libraries suitable for most platforms with language bindings available for C#, Java, Obj-C, Perl, PHP, Python, Ruby, and Tcl. It's particularly interesting in the world of syndication because it can read RSS 1.0, Tag Soup RSS 2.0, and Atom and output in true RSS 1.0 format.

Try It Out   **An iTQL Session**

Note that the location and naming of the jar files may vary according to the kind of download you obtained (CVS or one of the ready-built packages), and the version numbers are likely to be greater than those used at the time of writing. If in doubt, refer to the documentation provided with the download.

1.   Open a command window in the directory containing the Kowari jar files. Enter the following:

```
java -jar kowari-1.0.5.jar
```

This will start a Kowari server.

2. Open a separate command window in the same directory (leaving the other running), and enter this:

```
java -jar itql-1.0.5.jar
```

This will start a query session. You should see a prompt like this:

```
iTQL Command Line Interface

Copyright (C) 2001-2004 Tucana Technologies, Inc.

Type "help ;", then enter for help.

iTQL>
```

3. Type the following:

```
create <rmi://localhost/server1#Friends>;
```

You should see the following:

```
iTQL> create <rmi://localhost/server1#Friends>;
```

```
Successfully created model rmi://localhost/server1#Friends
```

4. Verify that you're connected to the Internet, and then enter the following:

```
load <http://journal.dajobe.org/journal/2003/07/semblogs/bloggers.rdf>
  into <rmi://localhost/server1#Friends>;
```

A moment or two later you should see something like:

```
iTQL> load <http://journal.dajobe.org/journal/2003/07/semblogs/bloggers.rdf>
      into <rmi://localhost/server1#Friends>;
```

```
Successfully loaded 177 statements from
http://journal.dajobe.org/journal/2003/07/semblogs/bloggers.rdf into
rmi://localhost/server1#Friends
```

5. Next enter each of the following lines:

```
alias <http://www.w3.org/1999/02/22-rdf-syntax-ns#> as rdf;
alias <http://purl.org/rss/1.0/> as rss;
alias <http://xmlns.com/foaf/0.1/> as foaf;
alias <http://purl.org/dc/elements/1.1/> as dc;
```

After each line you should get a confirmation message.

6. Now enter this:

```
select $subject
     from <rmi://localhost/server1#Friends>
     where $subject <rdf:type> <rss:channel>;
```

You should now see a long list of results, beginning something like this:

```
[ http://journal.dajobe.org/journal/comments.rdf ]

[ http://usefulinc.com/edd/blog/rss ]

[ http://www.mnot.net/blog/XML/index.rdf ]
...
```

How It Works

The iTQL query client communicates with the Kowari server through Java RMI (Remote Method Invocation). The default address of the server is rmi://localhost/server1. In the first operation you created a store (an RDF Model) identified as rmi://localhost/server1#Friends:

```
create <rmi://localhost/server1#Friends>;
```

The next command read RDF/XML data from the Web and loaded it into the named model:

```
load <http://journal.dajobe.org/journal/2003/07/semblogs/bloggers.rdf>
     into <rmi://localhost/server1#Friends>;
```

It can get tedious entering the full URIs for terms in well-known vocabularies, so iTQL provides an aliasing facility similar to the way XML allows the use of namespace prefixes. Here three common namespaces are associated with shorter names:

```
alias <http://www.w3.org/1999/02/22-rdf-syntax-ns#> as rdf;
alias <http://purl.org/rss/1.0/> as rss;
alias <http://xmlns.com/foaf/0.1/> as foaf;
alias <http://purl.org/dc/elements/1.1/> as dc;
```

The aliases are arbitrary, but it makes sense to use the usual abbreviations for the namespaces. The next command entered was a query, but to get an idea of how that worked, here's a snippet of the source data loaded from the Web:

```
<foaf:Agent rdf:nodeID="id2246451">
    <foaf:name>Uldis Bojars</foaf:name>
    <foaf:weblog>
        <foaf:Document rdf:about="http://captsolo.net/info/">
        <dc:title>Uldis Bojars (Captain Solo)</dc:title>
        <rdfs:seeAlso>
          <rss:channel
              rdf:about="http://captsolo.net/info/xmlsrv/rdf.php?blog=2">
            <foaf:maker rdf:nodeID="id2246451"/>
            <foaf:topic rdf:resource="http://www.w3.org/2001/sw/"/>
            <foaf:topic rdf:resource="http://www.w3.org/RDF/"/>
          </rss:channel>
        </rdfs:seeAlso>
      </foaf:Document>
    </foaf:weblog>
    <foaf:interest rdf:resource="http://www.w3.org/2001/sw/"/>
    <foaf:interest rdf:resource="http://www.w3.org/RDF/"/>
</foaf:Agent>
```

In English, this says that there's an agent (actually a human one) named Uldis Bojars that has a Weblog, which is the document at the given address. Local to this RDF/XML data, the agent (Uldis) is given an identifier ("id2246451"). The title of the Weblog is "Uldis Bojars (Captain Solo)." A resource related to the Weblog (rdfs:seeAlso) is an RSS channel, with the given URI. The maker of the channel has the local id "id2246451", which corresponds to the agent (Uldis). The rdf:nodeID makes it easy to cross reference graph nodes in the RDF/XML in a way that works inside XML's tree structure. The channel has two associated topics, one of these by incredible coincidence is RDF and the other is the Semantic Web (the URIs are the home pages of those two projects). Ok, perhaps not that much of a coincidence given that the source data came from Planet RDF. Farther down you can see that those are also interests of the agent (Uldis again).

The source file contains details of 40 or so individual agents, each with a Weblog and feed. The query used to get the feed URIs looks like this:

```
select $subject
      from <rmi://localhost/server1#Friends>
      where $subject <rdf:type> <rss:channel>;
```

The syntax is quite close to that of SQL, and in this case the semantics are very similar indeed. The from clause identifies which set of statements (model) the query should be looking at, and the where clause gives a statement pattern. In the pattern $subject acts as a variable and will take on the value of the subject of all statements with <rdf:type> as their predicate (property) and <rss:channel> as their object. In the previous snippet, there is a statement that will match this:

```
<rss:channel
            rdf:about="http://captsolo.net/info/xmlsrv/rdf.php?blog=2">
```

According to RDF/XML syntax, this *typed node* will be interpreted as meaning the same as the triple:

```
http://captsolo.net/info/xmlsrv/rdf.php?blog=2 rdf:type rss:channel
```

The value of the $subject variable is used in the select clause, so all resources that have the type rss:channel in the blogroll will be selected by the query. Thus the command-line iTQL interpreter tool lists all the feed URIs found in the source RDF.

Two important points are worth emphasizing here. First, in both the source RDF/XML and the iTQL query, prefixes are used as local abbreviations for URIs. So the predicates the query is looking for are actually identified with the URI www.w3.org/1999/02/22-rdf-syntax-ns#type, and the objects with the URI http://purl.org/rss/1.0/channel.

The other point has even more potential for confusion. The ChannelSetReader code in Chapter 23 reads the URIs of rss:channel elements from an RDF/XML file. However that matching was done *purely at the level of syntax*. The matching done here happens after the data has been loaded into the Kowari store and works at the semantic level, following the RDF model. The typed node is a typed node, irrespective of how it appears in the source format. The big difference is that XML-only tools don't see the RDF structure, just the way the elements and attributes fit together. If the statement is expressed in another way, either elsewhere in the XML structure or perhaps using an rdf:Description element it will appear completely differently to XML tools. What's more the source syntax doesn't even have to be XML to work with RDF, it could be one of the other RDF formats like Turtle or NTriples. But the meaning of the statement will be the same. This separation of syntax from semantics offers a versatility that doesn't exist when the semantics are locked in-step with the syntax, as is commonly found in XML-only languages.

Going Programmatic

The iTQL command-line interpreter is a great little utility for data store interaction, but most of the time you're likely to want to have your computer do some work for you. Kowari offers a wide range of interfaces to the data, including a JavaBean through which iTQL queries can be channeled. The following listing (`FriendlyFeeds.java`) is an example of the `ItqlInterpreterBean` in action. It will extract the channel URIs from Planet RDF's FOAF profile, and read each feed in turn from the Web. The list of channels from the FOAF along with any extra channel references found in the feeds is then saved to file. The source looks like this:

```java
package org.urss.social;

import java.io.File;
import java.net.URI;

import org.kowari.itql.ItqlInterpreterBean;
import org.kowari.query.Answer;
import org.urss.feeds.FeedConstants;


public class FriendlyFeeds {

    static final String SOURCE_FOAF =
"http://journal.dajobe.org/journal/2003/07/semblogs/bloggers.rdf";

    static final String RMI_HOST = "rmi://localhost/server1";

    static final String FRIENDS_MODEL = RMI_HOST + "#Friends";

    static final String CHANNELS_MODEL = RMI_HOST + "#ChannelList";

    public static void main(String[] args) {
        try {
            ItqlInterpreterBean itql = new ItqlInterpreterBean();

            //   itql.executeUpdate("drop <" + FRIENDS_MODEL + ">;");

            itql.executeUpdate("create <" + FRIENDS_MODEL + ">;");

            String loadQuery = "load<" + SOURCE_FOAF + "> " + "into <"
                    + FRIENDS_MODEL + ">;";

            itql.executeUpdate(loadQuery);

            String aliases = "alias <" + FeedConstants.RDF_NS + "> as rdf; "
                    + "alias <" + FeedConstants.RSS_NS + "> as rss; "
                    + "alias <" + FeedConstants.DC_NS + "> as dc; "
                    + "alias <" + FeedConstants.FOAF_NS + "> as foaf;";
```

```
            itql.executeUpdate(aliases);

        String channelsQuery = "select $subject " + "from <"
                + FRIENDS_MODEL + ">"
                + "where $subject <rdf:type> <rss:channel>;";

        Answer channelAnswer = itql.executeQuery(channelsQuery);

        String feedLoaderQuery;
        channelAnswer.beforeFirst();

        for (int i = 0; i < channelAnswer.getRowCount(); i++) {
            channelAnswer.next();
            System.out.println(i);

            feedLoaderQuery = "load <"
                    + channelAnswer.getObject(0).toString() + "> "
                    + " into <" + FRIENDS_MODEL + ">;";

            System.out.println(feedLoaderQuery);
            try {
                itql.executeUpdate(feedLoaderQuery);
            } catch (Exception syntaxException) {
                System.out.println("Error loading "
                        + channelAnswer.getObject(0).toString());
            }
        }

        channelAnswer.close();

//      itql.executeUpdate("drop <" + CHANNELS_MODEL + ">;");
        itql.executeUpdate("create <" + CHANNELS_MODEL + ">;");

        String shiftChannelsQuery =
                "insert select $subject <rdf:type> <rss:channel> "
                + "from <"
                + FRIENDS_MODEL
                + "> "
                + "where $subject <rdf:type> <rss:channel> "
                + "into <"
                + CHANNELS_MODEL + ">;";

        itql.executeUpdate(shiftChannelsQuery);

        URI channelsURI = new URI(CHANNELS_MODEL);
        itql.backup(channelsURI, new File("friendly-channels.rdf"));
        URI friendsURI = new URI(FRIENDS_MODEL);
        itql.backup(friendsURI, new File("friends.rdf"));
    } catch (Exception e) {
        e.printStackTrace();
    }
    System.out.println("Done.");
    }
}
```

This file will live in the existing Java source tree in a new package, `org.urss.social`. To compile it you'll probably prefer to prepare a batch file that looks something like this (`build-social.bat`):

```
set dist=C:\kowari\dist
javac -classpath .;%dist%\kowari-1.0.5.jar;%dist%\itql-1.0.5.jar;%dist%\
driver-1.0.5.jar org\urss\social\FriendlyFeeds.java
```

Save this file in the root of your `urss` source tree. You will need to modify the path given for `dist` according to where you have saved the Kowari downloads. To run the code you can also use a batch file, something like (`run-social.bat`):

```
set dist=C:\kowari\dist
set lib=C:\kowari\lib
java -classpath .;%dist%\kowari-1.0.5.jar;%dist%\itql-1.0.5.jar;%dist%\
driver-1.0.5.jar;%lib%\saaj-1.1.jar;%lib%\
log4j-1.2.8.jar;org.urss.social.FriendlyFeeds
```

Note that the classpath and other parts following `java` *or* `javac` *that run over several lines in these listings should actually be all on the same line in the batch files. Both of these batch files follow the directory layout obtained when Kowari is downloaded using CVS. See the Kowari.org site for details.*

Try It Out   Kowari Blogroll Channels

1.   Open a command window in the Kowari distribution directory and enter:

```
java -jar kowari-1.0.5.jar
```

This will start a Kowari server.

2.   Open a command window in your source directory and compile the files by entering:

```
build-social.bat
```

3.   In the same window, run the demonstration by entering:

```
run-social.bat
```

You may see a log4j initialization error — ignore it. It will be followed by something like this:

```
0
1
Error loading http://dannyayers.com/feed/rdf
2
3
...
41
Done.
```

Once this has run, you should find a file called `friendly-channels.rdf` in the same directory. When you open this file in a text editor, you will see the list of channels found in the blogroll. The list, again, is expressed in RDF/XML, but without all the additional information about the maker of the Weblog and so on.

Each number corresponds to a different feed being loaded. Here there has been a problem with the second feed, but the demonstration continues all the same.

How It Works

You've already seen the most important part of the operation of this demo, the iTQL query language. Here is a brief discussion of its use in code. To begin, a new instance of `ItqlInterpreterBean` is created:

```
ItqlInterpreterBean itql = new ItqlInterpreterBean();
```

Now a query is constructed as a string—this is exactly the same as you saw with the command-line interpreter tool, with a string constant used for the URI, and the interpreter bean's `executeUpdate` method is used to pass the query to the data store:

```
itql.executeUpdate("create <" + FRIENDS_MODEL + ">;");
```

Similarly the other commands/operations you used in the query tool are constructed as strings and passed to the bean:

```
String loadQuery = "load<" + SOURCE_FOAF + "> " + "into <"
        + FRIENDS_MODEL + ">;";

itql.executeUpdate(loadQuery);

String aliases = "alias <" + FeedConstants.RDF_NS + "> as rdf; "
        + "alias <" + FeedConstants.RSS_NS + "> as rss; "
        + "alias <" + FeedConstants.DC_NS + "> as dc; "
        + "alias <" + FeedConstants.FOAF_NS + "> as foaf;";

itql.executeUpdate(aliases);

String channelsQuery = "select $subject " + "from <"
        + FRIENDS_MODEL + ">"
        + "where $subject <rdf:type> <rss:channel>;";
```

When it comes to the query that gets the channel URIs, the `executeQuery` method is used. Unlike the `executeUpdate` queries, this returns some data of interest. The query results take the form of an `Answer` object:

```
Answer channelAnswer = itql.executeQuery(channelsQuery);
```

The results of this query, as in the command-line version, will be a list of channel URIs. However, this time those URIs are each going to be addressed in turn, and the contents of those feeds will be loaded into another RDF model. To get data out of an `Answer` object you can treat it like a list of records, looking at each record or row in turn, with individual values in the row being addressed by name or index. Here the results (passed through the variable `$subject`) form a simple column, and the URIs themselves are obtained by using the string representation of each row of the results. These URIs are put into another `load` query, to load the feed data from the Web. You can see the loop that steps through the rows found in the `Answer` object here:

```
String feedLoaderQuery;
channelAnswer.beforeFirst();

for (int i = 0; i < channelAnswer.getRowCount(); i++) {
```

```
        channelAnswer.next();
        System.out.println(i);

        feedLoaderQuery = "load <"
+ channelAnswer.getObject(0).toString() + "> "
+ " into <" + FRIENDS_MODEL + ">;";

        try {
            itql.executeUpdate(feedLoaderQuery);
        } catch (Exception syntaxException) {
            System.out.println("Error loading "
+ channelAnswer.getObject(0).toString());
        }
    }
channelAnswer.close();
```

To get at all the channel URIs in this combined data, a slightly different query is required, one which will pull out all the statements of the form:

```
<uri> <rdf:type> <rss:channel>
```

But that's not all. The results of this query will be placed into a completely different RDF model, which is created here:

```
itql.executeUpdate("create <" + CHANNELS_MODEL + ">;");
```

To insert the selected data into this new model, the whole query has the following shape:

```
insert selected items into <target model>
```

This is constructed as a string, with *selected items* being the query to select the channel URIs and *target model* being the newly created CHANNELS_MODEL. Here is the source code for this:

```
String shiftChannelsQuery = "insert select $subject <rdf:type> <rss:channel> "
                    + "from <"
                    + FRIENDS_MODEL
                    + "> "
                    + "where $subject <rdf:type> <rss:channel> "
                    + "into <"
                    + CHANNELS_MODEL + ">;";

itql.executeUpdate(shiftChannelsQuery);

URI uri = new URI(CHANNELS_MODEL);
```

Finally the `backup` method of the `ItqlInterpreterBean` is used to dump the models containing the channel URIs and all the data in the #Friends model to file:

```
                URI channelsURI = new URI(CHANNELS_MODEL);
                itql.backup(channelsURI, new File("friendly-channels.rdf"));
                URI friendsURI = new URI(FRIENDS_MODEL);
                itql.backup(friendsURI, new File("friends.rdf"));
```

If you look inside these two files, you might not recognize what you find until you scroll down somewhat. The backup format makes big use of XML entities, which will be used to substitute in the namespace URIs. Here's an excerpt of the code of `friendly-channels.rdf`:

```
<?xml version="1.0" encoding="WINDOWS-1252"?>

<!DOCTYPE rdf:RDF [
  <!ENTITY ns38 'http://www.ilrt.bristol.ac.uk/discovery/rdf/resources/'>
  <!ENTITY ns5 'http://www.w3.org/1999/02/22-rdf-syntax-ns#'>
  ...
  <!ENTITY ns33 'http://www.bnode.org/rdfxml/page/'>]>

<rdf:RDF
  xmlns:ns38="&ns38;"
  xmlns:ns5="&ns5;"
  ...
  xmlns:ns33="&ns33;">

  <rdf:Description rdf:about="http://www.hackdiary.com/">
    <ns5:type rdf:resource="http://purl.org/rss/1.0/channel"/>
  </rdf:Description>
  ...
</rdf:RDF>
```

The `rdf:Description` chunk here is the interesting part; it is in fact logically equivalent to the abbreviated form:

```
<rss:channel rdf:about="http://www.hackdiary.com/" />
```

All that's changed is the XML serialization.

If you look inside `friends.rdf` you should see something similar, but in there you may be able to spot the items taken from the feeds of Planet RDF's friends. Dumping this data to file has its uses, but being able to query the model offers some great potential for applications. When you open the iTQL interpreter utility (with the Kowari server running), you may like to try the following:

```
select $item $title $date from <rmi://localhost/server1#Friends>
    where $item <rdf:type> <rss:item>
        and $item <rss:title> $title
        and $item <dc:date> $date
    order by $date desc
    limit 10;
```

You should see 10 items, each looking similar to the following:

```
[ http://usefulinc.com/edd/blog/contents/2004/11/10-suspend/read,
    Suspend to RAM working on Sony TR1MP, 2004-11-10T20:23:18.00Z ]
```

If you compare these to the query, you can see how the values have been pulled out in a manner very much like that of a SQL database. You may like to check out the iTQL documentation and experiment with queries of your own. If you point a Web browser at `http://localhost:8080/webui` you will find another interface to the data store.

In an Ideal World...

So the `FriendlyFeeds` demo grabbed a FOAF profile from the Web, and downloaded the contents of all the feeds into a Kowari data store. However the FOAF profile used at the start was from Planet RDF — hardly your average person's profile. As it happens all the feeds listed in Planet RDF's profile are in RSS 1.0 format, that is, they are RDF/XML. Even with this cheating, you might have noticed there were a lot of error messages along the way. These were more than likely caused by ill-formed XML errors in the source feeds. There is always the option of limiting your reading to well-formed RSS 1.0 sources, but that would likely lead to a narrow, probably quite peculiar view of the world. A better approach is to broaden your horizons and welcome the full spectrum of formats. The benefits of the RDF model in a neat implementation like Kowari can still be used on RSS 2.0 and Atom source data without too much trouble.

Fetching and Normalizing

To be able to use syndication data in an RDF store, you must of course first get the data into that store. RDF/XML is the interchange format for RDF, so if you can get your data into that, then it can be read directly into the store. In earlier chapters you saw an aggregator subsystem in Java that could fetch data from the Web and pass it on to subsequent processing. Here the same subsystem will be reused, with the target this time being RDF/XML files. Figure 29-1 shows a conceptual block diagram of the revised fetching system.

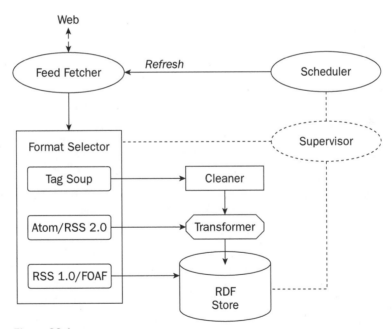

Figure 29-1

Note that Figure 29-1 doesn't correspond directly to the classes in the application code. For example, much of the functionality such as individual feed scheduling is associated with the feed classes themselves.

RDF to RDF

The classes that do the fetching of the feed data will remain the same as before. However, a new set of interpreters will take that raw data and convert it into RDF/XML ready for the store. Starting at the bottom left of Figure 29-1, incoming data such as RSS 1.0 or FOAF is already in RDF/XML format, so it can be passed to the store. Figure 29-1 does not show this, but there will be an additional stage in between the feed fetcher subsystem and the store itself to decouple the subsystems. Each feed fetcher will save the data it obtains to an RDF/XML file. A completely separate subsystem will read these files from the directory to which they have been saved, and load them into the RDF store. More on that in a moment.

XML to RDF

A large proportion of syndicated data will be in well-formed Atom or RSS 2.0 feeds. The mapping between this and the feed model as expressed in RDF is straightforward enough that an XSLT transformation can be used to convert this XML into RDF/XML. Any incoming plain-XML data will be passed through an XSLT processor, the Transformer in Figure 29-1, before it is saved to file.

Tag Soup to RDF

You have already seen code for a tag soup parser that can build objects corresponding to those of an RSS feed. We use this in Chapter 27 to serialize out as RSS 2.0, and via transformation RSS 1.0 and HTML. The same building blocks can be reused to take incoming tag soup and serialize it out as RDF/XML — because RSS 1.0 is RDF/XML. We will arrange the code of Chapter 27 a little, but the mechanisms are exactly the same.

Coupling the Store

The new fetcher design will dump files containing normalized feed data into a directory in the file system. A completely separate mini-application picks up these files and loads them into the RDF store. This is a fairly crude setup, and as it stands has drawbacks that prevent the approach from being more generally useful. If an attempt is made to read a file while it is being written, what happens will largely depend on the behavior of the operating system looking after the file system. There are ways of dealing with this situation allowing us to monitor the files somewhat reliably. Practical applications can monitor files, and either exploit any available native file change notification mechanism, or use a stack of heuristics to determine when the operation is safe. For example parts of Dashboard [www.nat.org/dashboard/] use the former approach, while the AntFlow system [http://antflow.onionnetworks.com/] follows the latter approach. But the current setup can work without such sophistication because of a factor at either end of the communication chain. The producer will re-present the feed data after any significant change, such as the addition of new entries; these will be forwarded into the file system directory by the feed fetcher. Given that there may be 10 or 20 entries in a feed, each individual entry is in effect published many times, providing a large degree of redundancy over time. At the receiver side, the RDF model is such that statements are in effect cumulative — one statement can't cancel out another, at least not at the logical level. Duplication of statements makes no difference to the subsequent interpretation. In practice it's easy enough to handle a file reading/parsing error by aborting the operation, but without the need to halt the system. RDF/XML inherits the strictness of XML, so either a statement will be passed on accurately or not at all. Overall, as much by luck as judgment, this represents a robust enough system.

The files used will all appear in the org.urss.social package. This package and the org.urss. planet packages are prime candidates for refactoring, but for the purposes of demonstration it's convenient to keep the code separate from the earlier implementations. The new classes are as follows:

- ❑ Supervisor: Top-level application runner

- ❑ FormatSniffer: Detects the format of a feed

- ❑ RDFInterpreterFactory: Creates interpreters for each feed

- ❑ CleanerInterpreter: An interpreter for ill-formed feeds

- ❑ TransformerInterpreter: An interpreter for well-formed, plain-XML feeds

- ❑ WriterInterpreter: An interpreter for RDF/XML feeds

- ❑ KowariLoader: Loads the normalized feed files into the data store

Supervisor

This class is a minor extension of the Planet.java file we show in Chapter 27. The source code begins
like this:

```
package org.urss.social;

import java.util.Iterator;
import java.util.Set;

import org.urss.feeds.EntryList;
import org.urss.feeds.EntryListImpl;
import org.urss.feeds.FeedConstants;
import org.urss.feeds.FeedFetcher;
import org.urss.feeds.FeedFetcherImpl;
    public static void main(String[] args) {
        Supervisor supervisor = new Supervisor();
        Set channelURIs = supervisor.loadChannelList("input/feedlist.rdf");
        FeedSet feeds = supervisor.initFeeds(channelURIs);

        while (true) {
            feeds.refreshAll();
        }
    }
    public Set loadChannelList(String filename) {
        ChannelSetReader reader = new ChannelSetReader();
        return reader.load(filename);
    }
}
```

The main method loads the list of feeds from file with the aid of a ChannelSetReader object created in
the loadChannelList method. The set of URIs is passed to a local method to initialize fetchers for each
of the feeds. When initialized, the system passes into an infinite loop with the purpose of keeping the
local data up-to-date forever. The rest of Supervisor.java is comprised by the initialization method,
which looks like this:

```
    public FeedSet initFeeds(Set channelURIs) {
        FeedSet feeds = new FeedSetImpl();
        Iterator channelIterator = channelURIs.iterator();
        FeedFetcher feedFetcher;
        Interpreter interpreter;
        String uriString;
```

```
            FormatSniffer sniffer = new FormatSniffer();
            HttpConnector connector;
            char format;
            while (channelIterator.hasNext()) {

                uriString = (String) channelIterator.next();

                //          added for Social
                connector = new HttpConnector(uriString);
                boolean streamAvailable = connector.load();
                if (streamAvailable) {
                    format = sniffer.sniff(connector.getInputStream());
                } else {
                    format = FeedConstants.UNKNOWN;
                }

                System.out.println(uriString + "\n"
                        + FeedConstants.formatName(format) + "\n");

                feedFetcher = new FeedFetcherImpl(uriString);
                feedFetcher.setFormatHint(format);
                interpreter = RDFInterpreterFactory.createInterpreter(format,
                        entries); // changed for Social
                feedFetcher.setInterpreter(interpreter);
                feedFetcher.setRefreshPeriod(REFRESH_PERIOD);
                feeds.addFeed(feedFetcher);
            }
            return feeds;
        }
    }
```

An extra section in this code uses `HttpConnector` objects to get feed data that is passed to an instance of `FormatSniffer` to detect which general category the format falls in. This code isn't particularly efficient or economical with system resources, but usually the sniffing only needs to occur once, so it doesn't really demand optimization. Here is the complete source code for `FormatSniffer.java`:

```
package org.urss.social;

import java.io.InputStream;

import javax.xml.parsers.SAXParserFactory;

import org.urss.feeds.FeedConstants;
import org.xml.sax.Attributes;
import org.xml.sax.InputSource;
import org.xml.sax.XMLReader;
import org.xml.sax.helpers.DefaultHandler;


public class FormatSniffer extends DefaultHandler {

    char format = FeedConstants.UNKNOWN;
```

```java
    public char sniff(InputStream inputStream) {

        SAXParserFactory parserFactory = SAXParserFactory.newInstance();
        parserFactory.setNamespaceAware(true);
        XMLReader reader = null;
        try {
            reader = parserFactory.newSAXParser().getXMLReader();
        } catch (Exception e) { // bad
            e.printStackTrace();
        }
        reader.setContentHandler(this);
        InputSource inputSource = new InputSource(inputStream);
        try {
            reader.parse(inputSource);
        } catch (Exception e) { // whatever the problem, there's no XML available
            return FeedConstants.RSS2_BOZO;
        }
        return format; //
    }

    public void startElement(String namespaceURI, String localName,
            String qName, Attributes attributes) {
        if(namespaceURI.equals(FeedConstants.RDF_NS) && localName.equals("RDF")){
            format = FeedConstants.RDF_OTHER;
        }
        if(namespaceURI.equals(FeedConstants.RSS_NS) && localName.equals("items")){
            format = FeedConstants.RSS1;
        }
        if(localName.equals("rss")){
            format = FeedConstants.RSS2;
        }
        if(namespaceURI.startsWith("http://purl.org/atom")
            && localName.equals("feed")){
            format = FeedConstants.ATOM;
        }
    }
}
```

The class acts as a SAX parser, with the parsing class itself (XMLReader) being created and applied to the feeds in the sniff method. The handler assigned to the parser is the instance of this class itself. The class extends SAX's base handler implementation DefaultHandler, only overriding the startElement method. When sniff is called, the parser will attempt to run through the data as XML. If it isn't, then an exception will be thrown and the format of the feed will be marked as type RSS2_BOZO, that is, ill-formed.

The startElement method detects the format of any well-formed XML using a sequence of simple tests. The first looks for a root element of <rdf:RDF>, with the rdf: prefix qualified to the RDF namespace. This will be found in most RDF/XML files (it's no longer essential for the RDF/XML format in general, but remains something of a convention). The next check is for an <rss:items> element (rss: with its usual qualification). This should be a pretty good indicator that the data is an RSS 1.0 feed, although many of the RSS vocabulary terms are used in non-RSS documents (for example, rss:channel in FOAF blogrolls), this particular term does indicate a sequence of items, which is pretty much the defining characteristic of an RSS feed. The next check is for an <rss> element, which will be the root of all plain-XML RSS family feeds. Only the local name is checked as Netscape's RSS 0.91 uses a namespace, whereas Userland RSS 0.91 and the rest of the family (including RSS 2.0) don't. All of these formats will be treated as RSS 2.0, with varying degrees of degeneration. The final check is a little sly, looking for an element called <feed> with a namespace that *begins with* http://purl.org/atom. This will hopefully catch all deployed versions of Atom—those that have appeared so far have had the same URI base with minor differences in the name at the end.

The RDFInterpreter class looks after the creation of interpreters for the various feed types, as detected by the sniffer. The code is very straightforward, following the same structure as the InterpreterFactory used in the previous incarnations of the feed fetcher application. The factory is given the hint of the format type and returns an instance of a class that will deal with the data as required. Here is the full source code for RDFInterpreterFactory.java:

```java
package org.urss.social;

import org.urss.feeds.EntryList;
import org.urss.feeds.FeedConstants;
import org.urss.feeds.FeedFetcher;
import org.urss.io.Interpreter;

public class RDFInterpreterFactory {

    public static Interpreter createInterpreter(char formatHint,
            EntryList entries) {
        Interpreter interpreter = null;

        switch (formatHint) {

        case FeedConstants.RSS2_BOZO:
            System.out.println("Creating BOZO interpreter...");
            interpreter = new CleanerInterpreter();
            return interpreter;

        case FeedConstants.RSS2:
        case FeedConstants.ATOM:
            System.out.println("Creating XML interpreter...");
            interpreter = new TransformerInterpreter();
            return interpreter;

        case FeedConstants.RSS1:
        case FeedConstants.RDF_OTHER:
            System.out.println("Creating RDF interpreter...");
            interpreter = new WriterInterpreter();
            return interpreter;

        default:
            return null;
        }
    }

    public static String getFilename(FeedFetcher feed) {
        String feedFilename = feed.getURIString();
```

```
            feedFilename = feedFilename.substring(7);
        return feedFilename.replace('/','_');
    }
}
```

The last little method there is a simple utility to convert the URI of a feed to a name that can act as a file name, for example, http://example.org/myblog will become example.org_myblog. Here is the source code for the different interpreters, starting with the simplest, WriterInterpreter.java:

```
package org.urss.social;

import org.urss.feeds.FeedConstants;
import org.urss.feeds.FeedFetcher;
import org.urss.io.Interpreter;


public class WriterInterpreter implements Interpreter {

    public void interpret(FeedFetcher feed) {
        System.out.println("\nFeed: "+feed.getURIString());
        System.out.println("type: "
            + FeedConstants.formatName(feed.getFormatHint()));
        System.out.println("Writing from RDFInterpreter...");
        feed.downloadToFile("data/"+RDFInterpreterFactory.getFilename(feed));
    }

}
```

If you refer back to Figure 29-1, this interpreter is the one for RSS 1.0/FOAF. All it does is write the source RDF/XML to file using the FeedFetcher method downloadToFile, which is described in Chapter 22. It gets a target file name with the help of the utility in RDFInterpreterFactory, and its operation is liberally interspersed with messages to the console.

You have also already seen a significant proportion of the code that does the processing of Atom/RSS 2.0 feeds in TransformerInterpreter:

```
package org.urss.social;

import java.io.File;
import java.io.InputStream;

import javax.xml.transform.Result;
import javax.xml.transform.Source;
import javax.xml.transform.Transformer;
import javax.xml.transform.stream.StreamResult;
import javax.xml.transform.stream.StreamSource;

import org.urss.feeds.FeedConstants;
import org.urss.feeds.FeedFetcher;
import org.urss.io.Interpreter;
import org.urss.planet.FileEntrySerializer;

/**
```

```
 * Transforms feed XML (RSS 2.0/Atom) into RDF/XML
 *
 */
public class TransformerInterpreter implements Interpreter {

    private WriterInterpreter rdfInterpreter;

    private Transformer transformer;

    private static final String xslFilename = "templates/feed-rss1.0.xsl";

    public TransformerInterpreter() {
        rdfInterpreter = new WriterInterpreter();

    }

    public void interpret(FeedFetcher feed) {
        InputStream inputStream = feed.getInputStream();
        String filename = "data/" + RDFInterpreterFactory.getFilename(feed);

        System.out.println("\nFeed: "+feed.getURIString());
        System.out.println("type: "+
          FeedConstants.formatName(feed.getFormatHint()));
        System.out.println("Writing from TransformerInterpreter...");

        writeXmlFile(inputStream, filename, xslFilename);
    }

    public static void writeXmlFile(InputStream inputStream, String outputFilename,
            String xslFilename) {
        try {
            Source source = new StreamSource(inputStream);

            Result result = new StreamResult(new File(outputFilename));

            Transformer transformer =
                FileEntrySerializer.getTransformer(xslFilename);

            transformer.transform(source, result);

        } catch (Exception e) {
            e.printStackTrace();
        }
    }
}
```

When the `interpret` method is passed a `FeedFetcher` instance, it gets a reference to the stream that will carry the source feed data, and uses the `RDFInterpreterFactory.getFilename` method to get a destination file name for the data. These two pieces of information are passed to the `writeXmlFile` method, along with the name of an XSLT file. The `writeXmlFile` method takes some input XML, applies an XSLT transformation and saves the result to file. This is a variation on the `writeXmlFile` method in `FileEntrySerializer` (and is another candidate for later refactoring).

Operationally, `CleanerInterpreter` is the most complex of the three interpreters. It takes ill-formed XML and creates well-formed RSS 2.0, which it then passes through an XSLT transformation. You've already encountered this sequence of operations in the Planet demonstration. Here is the source code (`CleanerInterpreter.java`):

```java
package org.urss.social;

import org.urss.feeds.EntryList;
import org.urss.feeds.EntryListImpl;
import org.urss.feeds.FeedConstants;
import org.urss.feeds.FeedFetcher;
import org.urss.io.Interpreter;
import org.urss.parsers.FeedParser;
import org.urss.parsers.ParserInterpreter;
import org.urss.parsers.Rss2Handler;
import org.urss.parsers.SoupParser;
import org.urss.planet.FileEntrySerializer;

public class CleanerInterpreter implements Interpreter {

    FeedParser feedParser = null;

    Rss2Handler rss2handler = null;

    EntryList entries;

    FileEntrySerializer serializer;

    public CleanerInterpreter() {
        entries = new EntryListImpl();
        initializeCleaner();
        serializer = new FileEntrySerializer();
        serializer.loadDocumentShell("input/shell.xml");
    }

    public void interpret(FeedFetcher feed) {
        serializer.clearEntries();

        for (int i = 0; i < entries.size(); i++) {
            serializer.addEntry(entries.getEntry(i));
        }
        String filename = "data/" + RDFInterpreterFactory.getFilename(feed);
        System.out.println("\nFeed: "+feed.getURIString());
        System.out.println("type: "+
            FeedConstants.formatName(feed.getFormatHint()));
        System.out.println("Writing from CleanerInterpreter...");

        serializer.transformWrite(filename, "templates/feed-rss1.0.xsl");
    }

    private void initializeCleaner() {
        FeedParser feedParser = new SoupParser();
        Interpreter interpreter = new ParserInterpreter(feedParser);
```

```
            rss2handler = new Rss2Handler();
            rss2handler.setEntryList(entries);
            feedParser.setContentHandler(rss2handler);
    }

}
```

The `CleanerInterpreter` class uses a `SoupParser` to fire events at an `Rss2Handler`, with the entries discovered in the feed being loaded into an `EntryList`. When the parser has finished reading the data, the entry objects are serialized out through the `transformWrite` method of a `FileEntrySerializer`, to produce the requisite RDF/XML file.

Try It Out   Fetching and Normalizing Feeds

1. Download and save the source files to your source tree. In the `input` directory you should have a file listing the channels you want to read, as described in Chapter 22 (`feedlist.rdf`).

2. Open a command window in the root of the tree and enter the following:

```
javac -classpath . org/urss/social/Supervisor.java
```

This compiles the source files.

3. Now enter:

```
java -classpath . org.urss.social.Supervisor
```

This will run the feed-fetching application.

You should now see a series of reports in the console, featuring lines like this:

```
D:\urss>java -classpath . org.urss.social.Supervisor

Creating XML interpreter...
http://martinfowler.com/bliki/bliki.rss
RSS 2.0
...
Checking: http://martinfowler.com/bliki/bliki.rss
Connected, interpreting...

Feed: http://martinfowler.com/bliki/bliki.rss
type: RSS 2.0
Writing from TransformerInterpreter...
...
```

Here only the details of one feed have been shown; similar messages should be seen for all the other feeds listed in `feedlist.rdf`.

How It Works

The details of operation have already been covered, but if you look at the console output you can see the sequence of events:

```
Creating XML interpreter...
http://martinfowler.com/bliki/bliki.rss
RSS 2.0
```

The sniffer has determined that this feed is RSS 2.0, and the interpreter factory has created a corresponding interpreter. Shortly this feed is revisited, the data being passed to the interpreter:

```
...
Checking: http://martinfowler.com/bliki/bliki.rss
Connected, interpreting...
```

The purpose of this interpreter is to convert the RSS 2.0 into RDF/XML, and save it to file. That operation is subsequently reported:

```
Feed: http://martinfowler.com/bliki/bliki.rss
type: RSS 2.0
Writing from TransformerInterpreter...
...
```

If you now look at the contents of the data directory you should see something similar the following:

```
martinfowler.com_bliki_bliki.rss
www.dehora.net_journal_index.rdf
danja.typepad.com_fecho_atom.xml
```

Looking inside these files you should see they're RDF/XML.

Loading the Data Store

The source code for the part of the application that will take the RDF/XML files delivered previously and load them into a Kowari model is as follows (KowariLoader.java):

```java
package org.urss.social;

import java.io.File;
import java.net.URI;
import java.net.URISyntaxException;

import org.kowari.itql.ItqlInterpreterBean;
import org.kowari.query.QueryException;

public class KowariLoader {

    static final String DATA_DIR = "data";

    public static void main(String[] args) {
        URI friendsData = null;
        try {
            friendsData = new URI(FriendlyFeeds.FRIENDS_MODEL);
        } catch (URISyntaxException e) {
            e.printStackTrace();
        }

        ItqlInterpreterBean itql = new ItqlInterpreterBean();
        File dataDir = new File(DATA_DIR);
        File[] files;
        while(true){
```

```
        files = dataDir.listFiles();

        if(files.length > 0){
            for(int i=0;i<files.length;i++){
                try {
                    System.out.println("Loading "+files[i]);
                    itql.load(files[i], friendsData);
                    System.out.println("Deleting "+files[i]);
                    files[i].delete();
                } catch (QueryException e1) {
                    e1.printStackTrace();
                }
            }
        }
        try {
            Thread.sleep(1000);
        } catch (InterruptedException e1) {
            e1.printStackTrace();
        }
    }
}
```

This source is fairly self-explanatory, the key part being the following lines:

```
itql.load(files[i], friendsData);
System.out.println("Deleting "+files[i]);
files[i].delete();
```

Here the named file is loaded into the identified model, and then the source file is deleted.

Assuming you have already run the sub-application that gets the feed data and saves it as RDF/XML files, you can now run this sub-application and get the data into the store.

Quite a few libraries are needed to run this, so you probably want a batch file looking something like the following two.

build-social.bat:
```
set dist=C:\kowari\cvs\kowari\dist
javac -classpath .;%dist%\kowari-1.0.5.jar;%dist%\itql-1.0.5.jar;%dist%\
driver-1.0.5.jar org\urss\social\FriendlyFeeds.java
org/urss/social/KowariLoader.java
```

run-kloader.bat:
```
set dist=C:\kowari\cvs\kowari\dist
set lib=C:\kowari\cvs\kowari\lib
java -classpath .;%dist%\kowari-1.0.5.jar;%dist%\itql-1.0.5.jar;%dist%\
driver-1.0.5.jar;%lib%\saaj-1.1.jar;%lib%\log4j-1.2.8.jar;
  org.urss.social.KowariLoader
```

Try It Out   Adding Normalized Data to Store

You will need to have the Kowari distribution extracted to a convenient directory, and batch files like those above prepared to reflect your own installation layout.

1. Open a command window in the root of your source tree.

2. Enter the following to compile the applications:

```
build-social.bat
```

If you encounter a problem here, check the paths in the batch file correspond to those of your installation.

3. If it isn't already running, start the Kowari server; in the distribution directory enter:

```
java -jar kowari-1.0.5.jar
```

4. Enter the following to run the application:

```
run-kloader.bat
```

You may again see a log4j error message, which again can safely be ignored. This should be followed by something like:

```
Loading data\danja.typepad.com_fecho_atom.xml
Deleting data\danja.typepad.com_fecho_atom.xml
Loading data\martinfowler.com_bliki_bliki.rss
Deleting data\martinfowler.com_bliki_bliki.rss
Loading data\www.dehora.net_journal_index.rdf
Deleting data\www.dehora.net_journal_index.rdf
```

If you check the data directory you will see that those files have been removed. If you run the feed fetcher and this loader concurrently, you will periodically see a file appear in the directory and then be removed by the loader. (If you are going to run these mini-applications for any length of time, you should increase the sleep time in the loops, as previously described.)

Now if you start up the iTQL console again, you can query the store on the data.

For example:

```
select $title
    from <rmi://localhost/server1#Friends>
    where $subject <http://purl.org/rss/1.0/title> $title
    and $subject <http://www.w3.org/1999/02/22-rdf-syntax-ns#type>
                            <http://purl.org/rss/1.0/item>;
```

This will return all the item titles in the store. The results look something like this:

```
[ Raptor 1.4.3 ]
[ Regular Sucking Schedule ]
[ How to create a REST Protocol ]
[ Why Lisp will be around for another 50 years ]
...
[ 502 Bad MVC Framework ]
41 rows returned.
```

This resembles the kind of result you might get from a SQL-oriented relational database. One immediate big difference is that you can load any RDF/XML into the store and query it in the same fashion. That data may use any mix of RSS 1.0, FOAF, the geographical or calendar vocabularies, even terms from a vocabulary you've designed yourself. There is no need to construct domain-specific tables up front, and so RDF stores can offer a more agile alternative to traditional relational database systems.

Summary

In this chapter you saw...

- ❑ An overview of various ideas relating to "social software."
- ❑ How to query feed and FOAF data in an RDF store manually.
- ❑ How to query feed and FOAF data programmatically.
- ❑ How an FOAF profile could provide a source list of channels.
- ❑ How assorted feed data could be fetched and normalized.

Systems that operate like the one described here are relatively straightforward to build, it's mostly a matter of bolting together conceptually simple components into a (probably) conceptually simple whole. Don't forget the user interface components described in Chapter 28 and the Wiki in Chapter 24 speak essentially the same language. All of these systems can interoperate thanks to the use of common protocols and models (despite the need for occasional format translation). By demonstrating that the mechanics aren't really all that difficult, this chapter will have done a little to release your imagination to produce far more interesting applications.

Exercise

1. Write an iTQL query to extract the names of the people featured in the blogroll.

    Hint: You want to extract the `foaf:name` values of the `foaf:Person` resources.

Additional Content

The Web supports data of all different kinds, and from a syndication point of view much of it is potential content for a feed. As an example of using media data alongside syndication, this chapter describes a small application that will enable you to record and publish audio on the Web.

In this chapter you look at:

❑ An introduction to *podcasting*

❑ An overview of digital audio

❑ The reason for compression

❑ An audio syndication tool called *Imp*

Syndicated Broadcasting

The latest craze in blogging goes by the name of *podcasting*, which is an automated approach to delivering audio to a personal stereo using a syndication feed. The name comes from the target device, the iPod. Rather than posting photographs of their cat, the blogger can now provide an audio recording describing the cat's antics. By automating the download, the user receives the audio in a form ready to play rather than having to wait for a real-time download. The trade-off is that the material won't be available until usually the day after it has been published.

In this scenario, publishers of a syndication feed will also provide audio files on their Web servers. As each new audio file is made available, an entry will be added to their syndication feeds referring to the audio file in a manner appropriate to the feed format. On the consumer side, a feed reader will pay special attention to references to audio files taking actions based on user preferences. Typically the address of the audio file will be passed into a queue for downloading when the computer is otherwise idle. After the file has been downloaded, the client application may present the local copy of the audio file linked from the blog entry as part of the regular view. A true "podcasting" application will pass the audio file directly onto an iPod, for listening at the user's leisure.

The consumer side of the publish/subscribe chain will depend on the facilities available to the reader, so as demonstration application you will now see how the production end of the chain can be implemented.

Publishing Audio

To publish speech or other audio with the aid of a syndication feed, you need to be able to carry out the following three steps:

1. Record the audio.
2. Upload the audio to a Web server.
3. Add an entry to a syndication feed.

Virtually all computers support audio recording (most laptops even have a microphone built in); uploading can be done through any standard FTP or HTTP client that supports PUT; and entries can be added to syndication feed file using a text editor and subsequent PUT. But this approach isn't exactly user-friendly, and there are complications relating to audio formats. But computers can make life easier, and the application described here covers these three steps with the minimum of user input. Before looking at practical code, here first is a quick overview of how digital audio works.

Digital Audio in Brief

Our perception of sound is the result of rapid pressure changes of the air around us being detected by the ear. The frequency of those changes corresponds to pitch in music, the more rapid the changes, the higher the pitch. The human ear can detect frequencies in the approximate range of 20 cycles per second (Hertz, Hz) to 20 kHz (kilohertz), although the top end of that range declines considerably with the listener's age. These figures refer to the fundamental (sine wave) periodic signals. Real-world audio can be viewed as a mix of many different simple signals of different frequencies, even though it may be perceived as a single sound. The listener's ears receive a complex waveform, which, after a little local processing, is passed to the brain for interpretation.

The purpose of microphones is similarly to change variations in air pressure into variations in electrical current for subsequent processing. The signal at this point is analog, like that of the changes in air pressure, changing smoothly over time. For it to be usable in a computer it needs to be *digitized*, that is, turned into a numeric representation. The electronic hardware to do this is built into practically every soundcard. The most basic digital representation is as a sequence of numbers corresponding to the level of the air pressure at a given instance in time. Such a representation is obtained by measuring the electrical signal from the microphone and recording the value at regular intervals over time. This measuring and digitizing process is known as *sampling*. A sample in common (dance music) parlance is a short chunk of audio represented in a digital form.

As with traditional analog audio, the primary benefit of measuring and recording the electrical output of a microphone is that it is possible to turn that data back into audio, through an amplifier and loudspeakers. Of course, in between it can be processed and mixed with other signals, which may have originated from microphones or musical instrument pickups, or have been generated algorithmically on the computer. Between producer and consumer, the data will usually have been packaged in a physical data storage medium such as CDs. The CD itself is fulfilling at least three functions: data storage, transmission, and distribution. In addition, it provides an anchor point on which commercial transactions can take place. Of course, the Internet is changing all that. Hard drives of Web servers can fulfill the storage role, protocols such as HTTP and others designed for file sharing such as BitTorrent can carry out the transmission. Lagging behind somewhat are the commercial systems to support the new media, causing the familiar legal conflicts between media corporations and users.

Compression Issues

One problem with digital media is that to represent things like audio and video in a form that people can enjoy takes a lot of data. To digitize audio at 20 kHz to cover the human hearing bandwidth you need to sample it at a rate of at least double that (a single cycle goes up and down, your sampler needs to see both peak and trough). A little leeway is needed to filter out any higher frequencies that a microphone may detect, which may interfere with the data. It was starting with figures like these that led to the sample rate for CD audio of 44.1 kHz. Now each sample is a numeric value, and the next question is how much precision is required there. Audio stored with 16-bit precision (65,536 possible values) is generally perceived as being faithful to the original, and that's what audio CDs use. A figure lower, say 8-bit (256 possible values), than this produces sounds with a definite crunchiness; the distortion can be perceived. (Distortion introduced by microphones and loudspeakers is often much greater than that of the digitization process, but artifacts introduced by the real-world system tend to be harmonically related in a way that the ear doesn't mind so much.)

This situation is comparable to image color ranges, where 8-bit color looks like a poor-quality print, whereas 16-bit looks acceptable. Recorded audio is usually stereo, which means two channels, which, in turn, means double the amount of data. The net result of all this is to digitize good-quality audio you need around 10MB per minute. Professional audio equipment ups all these figures. These demands obviously have serious implications when it comes to current computer technology, especially when it comes to bandwidth over the Internet.

Regular data compression techniques (such as gzip) are of limited use when it comes to digital audio. Zip algorithms tend to rely on simple repeated patterns, whereas audio data is usually very complex. A significant issue is that these techniques are non-lossy, it's possible to reconstitute the data exactly as before compression. Non-lossy algorithms designed specifically for audio can achieve reduction down to around 35 percent on fairly quiet orchestral music. It's not an issue in the context of the kind of syndication described here, but worth noting that many standard compression algorithms require all the compressed data to be present before decompression can take place, meaning they aren't suitable for streaming over the Internet.

Fortunately in practice things aren't as bad as they might seem. For example, the ear isn't a perfect receiver of audio. If you hear a loud noise at the same time as a quieter one, say a gunshot alongside a speaking voice, you probably won't notice the quieter sound (unless perhaps the voice says, "Duck!"). That's putting it crudely, but the idea of one part of a signal masking another is one of the keys to effective compression. This and other psycho-acoustical phenomena mean that it's possible to take away a large amount of the information found in an audio signal, and for it to be perceived as being the same, or very nearly the same as the original. It's these perceptual factors that enable serious level of data compression on audio. Undoubtedly the most popular compressed format is MP3 (officially MPEG-1/2 Audio Layer 3) from the Moving Picture Experts Group, an ISO/IEC working group. Typical compression ratios for MP3 are around 10:1, and that's with little or no perceptual change in the original audio.

What's more, all this is assuming that the audio should be top quality. That simply isn't necessary for one of the most common human uses for audio — talking or listening. Speech only needs a fraction of the audio bandwidth, and a little crunchiness won't affect understanding. So even before you start looking at compression there can be fairly massive reduction in requirements, for example telephone audio is usually sampled at 8 kHz, mono (1-channel), 8-bit.

An Imp for the Web

The practical application that we describe here is a little tool in Java for carrying out everything needed to publish audio through RSS feeds. The different parts of the application are relatively well separated from each other, so it could make a good starting point for a more sophisticated application. In fact, part of the code has already been listed in Chapters 22 and 23 — the feed modeling is a minor extension of what you've seen already.

User Interface of Imp

The operation of this little tool is probably best explained through some screen shots. This assumes you have a microphone plugged into your computer and microphone input enabled in the operating system (in Microsoft Windows these settings are to be found through the Sounds and Multimedia icon in Control Panel).

On running the application, you'll see the controller shown in Figure 30-1.

Figure 30-1

On clicking the Record button, the controller will change as shown in Figure 30-2.

Figure 30-2

While this screen is displayed, any sound picked up by the microphone will be recorded. The bar meter in the window displays the recording level. To help avoid recording long periods of silence, the application will automatically pause recording if the sound level drops below a preset value for more than a short period. Clicking the Stop button will stop the recording, and change the controller to look like Figure 30-3.

Figure 30-3

At this point the user has the options of starting the recording again (overwriting anything already recorded), playing back the recording, or publishing it to the Web. If the Play button is clicked then the display will look like that of Figure 30-2, except that the bar meter will display progress through the recorded sound rather than level. Clicking the Publish button will pop up another dialog box, as shown in Figure 30-4.

Figure 30-4

This window has three initially blank text areas in which the user can annotate the recording, giving a title and description and identifying the creator of the recording. On clicking OK, the audio data along with feed data including reference to the audio file will be uploaded to the user's Web site.

Application Classes

The new Java classes used in this application are as follows:

- ❑ `Imp`: Application entry point, main GUI
- ❑ `MeterBar`: Level meter component
- ❑ `Settings`: Application settings
- ❑ `AudioTool`: Common interface for audio classes
- ❑ `Recorder`: Records an audio file
- ❑ `Player`: Plays an audio file
- ❑ `Publisher`: Publishes a feed with enclosures to the Web
- ❑ `Uploader`: FTP utility used by `Publisher`

The following classes are exactly as listed in Chapters 22 and 23:

- ❑ `Entry`: Basic interface for modeling an item
- ❑ `EntryDateSorter`: Sorts an entry list
- ❑ `EntryImpl`: Basic implementation of an item
- ❑ `EntryList`: A list of entries (interface)
- ❑ `EntryListImpl`: A list of entries (implementation)
- ❑ `FeedEntity`: Common model of entry/feed
- ❑ `FeedEntityBase`: Implementation of `FeedEntity`
- ❑ `FileEntrySerializer`: Serializes a basic feed model to XML

The following two classes are simple extensions of `Entry` and `FileEntrySerializer`, customized to support the RSS 2.0 needed for advertising media files:

❑ `EnclosureEntry`: Models an item in a feed containing an enclosure

❑ `EnclosureSerialize`: Serializes an enclosure-containing feed model to XML

All the previous classes are in the `org.imp.*` package, including those originally included in the `org.urss.*` source tree, which have had the appropriate change made to their `package` declarations (generally not good practice, but for the sake of demonstration it avoids confusion with other classes from that tree).

AudioTool Interface

This is the glue that joins the main GUI class (`Imp`) to the `Recorder` and `Player` classes. The full source is as follows:

```
package org.imp;

public interface AudioTool {

    public void startActivity();

    public void stopActivity();

    public int getLevel();

    public boolean getLevelVisible();

    public long getLength();
}
```

This interface fulfills two basic functions, controlling activity and monitoring activity. It allows the GUI to trigger the starting and stopping of both recording and playback through the `startActivity` and `stopActivity` method. It enables access to descriptive information that will be used for a value that will be shown on the meter through `getLevel`, and whether or not the meter should be visible at all, through `getLevel`. The other piece of information it provides access to is the length of the data file, the value of which will be needed in the RSS feed.

Audio in Java

There are two primary ways to work with audio in Java. The most direct is through the JavaSound API, which is part of the standard Java distribution. The other approach is through the more generalized Java Media Framework (JMF). There are various pros and cons for each approach, and here it was felt that the JavaSound would make for a simpler system, and being lower level result in code that is more likely to resemble what would appear with other languages.

Out of the box, JavaSound only supports a very limited number of audio formats, a list that does not include MP3. Fortunately, suitable libraries are available as part of the open-source Tritonus JavaSound plug-in libraries (`www.tritonus.org/plugins.html`). An additional native binary (Microsoft Windows or Linux) is also needed for the MP3 encoder; the Tritonus site has the appropriate links.

We have been unable to confirm this with this specific code, but LAME and Tritonus will work on recent versions of OS X (10.2, 10.3). Tritonus will not work on OS 9 because OS 9 only runs up to Java 1.1.8. Both OS X 10.2.x (JVM 1.4.1) and OS X 10.3.x (JVM 1.4.2) must use the 1.4 compatible version of Tritonus, which can be found at JSResources (`www.jsresources.org/`). The Tritonus mailing list is also very helpful; to subscribe, go to: `http://lists.sourceforge.net/lists/listinfo/tritonus-user`*.*

The core classes for working with sampled sound are appropriately enough contained in `javax.sound.sampled.*`. There's also a set of Service Provider Interfaces (`javax.sound.sampled.spi.*`), which are used internally by the Tritonus code. This interface makes it possible to support transparently the MP3 format. In a nearby package (`javax.sound.midi.*`) there's also support for MIDI, the Musical Instrument Digital Interface, but that's concerned with musical instrument instructions rather than sampled audio.

Lines and Audio Formats

The `javax.sound.sampled.Line` interface is the parent of the most important sampled audio classes and acts as a path for data flow in real time. As a pipeline the line delivers audio data from one part of a system to another. The way in which a `Line` is connected to the rest of the system is visible in the `Line.Info` object (or one of its subclasses). Some types of `Line` can have built-in processors that exist as `Control` objects, for example, `GainControl` and `ReverbControl`. The parameters of these objects can be set using simple methods. The classes used here for audio input and output are `SourceDataLine` and `TargetDataLine`. These both deal with streamed data, the `SourceDataLine` being a line that acts as an origin of data (for example, for playback), the `TargetDataLine` acts as a destination for data (for example, for recording).

Associated with every `Line` is a data format as an `AudioFormat` object: the first thing you need to make a `Line`. The most extensive constructor is the following:

```
AudioFormat(encoding, samplerate, resolution, channels,
        framesize, framerate, bigendian)
```

The encoding is of type `Encoding`, a convenience wrapper with standard fields `PCM_SIGNED`, `PCM_UNSIGNED`, `ULAW`, and `ALAW`. The first two of these are pulse-code modulation, which is the fancy name for simple numeric encoding of the samples. The other two are also sample-by-sample encodings of the audio data, but a mathematical function is applied to make better use of the number of bits available for each sample. The Tritonus classes add `MPEG1L3` to the list of encodings. The sample rate is expressed in samples per second and the resolution in bits, this being known in the API as `sampleSizeInBits`. Channels currently specifies stereo (2) or mono (1). The frame size refers to the number of bytes needed for each unit of time, for example, a PCM stereo, 16-bit format would normally have 2 bytes for each of two channels, that is a frame size of four. With other encodings (from third-party service providers) the required value of frame size may not be so clear. The delightfully named `bigEndian` field is a boolean value which specifies the byte order (true for Sun `*.au`, false for Windows PCM `*.wav`).

Audio Recorder Class

The following is the full source code of `Recorder.java`, with blocks separated by a little explanation. Here you can see some of the standard I/O classes that are included along with quite a selection from the JavaSound package:

```
package org.imp;

import java.io.ByteArrayInputStream;
import java.io.ByteArrayOutputStream;
import java.io.File;

import javax.sound.sampled.AudioInputStream;
import javax.sound.sampled.AudioSystem;
import javax.sound.sampled.DataLine;
import javax.sound.sampled.LineUnavailableException;
import javax.sound.sampled.TargetDataLine;
```

The recorder is going to be started through a Swing button, and it's best that the GUI remain responsive after the button is clicked. Recording is a long-running process, so the operation is run in a separate thread, with the class extending Thread as follows:

```
public class Recorder extends Thread  implements AudioTool {

    private TargetDataLine targetDataLine;

    private AudioInputStream audioInputStream;

    private ByteArrayOutputStream byteArrayOutputStream =
                                new ByteArrayOutputStream();

    private int peak;
    private long length = -1;

    private File file;

    private boolean recording;
```

The first three member variables correspond to the path the audio data will take through the recording process, described next. The application will monitor the volume of the recorded audio, and the maximum level over a particular period of time will be held in peak. The boolean recording acts as a flag and allows the recording process thread to be stopped safely. When created, the Recorder object will do a little initialization in the form of deleting any existing audio file. The name of the file is provided by a member variable from the Settings class, which you'll see shortly. The constructor then looks like this:

```
public Recorder() {
    file = new File(Settings.audioFilename);
    file.delete();

}
```

A TargetDataLine is needed to capture audio from the microphone. The getTargetDataLine method first creates a DataLine.Info object that contains details of the format requirements (specified in Settings). The AudioSystem is then asked for the kind of Line required. To reserve system resources for a Line it is necessary to open it, and similarly these resources may be released by closing the Line.

```java
public TargetDataLine getTargetDataLine() {
    DataLine.Info info =
        new DataLine.Info(TargetDataLine.class, Settings.format);
    TargetDataLine tdline = null;
    try {
        tdline = (TargetDataLine) AudioSystem.getLine(info);
        tdline.open(Settings.format, Settings.bufferSize);
    } catch (LineUnavailableException e) {
        e.printStackTrace();
    }
    return tdline;
}
```

The data for the recorder picked up by the TargetDataLine will be pumped into a buffer that is set up at the start of the run method that follows. The number of frames in the buffer is then calculated, the Line delivers its data as these little snapshots. The recording flag is set and the loop that will capture data is started. The targetDataLine.read call loads the buffer with data from the soundcard (the zero is the offset). A loop then steps through the buffer array to find the maximum amplitude of the signal. To keep things simple, the code only looks at the most significant byte of the data, the peak value of which is used to set the level of the meter display.

If the peak amplitude of the audio data held in the buffer is above the threshold (that is, not silence), the data is then pushed into a ByteArrayOutputStream. The peak level is examined in each buffered block. The entire block is rejected if this is too low. The run method is thus:

```java
public void run() {
    byte[] buffer = new byte[Settings.bufferSize];
    int nBufferFrames = Settings.bufferSize / Settings.frameSize;

    recording = true;
    while (recording) {
        int nFramesRead = targetDataLine.read(buffer, 0, nBufferFrames);
        peak = 0;
        for (int i = 1; i < nFramesRead - 1; i += Settings.frameSize * 2) {
            peak = buffer[i] > peak ? buffer[i] : peak;
        }
        if (peak > Settings.threshold) {
            byteArrayOutputStream.write(buffer, 0, nFramesRead);
        }
    }
}
```

The following method is called when the Record button is clicked. First the TargetDataLine is obtained and started, then this thread (that is, the run method) is set running:

```java
public void startActivity() {
    targetDataLine = getTargetDataLine();
    targetDataLine.start();
    start();
}
```

When the Stop button is clicked the `stopActivity` method is called. This will allow the I/O to continue to pick up any data remaining in the `TargetDataLine`, which is emptied by the `drain` method. The line's resources are then cleaned up and the recording loop can be stopped. The method looks like this:

```
public void stopActivity() {
    targetDataLine.drain();
    targetDataLine.stop();
    targetDataLine.close();
    recording = false;
    try {
        byteArrayOutputStream.close();

        byte[] byteData = byteArrayOutputStream.toByteArray();
        ByteArrayInputStream byteArrayInputStream =
                        new ByteArrayInputStream(byteData);
        audioInputStream = new AudioInputStream(byteArrayInputStream,
                Settings.format, byteData.length / Settings.frameSize);

        length = writeAudioFile(audioInputStream, file);

        audioInputStream.close();
    } catch (Exception e) {
        e.printStackTrace();
    }

}
```

Although the `ByteArrayOutputStream` makes a perfectly good buffer for the data, the immediate aim is to get it down on disk. An additional complication is that the current PCM sample data needs to be converted into the MP3 format. To prepare for this the data is retrieved as a byte array, which is then pushed out again into a `ByteArrayInputStream` that is passed to the `writeAudioFile` method. That method returns the number of bytes written to disk, which is passed into the `length` field. Right on cue, here is the `writeAudioFile` method. It effectively passes the data through a pipeline to convert the format into the required encoding (MPEG1L3) which is then written to the disk in the required file format (MP3). To help with troubleshooting a call to `Settings.showProperties` is made to write the system's audio system details to the console. Here is the method:

```
public static int writeAudioFile(AudioInputStream inputStream, File outFile)
        throws Exception {

    AudioInputStream audioInputStream = AudioSystem.getAudioInputStream(
            Settings.MPEG1L3, inputStream);
    if (audioInputStream == null) {
        throw new Exception("Conversion not supported.");
    }
    int writtenBytes = AudioSystem.write(audioInputStream, Settings.MP3,
            outFile);

    Settings.showProperties(System.getProperties());
    return writtenBytes;
}
```

While recording, the level meter will show a value proportional to the peak level of the data, and it gets its value here:

```java
public int getLevel() {
    return peak;
}
```

The level meter should always be visible during recording:

```java
public boolean getLevelVisible() {
    return true;
}
```

The figure for the number of bytes written to disk will be needed when it comes to publishing the RSS, so that's made available here:

```java
public long getLength() {
    return length;
}
}
```

Audio Player Class

The `Player` class is very similar to the `Recorder` class. This time data will be passed to a `SourceDataLine`, which acts as a *source* to a mixer. There's nothing conceptually different here so in the interests of keeping the weight of this book down a little, please refer to the explanations for the `Recorder`.

```java
package org.imp;

import java.io.File;

import javax.sound.sampled.AudioFormat;
import javax.sound.sampled.AudioInputStream;
import javax.sound.sampled.AudioSystem;
import javax.sound.sampled.DataLine;
import javax.sound.sampled.SourceDataLine;

public class Player extends Thread implements AudioTool {

    private SourceDataLine sourceDataLine;

    private boolean playing;

    private int position;

    private long length = -1;

    private AudioInputStream audioInputStream;

    private int playLevel;

    private boolean end;
```

```
public Player() {
    end = false;
}

public void startActivity() {
    start();
}

public void run() {
    end = false;
    playing = true;
    File soundFile = new File(Settings.audioFilename);
    byte[] bytes = new byte[Settings.bufferSize];
    AudioInputStream audioInputStream = null;
    try {
        audioInputStream = AudioSystem.getAudioInputStream(soundFile);
        length = audioInputStream.getFrameLength()/Settings.frameSize;
        if (audioInputStream == null) {
            throw new Exception("Can't read file: "
                    + Settings.audioFilename);
        }
        AudioFormat sourceFormat = audioInputStream.getFormat();
        AudioFormat.Encoding targetEncoding = AudioFormat.Encoding.PCM_SIGNED;
        audioInputStream = AudioSystem.getAudioInputStream(targetEncoding,
                audioInputStream);
        AudioFormat audioFormat = audioInputStream.getFormat();

        sourceDataLine = null;
        DataLine.Info info = new DataLine.Info(SourceDataLine.class,
                audioFormat);

        sourceDataLine = (SourceDataLine) AudioSystem.getLine(info);
        sourceDataLine.open(audioFormat);
        sourceDataLine.start();
        int nBytesRead = 0;
        while (nBytesRead != -1) {
            nBytesRead = audioInputStream.read(bytes, 0, bytes.length);

            if (nBytesRead >= 0) {
                position = sourceDataLine.write(bytes, 0, nBytesRead);
                playLevel = (int) (128 * (float) position / (float) length);
            }
        }
        audioInputStream.close();

    } catch (Exception e) {
        e.printStackTrace();
    }
    stopActivity();
    end = true;
}

public void stopActivity() {
```

```
        sourceDataLine.drain();
        sourceDataLine.stop();
        sourceDataLine.close();
        playing = false;
    }

    public boolean isEnd() {
        return end;
    }

    public int getLevel() {
        return playLevel;
    }

    public boolean getLevelVisible() {
        return !end;
    }

    public long getLength() {
        return length;
    }
}
```

The meter display will follow the progress of playback, but isn't visually interesting. It only changes as blocks of data are chunked through the buffer, which will often mean it goes from a minimum reading to a maximum reading in a single step.

So far you've seen the audio subsystem of the application that is comprised of the `Recorder` and `Player` classes, along with their shared `AudioTool` interface.

Imp User Interface

Before getting on to the `Imp` class, which is the entry point of the application and looks after most of the user interface, here is the source of the component used for the level meter:

```
package org.imp;
import java.awt.Graphics;

import javax.swing.JProgressBar;

class MeterBar extends JProgressBar {
    private final AudioTool tool;

    public MeterBar(AudioTool tool, int min, int max) {
        super(min, max);
        this.tool = tool;
    }

    public void paint(Graphics g) {
        setValue(tool.getLevel());
        super.paint(g);
    }
}
```

As you can see, the `MeterBar` class is a fairly trivial extension of the standard Swing `JProgressBar` class. The only addition is that it's associated with an object that implements the `AudioTool` interface, from which it will obtain its value (the level) when called upon to repaint.

The primary UI for this application (the one with the buttons), is contained in `Imp.java` and is mostly comprised of a fairly conventional `JFrame` setup, with listeners on the buttons that dispatch instructions to the `Recorder` and `Player`. It also contains an inner class `LevelUpdate`, an instance of which is run as a separate thread when the level meter is active. To simplify method calls between the various classes, `Imp` also implements the `AudioTool` interface. The source is as follows:

```java
package org.imp;
import java.awt.BorderLayout;
import java.awt.Color;
import java.awt.Container;
import java.awt.Dimension;
import java.awt.SystemColor;
import java.awt.Toolkit;
import java.awt.Window;
import java.awt.event.ActionEvent;
import java.awt.event.ActionListener;

import javax.swing.JButton;
import javax.swing.JFrame;
import javax.swing.JPanel;
import javax.swing.JProgressBar;

public class Imp implements ActionListener, AudioTool {

    private JFrame window;
    private AudioTool audioTool;
    private JProgressBar meterBar;
    private JButton recordButton;
    private JButton stopButton;
    private JButton playButton;
    private JButton publishButton;
    private int level = 0;
    private boolean showLevel;
    private LevelUpdate levelUpdate;
    public static Settings settings;
    private long length = -1;

    public static void main(String[] args) {
        settings = new Settings();
        new Imp();
    }

    public Imp() {
        JFrame window = createWindow();

        Container contentPane = window.getContentPane();
        contentPane.setLayout(new BorderLayout());

        JPanel buttonPanel = createButtonPanel();
```

```
        contentPane.add(buttonPanel, BorderLayout.SOUTH);

        meterBar = createMeterBar();
        contentPane.add(meterBar, BorderLayout.CENTER);

        enableButtons(true, false, false, false);
//        enableButtons(true, false, true, true); //handy for testing
        window.setVisible(true);
    }

    private JFrame createWindow() {
        window = new JFrame("Imp");
        centerWindow(window,300,80);
        return window;
    }

    public static void centerWindow(Window window, int width, int height){
        Dimension screenSize = Toolkit.getDefaultToolkit().getScreenSize();
        Dimension size = new Dimension(width, height);
        window.setSize(size);
        window.setLocation((screenSize.width - size.width) / 2,
                (screenSize.height - size.height) / 2);
    }

    private JPanel createButtonPanel() {
        JPanel buttonPanel = new JPanel();

        recordButton = new JButton("Record");
        recordButton.addActionListener(this);
        buttonPanel.add(recordButton);

        stopButton = new JButton("Stop");
        stopButton.addActionListener(this);
        buttonPanel.add(stopButton);

        playButton = new JButton("Play");
        playButton.addActionListener(this);
        buttonPanel.add(playButton);

        publishButton = new JButton("Publish");
        publishButton.addActionListener(this);
        buttonPanel.add(publishButton);
        return buttonPanel;
    }

    private JProgressBar createMeterBar() {
        meterBar = new MeterBar(this, 0, 128);
        meterBar.setBorderPainted(true);
        meterBar.setForeground(Color.green);
        return meterBar;
    }

    private void enableButtons(boolean start, boolean stop,
```

```
                              boolean play, boolean publish){
    recordButton.setEnabled(start);
    stopButton.setEnabled(stop);
    playButton.setEnabled(play);
    publishButton.setEnabled(publish);
}

public void actionPerformed(ActionEvent e) {
    String command = e.getActionCommand();

    if (command.equals("Record")) {
        audioTool = new Recorder();
        audioTool.startActivity();
        startMeter();
        enableButtons(false, true, false, false);
    }

    else if (command.equals("Stop")) {
        stopActivity();

    } else if (command.equals("Play")) {
        //    captureMode = false;
        audioTool = new Player();
        levelUpdate.setMetered(audioTool);
        audioTool.startActivity();
        enableButtons(false, true, false, false);
        startMeter();
    } else if (command.equals("Publish")) {
        EnclosureEntry entry = new EnclosureEntry();

        entry.setLength(Integer.toString(getLength()));
        (new Publisher()).publish(entry);


    }
}

public void stopActivity() {
    showLevel = false;
    audioTool.stopActivity();
    length = audioTool.getLength();
    enableButtons(true, false, true, true);
}

public void startMeter() {
    levelUpdate = new LevelUpdate();
    levelUpdate.setMetered(audioTool);
    levelUpdate.start();
}


public long getLength() {
    return length;
}
```

```
class LevelUpdate extends Thread {
    float oldlevel = 0;

    AudioTool active;

    public void setMetered(AudioTool active) {
        this.active = active;
    }

    public void run() {
        level = 0;
        meterBar.setBackground(Settings.meterBackgroundColor);
        meterBar.repaint();
        while (active.getLevelVisible()) {
            //  level = captureMode ? rec.getLevel() : play.getLevel();
            level = active.getLevel();

            //      if (!captureMode && play.isEnd()) {
            //         showLevel = false;
            //  }
            if (level != oldlevel) {
                meterBar.repaint();
                oldlevel = level;
            }
            try {
                Thread.sleep(100);
            } catch (InterruptedException ie) {
                System.out.println(ie);
            }
        }
        enableButtons(true, false, true, false);
        meterBar.setBackground(SystemColor.control);
        meterBar.repaint();
        level = 0;
    }
}

public int getLevel() {
    return level;
}

public boolean getLevelVisible() {
    return audioTool.getLevelVisible();
}

public void startActivity() {
    // not used
}
}
```

Before moving onto the syndication-related code proper, you'd better see where the settings data used by the application comes from. A standard Java properties file is used for these, stored as settings.txt. The order of key/value pairs in this don't matter, but they are listed here according to which part of the application uses them, starting with the audio settings:

```
#Imp Properties
#Sun Nov 28 16:44:05 CET 2004
audioFilename=audio.mp3
bufferSize=16384
resolution=16
frameSize=2
samplerate=22050.0F
threshold=10
frameRate=22050.0F
nChannels=1
```

These audio settings are chosen to provide good enough quality for typical purposes. These values can be modified depending on the use of the application, as long as the encoder/decoder libraries support them (check the Tritonus documentation).

There are only two settings specific to the RSS data, the name of the file that will hold the feed data and the maximum number of <item> elements it should contain:

```
rssFilename=broadcast.xml
maxItems=5
```

The application will upload the audio data file and RSS data to a Web server using FTP. You will need to insert your own values here:

```
user=myusername
pass=mypassword
httpHost=http\://mywebserver.com
ftpHost=mywebserver.com
path=audio
```

The Settings class merely acts as a wrapper for values picked up from the settings.txt file. Its source is as follows:

```java
package org.imp;

import java.awt.Color;
import java.io.FileInputStream;
import java.io.FileOutputStream;
import java.util.Enumeration;
import java.util.Properties;

import javax.sound.sampled.AudioFileFormat;
import javax.sound.sampled.AudioFormat;
import javax.sound.sampled.AudioFormat.Encoding;

import org.tritonus.share.sampled.AudioFileTypes;
import org.tritonus.share.sampled.Encodings;

public class Settings {

    public static String SETTINGS_FILE = "settings.txt";
    public static Encoding encoding = Encoding.PCM_SIGNED;
```

```
public static final AudioFormat.Encoding MPEG1L3 = Encodings
        .getEncoding("MPEG1L3");
public static final AudioFileFormat.Type MP3 = AudioFileTypes.getType(
        "MP3", "mp3");
public static final Color meterBackgroundColor = Color.black;
private Properties properties;
public static float sampleRate;
public static int resolution;
public static int nChannels;
public static int frameSize;
public static float frameRate;
public static boolean bigEndian;
public static AudioFormat format;
public static int bufferSize;
public static int threshold;
public static String audioFilename;
public static String httpHost;
public static String path;
public static String rssFilename;
public static String user;
public static String pass;
public static int maxItems;
public static String ftpHost;

public Settings() {
    properties = new Properties();
    try {
        properties.load(new FileInputStream(SETTINGS_FILE));
    } catch (Exception e) {
        e.printStackTrace();
    }

    sampleRate = getFloat("sampleRate");
    resolution = getInt("resolution");
    nChannels = getInt("nChannels");
    frameSize = getInt("frameSize");
    frameRate = getFloat("frameRate");
    bigEndian = getBoolean("bigEndian");

    format = new AudioFormat(encoding, sampleRate, resolution, nChannels,
            frameSize, frameRate, bigEndian);

    bufferSize = getInt("bufferSize");
    threshold = getInt("threshold");
    audioFilename = getString("audioFilename");

    httpHost = getString("httpHost");
    ftpHost = getString("ftpHost");
    path = getString("path");
    rssFilename = getString("rssFilename");
    user = getString("user");
    pass = getString("pass");

    maxItems = getInt("maxItems");
```

```
        }

    public int getInt(String name) {
        String stringValue = properties.getProperty(name);
        return Integer.parseInt(stringValue);
    }

    public float getFloat(String name) {
        String stringValue = properties.getProperty(name);
        return Float.parseFloat(stringValue);
    }

    public boolean getBoolean(String name) {
        String stringValue = properties.getProperty(name);
        return Boolean.getBoolean(stringValue);
    }

    public String getString(String name) {
        return properties.getProperty(name);
    }

    public static void showProperties(Properties properties) {
        Enumeration keys = properties.keys();
        while (keys.hasMoreElements()) {
            String key = (String) keys.nextElement();
            String value = (String) properties.getProperty(key);
            if (key.startsWith("tritonus.lame.effective")) {
                System.out.println(key.substring(24) + " = " + value);
            }
        }
    }
}
```

Publishing to a Feed

The code listed so far in this chapter produces the audio data to be published, what remains is the small task of putting together a syndication feed and publishing it.

Syndication and Enclosures

In a sense there's nothing new about syndication audio and other media files over the Web. The M3U Playlist format is the default file list format of WinAMP and most other media programs. This has been employed on the Web for a while for the delivery of music. But there has been a surge of interest and publicity, primarily from bloggers, in using feed formats as playlists. Hype aside, the primary advantage is that existing syndication infrastructure can be repurposed for delivery of audio. The gain over traditional radio at the broadcasting side is that it's relatively easy for anyone to do it themselves. At the receiver side there is the opportunity to be far more selective with listening, and generally have more control. This is thanks not only to the metadata that can be provided along with the audio items, but to the fact that users can listen at their convenience rather than at the times decided by the broadcaster.

The approach to media files varies between the different syndication formats. Until recently RSS 1.0 had no specific support, although the Resource Description Framework (RDF) on which it is based is eminently suited to describing such resources. For example, Adobe has created the Extensible Metadata

Platform (XMP), which enables embedded RDF metadata in media files (all their products support this standard). However this is a step removed from the explicit RDF/XML found in feeds.

RSS 2.0 is the format that has received most attention in this area, with the early "podcasts" being expressed this way. The approach taken in RSS 2.0 with media files is similar to that of attachments with e-mail, each item can have an associated *enclosure*. Unlike e-mail, the enclosure isn't actually enclosed but referred to through a URI instead, relying on other subsystems to get the file. The following is how an enclosure appears in an RSS 2.0 feed:

```
<item>
  <guid>http://mysite/some_audio.mp3</guid>
  <title>Some Audio</title>
  <description>Something for the sake of demonstration</description>
  <pubDate>Tue, 30 Nov 2004 18:12:21 CET</pubDate>
  <enclosure url="http://mysite/some_audio.mp3"
                    length="654321" type="audio/mpeg"/>
</item>
```

The `<enclosure>` element appears as a child of an `<item>` element. The attributes of the `enclosure` element are `url`, which is the HTTP URI of the media file, `length`, which is the file's length in bytes and `type`, which is the MIME (Internet Media Type) of the data. All three attributes are required.

The latest proposal for RSS 1.0 is very similar to that of RSS 2.0, but taking advantage of namespace-based modularity for the vocabulary. A minimal item might look something like this:

```
<item rdf:about="http://mysite/some_audio.mp3">
  <title>Some Audio</title>
  <description>Something for the sake of demonstration</description>
  <enc:enclosure enc:url="http://mysite/some_audio.mp3"
                    enc:length="654321" type="audio/mpeg"/>
</item>
```

RSS 1.0 has a potential advantage when it comes to adding metadata to the enclosure as RDF in that it would also be possible to talk about the enclosure directly, for example, using syntax such as:

```
<rdf:Description rdf:about="http://mysite/some_audio.mp3">
  <foaf:maker>
     <foaf:Person foaf:name="Giovanni Tummarello" />
  </foaf:maker>
  <prism:copyright>Copyright (c) 2003, Giovanni</prism:copyright>
</rdf:Description>
```

Of course this would require a consumer that can receive arbitrary RDF/XML, but there is lots of potential for discovering items of interest or creating well-documented archives.

Atom, on the other hand, sees media content as nothing special — content is content. It remains to be seen what specific syntax will be used for enclosures, but it is likely to be based around the `<content>` element. Chances are it will also be possible to provide "true" enclosures, by serializing the binary data in the media file to Base64 encoding, and including it inline in the text. At first glance this seems both elegant and inefficient; Base64 material takes up a lot more space than binary data. However the expansion in the number of bytes used to express the content as text could likely be offset by gzip compression, which most Web servers support.

However, the podcasting world is still young, and many issues have yet to be resolved in all formats. The nearest thing to a deployed standard in this area is the use of the <enclosure> element to advertise the existence of an MP3 file, so that is the approach taken in the Imp application.

Supporting the Enclosure Element

The code in Chapter 23 includes an Entry interface and an EntryImpl class to model an item in a feed as an object. The Imp application uses a simple class that extends the EntryImpl class (and thus also implements Entry), which is as follows:

```java
package org.imp;

public class EnclosureEntry extends EntryImpl {

    private String url = "";
    private String length = "";
    private String type = "";

    public String getLength() {
        return length;
    }

    public void setLength(String length) {
        this.length = length;
    }

    public String getType() {
        return type;
    }

    public void setType(String type) {
        this.type = type;
    }

    public String getUrl() {
        return url;
    }

    public void setUrl(String url) {
        this.url = url;
    }

    public String toHTML() {
        String string = super.toHTML();
        string += "\n<p>Enclosure:";
        string += "\nurl = " + url;
        string += "\nlength = " + length;
        string += "\ntype = " + type+"</p>";
        return string;
    }
}
```

All this class does is add slots for the values associated with enclosures, and provide a method overriding that of its parent class to provide an HTML representation of itself (which, incidentally, isn't used here).

Serializing an Entry

Again, you've already seen a class that would serialize `Entry` objects to XML to build up an RSS feed, it is called `FileEntrySerializer`. It worked by initially loading an RSS shell (the outer elements) into a DOM document and adding items as required. The `Imp` application reuses this technique by extending that class and adding a method to turn the field values found in an `EnclosureEntry` object into appropriate parts of the DOM document. The source is as follows:

```
package org.imp;

import org.w3c.dom.Element;
import org.w3c.dom.NodeList;

public class EnclosureSerializer extends FileEntrySerializer {

    public void addEnclosureEntry(EnclosureEntry entry) {
        super.addEntry(entry);
        addEnclosure(entry);
    }

    private void addEnclosure(EnclosureEntry entry) {
        Element lastItem = (Element) getChannelElement().getLastChild();
        Element enclosureElement = lastItem.getOwnerDocument().createElement(
                "enclosure");
        enclosureElement.setAttribute("url", entry.getUrl());
        enclosureElement.setAttribute("length", entry.getLength());
        enclosureElement.setAttribute("type", entry.getType());
        lastItem.appendChild(enclosureElement);

    }

    public void trimItems() {
        NodeList items = getChannelElement().getElementsByTagName("item");
        if (items.getLength() > Settings.maxItems) {
            getChannelElement().removeChild(items.item(0));
        }
    }
}
```

Publisher Class

If you refer back to Figure 30-4, you will see the window that is triggered by the user clicking on the Publish button. In `Imp.java`, the code that will handle this event looks like this:

```
    } else if (command.equals("Publish")) {
EnclosureEntry entry = new EnclosureEntry();
entry.setLength(Integer.toString(getLength()));
(new Publisher()).publish(entry);
}
```

An `EnclosureEntry` object is created and its `setLength` method called, which will give a value to the variable that corresponds in the RSS to the `length` attribute inside the `<enclosure>` element. A new instance of `Publisher` is created and the entry passed to its `publish` method. The user will see a dialog box pop up, into which they can enter information about the enclosure. The source for the `Publisher` class is as follows:

```
package org.imp;

import java.awt.Container;
import java.awt.event.ActionEvent;
import java.awt.event.ActionListener;
import java.text.SimpleDateFormat;
import java.util.Date;

import javax.swing.BoxLayout;
import javax.swing.JButton;
import javax.swing.JDialog;
import javax.swing.JLabel;
import javax.swing.JTextField;

public class Publisher implements ActionListener {

    private JTextField titleField;
    private JTextField descriptionField;
    private JTextField authorField;
    private EnclosureEntry entry;
    private JDialog dialog;

    public static final SimpleDateFormat RFC822 = new SimpleDateFormat(
            "EEE, d MMM yyyy HH:mm:ss z");

    private String stampedAudioFilename;
```

Following the member fields which largely correspond to user interface components, here is the `publish` method, which passes the entry to a member variable before calling `createDialog`, the method which follows. As you can see, this is regular Swing code to produce a dialog box featuring three labeled text fields:

```
    public void publish(EnclosureEntry entry) {
        this.entry = entry;
        createDialog();
    }

    private void createDialog() {
        dialog = new JDialog();
        dialog.setModal(true);
        dialog.setTitle("Metadata");
        Imp.centerWindow(dialog, 300,200);
        Container container = dialog.getContentPane();
        container.setLayout(new BoxLayout(container, BoxLayout.Y_AXIS));
        JLabel titleLabel = new JLabel("Title");
        container.add(titleLabel);
        titleField = new JTextField();
```

```
        container.add(titleField);
        JLabel descriptionLabel = new JLabel("Description");
        container.add(descriptionLabel);
        descriptionField = new JTextField();
        container.add(descriptionField);

        JLabel authorLabel = new JLabel("Creator");
        container.add(authorLabel);
        authorField = new JTextField();
        container.add(authorField);

        JButton okButton = new JButton("OK");
        okButton.addActionListener(this);
        container.add(okButton);
        dialog.pack();
        dialog.show();
    }
```

Near the end of `createDialog`, this object is passed as a listener for the OK button. The handler for clicks on this button is as follows:

```
    public void actionPerformed(ActionEvent e) {
        dialog.dispose();
        doPublication();
    }
```

After getting rid of the dialog box, the `doPublication` method is called, which first calls a method to prepare the entry object using the information received from the dialog box. It then calls another method to create the whole feed file, and then another method to carry out the upload procedures:

```
    private void doPublication() {
        prepareEntry();
        createFeedFile();
        upload();
    }
```

Preparing the entry involves calling the setter methods of the `EnclosureEntry` object with suitable values. A nearby helper method, `getValue`, is used to provide default values if nothing appropriate has been found in the dialog box. The audio file is saved to disk as `audio.mp3`. Rather than overwrite the existing file on the server, a new name is created by prepending the current time (in milliseconds since 01/01/1970) to `audio.mp3`. This timestamped name is used along with the host name and path from `Settings`, to create the enclosure's `url` attribute and item's `guid` (in other words, the URI of the resource):

```
    private void prepareEntry() {
        Date now = new Date();
        String date = RFC822.format(now);
        entry.setDate(date);
        entry.setTitle(getValue(titleField.getText()));

        entry.setDescription(getValue(descriptionField.getText()));
        entry.setContent(getValue(descriptionField.getText()));
```

```
            entry.setAuthor(getValue(authorField.getText()));
            stampedAudioFilename =
                        now.getTime()+ "_" + Settings.audioFilename;
            String url = Settings.httpHost +"/"
                            + Settings.path+"/"+stampedAudioFilename;

            entry.setURIString(url);
            entry.setLink(url);
            entry.setUrl(url);
            entry.setType("audio/mpeg");
            entry.setSourceLink(Settings.httpHost);
            System.out.println(entry.toHTML());
        }

        private String getValue(String string){
            if((string == null) || (string.length()==0)){
                string = "not specified";
            }
            return string;
        }
```

Now that the entry object has been fully populated with values, it's time to add it to a feed. "Which feed?" you ask. Following the same strategy we use in Chapter 27 with the `FileEntrySerializer`, a pre-existing shell comprised of the outer RSS elements is loaded from file. Here the shell file will be the RSS feed file itself, with individual entries added using the DOM through `EnclosureSerializer`. If the number of items after adding this one is greater than that specified in settings, then an item is removed from the end of the feed. After the feed has been created (or more accurately, updated) it is saved to disk, as you can see here:

```
        private void createFeedFile() {
            EnclosureSerializer serializer = new EnclosureSerializer();
            serializer.loadDocumentShell(Settings.rssFilename);
            serializer.addEnclosureEntry(entry);
            serializer.trimItems();
            serializer.write(Settings.rssFilename);
        }
```

The action of uploading to the Web is carried out through an instance of the `Uploader` class. Ideally the user interface would give some indication of the progress, but to keep things simple, progress reports are passed to the console. The process of uploading begins by logging on to the server, then moving to the appropriate (remote) directory, and then uploading first the RSS feed file and then the audio file, both lifted from disk.

```
        public void upload() {
            try {
                Uploader uploader = new Uploader();
                System.out.println(Settings.ftpHost);
                String response = uploader.connect(Settings.ftpHost);
                System.out.println(response);
                uploader.login(Settings.user, Settings.pass);
                System.out.println(response);
                uploader.changeDirectory(Settings.path);
```

```
            System.out.println(response);
            uploader.uploadFile(Settings.rssFilename);
            System.out.println(response);
            uploader.uploadFile(Settings.audioFilename, stampedAudioFilename);
            uploader.disconnect();
            System.out.println("done");
        } catch (Exception e) {
            e.printStackTrace();
        }
    }
}
```

FTP Upload

The File Transfer Protocol (FTP) is supported by a very large proportion of servers on the Web. It offers a straightforward technique for passing a file from A to B. In an ideal world, it would probably have been preferable to use the HTTP PUT method here, but that is less well supported.

There is no official, documented support for FTP in Java, but support is there (at least in JDK 1.5), and has been for a long time. So rather than complicate matters by writing the socket code from scratch or bringing in a third-party library (such as the excellent Jakarta Commons-Net [http://jakarta .apache.org/commons/net/]), we use the Sun classes. In fact, the Uploader class is little more than a simple wrapper that delegates calls to an instance of sun.net.ftp.FtpClient, as you can see:

```java
package org.imp;

import java.io.BufferedOutputStream;
import java.io.FileInputStream;
import java.io.IOException;

import sun.net.ftp.FtpClient;

public class Uploader {

    private FtpClient client;

    public Uploader() {
        client = new FtpClient();
    }

    public String connect(String ftpHost) throws IOException {
        client.openServer(ftpHost);
        return client.getResponseString();
    }

    public String login(String user, String pass) throws IOException {
        client.login(user, pass);
        return client.getResponseString();
    }

    public String changeDirectory(String path) throws IOException {
        client.cd(path);
        return client.getResponseString();
```

```
    }

    public String getCurrentDirectory() throws IOException {
        client.pwd();
        return client.getResponseString();
    }

    public String uploadFile(String localFilename, String remoteFilename)
                throws Exception {
        int i = 0;
        byte[] bytesIn = new byte[1024];
        FileInputStream in = new FileInputStream(localFilename);
        BufferedOutputStream out = new BufferedOutputStream(client
                .put(remoteFilename));
        while ((i = in.read(bytesIn)) >= 0) {
            out.write(bytesIn, 0, i);
        }
        in.close();
        out.close();
        return client.getResponseString();
    }

    public String uploadFile(String filename) throws Exception{
        return uploadFile(filename,filename);
    }

    public String disconnect() throws IOException {
        client.closeServer();
        return client.getResponseString();
    }
}
```

The only method that does anything of note is uploadFile. It takes the local file name and from it creates an InputStream. An output stream is obtained with a call to the FtpClient.put on the destination file name, and this stream is wrapped in a buffer. The data is then read from the FileInputStream in blocks of 1024 bytes that are passed through FTP to the target server.

Building the Imp

The source files as listed at the start of this chapter should all be in the imp directory in the following tree:

```
[anywhere]\org\imp
```

In the root *anywhere* directory, you'll need to download some libraries from www.tritonus.org/plugins.html.

For use on Microsoft Windows, you need the following:

❑   tritonus_mp3.jar

❑   tritonus_share.jar

❑   javalayer.jar

Additionally, the following DLLs will need to be on the system path (for example, in `WINNT\System32`):

- ❏ `lametritonus.dll`
- ❏ `lame_enc.dll`

In the same directory you will also need an XML file called `broadcast.xml` to use as the shell for the RSS feed. At a minimum it should look something like this:

```
<rss version="2.0">
    <channel>
        <title>Yadda Yadda</title>
        <description>My Audio Rants</description>
        <language>en-us</language>
    </channel>
</rss>
```

Note the inclusion of the `<language>` element. This isn't a requirement of RSS 2.0 but applications might check for it.

Try It Out   Running the Imp

1. Open a command window in the root *anywhere* directory, and type:

```
javac -classpath .;tritonus_mp3.jar;tritonus_share.jar org\imp\*.java
```

This will compile the application.

2. Now type:

```
java -cp .;tritonus_mp3.jar;tritonus_share.jar org.imp.Imp
```

This will run the application, and you should see the controller shown in Figure 30-1.

How It Works

The description throughout the chapter is the long version. In short:

- ❏ Clicking Record causes the `Recorder` class to start transferring data from your soundcard to a buffer; clicking Stop converts it the data from PCM audio into an MP3 file.

- ❏ Clicking Record causes the `Player` class to read MP3-encoded data from the file, convert it to PCM, and pass this to the soundcard for playback.

- ❏ Clicking Publish causes the `Publisher` class to provide the Metadata input window. When you click OK, this data is added to an XML file using DOM. That file and the audio are then uploaded to a server using the FTP protocol.

Troubleshooting

If you run into problems along the way, you may find it useful to try some of the tools from `jsresources.org`. In particular their `JSInfo.jar` provides details of what audio facilities are available to Java on your machine. If everything seems to be working correctly, but the audio is silent, try recording and playing back with a different tool, such as the Sound Recorder found in accessories. On laptops an external microphone will give better results than the one that's built in. You should also try to keep audio leads clear of mains leads, which can cause hum, as can nearby fluorescent lights.

Developments in Syndicated Media

At the time of writing there's a lot of active development in this area, in particular to support the enclosures of RSS 2.0 to provide simple podcasting applications. However, it seems likely that while the current craze for audioblogging this way is likely to settle down before long, there is huge potential for future applications of syndication in media distribution.

There is a lot of crossover between the kind of applications enabled by RSS and Atom and file sharing applications. In the context of RSS 2.0 enclosures there is ongoing discussion about the distribution of media objects using the BitTorrent (`http://bittorrent.com/`) file-sharing protocol, with the media objects being identified in the RSS 2.0 feed.

At the time of writing, no single, preferred approach to expressing this kind of data in RSS 1.0 has emerged, but that's not for want of alternative proposals (mostly in the archives of the rss-dev mailing list at `http://groups.yahoo.com/group/rss-dev/`). A related RDF vocabulary, MusicBrainz, has been used for music description for several years now (`www.musicbrainz.org/MM/`).

For Atom, the question of enclosure support has been raised in the context of feature-parity with RSS 2.0 (that is, to simplify the migration path between these formats). It seems likely that it will be implemented using something like the following syntax:

```
<link rel="enclosure" href="http:/example.com/podcast.mp3" />
```

Although RSS 1.0 may be lagging behind when it comes to podcasting, it has a head start when it comes to managing metadata associated with media files. For example, the Kowari store/toolkit in Chapter 29 has a demo application called *MusiK*, which can be used to extract, store, and search MP3 metadata for an audio library (`www.kowari.org/`). Another example is the DBin project for peer-to-peer metadata sharing, which supports creation of MPEG-7 from audio data using neural networks (`http://dbin.org/`). It remains to be seen what will happen when developers in the media syndication space become aware of the work already done on RSS-compatible metadata.

At the time of writing a proposal from Yahoo! for a media-oriented module for RSS is also under review. For details go to `http://tools.search.yahoo.com/mrss/mrss.html`.

It seems likely that multimedia distribution assisted by syndication technologies will play a key role in the onset of *ubiquitous* and *pervasive* computing. These are two sides of the same coin, where networked devices appear everywhere in all different shapes and forms, and are familiar enough to merge in with regular human life. For example, one aspect that is likely to see a lot of attention in the next year or two is useful interoperation between the audio (and photographic) capabilities of mobile phones and their increasing support for the kind of software traditionally found on desktop PCs.

Summary

In this chapter you looked at...

- ❏   The basics of digital audio.
- ❏   How sound can be recorded using Java.
- ❏   How the resulting audio can be syndicated using RSS 2.0.

Recorded audio is only one possible use of syndication for distribution of large binary files. Video, software applications, and potentially interactive media and software designed to work with the syndication applications are other possibilities. However, the audio application provides a nice simple case, not least because there are syndication tools that already support it.

Loose Ends, Loosely Coupled

This chapter looks at various techniques closely associated with syndication, data access, information discovery, and event notification.

On the surface, syndication tools resemble traditional Web browsers. The advantages of using an RSS reader rather than a good browser aren't that obvious. A set of bookmarks opened in tabs in Firefox can provide an experience not unlike checking your RSS subscriptions.

Because you're reading this part of the book, chances are you're already aware of the various characteristics of syndication that can result in a qualitative difference to whoever assumes the role of content provider or user. The *microcontent* nature of feed items, the metadata inherent in feeds and the polling mechanism for keeping up-to-date all contribute to a diverse environment.

Used with a little forethought, all these aspects can be seen as a system that smoothly extends the capabilities of the basic HTTP + HTML Web. For systems to take advantage of network connectivity various pieces have to be in place. The Web is like a mesh of ant trails, lots of different paths carrying different messages of different relevance to different people at different times. Certain operations need to be possible in this communications infrastructure. In particular, there have to be appropriate access controls on resources (which is usually handled by authentication); discovery of related or new information and resources by *looking*; and notification, the event-driven discovery of resources, by being *told*.

In this chapter you will learn:

- ❑ How to find feeds from Web pages
- ❑ How virtually any XML format can provide RSS-compatible data
- ❑ How trackback works
- ❑ Some of the design issues behind RSS modules

Finding Feeds

It is possible to read RSS/Atom feeds through a browser using an online aggregator and some of the desktop aggregators use full-blown browser components, making it possible to surf the HTML Web from there. However, there is something of a disconnect between browser and aggregator. This is usually felt as a hassle for feed subscription, where it can be necessary to manually copy a feed link from a Web page into the aggregator. It's common practice for sites to link to their feeds using a little orange [XML] icon, but this usually does little more than signal the existence of the feed to users who know what the icon means. Given that it is questionable practice to link from a human-readable Web page to a feed intended for machine consumption, the first line of attack on this problem is to get rid of the visible link altogether.

Autodiscovery

RSS Autodiscovery (or Atom, FOAF Autodiscovery) is a way of finding resources associated with a Web page that can be processed by a machine. It's essentially just using the HTML <link> tag in a conventional fashion. This makes it easy for aggregators and similar client tools to visit someone's blog or home page and automatically pick up the URI of their feeds or other machine-friendly data.

Chapter 20 demonstrates another popular use of the <link> tag — identifying style sheets:

```
<link rel="stylesheet" type="text/css" href="pink.css">
```

The rel attribute provides the nature of the relationship between this place in this document and the remote file pink.css. The type attribute provides the MIME type of the file. A typical autodiscovery link might look like the highlighted line here:

```
<html>
  <head>
    <title>My Home Page</title>
    <link rel="alternate" type="application/rss+xml" title="RSS"
        href="http://example.org/my-feed.rss" />
  </head>
  <body>
  Front page text...
  </body>
</html>
```

The <link> element is generally very similar to the familiar (X)HTML anchor element, usually encountered in the form <a href="...">. In fact, some browsers (such as Lynx) will display any such link as a navigational element. Like anchors, the link describes some relationship between the point in the local document and the remote resource.

But the <link> element must only appear in the <head> of HTML documents, and <a> only in the <body>. The usual behavior associated with an anchor link is the retrieval of another Web resource. The interpretation of the autodiscovery link is essentially, "there's another representation of this page at this URI." There isn't any behavior as such associated with this link, although a typical usage scenario is that of the Bloglines (http://bloglines.com) bookmarklet. If you are viewing a Weblog that you find interesting in your browser, clicking the bookmarklet will give you the opportunity to subscribe to the linked feed in your online Bloglines aggregator.

A simple example of the Atom version of autodiscovery is:

```
<link rel="alternate" type="application/atom+xml"
                       href="http://example.org/index.atom">
```

The specification for use with Atom has been prepared as an IETF-style pre-draft and contains clear specification of what syntax is acceptable. Much of this is likely to be useful if you run into any problems using autodiscovery with the other syndication formats. You can access the draft spec is at `http://diveintomark.org/rfc/draft-pilgrim-atom-autodiscovery-02.html`.

Given that the autodiscovery link may be found in a Web page that uses any of the various (X)HTML versions, there's a lot of variation possible in the source document from which you want to extract the link.

Practical Approaches

There are several ways the feed autodiscovery information could be extracted from a Web page. Probably the most direct way is by using a regular expression. For example, the following is taken from a PHP autodiscovery routine:

```
preg_match_all('/<link\s+(.*?)\s*\/?>/si', $html, $matches);
$links = $matches[1];
```

The expression here will match all occurrences of the link construction in `$html` and place them in `$matches`. Later on, these constructions are broken down further and tests made on the attribute values. (The full code, written by Keith Devens, is in the public domain and can be found at `http://keithdevens.com/weblog/archive/2002/Jun/03/RSSAuto-DiscoveryPHP`.)

Another approach is to use standard XML tools (probably XPath-based) to extract the `<link>` information. The big drawback here is that the source pages may not be XHTML, they may be HTML, and even then there's no guarantee of spec-compliance. However, it is still a viable alternative as the source page can be preprocessed using a markup cleaner library like HTML Tidy or TagSoup.

The third alternative is to parse the page as HTML, and be forgiving about any errors it may contain. This is in effect the approach taken by Mark Pilgrim's Python Ultra-liberal RSS locator (`http://diveintomark.org/projects/misc/rssfinder.py.txt`). This uses Python's SGML parser libraries to look after the HTML parsing, and also contains code for few other feed location strategies such as querying Syndic8's database through XML-RPC.

Consommé Code

In the following code, we take the loose HTML parsing approach. This subsystem isn't as liberal as it could be, and still manages to lack sophistication, but works nicely in the majority of cases and should be straightforward to improve if necessary.

You saw the Java `SoupParser` in action in earlier chapters, where it was used to extract feed information from potentially ill-formed XML. It's built like SAX2, using a parser that generates calls to a handler class. The same basic `SoupParser` can be reused to extract the `<link>` elements from the `<head>` of a HTML page, rather a light application comparable to spooning croutons from French Onion soup. The following code defines these new classes:

- ❑   Link: A fairly trivial model of a `<link>` element
- ❑   HtmlHandler: Receives calls from the parser and creates Link objects
- ❑   HtmlParserDemo: A little class to run the parser

These classes will appear in the package `org.urss.parsers` along with the existing SoupParser class. The other important dependency not found in the standard Java package is the HttpConnector class also listed in an earlier chapter. This class is again used here as a utility to get a page from the Web.

To start the listings, here's the complete source to Link.java :

```java
package org.urss.parsers;

public class Link {

    public String rel = null;
    public String href = null;
    public String type = null;

    public String toString() {
        return "<link rel=\"" + rel + "\" href=\"" + href + "\" type=\""
                + type + "\"/>";
    }

    public boolean isAlternate() {
        if ((rel != null) && rel.equals("alternate")
                    && (href != null) && (type != null)) {
            return true;
        }
        return false;
    }
}
```

The code starts with three member variables corresponding to the attributes of interest being initialized to null. In the interests of simplicity these are declared as public, there's little that can go wrong here. You then have a replacement toString method that will return an XHTML representation of this link. It's a convenient way of displaying the data, and may be useful when you come to pass the data along to your application. The isAlternate method is a simple helper to check to see if the value of the rel attribute is the string "alternate". If this is the case, and values are available for the other two attributes found in autodiscovery links, the method will return true.

A SoupParser instance will be passed the location of the page of interest, and as it reads through the page will call the handler object assigned to it. For autodiscovery the handler will be an instance of the HtmlHandler class, the source of which looks like this:

```java
package org.urss.parsers;

import java.util.ArrayList;
import java.util.List;

import org.xml.sax.Attributes;
import org.xml.sax.helpers.DefaultHandler;
```

```
public class HtmlHandler extends DefaultHandler {

    private List links = new ArrayList();

    public void startElement(String namespaceURI, String localName,
            String qName, Attributes attributes) {
        if ("link".equalsIgnoreCase(localName)) {
            Link link = new Link();
            link.rel = attributes.getValue("rel");
            link.href = attributes.getValue("href");
            link.type = attributes.getValue("type");
            links.add(link);
        }
    }

    public List getLinks() {
        return links;
    }
}
```

This class extends the SAX2 convenience class `DefaultHandler` that provides dummy implementations of all the methods required by the parser. The only callback method needed to read the links is `startElement`, which is overridden here. If the parser is looking at an element named `link`, a new instance of the `Link` class listed previously is created. The next few lines assign its member values pulled from the `Attributes` object this handler has been passed. The newly populated `Link` object is then added to an `ArrayList` called `links`. When called, the `getLinks` method predictably returns this collection.

The real functionality of the feed autodiscovery subsystem is provided by the previous objects fuelled by a `SoupParser`, but the next listing will show how this subsystem can be constructed for use.

When given a URI as an argument the `main` method in this demo will get the identified page from the Web, run the `SoupParser` over it to extract any autodiscovery links, and then print the results to the console. The source of `HtmlParserDemo.java` now follows, with some description interleaved:

```
package org.urss.parsers;

import java.io.InputStream;
import java.util.List;

import org.urss.io.HttpConnector;

public class HtmlParserDemo {

    private List links;

    public List getLinks() {
        return links;
    }
```

The `parseHTML` method contains most of the interesting wiring in this subsystem. An instance of each of the `SoupParser` and `HtmlHandler` classes is created, and one assigned to the other. Next an instance of the `HttpConnector` class is constructed, taking the URI of the Web page of interest as a parameter.

The initial connection is set up with a call to `connector.load()`, which will return a `true` value if the connection operation has been successful. Assuming this is the case, the stream is obtained from the connector. This stream is then passed to the parser and the characters that flow through are parsed. Once the parser has done parsing, the handler will hold the links as a `List` in a parcel from the parser.

```java
public void parseHTML(String uriString) {

    try {
        SoupParser parser = new SoupParser();
        HtmlHandler handler = new HtmlHandler();

        parser.setContentHandler(handler);

        HttpConnector connector = new HttpConnector(uriString);
        boolean streamAvailable = connector.load();
        if (streamAvailable) {
            InputStream inputStream = connector.getInputStream();
            parser.parse(inputStream);
            links = handler.getLinks();
        }
    } catch (Exception e) {
        e.printStackTrace();
    }
}
```

The `main` method listed next creates a new instance of this class, and then calls the `parseHTML` previous method with the first string (the target URI) passed from the command line. The aforementioned links in a `List` as a parcel from the parser are then stepped through in turn, and if they look to be feed autodiscovery links they are printed to console.

```java
public static void main(String[] args) {
    HtmlParserDemo reader = new HtmlParserDemo();
    reader.parseHTML(args[0]);
    List links = reader.getLinks();

    for (int i = 0; i < links.size(); i++) {
        Link link = (Link) links.get(i);
        if (link.isAlternate()) {
            System.out.println(link);
        }
    }
}
```

Try It Out   Parsing HTML

Place the previous source files in the `[anywhere]\org\urss\parsers` source tree, and the follow these steps:

1.   Open a command window in the `[anywhere]` directory and enter:

```
javac -classpath . org/urss/parsers/HtmlParserDemo.java
```

This will compile the source code.

2. Verify that you're connected to the Internet, and enter:

```
java -classpath . org.urss.parsers.HtmlParserDemo http://mena.typepad.com/
```

You should now see something like the following:

```
C:\urss>java -classpath . org.urss.parsers.HtmlParserDemo http://mena.typepad.com/
<link rel="alternate" href="http://mena.typepad.com/dollarshort/atom.xml" type="
application/atom+xml"/>
<link rel="alternate" href="http://mena.typepad.com/dollarshort/index.rdf" type=
"application/rss+xml"/>
```

How It Works

The URI of the front page of a Weblog (`http://mena.typepad.com/`) is passed to the application on the command line. Before doing anything with that, the application sets up a parser/handler combination suitable for spotting `<link>` tags in HTML. Once these are initialized the URI is passed to HTTP communication objects which do an HTTP GET request on the given URI, receiving a response containing the data from the Web page identified by the URI. This response is passed through the parser to create the `Link` objects corresponding to the `<link>` tags in the page. After the page has been parsed, these objects are written to the console re-expressed as XML.

From Browser to Aggregator

A subsystem like the one described in the previous section would usually be called upon when a user sees an interesting news/blog page and wants to subscribe to a feed. In one way or another the URI of the page would be passed to that subsystem, which would find the feed URI(s) for subsequent processing, maybe beginning with a preview of the feed.

A typical scenario would be the use of a JavaScript bookmarklet to pass the URI to an aggregator. Bookmarklets are simply links that call upon a JavaScript program rather than using HTTP. The code is actually part of the link. A common way many tools do this is to have an HTTP server embedded in the aggregator that will run locally on a less-well-known port. Clicking the Bookmarklet will then pass the page URI in a call to the local server. You may have seen icons on sites that correspond to individual aggregator tools. Clicking some of these will have the effect of passing the feed URI directly to the aggregator. For example, you may find an icon for the BottomFeeder aggregator with the following in a hyperlink :

```
http://127.0.0.1:8666/btf?rss=http://example.org/blog/rss.xml
```

Here the site's RSS feed URI will be passed in an HTTP GET to BottomFeeder's Web server running on the local host (127.0.0.1) on port 8666. This approach bypasses the need for autodiscovery (the aggregator gets the feed URI). However, because there is no convention for which port, path, or even method to use it doesn't really work as a general solution. For a useful list of what details many well-known aggregators need, along with a subscription service tool go to `http://xml.mfd-consult.dk/syn-sub/`.

At present there isn't any single general solution to this browser-to-aggregator problem. However, there are a variety of possible approaches that may be suitable depending on how you want your application to operate.

There is at least one more direct approach. It is possible to use a non-standard URI scheme as an application trigger from the browser. As an example of how this can be done, here is a hack for Microsoft Windows operating systems that bypasses the need for a local HTTP server.

A Scheme Handler

The toy that is about to be described will use a completely fictional URI scheme, `look:`. To keep things simple, the handler will be a batch file running the command-line cURL tool to display the results of a HTTP HEAD call. You will need one of the Windows binary versions from `http://curl.haxx.se/`, and we assume that this executable (`curl.exe`) will be in your `C:\curl` folder. The handler application will be the following batch file, that is an executable text file (`gethead.bat`) saved in the `C:\curl` folder:

```
curl.exe --head %2
pause
```

Registering a URL Scheme in Windows

You now have to tell your system which application should deal with URLs (as Windows calls them) with the `look:` scheme. This involves making some minor additions to the Registry, which isn't difficult, but can cause havoc if anything goes wrong.

> *You should not edit your Windows Registry unless you are reasonably familiar with this activity or are prepared to risk a corrupted system. Make a backup of anything you don't want to lose before you proceed.*

The usual tool for editing the Windows Registry is `regedit.exe`, which you can start from the Start menu's Run option or from a command line. The first thing you should do after running this tool is to export a copy of the current Registry as a partial safeguard. This is on the Registry menu.

The data that needs to be added for the new URL scheme is as follows:

```
[HKEY_CLASSES_ROOT]
    [look]
        (Default) = "URL:look Protocol"
        URL Protocol = ""
        [DefaultIcon]
            (Default) = "C:\curl\curl.exe"
        [shell]
            [open]
                [command]
                    (Default) = "C:\curl\gethead.bat %1"
```

The `regedit` tool is a fairly straightforward albeit slightly clunky tree editor. The previous entry follows the same basic pattern as the Registry entry for the `mailto:` URL scheme, so if you explore that first you'll be able to get a picture of what you're aiming for. Be careful not to modify anything outside of this new entry. There are plenty of tutorial sites on the Web covering the Registry, and documentation at the Microsoft developer site (`http://msdn.microsoft.com/`).

Writing a Bookmarklet

Type the following into a text editor:

```
<a href="javascript:location.href='look: '+location.href">Pass to Aggregator</a>
```

Save the file on your local machine as if it were a complete HTML page; name it, for example, bookmark. htm. When you open this page in a browser, you will see a regular-looking hyperlink. Now either drag this link to your Favorites/Links (IE/Mozilla) toolbar, or right-click and select Add to Favorites/Bookmark This Link or use the Favorites/Bookmarks menu to add the link to your browser's toolbar.

Try It Out   **Using a Bookmarklet**

If you've followed the instructions so far, you're ready to go. Still in the browser, open any Web page anywhere else. Then click the Pass to Aggregator link on your browser's toolbar. It depends on the browser, but you should see a dialog box asking what you want to do. Figure 31-1 shows what this dialog box looks like in Firefox.

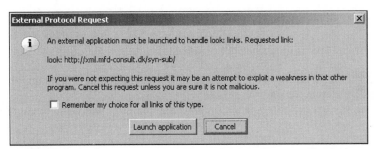

Figure 31-1

Assuming you click OK through any warning, and are online, within a few seconds you should see a command window (see Figure 31-2). Here you can see the result of an HTTP GET on the page that was in the browser when the Bookmarklet was clicked.

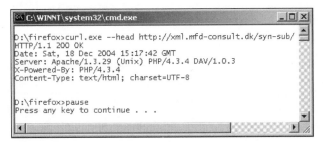

Figure 31-2

How It Works

The value given in the href part of the bookmarklet link was this:

```
javascript:location.href='look: '+location.href
```

That will run the browser's JavaScript interpreter on this part:

```
location.href='look: '+location.href
```

This simply passes the browser a new value for the current page location, the value being the URI of the current page preceded by the string `look:`, for example `look: http://mena.typepad.com/`. This causes the browser to launch whatever handler application it knows for the `look:` URI scheme — it wouldn't have known one, but after adding the Registry entry, it will. The action it will carry out is to run the command in Registry:

```
C:\curl\gethead.bat %1
```

The `%1` here is a DOS variable that will get the first value passed to the command. In this case that will be the full URL. The contents of `gethead.bat` is as follows:

```
curl.exe --head %2
pause
```

This will run cURL with the `--head` option (do an HTTP HEAD) on the URI that is the *second* (space-separated) argument this batch file has been passed. The thing is, this application is triggered with the whole of the URL sent from the browser. Had that been of the form `look:http://example.org` or similar then cURL would have thrown an error — it doesn't understand the `look:` URI scheme. This is worked around by getting the browser (through the Bookmarklet) to pass on a URL of the form `look: http://example.org` — note the space. So cURL is actually run on the string after the space, a URL of the form `http://example.org`, which is of course in a well-known scheme.

Registering a URI Scheme for Real

The previous trick only provides a work-around for the lack of a convenient method for communicating between browser and aggregator. Because it relates to quite a fundamental part of Web architecture, there is a registry of URI schemes managed by the IANA (Internet Assigned Numbers Authority) and best practices suggest that it isn't a good idea to use unregistered schemes in URIs. The bar to getting a new scheme added is high; you would need a very convincing case. To date there are only 30 or so schemes (listed at `www.iana.org/assignments/uri-schemes`), each of which is backed by a stable RFC. However, there are a great many unregistered schemes in use, either for proprietary purposes or for general use.

Most URI schemes relate to protocols (`http: ftp:`, and so on) but the browser/aggregator communication problem doesn't really fall into this category, because it's more about simple operating system event notification rather than really passing data around. The widely deployed `mailto:` scheme is an example of one scheme like this that did slip through; it usually carries out a similar function in launching an application on the user's desktop rather than handling the data directly.

So when the `feed:` scheme was proposed not long ago, there was significant division of opinion. The idea behind `feed:` was to carry out that browser/aggregator link-passing. There are good arguments against using a scheme in this way (for details see `www.w3.org/TR/2004/REC-webarch-20041215/#URI-scheme`). The most convincing of these arguments is that it is already possible to do the same kind of dispatching based on MIME types. Unfortunately this isn't altogether true with the current generation of Web browsers. When dispatching this way, they usually pass on the data itself rather than the URI of the data. The other objection that `feed:` wasn't a registered scheme complete with RFC was in part assuaged by the publication of a pre-draft specification (`www.25hoursaday.com/draft-obasanjo-feed-URI-scheme-02.html`). The approach doesn't gel well with other parts of the Web architecture, but it is relatively easy to follow an approach similar to that of `look:`, assuming everyone will only be working on a single operating system platform (not a very Web-friendly assumption). So it's not uncontroversial, but as many aggregators support `feed:`, it seems reasonable to use this approach as a solution where other approaches aren't viable.

Using MIME Types

Rather than using a URI scheme to trigger a browser to launch an appropriate handler such as an aggregator, a more Web Architecture-friendly approach is for the feed to be served with an appropriate MIME type. The browser can then dispatch the information to a handler registered for that type, as it would if it were to play, for example, audio files. However there are two practical problems with this approach.

The first problem is that many feeds (possibly the majority) aren't served with a suitable MIME type. There's general agreement that the best MIME type for simple RSS formats is `application/rss+xml` although attempts to register this with IANA have so far met with failure due to the apparent lack of normative specifications. The Atom type is definitely `application/atom+xml`, and new releases of both Apache and Microsoft IIS will serve files with the `.atom` extension with this type in the HTTP headers. There is some division over the MIME type for RSS 1.0. This is RSS, so the `application/rss+xml` type would be appropriate, but it is also RDF/XML, which would call for the `application/rdf+xml` type. There isn't really enough deployment of syndication-oriented MIME type handlers to decide which is the better approach.

The second practical problem with using MIME type dispatching for single-click subscription from a browser is that most current browsers only pass the target data (as a stream) to the handler, not the source URI. The URI is the one piece of data the aggregator needs for subscription. However it seems likely that Atom will include such a link within the feed XML, and such a link can easily be added to RSS feeds as a namespace-qualified extension.

The MIME-based approach has been written up as a draft specification, the "Universal Subscription Mechanism" (`www.kbcafe.com/rss/usm.html`). The specification proposes that RSS 2.0 feeds include something like the following as a child element of their `channel` element:

```
<atom:link
        rel="start"
        type="application/rss+xml"
        title="The RSS Blog"
        href="http://www.kbcafe.com/rss/rss.xml"
        xmlns:atom="http://purl.org/atom/ns#" />
```

As with many other proposals in the information feed space, it remains to be seen which approach will gain most adoption in the long term.

GRDDL

Gleaning Resource Descriptions from Dialects of Languages (GRDDL) (`www.w3.org/2004/01/rdxh/spec`) is a simple technique. Since the early days of the Web, we have had the opportunity to include metadata in HTML documents. However, even when the facility is used, there aren't that many tools that can make good use of the metadata. GRDDL is primarily about applying an XSLT transform to a

(X)HTML document to produce an RDF/XML expression of the metadata the original document contained. Like a lot of these techniques, it's easiest to demonstrate by example.

Take a document, on the Web, say it's called `http://example.org/sample.html`:

```
<html xmlns="http://www.w3.org/1999/xhtml">
  <head profile="http://www.w3.org/2003/g/data-view">
    <title>The Pretzel Communique</title>
    <link rel="transformation"
        href="http://www.w3.org/2000/06/dc-extract/dc-extract.xsl" />
    <meta name="DC.Subject" content="Role of the Pretzel in the 21st Century" />
  </head>
  <body>
    Here's the content of the page.
  </body>
</html>
```

The profile attribute in the head elements points to a specific XHTML profile, which indicates, according to the GRDDL notes: *"RDF statements that result from transformation of the HTML document to RDF by designated algorithms are part of the document's meaning."* The algorithm designated here performs a transformation using an XSLT style sheet.

If this document were linked to by a blogger, it would be possible for the RSS 1.0 feed to contain metadata mechanically extracted from the document; for example:

```
<item rdf:about="http://example.org/sample.html">
    <title>The Pretzel Communique</title>
    <dc:subject>A Role of the Pretzel in the 21st Century</dc:subject>
...
</item>
```

The same idea can be applied to practically any source data. In the context of syndication it would also make a good option for extracting RDF from Atom or RSS 2.0, either at the feed level or from any embedded content. XSLT was presented earlier in the book as a way of obtaining RDF/XML (as RSS 1.0) from other formats. So what's special about GRDDL? There are at least two tricks that it brings to the table. The first is that the use of profiles in this way offers an unambiguous, automatable, formal approach to getting the metadata out of the source documents — it's a lot more specified than a quick hack, although just as simple. Secondly, the mechanism is defined such that more than one transformation can be applied in a modular fashion. This example pulls out some Dublin Core material. Another style sheet might pull out material expressed as XFN (XHTML Friends Network) from the original document, producing RDF using the FOAF vocabulary. The statements obtained from each transformation can simply be added together.

Robots, Crawlers, Harvesters, and Scutters

It's worth mentioning here that many of the clients that visit Web servers are several steps removed from a human. Some of these are undesirables such as bots designed to collect e-mail addresses, the end result being inboxes full of unsolicited trash. There are also plenty of benign agents, such as those collecting data for search engine indexes — if you check your Web server access logs, you are sure to see records of visits by Googlebot (`www.google.com/bot.html`). If you want, you can request that visitors like this don't visit parts of your site using a `robots.txt` file.

When a bot visits a site, say `http://example.org/`, it should first check to see if `http://example.org/robots.txt` exists. If it does, it should read and interpret entries as follows:

```
# I don't want Google to list my personal stuff
User-agent: googlebot
Disallow: /private/

# There's no point in indexing these anyway
User-agent: *
Disallow: /cgi-bin/
Disallow: /tmp/

# These may change, I don't want them on record
User-agent: *
Disallow: /my-opinions/
```

If there's anything that would be wasting bandwidth for a crawler to visit, or maybe there's material you'd rather didn't appear in search engines, then a `robots.txt` in the root directory of your server is the answer. It can be educational to see what other people have in their `robots.txt` file, for example, `www.whitehouse.gov/robots.txt`.

Most crawlers and harvesters operate by following regular hyperlinks:

```
<a href="over-here.html">Another interesting page</a>
```

However, there's a new breed of bot on the Web born of the FOAF community. These "scutters" are designed to follow links in RDF/XML files to discover additional information about resources. In the RDF Schema specification the property `rdfs:seeAlso` is described as follows:

A triple of the form: S `rdfs:seeAlso` O states that the resource O may provide additional information about S. It may be possible to retrieve representations of O from the Web, but this is not required. When such representations may be retrieved, no constraints are placed on the format of those representations.

So there is really very little that is demanded of `rdfs:seeAlso`, making it ideal for creating hyperlink-like connections between RDF documents for scutters to follow. An unofficial, very loose convention is that the target of an `rdfs:seeAlso` will be another RDF/XML file. This property can be used to make a connection between any two resources, so, for example, if you wanted to flesh out a blog post with a reference to some background material, you could have an item in your RSS 1.0 feed like this:

```
<item rdf:about="http://example.org/pascals-wager">
    <title>My Lovely Sermon</title>
    <description>Writing a sermon isn't easy at the best of times...
    </description>
    <rdfs:seeAlso rdf:resource="http://akma.disseminary.org/foaf.rdf" />
</item>
```

Here the FOAF profile of someone who has a connection to the subject of the post is being referred to.

For more on scutters see `http://rdfweb.org/topic/ScutterSpec`, and the use of `rdfs:seeAlso` for this kind of data advertisement can be found at `http://esw.w3.org/topic/UsingSeeAlso`.

A recent development for search engine Web bots is the introduction of support for HTML anchor links with additional information in their `rel` attributes.

Inter-Site Communication

In addition to the client-server communication used in syndication, use of server-to-server and peer-to-peer communication has been on the increase in recent times. This can offer benefits in terms of increased efficiency through sharing of data between online aggregators, or enabling new forms of information provision through inter-service linkage.

Clouds

RSS 2.0 includes an element `<cloud>` that is specified as a sub-element (the examples show this as a child) of the `<channel>` element. This subelement provides support for a kind of event-driven *push* interface from a syndication server to the client (which may be acting as a server itself). The feed element will look something like this:

```
<cloud domain="example.org" port="80" path="/RPC2" registerProcedure="rssNotify"
       protocol="xml-rpc" />
```

On finding an element like this in a feed, the client can call back to the XML-RPC method described, supplying a list of feeds to watch. Subsequently, if one of those feeds changes then the server will send an XML-RPC message containing the URI of the updated feed back to the client. You can find more details of this protocol can be found at `http://blogs.law.harvard.edu/tech/soapMeetsRss`.

Outside of UserLand's products this approach doesn't really seem to have caught on. The need to try and minimize the bandwidth waste incurred by simple polling hasn't been forgotten though, and there is a strong possibility that syndication could move more towards a push-oriented system in the not-too-distant future. In the meantime, various other approaches to notification and push have been discussed in the context of the Atom protocol. More on those shortly.

Weblog Pings

One of the earliest services targeted specifically at blogs was Weblogs.com, which is set up to receive notification of site changes (that is, new posts) and supplies both a HTML and XML formatted list of the most recently updated Weblogs. This kind of setup can potentially be used to help in making syndication more efficient. Rather than polling a lot of individual sites to look for changes, it's possible, in principle at least, to watch for changes at a single location. The protocol for notification is XML-RPC, and calls will usually originate from method calls to an XML-RPC library in the blogging software. If this is already available, then only a couple of lines of code will be needed. However, it's interesting to see what's going on under the hood, which you can do with a telnet client.

> *You've probably got a telnet client installed already whether you know it or not, try typing **telnet** on the command line. If not, PuTTY (`www.chiark.greenend.org.uk/~sgtatham/putty/`) is a popular free client.*

First you need to connect to the host on port 80 — the usual HTTP port:

```
telnet rssrpc.weblogs.com 80
```

Then you need to pass along the HTTP header followed by a blank line and then the message body:

```
POST /RPC2 HTTP/1.1
Host: rssrpc.weblogs.com

<?xml version="1.0"?>
<methodCall>
    <methodName>rssUpdate</methodName>
    <params>
        <param>
            <value><string>Andrew's Blog</string></value>
        </param>
        <param>
            <value><string>http://www.tfosorcim.org/blog/</string></value>
        </param>
    </params>
</methodCall>
```

The service should respond with a confirmation message or an error message in XML, although you might get a raw HTTP 5xx error if there were lower-level problems.

> *There was work in progress on Weblogs.com at the time of writing so it wasn't possible to confirm operation. Hopefully by the time you read this, the service will have settled down again, although you will probably have to check details from the site. The original specification for the RSS-oriented service is at* http://www.xmlrpc.com/weblogsComForRss.

At some point not long after this action, a new entry should appear on the HTML list or in the XML data at Weblogs.com, the format of the XML looking like this:

```
<weblogUpdates version="1" updated="Sun, 19 Dec 2004 20:05:03 GMT" count="1177184">
    <weblog name="DeNine" url="http://denine.blogspirit.com/" when="1"/>
    <weblog name="[JUNK(IE) WRITINGS]" url="http://www.20six.fr/scavengershunt"
when="2"/>
    <weblog name="one glass, one song, one man" url="http://brookslampe.blogspot.com"
when="2"/>
    ...
</weblogUpdates>
```

This changes.xml file covers three hours, so the hour is presumably that's what the when attribute refers to.

There is another service available for *podcast* posts at http://audio.weblogs.com/, which also provides the list of fresh material in HTML and XML. Slightly more conveniently, this is provided in RSS 2.0 rather than the purpose-specific format presented previously.

Note that a lot more people are using the Weblog update call (weblogUpdates.ping) than use the RSS-oriented interface (rssUpdate). To get the most recent feeds for these you will have to get the blog HTML page and run autodiscovery on it to find the feed, although, of course, once done it's easy enough to keep a local map of blog HTML URIs/feed URIs.

A variation on the Weblogs.com approach has been taken at blo.gs which uses a single call to announce changes to both the HTML and RSS versions of a resource, supplying the two URIs as parameters (the method is `weblogUpdates.extendedPing`). An alternative was to send a direct HTTP GET with the site details as the query part of the URI, for example:

```
http://ping.blo.gs/?name=Andrew's Blog&url=http://www.tfosorcim.org/blog/
```

However the current blo.gs `changes.xml` service is being phased out, as the site (`http://blo.gs/cloud.php`) notes the new way will be to "simply connect to port 9999 on ping.blo.gs, feed the output through gzip decompression, and you will be receiving a streaming version of the old changes.xml files." The change file format is similar to the Weblogs.com example, with the notable addition of precise timestamp attributes. This will create a streaming feed over a persistent TCP/IP connection. If you want to take advantage of this, then check the site for documentation. Note that this service isn't intended for use as an update trigger in regular (selective) client applications, but for services that will provide information relating to all the blogs that use the service.

A simple way of taking advantage of the ping infrastructure that is in place on the Web is through services like Ping-O-Matic (`http://pingomatic.com/`). The idea is that you send them a ping either over XML-RPC or manually, and they distribute the message to any other services that may be interested as a fan-out kind of notification.

Publish/Subscribe Innovations

It may not come as a surprise that some of the most interesting developments in this field have come from a company called PubSub (`www.pubsub.com`). One area where they are playing a leading role is an initiative by some of the major ping consumers to improve the infrastructure to share data more efficiently between different services that receive pings. This group/initiative called FeedMesh has a mailing list at `http://groups.yahoo.com/group/feedmesh`.

In their own online service, pubsub.com provide a variety of facilities for end users, notably the ability to subscribe to a search query with the results being delivered as a syndication feed. Like several other RSS-oriented search services they have a fairly huge and constantly updated database pulled from syndication feeds. Unlike other services their focus is on the future, that is, the results come in as query-matching information appears on the Web, rather than looking at already published material. What's more, they also provide an instant notification service for this data using the open XMPP (Jabber) protocol. Support for this is built into the PubSub browser sidebar tools as well as the Gush newsreader/instant messenger tool (`www.2entwine.com/`). The PubSub site has code examples for client developers (`www.pubsub.com/tools.php`).

The use of XMPP as a transport for syndicated material is described in an IETF Internet-Draft (`www.xmpp.org/drafts/draft-saintandre-atompub-notify-01.html`).

Feed Deltas

Another related way in which PubSub are pushing the envelope is in their promotion of the use of RFC 3229 "Delta encoding in HTTP" with feeds. The specification describes how it is possible to communicate the changes in the representation of a resource by passing only the differences rather than the whole shebang. If a feed only has one extra entry added every day, what's the point in getting 15 entries every hour? When client syndication tools are only looking at a few dozen or even hundred feeds then the inefficiencies of traditional pull techniques aren't really a problem. Ok, use of HTTP conditional GET and similar techniques can compensate to a large extent. However, in situations where thousands, even millions of subscriptions are being maintained then the regular approach simply isn't up to the job. RFC 3229 with feeds offers a way of minimizing the passing of redundant data and making significant cuts in overall bandwidth requirements. The potential gain here is apparent if you consider that if inter-service communication can be achieved efficiently, then only a single service needs to subscribe to millions of feeds. The crucial "diff" material can be forwarded to other services with a net bandwidth use and overall complexity reduced to a fraction of what might otherwise be the case.

Bob Wyman of PubSub has documentation and links relating to RFC 3229 with feeds on his Weblog at `http://bobwyman.pubsub.com/main/2004/09/using_rfc3229_w.html`.

Trackback

Trackback is another way content management systems can communicate with each other. The protocol is used primarily as an automatic comment-placing system for Weblogs. Say you've seen a blog post that you find interesting. You write a blog post yourself, linking to the individual entry on the remote page and expressing your opinion. If both blogs have the necessary capabilities, then a reference to your post will appear by magic in the comments/trackbacks section of the remote site. This is the kind of magic that hides some non-trivial implementation.

The following description assumes that everything possible is automated, many tools need additional human intervention (usually pasting of the target URI in a text box). You can find the trackback specification at `www.movabletype.org/docs/mttrackback.html`.

Right Back to the Track

The trackback system works through a dialog between the two sites. When you post your opinion of the remote page, your blogging tool will extract from your post the link you supplied — that is the URI (permalink) of the remote item. Your tool will then retrieve the remote HTML page and look through the markup for embedded markup containing trackback data. The usual case is that for every visible entry on a blog there is a hidden block of markup. Your tool will attempt to match the URI you have linked to with one referred to in one of these blocks. After the correct block has been located, then another URI is extracted from that block; this is the all-important Trackback Ping URL.

Now your system has a target, it will send a trackback ping to it. These pings are RESTful, in other words they use standard HTTP directly, rather than tunneling through XML-RPC. The call is made using the POST method, and the HTTP header will typically look something like this:

```
POST http://example-target.org/mt-tb.cgi/item123
Content-Type: application/x-www-form-urlencoded
title=More+Sermon+Stuff&url=
            http://my-original-blog&excerpt=Here+we+go&blog_name=My+Igloo
```

The Content-Type is the same encoding as generally sent from HTML forms — this also happens to be the easiest (semi-manual) way of sending a trackback ping.

The possible parameters in the POST data are:

- ❏ title: The title of the local entry
- ❏ excerpt: An excerpt of the content of the local entry

❑   `url`: The URI (permalink) of the local entry

❑   `blog_name`: The name of the blog in which the local entry is posted

The response to a query like the previous one is a little chunk of XML (similar to XML-RPC confirmations) that helps support error detection above the HTTP layer. If everything's ok, the server will respond with:

```
<?xml version="1.0" encoding="iso-8859-1"?>
<response>
<error>0</error>
</response>
```

If something has gone wrong, either an HTTP-level error will appear (404, 5xx, and so on) or something like the following:

```
<?xml version="1.0" encoding="iso-8859-1"?>
<response>
<error>1</error>
<message>description of error</message>
</response>
```

At the communication level, that's all there is to it. The rest is a simple matter of programming. Figure 31-3 shows a standalone trackback ping form.

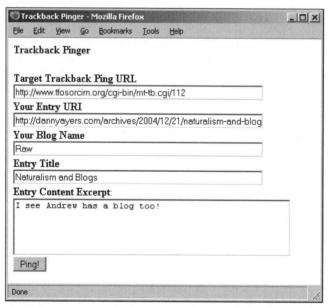

Figure 31-3

The source (`trackback.html`) is as follows:

```
<html xmlns="http://www.w3.org/1999/xhtml">
<head>
   <title>Trackback Pinger</title>
</head>
<body>
   <h4>Trackback Pinger</h4>
   <form action="" method="post"
       onsubmit="this.action = this.targetUrl.value; return true;">
       <b>Target Trackback Ping URL:</b>
<br/>
       <input name="targetUrl" size="60" />
<br/>
       <b>Your Entry URI:</b>
<br/>
       <input name="url" size="60" />
<br/>
       <b>Your Blog Name:</b>
<br/>
       <input name="blog_name" size="60" />
<br>
       <b>Entry Title:</b>
<br/>
       <input name="title" size="60" />
<br>
       <b>Entry Content Excerpt:</b>
<br/>
       <textarea name="excerpt" rows="4" cols="50"></textarea>
<br/>
       <input type="submit" value="Ping!"/>
   </form>
</body>
</html>
```

For the most part, this is ordinary HTML, where the names of the input fields will act as parameters in the HTTP POST. The only unusual part is this:

```
<form action="" method="post"
    onsubmit="this.action = this.targetUrl.value; return true;">
```

Normally when a form submit button is clicked, the specified HTTP method (GET or POST) will be applied to the URI in the `action` attribute. However, here that attribute is declared as an empty string. When the Ping! button is clicked, the tiny piece of JavaScript in the `onsubmit` attribute will copy the Trackback Ping URL from the `targetUrl` text field into the action slot of the form. This has the effect of the POST being done on the user-set value.

After filling in the form and clicking the Ping! button, in your browser you will either see an HTTP error (for example, due to using the wrong trackback URI) or a single *0*, which will be what the XML success message looks like in a browser, or an error message from the target site.

This form allows manual submission of trackback pings. Ideally, the entire automated process will go like this:

❑ Agnes posts an entry to her Weblog. This appears on HTML page P with permalink X, which also will contain a block of hidden markup associating permalink X with trackback link Y.

❑ Brenda posts an entry to their blog, commenting on entry X.

❑ Brenda's server visits page P, finds the reference to permalink X, and gets the trackback address Y.

❑ Brenda's server posts to Agnes's blog details of their entry using the trackback protocol.

❑ Agnes's blog adds the link and excerpt from Brenda's entry.

The trackback specification does also include a description of how a list of trackback pings can be retrieved from a server for a given trackback URL, although this isn't needed for the basic trackback communications.

More Autodiscovery

No individual aspect of trackback is especially difficult, even if the parts do fit together to make a confusing whole. One slightly tricky bit is getting the trackback info from the original (commented-on) blog's HTML page. The reason for this trickiness is that the creator of trackback decided it made sense to use RDF/XML, presumably to be consistent with the use of RSS 1.0 in feeds. Unfortunately, RDF/XML and HTML do not mix well.

> *The GRDDL approach to RDF in (X)HTML described earlier in this chapter is one of the few rays of sunshine on an otherwise fairly grim-looking heap of messy markup that has been piling up since the early days of RDF/XML. In a nutshell, there's no simple approach that doesn't break something or upset somebody. It's a long story; if you're interested, there's background at* `http://infomesh.net/ 2002/rdfinhtml/` *and more recent work by a W3C Task Force is described at* `www.w3.org/2003/ 03/rdf-in-xml.html`.

Typically a tool-generated blog front page will contain a series of entries, nicely marked up in (X)HTML, probably with CSS providing an attractive layout. Each entry might begin something like this:

```
<h3 class="storytitle">
 <a href="http://blog.pietrosperoni.it/index.php?p=20">My new phone,
                                             my new Moblog</a>
</h3>
```

There would then follow the body of the blog entry where you might see a section devoted to feedback, including a link to the appropriate URI to handle comments for this entry. But then, if trackback is supported, you have the fun part:

```
<!--
 <rdf:RDF
    xmlns:rdf="http://www.w3.org/1999/02/22-rdf-syntax-ns#"
    xmlns:dc="http://purl.org/dc/elements/1.1/"
    xmlns:trackback="http://madskills.com/public/xml/rss/module/trackback/">

    <rdf:Description
```

```
            rdf:about="http://blog.pietrosperoni.it/index.php?p=20"
            dc:identifier="http://blog.pietrosperoni.it/index.php?p=20"
            dc:title="My new phone, my new Moblog"
            trackback:ping="http://blog.pietrosperoni.it/wp-trackback.php/20" />

    </rdf:RDF>
-->
```

The RDF/XML in this code would be enough to bring a glow to any Semantic Web enthusiast's cheeks, especially as it was created by a widely deployed, fairly standard blog tool (this example was generated by WordPress). However, the problem of embedding RDF in HTML has been worked around by placing the trackback information in a comment section. It doesn't disturb the content markup, and in the absence of any better system, the specification designer made a reasonable choice. However, the XML specification makes it clear that on the XHTML train, comments aren't even the baggage compartments. XML comments are not considered character data, and any respectable processor is free to ignore their contents if it so wishes. So here we have undeniably important material, tucked away in an area labeled insignificant. This would lead even a moderately purist markup enthusiast to say very bad words.

Trackback is widely deployed in this form whatever the architectural aesthetics, and generally works very well. The RDF/XML describes a very simple set of properties of the entry resource. The URI in the rdf:about attribute is the same as that used in the (perma)link in the HTML of the title, this identifies the entry resource. The properties provide an identifier and title using the Dublin Core vocabulary, along with the trackback ping URI, the part essential for inter-blog dialog.

In practice most implementations of trackback ignore the RDF/XML nature of the embedded data and use simple regular expressions to retrieve the URI of interest. This approach is entirely understandable, because it's probably the quickest and simplest thing that might possibly work. In fact sample Perl code is provided along with the trackback specification that uses this technique. It should be noted that (comment-embedding aside) the use of regular expressions in this way is often likely to be more fragile than using a purpose-built parser, as the specification may be based on a grammar that is more complex than a simple regular expression may take into consideration.

Pulling Out the Comments

As it happens, the Java code described earlier in the chapter for extracting <link> elements is very close to what is required for extracting trackback comment blocks. The kind of treatment required isn't included in a standard SAX handler, so here an interface is defined for a single method:

```
package org.urss.parsers;

public interface CommentHandler {
    public void comment(String comment);
}
```

Then some small modification is needed in the SoupParser.java code to make these calls. This is the existing code from Chapter 23 that checks for comment blocks:

```
public boolean isComment() {
    Matcher match = commentRe.matcher(this.data.substring(this.charIndex));
    if (match.find()) {
        this.charIndex = this.charIndex + match.end();
        comment(match.group());
```

```
                return true;
        }
        return false;
    }
```

The `comment` method is called with the comment string beginning with `<!--` and ending with `-->`, so for convenience, before the handler is called the string has these trimmed off. The `comment` method looks like this:

```
    public void comment(String raw) {
        String comment = raw.substring(4, raw.length() - 4);
        if (contentHandler instanceof CommentHandler) {
            ((CommentHandler) contentHandler).comment(comment);
        }
    }
```

Reflection is used to check that the content handler object implements the `CommentHandler` interface, and if it does the `comment` method there is called with the text of the comment being passed over.

The handler for link extraction, `HtmlHandler`, needs to implement `CommentHandler` to be able to take advantage of this addition, so the class declaration in `HtmlHandler.java` needs a minor change:

```
    public class HtmlHandler extends DefaultHandler implements CommentHandler {
```

`HtmlHandler` has an `ArrayList` to collect the links, and a similar facility can easily be added for the comments (in `HtmlHandler.java`):

```
    private List comments = new ArrayList();

    public List getComments() {
        return comments;
    }
```

Of course, a method is also needed to catch the comments, implementing the method defined in `CommentHandler`. This method is very simple, and just adds the `String` containing the comment as another object in the `List`:

```
    public void comment(String comment) {
        comments.add(comment);
    }
```

To show this in action, a revised version of `HtmlParserDemo.java` is required. Here is the full source code:

```
package org.urss.parsers;

import java.io.InputStream;
import java.util.List;

import org.urss.io.HttpConnector;


public class HtmlParserDemo {
```

```
    private List links;

    private List comments;

    public List getComments() {
        return comments;
    }

    public List getLinks() {
        return links;
    }

    public void parseHTML(String uriString) {

        try {
            SoupParser parser = new SoupParser();
            HtmlHandler handler = new HtmlHandler();

            parser.setContentHandler(handler);

            HttpConnector connector = new HttpConnector(uriString);
            boolean streamAvailable = connector.load();
            if (streamAvailable) {
                InputStream inputStream = connector.getInputStream();
                parser.parse(inputStream);
                links = handler.getLinks();
                comments = handler.getComments();
            }
        } catch (Exception e) {
            e.printStackTrace();
        }
    }

    public static void main(String[] args) {
        HtmlParserDemo reader = new HtmlParserDemo();
        reader.parseHTML(args[0]);
        List links = reader.getLinks();

        for (int i = 0; i < links.size(); i++) {
            Link link = (Link) links.get(i);
            if (link.isAlternate()) {
                System.out.println(link);
            }
        }
        List comments = reader.getComments();
        for (int i = 0; i < comments.size(); i++) {
            System.out.println(comments.get(i));
        }
    }
}
```

After recompiling the modified code, it can be run again; for example:

```
java -classpath . org.urss.parsers.HtmlParserDemo http://mena.typepad.com/
```

This now produces the result:

```
<link rel="alternate" href="http://www.sixapart.com/corner/index.rdf"
      type="application/rss+xml"/>
<link rel="alternate" href="http://www.sixapart.com/corner/atom.xml"
      type="application/atom+xml"/>

<rdf:RDF xmlns:rdf="http://www.w3.org/1999/02/22-rdf-syntax-ns#"
         xmlns:trackback="http://madskills.com/public/xml/rss/module/trackback/"
         xmlns:dc="http://purl.org/dc/elements/1.1/">

<rdf:Description rdf:about=
         "http://www.sixapart.com/corner/archives/2004/12/upcoming_releas.shtml"
    trackback:ping="http://www.sixapart.com/mt/trackback/856"
    dc:title="Upcoming Release to address Spam Issues"
    dc:identifier=
         "http://www.sixapart.com/corner/archives/2004/12/upcoming_releas.shtml"
    dc:subject=""
    dc:description="As Anil said over at Six Log..."
    dc:creator="Mena"
    dc:date="2004-12-20T16:38:21-08:00" />
</rdf:RDF>

... lots more trackback blocks ...
```

You can now pass this block for extraction of the data into the rest of your system, perhaps using a regular expression to pull out the permalink and ping target URIs. This isn't an unreasonable approach, given that most producers will stick closely to this format (and that there has already been some heavy regexp action on the markup). However it may be more useful or reliable to pass these blocks onto either an XML parser or a true RDF/XML parser to read the data in the manner defined in the specification.

Defining Extension Modules

The names of elements and attributes in a syndication feed can be viewed as a vocabulary, which is used with the syntax conventions to describe pieces of information: feeds and the entries they contain. All the syndication format specifications describe a core vocabulary containing a mix of terms used to describe structure (for example, RSS 1.0's `channel` and `item`), content (such as Atom's `content` or RSS 2.0's `description`), as well as specific details (for example, `title` and `pubDate`). But what if the information you want to publish isn't adequately covered by these core terms?

All three leading syndication formats (RSS 1.0, RSS 2.0, and Atom) support custom extensions. These are additions to the core vocabulary usually designed for a specific purpose or domain of interest. For example, say you wanted to publish a feed containing weather reports giving the temperature, rainfall and so on for a particular region. It will be possible to put all this information in entry content as text. However, this is an old-media approach. In some cases this will be the best way, by virtue of its simplicity and the certainty that most aggregators/newsreaders would be able to display the information. However, you can be more explicit about the information you provide, and make it available in a machine-readable form.

There are two main phases in the design of an extension, creating a model of the information you wish to cover and working out the syntax. The model ideally will take into account the model underlying the syndication format, and work with the existing concepts like channel and item. The design *must* take into account the syntax of the underlying format simply to be valid, but also to express the information you want to convey in a way that will be easy for tools to generate or interpret.

Before going into details, here's a snippet of what a weather report extension might look like in practice:

```
<rss version="2.0"
    xmlns:weather="http://weather-reports-r-us/specs/ns#">
...
<item>
    <guid>http://weather-reports-r-us.com/2005-01-25/aberdeen</guid>
    <title>Weather in Aberdeen</title>
    <description>Bright but chilly</description>
    <weather:temperature>-9</weather:temperature>
    <weather:rainfall>0</weather:rainfall>
</item>
```

RSS, Atom, and XML Namespaces

Taking a step back in time to the RSS 0.91/1.0 fork, one of the main issues of disagreement was associated with support for XML namespaces. The history is rather a mess: RSS 0.9 had namespace support (through RDF/XML), RSS 0.91 dropped it, RSS 1.0 reintroduced it (through RDF/XML), RSS 2.0 reintroduced partial support. However, around the time of the original fork, a key aspect of the rss-dev group's design of RSS 1.0 was modularity, reusing existing vocabularies wherever possible. This approach is clear from the choice of RDF/XML, and to some extent reflects a view of the information feed being a flow of machine-oriented *data*.

The RSS 0.9x approach promoted by Dave Winer leaned more towards viewing the feed as a transport for human-oriented *content*, so application extensibility was less of a concern. Of course the machine-oriented data of RSS 1.0 could include material destined for human consumption, but it would be delivered possibly in a less directly rendered fashion. Rather than going down the path of modularity, the RSS 0.9x philosophy emphasized simplicity, especially in syntax. Rather than using accurately defined terms with the aid of extension vocabularies, the core terms were defined in a loose enough manner to enable their repurposing across a range of applications, with the view that content was content, period. (This helps explain why the RSS 2.0 <description> element doesn't actually describe anything, but rather hold the content.)

Moving closer to the present, in the period leading up to RSS 2.0, there was growing demand in the developer community for extensions to the simple branch of RSS. This led to the reintroduction of support for namespace-qualified extension vocabularies, although the core RSS 2.0 vocabulary itself remains without a namespace.

The Atom terms are in an XML namespace, and the format has support for extension data through namespaces. It is a little ironic that one of the key issues picked up by the Atom project was the ambiguity related to *content* found in the (now frozen) specification of RSS 2.0.

Expressing Things Clearly

The following snippet uses the weather extension, but this time in an RSS 1.0 feed:

```
<rdf:RDF
    xmlns:rdf="http://www.w3.org/1999/02/22-rdf-syntax-ns#"
    xmlns="http://purl.org/rss/1.0/"
    xmlns:weather="http://weather-reports-r-us/specs/ns#">
...
<item rdf:about="http://weather-reports-r-us.com/2005-01-25/aberdeen">
    <title>Weather in Aberdeen</title>
    <description>Bright but chilly</description>
    <weather:temperature>-9</weather:temperature>
    <weather:rainfall>0</weather:rainfall>
</item>
```

In its RDF interpretation, the semantics of this are unambiguous — the identified item has two properties, to give their fully qualified names:

```
http://weather-reports-r-us/specs/ns#temperature
http://weather-reports-r-us/specs/ns#rainfall
```

These two properties have literal values, -9 and 0, respectively. Those are the semantics, but what does it all mean? Here we are back with the issue of domain modeling. What this code snippet states is that the item has those properties, along with the properties of title and description. This may not be exactly what was intended. If the item in question is what us humans would call, "the weather in Aberdeen today," then this makes sense. But if the resource http://weather-reports-r-us.com/ 2005-01-25/aberdeen is actually a document providing the weather report, then this bit of RDF/XML is describing the document as cold and dry.

Looking back at the RSS 2.0 version of this, what does that mean? This version doesn't have any explicit semantics, apart from the syntax containership expressed by the XML. No logical relationships are defined; all you have are the item identified by the guid, the names of the elements, and the text inside them. In this case the definition is entirely up to what is contained. If you're looking after the weather vocabulary, you can make sure it says what you intend. The downside is that the partial understanding offered by RDF isn't available.

The easiest way to creating your own extension vocabularies is to look how other people have done it. For RSS 1.0 you can find many suitable vocabularies through the ESW Wiki:

```
http://esw.w3.org/topic/VocabularyMarket
```

For RSS 2.0, there's a list of modules here:

```
http://blogs.law.harvard.edu/tech/directory/5/specifications/rss20ModulesNamespaces
```

The RVW review format is defined for both RSS 1.0 and 2.0:

```
http://hublog.hubmed.org/archives/000307.html
```

Other Resources

Some other material relating to the "loosely coupled" Web can be found on the following sites:

- ❑ Internet Topic Exchange: `http://topicexchange.com/`

- ❑ Feedmesh (inter-site pinging): `http://groups.yahoo.com/group/feedmesh/`

- ❑ Using the `rel` tag for extra metadata: `http://developers.technorati.com/wiki/RelTag`

- ❑ Attention.xml (for watching what you're watching): `http://developers.technorati.com/wiki/attentionxml`

- ❑ The del.icio.us API (link-sharing system): `http://del.icio.us/doc/api`

- ❑ Flickr services (photo sharing): `www.flickr.com/services/api/`

Summary

In this chapter you learned...

- ❑ How feeds can be found using autodiscovery.

- ❑ How RDF can be gleaned from other XML formats.

- ❑ How inter-site communications can be enabled using a variety of protocols.

- ❑ How trackback works.

- ❑ What RSS modules look like.

What Lies Ahead in Information Management

The field of information feeds built around RSS and Atom is changing rapidly. One reason for that rapid change is that the usefulness of automated information feeds has thrown up new issues in how groups of information users can most efficiently and usefully manage the overwhelming volume of information that is available to anyone who has an Internet connection and a desktop or online aggregator. There are currently believed to be several million information feeds of which perhaps 4 or 5 million are active. No single human being can hope to process even a fraction of that flood of information. So, transforming the flood of information to a well-focused flow is important to an increasing number of users of information feeds.

Only a year or two ago, perhaps, the important questions were more basic: How can I create an RSS or Atom feed? Are there any tools that I can use to help me create an information feed? How can I find an aggregator that will let me use information feeds? For newcomers to the information feed area and for many developers, such questions won't go away. But other questions are, in my opinion, becoming more important. Just as we seldom think of our computing in terms of the binary zeroes and ones, so I anticipate that we, as users, will soon think less often of information feeds as such but will focus our interest on higher-level abstractions. It is still early to try to guess precisely what those abstractions might prove to be, but the issues raised and questions posed in this chapter may help to point you toward some possible solutions and next-generation approaches.

In this chapter you think about:

- ❑ Filtering the flood of information
- ❑ Moving toward a user-centric rather than feed-centric view of information
- ❑ How users can best access data originating from information feeds
- ❑ How to store relevant information
- ❑ How to retrieve information from storage
- ❑ What types of content might be available through information feeds

Filtering the Flood of Information

One fundamental question is, "How can I best use the huge amount of information that is available in information feeds?" Because everybody has a limited amount of time available, it is important to use aggregators (or the generation of tools that succeed them) to focus on the information you need.

When using desktop tools such as Abilon, it is possible to set up filters that include or exclude information feed items containing selected keywords or phrases. For some uses it might be more useful to be able to select such keywords globally. For other uses the granular approach of feed-by-feed filtering may be the best choice.

Flexibility in Subscribing

In our fast moving world of information feeds it is a distinct advantage if the user can quickly add and remove feeds. Most tools already provide this functionality, but some require the user to go looking for individual feed URLs while others support autodiscovery. Increasingly, we suspect, users will be reluctant to do the spade work, and autodiscovery will come to be an expected routine.

Autodiscovery on a single page is already desirable. But why not allow an aggregator to behave like a bot and navigate around a site to retrieve all feeds on the site, present those in an easy-to-use display (perhaps using check boxes), and then subscribe the user to their choice of feeds from that site? Such time-saving approaches are likely to differentiate successful aggregators from those whose following may decline.

Similarly, as the number of feeds rise that a typical user subscribes to, an improved user interface to allow review and changes in subscription might be advantageous.

Finding the Best Feeds

How do you find the best and most relevant feeds for topics that interest you? As a Web user you will, typically, have a range of sites that you visit regularly and may have some additional sites in your bookmarks folders. But are they the best sites as far as information feeds are concerned?

In our opinion, we need better, more convenient, tools to help us find the most relevant feeds, particularly for emerging topics. Searching sites like Technorati.com does help find feeds that include topics of interest. But can we find better ways? Time will tell.

Filtering by Personality

One approach that is already being informally adopted is what might be termed filtering by personality. If you subscribe to a feed from a blog whose author's opinion you respect, you are likely to have increased regard for information feeds to which that blog author subscribes. Aggregators that retrieve the blogroll of such subscribed feeds and allow the user to choose any feeds from that list might improve usability and efficiency.

Finding the Wanted Non-Core Information

If you, like us, have reasons for wanting to be aware of new technology trends, what is the best way to find those? If the technology or the use to which it is put is new, traditional search terms may completely miss the arrival or growth of new activity.

For the moment, we can't see a convenient way of getting past the techniques we currently use. Read the feeds for several people that we see as opinion formers or having cutting edge interests.

Point to Point or Hub and Spoke

Currently desktop aggregators retrieve feed information from individual servers where the feeds are created. In many other settings point-to-point connections scale poorly and hub-and-spoke connections become more efficient as the number of connection points rises. Perhaps desktop aggregators will move to a hub-and-spoke mode of operation.

Imagine that your desktop aggregator enables you to select topics that you want to subscribe to rather than individual feeds. You then choose some aggregator server from a list available so that you can easily switch from one aggregator server to another. Perhaps, too, the next generation aggregator enables you to weigh certain criteria, including personality associations, possibly using FOAF or OPML. From your desktop aggregator, you can then subscribe to the latest feeds on the topics of interest to you, with the criteria that are important to you weighted as you wish.

The approach just described could be much more efficient and effective than most of the current approaches.

New Technologies

The material covered in this book provides a fair sample of the techniques available today to developers working with information feeds. But change is the one certainty, and on the Web not only is the appearance of new formats and protocols to be expected, but major paradigm shifts are not uncommon. For example, until recently a certain proportion of online individuals would have a homepage or site, often facilitated by a service like GeoCities or AngelFire. But the recent past has seen an astronomical growth in the number of personal sites, thanks to blogging. Who could have predicted a minor change in format (from relatively static to journal-like) could make such a huge difference in adoption? Of course, this particular shift was due in part at least to the spread of RSS feeds.

There has been movement in developers' attitudes toward the technologies, alongside the growth of the Extreme Programming anti-methodology has been an increased awareness of scripting languages such as Python, and a shift away from Cathedral-like design. The open-source community is vast. While the stack of SOAP-oriented "official" Web services specifications grows in number and weight, many companies have found immediate benefit in moving to lightweight, RESTful HTTP plus XML designs.

Many of the technologies that date back to the early days of computing are finding new roles in the new interconnected environment. Statistics-based techniques for pattern matching, clustering, and data mining, which had their origins in the farthest fringes of artificial intelligence research in the last century, are now mainstream and powering the leading search engines. Techniques of logical reasoning (which also prospered in AI) have grown into languages that potentially offer a direct path to an improved Web. The uppercase, more formal Semantic Web is built of layers including URIs, HTTP, XML, RDF, and OWL, but nearby is the lowercase semantic web pile built of URLs, HTTP, HTML, tags, and quick-and-dirty services. Between these two lies a wide spectrum of potential for future development, and right near the center of all lie the information feed technologies.

A User-Centric View of Information

We believe that, as the basic techniques of creating and aggregating feeds become better understood and used, the focus will shift from the developer to the user. Typical users won't often be interested in seeing the raw information feeds. If they want to follow a selected topic, then it is likely to be the primary focus of interest. They may also be interested in the author of the feed to validate the opinions expressed.

Information for Projects

In the real world many of us work on projects that may last a few weeks or months. Occasionally, we may also participate in longer-term projects. That need to shift from one project to another lies behind the suggestion we made earlier in this chapter that we need an easier way to subscribe and unsubscribe from information feeds.

However, there are also other factors related to information feeds that are impacted by our participating in projects. For example, wouldn't it be useful to be able to view the information that flows to us through the varied information feeds that we subscribe to by the project that the information relates to?

Would an aggregator that allows users to subscribe by project offer real advantages? Or could the folder metaphor that many aggregators already support allow feeds to be grouped by project adequately for most needs?

Automated Publishing Using Information Feeds

Information feed specifications don't have a standard authentication mechanism yet beyond the low-level facilities offered by HTTP and the like. However, if it was possible to use authenticated subscriptions, the creator of feeds would know that only permitted subscribers could access the feed. This would open up the possibility of creating targeted feeds, including confidential information, analogous to an intranet, in what might be called an intrafeed. Without authentication the risk of unwanted access to a feed remains an inhibiting factor to potential growth in this direction.

Ownership of Data

Issues relating to who actually owns the data found in feeds and in general online have become more significant alongside the growth in personal and public sites and feeds. Laws haven't traditionally been designed for an environment like the Web, and rights management in particular has been thrust into the foreground, in part thanks to the ease in which data can now be shared. The often bizarre world of software patents provides considerable income for lawyers and can act as a significant deterrent to innovation.

Government actions in the "War on Terror" bring both a demand for suspicion and monitoring of communications and a renewed awareness of the need for privacy, especially online. What the future holds in terms of data ownership remains to be seen. The current trend for exposing as much as possible as widely as possible continues in personal, academic, and scientific areas and even to some extent in government. This all seems to support the claim, "information wants to be free." What better way of freeing it than making it accessible through feeds?

How Users Can Best Access Data

The interface that a user employs to access data will likely be of great importance. Already some tools like Omea and RSS Bandit provide useful and effective metaphors to navigate among Web pages linked from information feeds. Are there better ways to do this? Will we find some interface technique that is the equivalent of the Back button on a browser? We don't mean that it will have the same functionality as a Back button, but rather that it may change the interface in a way that enables the user to move around information of interest more effectively.

The variety of interfaces used by current aggregators suggests to me that the issue of how best to navigate around information feeds has not yet been fully understood.

How to Store Relevant Information

We have already discussed the issue of whether to store information derived from feeds. By now, you should be convinced that there are real situations where storing data and making it available to users in a way that is meaningful to them can be a much more useful approach than simply skimming information, either automatically or manually, and then discarding it.

If information, or at least a subset of information, is intended to be kept for significant periods of time by a significant proportion of users, then the additional metadata provided by RSS 1.0 through its RDF functionality potentially becomes significantly more important. When feeds contain such information of potentially enduring interest, can feed producers make more use of RSS 1.0 and add to the potential linkability of information that RDF can provide? Using RDF can certainly put additional demands on developers compared to the more traditional approach of RSS 0.9x and 2.0 or Atom 0.3. Is the additional effort worth it? Time will tell. Perhaps something like the approaches of the Friend of a Friend (FOAF) or de.licio.ous will attract sufficient user interest to encourage feed producers to include the relevant information in their feeds.

How to Retrieve Information from Storage

Easy-to-use, powerful search tools will, in my opinion, become a "must have" in next-generation aggregators or personal information centers. If the under-the-hood technology is a database engine, then full-text search capabilities are likely to be very useful. Of course, the full-text syntax will need to be hidden from typical end users, but the ability to search for multiple terms will become increasingly important as data volumes rise, and it is beyond the capacity of our memory (assuming we saw the information before it entered the information store) to remember where we saw particular pieces of interesting information.

In time, will we move to using visual ways to explore information that interests us? Will the display ideas like those exemplified in de.licio.us become the norm? At the moment, this approach is fairly slow to use but it's interesting and some aspects are intuitive. Will a next-generation interface be the approach of choice, at least in some information domains?

Revisions of Information Feed Formats

As was describe in Chapter 13, the Atom specifications remain under development at the IETF.

Immediately before this book went to press a first draft of the RSS 1.1 specification was published online at `http://inamidst.com/rss1.1/`. A guide to RSS 1.1 was published at `http://inamidst.com/rss1.1/guide`. RSS 1.1 is a potential successor to RSS 1.0. Like RSS 1.0 it uses RDF.

RSS 1.1, at least in its first draft, aims to clarify some ambiguities in the RSS 1.0 specification. The following is a summary of the changes proposed in the first draft.

> *The following description of possible changes in RSS 1.1 is subject to change. The preceding URLs are likely to be updated as RSS 1.1 proceeds through later drafts and seem likely to be the most appropriate place to look for definitive information.*

Elements and attributes from the RSS 1.0 namespace will not be allowed in RSS 1.1 extension modules. The `rdf:about` attribute will no longer be required on `item` elements. It is proposed that the `rss:items` element will be replaced by an `rdf:List` element. The `xml:lang` attribute will be allowed in more places in an RSS 1.1 feed document. The rarely used `rss:textinput` element will be removed. It is proposed that the namespace for RSS 1.1 elements will be `http://purl.org/net/rss1.1#`. The `version` attribute on the `rss:rss` element will be removed. RSS 1.1 will have a formal schema expressed in RELAX NG (for more details go to `www.oasis-open.org/committees/relax-ng/spec-20011203.html` and `http://www.oasis-open.org/committees/relax-ng/tutorial-20010810.html`).

Non-Text Information Delivered Through Information Feeds

Podcasting, discussed in Chapter 30, has become fashionable during the period in which this book has been written. Will it be a fashion that will pass off? Will it be generally available so that podcasting will, in a few years, be almost as natural as making a phone call?

Is there a need for the immediacy that podcasting can provide? Does it improve, for general topics, over the now traditional text-only or text-dominated blog?

Product Support Uses

Product support costs often make up a significant part of the real costs of software. Could blogs, possibly with sound or video content, provide off-the-shelf solutions to common problems?

Educational Uses

Some information feeds can be supplied on a paid subscription basis. Could information feeds be adapted to provide a means of delivery of course materials to registered students on distance learning courses? Would it offer real advantages over more traditional means of course delivery? Do we, for example, need large buildings for students to congregate in? Or are such approaches becoming out-dated, at least for some uses?

Summary

Information is pivotal to the way we work. Information feeds offer the potential of more effective and efficient access to and use of information. A user-centric approach seems likely to be the way that infor-mation feeds may move. It is an open question how best to meet the information needs of an increas-ingly demanding user population. We briefly discussed some possible future uses of information feeds to deliver information.

In this chapter you considered various issues, including...

❑ How information feeds can be abstracted in ways more relevant to the user.

❑ How users can filter feeds to exclude unwanted feed items.

❑ How a hub-and-spoke approach might offer advantages compared to the current point-to-point approach.

❑ How users can locally store information long term and retrieve it efficiently.

Answers to Exercises

Chapter 6

1. Is the following line of code part of a well-formed XML document?

```
<rdf:RDF xmlns:rdf="http://www.w3.org/1999/02/22-rdf-syntax-ns#'>
```

A. No, it's not well-formed XML. The delimiters of the attribute are a double quote (before the namespace URI) and a single quote (at the end of the namespace URI). Because the start tag is not well formed, the whole document cannot be well formed. Either paired apostrophes or paired double quotes are required in a well-formed XML document.

2. Can XML names begin with numbers?

A. No. XML names must begin with an alphabetic character or an underscore character.

3. Is the following well-formed XML?

```
<xmlDocument>
<!-- The content goes here. -- -->
</xmlDocument>
```

A. No, there are two reasons why this short document is not well-formed XML. You cannot begin an element name with the sequence of characters xml, and you cannot include two successive hyphens in an XML comment, except in the comment delimiters.

Chapter 8

1. Create a simple RSS 0.91 document and check its validity using the online validator located at http://feeds.archive.org/validator/. You will need to be able to upload the document to a publicly accessible URL using, for example, an FTP client.

A. There is no sample solution for this exercise. You will learn best by creating a document yourself and validating it.

2. Does RSS 0.91 use XML namespaces? Can you explain why the relevant design decision may have been taken?

A. RSS 0.91 does not use XML namespaces. At the time that RSS 0.91 was specified (June 2000), it was perceived that XML namespaces added complexity that might deter some potential users from using RSS.

Chapter 19

1. The first example of HTTP server code in this chapter was `InflexibleServer.py`, which served up the same string whatever page was requested. You also saw `ZippyClient.py`, an HTTP client that knew how to manage data from a server that supported compression. Your task is to create a modified version of `InflexibleServer.py` to gzip its data before serving it, so `ZippyClient.py` can talk to it. To get you started, here is a method that will take a string and gzip it:

```
def compress(self, data):
    zipBuffer = StringIO.StringIO()
    zipFile = gzip.GzipFile(mode = 'wb',
        fileobj = zipBuffer, compresslevel = 6)
    zipFile.write(data)
    zipFile.close()
    zipped = zipBuffer.getvalue()
    zipBuffer.close()
    self.content_length = len(zipped)
    return zipped
```

Note that you will need to import the `StringIO` and `gzip` packages to use this method. It is trivial to add a call to this method on the data being served, but you also have to set up the code to check whether the client accepts gzipped data, and also return appropriate HTTP response codes—not so trivial. You need to add code to look for a header in the HTTP request that will look something like this:

```
Accept-Encoding: gzip
```

Before compressing and returning the data, the server should add a header that looks like this:

```
Content-Encoding: gzip
```

Don't be afraid to insert lots of `print` statements to see what's happening in both the client and server code.

A. Here is one way of solving the problem:

```
# a single-minded HTTP server with gzip capability

import SocketServer
import BaseHTTPServer
import string
import StringIO
import gzip

PORT = 8008
```

```
DATA = \
"<rss version=\"2.0\">\n\
   <channel>\n\
      <title>My Channel</title>\n\
      <link>http://example.org/</link>\n\
      <description>A minimal feed</description>\n\
      <item>\n\
         <title>My First Item</title>\n\
         <description>This is the first post</description>\n\
      </item>\n\
      <item>\n\
         <title>My Second Item</title>\n\
         <description>This is the second post</description> \n\
      </item> \n\
      <item> \n\
         <title>My Third Item</title> \n\
         <description>This is the third post</description> \n\
      </item> \n\
   </channel> \n\
</rss>"

class InflexibleZipServer(BaseHTTPServer.BaseHTTPRequestHandler):
    def do_HEAD(self):
        self.send_head()

    def do_GET(self):
        self.send_head()
        print "Request Header:"
        print self.headers
        print "---"
        if self.canCompress:
            self.wfile.write(self.compress(DATA))
        else:
            self.wfile.write(DATA)
        self.wfile.close()

    def acceptsGzip(self):
        print self.headers
        encodings = self.headers.get('Accept-Encoding')
        if encodings != None:
            return (string.find(encodings, "gzip") != -1)
        return False

    def send_head(self):
        self.send_response(200)
        if self.acceptsGzip():
            self.canCompress = True
            self.send_header('Content-Encoding', 'gzip')
        else:
            self.canCompress = False
        self.send_header("Content-Type", "application/rss+xml")
        self.end_headers()

    def compress(self, data):
```

```
        print "Compressing!!"
        zipBuffer = StringIO.StringIO()
        zipFile = gzip.GzipFile(mode = 'wb',
            fileobj = zipBuffer, compresslevel = 6)
        zipFile.write(data)
        zipFile.close()
        zipped = zipBuffer.getvalue()
        zipBuffer.close()
        return zipped

httpd = SocketServer.ThreadingTCPServer(('', PORT), InflexibleZipServer)

print "serving at port", PORT
httpd.serve_forever()
```

As well as the addition of the compress method, an acceptsGzip method has been added and there have been significant changes to the send_head method and do_GET. The send_head method is called right after a request is made to the server, and in it a conditional block now checks if the client making a request supports gzip compressed data. The check is done by acceptsGzip:

```
def acceptsGzip(self):
    print self.headers
    encodings = self.headers.get('Accept-Encoding')
    if encodings != None:
        return (string.find(encodings, "gzip") != -1)
    else:
        return False
```

The parent class BaseHTTPServer.BaseHTTPRequestHandler will obtain the request headers, and for debugging purposes these are printed to the console. The key AcceptEncoding is used to find any corresponding value. You may have used a direct string comparison, for example:

```
if self.headers.get('Accept-Encoding') == "gzip":
...
```

This will work fine in this controlled example, but in the wild the 'Accept-Encoding' header may contain more information than is needed to simply confirm support, for example:

```
Accept-Encoding: compress;q=0.5, gzip;q=1.0
```

So in the code here the string module's find method is used to look for any occurrence of the string 'gzip'. If it's found, then acceptsGzip will return True, otherwise False. The send_head method records this Boolean in canCompress, as well as sending back the header:

```
Content-Encoding: gzip
```

If the value of canCompress is False then do_GET will send back the raw data as before. If the value is True, then the data will be run through the compress method. That method looks like this:

```
def compress(self, data):
    print "Compressing!!"
    zipBuffer = StringIO.StringIO()
    zipFile = gzip.GzipFile(mode = 'wb',
```

```
          fileobj = zipBuffer, compresslevel = 6)
      zipFile.write(data)
      zipFile.close()
      zipped = zipBuffer.getvalue()
      zipBuffer.close()
      self.content_length = len(zipped)
      return zipped
```

The gzip library is primarily designed to operate on files, so here a buffer that looks like a file is created using `StringIO.StringIO()`. This is used as the container in the `GzipFile` constructor, and given the arguments to make it writeable with binary data and have a compression level of 6. The raw feed data string is written into the `GzipFile` object, which is subsequently closed. The result of this is that the `zipBuffer` will now contain the data in a compressed form, and the value (a binary object) of this is obtained. As an extra convenience the length of this representation of the content is also recorded. Once returned to the `send_head` method, the compressed data is then served to the client. The new `InflexibleZipServer` can now be run by typing in a command window:

```
python InflexibleZipServer.py
```

To confirm everything is working as it should, `ZippyClient.py` needs a URI to reflect that of the local server:

```
URI = "http://127.0.0.1:8008/"
```

If you now run `ZippyClient.py` in another command window, in the server window you should see something like this:

```
D:\rss-book\19\code>python InflexibleZipServer.py
serving at port 8008
trotter - - [08/Aug/2004 23:29:05] "GET / HTTP/1.0" 200 -
Request Header:
Host: 127.0.0.1:8008
User-agent: Python-urllib/2.1
Accept-encoding: gzip


---
Host: 127.0.0.1:8008
User-agent: Python-urllib/2.1
Accept-encoding: gzip


Compressing!!
```

The first half of the console message says what the client has requested, the second half says what has been returned. Looking in the window in which `ZippyClient` was run, you should see the following:

```
D:\rss-book\19\code>python ZippyClient.py
connect: (127.0.0.1, 8008)
send: 'GET / HTTP/1.0\r\nHost: 127.0.0.1:8008\r\nUser-agent: Python-urllib/2.1\r
\nAccept-encoding: gzip\r\n\r\n'
reply: 'HTTP/1.0 200 OK\r\n'
header: Server: BaseHTTP/0.3 Python/2.3.3
header: Date: Sun, 08 Aug 2004 21:29:05 GMT
```

```
header: Content-Encoding: gzip
header: Content-Type: application/rss+xml
ZIPPED!
<rss version="2.0">
  <channel>
    <title>My Channel</title>
    <link>http://example.org/</link>
    <description>A minimal feed</description>
    <item>
       <title>My First Item</title>
       <description>This is the first post</description>
    </item>
    <item>
       <title>My Second Item</title>
       <description>This is the second post</description>
    </item>
    <item>
       <title>My Third Item</title>
       <description>This is the third post</description>
    </item>
  </channel>
</rss>
```

To confirm the server can still deliver data to clients that don't support gzip, you can comment out the line in `ZippyClient.py` that adds the header notifying the server of gzip support, for example:

```
# request.add_header('Accept-Encoding', 'gzip')
```

The client should print exactly the same feed data to the console as before.

Finally you might like to set the server running and point whatever Web browsers and aggregators you have at hand to `http://127.0.0.1:8008/` and observe the console to see whether the clients are using gzip.

Chapter 20

1. The following is an Atom 0.3 feed approximating the RSS 2.0 example:

```
<?xml version="1.0" encoding="UTF-8"?>
<?xml-stylesheet type="text/css" href="rss+atom.css"?>
<feed xmlns="http://purl.org/atom/ns#" version="0.3">
  <title>Tech Idol</title>
  <tagline>The hottest performers on the Net!</tagline>
  <link rel="alternate" type="text/html" href="http://example.org/idol/"/>
  <entry>
    <title>Shelley</title>
    <id>http://example.org/idol/shelley</id>
    <link rel="alternate" type="text/html"
            href="http://example.org/idol/shelley"/>
  <modified>2004-07-01T09:39:21Z</modified>
  <content type="text/html" mode="escaped">
            Shelley first impressed the judges with
```

```
                    her 3-line backup script, then trampled the opposition
                    with her cover of "These Boots Were Made for Walking".
            </content>
    </entry>
    <entry>
      <title>Sam</title>
      <id>http://example.org/idol/sam</id>
      <link rel="alternate" type="text/html" href="http://example.org/idol/sam"/>
      <modified>2004-07-01T 08:37:3Z</modified>
      <content type="text/html" mode="escaped">
                Test-driven development while plate-spinning?
                Sam's the man.
            </content>
    </entry>
    <entry>
      <title>Marc</title>
      <id>http://example.org/idol/marc</id>
      <link rel="alternate" type="text/html" href="http://example.org/idol/marc"/>
      <modified>2004-07-01T08:56:02Z</modified>
      <content type="text/html" mode="escaped">
            Marc's multimedia presentation of "O Sole Mio"
            served him well, but perhaps he should have kept those
            knees covered!
            </content>
    </entry>
  </feed>
```

Modify the CSS `rss.css` to style this document in a similar fashion to the RSS document.

A.   The following gives a reasonably readable view of both RSS 2.0 and Atom data:

```
rss:before, feed:before {
    content: "* This is an RSS feed and is
                    best viewed in an aggregator or newsreader *"
}

rss, feed {
    display:block;
    margin:1em;
    font-family: Arial;
}

channel, feed {
    display:block;
    border:1px solid #000;
    width: 30em;
    padding:1em;
    background-color:#fff;
}

item, entry {
    display:block;
    margin-bottom:1em;
    border:1px solid #000;
```

```
        background-color:#ddd;
        padding:1em;
}

title {
        display: block;
        padding:0.5em;
        border:1px solid #000;
        font-size:120%;
        font-weight:bold;
        margin:0.5em;
        background-color:#fff;
}

tagline {
        display: block;
        padding:0.5em;
        border:1px solid #000;
        font-size:100%;
        font-weight:bold;
        margin:0.5em;
        background-color:#fff;
}

description, content {
        display: block;
        padding:0.5em;
        border:1px solid #000;
        margin:0.5em;
        background-color:#fff;
}

pubDate, modified {
        display: block;
        padding:0.5em;
        border:1px solid #000;
        margin:0.5em;
        font-size:90%;
        background-color:#fff;
}

link {
        display: block;
        padding:0.5em;
        border:1px solid #000;
        font-size:80%;
        margin:0.5em;
        background-color:#fff;
}

language, managingEditor, generator, image, guid, ttl, skipHours, skipDays,
webMaster, lastBuildDate, updateBase, updateFrequency, updatePeriod, docs {
        display: none;
}
```

Most of the elements in Atom are being handled by the addition of their name to the CSS selector for the RSS 2.0 term, which most resembles them. The only addition is tagline, which here is almost the same as title, except displayed in a slightly smaller typeface.

2. While discussing the RDF model, a simple node and arc diagram of a single item was shown. Later you saw a larger diagram of blogroll data. Of course it's possible to represent the data in a full RSS 1.0 feed in this fashion. Here is part of the sample feed data rewritten in RSS 1.0. See if you can sketch out the node and arc diagram for this data:

```
<rdf:RDF
    xmlns="http://purl.org/rss/1.0/"
    xmlns:rdf="http://www.w3.org/1999/02/22-rdf-syntax-ns#"
    xmlns:content="http://purl.org/rss/1.0/modules/content/">

    <channel rdf:about="http://example.org/idol.rdf">
        <title>Tech Idol</title>
        <items>
            <rdf:Seq>
                <rdf:li rdf:resource="http://example.org/idol/shelley"/>
            </rdf:Seq>
        </items>
    </channel>

    <item rdf:about="http://example.org/idol/shelley">
        <title>Shelley</title>
        <link >http://example.org/idol/shelley</link>
        <content:encoded>
                Shelley first impressed the judges with her 3-line backup script,
                then trampled the opposition with her cover of "These Boots Were
                Made for Walking".
        </content:encoded>
    </item>
</rdf:RDF>
```

Hint: The W3C's validator provides graphic views at www.w3.org/RDF/Validator/.

A. Figure A-1 shows a graphic representation of the RDF/XML feed data.

In the interests of clarity the URIs here have been abbreviated. So http://../idol.rdf is actually:

```
http://example.org/idol.rdf
```

rss:channel is:

```
http://purl.org/rss/1.0/channel
```

rdf:type is:

```
http://www.w3.org/1999/02/22-rdf-syntax-ns#type
```

This isn't an insignificant point; it's the URIs that give the resources and properties globally unambiguous names.

Appendix A

Resources in Figure A-1 are represented as ovals; literals as rectangles. The oval labeled _:theitems is actually a blank node, it doesn't have a URI of its own. The label is only an arbitrary local name, used for convenience, following the convention for prefixing blank node names with _:.

Note that the nodes that provide the type for the RSS/RDF entities (rss:channel, rdf:Seq, rss:item) are resources in their own right and thus have URIs, as do all the relationships (the properties rdf:type, rss:title, and so on). The general use of the URI is a major reason the model and logic of RDF works well on the Web.

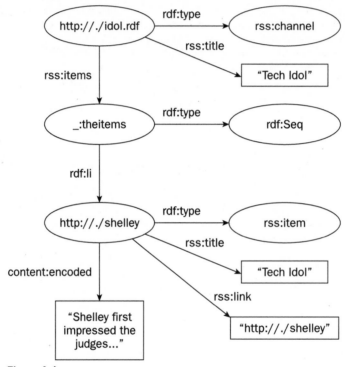

Figure A-1

Chapter 21

1. You have seen the SQL needed to create the Items and Persons tables. Your task is to work out the SQL needed to create a table to hold feed-related data. Refer to one or more of the format specification (RSS 1.0, RSS 2.0, or Atom) and choose the fields that you think you're likely to need. Your solution will fill in the blank here:

```
CREATE TABLE Feeds (
...
);
```

A. The following SQL will create a table to store most of the common pieces of data relating to feeds.

```
CREATE TABLE Feeds (
    id INTEGER PRIMARY KEY,
    editor_id INTEGER,
    url TEXT,
    title TEXT,
    description TEXT,
    pub_date TEXT,
    last_download_date TEXT,
    status TEXT
);
```

This would lead to an entity called something like *TextInfo*, with attributes perhaps something like *infotype* ("title" or "description"), *content* ("My First Post"), and *language* ("en-us").

2. There's a demonstration of an RDF query language (Squish) at www.ilrt.bris.ac.uk/discovery/2000/11/rss-query/.

The demo uses an RDF vocabulary for talking about jobs alongside RSS 1.0—job advertisements appear in feeds. Here is an example:

```
<item rdf:about="http://example.com/job1.html">
    <title>Digging a Big Hole</title>
        <link>http://example.com/job3.html</link>
        <description>
           The job involves going out into a busy road with a spade and
           digging for several years.
        </description>

        <job:advertises>
            <wn:Job job:title="Hole Digger"
                    job:salary="10000"
                    job:currency="GBP">
                <job:orgHomepage rdf:resource="http://example.com/"/>
            </wn:Job>
        </job:advertises>

</item>
```

The exercise is to use the Runner1.py code to load some of this data into the triplestore (for example, from www.ilrt.bris.ac.uk/discovery/2000/11/rss-query/jobs-rss.rdf), and then write a SQL view that will return a list of job titles and salaries from the data.

A. One possible solution is as follows:

```
CREATE VIEW jobs AS SELECT
JobTitles.object,
JobSalaries.object
FROM
triples Jobs,
triples JobTitles,
triples JobSalaries
WHERE
Jobs.property == "http://www.w3.org/1999/02/22-rdf-syntax-ns#type"
```

```
AND
Jobs.object == "http://xmlns.com/wordnet/1.6/Job"
AND
JobTitles.property ==
    "http://ilrt.org/discovery/2000/11/rss-query/jobvocab.rdf#title"
AND
JobTitles.subject == Jobs.subject
AND
JobSalaries.property ==
    "http://ilrt.org/discovery/2000/11/rss-query/jobvocab.rdf#salary"
AND
JobSalaries.subject == Jobs.subject;
```

Chapter 22

1. Make a copy of `ChannelSetReader.java` and modify it to read URIs from OPML subscription lists.

   Here is an example of source data (`feedlist.opml`):

```xml
<opml version="1.0">
   <head>
      <ownerName>John Doe</ownerName>
      <ownerEmail>jd@example.org</ownerEmail>
   </head>
   <body>
         <outline text="Bill de hÓra" type="rss"
                xmlUrl="http://www.dehora.net/journal/index.rdf"/>
         <outline text="Martin Fowler's Bliki" type="rss"
                xmlUrl="http://martinfowler.com/bliki/bliki.rss"/>
         <outline text="Finally Atom" type="rss"
                xmlUrl="http://dannyayers.com/feed/rss2"/>
         <outline text="Raw" type="rss"
                xmlUrl="http://danja.typepad.com/fecho/atom.xml"/>
   </body>
</opml>
```

   Note: The guidelines suggest using `type="rss"` for every kind of syndication feed.

   Hint: OPML doesn't use namespaces. This means that an element type can be identified by its local name alone. You can examine the data sent to `startElement` when parsing a document by replacing that method with something like this:

```java
public void startElement(String namespaceURI, String localName,
                         String qName, Attributes attributes) {

    System.out.println("\nnamespaceURI:" + namespaceURI);
    System.out.println("localName:" + localName);
    System.out.println("qName:" + qName);

    for(int i=0;i<attributes.getLength();i++){
       System.out.println("    attribute "+
             attributes.getLocalName(i)+
```

```
                              " = "+
                    attributes.getValue(i));
          }
    }
```

Also note that the `Attributes` class includes a method `attributes.getValue` that takes as a single (string) parameter the local name of the attribute and returns the value.

A. Assuming the rest of the code is the same as `ChannelSetReader.java` except for its class name (and the use of the class name in the `main` method), the only modification needed to parse simple OPML subscription lists is to replace `startElement` with the following:

```
public void startElement(String namespaceURI, String localName,
        String qName, Attributes attributes) {

    if (localName.equals("outline")) {
        String uriString = attributes.getValue("xmlUrl");
        feedURIs.add(uriString);
    }
}
```

2. See if you can come up with a good strategy for keeping track of feeds that aren't providing data as they should. For example, the consumer code in this chapter managed errors in feeds by deducting a "life" every time something went wrong, and unsubscribing when a `FeedFetcher` had no lives left. A big drawback of this approach is that a subscription list will fairly rapidly get emptied if the connection to the Internet is lost. Can you think of a better approach? There is no single solution to this problem, and it will depend to some extent on how you intend your application to interact with end users.

A. There is no single solution to this problem, and it will depend to some extent on how you intend your application to interact with end users.

Chapter 23

1. Modify the `SoupParser` to provide support for XML comments.

The `SoupParser` as listed was missing various bits of functionality that could be useful in syndication applications, among these are support for comments and processing instructions. A typical XML comment looks like this:

```
<!-- Some text -->
```

There isn't a standard SAX handler for these, but (regrettably) they are sometimes used to contain useful information. A case in point is Trackback, the inter-Weblog notification mechanism that uses blocks of RDF/XML hidden in comments on the (X)HTML page.

The `SoupParser` code already includes a suitable regular expression; this is it (early on in the source):

```
private static Pattern commentRe = Pattern.compile("^<!--.+?-->",
Pattern.DOTALL);
```

The `isComment` method is already being called at appropriate times; all your code needs to do is recognize the comment syntax and print the contents to the console.

Hint: The code for `isComment` will be like the existing `isCDATA` method, but quite a lot simpler.

A. The following will recognize XML comments and print them to the console:

```
public boolean isComment() {
    Matcher match = commentRe.matcher(this.data.substring(this.charIndex));

    if (match.find()) {
        System.out.println("MATCH");
        this.charIndex = this.charIndex + match.end();
            System.out.println(match.group());
        return true;
    }
    return false;
}
```

2. Modify the `SoupParser` to provide support for XML Processing Instructions.

XML can use Processing Instructions to associate a CSS (cascading style sheet) or XSL (XML Stylesheet Language) with the document. This may be needed for re-rendering an XHTML page or transforming an XML document. The following is a typical example:

```
<?xml-stylesheet href="lurid.css" type="text/css"?>
```

The SAX2 specification includes a listener in the `ContentHandler` interface:

```
void processingInstruction(String target, String data)
```

The target part of the PI is the first text chunk after `<?`, in the previous example `xml-stylesheet`. The data part is the rest of the material up to the closing `?>`. Note that although `xml-stylesheet` and some other common PIs use what appear to be attributes, these have no individual meaning for SAX and are usually referred to as pseudo-attributes. The data string is just the whole chunk of text.

The source of `SoupParser` already contains a suitable regular expression pattern for recognizing PIs, it looks like this:

```
private static Pattern piRe = Pattern.compile("^<\\?.+?\\?>", Pattern.DOTALL);
```

Note that the pattern misses the starting `<`; it has a start-of-string marker `^` instead, as the test will be made immediately after the parser has encountered a `<`.

What your code has to do is to implement the `isProcessingInstruction` method so that it checks to see whether the data at this point is a PI, and if it is, you should make a call to the SAX method passing the appropriate arguments, for example:

```
this.contentHandler.processingInstruction( target, data);
```

Hint: The code for `isProcessingInstruction` will be similar to the existing `isCDATA` method.

A. The following will allow `SoupParser` to recognize processing instructions and make the appropriate call to the SAX listener:

```java
    public boolean isProcessingInstruction() {

        Matcher match = piRe.matcher(this.data.substring(this.charIndex));

        if (match.find()) {
            this.charIndex = this.charIndex + match.end()-1;
            String raw = match.group();
            raw = raw.trim();
            int space = raw.indexOf(' ');
            String target = raw.substring(2, space);
            String data = raw.substring(space+1, raw.length()-2).trim();
            try {
                this.contentHandler.processingInstruction(target, data);
            } catch (SAXException e) {
                e.printStackTrace();
            }
            return true;
        }
        return false;
    }
}
```

Chapter 24

1. Create a module for SynWiki called `module_rss2.php` to deliver RSS 2.0 formatted data. The data you're aiming for will look something like this:

```xml
<rss version="2.0">
  <channel>
    <title>Wiki News</title>
    <link>http://localhost/synwiki/</link>
    <description>New stuff on the Wiki</description>
    <language>en-us</language>
    <pubDate>Mon, 27 Sep 2004 12:45:38 +0200</pubDate>
    <lastBuildDate>Mon, 27 Sep 2004 12:45:38 +0200</lastBuildDate>
    <docs>http://example.org/docs</docs>
    <generator>SynWiki</generator>
    <managingEditor>synwiki@example.org</managingEditor>
    <webMaster>webmaster@example.org</webMaster>

  <item>
    <guid>http://localhost/synwiki/view.php?PageTwo</guid>
    <title>Page two</title>
    <description>this is page two</description>
    <pubDate>Sun, 26 Sep 2004 20:31:35 +0200</pubDate>
  </item>

  <item>
    <guid>http://localhost/synwiki/view.php?PageOne</guid>
    <title>A title</title>
    <description>This is page one.</description>
    <pubDate>Sat, 25 Sep 2004 15:45:00 +0200</pubDate>
  </item>

  </channel>
```

A. The following (`module_rss2.php`) will produce an RSS 2.0 feed:

```php
<?php

include("config.php");
include("dbconnect.php");
include("util.php");

header("Content-type: text/xml;charset=utf-8");

dbConnect();
$query = "SELECT * FROM syn_content ORDER BY date DESC LIMIT 3";
$result = mysql_query($query);

$pubDate = convertDateW3CtoRFC2822(getDateString());
?>

<rss version="2.0">
    <channel>
        <title>Wiki News</title>
        <link><?php echo $URI_BASE ?></link>
        <description>New stuff on the Wiki</description>
        <language>en-us</language>
        <pubDate><?php echo $pubDate; ?></pubDate>
        <lastBuildDate><?php echo $pubDate; ?></lastBuildDate>
        <docs>http://example.org/docs</docs>
        <generator>SynWiki</generator>
        <managingEditor>synwiki@example.org</managingEditor>
        <webMaster>webmaster@example.org</webMaster>
<?php
if ($result) {
    while ($row = mysql_fetch_array($result)) {
        $rss2Date = convertDateW3CtoRFC2822($row["date"]);
        $content = $row["content"];
        $content = replaceExpressions($content);
        $content = escapeChars($content);
?>
    <item>
    <guid><?php echo $URI_BASE."view.php?".$row["entry_id"]; ?></guid>
    <title><?php echo $row["title"]; ?></title>
    <description><?php echo $content; ?></description>
    <pubDate><?php echo $rss2Date; ?></pubDate>
    </item>
<?php
    }
}
?>
    </channel>
</rss>
```

Chapter 25

1. In the examples in the text you saw how the DocBook-like format of book.xml could be transformed into RSS 2.0. Later, the resulting RSS was converted into XHTML. See whether you can shorten this sequence by creating a single book2html.xslt style sheet, which will take book.xml as input and output an XHTML representation like that listed in the text.

A. book2html.xslt:

```xml
<?xml version="1.0" encoding="UTF-8"?>
<xsl:stylesheet version="1.0" xmlns:xsl="http://www.w3.org/1999/XSL/Transform">

    <xsl:output method="xml" indent="yes"/>

    <xsl:template match="/">
        <xsl:apply-templates/>
    </xsl:template>

    <xsl:template match="book">
        <xsl:text disable-output-escaping="yes">
&lt;!DOCTYPE html PUBLIC "-//W3C//DTD XHTML 1.0 Strict//EN"
 "http://www.w3.org/TR/xhtml1/DTD/xhtml1-strict.dtd"&gt;
  </xsl:text>
        <html>
            <head>
                <title>
                    <xsl:value-of select="bookinfo/title"/>
                </title>
            </head>
            <body xml:lang="{@lang}" lang="{@lang}">
                <xsl:apply-templates/>
            </body>
        </html>
    </xsl:template>

    <xsl:template match="article">
        <div class="item">
            <h1>
                <xsl:value-of select="articleinfo/title"/>
            </h1>
            <p>
                <xsl:value-of select="para"/>
            </p>
        </div>
    </xsl:template>

    <xsl:template match="text()"/>

</xsl:stylesheet>
```

Chapter 26

1. Add code to `BlogClient.cs` that will implement the `blogger.editPost` method.

A. In `BlogClient.cs`, add the following code:

```
public Hashtable editPost(string appKey, string postID, string userName, string
password, string entryText, string publish){

    MethodCall call = new MethodCall("blogger.editPost");

    call.addParam("string", appKey);
    call.addParam("string", postID);
    call.addParam("string", userName);
    call.addParam("string", password);
    call.addParam("string", entryText);
    call.addParam("boolean", publish);

    Stream  responseStream = call.call(targetURI);
    XmlDocument responseDocument = new XmlDocument();
    responseDocument.Load(responseStream);

    Hashtable results;
    XmlNode fault = responseDocument.SelectSingleNode("//fault");

    if(fault != null){
      results = extractStructValues(responseDocument);
    } else {
      Console.WriteLine(responseDocument.DocumentElement.OuterXml);
      results = new Hashtable();
      string responseValue =
        responseDocument.SelectSingleNode("//value").InnerText;
      results.Add("value", responseValue);
    }
    return results;
  }
```

In `Main.cs`, add the following code:

```
if(args.Length == 2){
   Hashtable results = client.editPost(account.appKey, args[0], account.userName,
account.password,
                                       args[1], "1");
   displayHashtable(results);
}
```

Chapter 29

1. Write an iTQL query to extract the names of the people featured in the blogroll.

Hint: You want to extract the `foaf:name` values of the `foaf:Person` resources.

A. The solution is:

```
select $object
    from <rmi://localhost/server1#Friends>
    where $subject <rdf:type> <foaf:Agent>
    and $subject <foaf:name> $object;
```

If you run this you should see something like the following (list shortened here):

```
iTQL> select $object
    from <rmi://localhost/server1#Friends>
    where $subject <rdf:type> <foaf:Agent>
    and $subject <foaf:name> $object;

[ @semantics ]
[ Danny Ayers ]
[ Dave Beckett ]
...
[ Jo Walsh ]
[ Norm Walsh ]

42 rows returned.
iTQL>
```

Useful Online Resources

Many online resources relating to developer tools to create and manipulate information feeds are covered in Chapter 18 and in the chapters that discuss the use of individual tools. In this appendix we provide you with a list of further resources that you might find useful.

Specification Documents for Information Feeds

The following are the specification documents for the information feed formats discussed in this book:

- ❑ Atom Format 0.3: www.mnot.net/drafts/draft-nottingham-atom-format-02.html
- ❑ Atom 1.0: www.ietf.org/ids.by.wg/atompub.html
- ❑ RSS 0.91: http://backend.userland.com/rss091
- ❑ RSS 0.92: http://backend.userland.com/rss092
- ❑ RSS 1.0: http://web.resource.org/rss/1.0/spec
- ❑ RSS 2.0: http://blogs.law.harvard.edu/tech/rss

The following are specification documents relating to authoring or notification protocols:

- ❑ Atom Protocol Working Drafts: http://bitworking.org/projects/atom/
- ❑ Blogger API: www.blogger.com/developers/api/1_docs/
- ❑ MetaWeblog API: www.xmlrpc.com/metaWeblogApi
- ❑ Transporting Atom Notifications over XMPP: www.ietf.org/internet-drafts/draft-saintandre-atompub-notify-02.txt

The Atom Working Group Charter includes target dates for finalization of the Atom Syndication Format and Atom Publishing Protocol specifications in March/April 2005. The finished versions should be available through the Atom 1.0 link around that time; if not, further information is available on the Wiki at www.intertwingly.net/wiki/pie/FrontPage.

Some of the specifications on which the information feed formats and protocols depend can be found through these links:

- ❑   Uniform Resource Identifiers (URIs): http://gbiv.com/protocols/uri/rev-2002/rfc2396bis.html

- ❑   HTTP: www.w3.org/Protocols/

- ❑   XML: www.w3.org/TR/REC-xml/

- ❑   XML namespaces: www.w3.org/TR/REC-xml-names/

- ❑   XML media types: www.ietf.org/rfc/rfc3023.txt

- ❑   HTML: www.w3.org/MarkUp/

- ❑   XML-RPC: www.xmlrpc.com/spec

- ❑   SOAP: www.w3.org/TR/soap/

The URI specification (RFC 2396) has been revised but has yet to receive an RFC number of its own. The link above is a temporary address.

Resource Description Framework

The Resource Description Framework is the foundation of RSS 1.0. It has several specification documents on the World Wide Web Consortium Web site that contain the specifications of the revised documents finalised in 2004:

- ❑   RDF Primer: www.w3.org/TR/rdf-primer/

- ❑   RDF Concepts and Abstract Syntax: www.w3.org/TR/rdf-concepts/

- ❑   RDF Semantics: www.w3.org/TR/rdf-mt/

- ❑   RDF Syntax: www.w3.org/TR/rdf-syntax-grammar/

- ❑   RDF Schema: www.w3.org/TR/rdf-schema/

The 1999 RDF Model and Syntax recommendation is located at www.w3.org/TR/REC-rdf-syntax:

- ❑   RDF Model and Syntax: www.w3.org/TR/1999/REC-rdf-syntax-19990222

- ❑   RDF Schema: www.w3.org/TR/1999/PR-rdf-schema-19990303/

For anyone wanting to dig deeper into Semantic Web technologies, there are also the OWL Web Ontology Language specifications:

❑ OWL Overview: www.w3.org/TR/owl-features/

❑ OWL Guide: www.w3.org/TR/owl-guide/

Modules and Other Related Resources

❑ RSS 1.0 Modules Overview: http://purl.org/rss/1.0/modules/

❑ RSS 2.0 modules: http://blogs.law.harvard.edu/tech/directory/5/specifications/rss20ModulesNamespaces

❑ Creative Commons (licensing module): www.creativecommons.org

❑ PRISM (Publishing Industry Metadata Specification): www.prismstandard.org/

❑ Dublin Core Metadata Initiative: http://dublincore.org/

❑ FOAF (Friend of a Friend): www.foaf-project.org/

❑ Trackback: www.movabletype.org/trackback/

❑ Easy News Topics: www.purl.org/NET/ENT/1.0/

❑ OPML: www.opml.org/spec

❑ SIAM: www.25hoursaday.com/draft-obasanjo-siam-01.html

❑ Attention.xml: http://developers.technorati.com/wiki/attentionxml

Online Validators and Other Tools

The most useful validator is located at http://feedvalidator.org/.

UserLand has an RSS validator located at http://rss.scripting.com/.

The W3C have an online RDF validator located at www.w3.org/RDF/Validator/ and an HTML validator at http://validator.w3.org/

Syndic8, located at www.syndic8.com/, is a feed catalog site with various tools and statistics useful for the RSS/Atom developer.

The following are information feed–related search services that may be of particular interest to the developer:

❑ PubSub: http://pubsub.com

❑ Technorati: http://technorati.com

❑ Feedster: http://feedster.com

Resources Looking at the Bigger Picture

The following resources look at the bigger picture of networks and the Web:

❑ Architecture of the World Wide Web: www.w3.org/TR/webarch/

❑ Web Architecture Design Issues: www.w3.org/DesignIssues/Overview.html

❑ Architectural Styles and the Design of Network-based Software Architectures (REST): www.ics.uci.edu/~fielding/pubs/dissertation/top.htm

❑ RSS in Science Publishing: www.dlib.org/dlib/december04/hammond/12hammond.html

Mailing Lists

The following mailing lists are relevant to the content of this book:

❑ RSS-Dev: http://groups.yahoo.com/group/rss-dev/

❑ RDF/Semantic Web Interest Group: www.w3.org/2001/sw/interest/

❑ RSS 2.0 Support: http://groups.yahoo.com/group/RSS2-Support/

❑ Atom Syntax: www.imc.org/atom-syntax/index.html

❑ Atom Protocol: www.imc.org/atom-protocol/

❑ XML-Dev: http://xml.org/xml/xmldev.shtml

❑ Syndication List: http://groups.yahoo.com/group/syndication/

❑ Atom-OWL: http://groups-beta.google.com/group/atom-owl

❑ RDFWeb-Dev (FOAF): http://rdfweb.org/mailman/listinfo/rdfweb-dev

❑ BloggerDev: http://groups-beta.google.com/group/bloggerDev

❑ Jena-Dev: http://groups.yahoo.com/group/jena-dev/

❑ FeedMesh: http://groups.yahoo.com/group/feedmesh/

❑ iPodder-Dev: http://groups.yahoo.com/group/ipodder-dev/

Glossary

aggregation: The process of retrieving and displaying items from one or more information feeds.

aggregator: A desktop tool that displays the items from one or more information feeds.

Atom: A project at the IETF that aims to produce an information feed format and a publication protocol.

autodiscovery: A mechanism that enables an aggregator to locate the URL for an information feed by using information in the head of an HTML/XHTML Web page.

blog: An online method of publication, often used to publish an online diary on technical or personal topics of interest to the blog's author. Abbreviation of *weblog*.

blogroll: A list of blogs to which a blog author subscribes.

channel: A term sometimes used for an information feed.

Channel Definition Format: A precursor technology to RSS and Atom, proprietary to Microsoft. Typically abbreviated as CDF.

content: The non-metadata parts of an information feed.

content syndication: Distribution of content to multiple users. Often used to refer to the use of content on multiple Web sites.

Dublin Core: An initiative that attempts to standardize aspects of metadata related to the publication of documents. Also used to refer to an RSS 1.0 module that includes elements from the Dublin Core Metadata Initiative.

feed: A commonly used abbreviation for an information feed.

FOAF: Friend of a Friend. An extension module that attempts to express relationships among several human beings.

HotSauce: A product of historical interest that implemented the Meta Content Framework.

IETF: Internet Engineering Task Force. Development of the Atom specifications, at the time of writing, is being taken forward by an IETF working group.

information feed: An XML document (expressed, typically, in a flavor of RSS or Atom) that is made available to aggregators.

MCF: Meta Content Framework. An early information feed technology sponsored by Apple.

Meta Content Framework: An early information feed technology that became the basis for HotSauce.

metadata: Data about other data.

namespace: A collection of XML elements and attributes, typically associated with a URI (the "namespace URI").

news feed: A term used to refer to information feeds where the items relate to news.

Newsgator: A commercial aggregator product that is used inside Microsoft Outlook.

NewsML: News Markup Language.

OneNote: A commercial product that can be used to store information long term.

Onfolio: A commercial product that can be used to subscribe to feeds and to store information long term.

OPML: Outline Processor Markup Language. Used, for example, to create blogrolls.

OWL: Web Ontology Language, a specification being developed by the World Wide Web Consortium as part of the Semantic Web activity.

podcasting: Audio blogging.

RDF: Resource Description Framework. A framework to capture metadata. Used in RSS 1.0.

RDF Site Summary: One of the terms for which RSS can stand.

Really Simple Syndication: One of the terms for which RSS can stand.

Rich Site Summary: One of the terms for which RSS can stand.

RSS: An acronym with three possible expansions — RDF Site Summary, Really Simple Syndication, and Rich Site Summary.

RSS 0.9x: This refers to RSS versions 0.9, 0.91 and 0.92. In this context RSS can stand for either RDF Site Summary or Really Simple Syndication.

RSS 1.0: In RSS 1.0 the term RSS stands for RDF Site Summary.

RSS 2.0: The descendant of RSS 0.9*x*.

RSS Feed: An information feed expressed in a flavor of RSS.

RSS Modules: A term used to refer to a module that extends RSS 1.0.

Semantic Web: A framework to allow data to be shared across the Web, with shared understanding of semantics.

SOAP: Simple Object Access Protocol.

Syndic8: A Web site that aggregates information feeds and information from them.

syndication: The process of distributing information to multiple users. Often called *content syndication*.

Weblog: *See* blog.

XML: Extensible Markup Language. The markup metalanguage in which Atom and some RSS versions are written.

XML namespace: A collection of XML elements and attributes associated with a URI (the "namespace URI").

XML-RPC: A remote procedure call mechanism. One use is in the publication-subscription metaphor.

XML Schema: A specification that defines the structure of a class of XML documents.

XHTML: Extensible Hypertext Markup Language. HTML rewritten to comply with XML syntax rules.

Index

S